Corporate Governance

Corporate Governance

Principles, policies, and practices

FOURTH EDITION

Bob Tricker

OXFORD
UNIVERSITY PRESS

OXFORD
UNIVERSITY PRESS

Great Clarendon Street, Oxford, OX2 6DP,
United Kingdom

Oxford University Press is a department of the University of Oxford.
It furthers the University's objective of excellence in research, scholarship,
and education by publishing worldwide. Oxford is a registered trade mark of
Oxford University Press in the UK and in certain other countries

First edition 2009
Second edition 2012
Third edition 2015

Impression: 1

Published in the United States of America by Oxford University Press
198 Madison Avenue, New York, NY 10016, United States of America

British Library Cataloguing in Publication Data
Data available

Library of Congress Control Number: 2019938777

ISBN 978-0-19-880986-9

Printed in Italy by L.E.G.O. S.p.A.

Dedicated to the memory of Gretchen Tricker (1945–2018), wife, mother, free spirit, author, and editor of countless journal articles and books on corporate governance, including this one.

Preface

What is new in this edition

Since the first edition of this book was published in 2009, corporate governance has grown dramatically in both scope and significance. Each subsequent edition reflected new theoretical insights, changing governance processes, and wider dimensions to the subject.

The first edition focused primarily on practices reflected in corporate regulation and corporate governance codes, which called for independent non-executive directors in listed companies, audit committees, remuneration committees, and nomination committees of the main board, the separation of board chair from chief executive officer (CEO), and reporting to shareholders that these requirements had been met.

The global financial crisis around 2008 faced some countries with economic collapse; in others companies needed government bail-out or were nationalized. The crisis focused attention on the culture of some financial institutions, their directors' cavalier attitudes to growth, and a failure to recognize risk. Changes in company law and regulation followed, which were introduced in the second edition of the book. Now institutional investors increasingly challenged boards; investor relation activities increased in response. Another theme that emerged in the second edition was the need for boards to recognize a responsibility for creating their company's ethical culture, determining its corporate social responsibility, and integrating economic, social, and environmental factors.

The third edition, in 2015, highlighted some on-going corporate governance concerns, including issues such as 'aggressive' tax avoidance strategies, allegedly excessive top management remuneration, corporate responses to whistle blowers who published companies' shortcomings, and other issues of corporate culture and business ethics. Relations with auditors and their independence, corporate social responsibility, approaches to risk, board diversity (in particular women on boards), and shareholder involvement all arose. It was also increasingly recognized that corporate governance was an important issue, not only in listed companies covered by the corporate governance codes, but in private companies and corporate entities that do not have shareholders.

This fourth edition provides a new focus for understanding corporate governance that goes far beyond the emphasis on regulation, rules, and voluntary codes of the first. The culture of a country, embracing its historical, religious, social, economic, environmental, and legal contexts, determines that country's approach to corporate governance. Further, the culture of each company, particularly the board-level culture, determines how corporate governance ideas are applied.

For the first time, a distinction is drawn between Western and Eastern perceptions of corporate governance. In the West, including the United States, Great Britain and countries in the British Commonwealth, and Continental European countries, corporate governance is perceived as a way to regulate companies and avoid unacceptable behaviour. In the East, including China, Japan, South Korea, and countries in the Far East influenced by the Chinese diaspora over the years, corporate governance is seen as a means to support the creation of wealth for the benefit of owners, employees, and, ultimately, society. Whereas the West tends to see corporate governance as a means of controlling and regulating companies, China uses it flexibly to benefit the economy, in the interests of the people and the party. A new chapter expands the focus on the governance of corporate entities other than listed companies, which was the focus of all the early corporate governance codes.

When the first edition was published, it was widely assumed that globalization and the free movement of executives, money, goods, and services was the way of the future. Today that is not so clear. In previous editions, one definition of corporate governance was about the way power is exercised over corporate entities in society. But in many Western countries the power and privileges enjoyed by elites, in politics, finance, and business, are being challenged. This so-called 'populism' led to the election of President Trump in the United States and the British referendum decision to leave the European Union. The effect is also being felt in boardrooms, as increasingly active institutional shareholders, and an investigative media, challenge the governance of companies.

Confidence in international organizations such as the United Nations, the European Union, the World Bank, and the International Monetary Fund has diminished. International trade agreements have been threatened. For nearly forty years, corporate governance has evolved under the belief that free trade, globalization, and the resultant multinational companies were desirable. Such assumptions have been challenged. The continuing influence of corporate governance, rooted in Western institutions, influence, and values, can no longer be assumed. Other countries and cultures now have the potential to contribute to corporate governance thinking and practice.

Some striking changes to the governance of international companies have occurred during the decade since this book was first published. Sovereign funds from countries that include some Arab oil states, China, Singapore, and Sweden have acquired significant stakes in some multinational companies. Mergers and acquisitions across national boundaries have seen the ownership and the governance of major companies pass to other jurisdictions. British Airways, for example, is now a subsidiary of a Spanish company. Some American companies have moved their domicile overseas as part of their international tax planning strategy, sometimes by reversing into an overseas company they acquired. Such changes realign the way companies are governed around the world.

This edition maintains an international perspective on the governance of public listed companies, subsidiary companies in corporate groups, family firms, public bodies, and many other types of corporate entity that need to be governed as well as managed.

Many of the older cases have been replaced for this edition, although a few of the stalwarts remain, now noted as 'classic corporate governance cases'. The international spread of cases has been maintained, with many from the USA, the UK, and the rest of the world, including some new cases about corporate governance in China.

Self-test questions are still included at the end of each chapter to reinforce the learning process, but in this edition the answers are included in the online resources.

It is nearly fifty years since I began my studies of what I subsequently called corporate governance. Its focus, practices, and significance have changed beyond belief. I hope that readers will continue working to improve the governance of the organizations with which they are involved, and that some will contribute to the further development of this fascinating and vital subject.

Bob Tricker
Devon, UK, 2019

Acknowledgements

I owe a considerable debt to the many colleagues, researchers, students, regulators, and company directors and chairmen who, over the years, have contributed to my knowledge and understanding of corporate governance. Gratitude is clearly owed to the directors of the ten organizations who supported my original research in the Corporate Policy Group at Nuffield College, Oxford, from 1979 to 1983, which led to the publication of *Corporate Governance* in 1984.

Since the publication of the third edition of this book, I have been working closely with Dr Gregg Li from Hong Kong on *Understanding Corporate Governance in China* (Hong Kong University Press, 2018). His research in mainland China has greatly increased my knowledge, which is reflected in new material in this edition.

Kate Gilks, my editor, and her colleagues at the Oxford University Press have been a constant source of support, and the anonymous reviewers made suggestions that significantly improved the book. I am grateful to them all. The opportunity to draw material from the websites of companies, regulators, and other institutions is also much appreciated.

Chapter 1 has been adapted by permission of the publishers from *Corporate Governance*, seminal readings in the History of Management Thought series, R. I. Tricker (ed.), Ashgate, Aldershot, UK, and Burlington, Vermont, USA, 2000.

Figures (2.1, 2.5, 2.6, 2.7, 2.8, 2.9, and 13.1) and case studies (Tyco and Robert Maxwell) are based on material that first appeared in *The Economist Essential Director*, by Bob Tricker, Profile Books, London, 2003, and reproduced with kind permission. I also acknowledge the approval of Routledge to include some new cases, which appeared in Bob and Gretchen Tricker, *Business Ethics—a stakeholder, risk, and governance approach* (2014). The Tencent Holdings, Yum China Holdings, and Alibaba case studies and Chapter 13 were adapted from material written by the author for Tricker and Li, *Understanding Corporate Governance in China*, Hong Kong University Press, 2018.

Finally, thanks to my late wife, Gretchen, not only, as so many authors say, for her support during the writing, but for her direct contribution. Being an editor and writer herself, among other things she wrote the centennial history of the Hong Kong Stock Exchange; she undoubtedly added significantly to this edition.

Bob Tricker, 2019

Contents

PART 3 **Practices**

List of case studies

Case studies

Corporate Governance in Action

List of abbreviations

AGM	annual general meeting
AIM	(London) Alternative Investment Market
ALI	American Law Institute
ASX	Australian Securities Exchange
BBA	British Bankers' Association
CACG	Commonwealth Association for Corporate Governance
CalPERS	Californian State Employees' Pension Fund
CDO	collateralized debt obligations (pools of bonds backed by bundles of mortgages)
CEO	chief executive officer
CFO	chief financial officer
CFTC	(US) Commodity Futures Trading Commission
CIC	(UK) community interest company
CII	(US) Council of Institutional Investors
CIPFA	(UK) Chartered Institute of Public Finance and Accounting
CNED	connected non-executive director (also called 'affiliate non-executive director')
COO	chief operating officer
COSO	(US) Committee of Sponsoring Organizations of the Treadway Commission
CRO	chief risk officer
CSIA	Corporate Secretaries International Association
CSR	corporate social responsibility
CSRC	China Securities Regulatory Commission of the State Council
D&O	directors' and officers' liability insurance
EEA	European Economic Area (EU countries plus Iceland, Liechtenstein, and Norway)
EEC	European Economic Community (later European Union)
EFRAG	European Financial Reporting Advisory Group
EGM	extraordinary general meeting
ERM(S)	enterprise risk management (system)
ESG	environmental, social and governance (reporting)
ESV	enlightened shareholder value
EU	European Union
Fannie Mae	(US) Federal National Mortgage Association

FCA	(UK) Financial Conduct Authority
FRC	(UK) Financial Reporting Council
Freddie Mac	(US) Federal Home Loan Mortgage Corporation
GAAP	generally accepted accounting principles
GAAS	generally accepted auditing standards
GEM	(Hong Kong) Growth Enterprise Market
GRI	Global Reporting Initiative
HKICPA	Hong Kong Institute of Certified Public Accountants
IASC	International Accounting Standards Committee
ICGN	International Corporate Governance Network
ICSA	(UK) Institute of Chartered Secretaries and Administrators
IFC	International Finance Corporation
IFRS	International Financial Reporting Standards
IOSCO	International Organization of Securities Commissions
INED	independent non-executive director
IPAC	International Auditing Practices Committee
IPO	initial public offering (of shares)
ISO	International Standards Organization
IT	information technology
LBS	London Business School
LIBOR	London Interbank Offer Rate (on inter-bank loans)
MMS	(US) Minerals Management Service
NACD	(US) National Association of Corporate Directors
NASDAQ	(US) National Association of Securities Dealers Automated Quotations (also Nasdaq Composite Index)
NED	non-executive director
NGO	non-governmental organization
NHS	(UK) National Health Service
NYSE	New York Stock Exchange
NYX	NYSE Euronext
OECD	Organisation for Economic Co-operation and Development
PCAOB	(US) Public Company Accounting Oversight Board
PLA	(Chinese) People's Liberation Army
PRA	(UK) Prudential Regulation Authority, banking regulator
PRC	People's Republic of China
PwC	PriceWaterhouseCoopers
quango	quasi-autonomous non-governmental organization; (UK and Australia) quasi-autonomous national governmental organization
R&D	research and development

ROI	return on investment
ROSC	(World Bank/IMF) Reports on the Observance of Standards and Codes
SAR	(Hong Kong) Special Administrative Region (of China)
Sarbox	see SOX
SASAC	(China) State-owned Assets Supervision and Administration Commission of the State Council
SE	*Societas Europaea*
SEBI	Securities and Exchange Board of India
SEC	(US) Securities and Exchange Commission
SFC	(Hong Kong) Securities and Futures Commission
SME	small and medium-sized enterprises
SOE	state-owned enterprises
SOX	(US) Sarbanes-Oxley Act of 2002
SPE	special purpose entity
SWF	sovereign wealth fund
SWOT	strengths, weaknesses, opportunities, threats (analysis)
TEPCO	Tokyo Electric Power Company
UNEP FI	United Nations Environment Programme Finance Initiative
WBCSD	World Business Council for Sustainable Development
WEF	World Economic Forum
XBRL	eXtensible Business Reporting Language

Guide to the book

 Learning Outcomes

This chapter enables us to:

- Acknowledge that *all* corporate entities need governing.
- Realize how corporate governance has evolved.
- Appreciate the significance of the invention of the limited-liability co
- Realize the cultural component of corporate governance.
- Recognize recent developments and current frontiers of the subject.

Learning outcomes

Introducing you to every chapter, learning outcomes list the main concepts and themes covered in each chapter to help you clearly identify what you can expect to learn. They can also be used to review your learning and effectively plan your revision.

Corporate Governance in Action 2.1 The role of the US S and XBRL reporting

The SEC was created following the Great Crash of 1929. Previously, there had b federal involvement in corporate matters. During the 1920s, over 20 million sha make their fortunes on the stock market. Of around US$50 million in new secur worthless. Countless fortunes were lost. Many banks failed. Depression followe markets collapsed.

Corporate governance in action

These are real-life examples of codes, policies, and statements from companies around the world which help to illustrate the ideas discussed in the text. They will prompt you to analyse how organizations apply these ideas in practice.

Case studies

 Case study 2.1 Sir Philip Green and the collapse

Sir Philip Green

Green is a flamboyant and confrontational billionaire. Many reporters have temper. He is not one to give interviews. So he was unlikely to provide inforr

Case studies

Longer case studies are at the end of each chapter and they explore a variety of contemporary issues in a range of organizations. They are accompanied by discussion questions which will help you apply corporate governance principles to real-world business scenarios, and reinforce your learning. Over half of the case studies are brand new for this edition!

Self-test questions

To confirm your grasp of the key points in this chapter, try answering t

1. Why does a corporate entity need a constitution?
2. What is the principal difference between a private and a public cor
3. Explain the difference between governance and management.
4. What are the two aspects of the board's work that can provide a para
5. Describe the scope of corporate governance.

Self-test questions

Check your progress and test your knowledge with the end of chapter self-test questions. You can also visit the online resources to read suggested answers.

Projects and exercises

1. The European Union has passed legislation permitting the incorpor company' transcending the borders of its member states. Would it companies were able to be incorporated in the United States at the
2. Chart the governance and management structure of a corporate en familiar, using the circle and triangle schematic. Academic, sporting could be covered, as well as public or private companies. Does the the potential to exercise power in that organization?

Projects and exercises

Develop your analytical and research skills by completing the projects and exercises at the end of each chapter. These exercises are varied in nature and designed to help you reflect on key issues and think in practical terms.

References and further reading

Blair, Margaret (1995) *Ownership and Control: Rethinking Corporate Governance for the Twenty-First Century.* The Brookings Institute, Washington DC.

Cadbury, Sir Adrian (1992) The Financial Aspects of Corporate Governance: A report of the committee on corporate governance. Gee & Co., London.

Clarke, T. (2004) *Theories of Corporate Governance.*

Demb, Ada and Frederic *Corporate Board: Con* University Press, New

Financial Conduct Autho independently togeth about diversity', speed 30 October. Available speeches/art-thinking

References and further reading

Full references to sources used in the chapter are provided at the end of each chapter, allowing you to read in more detail or aid your research.

Guide to the online resources

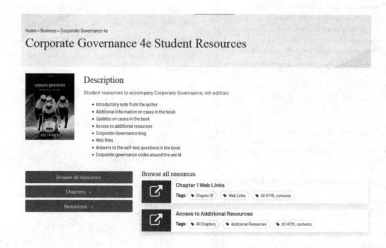

Supporting content for both students and registered lecturers of the book is available in the online resources. Students can find additional information and updates on the cases in the book or explore the subject further with new web links to additional content. Lecturers can download additional case studies, PowerPoint slides, group activities, and access teaching notes for the case studies for use in their teaching.

There is also a link to the **Corporate Governance blog**, regularly updated by Bob Tricker and Chris Mallin, offering comment on current events in the world of business, economics, and finance, from the perspective of corporate governance.

Visit **www.oup.com/uk/tricker4e/** to find out more.

Introduction

What the book is about

This book will enable readers to:

- appreciate the nature, functions, and realities of boards of directors and other governing bodies;
- analyse board structures, systems, and procedures, including board committees, chairmen and chief executives, board remuneration, board leadership, and board effectiveness;
- understand major aspects of corporate governance, including:
  - corporate governance principles and codes of practice;
  - the board's performance roles: strategy formulation and policy-making;
  - the board's conformance roles: executive supervision and accountability;
  - the board's responsibility for handling corporate risk:
    - o the significance of board-level cultures and the leadership role of the board chair;
  - assessment of board and director performance;
  - corporate governance rating systems;
- understand various theories of corporate governance;
- appreciate corporate governance processes around the world, including:
  - recognizing the significance of national cultures in corporate governance practices:
    - o adopting an international and comparative perspective on the subject;
- recognize the issues that are influencing corporate governance and board thinking, including strategic risk management, cyber risk, corporate social responsibility, sustainability, board diversity, and business ethics;
- consider the future direction of corporate governance around the world and the drivers of change.

How to use the book

The textbook provides the basis for understanding the subject. The boxed material provides further illustration and examples. Case studies, at the end of each chapter, tell stories to illustrate issues in that chapter. Considering and, where possible, discussing, the cases reinforces the learning. More case studies and supportive material can be found in the online resources.[1]

The internet now holds a vast amount of information about corporate governance. All listed companies have websites, most with extensive material on their corporate governance and investor relations. Regulators and professional bodies provide relevant information and there are a number of useful sites devoted specifically to corporate governance matters. The text references many websites to supplement the book. Because the addresses of many sites are long, it is easy to make mistakes. So a list of addresses is provided in the students' materials associated with the book, to 'cut and paste'. Each chapter has a set of self-test questions (with answers in the online resources) to enable readers to check what they have learned.

Experience has shown that the book has been used in various graduate, undergraduate, and professional courses and as a set text for professional examinations.

The basis of the book

The book is based on material that the author has developed over the years for directors' courses at the Institutes of Directors in London and Sydney, the MBA programme at the Australian Graduate School of Management, executive Masters at Hong Kong University, Melbourne University, Hong Kong Baptist University, and an open-learning course for Hong Kong Open University, as well as corporate governance courses for Russian university teachers sponsored by the Canadian Government at the Schulich School of Business in Toronto. Subsequently, I have continued to write regularly for the Oxford University Press Corporate Governance blog, which I share with Professor Christine Mallin. Most recently, I have been working on corporate governance in China with my colleague Dr Gregg Li.

My interest in boards and their behaviour was really kindled, however, in the 1970s, when I was head of the Oxford Centre for Management Studies, subsequently to become Templeton College, and then part of the Saïd Business School, Oxford. The Management Centre was incorporated as a company limited by guarantee and its large governing council comprised heads of Oxford colleges and leaders of major British companies. Council members outnumbered the academic staff. Its divisive cliques, political power plays, and unpredictable interpersonal relations astounded me. This was not the behaviour of the classical organization theories, analytical decision-making, and basic management concepts that we were teaching in the Management Centre.

It occurred to me that governance was different from management. Throughout the 20th century, the focus had been on management. But where was the board on the management

---

[1] More material, including the OUP Corporate Governance blog, can be found on my own website: www.BobTricker.com

organization chart? Clearly, the governance of corporate entities and the processes of their governing bodies was a subject that deserved study. The subsequent opportunity to research at Nuffield College, Oxford, led to the book *Corporate Governance*, published in 1984.[2] I remember agonizing over the term 'corporate governance' in the title. Although 'governance' was an ancient concept, *corporate* governance was not a phrase then in use. Indeed, I had named the trust that funded my research at Nuffield College the Corporate *Policy* Group, not the Corporate *Governance* Group. However, the book did introduce the subject and the phrase 'corporate governance'. It identified some issues that remain pertinent to this day: the structure of boards; the role of independent non-executive directors; the governance of complex groups; the board's supervision of management; accountability; corporate regulation; and corporate social responsibility. In those days, board-level participation by employees was also an important topic.

Subsequently, of course, the subject has moved centre stage. Indeed, it may be that the 21st century has become the era of corporate governance, just as the 20th century had been that of management.

---

[2] Latest edition: *Corporate Governance*, seminal readings in the History of Management Thought series, R. I. Tricker (ed.), Ashgate, Aldershot, UK, and Burlington, Vermont, USA, 2000.

Part 1

Principles

Corporate Governance: A Frontier Subject

 Learning Outcomes

This chapter enables us to:

- Acknowledge that *all* corporate entities need governing.
- Realize how corporate governance has evolved.
- Appreciate the significance of the invention of the limited-liability company.
- Realize the cultural component of corporate governance.
- Recognize recent developments and current frontiers of the subject.

All corporate entities need governing

The 20th century saw massive growth in serious management thought. Organization theories acquired new significance, although the board of directors seldom appeared on company organization charts. Strategic management made great strides, but the contribution of company directors was seldom mentioned. Important theories and practices were developed for the management of finance, marketing, and operations, although little concern was shown for the role of the board of directors. This was the era of management: management theories, management consultants, management gurus, and management teaching. The preoccupation was with management.

However, if management was the focal point for the 20th century, corporate governance has become the primary focus in the 21st. Most advanced and emerging economies have introduced corporate governance codes. Many have updated company law. In the United States, following the Enron debacle,[1] stringent new law was enacted to control corporate behaviour, reporting, and audit. The global financial crisis starting in 2007 added further strands to corporate governance policy and practice.

All corporate entities need to be governed. That includes profit-orientated companies, both public and private, joint ventures, cooperatives, partnerships, and not-for-profit organizations such as community organizations, charities, and academic institutions, as well as governmental corporate entities and quangos.[2] All need a governing body, whatever it may be called. For most companies this is their board of directors. Other corporate entities may call their governing body a council, a court, a committee, a board of governors, or, in the case of some Oxford colleges, simply the governing body. To avoid repetition, from now on we will

---

[1] See Case study 1.2.
[2] QUANGO—an acronym for quasi-autonomous non-governmental organization.

refer to all governing bodies as 'boards' and their members as 'directors', since many of the essential principles and practices apply, whatever names are used.

Essentially, corporate governance is about the way power is exercised over corporate entities. It covers the activities of the board and its relationships with those managing the enterprise, and with the shareholders or members, as well as with the external auditors, regulators, and other legitimate stakeholders.

Corporate governance is different from management. Executive management is responsible for running the enterprise, but the governing body ensures that it is running in the right direction and being run well. Directors are so called because they are responsible for setting the organization's direction, formulating strategy, and policy-making. Further, the board is responsible for supervising management and being accountable. Overall, the board is responsible for their organization's decisions and its performance.

Corporate governance is old, only the phrase is new

The idea of governance at the level of national government is ancient. Chaucer (c.1343–1400), the English writer, philosopher, and courtier, used the word, although he could not decide how it should be spelt ('gouernance', 'governaunce'). But the phrase *corporate governance* did not come into use until the 1980s. However, it was quickly adopted worldwide. In 1988, Cochran and Wartick published an annotated bibliography of corporate governance publications; it had 74 pages. Today, Google accesses over 64 million references to corporate governance. Research into corporate governance also began to develop in the late 1980s. The research journal *Corporate Governance—An International Review* was founded in 1992.

Yet, although the theoretical exploration of the subject is relatively new, the practice of corporate governance is as old as trade. Shakespeare (1564–1616) understood the problem. In his play *The Merchant of Venice*, Antonio the merchant agonized as he watched his ships sail out of sight, with his fortune entrusted to others. Whenever a principal has to rely on agents to handle their business, governance issues arise. This agency issue has long been recognized and is a central challenge in the running and regulating of modern enterprises. With a sole trader or in a small family firm, there is seldom any real separation between management and governance; changes in strategic direction merge with the day-to-day running.

In this chapter, we trace the evolution of corporate governance ideas and practices over the years from the governance of merchant ventures, through companies set up by trading empires, to the brilliant invention of the limited-liability company in the 19th century, which opened the door to the burgeoning ambiguity, complexity, and rapid changes in corporate governance today. The underlying ideas and concepts of corporate governance have been slow to evolve, with the underpinning legal frameworks still owing more to mid-19th-century thinking than to the realities of complex modern business. We shall see how changes are often responses to critical situations rather than developments in theory. We shall also see how national cultures play a dominant role in corporate governance in different countries.

The early days: merchants and monopolists

In medieval Europe, craft guilds for each trade, such as weavers, tailors, and wheelwrights, enforced standards, regulated prices, and controlled training and entry to their trade. Guilds were incorporated through legal processes, usually a charter, by cities and states. Only masters of the trade could be members of the guild and only guild members could practise that trade. Guild members elected the guild's governing body.

By the 17th century, economic, political, and military competition was growing between the empires of Britain, Holland, Portugal, and Spain. Companies, created by charter from the monarch or the state, pursued trading interests under rules set in the charter. In 1600, England's Queen Elizabeth I granted a royal charter to the East India Company, giving it a monopoly over all trade between England and Asia. The company was a joint-stock company, with over 1,000 stockholders, who elected a governing board of 24 directors each year. The company traded principally with India and China in cotton, silk, tea, and opium, at one time administering parts of the British Indian Empire with a private army. The Hudson Bay Company received its royal charter in 1670, when Prince Rupert, cousin of King Charles II, saw the opportunities for fur trading in the Hudson Bay area of what is now Canada.

As we shall see, the story of corporate governance has many over-ambitious and dominant business people with unrealistic expectations, leading to corporate collapse and, sometimes, fraud. The South Sea Company was incorporated in 1711, to trade with Spain's South American colonies, mainly in slaves. In 1718, King George I of England became governor of the company, bringing prestige and confidence. Then, Adam Smith (1723–1790), a moral philosopher at the University of Glasgow, argued that society benefits when individuals pursue their own self-interest, because the free market then produces the goods and services needed at low prices. He is considered by many to be the father of modern economics.[3] But he was suspicious of businessmen, as many academics are to this day. His oft-quoted comment on their behaviour offers a classic corporate governance perspective:

> The directors of companies, being the managers of other people's money rather than their own, cannot well be expected to watch over it with the same anxious vigilance with which (they) watch over their own.

(Smith, 1776)

The invention of the limited-liability company

At the start of the 19th century, apart from corporations created by the crown or the state, there were basically three ways in which people could engage in business: as a sole trader, in a partnership, or as an unincorporated body in which some managed the firm while sleeping partners just provided finance. In each case, if the business became insolvent, the creditors could pursue their debts with any and all of the owners until ultimately they became bankrupt. In those days, not paying your debts was a crime leading to debtors' prison, with the possibility of your wife and children being sent to the parish workhouse. This was quite

[3] Adam Smith ([1776] 1976) *The Wealth of Nations*, revised edn, George J. Stigler (ed.), University of Chicago Press, Chicago.

a disincentive to invest unless people were directly involved in the management activities. But this was a period of great economic growth, generated by the industrial revolution. Firms needed external capital to expand faster than ploughed-back profits would allow. Moreover, the emerging middle classes had funds available.

The French were the first to create a form of corporate incorporation, which restricted shareholders' liability for corporate debts. From 1807, the *Société en commandité par actions* limited the liability of external investors. However, executive directors, who managed the enterprise, still remained personally exposed to their companies' debts. Meanwhile, in Britain, the need for companies to access capital without exposing external investors to the threat of bankruptcy was debated in Parliament. Some members of Parliament called for a form of incorporation that mirrored the French system. But in the event, the British Companies Acts of 1855 and 1862 gave limited liability to *all* shareholders, whether they were involved in the management of the company or not.

The joint-stock, limited-liability company proved to be one of the finest systems ever designed. The key concept was the incorporation of a legal entity, separate from the owners, which nevertheless had many of the legal property rights of a real person—to contract, to sue and be sued, to own property, and to employ. Yet the shareholders were no longer responsible for the company's debts. The company had a life of its own, giving continuity beyond the life of its founders, who could transfer their shares in the company. Nevertheless, ownership remained the basis of power. Shareholders elected their directors, who owed a stewardship duty and reported to them. The concept of ownership and shareholder rights still underpins modern company law, although the reality of power over many large companies is now very different.

During the late 19th century, some states in the United States passed legislation allowing the incorporation of companies. In New York, Wall Street financial institutions financed and handled the shares of companies formed to build railways and to develop industry in the growth years that followed the American Civil War (1861–5). But legislators were suspicious of limiting shareholders' responsibility for their companies' debts. Moreover, the objectives of each company and its life span had to be defined, and one company could not own another. The industrial age brought great wealth to some American companies and their owners.

Subsequently, state constitutions were amended and laws rewritten to be more amenable to these powerful companies. Shareholder limited liability was introduced. Charter battles were fought to allow conglomerates, in which companies owned other companies. Eventually, corporate charters no longer limited the range of companies' activities and their life spans. To this day, companies in the United States are incorporated at the state not the federal level.

The concept of the limited-liability company spread throughout the British Empire of the late 19th century. The company laws of Australia, Canada, some Caribbean islands that are now tax havens, India, Malaysia, New Zealand, Singapore, South Africa, and other African countries still reflect those origins, although they have subsequently evolved to reflect changing local circumstances. However, in many cases Commonwealth case law can provide precedents. Hong Kong, while now a special administrative region of China, still retains its British-orientated company law and legal system, although the right of final appeal has passed from London to Beijing.

The notion of the limited-liability company was simple and successful, leading to huge industrial growth around the world, and the creation of untold employment and wealth.

Unfortunately, the simplicity of the mid-19th-century model now bears about as much relationship to reality as a hang-glider does to a fleet of jumbo-jets. Nevertheless, the original corporate concept remains the essential basis of contemporary company law.

Initially, all joint-stock, limited-liability companies were public companies—that is, they could invite the public to subscribe for their shares. Their main purpose was to raise capital from the public, who would not be responsible for their company's debts. By the early 20th century, however, business people saw that the model could be used to give limited liability to family firms and other private businesses, even though they did not need access to capital from outside investors. Such private companies, incorporated in jurisdictions around the world, now far outnumber public companies, which can invite the public to subscribe for their shares.

The separation of ownership from operations

In the early days, limited-liability companies were relatively small and uncomplicated. Shareholders were drawn from the wealthier classes and could attend or be represented in annual general meetings of the company. They were relatively close to the companies in which they had invested. In those days, there were no chains of financial institutions, pension funds, hedge funds, brokers, or agents between investors and the boardroom.

But by the early years of the 20th century things were changing. In the United States, the United Kingdom, and other economically advancing countries, many companies had become large and complex. Their shareholders were now numerous, geographically widespread, and differed in both their time horizons and their expectations about dividends and capital growth. Shares in most public companies were now listed on stock exchanges. Chains of financial institutions and other intermediaries stood between companies and the votes of their shareholders in company meetings. Links between management and investors in their companies were becoming distant.

Using data from companies in the United States, Berle and Means (1932) drew attention to the growing separation of power between the executive management of major public companies and their increasingly diverse and remote shareholders. They realized the significance of corporate power, observing that:

> [t]he rise of the modern corporation has brought a concentration of economic power which can compete on equal terms with the modern state—economic power *versus* political power, each strong in its own field. The state seeks in some aspects to regulate the corporation, while the corporation, steadily becoming more powerful, makes every effort to avoid such regulation ... The future may see the economic organism, now typified by the corporation, not only on an equal plane with the state, but possibly even superseding it as the dominant form of social organization.

> (Berle and Means, 1932, revised edn 1967)

This was a seminal work of corporate governance (although that was not a phrase Berle and Means used). The recognition of issues they had raised was instrumental in the creation of the US Securities and Exchange Commission (SEC). Berle and Means left a vital intellectual inheritance for corporate governance: it is surprising that it took so long before it was taken up.

For the next 40 years, the work of directors and boards remained the province of jurisprudence, enlivened with anecdote and exhortation. In 1971, a pioneering work by Mace, based on research in US companies, sought to discover what directors really did and, in the process, challenged the conventional wisdom:

> In most companies, boards of directors serve as a source of advice and counsel, serve as some sort of discipline, and act in crisis situations if the president dies suddenly or is asked to resign because of unsatisfactory management performance.
>
> The business literature describing the classical functions of boards of directors typically includes three important roles: (1) establishing basic objectives, corporate strategies, and board policies; (2) asking discerning questions; and (3) selecting the president.
>
> (Instead) I found that boards of directors of most large and medium-sized companies do not establish objectives, strategies, and policies however defined. These roles are performed by company management. Presidents and outside directors generally agreed that only management can and should have these responsibilities.
>
> A second classical role assigned to boards of directors is that of asking discerning questions—inside and outside the board meetings. Again it was found that directors do not, in fact, do this. Board meetings are not regarded as proper forums for discussions arising out of questions asked by board members.
>
> A third classical role usually regarded as a responsibility of the board of directors is the selection of the president. Yet it was found that in most companies directors do not in fact select the president, except in ... crisis situations ...

(Mace, 1971)

Developments in the 1970s: audit committees, and two-tier boards

Two significant developments occurred in corporate governance thinking in the 1970s. In 1972, in the United States, the SEC required listed companies to create audit committees, as standing committees of the main board comprising independent outside directors. These audit committees were to provide a bridge between the external auditor and the main board, ensuring that directors were made aware of any issues that had arisen between the auditor and the company's finance department.

An increasingly litigious climate in the United States, with shareholders of failed companies seeking recompense from directors, boards, and, in particular, auditors (whose indemnity insurance was seen to provide a 'deep pocket' to be emptied for shareholders' benefit), led to more emphasis on checks and balances at board level. Auerbach (1973) wrote of the audit committee as a new corporate institution. Mautz and Neumann (1970, 1977) discussed the practicalities of audit committees. In the UK, Tricker (1978) undertook a study of British board structures, membership, and processes, intending to advocate audit committees in the UK, but concluded that, although many listed-company boards did have non-executive directors, the concept of director independence was not understood in Britain. Sir Brandon Rhys-Williams, a member of the British Parliament, also called for non-executive directors and audit committees in the UK, a proposal that led to a green paper *The Conduct of Company Directors* (1977) and a Parliamentary bill calling for audit committees, which ultimately failed.

The European Economic Community (EEC)[4] issued a series of draft directives on the harmonization of company law throughout the member states. The EEC draft fifth directive (1972) proposed that unitary boards, in which both executive and outside directors were responsible for seeing that the business was being run well and in the right direction, be replaced by the two-tier board form of governance practised in Germany and Holland. In this form of governance, companies have two distinct boards, with no common membership. The upper, supervisory board monitors and oversees the work of the executive or management board, which runs the business. The supervisory board has the power to hire and fire the members of the executive board.

The idea of the two-tier board was not well received in Britain—partly because it would replace the unitary board, which was seen, at least by directors, as a viable system of governance. Moreover, in addition to the separation of powers, the directive included co-determination ideas then practised in Germany, in which the company was seen as a social partnership between capital and labour with the supervisory board made up of equal numbers of representatives of the shareholders and employees. The UK's response was the report of the Committee chaired by Lord Bullock. *The Report of the Committee of Inquiry on Industrial Democracy (1977)* and the research papers (1976) associated with it reflected the first serious corporate governance study in Britain. The Committee's proposal, for a continuation of the unitary board, but with some directors representing the employees, was not well received in Britain's boardrooms either.

The 1970s also saw a questioning of the role of the major corporation in society. Broadly, the argument was made that public companies have responsibilities beyond their prime legal duty to their shareholders. Given the scale and significance of such companies, boards should report and, some argued, be accountable to a range of stakeholders who could be affected by board decisions—customers, suppliers, and others in the added-value chain, employees, the local community, and the state. In the United States, there was an important dialogue between the American Bar Association, looking for an alternative basis of power over companies, and the Corporate Roundtable representing directors' convictions of the value of the existing model. Consumer advocate Ralph Nader offered a specification for a model corporation rooted in stakeholder thinking. Jensen and Meckling (1976), whose work was subsequently to become crucial to the development of agency theory, asked whether the original concept of the company could survive.

The debate was picked up in the UK. A committee of the Confederation of British Industry, chaired by Lord Watkinson (1973), reported on the wider responsibilities of the British public company. A report by Fogarty (1975) discussed companies' responsibilities and stakeholder participation. The Accounting Standards Steering Committee produced *The Corporate Report* (1975), which called for all economic entities to report publicly and accept accountability to all those whose interests were affected by the directors' decisions. The political implications of these proposals for the widening of accountability and control over companies, and the related erosion of managerial power, soon consigned this report to the archives.

Meanwhile, a number of corporate governance problems featured in the reports of inspectors appointed by the UK government Department of Trade. The inspectors at Pergamon

---

[4] Subsequently renamed the European Union.

Press (1971) concluded that owner Robert Maxwell should not again run a public company—advice that was subsequently ignored, enabling him to build a media empire that collapsed dramatically 20 years later.[5] Other inquires, which examined board-level problems at Rolls Royce (1973), London and County Securities (1976), Lonrho Ltd (1976), and others, all added to the interest in the way companies were governed, although commentators still spoke of the way they were managed.

Developments in the 1980s: more corporate collapses

In the 1980s, broader stakeholder concerns became overshadowed by the market-driven, growth-orientated attitudes of Reaganite and Thatcherite economics. Directors' responsibility to increase shareholder value was reinforced. The profit performance model became the basis for the privatization of state-run entities—rail, coal, electricity, gas, and water enterprises were all privatized in the UK and, gradually, around the world. The threat of predator takeover bids (the market for control) was presented in Anglo-American circles as an essential incentive for strong board-level performance. Hostile bids, at this time, were often financed through the newly available high-risk, high-rate 'junk' bonds.

By the late 1980s, the downside of such thinking was becoming apparent. In the United States, the names Ivan Boesky, Michael Levine, and Michael Milken were to go down in the annals of corporate governance with the massive, junk-bond-financed, insider information deals through Drexel, Burnham, and Lambert. In Australia, the names Alan Bond, Laurie Connell of Rothwells, and the Girvan Corporation were being associated with questionable governance practices. In Japan, Nomura Securities was accused of having too close links with its regulator, having offered well-paid sinecures to senior bureaucrats on retirement (called *amakudari*—literally 'descent from heaven'). Lavish payouts to major institutional clients to cover losses and links with a *yakuza* underworld syndicate were also alleged.

In Australia, a 1989 report from the National Companies and Securities Commission on the collapse of Rothwells Ltd, a listed financial institution,[6] commented that 'at no time did the board of Rothwells perform its duties satisfactorily'. The company was dominated by an entrepreneurial figure, Laurie Connell, who expanded the company with acquisitions providing loans to many companies on the second board of the Western Australia Stock Exchange.

In the UK, it was the Guinness case and, subsequently, the collapse of Robert Maxwell's companies.[7] Boards dominated by powerful executive directors were now seen to need checks and balances, particularly where the posts of chief executive and chair of the board were combined and the outside directors were weak. The concepts of corporate governance were at last to become the focus of attention; indeed, the phrase itself was about to appear.

In the mid-1980s, research into governance issues expanded: for example, Baysinger and Butler (1985), using the phrase 'corporate governance', looked at the effects on corporate performance of changes in board composition, and Mintzberg (1984) posed the question 'who should control the corporation?' But the subject came centre stage less as the result of academic, research-based deliberations, and more as a result of official inquiries set up in

[5] See Case study 1.1.
[6] National Companies and Securities Commission is now the Australian Securities Commission.
[7] See Case study 1.1.

response to the corporate collapses, perceived board-level excesses, and apparently domi-nant chief executives.

In the United States, boards and their directors were coming under pressure. Institutional investors became increasingly proactive, demanding more strategic information and better corporate performance. Drucker (1991) drew attention to the potential governance power in shareholders' proxy votes. Companies needed to influence their share prices and to tap the ever-increasing pension funding and savings around the world. Expectations of institutional investors for performance improvement grew, along with pressure to end corporate govern-ance practices that benefited incumbent boards and reduced the probability of the company being subjected to hostile bid. Investigative media and the threat of litigation added to the pressure on directors. The directors of American Express, General Motors, and IBM all had cause to regret the power of institutional fund managers to vote their shares against incum-bent members of boards whom they considered to be performing badly.

The US Treadway Commission had been formed in 1985, to consider fraudulent corporate financial reporting. Its first report (1987) led to the creation of the Committee of Sponsoring Organizations of the Treadway Commission (COSO),[8] a private sector initiative to encourage executive management and boards towards more effective business activities.

Developments in the 1990s: voluntary codes or regulations

In the 1990s, corporate governance codes arrived. The first was the UK's Cadbury Report (1992), produced by a committee chaired by Sir Adrian Cadbury, on the financial aspects of corporate governance. Based on what was considered good practice, the code was addressed to the governance of public, listed companies.

The code called for:

- the wider use of independent non-executive directors, with 'independence' defined as being 'independent of management and free from any business or other relationship which could materially interfere with the exercise of independent judgement, apart from their fees and shareholding';

- the introduction of an audit committee of the board with independent members;

- the division of responsibilities between the chair of the board and the chief executive, or, if the roles were combined, strong independent directors;

- the use of a remuneration committee of the board to oversee executive rewards;

- the introduction of a nomination committee with independent directors to propose new board members.

---

[8] Originally formed to sponsor the National Commission on Fraudulent Financial Reporting, the Committee of Sponsoring Organizations (COSO) of the Treadway Commission is a voluntary, private sector organization dedicated to guiding executive management and governance participants towards the establishment of more effective, efficient, and ethical business operations on a global basis. It sponsors and disseminates frameworks and guidance based on in-depth research, analysis, and best practices. The following organizations take part:
The Institute of Management Accountants;
The American Institute of Certified Public Accountants;
The Institute of Internal Auditors; and
The Financial Executives International.

The Cadbury corporate governance code was voluntary; companies did not have to follow it. But they were required to report publicly that they had complied with the code or, if they had not, to explain why. The only sanction the Report proposed was the threat of a delisting from the stock exchange.

Some critics of the Cadbury Report argued that it went too far—'the emphasis on the importance of non-executive directors would introduce the controls of the European two-tier supervisory board by the back door,' they said. Others felt that the report did not go far enough—it lacked teeth by proposing delisting for defaulters rather than legally enforceable sanctions.

In the United States, companies must follow the company law of the state in which they are incorporated, and comply with US generally accepted accounting principles (GAAP). In addition, companies must meet the demands of the SEC, and the rules of any stock exchange if their shares are listed.

In 1997, the US Business Roundtable, which takes a pro-business perspective, produced a Statement on Corporate Governance, which was updated in 2002, listing the following guiding principles of sound corporate governance:

- the paramount duty of the board of directors of a public corporation is to select a chief executive officer (CEO) and to oversee the CEO and other senior management in the competent and ethical operation of the corporation on a day-to-day basis;
- it is the responsibility of management to operate the corporation in an effective and ethical manner in order to produce value for stockholders;
- it is the responsibility of management, under the oversight of the board and its audit committee, to produce financial statements that fairly present the financial condition and results of operations of the corporation;
- it is the responsibility of the board and its audit committee to engage an independent accounting firm to audit the financial statements prepared by management and to issue an opinion on those statements based on GAAP;
- it is the responsibility of the independent accounting firm to ensure that it is in fact independent, is without conflicts of interest, employs highly competent staff, and carries out its work in accordance with generally accepted auditing standards (GAAS);
- the corporation has a responsibility to deal with its employees in a fair and equitable manner.

But corporate governance in the United States tends to be based on mandatory compliance with regulation and law,[9] rather than the discretionary 'comply or explain' approach of voluntary codes elsewhere.

The Cadbury Report was significant in influencing thinking around the world. Other countries followed with their own reports on corporate governance. These included the Viénot Report (1995) from France, the King Report (1995) from South Africa, the Toronto Stock Exchange recommendations on Canadian Board practices (1995), the Netherlands Report (1997), and a report on corporate governance from the Hong Kong Society of Accountants (1996).[10]

---

[9] This was reinforced by the 2002 post-Enron Sarbanes-Oxley Act.
[10] We will study these codes in more detail in Chapter 5: The Regulatory Framework.

As with the Cadbury Report (1992), these reports were particularly concerned about the potential for abuse of corporate power. Similarly, they called for greater conformance and compliance at board level, recommending the use of audit committees as a bridge between board and external auditor, the wider use of independent, outside, non-executive directors, and the separation of the role of chair of the board from that of chief executive. The theme was more checks and balances to avoid executive domination of decision-making and to protect the rights of shareholders, particularly minority shareholders.

An Australian Committee on corporate governance (1993), chaired by Professor Fred Hilmer of the Australian Graduate School of Management, advanced a view that added a new dimension to the conformance and compliance emphasis of the Cadbury and the other reports, however. Governance is about performance as well as conformance, his report argued: 'The board's key role is to ensure that corporate management is continuously and effectively striving for above-average performance, taking account of risk.' It adds, almost as an afterthought, 'this is not to deny the board's additional role with respect to shareholder protection'.

Hilmer gave his report the splendid title *Strictly Boardroom*—after the film *Strictly Ballroom*, which portrays the world of competitive ballroom dancing, in which originality, creativity, and innovation had been sacrificed to inflexible and inhibiting rules and regulations. This is the danger facing current governance practices, argued Hilmer, with conformance and compliance overshadowing improved corporate performance.

In 1998, the Organisation for Economic Co-operation and Development (OECD) proposed the development of global guidelines on corporate governance and encouraged states to introduce such guidelines. The report usefully emphasized the contrast between the strong external investment and firm corporate governance practices in America and Britain and those in Japan, France, and Germany, which had less-demanding governance requirements. In these countries, other constituencies, such as employees, receive more deference, the regulatory structures are less obtrusive, directors are seldom truly independent, and investors seem prepared to take a longer-term view.

Institutional investors were also active. In the USA, Institutional Shareholder Services and the Investor Responsibility Research Center emerged to inform institutional fund managers on governance issues. In the UK, the Association of British Insurers and the National Association of Pension Funds also actively advised their members on proxy voting issues. In Australia, it was the Australian Investment Managers' Association. The Californian State Employees' pension fund (CalPERS) was particularly active, producing global principles for corporate governance, intended to benchmark corporate governance practices in companies in its portfolio around the world. In response, some companies, such as General Motors (1996), published their own board governance guidelines on significant governance issues.

However, probably the most telling driver of change in corporate governance in the 1990s was the dynamic, flexible new corporate structures, often global, that were replacing the stable, often regional, corporate groups of the post-war years—massively complex networks of subsidiary companies and strategic alliances with cross-holdings of shares, cross-directorships, chains of leveraged funding, and dynamic and ever-changing operational and financial linkages throughout the added-value chain. These were networks that operated in multiple jurisdictions, cultures, and currencies—groupings with voracious appetites for growth. Top management of major corporations around the world now wielded enormous power. While claiming to reflect owners' interests, directors were seen to be pursuing their own agendas and expecting huge rewards—privileges reserved in earlier generations for kings and their courtiers.

The cultural component of corporate governance

Although the underlying principles are broadly similar, the policies and practices of corporate governance vary considerably around the world. We have already seen three distinct models:

- *The United States rule-based model*, which relies on regulation and the law to ensure that companies adhere to the requirements of state and federal policies and regulator's requirements. This model uses the unitary board, with both executive and outside, non-executive directors.
- *The UK/Commonwealth principles model*, which requires companies to report that they have voluntarily followed a corporate governance code or explain why they have not. This model also adopts a unitary board.
- *The continental European two-tier model*, in which the roles of the executive directors form the executive board, which is overseen by the supervisory board of non-executive directors representing shareholder and employee interests.

These three can be thought of as Western approaches to corporate governance, even though practised in countries such as Australia, India, and South Africa. However, although Western ideas have influenced their development, there are other forms of corporate governance that could be considered Eastern approaches. These include:

- The Japanese *keiretsu* model, reflecting the networks of inter-connected companies with cross-directorships of mainly executive directors.
- The South Korean *chaebol* model, in which conglomerate groups are connected by family interests.
- China's unique approach to corporate governance, which has adapted the unitary board and supervisory boards, and included representatives of the Communist Party to create wealth and serve the interests of the people and the state.
- The Asia family-based business model, which is found throughout East Asia following the diaspora of entrepreneurial business people from mainland China over the years.

We will explore each of these models in detail later, but it is worth noting, at this stage, the significance of culture to policies and practices of corporate governance. Culture can be thought of as the social heritage of beliefs, expectations, and values that people share. Over the years, the culture of a country is influenced by its geography, its history of social, economic, and political change, and its religion. Culture is moulded by situations that affect relations between individuals, institutions, and the state. Culture influenced by experience, education, and law is reflected in the language, and is passed on by life in families and organizations.

The culture of a country influences what is thought of as acceptable, important, and right or wrong. It affects how people think and act. For companies, culture means the way things have been and are done around the company. Often nebulous and unclear, culture would come to reinforce or slow down any corporate governance practices introduced by a board of directors.

An appreciation of culture is fundamental to understanding corporate governance.

In the late 20th century, when ideas about corporate governance began to be discussed, much of the thinking and practice was influenced by countries that shared Anglo-American culture—a belief in the rule of law; the importance of the rights of individuals to personal freedom and ownership of property; individual accountability; and the existence of account-able, democratic institutions, including an independent judiciary. As we shall see, that is not the underlying culture of some other countries that are significant in today's global economy.

Developments in corporate governance in the early 21st century

As the 21st century dawned, corporate governance seemed to be developing well around the world. The importance of good corporate governance was well recognized. Codes of principles or best practice in corporate governance for listed companies were in place in most countries with stock markets. Many of the corporate governance codes now called for director appraisal, training, and development, and for board-level performance reviews. Many felt that markets were offering a premium for shares in well-governed companies. This was particularly the case in the United States. Indeed, there was a widespread expectation in the USA that the rest of the world would gradually converge with the American approach to corporate governance and the US GAAP, not least because the world, it was felt, needed access to American funds.

But the new century had scarcely begun when disaster struck. Enron, one of the largest companies in the USA, collapsed on the back of heavy, unreported indebtedness and dubious corporate governance attitudes among the executive directors. In addition to Enron, Waste Man-agement, Worldcom, and Tyco also collapsed. So did their auditor, Arthur Andersen, one of the big five global accounting firms, as their clients changed auditors and partners changed firms. Corporate governance problems appeared in companies in other parts of the world as well. In the UK, Marconi, British Rail, Independent Insurance, and Tomkins faced governance problems, as did HIH Insurance in Australia, Parmalat in Italy, and Vodaphone Mannesmann in Germany.

The US GAAP were now pilloried as being based on rules that could be manipulated, rather than on the principles of overall fairness required in international accounting standards. Finan-cial transparency, governance processes, and, most significantly, attitudes toward corporate governance were questioned. Confidence in the financial markets was shaken. Suddenly, from being the leaders of economic success, entrepreneurial risk-taking, and sound corporate gov-ernance, directors were depicted as greedy, short-sighted, and more interested in their personal wealth and share options than in creating sustainable wealth for the benefit of the shareholders. The response in the United States was a Blue Ribbon Commission and more legislation.

In 2001, a Blue Ribbon Commission, set up in the United States by the National Associa-tion of Corporate Directors (NACD), published a report on director professionalism, the key recommendations of which were:

● boards should be composed of a substantial majority of independent directors;

- boards should require that key committees—including, but not limited to, audit, compensation, and governance/nominating—be composed entirely of independent directors, and be free to hire independent advisers as necessary;
- each key committee should have a written, board-approved charter detailing its duties. Audit committee duties, at a minimum, should include two key elements:
  a. oversight of the quality and integrity of financial reports and the process that produces them; and
  b. oversight of the management of risk.

A year later, the American Law Institute published a set of general principles on corporate governance, which generated a debate on the regulation of boards and directors. In November 2003, the SEC approved new listing requirements reflecting many of the NACD's recommendations.

In 2002, the US Sarbanes-Oxley Act was rushed through, placing new stringent demands for the governance of all companies listed in the United States. This Act, now nicknamed 'Sox' or 'Sarbox', significantly raised the requirements and the costs of corporate governance. The New York Stock Exchange (NYSE) and Nasdaq reflected the changes in their listing rules. Only independent directors could *now* serve on audit and remuneration committees, shareholders had to approve plans for directors' stock options, and subsidized loans to directors were forbidden. A new institution was created to oversee audit firms, which must rotate their audit partners, to prevent an over-familiarity between auditors and the client's finance staff. Auditors were also forbidden to sell some non-audit services to audit clients, and audit staff were to serve a cooling-off period before joining the staff of an audit client—all of which had happened in Enron.

Towards the end of the 20th century, the main emphasis in the field of corporate governance had been on listed companies. But a parallel development had occurred during the 1990s, accelerating into the 2000s: the concepts and principles of corporate governance developed for listed companies were also seen to be relevant to unlisted private companies and to many other corporate entities. Corporate governance policies and procedures were developed for charities, educational, sports, and medical bodies, professional institutions, government corporations, and quangos. Corporate governance codes and best governance practices were published for some not-for-profit sectors.

Corporate governance implications of the global financial crisis

In 2007, in the United States, after more than a decade of substantial growth, house prices began to fall, leaving some owners in negative equity, their mortgage loans greater than the value of their homes. Worse, it emerged that many of these loans had been made to people who were not good credit risks—the so-called sub-prime market. Foreclosures escalated, driving house prices down further.

For a decade, lax monetary policies, cheap money, and massive liquidity had produced a lending-and-asset bubble in the Western world. Companies used low-interest loans to leverage their financial strategies. World trade had boomed, with some countries facing vast trade imbalances. Personal borrowing soared, some secured on inflating house prices, some on extended credit card debt.

The catalyst for the subsequent chaos was financial engineering. Financial institutions had bundled their loan assets into securities, which they then sold on to other financial institutions. This securitization of debt spread the risk around the world's financial systems, but, because these instruments were complex and sophisticated, there were problems matching exposure to security. Moreover, not all bank directors appreciated the extent of their banks' exposure to risk. Rumours of banks' over-exposure to sub-prime debt circulated, lowering confidence, which is the basis of every financial system: confidence that credit will be available when needed and trust that debts will be repaid when due. Facing uncertainty, banks began to tighten their lending policies. Funds became scarce. Central banks had to make special arrangements to provide money to meet some institutions' liabilities.

In 2007, the first run on a UK bank for over a century occurred at the Northern Rock bank,[11] which had to be taken over by the British government. In the USA, Bear Stearns, a financial institution, was bailed out by the US government. Then, dramatically, the two huge American mortgage organizations, Fannie Mae and Freddie Mac, which account for a large part of all mortgages to homeowners in the United States, were given government guarantees of up to US$5 trillion. Next, American International Group (AIG), the world's biggest insurer and provider of hedging cover to the banking system, imploded. The US government, believing that it could not countenance the adverse economic effects of the failure of AIG, provided a loan facility of US$85 billion to protect the interests of its taxpayers, secured on AIG assets, taking an 80 per cent equity stake in the company. Lehman Brothers was not so fortunate: the Federal Reserve System refused to provide support and, after 158 years, the firm became bankrupt, which drove down market confidence still further.

In September 2008, the US Federal Reserve and the US Treasury tried to restore confidence. They proposed a bail-out in which the American government would take on banks' bad debts, including the sub-prime loans, with the underlying collateral security. Some complained that this would allow the financial executives, whose reckless investments had caused the crisis in the first place, to unload their risky assets and then walk away with their bonuses and golden parachutes intact. Some commentators, in both the United States and Europe, argue to this day that some senior bankers should have faced criminal charges for taking excessive risk and exposing shareholders, and ultimately the public, to loss.

Other countries around the world also experienced liquidity problems. In September 2008 there was a run on the Bank of East Asia in Hong Kong, which was quickly met by reassurances from Hong Kong's financial authorities. In October 2008, all of the banks and the stock exchange in Iceland were closed when depositors' demands for cash could not be met. Iceland, a country of around 300,000 people, which had previously relied on fishing and tourism, had been led by a handful of financial entrepreneurs to engage in international finance way beyond its economic potential.

In the United States, plans were announced for the government to take a US$700 billion equity stake in its banks. In the UK, the government effectively nationalized three banks—Royal Bank of Scotland, HBOS, and Lloyds TSB. Some senior bankers lost their jobs. In both the United States and the UK, the government had now become the largest provider of

---

[11] We will study the Northern Rock case in Chapter 5.

mortgages. Iceland, meanwhile, its banks and stock exchange still closed and its currency unacceptable, appealed to the International Monetary Fund for help.

The global financial crisis raised some fundamental corporate governance issues:

- *Where were the directors of the failed financial institutions*—particularly the independent, outside directors who were supposed to provide a check on over-enthusiastic executive directors? Did they really understand the strategic business models and sophisticated securitized instruments involved? In other words, did they appreciate the risk inherent in their companies' strategic profile?

- *Where were the banking regulators?* Although the extent of the crisis was unprecedented, the regulators seem to have been beguiled into complacency, perhaps taken over by the industry they were there to regulate.

- *Where were the auditors?* In approving the accounts of client financial institutions, did they fully appreciate and ensure the reporting of exposure to risk?

- *Did the credit agencies contribute to the problem* by awarding high credit ratings to companies over-exposed to significant risk?

- Government bail-outs also raised the question of so-called *moral hazard*—by protecting bankers from their past reckless decisions, would others be encouraged to take excessive risks in the future?

- *Will the experts who designed the sophisticated loan securitization vehicles and other financial engineering systems be held to account?* Are their ideas and enthusiasms now under control?

- *Were any of the financial institutions' activities illegal?* Compare the situation with Enron, in which some top executives continued to believe that nothing they had done was illegal, even after they were in jail.

- And, not least, *did excessive bonuses and share options encourage short-term and unrealistic risk-taking with shareholders' funds?* The news that some bankers had lost their fortunes as share prices collapsed was cold comfort to mortgagees who lost their homes, shareholders who lost their savings, and employees who lost their livelihoods.

Predictably, regulatory authorities sought to improve corporate regulation to avoid further problems. In the United States, the SEC proposed changes to regulatory procedures for listed companies including obligatory (although non-binding) shareholder votes on top executive remuneration, the annual election of directors, and the creation of board-level committees to focus on enterprise risk exposure. The separation of the CEO role from that of the board chair, as called for in corporate governance codes in other countries, was suggested. In July 2010, the US Federal Government enacted the Dodd-Frank Wall Street Reform and Consumer Protection Act, regulating the financial sector, and requiring greater accountability and transparency.

In the United Kingdom, although the Financial Review Council did not find evidence of serious failings in the governance of British businesses outside the banking sector, it did propose changes to the UK Code to improve governance in major companies. The proposed changes were intended to enhance accountability to shareholders, to ensure that boards are well balanced and challenging, to improve a board's performance and to deepen awareness of its strengths and weaknesses, to strengthen risk management, and to emphasize that perfor-mance-related pay should be aligned with the company's long-term interests and risk policy.

In 2010, the existing UK Combined Code was renamed the UK Corporate Governance Code,[12] a name some thought would have been more appropriate all along. The main pro-posals for change were:

- annual re-election of the chair or the whole board;
- new principles on the leadership of the chair, and the roles, skills, and independence of non-executive directors and their level of time commitment;
- board evaluation reviews to be externally facilitated at least every three years;
- regular personal performance and development reviews by the chair with each director;
- new principles on the board's responsibility for risk management;
- performance-related pay should be aligned to the company's long-term interests and its risk policy;
- companies to report on their business model and overall financial strategy.

In 2018 The UK Corporate Governance Code was updated, keeping the major principles but simplifying the format. We will explore this latest version of the code in Chapter 5.

New frontiers for corporate governance

Corporate governance thinking and practice continue to evolve. We will be exploring these new frontiers throughout this book, but for now let us consider some of the more significant.

Growing corporate complexity

Research from the Harvard Business School,[13] following the global financial crisis, concluded that recent boardroom failures had differed from the previous corporate failings, such as Enron, WorldCom, and other corporate collapses, which were rooted in management mal-feasance and led to the US Sarbanes-Oxley Act. Recent corporate governance problems, the researchers found, were primarily attributable to the growing complexity of the companies that boards governed. The research also found a strong consensus among directors that the key to improving boards' performance was not government action, but action by each board. Moreover, it emphasized the differences between companies and concluded that boards needed to develop appropriate structures, processes, and practices. The notion that 'one size fits all' was viewed with scepticism. The Harvard research identified six areas for improvement at board level:

- clarifying the board's role;

---

[12] Proposed reforms to the *UK Corporate Governance Code* (2009) FRC PN 287, 1 December. Available at: www.frc.org.uk/corporate/reviewCombined.cfm

[13] Lorsch, Jay with Joe Bower, Clayton Rose, and Suraj Sriinivasan (2009) *Perspectives from the Boardroom*, Harvard Business School, Cambridge, MA, USA.

- acquiring better information and deeper understanding of the company;
- maintaining a sound relationship with management;
- providing oversight of company strategy;
- assuring management development and succession;
- improving risk management.

Changes in ownership patterns

In the early days of the corporate concept, the shareholding owners of the company were just once removed from the board of directors they elected to run their company. This can still be the case in small companies and start-up situations. But elsewhere the position has become strikingly different. A complex chain of intermediaries and agents can lie between investors and the company in which they are ultimately investing. For example, an individual might invest in a pension fund, which invests in a highly geared hedge fund, which includes an index-tracking fund, which invests in the shares on a given stock market index. More-over, shares in the chain could be lent to cover other transactions of the financial institution involved. Consequently, it can be difficult for ultimate owners to exercise any influence over the governance of the company in which their funds have been invested, which was the original intention of the corporate concept. Further, private equity deals, in which financial institutions take major stakes in listed companies, often with highly leveraged financial posi-tions, have added to corporate governance issues, particularly accountability and transpar-ency. Encouraging and responding to shareholder involvement can be a significant challenge to investor relations.

Board responsibility for enterprise risk management and business continuity

Companies add value in different ways to achieve their corporate goals. In some busi-nesses, added value might lie in the global upstream supply chain, their technological expertise, product uniqueness, and brand image. In other cases their market position, the downstream distribution network, access to finance, managerial expertise, or repu-tation might be the foremost consideration. Failure in a critical area can expose a com-pany to strategic risk and even threaten business continuity. The catastrophic collapse of BP's Deepwater Horizon oil rig badly damaged the company's finances, share price, and reputation.[14]

Surprisingly, studies have shown that some outside directors do not know where value is added in their company. Consequently, they cannot know whether the company is exposed to strategic risk. So the most significant risks that companies face may be the least well under-stood by boards. In the global financial crisis, it was apparent that many directors of financial institutions did not understand their firms' exposure to strategic risk. Directors need to under-stand how value is added within their business, where the company is critically exposed to

---

[14] The case of the BP Deepwater Horizon disaster is studied in Chapter 8.

risk, and what policies are in place to manage those risks. Identifying and assessing critical risk needs to be a board-level activity.

Corporate governance by rule or by principle

Many commentators refer to the 'Anglo-American' approach to corporate governance. They contrast the Anglo-American governance traditions of the unitary board, which has both executive and non-executive directors, with the continental European, two-tier, supervisory board and executive board. They compare the company law approach of the Anglo-American common law jurisdictions with that of civil law countries.

But actually a schism has appeared between American and British concepts of corporate governance. American practice relies on a prescriptive, rules-based, legal approach to governance; the British approach prefers a voluntary, non-prescriptive, principles-based, more self-regulatory approach. The underpinning of American corporate governance has become mandatory governance determined by regulation and law, such as the Sarbanes-Oxley Act. In other words, 'obey the legal requirements or risk the penalties', which can include unlimited fines and jail. By contrast, the basis of corporate governance in Britain and many other countries,[15] whose company law has been influenced over the years by UK common law traditions, involves a discretionary approach to governance by principle. In other words, 'comply with the corporate governance code or explain why you have not'. This frontier is really a fundamental philosophical debate of considerable significance for the future of the subject. The European Union is again reviewing the basis of corporate governance in member states and may opt for the more rule-orientated continental European model of company law. The dilemma remains unresolved.

Unitary boards marking their own exam papers

Another dilemma concerns the workings of the unitary board, in which directors are responsible for both the strategic direction and the success of the business, while also being responsible for overseeing the activities of executive management. In other words, the board is expected to be involved in strategy formulation and planning while also supervising management performance. It has been suggested that this means the unitary board is effectively trying to mark its own examination papers. Of course, the two-tier board structure avoids this problem by having the executive board responsible for performance and the supervisory board for ensuring conformance, common membership between the two boards being forbidden.

To overcome this dilemma, corporate governance codes call for independent, outside (non-executive) directors to play a vital role. Independence is precisely defined to ensure that these directors have no interest in the company that might, or might be seen to, adversely affect genuine independent and objective judgement. The minimum number or percentage of independent board members is usually specified.

[15] Including Australia, Canada, New Zealand, Hong Kong, India, Malaysia, South Africa, and Singapore.

Independent directors who do not know enough about the business

But director independence can create another dilemma. The more independent directors are, the less likely they are to know about the company and its industry. The more non-executive directors know about a company's business, organization, strategies, markets, competitors, and technologies, the less independent they can become. Yet the knowledge and experience of such people are exactly what top management needs to contribute to its strategy, policy-making, and risk assessment.

The NYSE sponsored a Commission that published ten core principles of corporate governance.[16] While the Commission supported the NYSE's listing requirements, which call for a majority of independent directors, it also pointed out that companies can have additional, non-independent, outside directors so that there is an appropriate range and mix of expertise, diversity, and knowledge. The Commission pointed out that while independence is an important attribute for board members, the NYSE's Listing Standards do not limit a board to just one non-independent director and boards should seek an appropriate balance between independent and non-independent directors. The Commission's ten core principles were:

1. The board's fundamental objective should be to build long-term sustainable growth in shareholder value for the corporation.

2. Successful corporate governance depends upon successful management of the company, because management has the primary responsibility for creating a culture of performance with integrity and ethical behaviour.

3. Good corporate governance should be integrated with the company's business strategy and not viewed as simply a compliance obligation.

4. Shareholders have a responsibility and long-term economic interest to vote their shares in a reasoned and responsible manner, and should engage in a dialogue with companies in a thoughtful manner.

5. While legislation and agency rule-making are important to establish the basic tenets of corporate governance, corporate governance issues are generally best solved through collaboration and market-based reforms.

6. A critical component of good governance is transparency, because well-governed companies should ensure that they have appropriate disclosure policies, and practices, and investors should also be held to appropriate levels of transparency, including disclosure of derivative or other security ownership on a timely basis.

7. The Commission supports the NYSE's listing requirements generally providing for a majority of independent directors, but also believes that companies can have additional non-independent directors so that there is an appropriate range and mix of expertise, diversity, and knowledge on the board.

---

[16] New York Stock Exchange: sponsored Commission on corporate governance, 10 Core Principles of Corporate Governance, October 2010—a commission representing investors, issuers, broker-dealers, and governance experts.

8. The Commission recognizes the influence that proxy advisory firms have on the markets, and believes that it is important that such firms be held to appropriate standards of transparency and accountability.

9. The SEC should work with exchanges to ease the burden of proxy voting, while encouraging greater participation by individual investors in the proxy voting process.

10. The SEC and/or the NYSE should periodically assess the impact of major governance reforms to determine if these reforms are achieving their goals.

Board diversity

Diversity in board membership has become a major interest around the world in recent years. Mainly, board diversity has referred to gender diversity, driven by a concern for greater equality between men and women at the top of large corporations. Some countries have introduced quotas, as we will discuss in Chapter 2. The European Union has called for equality between men and women, and in particular 40 per cent female board membership by 2020. However, not all member states have accepted the requirement. Many companies are also opposed to quotas, arguing that they do not guarantee that the most appropriate people become directors and, if mandated, the female board members could become 'token directors', with decision-making done outside the boardroom.

In addition to gender diversity, however, some commentators have called for greater diversity of business experience and skills, for boards to reflect stakeholders' interests, and even to mirror the diversity of society. We will explore the implications of such notions in Chapter 2.

Shareholders' changing expectations of directors and boards

Once upon a time, a directorship was a sinecure—an occasional meeting between friends, maybe a few supportive questions, then a fee and probably lunch. Not now. Today, more is expected of company directors, indeed of the members of all governing bodies, than ever before. In listed companies, shareholders are no longer compliant. They expect their directors to increase shareholder value. They challenge director remuneration they consider excessive. Institutional investors—insurance companies, pension funds, and other financial institutions—can put pressure on poorly performing boards, complain publicly about allegedly excessive directors' remuneration, and demand high standards of corporate governance. The requirements on listed companies and their directors, from financial regulators, stock exchanges, and an increasingly investigative media around the world, have also increased. The threat of litigation against companies, boards, and individual directors has introduced the risk of serious financial exposure as well as the potential for public derision.

Directors of private companies, that is, those without public investors, including entrepreneurial businesses, subsidiary companies, joint venture entities, and family firms, can also find themselves under the corporate governance spotlight. The interests of minority shareholders must be protected. In certain circumstances, directors can become personally responsible for their company's debts. They can also be fined heavily if the company fails to meet its statutory obligations. Moreover, like their public company counterparts, shareholders in private companies now expect their directors to set high standards of governance and to deliver improving corporate performance.

Members of the governing bodies of not-for-profit institutions, including hospital trusts, charities, professional bodies, cooperatives, colleges, and community organizations, also face demands for better governance. Members of their governing bodies are expected to act professionally, and to be accountable, with their activities transparent.

Society's changing expectations of directors and boards

Society's expectations of companies, boards, and directors are changing, too. The movement we saw in the 1970s, expecting more of companies than just making a profit for their shareholders while remaining within the law, has reappeared with new force. Company collapses in the late 20th and early 21st centuries, and growing criticism of directors' behaviour, reinforced by the trauma caused by the global financial crisis, have led to renewed concern about business ethics. The original 19th-century concept of the limited-liability company was founded on trust and stewardship. But the ethical framework enshrined in the original concept has been overshadowed as power shifted from owners to directors. Now pressures for sound governance, director-level stewardship, and ethical business behaviour have emerged.

Public dissatisfaction with the globalization of trade and the free movement of people across borders could be seen in the election of President Donald Trump and the British voters' decision to leave the European Union. The media outcry against companies' aggressive tax avoidance and the use of tax havens also reflects a changing public attitude to corporate behaviour. In a world affected by global finance, trading, and services, the need for socially responsible behaviour by companies has acquired new momentum. Calls have increased for companies to show concern for the effects of their actions on all stakeholders including the communities they affect. Corporate social responsibility, or CSR as it is now widely known, has become a major concern of many companies, as we shall see. The concern for ecology and the conservation of the planet's resources, taking corporate decisions that do not deplete the world's resources to the detriment of future generations, has brought sustainable development to the corporate governance agenda. Corporate governance has acquired some new dimensions.

Case studies

 Case study 1.1   Robert Maxwell: a classic corporate governance case

Robert Maxwell, then Jan Ludvik Hoch, was born in Czechoslovakia in 1923, grew up in poverty, fought with the Free Czech army in the Second World War, and received the British Military Cross. He became an international publishing baron. In the early 1970s, inspectors appointed by the UK government led an inquiry into the failure of his company Pergamon Press and concluded that he was not 'a person who can be relied on to exercise stewardship of a publicly-quoted company'. Nevertheless, he subsequently succeeded in building a media empire including two public companies—Maxwell Communication Corporation and Mirror Group Newspapers. Following his death in 1991, falling overboard from his yacht with a heart attack—rumours that he had committed suicide or been murdered because he had been a spy were disproved by four coroners—it was alleged that he had used his dominant position as chair of the trustees of the group's pension funds to siphon off funds to support his other interests and that he had been involved in an illegal scheme to bolster the price of companies in the group. Eventually, the lead companies were declared insolvent, banks called in loans that could not be repaid, and the group collapsed. Investigators estimated that £763 million had been plundered from the two public companies and their pension funds to prop up Maxwell's private interests.

There are many lessons for directors in the Maxwell affair. Maxwell's leadership style was dominant: he reserved considerable power for himself and kept his top executives in the dark. An impressive set of independent non-executive directors added respectability to the public company boards, but they were ill-informed. Maxwell threatened litigation to prevent criticism of his corporate affairs: many investigative journalists and one doctoral student received writs. The complexity of the group's organizational network, which included private companies incorporated in tax havens with limited disclosure requirements, made it difficult to obtain a comprehensive overview of group affairs. The auditors were criticized. In a revealing internal memo (discovered by Persaud and Plender, 2006), the senior partner of CoopersLybrandDeloittes wrote:

> The first requirement is to continue to be at the beck and call of Robert Maxwell, his sons, and his staff, appear when wanted, and provide whatever is required.

The failings of the trustees of the Maxwell group pension fund and the regulatory bodies were all recognized.

Involvement with his father's empire left Robert Maxwell's son Kevin bankrupt. Two decades later, in 2011, he was disqualified as a director for eight years by the UK Department for Business Innovation and Skills. The Department found that he and two other directors had diverted more than £2 million out of the bankrupt construction company Syncro Ltd ahead of liquidation. He had also failed to preserve accurate records in a 'disregard for a director's duty'.

Discussion questions

1. What would you say are the crucial questions in the Maxwell affair?

2. How might they have been answered?

 Case study 1.2   Enron: another classic corporate governance case

The merger of Houston Natural Gas and InterNorth in 1985 created a new Texas energy company called Enron. In 1989, Enron began trading in commodities—buying and selling wholesale contracts in energy. By 2000, turnover was growing at a fantastic rate, from US$40 billion in 1999 to US$101 billion in 2000, with the increased revenues coming from the broking of energy commodities. The rapid rate of growth suggested a dynamic company and Enron's share price rocketed. Top executives reaped large rewards from their share options. The company's bankers, who received substantial fees from the company, also employed analysts who encouraged others to invest in Enron. But the cash flow statement included an unusual item: *'other operating activities $1.1 billion'*. The accounts for 2000 were the last Enron was to publish.

The chief executive of Enron, Jeffrey Skilling, believed that old asset-based businesses would be dominated by trading enterprises such as Enron making markets for their output. Enron was credited with 'aggressive earnings management'. To support its growth, hundreds of special purpose entities (SPEs) were created. These were separate partnerships that traded with Enron, with names such as Cayman, Condor and Raptor, Jedi and Chewco, often based in tax havens. Enron marked long-term energy supply contracts with these SPEs at market prices, taking the profit in its own accounts immediately. The SPEs also provided lucrative fees for Enron top executives. Further, they gave the appearance that Enron had hedged its financial exposures with third parties, whereas the third parties were, in fact, contingent liabilities on Enron. The contemporary American GAAP did not require such SPEs to be consolidated with partners' group accounts, so billions of dollars were kept off Enron's balance sheet.

In 2000, Enron had US$100 billion in annual revenues and was valued by the stock market at nearly US$80 billion. It was ranked seventh in *Fortune*'s list of the largest US firms. Enron then had three principal divisions, with over 3,500 subsidiaries: Enron Global Services, owning physical assets such as power stations and pipelines; Enron Energy Services, providing management and outsourcing services; and Enron Wholesale Services, the commodities and trading business. Enron was the largest trader in the energy market created by the deregulation of energy in the USA.

The company had many admirers. As the authors of the book *The War for Talent* (Harvard Business School Press, 2001) wrote, 'few companies will be able to achieve the excitement extravaganza that Enron has in its remarkable business transformation, but many could apply some of the principles'.

Enron's auditor was Arthur Andersen, whose audit and consultancy fees from Enron were running around US$52 million a year. Enron also employed several former Andersen partners as senior financial executives. In February 2001, partners of Andersen discussed dropping their client because of Enron's accounting policies, including accounting for the SPEs and the apparent conflicts of interest of Enron's chief financial officer, Andrew Fastow, who had set up and was benefiting from the SPEs.

In August 2001, Skilling resigned 'for personal reasons'. Kenneth Lay, the chairman, took over executive control. Lay was a close friend of US President George W. Bush and was his adviser on energy matters. His name had been mentioned as a future US Energy Secretary. In 2000, Lay made £123 million from the exercise of share options in Enron.

A week after Skilling resigned, Chung Wu, a broker with UBS Paine Webber US (a subsidiary of Swiss bank UBS), emailed his clients advising them to sell Enron. He was sacked and escorted out of his office. The same day Lay sold US$4 million worth of his own Enron shares, while telling employees of the high priority he placed on restoring investor confidence, which 'should result in a higher share price'. Other UBS analysts were still recommending a 'strong buy' on Enron. UBS Paine Webber received substantial brokerage fees from administering the Enron employee stock option programme. Lord Wakeham, a former UK cabinet minister, was a director of Enron and chair of its nominating committee. Wakeham, who was also a chartered accountant and chair of the British Press Complaints Council, was paid an annual consultancy fee of US$50,000 by Enron, plus a US$4,600 monthly retainer and US$1,250 attendance fee for each meeting.

A warning about the company's accounting techniques was given to Lay in mid-2001 by Sherron Watkins, an Enron executive, who wrote: 'I am nervous that we will implode in a wave of accounting scandals.'[17] She also advised Andersen of potential problems. In October 2001, a crisis developed, when the company revised its earlier financial statements revealing massive losses attributable to hedging risks taken as energy prices fell, which had wiped out US$600 million of profits. A SEC investigation into this restatement of profits for the past five years revealed massive, complex derivative positions and the transactions between Enron and the SPEs. Debts were understated by US$2.6 billion. Fastow was alleged to have received more than US$30 million for his management of the partnerships. Eventually, he was indicted on 78 counts involving the complex financial schemes

[17] McLean, Bethany and Peter Elkind (2003) *The Smartest Guys in the Room—the Amazing Rise and Scandalous Fall of Enron*. Penguin Publishing Group, London.

that produced phantom profits, enriched him, and doomed the company. He claimed that he did not believe he had committed any crimes.

The FBI began an investigation into possible fraud at Enron three months later, by which time files had been shredded. In a subsequent criminal trial, Andersen was found guilty of destroying key documents, as part of an effort to impede an official inquiry into the energy company's collapse. Lawsuits against Andersen followed. The Enron employees' pension fund sued for US$1 billion, plus the return of US$1 million per week fees, seeing the firm as its best chance of recovering some of the US$80 billion lost in the Enron debacle. Many Enron employees held their retirement plans in Enron stock: some had lost their entire retirement savings. The US Labor Department alleged that Enron had illegally prohibited employees from selling company stock in their '401k' retirement plans as the share price fell. The Andersen firm subsequently collapsed, with partners around the world joining other 'Big Four' firms.

In November 2001, Fastow was fired. Standard and Poor's, the credit-rating agency, downgraded Enron stock to junk bond status, triggering interest rate penalties and other clauses. Merger negotiations with Dynergy, which might have saved Enron, failed.

Enron filed for Chapter 11 bankruptcy in December 2001. This was the largest corporate collapse in US history up until then: Worldcom was to exceed it. The NYSE suspended Enron shares. John Clifford Baxter, a vice-chair of Enron until his resignation in May 2001, was found shot dead. He had been one of the first to see the problems at Enron and had heated arguments about the accounting for off-balance-sheet financing, which he found unacceptable. Two outside directors, Herbert Weinokur and Robert Jaedicke, members of the Enron audit committee, claimed that the board either was not informed or was deceived about deals involving the SPEs.

Early in 2002, Duncan, the former lead partner on Enron's audit, who had allegedly shredded Enron files and been fired by Andersen, cooperated with the Justice Department's criminal indictment, becoming a whistle blower and pleading guilty to charges that he had 'knowingly, intentionally and corruptly persuade[d] and attempt[ed] to persuade Andersen partners and employees to shred documents'.

Why did it happen? Three fundamental reasons can be suggested: Enron switched strategy from energy supplier to energy trader, effectively becoming a financial institution with an increased risk profile; Enron's financial strategy hid corporate debt and exaggerated performance; US accounting standards permitted the off-balance-sheet treatment of the SPEs.

What are the implications of the Enron case? First, important questions are raised about corporate governance in the United States, including the roles of the CEO and board of directors, and the issue of duality; the independence of outside, non-executive directors; the functions and membership of the audit committee; and the oversight role of institutional shareholders. Second, issues of regulation in American financial markets arise, including the regulation of industrial companies with financial trading arms like Enron, the responsibilities of the independent credit-rating agencies, the regulation of US pension funds, and the effect on capital markets worldwide. Third, there are implications for accounting standards, particularly the accounting for off-balance-sheet SPEs, the regulation of the US accounting profession, and the convergence of US GAAP with international accounting standards. Last, auditing issues include auditor independence, auditors' right to undertake non-audit work for audit clients, the rotation of audit partners, audit firms or government involvement in audit, and the need for a cooling-off period before an auditor joins the staff of a client company.

Some British banks were caught in the Enron net. Andrew Fastow, the former CFO, produced an insider account of how the banks had helped to prop up the house of cards. Three British bankers were extradited to the United States to stand trial, under legislation designed to repatriate terrorists.

Jeffrey Skilling, the former CEO, was sentenced to 24 years' prison and to pay US$45 million restitution in October 2006. Claiming innocence, he appealed. Kenneth Lay (aged 64) was also found guilty, but died of a heart attack in July 2006, protesting his innocence and believing he would be exonerated.

Although Enron collapsed with such dramatic results, international corporate governance guidelines had in fact been followed, with a separate chair and CEO, an audit committee chaired by a leading independent accounting academic, and a raft of eminent independent non-executive directors. However, the subsequent collapse owes more to abuse of their power by top managers and their ambivalent attitudes towards honest and balanced corporate governance.

Discussion questions

1. Should a company's bankers, who receive substantial fees from that company, also employ analysts who encourage investment in that company?

2. Enron's external auditor, Arthur Andersen, earned substantial consultancy fees from the company as well as the audit fee. Enron also employed several former Andersen partners as senior financial executives. Could the external auditors really be considered independent?

3. What does this case suggest about corporate governance in the United States at the time? Consider the roles of the CEO and board of directors, the duality of chair and CEO, the independence of outside, non-executive directors; the functions and membership of the audit committee; and the oversight role of institutional shareholders.

Self-test questions

To confirm your grasp of the key points in this chapter, try answering the following questions.

1. Define corporate governance.
2. What are the main attributes of the limited-liability company?
3. What is the basis of corporate power?
4. What did the classical Berle and Means (1932) study emphasize?
5. What was the response of the UK Bullock Committee Report (1977)?
6. What did the Corporate Report (1975) from the UK Accounting Standards Committee propose?
7. Name some corporate collapses in the 1980s that led to the first studies of corporate governance.
8. What was the first official report on corporate governance and why was it commissioned? What were the major recommendations of the Cadbury Report?
9. Name some financial institutions in the USA that failed during the global financial crisis.
10. What additional dimension did the Australian Hilmer report add to the conformance and compliance concepts of corporate governance?

 For suggested answers to these self-test questions visit the online resources at: **www.oup.com/uk/tricker4e/**

Projects and exercises

1. Prepare a report on why the underlying ideas and concepts of corporate governance were slow to evolve. Why was the phrase 'corporate governance' not used until the 1980s and

the subject scarcely studied during the latter half of the 20th century when the study of management was at its height?

2. Research one or more of the cases of early corporate collapse mentioned in the text: in Australia, Alan Bond, Laurie Connell of Rothwells, and the Girvan Corporation; in Japan, Nomura Securities and the Recruit Corporation; in the United States, Ivan Boesky, Michael Levine, and Michael Milken of Drexel, Burnham, and Lambert; in the UK, Guinness and the Robert Maxwell companies. Prepare a report or class presentation outlining the case(s). What was the underlying reason for the failure? Would today's corporate governance codes, rules, and regulations have prevented these outcomes?

3. Explore the cases of corporate collapse mentioned in the text. Is there an underlying explanation for their failure? Prepare a report or a class presentation.

4. Explore the collapse of financial institutions mentioned in the chapter. Prepare a report or a class presentation on corporate governance implications stemming from the global financial crisis.

References and further reading

Accounting Standards Steering Committee (1975) *The Corporate Report: A Discussion Paper*. London.

American Law Institute (1984) *Principles of Corporate Governance*, in three parts. Philadelphia, PA.

Auerbach, Norman E. (1973) 'Audit Committees: New Corporate Institution', *Financial Executive*, September, pp 96–7, 102, 104.

Baysinger, Barry D. and Henry N. Butler (1985) 'Corporate Governance and the Board of Directors: Performance Effects of Changes in Board Composition', *Journal of Law, Economics and Organization*, 1, pp 101–24.

Berle, Adolf A. and Gardiner C. Means (1932) *The Modern Corporation and Private Property*. Macmillan, edn revised by Adolf Berle (1967) Columbia University, Harcourt, Brace and World, New York.

Bullock, Lord (1977) Industrial Democracy: a report of the Committee of Inquiry on Industrial Democracy. HMSO Cmnd 6706, 1977 [with European Experience—reports prepared for the Industrial Democracy Committee (1976) Eric Batstone and P. L. Davies, HMSO].

Cadbury, Sir Adrian (1992) The Financial Aspects of Corporate Governance: A report of the committee on corporate governance. Gee & Co., London.

Chaucer, Geoffrey (c.1483 and 1476) *The Canterbury Tales*. Caxton.

Cochran, Philip L. and Steven L. Wartick (1988) *Corporate Governance: A Review of the Literature*. Morristown, Financial Executives Research Foundation.

Corporate Governance: An International Review. Wiley-Blackwell, Malden, MA.

Cruver, Brian (2002) *Enron—Anatomy of Greed, the Unshredded Truth from an Insider*, Random House, London.

Dimma, William A. (2006) *Tougher Boards for Tougher Times—corporate governance in the post-Enron era*, John Wiley, Ontario.

Drucker, Peter F. (1991) 'Reckoning with the Pension Fund Revolution', *Harvard Business Review*, March–April, pp 106–14.

Earl, Michael J. (ed.) (1983) *Perspectives on Management*. Oxford University Press, Oxford.

Estes, Robert M. (1973) 'Outside Directors: More Vulnerable than Ever', *Harvard Business Review*, January/February, pp 107–14.

European Economic Community (1972) Proposal for a fifth directive on the structure of companies, Strasbourg.

Fogarty, Michael P. (1975) *Company Responsibility and Participation: a new agenda*. PEP Broadsheet Number 554, Volume XLI, London, August.

Friedman, L. M. (1973) *A History of American Law*. Simon and Schuster, New York.

Friedman, Milton (2002) *Capitalism and Freedom*. University of Chicago Press.

Friedman, Milton (2008) *Milton Friedman on Economics: selected papers*. University of Chicago Press Journals.

Greenbury, Sir Richard (1995) Directors' Remuneration: the Report of a Study Group. Gee & Co., London.

Hadden, Tom (1972) *Company Law and Capitalism*. Weidenfeld & Nicolson, London.

Hampel, Sir Ronald (1998) *Committee on Corporate Governance: Final Report*. Gee & Co., London, January.

HMSO (1977) *The Conduct of Company Directors*. White Paper, UK Cmnd 7037 presented to Parliament.

Hilmer, Frederick G. (1993) *Strictly Boardroom: Improving Governance to Enhance Company Performance*. Information Australia, Melbourne, Australia.

Jensen, Michael C. and William H. Meckling (1976) *Can the Corporation Survive?* Centre for Research in Government Policy and Business, University of Rochester, US, May.

Mace, Myles L. (1971) *Directors: Myth and Reality*. Graduate School of Business Administration, Harvard University, Boston, Mass.

Mautz, R. K. and F. L. Neumann (1970) 'The Effective Corporate Audit Committee', *Harvard Business Review*, November/December.

Mautz, R. K. and F. L. Neumann (1977) *Corporate Audit Committees: Policies and Practices*. Ernst and Ernst, New York.

Mintzberg, Henry (1984) 'Who Should Control the Corporation?', *California Management Review*, XXVII, pp 90–115.

National Association of Corporate Directors (1996/2001/2005) Report of the NACD Blue Ribbon Commission on Director Professionalism for Public Company Governance. Washington, DC.

Persaud, Avinash D. and John Plender (2006) *All You Need to Know about Ethics and Finance*. Longtail Publishing, London.

RSA (The Royal Society for the Encouragement of Arts, Manufactures and Commerce) (1995) *Tomorrow's Company: the Role of Business in a Changing World*. London.

Securities and Exchange Commission (1972) 'Standing Audit Committees composed of Outside Directors', Release No. 123, March, *SEC Accounting Rules*.

Shakespeare, William (1596/8) *The Merchant of Venice*, Act 1 Scene 1, first folio.

Smith, Adam ([1759] 2018) *The Theory of Moral Sentiments*. Kartindo Classics Press, India.

Smith, Adam ([1776] 1976) *The Wealth of Nations*. Revised edn, George J. Stigler (ed.), University of Chicago Press, Chicago.

Tricker, R. I. (1978) *The Independent Director: A Study of the Non-executive Director and of the Audit Committee*. Tolley with Deloitte, Haskins & Sells, London.

Tricker, R. I. (1984) *Corporate Governance*. Gower Publishing, Aldershot, UK.

Watkinson, Lord (1973) Responsibilities of the British Public Company: Report of the Company Affairs Committee of the Confederation of British Industry. London, September.

Useful websites

'Corporate board: role, duties and composition', journal open access from 2018:

www.virtusinterpress.org/Corporate-Board-role-duties-and,5247.html

www.corpgov.net

A valuable site, full of vital corporate governance information by company, country, and topic, reviews, updates, and library, plus vital links to other relevant corporate governance sites.

2 Governance and Management

 Learning Outcomes

This chapter enables us to:

- Be aware of different definitions of corporate governance.
- Appreciate the scope of corporate governance.
- Accept the significance of corporate constitutions.
- Recognize the difference between governance and management.
- Understand performance and conformance roles in corporate governance.
- Review different board structures.

Definitions of corporate governance

In Chapter 1, we suggested that corporate governance is concerned with the exercise of power over corporate entities. While this is true, it is an overarching view that does not help in understanding the boundaries, levels, and processes of the subject. We now need to explore other definitions of corporate governance. Notice how the different definitions reflect alternative viewpoints on the subject.

The operational perspective

The definitions adopted by some authorities focus on governance structures, processes, and practices. The first corporate governance report, Sir Adrian Cadbury's *Report on the Financial Aspects of Corporate Governance* (1992), took such a view. This report defined corporate governance as 'the system by which companies are directed and controlled'. Cadbury also explained that boards of directors are responsible for the governance of their companies, while the shareholders' role in governance is to appoint the directors and the auditors, and to satisfy themselves that an appropriate governance structure is in place.

Hilmer (1993), writing in the Australian context, emphasized the strategic responsibility of the board, suggesting that:

> the board's key role is to ensure that corporate management is continuously and effectively striving for above average performance, taking account of risk, (which) is not to deny the board's additional role with respect to shareholder protection.

The operational perspective was also adopted in the corporate governance code developed by the Organisation for Economic Co-operation and Development (OECD) (2001): 'Corporate governance is about the procedures and processes according to which an organization is directed and controlled.'

The operational perspective, focusing on the roles and interactions between the shareholders, the board, and the management, has been the basis for much work in corporate governance.

A relationship perspective

The OECD report strengthened its operational perspective by including the relationship among various participants:

> The corporate governance structure specifies the distribution of rights and responsibilities among the different participants in the organization—such as the board, managers, shareholders, and other stakeholders—and lays down the rules and procedures for decision-making.

The Corporate Library, an influential website (www.thecorporatelibrary.com), described corporate governance as: 'the relationship among the shareholders, directors and management of a company, as defined by the corporate charter, by-laws, formal policy, and rule of law'.

This relationship perspective was reinforced by the California Public Employees Retirement System (CalPERS), a significant institutional investor, which included in its definition 'the primary participants are: shareholders, company management (led by the chief executive officer), and the board of directors'. Monks and Minow (1995) agreed, but added the employees: 'Corporate governance involves the relationship among various participants, including the chief executive officer, management, shareholders, and employees, in determining the direction and performance of corporations'.

A stakeholder perspective

Notice that the OECD definition includes 'other stakeholders', as well as the shareholders, board, and management. It takes a wider view of those involved in and affected by corporate governance. Demb and Neubauer (1992) also took the stakeholder view: 'Corporate governance is the process by which corporations are made responsive to the rights and wishes of stakeholders'.

We will consider later who the stakeholders in a modern corporation might be.

A financial economics perspective

Financial economists tend to see corporate governance through a different lens from that of the lawyer and management expert: 'Corporate governance deals with the way suppliers of finance assure themselves of getting a return on their investment' (Shleifer and Vishny, 1997).

Their principal concern is with the ownership concentration in corporate governance systems around the world and the legal protection available to investors. Nevertheless, financial economics has been the dominant contributor of scholarly research into corporate governance, applying agency theory to board-level activities, as we shall see in Chapter 3.

A societal perspective

Finally, we come to a perspective that places the corporate entity in society. In 1995, Blair set corporate governance in this context as 'the whole set of legal, cultural, and institutional arrangements that determine what public corporations can do, who controls them, how that control is exercised, and how the risks and return from the activities they undertake are allocated'. Many would now include all corporate entities, as well as 'public corporations'.

Sir Adrian Cadbury, addressing the Global Corporate Governance Forum of the World Bank in 2000, took such a viewpoint when he said:

> Corporate governance is concerned with holding the balance between economic and social goals and between individual and communal goals. The corporate governance framework is there to encourage the efficient use of resources and equally to require accountability for the stewardship of those resources. The aim is to align as nearly as possible the interests of individuals, corporations and society.

Such a perspective sets corporate governance at a high level of abstraction. It includes all of the stakeholders involved with the company, including the contractual stakeholders such as the shareholders, managers, and other employees, suppliers, customers, consumers, bankers, but also other stakeholders outside the company whose interests could be affected by corporate behaviour, including the local, national, and international societal interests. Such a perspective can raise interesting philosophical issues about relationships between the individual, the enterprise, and the state. The societal perspective is reflected in the growing interest in stakeholder theory, and corporate social responsibility.

Of course, these different perspectives are not mutually exclusive; they overlap. None are all-inclusive; each can be relevant in context. The vital issue is to adopt the perspective that is appropriate to the matter under review.

The scope of corporate governance

Central to corporate governance thinking and practice are the shareholders, the board of directors, and the management. The corporate governance codes focus on this set of players, as does much company law. External auditors play a crucial role in corporate governance, although they are not often presented as central to its study. In the original 19th-century concept of the corporation, the shareholders appointed some of their own members to act as auditors, to check on the reports presented to them by their directors. Subsequently, they were replaced by professional auditors, as the accounting profession developed in the later years of that century. Later, we shall consider the implications of audit in the modern, global world, with just four massive, international firms of accountants, following the demise of the fifth, Arthur Andersen, after the Enron debacle, which we will study in Chapter 11 (Corporate Governance in Action 11.2) and 15 (Corporate Governance in Action 15.4). The importance of audit committees—standing committees of the main board, which are now required by all the codes of good practice in corporate governance—will also be studied in depth in Chapter 15.

For public, listed companies, the stock markets and their listing rules are, clearly, vitally significant to corporate governance. The rules that govern the stock market on which the company's shares are listed and in particular the requirements laid down for listing are fundamental to the effective governance of listed companies. Stock markets around the world also play an important role in the creation and policing of corporate governance codes.

Another viewpoint focuses on the interrelations between the company and its shareholders, including any dominant owners, institutional investors, and minority shareholders. In public companies, market intermediaries play an increasingly important role in modern corporate governance. In the original model of the corporation, shares were held by individual shareholders who interacted directly with their company. Today, although individual investors do have a significant share in some markets, institutional investors play a very significant part in most. The institutional investors may include an array of financial institutions such as pension funds, investment funds, life assurance funds, unit trusts, hedge funds, and other investment houses. There can be a raft of intermediary institutions between the company and the ultimate investor in its shares. Investment bankers may act as underwriters in launching shares in an initial public offering (IPO) of shares. Brokers, merchant bankers, and other institutions can hold shares on behalf of others. A further complication can arise if the financial institution holding shares lends them as security for other transactions. This situation can make it difficult for companies to know who their voting shareholders are, and for those shareholders to exercise their proxy votes and to take part in the governance of the company. Figure 2.1 depicts the circles of influence and the scope of corporate governance.

Governments obviously provide the underpinning for corporate governance by enacting the legislation that facilitates, regulates, and constrains the activities of corporate entities registered in their jurisdiction. The creation and updating of Companies Acts are obvious examples. The registration of companies and the filing and access to corporate documents is also a function of the relevant government department. The relationship between government, which in effect allows the corporate entity to be created and to operate in its jurisdiction, and companies is an important element of corporate governance.

Corporate regulators play an ever-increasing role in corporate governance. Many company jurisdictions now have a separate regulatory authority that monitors stock market activity, determines and requires compliance with corporate governance codes, and has the power to ensure compliance.

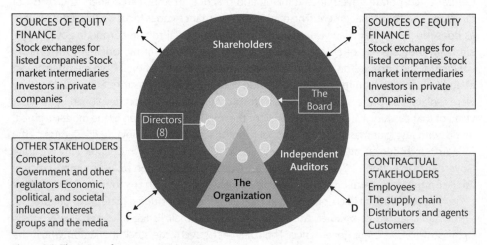

Figure 2.1 The scope of corporate governance

In the United States, the US Securities and Exchange Commission (SEC) exists to protect investors, to maintain fair, orderly, and efficient markets, and to facilitate capital formation. The SEC oversees the key participants in the securities world, including securities exchanges, securities brokers and dealers, investment advisers, and mutual funds. Crucial to the SEC's effectiveness in each of these areas is its enforcement authority, being able to take legal action against insider trading, accounting fraud, and the provision of false information.

Some commentators and researchers widen the focus of corporate governance to include contractual stakeholders—that is, those with whom the company has contractual relations, including employees, suppliers, and all those in the upstream and downstream added-value chains from suppliers of original goods and services, other contractors, and supply firms, through distributors, wholesalers, and retailers, to the final customer and consumer. Government and other corporate regulators are also basic components of the corporate governance system. This includes the effect of the company law, the legal institutions, and the regulatory mechanisms of the country concerned. Previously, the press showed little interest in business affairs unless there were major catastrophes. But in recent years the media have shone a spotlight on corporate activities, and the investigative media now play a useful role in the corporate governance process and have to be considered by practitioners.

Finally, the growing importance of societal influences and other stakeholders in corporate governance needs emphasis. In earlier days, companies tended to be left alone to carry on their activities in the pursuit of profit without interference, provided that they abided by the laws of the jurisdictions in which they operated. This is no longer the case. Today, many people expect companies to adopt a socially responsible attitude to their activities, for example by not doing objectionable things, such as exploiting workers, polluting the environment, or wasting energy.

Corporate social responsibility (CSR) reflects what some commentators see as companies' obligations to everyone who might be affected by the company's activities (the stakeholders): not only contractual stakeholders, such as employees, suppliers, and customers, but local neighbourhoods that could be affected by a plant closure, cities and states affected by the loss of jobs and tax revenues stemming from a company's strategy to move activities elsewhere, and even larger international society for companies' employment policies, environmental impacts, or marketing policies around the world.

At this stage it may be useful to consider the role of regulatory bodies such as the US Securities and Futures Exchange, the UK Companies House, the listing requirements of the Australian Securities Exchange, and the role of the Hong Kong Securities and Futures Commission. This information, in the Corporate Governance in Action boxes that follow, will give you an insight into the regulatory process and encourage you to explore the way the regulatory institutions operate in your own country.

Corporate Governance in Action 2.1   The role of the US SEC and EDGAR and XBRL reporting

The SEC was created following the Great Crash of 1929. Previously, there had been little support for federal involvement in corporate matters. During the 1920s, over 20 million shareholders set out to make their fortunes on the stock market. Of around US$50 million in new securities issued, half became worthless. Countless fortunes were lost. Many banks failed. Depression followed and confidence in the markets collapsed.

Congress passed the 1933 Securities Act to restore investor confidence. The Securities and Exchange Commission (SEC) was set up to enforce the new laws designed to promote security in the market by requiring public companies to tell the truth about their business, their securities, and the risks involved, and requiring security dealers to treat investors fairly and honestly.

The mission of the SEC is to protect investors, to maintain fair, orderly, and efficient markets, and to facilitate capital formation. Unlike the banking world, where deposits are guaranteed by the federal government, stocks, bonds, and other securities can lose value. The laws and rules that govern the securities industry in the United States derive from a simple and straightforward concept: all investors, whether large institutions or private individuals, should have access to certain basic facts about an investment prior to buying it, and as long as they hold it. To achieve this, the SEC requires public companies to disclose meaningful financial and other information to the public. This provides a common pool of knowledge for all investors to use to judge for themselves whether to buy, sell, or hold a particular security.

The SEC oversees the key participants in the securities world, including securities exchanges, securities brokers and dealers, investment advisers, and mutual funds. Crucial to the SEC's effectiveness in each of these areas is its enforcement authority. Each year, the SEC brings hundreds of civil enforcement actions against individuals and companies for violation of the securities laws. Typical infractions include insider trading, accounting fraud, and providing false or misleading information about securities and the companies that issue them.

To support investors, the SEC provides a mass of information, including the EDGAR database of disclosure documents that public companies are required to file with the Commission. From 2011, the SEC required filings of all necessary corporate documents to be XBRL-based. XBRL (eXtensible Business Reporting Language) is an open, free, global, standard system covering financial data and facilitates the creation, distribution, and use of business reports.

The SEC is the primary overseer and regulator of the US securities markets, and works closely with many other institutions including Congress, other federal departments and agencies, the self-regulatory organizations (e.g. the stock exchanges), state securities regulators, and various private sector organizations. In particular, the Chair of the SEC, together with the Chair of the Federal Reserve, the Secretary of the Treasury, and the Chair of the Commodities Futures Trading Commission, serves as a member of the President's Working Group on Financial Markets.

(For more information, see www.sec.gov and www.xbrl.org/uk.)

Corporate Governance in Action 2.2   Companies House: the UK company registration service

In the United Kingdom, Companies House is the central registry for all companies registered in the UK—private, public, and limited by guarantee. All companies in the UK have to be formally incorporated through Companies House, and must file the required documents and financial accounts, annually and whenever changes occur. These documents are then available for public scrutiny.

Companies House WebFiling Service allows companies to file the required forms online. The option of filing hard copies was withdrawn from 2013, being replaced by electronic reporting using XBRL (eXtensible Business Reporting Language).

Companies House provides a free searchable index of company names and addresses on over 2 million companies registered in the UK. Companies House WebCheck is an online search tool, for accessing and downloading company information from over 250 million company documents including company accounts. Copies of a company's latest accounts and annual return and some company reports can be bought online.

(For more information, see www.companieshouse.gov.uk.)

Corporate Governance in Action 2.3   The role of the Australian Securities Exchange (ASX)

The ASX has two basic functions, as follows:

1. To operate Australia's primary national stock exchange for equities, derivatives, and fixed-interest securities, including settlement facilities. It also provides comprehensive information on the Australian stock market, including share prices. Under the Australian Corporations Act, ASX is required to operate markets that are fair, orderly, and transparent.

2. To supervise the market, including monitoring participants' conduct and enforcing compliance with the rules. To protect the integrity of the market, ASX sets standards for the behaviour of listed companies through its Listing Rules.

In 2006, to overcome concerns about conflict between its regulatory and commercial functions, and to provide greater transparency and accountability, ASX placed its supervisory function in a separate subsidiary called ASX Markets Supervision, with its own board. ASX Markets Supervision processes applications for listing on the ASX, monitors compliance with the Listing Rules, and reviews proposals from listed entities for significant restructures, reorganizations, and new issues.

The ASX Corporate Governance Council has developed a set of guidelines: Principles of Good Corporate Governance and Best Practice Recommendations.

(For more information, see www.asx.com.au.)

Corporate Governance in Action 2.4   The Listing Rules of the ASX

To protect the integrity of the market, ASX sets standards for the behaviour of listed companies through its Listing Rules. These Listing Rules cover the following matters:

- admission of companies to the ASX Official List;
- market quotation;
- continuous disclosure of relevant information;
- periodic disclosure of specific information;
- additional reporting for mining and exploration firms;
- securities trading;
- changes in capital and new issues of shares;
- transfers and registration of share transactions;
- restricted securities;
- transactions with persons in a position of influence;
- significant transactions;
- on-going requirements;
- additional requirements for trusts;
- meetings required;
- documents required;
- fees;
- the halting of trading, suspension, and removal of companies;
- application of the listing rules.

The ASX Listing Rules, Appendices, and Guidance Notes are available in electronic format.

(For more information, see www.asx.com.au.)

Corporate Governance in Action 2.5   The role of the Hong Kong Securities and Futures Commission

The Securities and Futures Commission (SFC) is an independent, non-governmental, statutory body outside the civil service, responsible for regulating the securities and futures markets in Hong Kong, for administering the laws governing the securities and futures markets in Hong Kong, and for facilitating and encouraging the development of these markets.

The statutory duties of the SFC are:

- to maintain and promote the fairness, efficiency, competitiveness, transparency, and orderliness of the securities and futures industry;
- to promote understanding by the public of the operation and functioning of the securities and futures industry;
- to provide protection for members of the public investing in or holding financial products;
- to minimize crime and misconduct in the securities and futures industry;
- to reduce systemic risks in the securities and futures industry;
- to assist the Financial Secretary in maintaining the financial stability of Hong Kong by taking appropriate steps in relation to the securities and futures industry.

As the statutory regulator of the securities and futures markets in Hong Kong, the Commission places great importance on corporate governance: 'We always strive to enhance our accountability to the public and the transparency of our work. We adopt and implement corporate governance practices commensurate with the best standards applicable to public bodies.' All important policies and decisions are discussed and approved by the board, which meets regularly every month and holds additional meetings as necessary. Divisional staff attend board meetings to explain policy proposals, reporting on important operational matters and regulatory issues. Members are also briefed on the financial positions of the Commission and provided with monthly financial statements.

(For more information, see www.sfc.hk.)

The significance of constitutions for corporate entities

Every corporate entity needs a constitution

A corporate entity is formed whenever a group of members organize a company, institution, society, association, or other entity to serve their purpose. Being artificial, corporate entities have to be created. For that, they need some form of constitution, which may be formal under the law, for example under company law or the law registering cooperatives, or informal, consisting of little more than a name, a purpose, and a set of rules. As the name indicates, corporate governance is about the way in which these corporate entities are governed.

In each case, the entity has an existence separate from its members, runs activities, and needs to keep separate financial accounts. Its constitution should provide the organization's name and purpose, define the rights and duties of its members, and lay down the way in which it is to be governed. Typically, the constitution will define the nature of the governing body, its role, and how its members are elected or chosen.

Corporate entity	Members	Constitution	Governing body
Limited-liability company	Shareholders	Memorandum and articles of association	Board of directors
Professional organization	Qualified members of the profession	Charter and membership rules	Council
Local football club	Club members	Rules	Committee
Trades union	Registered members	Constitution and Branch rule books	General Executive Council
Oxford college	Fellows of the college	Founding statute or Royal charter	The Governing Body

Figure 2.2 Examples of the governance arrangements in different corporate entities

Figure 2.2 provides some comparisons of corporate entities, showing the separation between corporate entities and their members, with examples of different constitutions and governing bodies.

The governing body usually wields governance power over the corporate entity. However, in the case of companies, particularly public companies, other drivers of governance power can include shareholder activists, institutional investors, corporate raiders, and holders of blocks of shares, as well as threats of hostile takeover bids.

Whether the constitution is formal, as required under law, or an informal set of rules, it is a fundamental underpinning of the corporate entity and, hence, its governance. Yet, amazingly, many people appointed as directors of limited companies or elected to councils or committees of other bodies have never read that entity's constitution. An important part of the induction of every company director should be to study and understand the company's articles of association, particularly the rules about its governance.

Incorporating a joint-stock, limited-liability company

The incorporation of a limited-liability company involves the registration of formal documents, in line with the company laws of the jurisdiction in which the company is to be incorporated. Typically, the founding members (shareholders) of the company have to prepare and submit the articles of association for the proposed company to the companies' registrar. In some jurisdictions a memorandum is also required stating the company's name, share capital, registered office, and, sometimes, its purpose. Alternatively, the promoters of the company may buy a company 'off the shelf', from a business that specializes in setting up companies, and simply change the name of the company to the one they want.

The companies' registrar will check the proposed company name to ensure that there is no duplication and that the name is not undesirable (for example, in the UK names that suggest a connection with the royal family or involvement with unacceptable activities are not allowed). On incorporation, the company's name is entered on the companies' register and the articles of association become public documents, available for scrutiny by anyone.

Other statutory documents, such as an annual return with the details of the shareholders, officers, and directors, changes to company details and changes to the capital structure have to be filed together with, in some jurisdictions, financial accounts.

In the United States, companies are incorporated under the laws of a specific state. As we saw in Chapter 1, unlike most other countries, there is no provision for the formation of a company at the federal level in the United States, although the SEC provides federal-level oversight of public companies listed on US stock markets. Many public companies, with shares listed on a US stock market, are incorporated in the state of Delaware, where corporate laws offer more flexibility in conducting business than in many other states. Delaware also has a highly respected business court, the Delaware Court of Chancery, which is considered by some to be sympathetic to boards of directors.

In the European Union, however, it is now possible to incorporate companies not only in the country of origin, but also at the European level. The European company, known by the Latin term *Societas Europaea* (SE), enables companies incorporated in different member states of the European Union to merge or to form a holding company at the European level. In other words, it provides firms with the option of incorporating in other member states. Formation of an SE holding company is available to both public and private companies with registered offices or branches in different member states. One-tier or two-tier boards are permitted. Provisions also call for the participation of employees in company matters.

Companies incorporated for profit-making purposes with shareholders who have limited liability can be classified, broadly, into two groups—public and private.

1. The public limited company may offer its shares to the general public. Shareholder members are not liable for the company's debts. In the UK, public limited companies must add the designation 'PLC' to their names; elsewhere, they are required to add the word 'limited' or 'incorporated' to their name, so that those contracting with them understand that the shareholders' liability is limited. Not all public companies are listed on a stock exchange, but all listed companies must be public companies. To obtain a listing on a stock exchange, a company must meet the listing requirements of that exchange. In most jurisdictions, the company must also pass the scrutiny of the securities regulatory authority. Typically, a listing requires the preparation of a prospectus, which is a legal document that reviews the company, and its history, business, and financial situation. The prospectus provides prospective investors with the information that they will need to decide whether they wish to risk their funds.

2. The private limited company may not offer its shares to the general public. This is by far the most common form of incorporation. Private limited companies are required to add 'Limited' ('Ltd') or 'Incorporated' (Inc.) to their names. In most jurisdictions, the number of members of a private company is limited and the requirements for filing documents with the registrar are not as demanding as those for public companies.

A third category covers corporate entities created for the public benefit or community interest rather than private advantage and profit-making. In the United States, public benefit corporations are incorporated within states for the delivery of public services, for example transportation authorities, port authorities, and community organizations. Such entities have no shareholders, and raise their funds through bonds that pay interest, which is a charge against profits, rather than pay dividends, which would take a share of profits. In the United Kingdom, private companies incorporated by guarantee have guarantor members whose liability is limited to the amount they agree to contribute on a winding-up, often quite a nominal sum. A 2004 UK Act created the community interest company (CIC) for activities that benefit the community rather than private interests. Examples include companies limited by guarantee, charities, and other not-for-profit entities, National Health Service foundation trusts, companies providing services with an element of public subsidy (see Case study 3.1 Network Rail), as well as organizations linking the public and private sectors, such as regeneration projects. A state regulator ensures that the CIC has been established for community benefit and that all assets and profits are used for these purposes.

We will study the governance of subsidiary and associated companies, joint ventures, public interest companies, and complex groups of companies in Chapter 11.

The memorandum and articles of association

A company's memorandum is a short document that states the company's name, outlines the purposes for which it has been created, gives the address of its registered office, lists the nominal amount and classes of shares with which it is being formed, and states that the liability of its members is limited to the equity capital subscribed. In most jurisdictions, details of the initial subscribing members are included. A registered office is needed because the company is not a person and anyone dealing with the company needs to know where to find it. The objects clause in a memorandum defines its purposes. In the early days, this was, in effect, a constraint imposed by the community for allowing the company to trade with limited liability. Action taken by a company outside its objects would be invalid. Subsequently, this clause has often been drawn very widely, so that the company is free to carry on a wide range of activities. Because of the breadth of activities now included, some company laws no longer require an objects clause, and some no longer call for a memorandum.

The articles of association are, in effect, the rules by which the company is governed. Companies' Acts in many jurisdictions contain a draft memorandum for guidance. Corporate Governance in Action 2.6 provides an example of the contents of a simple set of articles. Memorandum and articles are public documents and anyone may request copies. Many companies now make them available on their websites. Most jurisdictions require companies to file registration documents, periodic financial and other reports to help investors, creditors, and other interested parties find relevant information. For links to a complete list of filings and instructions for searching the EDGAR database, go to: www.sec.gov/edgar/searchedgar/webusers.htm

Corporate Governance in Action 2.6   Example of the contents of articles of association

A typical set of articles might contain detailed rules on the following.

Share capital

Details of the share capital, including any class of shares with special rights, such as voting rights or preferential status for dividends, also the means of varying such rights; if the shares are not fully paid up on issue, the way in which calls may be made; the way in which shares may be transferred from one shareholder to another; the type of meeting and resolution of the members required to alter the company's capital.

General meetings of the company

The requirement to hold an annual meeting of the shareholder members; the rules governing special or extraordinary meetings of members; the notice required for meetings; proceedings at general meetings, including the necessary quorum, the appointment of the chair, and voting on resolutions by a show of hands of those present or by a poll based on shareholdings.

Directors

The number of directors, any shareholding qualification for directors, the determination of the remuneration of directors; the powers and duties of directors; the disqualification of directors, for example by becoming bankrupt, of unsound mind, missing meetings, or prohibited by the courts or companies registrar from acting as a director; the length of service and the rotation of directors, for example with one-third retiring every year (known as a staggered board); the proceedings at directors' meetings, including notice of meetings, quorum, election of chair, delegation of powers to committees of the board.

Officers of the company

The board's power to appoint a managing director or chief executive officer (CEO), a company secretary, and other officers such as a chief finance officer (CFO).

Dividend policy and reserves

The powers of the members in general meetings to agree policies on reserves and the payment of dividends. (Typically, on such matters, the general meeting will follow the proposals put before it by the board.)

Requirements for accounts and audit

The requirement for the directors to keep proper financial records for the company and to provide regular accounts, including a profit and loss account and balance sheet to the members periodically; the appointment of auditors in line with the Companies Acts.

Provisions for winding up the company

The procedures for winding up the company with the members' agreement or on enforced liquidation.

Other forms of incorporation

We have looked at the incorporation of limited-liability companies (private companies limited by shares, private companies limited by guarantee, and public companies limited by shares) under the Companies' Acts of the jurisdiction in which the companies are registered. But there are other ways in which corporate entities can be formally created, as we saw in Figure 2.2.

Some sectors—for example, savings and loan associations in the United States, building societies in the UK and Commonwealth countries, cooperatives for farmers and other suppliers in Canada, and consumer cooperatives in the UK—are incorporated under legislation designed to facilitate and regulate that specific sector.

Incorporation of specific corporate entities by the state is also common in many countries. The legislature provides the new organization with its own facilitating legislation, which defines and creates the entity and determines its governance processes, including its mission and accountability, the form of its governing body, and how the directors are appointed, which is often by the government or state agencies. For example, the Federal National Mortgage Association (Fannie Mae) was created by the US government to provide government backing for financial products and services that make it possible for low- and middle-income families to buy homes of their own. Such entities are sometimes referred to as quangos, which is an acronym for quasi-autonomous non-governmental organization, because, although they have a life and mission separate from the state, the state maintains an arm's-length interest in them. Indeed, during the global financial crisis, Fannie Mae and its sister institution, Freddie Mac, had to be bailed out by the US government.

To add a degree of confusion, 'quango' is also used, particularly in the United Kingdom and Australia, as an acronym for quasi-autonomous *national* governmental organization to describe organizations to which governments have devolved power, but in which they retain a direct influence. Examples include the Risk Management Agency of the US Department of Agriculture, the Adult Learning Inspectorate of the UK Department of Education and Skills, and the Australian Communications and Media Authority.

Charities are often set up as not-for-profit, incorporated bodies and registered under the charities law in the relevant jurisdiction. Most of the principles and practices discussed in this book apply to the governance of such entities, although those serving on their governing bodies may also be trustees and subject to additional requirements of trust law. In some countries, the charity and other not-for-profit sector bodies have developed their own corporate governance principles, codes, and best practice guidelines, as we will see in Chapter 11.

Partnerships provide another form of corporate entity. Typically, in a partnership, all partners are liable for the partnership debts in line with the agreement between the partners. But in some jurisdictions it is now possible to incorporate limited-liability partnerships, which have proved attractive to some audit firms to provide a cap to an individual partner's liability.

Professional bodies provide some interesting cases of alternative approaches to incorporation and governance. In some countries, professional bodies are incorporated under their own statute by the state authorities. In the UK and some other Commonwealth countries, many professional bodies have been created by a royal charter. Such chartered professional bodies have sovereignty over their own affairs, including the examination and admission to membership, the maintaining of standards, and the disciplining of members.

The engineering profession in both the United States and the UK has developed with constitutionally separate professional bodies to represent the interests of the various branches—electrical, civil, mechanical, and so on. Subsequently, in Britain, the Engineering Council was created by royal charter to oversee an effective federation of the separate bodies. Unlike the engineers, the UK accountancy profession has not managed to agree a federation and has a number of separate professional bodies. In the United States, criticisms following the collapse of Enron and Arthur Andersen, its auditor, led to the creation of the Public Company Accounting Oversight Board (PCAOB). In the UK, standards and oversight of the accounting profession are maintained by a number of independent bodies. In Canada, by contrast, there are provincial institutes of chartered accountants with a Co-ordinating Council of Institutes of Chartered Accountants of Canada. The governance of professional bodies, many of which have relatively large governing bodies (often called councils), can be intriguing.

Finally, we should note that a vast number of small corporate entities are created simply by agreement between interested parties. Sports clubs, drama groups, arts societies, and religious organizations all provide examples. Nevertheless, all such entities need governing as well as managing, and, consequently, need some form of constitution, which should be written if unnecessary disputes are to be avoided.

In this chapter, we have distinguished many different forms of incorporation. The principles and practices of corporate governance apply to them all, although obviously they need adapting to the circumstances. This book focuses on the governance of companies, recognizing that all other corporate entities need corporate governance, and that the methods of governing companies can be adapted to the not-for-profit and other non-company sectors.

The difference between governance and management

As we saw in Chapter 1, professional management was the major focus in business throughout the 20th century. Today, the way companies are governed has become more important than the way they are managed. Yet some people fail to make the distinction between governance and management. The notion of management as a hierarchy is commonplace—as in the classical pyramid of Figure 2.3.

A CEO, or managing director, has overall managerial responsibility, with other managers reporting to them and so on down the management hierarchy. Authority and responsibility are delegated downwards, with matching accountability expected upwards in return. The classical theory enables functional departments to be shown, and distinctions drawn, between line management responsible for executive action and staff management responsible for advising the line. We understand that this is an inadequate picture of the realities of management, but we generally accept that management operates through hierarchies. We know who reports to whom in the organization.

Figure 2.3 The classical depiction of management

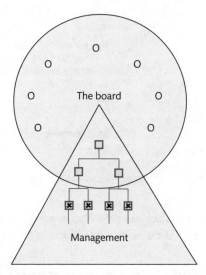

Figure 2.4 The board and management

But where is the board in classical management theory? Boards seldom appear on organization charts. The board is not part of the management structure; nor is it a hierarchy. Each director has equal responsibility and similar duties and powers under the law. There is no executive 'boss' of a board.

In Figure 2.4, the board has been superimposed on the management structure.

In a unitary board—that is, a board with both executive and non-executive, outside directors—the executive directors hold a managerial role in addition to their responsibilities as members of the board of directors. Shown in Figure 2.4, they sit in both the board circle and the management triangle. As executives, they are employees of the company and covered by employment law. Directors, as such, are not employees and are subject to company law. The other directors shown in the figure are the non-executive or outside directors—members of the board circle, but not part of the management hierarchy (triangle). Other managers, who are within the management hierarchy but not on the board, are shown with a cross.

A further important distinction can be drawn between non-executive directors who are independent of the entity, and non-executive directors who, although they are not executives of the company, have some link with it. Independent non-executive directors have no relationship with the company that could affect the exercise of independent and objective judgement. Those who are not independent have some link with the company, such as close family ties to the chair, being a representative of a dominant shareholder, having previously served as an executive of that company, having links with major trading partners of the company, and so on.

Such connections raise questions about these directors' independence. There may be good reasons for having them on the board, but we shall refer to them as 'connected' non-executive directors. These issues will be explored in more depth in Chapter 4. In the United States, the common practice is to refer to non-executive directors as 'outside directors'. For consistency, we will use the abbreviations INED (independent non-executive director) and CNED (connected non-executive director). Some authorities refer to a CNED as an affiliated non-executive director.

Governance—the work of the board of directors or other governing body

Management—the work of the executive management team

Figure 2.5 Governance distinguished from management

We now have a model that enables us to distinguish governance from management—see Figure 2.5—the board ensures that it is being run well and in the right direction.

The performance and conformance aspects of governance

Board responsibilities

We can now explore what the board does. Overall, the board's task is to direct the company, which is why directors are given that title. This activity can be seen to involve four basic elements—strategy formulation; policy-making; supervision of executive management; and accountability to shareholders and others.

In fulfilling their duties, directors have to consider the future of the company as well as its present position and recent results. They also need to look inwards at the organization and its component parts, and externally at the company in its competitive market position and in its broader economic, political, and social context. These basic perspectives and processes are shown in Figure 2.6.

In formulating strategy, the board works with top management, looking ahead in time and seeing the firm in its strategic external environment. Strategies then need to be translated into

	Past- and present-focused	Future-focused
Outward-looking	Accountability	Strategy formulation
Inward-looking	Supervising executive activities	Policy-making

Figure 2.6 The basic board perspectives and processes

policies to guide top management action and to provide plans for subsequent control. The board then needs to monitor and supervise the activities of executive management, looking inwards at the current managerial situation and at recent performance. Accountability involves responding externally, reflecting corporate activities and performance to the shareholders and other stakeholders with legitimate claims to accountability. Of course, a simple 2x2 matrix inevitably presents a simplified view of board processes—but at least by looking forwards and backwards in time and internally and externally in space, it is all-embracing.

The Cadbury Report (1992) supports this framework, commenting that 'the responsibilities of the board include setting the company's strategic aims, providing the leadership to put them in effect, supervising the management of the business and reporting to shareholders on their stewardship'.

Boards vary in the extent to which the board as a whole engages in these functions or delegates work to the CEO and the management team, while ensuring that the necessary monitoring and control processes are in place. An extension of the basic quadrant of board processes recognizes this by introducing a central cell showing that boards work with management, through their chief executives or managing directors.[1] Figure 2.7 depicts this process. Boards can choose the extent to which they delegate functions to the management. In some cases, for example, boards play a major part in the formulation of the company's strategy; in others, this is delegated to top management, with the board receiving, questioning, and finally approving management's strategic proposals.

Figure 2.7 can also highlight a potential dilemma for the unitary board. The roles in the right-hand column—strategy formulation and policy-making—are performance roles, concerned with the board's contribution to corporate direction. Those on the left—executive supervision and accountability—are essentially concerned with ensuring conformance. Figure 2.8 shows this important distinction.

As Lord Caldecote, a very experienced board chairman, once commented: 'a problem with the unitary board is that directors are marking their own examination papers'. In a two-tier board the roles are separated, with the executive board responsible for performance and the supervisory board responsible for conformance.

Figure 2.7 Framework for analysing board activities

[1] Hilmer, Frederick G. (1993) *Strictly Boardroom*. Sydney: Information Australia.

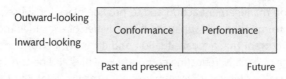

Figure 2.8 The performance and conformance aspects of a board's work

Alternative board structures

Unitary boards

When a company has a single governing body, the board is known as a 'unitary board', in contrast to the two-tier board. The formal structure of such boards has been widely written about in corporate governance. What is the appropriate balance between executive and non-executive members? What is the appropriate size for the board? Intuitively, there are four possible structures: a board with only executive directors; a board with a majority of executive directors; a board with a majority of non-executive directors; and a board with only non-executive directors.

The all-executive-director board

In the *all-executive-director board*, the top managers are also the directors. There are no outside, non-executive directors (see Figure 2.9). This structure can be found in many small family firms and start-up businesses. Typically, the company has not reached the stage at which it needs non-executive directors. Directors on such boards seldom draw a distinction between their duties as directors and their roles as managers. In their minds, the company is a legal convenience, perhaps with taxation advantages and limiting personal liability, rather than a distinct legal entity. Bankers providing finance to such companies often require personal guarantees from individual directors to cover loans made to the company. As we will see later, the all-executive-director board is also found frequently in the board structures of subsidiary companies operating in corporate groups.

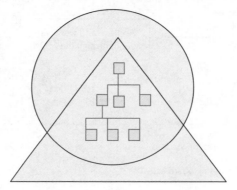

Figure 2.9 The all-executive-director board

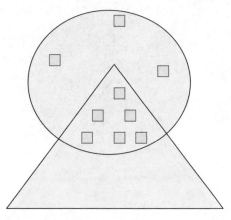

Figure 2.10 The majority-executive-director board

The majority-executive-director board

In the *majority-executive-director board*, some non-executive directors have been invited to join the board, although they remain in the minority (see Figure 2.10). The addition of non-executive directors to a board can arise for various reasons. The executive directors of a successful, growing company may feel the need for additional expertise to back up their own experience, perhaps as they enter new markets, get involved in new technologies, or face more complex managerial or financial issues. The price of accepting significant growth capital from an outside source may also be the requirement to allow a non-executive director to represent the interests of the lender. A family firm moving into the second generation may find that, while some family members continue to be directly involved in the management of the firm, others are now outside the firm and shareholders only. Calls for non-executive directors to represent the non-management family shareholders on the board may now arise. The challenges of governance in family firms will be discussed in Chapter 11.

However, in the majority-executive board, the executive directors, being in the majority, typically continue to exercise considerable power over the company. Some authorities refer to such boards as 'executive boards'. This model reflected the typical structure of the British public listed company until the 1970s. Research has shown that, at that time, the boards of even major companies had a majority of executive directors. The conventional wisdom was that non-executive directors could be quite useful on a board, adding additional experience, perspective, and insight to discussions, that about one-third non-executive directors was about right, but that the non-executives should never be in the majority. In those days, executive directors wielded the power over what they perceived as 'their' company.

The majority-non-executive-director board

However, in the United States, the United Kingdom, and similar advanced economies, the boards of most significant listed companies now have a *majority of non-executive directors* and many of these non-executive directors are likely to be independent directors. Indeed, as we shall see, many corporate governance codes now demand this structure for listed companies.

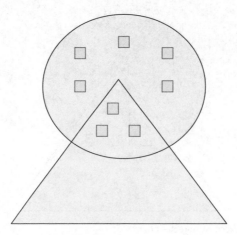

Figure 2.11 The majority-non-executive-director board

Clearly, when non-executive directors are in the majority, the culture of the board, its internal relationships, and, indeed, its activities are likely to be different from those of boards dominated by executive directors. Some authorities refer to such boards as 'professional boards' (see Figure 2.11).

The typical board of a company listed in the United States will have only one or two executive directors—the chair or CEO, the CFO, and perhaps the chief operating officer (COO)—with three or four times that number of outside directors. Nevertheless, the chair/CEO continues to wield considerable power, because in the United States these roles are often combined in a single person. Consequently, the outside directors are expected to provide oversight and supervision of executive activities, the achievement of corporate objectives, and assure compliance with corporate governance requirements. Since independence criteria require outside directors to have no relationship with the company, other than the directorship, which can mean that such directors have relatively little knowledge of the company's industry or markets, the formulation of strategy has to be led by the CEO supported by the top management team, with the board questioning to ensure that strategic developments are in an appropriate direction and that business risks have been appropriately assessed. Critics of this type of board structure suggest that, in practice, it gives too much power to the executive directors by making them responsible for strategy as well as the day-to-day running of the enterprise. The outside directors, they suggest, are inevitably pushed into a conformance and compliance mode, rather than contributing positively to the performance aspects of strategy formulation and policy-making. 'Such board structures are pushing us towards the European two-tier board system', one experienced director of a British public company has argued.

The all-non-executive-director board

Finally, there is an obvious fourth category of board structure: the *board composed entirely of non-executive directors* (see Figure 2.12). Such board structures are seldom found in listed public companies, but frequently in the boards of not-for-profit entities, such as charitable organizations, arts, health, and sports organizations, and quangos. Frequently, the

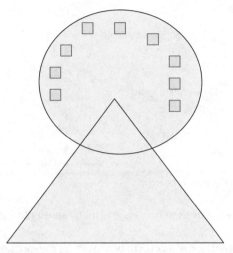

Figure 2.12 The all-non-executive-director board

constitutions of such organizations call for a proportion of the board members to be drawn from interest groups involved; in a hospital, for example, this means medical staff, administrators, funding bodies, patients, and the local community. Some authorities refer to such boards as 'stakeholder boards'.

The boards of some subsidiary companies in corporate groups may also have such a structure, in which the board consists of senior executives from elsewhere in the corporate organization. When boards have this structure, the CEO and, perhaps, members of the management team typically attend board meetings, but are there to provide information and to answer directors' questions, not to be formally involved in the taking of decisions. Indeed, in most cases, the constitution will provide for the board to invite managers to attend meetings, either for the entire agenda or for specific items, but reserving the right to ask them to leave and for the board to take decisions *in camera*.

Two-tier boards

It is apparent that, conceptually, the all-non-executive board has the same structure as the European two-tier or supervisory board architecture. Figure 2.12 can be redrafted to show this, as in Figure 2.13.

In the German approach to corporate governance, large and public companies are required to have a two-tier board structure: the upper, supervisory board, called the *Aufsichtsrat*, and the lower, management board or committee, called the *Vorstand*. The supervisory board is composed entirely of outside directors and the management board entirely of executive directors.

Germany has long believed that the management of large companies should involve a close relationship between the workers and the company, an informal partnership between labour and capital. This process, referred to as 'co-determination', is enshrined in law. As a result, half of the members of supervisory boards represent the interests of the employees and are appointed through the trades union organizations. The remaining supervisory board members represent the interest of the shareholders and are appointed by them. In Germany

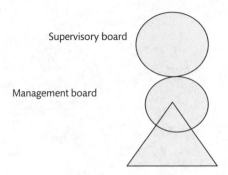

Supervisory board

Management board

Figure 2.13 The two-tier or supervisory board

financial institutions are major shareholders and their representatives are often members of supervisory boards.

In practice, members of the management board attend meetings of the supervisory board, but have no vote. The executive members present their strategies, management plans, and budgets to the supervisory board for comment and approval. If necessary, the supervisory board refers matters back to the executives for further consideration. The supervisory board can then review and assess subsequent managerial performance. The power of the supervisory board lies in its ability to appoint to and remove members from the executive board.

The German Corporate Governance Commission launched a code of best practice (Kodex) in 2002, which provided supervisory boards with more powers over management and external audit, required details of directors' remuneration (including the criteria for performance-based rewards), and gave investors more timely information. While technically voluntary, some of the provisions have been enshrined in company law. Since 2003, German companies have had to issue an annual statement published online, showing whether they have complied with the code and explaining any discrepancies.

The corporate governance architecture of Dutch companies also adopts the two-tier board. But the structure of the Dutch supervisory board is tripartite—one-third representing capital, one-third employees, and the other third society at large. A companies' court resolves questions about the suitability of members to represent the three interest groups.

As we saw earlier, at one time the Commission of the European Union (or EEC as it then was) believed that the two-tier board should be adopted in all member states, but subsequently adopted a more adaptable approach reflecting practices in the member states. The legal framework in those countries that adopt the two-tier board model is typically based on continental European Napoleonic civil law, which is typically highly prescriptive. By contrast, in the United States, the United Kingdom, and many Commonwealth countries with law derived originally from British law, the legal framework is rooted in common law that evolves as decided cases set precedents. Corporate Governance in Action 2.7 shows the practical effects of a two-tier board.

Corporate Governance in Action 2.7   Volkswagen's supervisory board

German company Volkswagen, Europe's largest car-maker, had a supervisory board. Institutional investors demanded that the chairman of the supervisory board, Herr Piëch, resign because of alleged conflicts of interest. They claimed that Herr Piëch and his family held significant shares in Porsche, which held a near 20 per cent stake in Volkswagen.

Germany's voluntary corporate governance code states that conflicts of interest should result in the termination of a supervisory board member's mandate. Herr Piëch claimed that the conflict would be managed by his leaving the room whenever any Porsche-related matter was discussed. Some American institutional investors called this 'naive'. Herr Piëch was strongly supported by the ten employee representatives on the 20-strong board.

Taiwan also uses two-tier boards. In mainland China, the authorities, in creating the corporate governance structures and processes for their newly privatized and listed companies, require a two-tier structure with a supervisory board and a main board, but, quite unlike the continental European model, also call for independent outside directors on the main board.

Table 2.1 compares corporate governance board structures in various countries. Please note: France has both unitary and two-tier boards.

Advisory boards

Advisory boards, sometimes called advisory committees, may be created by companies operating in various parts of the world, to give advice to the corporate directors about matters in overseas places. Typically, business leaders and/or influential politicians from the region are

Table 2.1 Comparison of corporate governance board structures

Country	Chair/CEO separation	Average board size	% outside directors
Unitary board model			
Australia	Very high	8	High
Belgium	High	15	High
Brazil	Low	6	Moderate
Canada	High	13	Very high
France	Nil	13	High
Italy	Total	11	High
Spain	Low	12	High
Sweden	High	9	Very high
Switzerland	High	5	Very high
UK	Very high	12	High
US	Low	13	Very high
Two-tier board model			
France	Total	12	Very high
Germany	Total	15	Total
Netherlands	Total	7	Total
Business network model			
Japan	Total	Large	Very low

invited to serve, but are not given executive powers. Advisory boards were more prevalent in the 1970s and 1980s. Subsequently, companies found that the advice they needed could be obtained more cheaply from consultants, who need to be retained only as long as their advice is wanted. Some also found that advisory boards, although they had no formal executive authority, assumed an independence that created complications by making policy recommendations, which were inconsistent with group-wide needs. An advisory board might, for example, call for more investment in a given country, when the board's global strategy called for disinvestment there. Business start-up entrepreneurs and small companies may also create advisory boards to get advice and counsel from an impartial and experienced group. Again, such advisory boards have no executive power.

Board diversity

Obviously, as well as the structure of the board, the knowledge, experience, and skills of each individual member is fundamental. We will study what qualities a director needs and what makes for an effective board in Chapter 13. But a matter of principle has arisen in recent years, which needs to be considered now—the issue of board diversity. As we noted in Chapter 1, the predominant interest in the diversity of board membership has been in gender diversity. But recently some commentators have also called for a broader representation of different constituencies on boards, to reflect the interests of, for example, customers, young people, or minorities.

Gender diversity

The case for gender diversity is now widely accepted. The low percentage of women on many boards suggests that a significant potential asset is being overlooked. But the response of some, admittedly male-dominated, board nomination committees is that they find relatively

Table 2.2 Percentage of women on listed company boards by country

Country	Estimate end-2014 of women serving on the boards of listed companies and state corporations
Denmark	41%
Sweden and France	25% or more
UK	20%
France	18%
USA	17%
Germany	14%
Australia	12%
Japan and United Arab Emirates	Slightly over 1%
Saudi Arabia	Virtually 0

Source: www.catalyst.org/knowledge/women-corporate-boards-globally

few women in senior executive positions with appropriate experience: that challenge has to be met first. However, experience differs around the world (see Table 2.2).

To redress the gender imbalance, some governments have advocated quotas for women to be appointed to boards. Norway introduced a quota in 2005. India, Malaysia, and South Africa have also called for quotas. In 2009, the US SEC passed a rule that required companies to explain their policies on nominating directors; in other words, companies have to explain their own attitudes towards gender diversity. In 2011, a UK-government-commissioned report by Lord Davies called for 25 per cent women on boards by 2015, which was not achieved though the percentage rose. The Davies Report also called for listed companies to explain their policies on gender diversity.

Calls for more women on boards and the use of quotas have tended to come from governments, regulators, and interest groups. Board members and shareholders, including institutional investors, have tended to be unenthusiastic, despite the obvious missed talent and opportunities for the female perspective.

Stakeholder diversity

This rationale calls for boards to have representatives of those with contractual links to the company, such as customers, contractors and distributors, suppliers, shareholders and other sources of finance, and so on. Proponents of such ideas point out that boards need reliable intelligence from all stakeholder sources in order to make valid judgements. Whilst agreeing with the need for reliable information, opponents of stakeholder diversity claim that there are time-honoured ways for directors to be informed about their stakeholders' needs and the likely effect of the board's decisions on them. Giving stakeholders board membership could promote conflicts of interest between the different interest groups.

Such a notion, of course, also includes employees of the company. This suggestion was discussed *ad nauseam* in the UK in 1977, when the EEC (as it then was) called, in their draft fifth directive, for two-tier boards with worker members appointed to the supervisory board. This was followed by Lord Bullock's report on industrial democracy in Britain, which argued that unitary boards were perfectly adequate but proposed that they should include worker representatives. In the event neither proposal got off the starting line.

Societal diversity

This idea is based on the belief that board members should reflect the impact a company might have on society at large. A board should include members capable of recognizing the needs and interests of society, age, gender, minority interests including ethnic, disability, or social minorities, and environmental, cultural, or societal interests. The intention would be for boards to balance corporate decisions with the interests of society.

A representative of the UK's Financial Reporting Council (FRC) explained the FRC's support of diverse boards:

> Real diversity is about a wide group of people bringing their broad range of experiences to the table; experiences which cause them to ask different questions, consider an issue from a different angle, or raise doubts that would otherwise never be considered.

The full text of the FCA document (precursor of the FRC) and a blog in response is in Case study 2.2: Do boards need diversity?

Obviously, the more diverse the background of board members, the more conflicts of opinion may arise. Board chairs might have to face more challenges than would be the case if the board were composed of like-minded people. Inevitably such a governance system would result in competing and potentially conflicting goals, and could ultimately challenge the concept of the joint-stock, limited-liability company.

Case studies

 Case study 2.1   Sir Philip Green and the collapse of BHS

Sir Philip Green

Green is a flamboyant and confrontational billionaire. Many reporters have experienced his explosive temper. He is not one to give interviews. So he was unlikely to provide information to your case writer, who has relied on company accounts, published reports, and newspaper commentary.

Over the years, Green built up a network of retail stores within the Arcadia Group, principally in clothing, both in Britain and abroad, through acquisition, merger, and restructuring. He received his knighthood for contributions to retailing.

Green and his family own and dominate Arcadia Group. Therefore, Green felt that Arcadia was his own company: so he and his family were entitled to pay themselves substantial dividends and fees. He is reported to have said 'It's my money, I can do what I like with it'.

The wealth of Sir Philip was ranked number 41 in the *Sunday Times* Rich List 2017. He and his family own a number of yachts.

Arcadia Group Ltd

The Arcadia Group Ltd is an investment company running a network of subsidiary companies mainly in clothes retailing under the brand names Topshop, Topman, Dorothy Perkins, Burtons Menswear, Wallis, Evans, Miss Selfridge, and Outfit. Arcadia had over 3,000 retail outlets and nearly 7 million square feet of space. The Arcadia accounts list 77 wholly owned subsidiaries, some of them with their own chain of subsidiaries.

The majority of the Arcadia Group Ltd is owned by Taveta Investments (No. 2) Ltd, which itself is owned by Tina Green, the wife of Sir Philip Green. Lady Green is a British citizen resident in the Principality of Monaco, a Mediterranean tax haven. Taveta Investments is the first link in a network of trusts and companies, many registered in Jersey, a Channel Islands tax haven. The Arcadia Group was dominated by Sir Philip Green up to his resignation from the board on 15 December 2015.

Carmen Ltd, a property company owned by the Green family, received over £10 million in rent on BHS stores in 2014/15. (For more information on Arcadia see www.arcadiagroup.co.uk.)

The business and ownership of BHS

British Home Stores was founded in 1928, by retailers from the United States. At the height of its success the retail chain had a department store in the high street of most major towns and cities in Britain, with departments selling furniture, clothing, lighting, toys, and kitchen appliances, for example. Eventually, British Home Stores became so well known that it shortened its name to BHS.

BHS was originally a public company, listed on the London Stock Exchange. Indeed, it was large enough to be a constituent stock in the FTSE 100 index; but in 2000 BHS was taken over by Sir Philip Green through Arcadia and became a private unlisted company.

Fifteen years later, in March 2015, Green agreed to sell BHS to Retail Acquisitions Ltd, a company run by Dominic Chappell, a three-times-bankrupt former racing driver. A nominal sum of £1 was paid to seal the contract. At the time, Mr Chappell was said to be personally insolvent.

According to the *Guardian* newspaper, Arcadia insisted on three protective covenants before selling BHS:

1. All monies available to BHS at the time of sale shall be used for the day-to-day running of BHS.

2. All proceeds realised from the sale of BHS properties shall be used to operate BHS as a going concern and to pay its debts.

3. No steps are to be taken by the buyer that would adversely affect the ability of BHS to continue as a going concern.

Arcadia Finance Director Paul Budge explained that this was to ensure that all funds available to BHS should be used for that company's business and not drawn down by the new owners.

The financial impacts of the BHS sale are clear in the Arcadia accounts for 2014/15. £216 million due to Arcadia Group Ltd were waived. Provisions relating to BHS disposal and cash transferred by Arcadia to BHS totalled £88 million. The cash costs of the BHS disposal included £2.3 million for professional fees.

The collapse of BHS and its aftermath

By April 2016, BHS was insolvent and unable to continue trading. The company was then put into winding-up administration. The international operations were shortly afterwards acquired by the Al Mana Group and still trade. But, unable to find a buyer, the British operations were liquidated in early 2017. This was the largest failure of a British retail chain since the collapse of Woolworths in 2008.

A spokesperson for Chappell said that 'the company just ran out of time and money'. Others were less supportive when it transpired that Chappell had taken a salary of half a million pounds from the company. Challenged about the loss of jobs at BHS, Green said that he was not responsible for what had happened at the company.

The BHS pension fund had more than 20,000 members including pensioners and current employees. Documents released after the crash suggested that the fund had faced a current deficit of over £500 million. In other words, estimated future liabilities of the fund exceeded its assets by half a million pounds. Many other company pension funds also faced deficits at the time, owing to increasing life expectancy (and therefore costs of pensions), low interest rates, and poor equity and bond market performance. But in liquidation BHS had no chance to make good its deficit.

The British government had created a Pension Protection Fund (PPF) in 2004 to protect pensioners in the private sector should their employer be liquidated. The PPF is funded by a levy on existing registered pension funds. However, it does not automatically guarantee the same benefits as the original fund. Moreover, in the BHS case questions were asked whether Green and the Arcadia Group had any liability, given the sale of the company for £1 a year earlier, without making good any pension deficit. The UK Pensions Regulator and the PPF do have the power to call on previous owners of a company for a contribution to a pension fund deficit, for the period reflecting their ownership.

A few commentators felt that the Arcadia shareholders had already lost their original substantial investment in BHS. But others pointed out that, during Green's 15-year control of the company, he and other family members had received substantial dividends and directors' fees from BHS.

Moreover, since much of that income had gone to the Monaco tax haven no British tax had been paid on it. There were calls for Green to lose his knighthood.

An inquiry was launched by the British parliament. Members of Parliament from the select committees for Work and Pensions, and Business Innovation and Skills, called for evidence to probe the BHS collapse. The Chairman of the Work and Pensions select committee, Frank Field, suggested that Green himself should fund the deficit. Green responded aggressively, claiming that he had offered to support the pension fund but his offer had been rejected. He also suggested that Field was biased against him. In his defence, Green said:

> Any fair review of the BHS balance sheet would show the support we had provided to the BHS business throughout. It is clear that we invested substantially in the business. We lent substantial sums to the business and we gave Retail Acquisitions every chance, with a solid platform to take the business forward.

The Chairman of the BHS pension fund trustees, Chris Martin, told the MPs that he had raised concerns about the deficit in the BHS pension fund after meeting Chappell. He felt that Retail Acquisitions had done little due diligence during their acquisition.

Business select committee member Richard Fuller called for an investigation by the FRC into the conduct of the directors and professional advisers involved. The FRC launched a probe into the involvement as BHS auditor of one of the Big Four audit firms, PriceWaterhouseCoopers (PwC). MPs called for Lady Green to shed light on the complex web of companies registered in her name in tax havens, and on their profits. They also wanted to know more about the relationship between the Greens and Goldman Sachs.

More critical comments followed. The Institute of Directors said that the action of Green:

> has the potential to be deeply damaging to British business. We spend a lot of time agonizing over the loss of trust in the business community and I think we can see why ... When someone ends up behaving like this people think that is how business is: and it is not.

Discussion questions

1. Why do you think Green sold BHS for £1? Why did Chappell buy the company?

2. Should the UK tax laws be changed to make non-residents liable to tax on dividends or other payments made by British companies out of profits earned in the UK?

3. Should there be a corporate governance code for private companies? Should it apply only to companies over a certain size (by turnover, number of employees, or profit, for example) and could sanctions be applied for failure to conform (listed companies might face the threat of delisting, for example)?

4. Should independent auditors provide non-audit services and advice to their audit clients? (In 2014/15 PwC were paid £355,000 in audit fees plus fees for non-audit services of £1,798,000.)

5. The UK Companies Act 2006 applies to all limited-liability companies in the UK—public and private. It therefore applied to the Arcadia Group Ltd and to BHS Ltd. The Companies Act specifically spells out a statutory duty to recognize the effect of board decisions on a wider public, including 'the interests of the company's employees', and 'the need to foster the company's business relations with suppliers, customers and others'. Did the decisions that led to the liquidation of BHS meet these requirements? If not, how might the Act be enforced?

Case study 2.2   Do boards need diversity?

The Financial Reporting Council (FRC) is the UK's independent regulator responsible for promoting transparency and integrity in business. The FRC sets the UK Corporate Governance and Stewardship Codes and UK standards for accounting and actuarial work, monitors compliance, and takes action to promote the quality of corporate reporting.

The following extract is from a speech by Christopher Woolard, Executive Director of Strategy and Competition at the Financial Conduct Authority (FCA—another major UK regulator), delivered at the Financial Services Industry Summit 2017.

The art of thinking independently together—why regulators care about diversity

I like to say I cared about diversity and inclusion long before it became the focus of attention in our workplaces—and indeed society as a whole. Growing up in the '70s my grandfather, who was a wonderful, talented man, used a wheelchair. If you wanted a masterclass in casual prejudice you just had to stick around him for a while and see how many people saw the chair and not the man.

But if you want to put a label on me, maybe the best one is social mobility ... Hard as it is to believe, for a while I appeared as a poster child. My graduate action learning set was chosen as the face of my employer—two white people, two BAME [black or minority ethnic] people, two men, two women ... of us four I was the only one to attend state school, grow up on a council estate and not be Oxbridge. The reality was we were all diverse in our own ways. But it was an unusual introduction to the feeling in your gut of standing in a room where there is an 'in group' and you aren't really part of it ... I believe that if you've ever had that feeling of being the one who is excluded, you have a responsibility to do something about it for others.

The other label is I occasionally get a knowing look when talking about gender. 'Ah, ha, you are a convert to the cause, you have daughters' someone will say. Well yes, I absolutely want my two daughters to be able to go into a workplace where they are treated with respect and as equals ... But I also want that equality for my son when he goes to work. I want those who manage him and make decisions about his future to have the kind of balanced judgement I talked about a few moments ago. The workplace that is going to be right for his sisters is also going to be right for him.

For the FCA as a regulator, diversity and inclusion isn't just an issue of moral conscience—it's an absolutely vital part of our social contract with the public.

We represent the interests of consumers across the UK. These are not one homogeneous mass of financial service users—they are utterly diverse, with differing needs, differing priorities and differing levels of financial education and ability.

In order to be truly effective, we have to reflect the society we serve. As insightful and broad minded as we all like to think we are our outlooks and perspectives are limited by our own experiences.

So we have to have diverse voices around the table. It is central to our ability to provide public value.

The same is also true of the firms we regulate.

Time and time again studies show that the inclusion of a diverse range of voices improves performance ... analysis by McKinsey showed that companies in the top quartile for racial and ethnic diversity are 35% more likely to have financial returns above their respective national industry medians.

(FCA, 2017)

In 2018, the FRC published a video and blog by the Chief Executive, Stephen Haddrill, on board diversity; see: https://frc.org.uk/news/march-2018/frc-publishes-video-and-blog-on-diversity

Boards need ability not diversity

Corporate governance thinking does not evolve: it skips from one topic to the next. Ideas in corporate governance are like memes: they convey ideas just as genes convey physical characteristics, as I wrote on this blog some time ago. These memes permeate thinking, and with today's instant communication flash around the world, become the conventional wisdom.

A couple of years ago the theme was risk. Cadbury and the early corporate governance codes had nothing to say about risk. Now boards needed to recognize their responsibility for identifying their company's risk profile, assessing long-term strategic risk, and ensuring that appropriate risk policies were in place and working. Risk had become a central issue in corporate governance.

More recently, it was culture—although commentators seemed unable to agree on what they meant by culture. However, culture can be thought of as 'the beliefs, expectations and values that people share'. Like the skins of an onion, culture has many layers—national, regional, corporate cultures, and the culture of the board room. Recent commentary about culture in corporate governance thinking has focused on board-level culture, which sets the tone throughout the organization and provides its moral compass. Board-level culture reflects the experience, beliefs and expectations of the board members, particularly the leadership style of the board chair and the effect of any dominant personalities on the board.

On board diversity

Now the focus has shifted again: board diversity has come into the spotlight. Again, however, ideas differ on what board diversity means. The time has come for some clearer thinking.

It seems that most people, when talking about board diversity, mean gender diversity: the need to have more women directors. That case seems clear and, around the world, efforts are being made to increase the proportion of women on boards through mandatory quotas or voluntary targets. The challenge is to increase the pool of women with executive management experience. The BEIS report, mentioned above, recommends that 'the UK Government should set a target that from 2020, at least half of all new appointments to senior and executive management level positions in all listed companies should be women'.

To others, however, board diversity means something quite different.

The UK's Financial Reporting Council, welcoming the Hampton/Alexander report in November 2016, wrote that it:

looked forward to working with the review team to improve reporting on diversity. In light of the current public debate on corporate governance, we stand ready to revise the UK Corporate Governance Code following the Government consultation. Our work on succession planning this year suggested that nomination committees should take a more active interest in talent management, in particular that initiatives are in place to develop the talent pipeline and to promote diversity in board and executive appointments. To better inform boards about the link between diversity, strategy and developing the business, more consideration should be given to the nature, variety and frequency of interaction between the board and aspiring candidates at all levels.

The BEIS report also refers explicitly to 'ethnic diversity' and recommends further measures 'to ensure that diversity is promoted at all stages of careers to broaden the pool of talent at the executive level'. The report further calls for 'companies [to] recruit executive and non-executive directors from the widest possible base'. The report concludes with a rallying cry: 'Overall, [our] recommendations are aimed at permanently ingraining the values and behaviours of excellent corporate governance into the culture of British business.'

Before we all rally to this banner, more clarity of thought is needed.

What is the purpose of the board of directors?

The role of the board of directors, indeed the role of the governing body of every organization, is to govern. To put it in the vernacular, corporate governance means ensuring that the enterprise is being well run and that it is running in the right direction. This is quite different from managing the business. In essence, the governance of a company includes overseeing the formulation of its strategy and policy-making, supervision of executive performance, and ensuring corporate accountability. Overall, the purpose of the board is to ensure that the company meets its objectives.

But that exposes a deeper question: what is the real purpose of a profit-orientated company? The answer has not changed since the classical 19th-century model of the joint-stock, limited-liability company was invented: to create wealth by providing employment, offering opportunities to suppliers, satisfying customers, and meeting shareholders' expectations.

Companies meet their societal obligations by paying taxes, adopting socially responsible policies, and obeying the law of the lands in which they operate. Companies should not be seen as vehicles for social engineering. The board does not need to reflect the structure of society.

Admittedly, the UK Companies Act does call for companies to recognize the interests of other stakeholders, including employees, suppliers, and customers: though it is hard to see how a company could survive by ignoring them. Stakeholder Senates, which could provide employee, market, and societal input to board deliberations, could include representatives of young and old, poor and rich, ethic and other minorities.

To fulfil the company's primary purpose of creating wealth, a board does not need to reflect society. It needs people who can contribute effectively to its governance. In other words, the qualities needed to be a director are the experience, knowledge, and ability relevant to governing that company, backed up in a fast-moving business environment with the ability to continue to learn and adapt. Companies are often competing with other companies around the world, whose directors are experienced professionals; in China for example.

....

Discussion questions

1. Marshal the arguments for and against board diversity. On balance which has the stronger case? Is a compromise feasible?

2. Will the FCA call for more diverse boards make British companies more or less able to compete with companies in other countries?

Self-test questions

To confirm your grasp of the key points in this chapter, try answering the following questions.

1. Why does a corporate entity need a constitution?

2. What is the principal difference between a private and a public company?

3. Explain the difference between governance and management.

4. What are the two aspects of the board's work that can provide a paradox for the unitary board?

5. Describe the scope of corporate governance.

6. Where can one inspect company accounts, annual returns, and other documents filed under the UK Companies Acts?

7. What led to the creation of the US Securities and Exchange Commission? When? What is its mission?

8. What sort of companies might have an all-executive board?

9. What is the typical structure of the board of companies listed in the United States?

10. What is a two-tier board? Outline how it works in Germany.

 For suggested answers to these self-test questions visit the online resources at: www.oup.com/uk/tricker4e/

Projects and exercises

1. The European Union has passed legislation permitting the incorporation of a 'European company' transcending the borders of its member states. Would it be a good idea if companies were able to be incorporated in the United States at the federal level?

2. Chart the governance and management structure of a corporate entity with which you are familiar, using the circle and triangle schematic. Academic, sporting, or professional bodies could be covered, as well as public or private companies. Does the diagram help to depict the potential to exercise power in that organization?

3. Consider the scope of corporate governance outlined in Figure 2.1. In your opinion, does this adequately cover the extent of the subject? What would you add or change to give a better perspective?

4. Research the state of gender diversity around the world. What are the pros and cons of moves towards greater equality between men and women on the boards of listed and government corporations?

References and further reading

Blair, Margaret (1995) *Ownership and Control: Rethinking Corporate Governance for the Twenty-First Century.* The Brookings Institute, Washington DC.

Cadbury, Sir Adrian (1992) The Financial Aspects of Corporate Governance: A report of the committee on corporate governance. Gee & Co., London.

Clarke, T. (2004) *Theories of Corporate Governance.* Routledge, London and New York.

Colley, John L. et al. (2003) *Corporate Governance?* McGraw-Hill Executive MBA series, New York.

Colley, John L. et al. (2005) *What is Corporate Governance?* McGraw-Hill, New York.

Davies, Adrian (1999) *A Strategic Approach to Corporate Governance.* Gower, London.

Demb, Ada and Frederich Neubauer (1992) *The Corporate Board: Confronting the Paradoxes.* Oxford University Press, New York.

Financial Conduct Authority (2017) 'The art of thinking independently together—why the regulator cares about diversity', speech by Christopher Woolard, 30 October. Available at: www.fca.org.uk/news/speeches/art-thinking-independently-together-why-regulator-cares-about-diversity

Hilmer, Frederick G. (1993) *Strictly Boardroom: Improving Governance to Enhance Company Performance.* The Sydney Institute and Information Australia, Melbourne, Australia.

Mallin, Chris ([2004] 2010) *International Handbook on Corporate Governance.* 3rd edn, Edward Elgar Publishing, London.

Monks, Robert A. G. and Nell Minow ([1995] 2011)
    Corporate Governance. 4th edn, Wiley, Chichester.

Nordberg, Donald (2011) *Corporate Governance:
    Principles and Issues*, Sage Publications, London.

Shleifer, Andrei and Robert W. Vishny (1997) 'A Survey
    of Corporate Governance', *The Journal of Finance*,
    LII, 2, June.

Useful websites

www.sec.gov

The US Securities and Exchange Commission—its role, latest regulations, and filing requirements, including a tutorial on the 'EDGAR' filing system.

www.icgn.org

The International Corporate Governance Network—exchanging corporate governance information internationally and raising standards.

www.oecd.org (follow links by topic or country to corporate governance)

The Organisation for Economic Co-operation and Development—corporate governance principles and discussion of corporate governance topics.

www.governance.co.uk

Governance—an international monthly newsletter on issues of corporate governance, boardroom performance, and shareholder activism.

3

Theories, Philosophies, and Concepts of Corporate Governance

 Learning Outcomes

This chapter enables us to:

- Study the various theories of corporate governance, including:
  - agency theory
  - transaction cost economics
  - stewardship theory
  - resource dependency theory
  - managerial and class hegemony
  - psychological and organizational perspectives.
- Discuss stakeholder perspectives (enlightened shareholder theory) and cultural aspects.
- Utilize a systems perspective on corporate governance issues.
- Realize that corporate governance still needs a paradigm.

This chapter is important for students studying corporate governance theory. Directors seeking information to improve their board-level contributions and those studying for professional examinations in corporate governance may not need this level of theoretical background. However, the material on the cultural component of corporate governance does have some relevance to practice.

The agency dilemma

A fundamental challenge underlying all corporate governance is not new.

> The directors of companies, being managers of other people's money, cannot be expected to watch over it with the same vigilance with which they watch over their own.
>
> (Smith, 1776)

This is the agency problem. In its simplest form, whenever the owner of wealth (the principal) contracts with someone else (the agent) to manage his or her affairs, the agency dilemma arises. How to ensure that the agent acts solely in the interest of the principal is the challenge. In the 18th and 19th centuries, many contracts were, indeed, between a single principal and a single agent, for example involving trading ventures, a construction project, or running a factory.

The arrival of the joint-stock, limited-liability company in the mid-19th century increased the number of principals (shareholders) and their agents (directors). The number and increasing diversity of the shareholders in public companies meant, moreover, that the interests of shareholders were no longer homogeneous. As Berle and Means (1932) showed in their influential analysis, when listed companies grew and their shareholders became more diverse, the separation between owners and directors increased and power shifted towards the directors.

Today, agency relationships in public companies can be complex. For example, an individual owner might invest their funds through a financial adviser, who places the funds in a mutual fund or investment trust, which in turn seeks to gear its portfolio by investing in a hedge fund, which spreads its resources across a range of equities, property, commodities, and other hedge funds. Tracing the agency chain in such cases can be difficult, and establishing the exposure to agency risk well-nigh impossible. However, the agency dilemma potential exists throughout the chain. The demands for transparency, reporting, accountability, audit, independent directors, and the other requirements of company law and securities legislation, plus the requirements of regulators and stock exchange rules, and the demands of the corporate governance codes, are all responses to the agency dilemma. Indeed, the concept underpinning corporate governance codes around the world and the demands of company law for checks and balances is the need to respond to the agency problem.

Sophisticated investors can profit if they believe the price of a share will fall. They borrow a batch of those shares and sell them. They are now 'short' of the shares which they borrowed. When the term of the borrowing ends the investor then buys shares on the market at the price to which they have fallen. But 'selling short' can also give the investor the shares' voting rights. This can thus build up a significant stake, in fact up to the level at which it, and any other fund acting in concert with it, would be required to make a public offer for the company. In other words, it is possible to acquire voting rights in a company without owning or investing in its stock. This is a long way from the original concept of the joint-stock company. It also raises a potential dilemma for directors: are they the stewards of the interests of the long-term traditional shareholders, or of those of the short-term activist institutions? The interests of the two groups are unlikely to be the same.

Nor is the agency problem limited to relations between investors in listed companies and their agents. The agency dilemma can occur in private companies, joint ventures, not-for-profit organizations, professional institutions, and governmental bodies. Wherever a separation between the members and the governing body has been put in place to protect their interests and to deliver the required outcomes, the agency dilemma will arise and corporate governance issues occur. The members could be the shareholders in a company, the members of a professional institution or a trade union, a group of owners in a cooperative, or the holding company in a corporate group; the governing body might be called the board of directors, the council, the committee, the governing body, or the holding company. But whatever names are used, whenever responsibility for activities and assets is delegated by those in the principal position to those in the agent situation, the agency dilemma will occur.

For example, consider a pyramid group of companies. The board of the holding company decides to operate the group with profit-responsible subsidiary companies in organizational divisions. The board believes that motivation and commitment will be maximized if the directors of each subsidiary are held responsible for generating profits and are measured by their company's annual return on investment (ROI). The opportunities for the subsidiary company directors to take decisions beneficial to the subsidiary, but detrimental to the group, are legion—for example by postponing longer-term decisions on research and development, management development, or maintenance to improve the short-term profit, or by manipulating the asset base in the ROI calculation. If the subsidiaries inter-trade, the opportunities multiply. Take a simple example: subsidiary company A manufactures a component that is incorporated into subsidiary company B's product. Company A needs a transfer price at which to sell to company B. Of course, A wants the highest price to maximize its own profits, while B wants the lowest to maximize its returns. If they cannot agree, company B may buy in the open market, leaving A with under-recovered overheads. Conversely, company A may sell to the market, leaving B with an insecure supply. Referring the transfer price decision to the holding company might resolve the dilemma, but at the cost of removing the decision-making authority of the directors of A and B. This situation is typical in decentralized groups and is called 'sub-optimization' by some authorities. In essence, it reflects the agency dilemma.

The agency problem can also arise in not-for-profit entities. Consider the British National Health Service (NHS): the responsible government ministry contracts with the providers of medical services to deliver the services through local doctors, hospitals, and other institutions. The authorities set standards and targets to measure achievement. For example, they might call for a hospital to improve its bed occupancy rate, thus encouraging the hospital governors to keep patients in for longer than is really necessary. Conversely, the authority might call for a speedy return of patients to the street, resulting in rising emergency readmissions. In fact, the NHS promulgates a large list of performance measures with quantifiable outputs in an attempt to reduce the agency dilemma. But success is only partial because agents always find ways of benefiting their entity to the detriment of the system as a whole.

Essentially, in agency situations, the parties have asymmetrical access to information. The directors know far more about the corporate situation than the shareholders, who must trust them. Indeed, shareholders have to rely on the directors to decide what information they should have, over and above the minimum required by regulation and company law. This is the underpinning concept of the joint-stock, limited-liability company: the shareholders trust the directors to be stewards of their funds. The agency theory of corporate governance takes a less sanguine view of directors' behaviour.

Agency theory

Agency theory, or principal–agent theory as some writers refer to it, looks at corporate governance practices and behaviour through the lens of the agency dilemma. In essence, the theory perceives the governance relationship as a contract between shareholder (the principal) and director (the agent). Directors, it is argued, seek to maximize their own personal benefit, to take actions that are advantageous to themselves, but detrimental to the shareholders (see Figure 3.1).

Figure 3.1 The governance relationship

As the early proponents of agency theory, Jensen and Meckling (1976), explained:

> agency theory involves a contract under which one or more persons (the shareholders) engage other persons (the directors) to perform some service on their behalf which includes delegating some decision-making authority to the agent. If both parties to the relationship are utility maximizers there is good reason to believe the agent will not always act in the best interests of the principal.

Anecdotal evidence of such behaviour is not hard to find. There are myriad cases in which directors treat a listed public company as though it were their own property, exploiting their position, receiving unsanctioned benefits, and taking remuneration unrelated to their performance, to the shareholders' detriment. Bob Monks (2008), a shareholder activist, reckoned that trillions of dollars of shareholders' wealth have been wrongly extracted from US corporations over the years by directors abusing their power.

Directors may also take a different view from their shareholders on corporate risk. After all, it is not their money they are risking. Of course, successful management involves taking controlled risks. But directors might hazard corporate funds on riskier ventures, a hostile takeover bid for example, than many of their shareholders would expect or want. Potential investors can only judge the ability of the board-level decision-makers and their risk profile from the company prospectus, reports, and past performance.

Most scholarly research into corporate governance has used agency theory, which has been developed within the discipline of financial economics (Fama and Jensen, 1983). Looking at corporate governance through the agency lens, researchers have explored links between corporate governance processes and corporate performance. In other words, they have looked for causal links between governance systems and their effects. For example, a study might test whether there is a correlation between board structure (the proportion of independent directors to executive directors) and long-term corporate performance.

Agency theory focuses at the level of shareholders and boards as entities. Board-level processes, political activities, and interpersonal relations between directors are outside their scan.[1] Consequently, researchers do not need access to the boardroom or to individual

---

[1] Some authorities refer to this as being treated as a 'black box', but that can confuse since the black box on an aircraft contains all of the vital data.

directors. Most agency theoretical research uses data about governance practices and company performance that are readily available in the public domain such as, for example, directors' reports and audited company accounts. Agency theory offers a statistically rigorous insight into corporate governance processes. Because of its simplicity and the availability of both reliable data and statistical tests, agency theory has provided a powerful approach to corporate governance theory building.

Criticisms of agency theory

Some critics of agency theory emphasize its relatively narrow theoretical scope. To study the intricacies of corporate governance in terms of contracts between principals and agents, they argue, is naive. They criticize the focus on purely quantitative metrics, such as board structure or corporate compensation packages, or on the building of a governance index through a 'box-ticking approach' where compliance with governance criteria mechanically feeds into a broad governance index, which is then compared with some measure(s) of corporate performance. Such critics believe that board behaviour does not consist of sets of contractual relationships, but is influenced by interpersonal behaviour, group dynamics, and political intrigue. They question whether the subtle and complex dynamics of board behaviour lend themselves to measurement and numerical analysis. As Ada Demb wrote in 1992, 'statistical methods will not explain the reality of the boardroom'.

Other contemporary scholarship has discovered that not only does increasing governance conformance and compliance not necessarily add to corporate performance, but it can actually detract from it. Muth and Donaldson (1998) challenged the findings of other agency theoretical research. Boards with well-connected executive directors perform better, they found, than those that followed corporate governance codes on the use of independent directors.

Other critics have challenged the shareholder/director agency model as simplistic in practice. These days, they suggest, pension funds, hedge funds, and other institutional investors can behave like imperial traders, even corporate raiders, rather than the long-term investors perceived by the agency paradigm. Also, the short-term outlook of stock markets in the UK and USA may produce different agency relationships from the longer-term and bank-related investment seen in countries such as Germany and Japan.

But there is also a deeper issue: inherent in agency theory is a philosophical, moral assumption about the nature of man. The theory assumes that people are self-interested, not altruistic; they cannot be expected to look after the interests of others. In other words, directors cannot be trusted. The legal concept of the corporation, and the basis of stewardship theory, as we shall see, takes the opposite view.

In summary, critics of agency theory argue that it has been erected on a single, questionable abstraction that governance involves a contract between two parties, and is based on a dubious conjectural morality that people maximize their personal utility. Nevertheless, agency theoretical research has remained the mainstay of published papers in corporate governance. An interesting research frontier of the subject bridges the disciplines of economics and law, applying the agency theoretical insights of economics to the legal context of the corporation.

Does good corporate governance produce better corporate performance?

Agency theoretical research has shown some linkages between company performance and various attributes of governance, such as women on boards, board structure and size, or audit committee activities. However, it has to be said that, so far, most conclusions are weak.

Indeed, in some cases in which a positive relationship has been shown between good governance and better performance, other scholars have reworked the data to draw contrary conclusions. More convincing evidence of a relationship between good corporate governance practices and company performance comes from the behaviour of institutional investors who are prepared to pay a premium for companies they judge to have good governance because they feel it reduces their exposure to risk.

However, a significant study was published by the Association of British Insurers (ABI) in 2008 (Selvaggi and Upton, 2008),[2] which suggests that there is a robust causal relationship between good corporate governance and superior company performance. ABI represents the interest of insurance companies in the UK, which tend to invest long-term, reflecting their need to meet long-term obligations. The ABI Institutional Voting Service database shows the extent to which listed UK companies comply with the provisions of the UK Combined Code, and adds expert judgements on other aspects of governance practices. The study showed a clear connection between good governance and both good company performance and share price levels.[3] Companies with poor governance showed a strong negative impact on performance. Moreover, companies that were red-topped repeatedly underperformed by 2–5 per cent a year in terms of industry-adjusted return on assets. The study also suggested that it was good corporate governance that led to better performance, not the other way around. Further, well-governed companies delivered higher returns when adjusted for risk, and the volatility of their share price returns was lower. The study also discovered that the impact of governance on performance was long-term.

However, the issue is not yet determined, as Bhagat, Bolton, and Romano (2007) explain, citing methodological shortcomings in existing papers:

> Financial economists and commercial providers of governance services have in recent years created measures of the quality of firms' corporate governance . . . there is no consistent relation between governance indices and measures of corporate performance. Namely, there is no one 'best' measure of corporate governance: the most effective governance institution appears to depend on context, and on firms' specific circumstances.

Transaction cost economics

Closely related to agency theory, transaction cost economics was derived from original work in 1937, by Coase. He recognized that a firm could save costs by undertaking activities within the organization rather than externally. In other words, the firm would get goods or services at

---

[2] http://www.ourcommunity.com.au/files/aicr/Fact_Sheets/Governance_Performance_Corporate_Britain.pdf
[3] Regression analysis was used to test relationships between the corporate governance criteria and corporate performance. The multivariate econometric methodology used allowed the determination of relationships between various factors simultaneously.

a lower price than in the marketplace. However, as a firm grows, there comes a point at which the external market becomes cheaper. Williamson (1975 and 1988) built on Coase's work, arguing that large corporate groups could overcome disadvantages of scale by 'the choice of governance structures'.

Transaction cost economics, therefore, focuses on the cost of enforcement or check-and-balance mechanisms, such as internal and external audit controls, information disclosure, independent outside directors, the separation of board chair from CEO, risk analysis, and audit, nomination, and remuneration committees. The argument is then advanced that such enforcement costs should be incurred to the point at which the increase in costs equals the reduction of the potential loss from non-compliance.

Stiles and Taylor (2001) observed that 'both transaction cost economics and agency theories are concerned with managerial discretion and both assume that managers are given to opportunism (self-interest seeking) and moral hazard, and that managers operate under bounded rationality'. In other words, directors and top management act in their own best interests, not necessarily in those of the shareholders. But transaction cost analysis focuses on governance structures and mechanisms, whereas agency theory sees the firm as a set of contracts.

The underlying discipline of transaction cost economics, like agency theory, is financial economics. Although the focus is different, the level of abstraction is similar, being at the level of the firm and its governance structures rather than board-level behaviour. Again, research results have been inconclusive, possibly because the complexity within organizations is ignored. For a seminal review of the earlier contributions of financial economics to corporate governance knowledge, see Shleifer and Vishny (1997).

Stewardship theory

Stewardship theory looks at governance through a different lens from agency theory, reflecting the original legal view of the corporation. The joint-stock company with limited liability for its shareholding investors was a simple and eminently successful development of the mid-19th century. The limited-liability company has provided capital, encouraged business growth, secured employment, provided innovation in industry and commerce, and created untold wealth over more than 150 years. This model proved robust and adaptable. Indeed, its great flexibility has led to the huge proliferation, diversity, and complexity of corporate types and structures today.

In essence, each company is incorporated as a separate legal entity. The shareholding members of the company nominate and appoint the directors, who then act as stewards for their interests. The directors report to them on the results of that stewardship, subject to a report from an independent auditor that the accounts show a true and fair view. Ownership is the basis of power over the corporation. Directors have a fiduciary duty to act as stewards of the shareholders' interest. Inherent in the concept of the company is the belief that directors can be trusted.

Stewardship theory reflects the classical ideas of corporate governance. Directors' legal duty is to their shareholders not to themselves, nor to other interest groups (see Figure 3.2). Contrary to agency theory, stewardship theory believes that directors do not inevitably act

Figure 3.2 The shareholder–director relationship

in a way that maximizes their own personal interests: they can and do act responsibly with independence and integrity. Of course, some fail, but this does not invalidate the basic concept.

Stewardship exponents recognize that directors need to identify the interests of customers, employees, suppliers, and other legitimate stakeholders, but under the law their first responsibility is to the shareholders. They argue that conflicts of interest between stakeholder groups and the company should be met by competitive pressures in free markets, backed by legislation and legal controls to protect customers (monopoly and competition law), employees (employment law; health and safety law), consumers (product safety law; consumer protection law), suppliers (contract law; credit payment law), and society (environmental law; health and safety law; taxation law). We will explore so-called stakeholder theory later in this chapter, and the growing interest in corporate social responsibility and a wider range of responsibilities for boards in Chapter 9.

The underpinning disciplines in stewardship theory are legal and organizational studies. By reflecting the legal model, stewardship theory provides precise boundaries for the company, clearly identifying its assets and liabilities, its shareholders and its directors. Stewardship theory emphasizes the responsibility of boards to maximize shareholder value sustainably in the long term.

Criticisms of stewardship theory

Critics of stewardship theory point out that the *de facto* situation in modern corporations is quite different from the 19th-century model. They argue that the concept of a set of shareholders owning a single company and appointing its directors is naive in modern circumstances, except for smaller companies. In listed companies they point out that shareholders have become remote from the company and do not nominate the directors. Financial reports, they suggest, have become intelligible only to experts. Consolidated group accounts, recording the finances of modern entities, complicate rather than explain complex groups, which lack transparency, with directors who are not readily accountable to shareholders.

Other critics of stewardship theory point out that because the theory is rooted in law, it is normative. It emphasizes what should be done, or even exhorts. It is not, they argue, predictive and is unable to show causal relationships between specific behaviours and corporate performance. Mallin (2007) made a further important point on the relevance of stewardship thinking. The fundamental concept of the joint-stock, limited-liability company provides the conceptual underpinning for company law in the USA, the UK, and many other jurisdictions around the world where common law prevails—that is, law based on legal principles enhanced by the precedents from subsequent cases relying on independent judges and juries. As a result, the rights of shareholders, particularly minorities, have been protected and in these countries the shareholder base in many public companies is diversified. In other countries, in continental Europe and Latin America for example, civil law prevails, which has less flexibility, does not learn from precedent, and is often administered by judges who are civil servants. As a result, laws are more codified and there is less protection for minorities; consequently share ownership is less widespread, with many companies still influenced by dominant shareholder and family interests.

After major corporate collapses in the late 20th and early 21st centuries, many commentators felt that the trust directors owed under the stewardship model had been undermined, and that this erosion of trust had adversely affected the well-being of investors, employees, and communities. Questions about the commitment of boards to members' interests surfaced. Nevertheless, stewardship theory remains the legal foundation for companies legislation all around the world.

The global financial crisis and the resultant dissatisfaction with companies and their boards led to calls for shareholder empowerment. A return to shareholder democracy, it was suggested, could redress the balance of power in favour of owners. Investors, particularly pension funds, hedge funds, and other institutional investors, should be more active. Such shareholder activism could include, for example, individual negotiations with management, or working collectively to develop strategies to influence companies with specific proposals and, if necessary, litigation, while voting all of the shares they held.

Sceptics of shareholder empowerment have argued that boards, elected by investors, should still have primacy. Only the directors are in a position to take into account relevant factors in business decisions. Giving more power to investors, the sceptics suggested, would increase investor costs and reduce returns. Involvement by investors in the governance of companies changes relationships and no longer being at arm's length might limit freedom to deal in the shares. Moreover, involvement could lead investors to advance special interests, promote narrow self-interests, and realize short-term gains. Further, they pointed out that the interests of pension fund members and investors in other funds are not homogeneous; they may have diverse needs, and could disagree with decisions of the fund.

A recent theoretical development recognizes the naivety, in the modern investment world, of the 19th-century model of shareholder capitalism in which joint-stock, limited-liability companies are owned by a handful of individual shareholders. Referred to as a theory of universal ownership, this view of fiduciary capitalism recognizes that modern listed companies, particularly in liquid markets such as the USA and the UK, are typically held by a highly diversified set of equity holders, including holdings concentrated in the hands of a few large institutional investors.

In the USA, the hundred largest financial institutions hold over 50 per cent of all publicly held equity. In the UK, there is a similar concentration of ownership. Since these large institutions have massive funds to invest, they need to buy shares across the board, effectively indexing the market as a whole. They are also likely to be investing in a wide range of equities, across geographical and emerging markets, and through a range of investment instruments, including hedge funds. Consequently, such institutional investors, the theory argues, now play an essential role in corporate governance and should assume a responsibility for overseeing governance issues, and abide by principles of responsible investment, including collective action if necessary. Critics of this approach point out that institutional investors such as pension funds are run by trustees whose accountability is not always apparent and is seldom challenged, whose interests do not align with those of fund beneficiaries, and who may use investment funds to protect themselves from claims for negligence.

Resource dependency theory

Resource dependency theory takes a strategic view of corporate governance. It sees the governing body of a corporate entity as the linchpin between the company and the resources it needs to achieve its objectives. These resources could include, for example, links to relevant markets including potential customers and competitors, access to capital and other sources of finance, provision of know-how and technology, and relationships with business, political, and other societal networks and elites. The directors are viewed as boundary-spanning nodes of networks able to connect the business to its strategic environment. Studies from this perspective focus on the interdependence of companies in a market and can serve to reduce uncertainty in corporate decisions. The theory finds its roots in organization theories, for example Pfeffer (1972).

The theory of social networks recognizes that those involved in corporate governance processes are often linked through networks. Individuals at the nodes may have things in common including, perhaps, social standing, class, income, education, institutional or corporate links, and so on. Lifestyle theory, focusing on the backgrounds of key players, has also been used. Some individuals in the networks, such as the chair or CEO, may be pivotal nodes in a number of networks, increasing their communication leverage. Such social networks can enhance or adversely interfere with independent and objective governance activities. Identifying such networks and monitoring their activities provides another insight into governance processes and powers.

Managerial and class hegemony

This perspective on the governance of companies focuses on the view that directors have of themselves and its impact on their behaviour on corporate governance. Directors in some companies perceive themselves as an elite group. This self-perception encourages them to behave in an elite way, dominating both the company organization and its external linkages. Top management appointments ensure that newcomers fit into that elite and sustain its image. Similarly, new independent directors are likely to be nominated and appointed only if they sustain the dominance of the ruling group. Calls for board diversity, quotas to increase the proportion of women directors, or for more representative boards, challenge such attitudes.

Class hegemony recognizes that directors' self-image can affect board behaviour and performance. Further, executive directors, with their own self-image bolstered by access to information, knowledge of on-going operations, and executive decision-making power, may dominate board decisions.

The theories of managerial and class hegemony are rooted in the socio-political disciplines, but have used case research, allied with biographical analysis, to produce some penetrating insights into corporate governance. Essentially, these studies see corporate governance as an interpersonal, political process.

Research using this approach requires access to individual directors. In one of the few books that successfully explored board behaviour through interviews, *Inside the Boardroom* by LeBlanc and Gillies (2005) provided sets of quotations from different directors, grouped by topic. Earlier works focusing on realities that are not illuminated by either agency or stewardship theories include Lorsch and McIver (1989), Demb and Neubauer (1992), Monks and Minow (1995), and Monks (1998).

Critics of the case approach to the study of corporate governance complain that the evidence is statistically irrelevant, largely anecdotal, and can be influenced by prejudice, self-centred reporting, and biased insights. The counterargument is that corporate governance involves a political process, not a statistically controlled group activity.

Psychological and organizational perspectives

Both agency and stewardship theories view corporate governance at the level of the firm, being concerned with relationships between owners and directors. Resource dependency and class/managerial hegemony theories again take a firm-level focus. Individual players, with their different mindsets, personalities, and foibles, do not appear in these theoretical paradigms.

But practitioners recognize that knowing what goes on in the boardroom and during interactions between directors is vital to understanding corporate governance. Empirical investigation is obviously needed. But access to directors and boards can be difficult. Directors may believe that secrecy is vital to protect strategic plans, to guard trade secrets, and, for the listed company, to avoid a leak of stock-market price-sensitive information. Some boards may also resist access from investigators to preserve interpersonal relationships within the board, to prevent the presence of an outsider changing board-level interactions, and to avoid unwanted media interest. Individual directors might also be concerned to prevent damaging information leaking out, affecting their reputations or, worse, generating lawsuits.

Corporate governance research from a psychological perspective seeks to understand how individual directors perceive their board-level work and what they believe leads to effective performance. Cognitive maps, produced by repertory grid techniques (Kelly, 1955, 1963), can be used to chart directors' mindsets. Constructs of language, using the language of the director, not words imposed by the researcher, can help to describe and interpret board-level experiences. If words such as 'involvement', 'leadership', 'participation', 'reputation', or 'teamwork' are used by the director, or moral values such as trust, harmony, or ethical standards mentioned, these become the frame of reference for the researcher. Psychological theories have yet to make a significant impact in understanding corporate governance, but the relevance of individuals at board level in the overall governance process suggests that this field has potential.

Viewing corporate governance from a longitudinal perspective has also provided some insights. Filatotchev and Wright (2005) collected material looking at the evolution of corporate governance practices over the life cycles of enterprises and institutions. Further light has been thrown onto corporate governance from the perspective of political economics. Roe (2003), writing about political and social conflict in corporations and the institutions of corporate governance, showed how a nation's political economy interacts with its legal structures and financial markets. Game theory has also been applied to corporate governance issues.

The societal perspective: stakeholder philosophies

Finally, we turn to perspectives on corporate governance at a societal level: so-called stakeholder theory. 'Stakeholder', a word coined to stand in juxtaposition to 'shareholder', recognizes the interests of all those affected by companies' decisions, including customers, employees, and managers, partners in the supply chain, bankers, shareholders, the local community, broader societal interests for the environment, and the state. Companies, stakeholder advocates suggest, owe a duty to all those affected by their behaviour. Some advocates go further and call for directors to be accountable and responsible to a wide range of stakeholders far beyond companies' current company law responsibility to shareholders. Such responsible behaviour, the stakeholder advocates argue, should be the price society demands from companies for the privilege of incorporation, granting shareholders limited liability for the company's debts.

Stakeholder thinking is concerned with values and beliefs about the appropriate relationships between the individual, the enterprise, and the state. It involves a discourse on the balance of responsibility, accountability, and power throughout society. It is not a predictive theory. Consequently, this societal view of corporate governance is probably better thought of as a philosophy rather than a theory.

In 1975, the UK Accounting Standards Steering Committee produced a discussion paper, the Corporate Report, which recommended that all large economic entities should produce regular accountability reports to all stakeholder groups whose interests might be affected by the decisions of that entity. The political implications of such a heroic idea quickly relegated the report to the archives.

In the United States, proposals for new company ordinances, including stakeholder accountability, came from Ralph Nader, who tussled with the boardroom-orientated Business Roundtable in 1970. In 1976, Nader, Green, and Seligman argued, emotively, that:

> (Giant corporations) can spend decisive amounts to determine which towns thrive and which gather cobwebs, corrupt or help overthrow foreign governments, develop technology that takes lives or saves lives . . . (The giant corporation) is largely unaccountable to its constituencies—shareholders, workers, consumers, local communities, taxpayers, small businesses, future generations.

Stakeholder thinking faded in the free-market, 'growth and greed' attitudes of the 1980s. But in the more environmentally and socially concerned world of the late 20th and early 21st centuries, corporate social responsibility and sustainability reporting were taken seriously again. The interest is also reflected in socially aware mutual funds, which limit their investment to companies deemed to adopt suitable business strategies, for example by not dealing in tobacco, gambling, or armaments. The Royal Society of Arts in England published a report in 1999, titled Tomorrow's Company, which advocated wider recognition of corporate responsibility to stakeholders such as suppliers, customers, and employees. The chair of the committee producing this report, Sir Stuart Hampson, who was also chair of the John Lewis Partnership—a company run as an employees' partnership—wrote:

> Shareholder value is the imperative commanding a lot of attention, but you cannot create shareholder value by talking to your shareholders. You create it by looking at the four drivers of a successful business: how good you are at involving and motivating your staff; how close you are to your customers; how good you are at removing wastage from the supply chain and maintaining good relations with suppliers; what your reputation is in the community at large. We don't believe that the board is there purely to create shareholder value. I'm sure nobody leaps out of bed in the morning and says 'I want to create shareholder value!' It's unrealistic.

The challenge to boards trying to adopt a stakeholder approach is that they no longer have a single constituency, the shareholders, to satisfy, but need to balance the potentially conflicting interests of a diverse set of stakeholders.

Sternberg (2000) argued that stakeholder ideas are fundamentally flawed, strongly advocating the ownership rights perspective. Potential conflicts between the expectations of different stakeholders were irreconcilable, she argued: boards need a single responsibility—to their shareholders. Turnbull (1997) took the opposite view, calling for a systems perspective that includes all of the components in the corporate situation. Expectations of companies around the world are changing, with growing demands for better consumer, environmental, and societal behaviour.

In 1998, the UK Hampel Committee dismissed stakeholder notions, saying 'directors are responsible for relations with stakeholders, but are accountable to the shareholders'—a view reflecting the conventional wisdom in boardrooms in both the UK and the USA. Roberto Goizuetta, a former head of Coca-Cola, captured the issue:

> Saying that we work for our shareholders may sound simplistic—but we frequently see companies that have forgotten the reason they exist. They may even try to be all things to all people and serve many masters in many different ways. In any event they miss their primary calling, which is to stick to the business of creating value for their owners.

But overshadowing agency, stewardship, stakeholder, and the other theoretical perspectives are also some basic unresolved issues at a meta-philosophical level. Every theory of corporate governance needs to be founded on a view of the legitimate relationship between the individual and society. Where does the desirable balance lie between the rights, responsibilities, and powers of the individual, the enterprise, and the state? Opinions vary significantly by culture, political context, and social system. Moreover, they have been evolving throughout history. All systems of governance must seek an appropriate balance between the interests of self and society. That applies to corporate governance just as it does to governance in other areas of society.

Enlightened shareholder theory

The stakeholder approach to corporate governance calls for boards to take into account the interests of a diverse and wide range of stakeholder groups, including shareholders, rather than to act solely in the interest of the shareholders, as called for in stewardship theory. Critics of stakeholder ideas say that dual legitimacy—meeting the needs of stakeholders and shareholders—is not feasible because:

- the interests of stakeholders are potentially in conflict—what benefits one group disadvantages another (e.g. higher wages, lower selling prices, or community contributions reduce the funds available for the other stakeholders, including the shareholders);
- it is impossible to maximize all stakeholder interests simultaneously;
- within stakeholder groups, interests vary (e.g. some employees may prefer higher wages, others better pension conditions);
- who establishes the interests of each stakeholder group is undefined;
- if directors represent stakeholder interests, they face conflicts of interest between constituencies.

A recent theoretical development has attempted to go beyond this shareholder versus stakeholder debate. Enlightened shareholder theory recognizes that the satisfaction of stakeholder needs and interests is crucial to corporate success and the creation of long-term wealth. The theory recognizes that companies generate profits and increase shareholder wealth only by satisfying stakeholder needs and responding to their interests. Shareholders benefit when boards satisfy stakeholder interests, because profits are made and they are primary stakeholders. The theory is grounded in continuing shareholder primacy, but differs from classical stewardship theory because boards are required to take stakeholder interests into account, explaining their actions to all stakeholders, including the way in which their decisions have exposed the company to risk.

In Chapter 9, on corporate social responsibility, we will see how the call for directors to recognize stakeholders is being pursued in statutory requirements (UK Companies Act 2006), in exhortatory guidance (the UN Principles for Responsible Investment), and in initiatives from institutional investors.

The cultural component of corporate governance

When Sir Adrian Cadbury presented his report on corporate governance, which was to prove so influential around the world, he emphasized that his report was about the financial aspects of corporate governance and was not a comprehensive exposé of the topic. He appreciated that his proposals were organizational (independent directors; board audit, remuneration, and nomination committees; and separate CEO and board chair) and presentational (corporate governance reports, etc.). He knew from his experience on the boards of Cadbury Chocolate and other companies that the activities of boards involve behavioural, contextual, and political aspects.

In recent years, these other aspects have come to the fore in what is often called the cultural aspects of corporate governance. For example, Peter Bartha of the Schulich School, York University, Toronto wrote 'corporate governance is greatly influenced by the contextual nature of the socio-ecosystem'. Unfortunately, 'ecosystem', a word borrowed from the natural sciences like the word 'culture', is a portmanteau word, carrying a bundle of different meanings.

Commentators frequently mention the importance of culture in corporate governance. They recognize that neither the 'comply or explain' regime of adherence to corporate governance codes nor corporate regulation capture the reality of corporate behaviour. But there is some confusion about what is meant by culture and why it is really relevant to corporate governance.

What is culture?

Culture can be thought of as the beliefs, expectations, and values that people share. Like the skins of an onion, culture has many layers—national cultures, regional cultures, the culture of a company, and the culture of each boardroom in which it is practised—hence it is in a sense an art as much as a science and in a state of continuous evolution.

The culture of a country is influenced by its social, economic, and political heritage, its geography, and its religion. Culture is moulded by situations that affect relations between individuals, institutions, and states. Culture is influenced by law, is reflected in the language, and is passed on by experience in families, schools, and organizations. It is culture that determines values, what is thought of as acceptable, important, and right or wrong. Culture affects how people think and act. It is fundamental to understanding corporate governance.

In the late 20th century, when ideas about corporate governance began to be discussed, much of the thinking and practice was influenced by countries that shared Anglo-American cultures—a belief in the rule of law; the importance of the rights of individuals to personal freedom and the ownership of property, in the context of accountable, democratic institutions, including an independent judiciary.

In the United States, corporate governance practices stemmed from the rule of company law laid down by state jurisdictions and at the federal level by regulation from the US SEC.

In the UK, and subsequently in most Commonwealth countries associated with the UK, the governance of companies was determined by Companies Acts and, for listed companies, by corporate governance codes, reinforced by Stock Exchange rules, which required companies to report compliance with the code or explain why they had not.

The influence of religion on corporate governance

Religious beliefs are part of the culture of every country and affect personal values, relationships, and attitudes to authority. They influence morality, ethical standards, and what business behaviour is considered acceptable. Underpinning beliefs are reflected in the way business decisions are made, corporate entities operate, and corporate governance practices develop in different countries.

The United States was founded by Puritans seeking religious freedom. The founding fathers, the majority of whom were lawyers, placed great emphasis on their constitution, the rule of law, and democratic rights. Those same traits are reflected in the governance of American companies to this day. Legal contracts, litigation, and shareholder rights are still at the forefront of business issues.

In the United Kingdom, on the other hand, the approach to corporate governance was more flexible, less rule-based and litigious, reflecting the broader traditions of Britain's religious inheritance. The Church of England, rejecting control from Rome, established a freedom of expression and tolerated other non-conformist religious traditions, which became embedded in British culture. The voluntary approach to corporate governance—'conform or explain why not'—reflects this more flexible, voluntary approach.

Other countries influenced by Britain during the days of the British Empire (including Australia, Canada, South Africa, other countries in Africa and the West Indies, as well as Hong Kong and Singapore) shared these corporate governance influences.

In Germany, the teachings of Martin Luther, 500 years ago, shaped the country's language and changed its way of life. Luther influenced belief in the moral imperative to seek principle and order, to be prudent with money, and to avoid debt. Southern European nations, on the other hand, influenced by Roman Catholicism, took a less austere approach: a distinction that is still being played out among the nations that adopted the euro as their national currency.

Northern European nations were also affected by the teaching of John Calvin, which emphasized the importance of working for the community, not just for their families and themselves. Germany's co-determination laws view companies as partnerships between labour and capital. In the two-tier board governance structure, the supervisory board contains representatives of workers as well as investors.

The influence of religion on corporate governance practices can be seen strikingly in Japan. Buddhism and Shinto, the national religion, have been dominant religious influences. Even though relatively few Japanese now identify with either religion, belief in spirits is widespread. Shrines to spirit deities are commonplace. Social cohesion is a dominant feature of Japanese business life, with high levels of unity throughout the organization, non-adversarial relationships, lifetime employment, enterprise unions, personnel policies emphasizing commitment, initiation into the corporate family, decision-making by consensus, cross-functional training, and with promotion based on loyalty and social compatibility as well as performance.

The Japanese *keiretsu* networks connect groups of Japanese companies through cross-holdings and interlocking directorships. Chairs and senior directors of companies in the *keiretsu* have close, informal relationships. Although the paternalistic relationship between company and lifetime 'salary-man' is under economic pressure, boards still tend to be decision-ratifying bodies rather than Western-style decision-making forums.

Although there have been recent efforts to require independent non-executive directors, as in the Western corporate governance model, Japanese top management remains rather sceptical. Many Japanese do not see the need for such intervention 'from the outside'. Indeed, they have difficulty in understanding how outside directors function. 'How can outsiders possibly know enough about the company to make a contribution,' they wonder, when they themselves have spent their lives working for it? How can an outsider be sensitive to the ingrained corporate culture?

Of course, the cultural significance of religion does not mean that religion or religious organizations played a part in the development of corporate governance norms. Indeed in some countries, the UK, China, and Japan for example, many people no longer claim any religious affiliation. But the religious culture provided the ethical context, the moral influence in creating law, running business, and influencing approaches to corporate governance.

Culture and the future of corporate governance

When corporate governance norms were first discussed in the 1980s, many thought that corporate governance in countries around the world would gradually converge with Western practices. They believed that because these countries needed to raise capital, trade in securities, and do business globally they would adopt Western practices. Institutions such as the

World Bank and the OECD put considerable effort into advising developing countries about modern corporate governance practice.

Globalization became a dominant feature in world trade because some countries offered significantly lower costs to developed markets. Some thought that globalization of the movement of goods, services, money, people, ideas, and information would inevitably lead to a convergence of intellectual insights, politics, and ideology. Such arguments are seldom heard these days. Capital can be raised in the East as well as the West. Securities can be traded on many stock exchanges. The notion, which might be termed 'globalism', seems unlikely to survive. Attempts by countries to protect their own industry and labour markets, and/or control the flow of people, money, and information across their borders, challenge the onrush of globalization.

Now, as the 21st century moves forward, discussion about corporate governance increasingly recognizes the significance of culture—national, regional, corporate, and board-level—to successful corporate governance. The governance of companies within a country needs to be consistent with that country's culture.

Differing boundaries and levels: systems theory

The disciplines contributing to the study of corporate governance to date include financial economics, law, accountancy, management studies, organizational behaviour, sociology, politics, and, perhaps, philosophy. The two dominant contenders for theoretical insight, agency and stewardship theories, are properly based on bounded models of reality: agency theory on an economic perspective; stewardship theory on a legal one. Inevitably, each perspective is limited. Each theory sees the world through a different lens.

Changing the metaphor, each of the various theoretical perspectives on corporate governance can be visualized as a spotlight lighting up part of the stage on which the corporate governance action is being played (Figure 3.3). Some spotlights illuminate one part of the stage; others throw light on other areas and from different angles. Each theoretical spotlight leaves some players and part of the action in darkness.

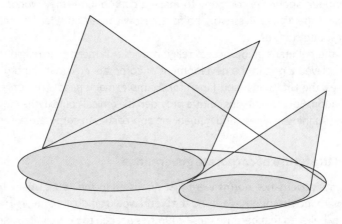

Figure 3.3 Spotlights on the corporate governance stage

Some theories focus on the shareholders and the board as a whole with its standing committees, perhaps including the external auditors; other theories focus on individual directors on the board and the interactions between them; yet other theories take the perspective of the stock markets, investors, and regulators; at the highest level, the political situation, the economic impact, and the cultural context come into view, along with legislatures, states, and international agencies. As yet, there is no theoretical floodlight that adequately lights the whole stage, illuminating all of the players, and showing their relationships and the action.

Systems theory takes a similar approach to understanding situations. All phenomena can be thought of as a hierarchy of systems. Take a car, for example: there are molecules in the steel washer, which is a component of the carburettor, which is part of the engine, which is a feature of the car, which can also be viewed as part of a traffic system. Each is useful in context; none tells the whole story.

Systems theory offers a useful way of looking at a situation. The classical view of systems uses three criteria to identify a system:

- the system's boundaries—that is, determining what is to be considered as within the system itself and what in the system's environment (systems are man-made artefacts to help us to understand a situation; moreover, each system can be further broken down to suit the needs of the user);

- the system's level of abstraction—that is, the level at which the system is perceived and the amount of detail treated within it;

- the system's function—that is, what occurs between the system's inputs and outputs.

So what are the boundaries of corporate governance? Cochran and Wartick, in the first bibliography of corporate governance (published in 1988), suggested that:

> Corporate governance is an umbrella term that includes specific issues arising from interactions among senior management, shareholders, boards of directors, and other corporate stakeholders.

Earlier, we adopted the simple expedient of defining corporate governance as being about the way power is exercised over corporate entities. In this way, we did not have to identify the players, nor define boundaries for their action. In Chapter 2, we saw how different authorities had produced other definitions of corporate governance. But what should be within the system and what should be its boundaries? We have a choice—individual directors, corporate entities, their owners or members, their governing bodies, intermediaries in the governance chain, auditors, regulators, laws, culture, national and international organizations, and all of the other stakeholders affected by the actions of those corporate entities.

Judging from the reams of academic literature, views clearly differ on the scope of corporate governance. As we have seen, for some, it is about principles and good practice on matters such as board structures and membership, the independence of directors, the use of audit, remuneration and nominating committees, and generally about board-level effectiveness. For others, corporate governance is about the relationship between owners and corporations, about the exercise of power by shareholders, particularly institutional investors who, in recent years, have shown themselves capable of removing dominant executive directors, restructuring boards, and influencing strategic direction. For still others, corporate governance is about the social responsibilities that corporations owe to a wide set of stake-holders beyond the board's classical fiduciary duty to the shareholders—responsibilities and accountabilities to employees, customers, lenders, suppliers, the local community, and society at large.

The approach we adopt in this book was well described by Clarke (2007), when he suggested that theoretical perspectives on boards and governance can best be seen as 'multiple theoretical lenses' through which to view the subject.

A subject in search of its paradigm

Agency theory is rooted in the belief that agents are utility maximizers, and therefore cannot be relied on to act in the best interests of their principals. Put simply: directors cannot be trusted. Stewardship theory is rooted in the belief that directors accept a fiduciary duty to act in the best interest of the owners who have entrusted their funds to them. In other words: directors can be trusted. Which is true? Karl Popper, in his influential work on scientific proof, argued that a scientific proposition could not be proved to be absolutely true, but a single contrary result would show it to be false. Both agency and stewardship theories fail Popper's test of scientific truth because each can readily be shown to be false in specific circumstances.

Corporate governance, as yet, does not have a single widely accepted theoretical base nor a commonly accepted paradigm. In the words of Pettigrew (1992), '[c]orporate governance lacks any form of coherence, either empirically, methodologically or theoretically with only piecemeal attempts to try and understand and explain how the modern corporation is run'. The subject has progressed some way since 1992, but is still in search of its paradigm.

In the original concept of the corporation, directors were appointed by, and were usually in direct contact with, their shareholders. Shareholder democracy had meaning and share-holders could participate. (Admittedly, some rogue entrepreneurs took advantage of their shareholders, but investment always involves risk.) But the concept of the corporation no longer works in that way. Directors in many large companies have become distant from the ultimate owners. Layers of brokers, agents, share-holding companies, institutional investors, pension funds, mutual funds, and banks come between boards and their companies' ultimate owners. In Western cultures a new governing elite has emerged. Self-enriching and self-perpetuating, these corporate directors wield the power, and reap the rewards, that were previously reserved for ruling monarchs and their aristocracy.

The 1990s saw a dramatic surge in academic interest in corporate governance. Unfortunately, research has so far failed to offer a convincing explanation as to how corporate governance works and has not contributed much to the practice of the subject. Significant professional developments have been responses to corporate corruption and collapse, not to research findings and theory building. The Sarbanes-Oxley Act of 2002 in the United States, the corporate governance codes in all economically developed nations, and the corporate governance institutions formed in many emerging economies have been based on the experience and conventional wisdom of company directors and their advisers, not on the conclusions of rigorous academic research.

Both agency theory and stewardship theory reflect the Anglo-Saxon case-law-based legal situation and financial markets with widely dispersed shareholders providing relative management autonomy. Some jurisdictions and markets do not have these characteristics. A more general theory of corporate governance would need to recognize the reality of company law, and ownership and control, in relevant jurisdictions and markets.

Corporate governance codes reflect the conventional wisdom of best practice in listed companies in that jurisdiction. There is a paucity of new conceptual thinking about corporate governance. Scholars need to break out of their preconceptions of corporate entities seen as legal entities or in terms of relationships between corporate entity and stakeholders, or of man as a utility-maximizing contract-maker, and build a theory that adequately reflects the world experienced by those actually involved at board level.

To present a comprehensive and coherent view of governance arrangements and structures around the world, corporate governance theory first needs a taxonomy of organizational types—public, private, family, subsidiary, associate, joint venture, non-profit, and so on—and complex ownership structures—pyramids, chains, nets, and the rest—to distinguish very different power bases and governance systems. Systems theory and cybernetics-based control-system concepts such as networks, system boundaries, goals, and sub-optimization might provide insights.

The creation of a general theory of corporate governance is certainly premature and probably overly optimistic, but such a theory would need to embrace:

- the relationship between individual, enterprise, and state;
- a broader definition of corporate entities to cover every organization in which governance and management are separate from the members;
- a mapping of all of the elements that affect and are affected by the governance of such organizations;
- the expectations, requirements, and demands of each participant;
- the duties and responsibilities of each participant;
- the powers, sanctions, and accountabilities of each participant.

At the moment, various theoretical insights cast light on different aspects of the play, highlighting some and leaving others in shadow. We need a viewpoint that will light up the entire stage, all of the players, and the entire action.

To return to our earlier traffic-system analogy, the overall operation of such a system depends on controls at three levels:

1. The regulatory level, with laws, regulations, and rules. At this level, conformance is mandatory: for example, in the UK, 'keep to the left of the road and at a roundabout give way to traffic coming from the right'. The actions of those involved are policed. There are sanctions and penalties for failing to obey. Notice the legal and cultural dependency at this level: for example, in the USA, a reader might say 'keep to the right of the road' and 'what is a roundabout?'.

2. The advisory level involving voluntary codes of conduct. At this level, the responsibility becomes a matter of generally accepted responsible behaviour, for example 'respect other road users' and 'look out for hazards—children, dogs, or obstacles in the road'.

3. The personal level, concerning individual beliefs and behaviour. At this level, personal value systems are involved, including courtesy, concern for others, socially aware behaviour, and trust.

The practice of corporate governance needs controls at similar levels. But to date the emphasis has been on levels one and two:

- the regulatory level—laws, regulations, mandatory rules;
- the advisory level—voluntary codes of conduct, corporate policies.

What has been missing is any focus on personal behaviour rooted in basic values—morality, honesty, integrity, decency, concern for others, respect, and trust. The challenge for research and writing on corporate governance, while extending knowledge at the regulatory and advisory levels, is to break into the black box of the boardroom and to focus on board-level activities, directors' behaviour, and board leadership: in other words to know what 'the culture of a company and its board' really means.

Case studies

 Case study 3.1   Network Rail

Before 1948, the railways in Britain were owned and run by different companies. Then they were nationalized and run by the state enterprise British Railways. In 1994, the UK's Conservative Government privatized the railway system again. New companies were incorporated with the right to run train services over various routes. The government recognized that some public subsidy would be needed to cover unprofitable services and routes, but believed that with financial incentives and private sector managerial efficiencies, services would improve. Railtrack PLC, a public company listed on the London Stock Exchange, was incorporated to control the entire railway infrastructure (tracks, signals, bridges, tunnels, and some stations), with the Rail Regulator setting charges for access to the tracks by the franchised train operating companies.

Over the following years, Railtrack was criticized for the spiralling costs of new projects, its poor performance in maintaining and developing rail infrastructure, and particularly for its poor safety record. Fatal crashes occurred. Railtrack's use of contractors on maintenance work allegedly had led to loss of control and lower safety. The strategy of having a single company run the entire rail network, used by all the train operators, was questioned. In the old days, each railway company had run on its own tracks.

In May 1997, the government changed. The Conservatives were replaced by New Labour, with Tony Blair as Prime Minister.

Following a major crash with many fatalities, the Railtrack board of directors was said to have panicked. Emergency tests showed dangerous faults on many lines and speed restrictions were imposed around the system, causing long delays for passengers and major losses to the train operators. The Railtrack board launched a massive investment programme, but by 2001 the company's debts were so large that the company needed repeated subsidy from the taxpayer to remain financially viable. Controversially, some government funding was used to pay a dividend to Railtrack shareholders.

In October 2001, the Secretary of State for Transport, Stephen Byers, called for Railtrack to be put into administration, claiming it was insolvent. Critics accused the government of deliberately bankrupting the company to begin the re-nationalization of the railway system, bringing the infrastructure back under state control. The government replied that the private sector would continue to run the railways but offered no compensation to Railtrack shareholders, arguing that the company was bankrupt.

In 2002, the government created a new company to run Britain's rail infrastructure. Called Network Rail, it was incorporated as a private company limited by guarantee, although the government claimed that governance would meet the standards of a PLC. Although the bulk of its funding would come from public funds, it was free from interference by government ministers. Moreover, it was exempted from the Freedom of Information Act, applicable to all public bodies.

The company's constitution provided for 'guarantor members' (not shareholders), who would receive the annual report and accounts, attend the AGM, and approve the appointment of directors and auditors. The members could also remove top executives. Over 100 members were appointed, representing various stakeholders such as the railway industry, the Department of Transport, and the public. The company explained that it operated as a commercial business directly accountable to its members, but that it was a 'not-for-dividend company', and any profits would be ploughed back into investment. Its board of directors had twelve members—five executives, six outside non-executives, and a non-executive chair.

A consulting firm, Coucher Pender (founded in 1999, by Iain Coucher and Victoria Pender), was retained by the Strategic Rail Authority to set up the new company for an undisclosed fee, with a further £484,000 paid by Network Rail. In 2004, Coucher was employed by the company as deputy chief executive. Pender was subsequently appointed director of corporate and government affairs.

Some of the weaknesses of the new company's governance were seen in 2008, when significant overruns on maintenance work left hundreds of thousands of travellers stranded over the New Year holidays. Governing members complained that management was not really accountable to anyone. 'There is a democratic deficit,' wrote Lord Berkeley, a member representing the rail freight industry. He called for a new board with fewer 'governors' who would have wider powers to supervise management. Further complaints were that members had conflicting interests: those drawn from the travelling public wanted low fares and improved services, employee representatives wanted better wages and employment terms, whilst those representing the public interest wanted lower subsidies from taxpayers.

In 2009, the chief executive, Iain Coucher, was said to be the highest paid public official in Britain, with remuneration of over £1 million. In his defence, it was argued that Network Rail was independent of the state; although others pointed out that the company was publicly funded.

An independent inquiry paid for by the company was set up in 2011, led by Anthony White, a leading Queen's Counsel, to investigate allegations of the misuse of state funding, of up to £4 billion a year. Further claims were made that cases of alleged sexual harassment and race discrimination from ex-employees had been silenced with huge pay-offs before the complaints could be heard by an employment tribunal.

Coucher left the company in October 2010, after eight years, three as chief executive and five as deputy. He received a £1.6 million 'golden goodbye', which the press described as a 'reward for failure'. The incoming chair, Rick Haythornthwaite, suggested that Coucher was secretive and had a 'militaristic' management style. In May 2011, the official inquiry dismissed allegations of the misuse of public funds and 'serious financial impropriety'.

Strategic proposals for another reorganization of the British rail industry surfaced in 2011. A 'vertical re-integration' was suggested, with train operating companies owning and running tracks and stations. Such a strategy, it was suggested, would make the companies more profitable, and might attract capital from international asset management companies and private equity funds.

In June 2015, the government suspended work upgrading two of the country's most congested rail lines—Mainline Midland and the Trans-Pennine route—because of cost overruns and missed targets. The decision came from the Treasury, which took over responsibility for Network Rail funding and therefore its debt after Network Rail was reorganized into a state-owned company.

Three months later, the rail regulator, the Office of Rail and Road, warned that the company might be in breach of its licence after they found flaws in the way it handled major projects. But the government refused to release a critical report, which spelt out serious problems with Network Rail and might have undermined government pledges, because of pending elections.

In July 2015, the government replaced the Chairman of Network Rail, Richard Parry-Jones, with Sir Peter Hendy. It also appointed Nicola Shaw, head of HS1 (the company known as High Speed 1, which runs the successful Channel Tunnel rail link),[4] to draw up plans for Network Rail's structure and funding. 'Network Rail is not working,' she said. 'There was a big change last year when its debt (then £38bn) was taken over by the Government. When you have a big change you ought to think about what you want to do from here.' The options she was considering included:

1. government continuing to fund the operation;

2. auctioning various routes (sections of track) as concessions to pension funds and sovereign wealth funds;

3. privatizing the entire operation through a public listing.

Shaw said that she would stop short of considering reuniting track and train operations, as had been the practice under the previously nationalized British Rail. In September 2015, government ministers moved closer to breaking up and selling off Network Rail with plans for a radical overhaul of operations, shifting decisions on track maintenance and new projects to regional line managers. By February 2016, Shaw was suggesting spinning off individual lines to investors and introducing an agency to oversee the industry at arm's length from government.

In October 2015, the Regulator issued a damning report naming 'systemic failings': one-third of railway upgrades—new stations, extra track capacity, electrification of lines—were running late, and key project costs were spiralling out of control. In November 2015, the Regulator fined Network Rail £2 million for delays and cancellations that constituted a breach of its licence. By that time, Network Rail had admitted that train punctuality was not good enough as its debts mounted and six-month pre-tax profits fell by 23 per cent to £246 million while operating costs rose by £88 million.

Meanwhile, Jeremy Corbyn, unexpectedly elected leader of the Labour Party in May 2015, put forward detailed proposals for the re-nationalization of the 15 independent train operating companies. Citing the continuing increases in rail fares, he said that bringing the entire network, including Network Rail, back under government control had widespread support. Legal experts pointed out the potential difficulties, not least European Union law which requires member states to open up their transport networks to cross-border competition, which would rule out UK nationalization. But in June 2016 the electorate decided in a referendum (Brexit) that the UK should leave the European Union.

Meanwhile the problems of the British railway system continue unabated. Blaming labour disputes, old rolling stock, and track delays, the Southern Railway network cut over 300 trains a day claiming this would make their services more 'resilient'. Plans to re-route the new high-speed line from London to the North ran through a newly built housing estate. Delays to rail, signalling, and electrification upgrades led to further late running and cancelled trains.

The Times wrote in an editorial that:

Thirteen years after its creation, Network Rail remains a byword for botched corporate governance. Without shareholders, ministerial oversight or direct contact with passengers, it is accountable chiefly to itself. It carries an unsustainable £38 billion debt burden but as a public body it has little incentive to pay this down or force on its staff the efficiencies that would cut costs.

[4] HS1 is owned by the Canadian investment funds Borealis Infrastructure and the Ontario Teachers' Pension Plan. It has a 30-year concession to run the Channel Tunnel rail link.

In July 2017 the government Department for Transport, recognizing problems of late-running trains and high costs, produced a confidential report suggesting the re-creation of a Strategic Rail Authority to oversee the activities of the railway operating companies. At the same time, a funding crisis caused the government to stop rail improvement projects on the East Coast main line and Western and Midland routes.

In 2018, regular travellers with season tickets faced a price increase averaging 3.4 per cent, significantly higher than the rate of inflation and much higher than increases in average wages. Their outcry was reinforced by media criticism of senior management remuneration in some operating companies and the levels of dividend taken by some operating companies, themselves owned by companies abroad.

This has to be one of the longest-running, unresolved corporate governance cases in the world.

Discussion questions

The case raises some interesting philosophical questions about the appropriate relationship between individuals, enterprises, and the state. The people in this case are British train travellers and taxpayers; the enterprises are the state-controlled Network Rail and private train operating companies; the state is the UK government.

1. Where should power and accountability lie?

2. What is the most appropriate governance structure—a nationalized entity like the previous British Rail; individual private, profit-orientated train operating companies as now, with Railtrack PLC responsible for the tracks, stations and signalling, selling its services to the operating companies; or a re-classified, state-owned corporation, with the national Treasury responsible for its debt?

3. Identify the corporate governance issues in this case. Which corporate governance theories could be used to explore each of them?

 Case study 3.2   Tencent Holdings Limited

Tencent Holdings is a highly successful provider of internet value-added services in China. These services include access to films, books, entertainment, smartphone gaming, advertising, financial services, internet cloud services, and many other features. Founded in 1998, Tencent has maintained steady growth. In 2004, Tencent Holdings was listed on the main board of the Hong Kong Stock Exchange Board (SEHK 700).

Discussing recent results, Chairman and CEO of Tencent, Ma Huateng, said:

> . . . we delivered strong revenue growth from multiple businesses, which enabled us to reinvest in innovations and new technologies in an increasingly competitive industry. While our games business continued to grow, we have stepped up our effort to ensure users play games in a healthy manner. Successful licensed drama serials and self-commissioned variety shows boosted user engagement and advertising revenue for our video platform.
>
> Our payment business continued to make everyday life easier for Internet users, with increased adoption of Weixin Payment for offline transactions. We have also been increasing

our investment in cloud services and AI (Artificial Intelligence) technologies, which will enable us to serve our users and business partners even better into the future.

Underlying the forward-looking statements is a large number of risks and uncertainties. Further information regarding these risks and uncertainties is included in our other public disclosure documents on our corporate website.

(Tencent, 2017)

Tencent has published a statement of its vision and values, as well as other corporate governance information.

The company's vision and values

Tencent states that its mission is 'to become the most respected Internet enterprise'.[5] Further, we have a 'steadfast commitment to corporate citizenship, our public charity programs, and the promotion of respectful Internet communities on our user platforms'.[6]

Corporate governance

Corporate governance can be defined as a set of processes, customs, policies, laws, and institutions affecting the way a company is directed, administered or controlled. Corporate governance also includes the relationships among the many stakeholders involved and the goals for which the corporation is governed. The principal stakeholders are the shareholders, the board of directors, executives, employees, customers, creditors, suppliers, and the community at large.[7]

The 'governance documents' section of the company's investor relations website provides access to the Corporate Governance Statement and Corporate Governance Charter.

The board of directors

Tencent has a unitary board, consistent with the Hong Kong Corporate Governance Code and the listing rules of the Hong Kong Stock Exchange. Currently, the members of the board are:

Ma Huateng (45)
Chairman of the Board and Chief Executive Officer

Mr Ma joined the company in 1999 and is one of its co-founders. Today he is responsible for strategic planning and positioning, and the overall management of the Group.

He has more than 23 years of experience in the telecommunications and internet industries, having been head of R&D for internet paging development at China Motion Telecom Development Ltd, a supplier of telecommunications services and products in China. Mr Ma is a delegate to the 12th National People's Congress. He has a BSc degree in computer science from Shenzhen University.

---

[5] www.tencent.com/en-us/investor.html
[6] www.tencent.com/en-us/index.html
[7] http://investors.telenet.be/phoenix.zhtml?c=241896&p=irol-irhome

Lau Chi Ping Martin (44)

Executive Director and President of the Company

Mr Lau joined the company in 2005, responsible for corporate strategies, investments, mergers and acquisitions, and investor relations. In 2006, he was appointed president to manage the day-to-day operations. He was made an executive director in 2007. Previously, Mr Lau had been an executive director at Goldman Sachs (Asia), investment banking division and the Chief Operating Officer of its Telecom, Media, and Technology Group. Earlier, he had worked for management consultants McKinsey & Company. Mr Lau has a BSc in Electrical Engineering from the University of Michigan, a MS in Electrical Engineering from Stanford University, and an MBA from the Kellogg Graduate School of Management (USA). Mr Lau is a non-executive director of Kingsoft Corporation, an internet software house listed in Hong Kong; a non-executive director of Nasdaq-listed JD.com, Inc., an online direct sales company in China; and a non-executive director of NYSE-listed Leju Holdings Ltd, an online-to-offline real estate services provider in China.

Jacobus Petrus (Koos) Bekker (64)

Non-executive director

In 1995, Mr Koos led the development of M-Net/MultiChoice pay-television business, and was a founder director of MTN in cellular telephony. In 1997, he became chief executive of Naspers, and served on the boards of other companies in the group. He holds a BA Hons and honorary doctorate in commerce from Stellenbosch University, an LLB from the University of the Witwatersrand, South Africa, and an MBA from Columbia University, New York.

Charles St Leger Searle (53)

Non-executive director

Mr Searle is the CEO of Naspers Internet Listed Assets. He serves on the board of a number of companies associated with the Naspers Group, including London Stock Exchange-listed Mail.ru Group Limited (the largest internet business in Russia) and Nasdaq-listed MakeMyTrip Ltd. Previously, Mr Searle was with Cable & Wireless PLC and Deloitte & Touche in London and Sydney. Mr Searle holds a degree from the University of Cape Town and is a member of the Institute of Chartered Accountants in Australia and New Zealand.

Li Dong Sheng (59)

Independent non-executive director

Mr Li is the Chairman and CEO of TCL Corporation and the Chairman of the Hong Kong-listed TCL Multimedia Technology Holdings Ltd, both of which produce consumer electronic products. Mr Li is a non-executive director of Fantasia Holdings Group Co., Ltd, a Hong Kong-listed property developer in China. Mr Li is also an independent director of New York-listed Legrand, the global specialist in electrical and digital building infrastructures. Mr Li holds a Bachelor's degree in radio technology from South China University of Technology.

Iain Ferguson Bruce (76)

Independent non-executive director

Mr Bruce joined KPMG, Hong Kong in 1964, and became Senior Partner in 1991, retiring in 1996. He was Chairman of KPMG Asia Pacific from 1993 to 1997. He is a fellow of The Hong Kong Institute of Directors and the Hong Kong Securities and Investment Institute. Mr Bruce is an independent non-executive director of Citibank (Hong Kong), MSIG Insurance (Hong Kong), Goodbaby International Holdings (a manufacturing company), 13 Holdings (a construction development company), and Wing On Company

International (a department store in Hong Kong operating as a property investment company). Each of these companies is listed on the Hong Kong Stock Exchange. Mr Bruce is also an independent non-executive director of Noble Group Limited, a commodity company listed on The Singapore Exchange.

Ian Charles Stone (66)
Independent non-executive director

Mr Stone held senior roles in accountants PCCW for 27 years, retiring in 2011. During that time, he advised many telecoms, wireless, and internet companies, including SmarTone, First Pacific, and Hong Kong Telecom. He acted as a Chief Executive of CSL, primarily in Hong Kong, but also in London and Manila. Following his retirement, Mr Stone has provided telecoms advice to telecom companies and investors in Hong Kong, China, Southeast Asia, and the Middle East. He is an independent non-executive director of a subsidiary of Tencent Holdings and a Fellow of The Hong Kong Institute of Directors.

Yang Siu Shun (61)
Independent non-executive director

Mr Yang was Chairman and Senior Partner of accountants PwC (PriceWaterhouseCoopers) Hong Kong, Executive Chairman of PwC China and Chairman of PwC Asia Pacific, before retiring in 2015. He was also one of the five members of the Global Network Leadership Team of PwC. Mr Yang is a Member of the National Committee of the Chinese People's Political Consultative Conference, a Justice of the Peace in Hong Kong, a Member of the Exchange Fund Advisory Committee of the Hong Kong Monetary Authority, a Steward of the Hong Kong Jockey Club, the Deputy Chair of the Council of the Open University of Hong Kong, and a Board Member and Audit Committee Chair of the Hang Seng Management College. Mr Yang is also an independent non-executive director of Hong Kong and Shanghai-listed Industrial and Commercial Bank of China. Mr Yang is a graduate of the London School of Economics, and is a Fellow of the Institute of Chartered Accountants in England and Wales, the Hong Kong Institute of Certified Public Accountants, and the Chartered Institute of Management Accountants.

The board has established the following sub-committees:

- audit committee;
- corporate governance committee;
- investment committee;
- nomination committee;
- remuneration committee.

Each committee acts within agreed terms of reference, which are available on the company's website.

A Tencent acquisition

In 2016, a 50:50 merger of equals was signed between China Music, a music streaming business in mainland China, and a far smaller rival, QQ Music, which had less than half the revenues and active users of China Music.

The founder of China Music, Xie Guomin, explained his strategy. For a decade he had been acquiring licences for thousands of songs, eventually building a giant library that gave his music app a dominant position in the China market. Xie discussed the situation with his private equity partner, Shan Weijian, who ran Hong Kong-based investment company PAG. They realized there was little option other than merging with the smaller and less successful rival, because QQ Music was a subsidiary of Tencent Holdings. Xie knew that when the rights to China Music's library came up for renewal, Tencent had the resources to outbid him, destroying the underlying value of his business.

Explaining the rationale behind the merger deal, Xie explained that although his business was more successful than his rival, Tencent 'doesn't care about the money. They can pay ten times more than we can for content and that would quickly change their market share.'

Discussion questions

1. What is your opinion of the structure and membership of the Tencent board? Does it meet contemporary Western opinions on board diversity? Is that good or bad?

2. Is it a sound idea to combine the roles of chair of the board and CEO?

3. How many non-executive directorships can one person sensibly hold?

4. Does the merger with China Music raise any strategic issues for Tencent or the Chinese economy?

Self-test questions

1. How would you explain the agency problem simply?

2. In essence, how does agency theory perceive the governance relationship?

3. How did Jensen and Meckling explain agency theory in 1976?

4. What criticisms are sometimes raised about agency theory?

5. In a few words outline the basis of stewardship theory.

6. What criticisms are sometimes heard about stewardship theory?

7. What is the fundamental difference between agency theory and stewardship theory?

8. What is culture?

9. What is the significance of culture to corporate governance?

10. How might a systems perspective help in comparing corporate governance theories?

 For suggested answers to these self-test questions visit the online resources at: **www.oup.com/uk/tricker4e/**

Projects and exercises

1. Prepare a paper or presentation analysing the various theories that have been applied to an understanding of corporate governance. Are they in conflict or are they, rather, different perspectives on the basic phenomena?

2. The text suggests that: 'All major developments in the field (of corporate governance), including the codes of good practice and the American Sarbanes-Oxley Act, have been responses to corporate crises. The codes and principles of corporate governance have been created by business leaders based on their experience and conventional wisdom about

what counts as good practice.' Do you agree? Is this a sound approach? What might be the drawbacks?

3. Do you agree or disagree that Roberto Goizuetta, a former head of Coca-Cola, captured the issue, when he said: 'Saying that we work for our shareholders may sound simplistic—but we frequently see companies that have forgotten the reason they exist. They may even try to be all things to all people and serve many masters in many different ways. In any event they miss their primary calling, which is to stick to the business of creating value for their owners.'

References and further reading

Aoki, Masahiko (2001) *Toward a Comparative Institutional Analysis*. MIT Press, Cambridge, MA.

Berle, Adolf A. and Gardiner C. Means (1932) *The Modern Corporation and Private Property*. Macmillan, edn revised by Adolf Berle (1967) Columbia University, Harcourt, Brace and World, New York.

Bhagat, Sanjai, Brian J. Bolton, and Roberta Romano (2007) 'The Promise and Peril in Corporate Governance Indices', 7 October, ECGI working paper No. 89/2007, Social Science Research Network (www.ssrn.com/abstract=1019921).

Clarke, Thomas (2004) *Theories of Corporate Governance: The Philosophical Foundations of Corporate Governance*. Routledge, New York.

Clarke, Thomas (2007) *International Corporate Governance: A Comparative Approach*. Routledge, London and New York.

Coase, Ronald H. (1937) 'The Nature of the Firm', *Economica* N.S.4, reprinted in Stigler, G. J. and K. E. Boulding (eds) (1952) *Readings in Price Theory*. Irwin, Homewood, IL.

Cochran, Philip L. and Steven L. Wartick (1988) *Corporate Governance: A Review of the Literature*. Financial Executives Research Foundation, Morristown, NJ.

Demb, Ada (1992) 'The Corporate Board: Confronting the Paradoxes', *Journal of Long Range Planning*, July.

Demb, Ada and Frederich Neubauer (1992) *The Corporate Board: Confronting the Paradoxes*. Oxford University Press, New York.

Demsetz, Harold (1988) 'The Theory of the Firm revisited', *Journal of Law, Economics and Organization*, spring.

Donaldson, L. and J. H. Davis (1992) 'Stewardship Theory or Agency Theory: CEO Governance and Shareholder Returns', *Australian Journal of Management*, 16, 1.

El-Mahdy, Dina Faisal and Carolyn Strand Norman (2011) *Corporate Governance and the US Firm: A Review and Directions for Future Research*. MWA Publishing, Swindon.

Fama, Eugene and Michael Jensen (1983) 'Separation of Ownership and Control', *Journal of Law and Economics*, 26, June.

Filatotchev, Igor and Mike Wright (eds) (2005) *The Life Cycle of Corporate Governance*. Edward Elgar, Cheltenham and Northampton, MA.

Gomez, Pierre-Yves and Harry Korine (2008) *Entrepreneurs and Democracy: A Political Theory of Corporate Governance*. Cambridge University Press, Cambridge.

Huse, Morten, Boards (2007) *Governance and Value Creation: The Human Side of Corporate Governance*. Cambridge University Press, New York.

Jensen, Michael C. (1986) 'Agency Costs of Free Cash Flow, Corporate Finance and Takeovers', *American Economic Review*, No. 76, May.

Jensen, Michael C. (2000) *A Theory of the Firm: Governance, Residual Claims and Organizational Forms*. Harvard University Press, Cambridge, MA.

Jensen, Michael and William Meckling (1976) 'Theory of the Firm: Managerial Behavior, Agency Costs and Ownership Structure', *Journal of Financial Economics*, No. 3/4, October.

Kelly, G. A. ([1955] 1963) *The Psychology of Personal Constructs (A Theory of Personality)*. Norton, New York.

Lan, Luh Luh and Loizos Hereacleous (2010) 'Rethinking Agency Theory: The View from Law', *Academy of Management Review*, 35, 2.

LeBlanc, Richard and James Gillies (2005) *Inside the Boardroom*. Wiley, Canada.

Lorsch, J. W. and E. McIver (1989) *Pawns or Potentates: The Reality of America's Corporate Boards*. Harvard Business School Press, Boston, MA.

Mallin, Christine A. ([2004] 2007) *Corporate Governance*. Oxford University Press, Oxford.

Millstein, Ira M. and S. M. Katsch (1981) *The Limits of Corporate Power: Existing Constraints on the Exercise of Corporate Discretion*. Macmillan, New York.

Mintzberg, Henry (1983) *Power In and Around Organizations*. Prentice-Hall, Englewood Cliffs, NJ.

Mintzberg, Henry (1984) 'Who Should Control the Corporation?', *California Management Review*, XXVII, Fall.

Monks, Robert A. G. (1998) *The Emperor's Nightingale: Restoring the Integrity of the Corporation*. Capstone Publishing, Oxford.

Monks, Robert A. G. (2008) *Corpocracy: How CEOs and the Business Roundtable Hijacked the World's Greatest Wealth Machine*. Wiley, Hoboken, NJ.

Monks, Robert A. G. and Nell Minow ([1995] 2011) *Corporate Governance*. 4th edn, Wiley, Chichester.

Muth, Melinda M. and Lex Donaldson (1998) 'Stewardship Theory and Board Structure: A Contingency Approach', *Corporate Governance: An International Review*, 6, 1, January, pp 5–28.

Nader, Ralph, Mark Green, and Joel Seligman (1976) *Taming The Giant Corporation*. W.W. Norton Co., Inc., New York.

Norberg, Donald (2011) *Corporate Governance: Principles and Issues*. Sage Publishing, London.

Pettigrew, Andrew (1992) 'On Studying Managerial Elites', *Strategic Management Journal*, 13.

Pfeffer, Jeffrey (1972) 'Size and Composition of Corporate Boards of Directors: The Organization and its Environment', *Administrative Science Quarterly*, 17, p. 218.

Roe, Mark J. (2003) *Political Determinants of Corporate Governance, Clarendon Lectures in Management Studies Series*. Oxford University Press, Oxford.

Selvaggi, Mariano and James Upton (2008) Governance and Performance in Corporate Britain, ABI research paper 7, Association of British Insurers, Gresham Street, London, February.

Shleifer, A. and R. Vishny, (1997) 'A Survey of Corporate Governance', *Journal of Finance*, 52, 2, June, pp 737–83.

Smith, Adam ([1776] 1976) *The Wealth of Nations*. Revised edn, George J. Stigler (ed.), University of Chicago Press, Chicago.

Sternberg, Elaine (2000) *Just Business: Ethics in Action*. 2nd edn, Oxford University Press, Oxford.

Stewart, James B. (2005) *Disney War*. Simon & Schuster, New York.

Stiles, P. and B. Taylor (2001) *Boards at Work: How Directors View Their Roles and Responsibilities*. Oxford University Press, Oxford.

Tencent (2017) 'Tencent announces 2017 second quarter and interim results', 16 August. Available at: www.tencent.com/en-us/articles/8003451502937229.pdf.

Thomsen, Steen (2008) *Introduction to Corporate Governance*. DJOF Publishing, Copenhagen.

Tirole, Jean (1996) *The Theory of Corporate Finance*. Princeton University Press, Princeton, NJ.

Tricker, R. I. (ed.) (2000) *Corporate Governance: History of Management Thought*. Ashgate, Dartmouth, UK.

Turnbull, Shann (1997) 'Stakeholder Governance: A Cybernetic and Property Rights Analysis in Corporate Governance', *Corporate Governance: An International Review*, 5, 1, pp 11–23; also in Tricker, R. I. (ed.) (2000) *Corporate Governance*, The History of Management Thought series. Ashgate Publishing, London.

Turnbull, Shann (2000) Corporate Governance: Theories, Challenges and Paradigms, Macquarie University, Sydney, see UK Social Science Research Electronic Paper collection.

Williamson, Oliver E. (1975) *Markets and Hierarchy*. Free Press, New York.

Williamson, Oliver E. (1988) 'The Logic of Economic Organization', *Journal of Law, Economics and Organization*, No. 4, Spring.

Williamson, Oliver E. (1996) *The Mechanisms of Governance*. Oxford University Press, New York.

Useful websites

www.conference-board.org

The Conference Board (USA) Corporate Governance Center.

www.business.bham.ac.uk/ccgrg

Centre for Corporate Governance Research, Birmingham University Business School.

www.ecgi.org

European Corporate Governance Institute.

https://www2.deloitte.com/.../audit/topics/corporate-governance.html

The Deloitte Center for Corporate Governance.

www.london.edu/facultyandresearch/researchactivities/centreforcorporategovernance.html

London Business School, Centre for Corporate Governance.

www.berr.gov.uk/bbf/corp-gov-research/page15049.html

UK government initiative on research into corporate governance.

www.unpri.org

Universal Principles for Responsible Investment (UNEP Finance Initiative and the UN Global Compact).

www.wiley.com/bw/journal.asp? ref=0964-8410

Corporate Governance—an international review.

4 The Governance Partnership: Investors, Companies, and Directors

 Learning Outcomes

This chapter enables us to:

- Understand shareholder rights, stewardship and activism.
- Appreciate the different types of director.
- Learn about directors' legal duties and rights.
- Grasp the leadership role of the board chair.
- Recognize the corporate officers.

A central concern of corporate governance is the relationship between members and the corporate entities of which they are members. In limited-liability companies, that is the relationship between the shareholders and the boards of the companies in which they invest. In not-for-profit corporate entities, professional bodies, and trades unions, for example, the crucial relationship is between the voting members and the governing body of the organization. In this chapter, we consider the essential relationships in limited-liability companies.

Shareholder rights

Shareholder rights are determined by the company's articles of association and company law, predominantly the Companies Acts or ordinances. With the ownership of shares come rights: the right to receive notice of, attend, and vote at shareholders' meetings, the right to inspect the shareholder register and the register of directors and officers, and the right to regular statutory information. But, having elected directors to govern the company, shareholders do not have the right to be involved in the day-to-day management of the business, nor to inspect company records or management accounts.

Obviously, the more voting shares held, the greater the potential power of the shareholder. Typically, a holding of more than 50 per cent provides majority control, with the ultimate right to nominate and elect directors, and to influence the direction of the business. However, companies must respect the rights of any minority shareholders.

In the 19th-century model of the joint-stock, limited-liability company shareholders had the right to nominate and elect the directors of their company. This is still the case in most small companies. But in public companies, listed on a stock exchange, the scale and diversity of share-holders means that it is difficult to exercise such rights. Consequently, company law in many jurisdictions has laid down rules for the election of directors, which differ between jurisdictions.

The European Union (EU) introduced the Shareholder Rights Directive in 2009, which aimed to encourage effective shareholder control in EU listed companies. Member states were required to incorporate the Directive into their national law. The UK, for example, passed the Companies (Shareholder Rights) Regulations in 2009,[1] which amended the provisions of the Companies Act 2006 regarding resolutions, voting, and calling meetings. The use of electronic means of share-holder voting, the appointment of proxies, and the use of websites to communicate with share-holders were covered. Holders of 5 per cent of the voting shares can now require the directors to call a shareholders' general meeting (previously it was 10 per cent). A simple majority is all that is needed to remove a director or, indeed, the entire board. The EU also tried to rule that com-panies in all member states should apply the principle 'one share, one vote', but failed to obtain agreement. Opposition came from countries such as Sweden, which permit dual-class shares, with different voting rights.

In the United States, the incumbent board has considerable influence in the election of direc-tors, sending a list of its preferred candidates to shareholders prior to voting at the shareholders' meeting. If shareholders want to nominate alternatives, they have to bear the cost of distributing the rival nomination forms themselves, which can be prohibitively expensive in a large company. Consequently, contested elections are rare, although internet communication may reduce costs. Proposals for companies to cover the costs of dissident shareholders wanting to nominate their own candidates have been around for many years. The 2004 Report from the Committee on Capital Markets Regulation (known as the Scott Report)[2] called for 'majority voting' in which directors are elected with a majority of votes cast and for shareholders to put forward candi-dates for the board of directors by simply having their names added to the company's nomin-ation proxy form. The US Securities and Exchange Commission (SEC) has tried to make it easier for shareholders to nominate their own candidates, but implementation has been delayed by pressure from business groups and directors, arguing that companies are protecting their share-holders from vested interests such as trades unions, hedge funds, and single-issue lobbyists who might want to have their representatives on the board. Attempts to force companies to change through class-action lawsuits on behalf of the shareholders, notably by Bob Monks the founder of Institutional Shareholder Services,[3] also failed.

The right of shareholders to have questions answered at shareholders' general meetings was also codified. The company must answer any questions relating to the business put by a member, unless it can be shown that it is not in the interests of the company, for example because it would mean disclosing confidential information, be against the good order of the meeting, or the question had already been answered on the company's website. Sharehold-ers also acquired a new right to have matters included on the agenda of the annual general meeting if they hold 5 per cent of the voting shares or have the support of 100 members enti-tled to vote. The company must bear the cost of circulating such requisitioned resolutions.

---

[1] Guidance on the implementation of the Shareholder Rights Directive can be found online at www.icsa.org.uk

[2] Chaired by Harvard University Law School Professor Hal S. Scott.

[3] See www.issgovernance.com

Corporate Governance in Action 4.1 Protecting minority shareholders' rights in Hong Kong

A Hong Kong-based company, which produced and marketed artificial Christmas trees, was listed on the Hong Kong Stock Exchange. The board proposed the sale of almost all of its business to parties linked with the majority shareholders, through a management buyout. A group of minority shareholders felt that the sale price was unreasonably low and tried to block the deal. Hong Kong is a common law country with well-established principles and a regulatory mechanism for the protection of minority shareholders from domination by majority shareholders, with the rights of minority shareholders codified in the Hong Kong Companies Ordinance (2014). However, in the event, the authorities decided that the rights of the minority shareholders had been met.

In the original limited-liability model, the company was in effect the shareholders acting together in a properly convened meeting. They could select the directors, influence the company direction, and agree directors' remuneration, termination, and severance pay. Some commentators call this 'shareholder democracy'. But some parts of the world have moved a long way away from the original notion of shareholder democracy. Many companies have attempted to improve communication with shareholders. But real shareholder democracy, in large companies with many and diverse shareholders, has not yet proved feasible.

Shareholder stewardship and activism

Advocates of shareholder democracy believe that with the rights of share ownership come corporate governance responsibilities. Shareholders, particularly institutional shareholders, they argue, have a duty to act as watchdogs over corporate activities and possible excesses. Such shareholder stewardship sounds desirable, for example challenging excessive director remuneration, opposing schemes to protect the company and the incumbent directors from predators, and highlighting unsatisfactory performance. Indeed, corporate governance codes in some countries call for such a commitment.

Shareholder pressure has been shown to be effective: in 2006, the CEO of Home Depot in the United States, Bob Nardelli, nicknamed 'Home Despot', was ousted; Hewlett-Packard had to amend its poison pill protection against predators; and McGraw-Hill and other companies had to eliminate 'staggered boards', in which one-third of the directors were elected every year, to a system that forced every director to stand for election each year, thus making the replacement of the entire board easier.

But shareholder activists can also leave the company in a worse position than before. With control, activist shareholders are able to dictate the direction of the company for their own advantage. In underperforming companies, they can press management to sell corporate assets, cut costs leading to redundancies, or divest subsidiaries at a profit. The intention of such activism is short-term, trying to engineer a rise in the share price before selling out at a profit. Although such activities are damaging to the incumbent board and may disadvantage long-term investors, advocates argue that the market for control provides a desirable force for change and that all shareholders benefit from a rising share price.

The need to differentiate between shareholders with a short-term, profit-orientated interest in a company and genuine long-term investors has been recognized. An advisory committee in the Netherlands suggested loyalty bonuses, such as higher dividends, for those holding their shares for four years. In the UK, Lord Myners, a government adviser, has suggested that share voting rights should be related to the period for which the shares have been held. Another suggestion is that investors who bought their shares after the announcement of a takeover bid should not be able to vote their shares on that issue. The argument behind such proposals is that those who hold their shares for the long term are likely to behave as owners, concerned about shareholder stewardship, rather than as short-term speculators, benefiting from movements in share prices.

However, an unintended consequence of changes to tax law and corporate regulation in the UK has been a shift from a longer-term owner's market to a shorter-term trader's market. In the past, institutional investors owned up to 80 per cent of the shares in the London market. Pension funds and insurance companies have been heavy sellers of equities to overseas institutional investors, hedge funds, and sovereign wealth funds. Now, they account for less than 30 per cent of UK share ownership. At this point, their leverage over companies' behaviour begins to wane. However, some foreign hedge funds can be supportive of well-managed companies, continuously keeping in touch, whereas some British investment houses have taken their compliance responsibilities too lightly, voting only for management resolutions.

Should shareholders in listed companies, particularly institutional investors, take a more proactive role in corporate governance? The danger for the investor might be that they become locked into the company, unable, as the Americans say, 'to do the Wall Street walk' or, as the English say, 'to vote with their feet'. But if an institution is tracking a stock exchange index, it may need to hold shares in specific companies anyway: better that it engages with the board to improve long-term shareholder value. As Anne Simpson of the US CalPERS fund has commented: 'Shareholders do need more say in the way that boards are run, but that should be balanced out by shareholders being held responsible for their actions—just as directors are. International discussion about shareholder rights and responsibilities needs to be taken forward on a balanced ticket.'

In 2010, the UK Financial Reporting Council (FRC) introduced an institutional investor Stewardship Code. The Stewardship Code should be applied on a 'comply or explain' basis: in other words reporting how the principles of the Code have been applied or explaining why if they have not been met. The FRC emphasizes that compliance with the Code is not an invitation to manage the affairs of companies, and does not preclude a decision to sell a holding, if this is considered in the best interest of investors.

Corporate Governance in Action 4.2 The UK Financial Reporting Council (FRC) Stewardship Code

Principle 1

Institutional investors should publicly disclose their policy on how they will discharge their stewardship responsibilities.

The disclosure should include:

- how investee companies will be monitored—in order for monitoring to be effective an active dialogue may, where necessary, need to be entered into with the investee company's board;
- the strategy on intervention;
- internal arrangements, including how stewardship is integrated with the wider investment process;
- the policy on voting and the use, if any, made of proxy voting or other voting advisory service(s), including information on how they are used; and
- the policy on considering explanations made in relation to the UK Corporate Governance Code.

Principle 2

Institutional investors should have a robust policy on managing conflicts of interest in relation to stewardship and this policy should be publicly disclosed.

An institutional investor's duty is to act in the interests of all clients and/or beneficiaries when considering matters such as engagement and voting.

Conflicts of interest will inevitably arise from time to time, which may include when voting on matters affecting a parent company or client.

Institutional investors should put in place and maintain a policy for managing conflicts of interest.

Principle 3

Institutional investors should monitor their investee companies.

Investee companies should be monitored to determine when it is necessary to enter into an active dialogue with their boards. This monitoring should be regular, and the process clearly communicable and checked periodically for its effectiveness.

As part of this monitoring, institutional investors should:

- seek to satisfy themselves, to the extent possible, that the investee company's board and committee structures are effective, and that independent directors provide adequate oversight, including by meeting the chair and, where appropriate, other board members;
- maintain a clear audit trail, for example records of private meetings held with companies, of votes cast, and of reasons for voting against the investee company's management, for abstaining, or for voting with management in a contentious situation; and
- attend the general meetings of companies in which they have a major holding, where appropriate and practicable.

Institutional investors should consider carefully explanations given for departure from the UK Corporate Governance Code and make reasoned judgements in each case. They should give a timely explanation to the company, in writing where appropriate, and be prepared to enter a dialogue if they do not accept the company's position.

Institutional investors should endeavour to identify problems at an early stage, to minimize any loss of shareholder value. If they have concerns they should seek to ensure that the appropriate members of the investee company's board are made aware of them.

Institutional investors may not wish to be made insiders. They will expect investee companies and their advisers to ensure that information that could affect their ability to deal in the shares of the company concerned is not conveyed to them without their agreement.

Principle 4

Institutional investors should establish clear guidelines on when and how they will escalate their activities as a method of protecting and enhancing shareholder value.

Institutional investors should set out the circumstances in which they will actively intervene and regularly assess the outcomes of doing so. Intervention should be considered regardless of whether an active or passive investment policy is followed. In addition, being underweight (having a low investment) is not, of itself, a reason for not intervening. Instances when institutional investors may want to intervene include when they have concerns about the company's strategy and performance, its governance, or its approach to the risks arising from social and environmental matters.

Initial discussions should take place on a confidential basis. However, if boards do not respond constructively when institutional investors intervene, then institutional investors will consider whether to escalate their action, for example, by:

- holding additional meetings with management specifically to discuss concerns;
- expressing concerns through the company's advisers;
- meeting with the chair, senior independent director, or with all independent directors;
- intervening jointly with other institutions on particular issues;
- making a public statement in advance of the annual general meeting (AGM) or an extraordinary general meeting (EGM);
- submitting resolutions at shareholders' meetings; and
- requisitioning an EGM, in some cases proposing to change board membership;

Principle 5

Institutional investors should be willing to act collectively with other investors where appropriate. At times collaboration with other investors may be the most effective manner in which to engage. Collaborative engagement may be most appropriate at times of significant corporate or wider economic stress, or when the risks posed threaten the ability of the company to continue. Institutional investors should disclose their policy on collective engagement. When participating in collective engagement, institutional investors should have due regard to their policies on conflicts of interest and insider information.

Principle 6

Institutional investors should have a clear policy on voting and disclosure of voting activity.

Institutional investors should seek to vote all shares held. They should not automatically support the board.

If they have been unable to reach a satisfactory outcome through active dialogue then they should register an abstention or vote against the resolution. In both instances, it is good practice to inform the company in advance of their intention and the reasons why.

Institutional investors should disclose voting records publicly and if they do not explain why.

Principle 7

Institutional investors should report periodically on their stewardship and voting activities.

Those that act as agents should regularly report to their clients details of how they have discharged their responsibilities. Such reports will be likely to contain both qualitative and quantitative information. The particular information reported, including the format in which details of how votes have been cast are presented, should be a matter for agreement between agents and their principals.

Transparency is an important feature of effective stewardship. Institutional investors should not, however, be expected to make disclosures that might be counterproductive. Confidentiality in specific situations may well be crucial to achieving a positive outcome.

Those that act as principals, or represent the interests of the end-investor, should report at least annually to those to whom they are accountable on their policy and its execution.

Those that sign up to this Code should consider obtaining an independent audit opinion on their engagement and voting processes . . . The existence of such assurance certification should be publicly disclosed.

Source: Financial Reporting Council (2012) *The UK Stewardship Code,* September. Available at: www.frc.org.uk/investors/uk-stewardship-code

Shareholder information

Most company law and corporate governance codes encourage transparency in corporate matters and require the reporting of specific information. For example, the OECD corporate governance principles call for timely and accurate disclosure of all material matters regarding the company, its financial situation, performance, ownership, and governance. Such transparency requires accurate accounting methods, full and prompt disclosure of information regarding the company, and the disclosure of conflicts of interest that directors or controlling shareholders might have.

Investor relations are a fundamental responsibility of the a board of listed company, one often delegated to the finance director or CFO. The primary vehicles for communication with shareholders and potential shareholders are a company's reports and shareholder members' meetings. Annual reports and, in some jurisdictions, half-yearly or quarterly reports, provide the chair and board with the opportunity to report on company operations, significant developments, and its financial position. Company law and stock exchange listing regulations require the disclosure of specific matters of corporate and financial information. Under the UK Corporate Governance Code (2008), companies also have to explain the company's business model and overall financial strategy, and show that remuneration incentives are compatible with the company's risk profile. Most listed companies now use websites as well as hard-copy reports to convey shareholder information.

Concern has been expressed recently that financial statements have become too complex for many users to understand. A 2014 bulletin from the European Financial Reporting Advisory Group (EFRAG) and the national standard-setting authorities in France, Germany, Italy, and the UK recognized that some of this complexity arose from increasingly complex transactions, but noted that another possible cause was the increasing complexity of international financial reporting standards.

In the UK, listed companies are required to present shareholders with an enhanced business review. The board is responsible for reporting on the company's strategy, risk management, and governance procedures. Companies do not need to follow a specific template in their presentation. Their reports should offer an honest and open description of the company's exposure to risk, explain how this is identified, and outline the risk management systems in place. Companies can report operational performance in terms of their key performance indicators against industry benchmarks. The business review should also note any contractual relations that are essential to the business, including key licences to operate, significant financial arrangements, and reliance on dominant sources of supply or crucial customers.

The regulations for holding company meetings are provided by company law and companies' articles of association. Some companies now use road shows, conference calls, webcasts, and other opportunities provided by social media to communicate with shareholders and the public. A few have developed sophisticated online tools that allow readers to build their own reports. Others have realized that regularly updated standing information about the company, its activities, and its personalities can be used to simplify the annual company report. An online stock exchange announcement by a company can now trigger email alerts, media feeds, and the updating of Facebook, YouTube, and Twitter pages.

Unlike corporate reports, which are a one-way means of communication, these alternative methods provide opportunities for many-way communication, enabling the company to communicate genuinely, listening to its shareholders, the market, and the public, as well as telling them what the company wants them to hear. Shareholder relations then become shareholder engagement.

Most companies provide more than the minimum information required by the regulations, going beyond mere compliance to voluntary disclosure that enhances the company image. Various annual competitions have been launched to encourage better disclosure, such as the ICSA Hermes Transparency in Governance awards in the UK and the Hong Kong Institute of CPAs Best Corporate Governance Awards.

However, concerns have been expressed that some accounting reports have become too difficult to understand. Some argue that this is inevitable because international business itself has become more diverse. Others blame the growing complication of international accounting standards. The 2014 EFRAG bulletin referred to above,[4] which it issued together with the national accounting standard-setters in the UK, France, Germany, and Italy, provides guidance on minimizing complexity in accounts.

There is also potential hazard in disclosing information to shareholders and the market. Insider dealing, that is buying or selling shares on the basis of information that is not in the public domain, is wrong and a criminal offence in most jurisdictions. Companies need to take care that they do not disclose confidential information to one party that is not available to others. Stock exchange regulations typically require all significant company announcements to be filed with them before being made public.

A relatively new problem for companies in communicating with their shareholders is identifying who they are. Electronic share transfers through nominee accounts can cloak the ultimate beneficiaries. Companies do not know whether the intermediaries have passed on the information they want to give to their ultimate shareholders. Nominee accounts also prevent companies from knowing the scale and composition of their shareholder base. The company law in some jurisdictions has been extended to respond to this issue.

---

[4] EFRAG was established in 2001 by the European accounting profession, account preparers and users, and national accounting standard-setters to provide an international forum to discuss financial reporting issues.

Different types of director

We turn now to the other side of the governance partnership—the company, as represented by its board of directors. The architecture of corporate governance is concerned with the design and style of governance and the way in which its structures match form with function. But before we proceed, we should note that the title 'director' needs to be used with care.

Company law in most jurisdictions refers to 'directors', but does not distinguish between different types of director. In company law, all directors have similar roles and responsibilities. Moreover, any person occupying the position of director may be treated in law as a director, although given another title, such as 'governor'. A director *de jure* has been duly nominated and appointed as a director, in line with the company law. A director, *de facto*, acts as though he or she is a director, without having been so appointed. Whether a person is a *de facto* director depends on the circumstances, but in such cases all of the duties and responsibilities of a director apply. But there are other, potentially confusing uses of the title 'director'.

An executive director is a member of the board of directors who is also an executive manager of the company. In the wording of our governance and management model introduced in Chapter 2, an executive director is a member of both the board circle and the management triangle. The chief executive officer (CEO), sometimes known as the managing director in Commonwealth law jurisdictions, is likely to be a member of the board, but does not have to be. Similarly, the chief finance officer (CFO), the chief operating officer (COO), and other members of what is sometimes called the 'C' suite of top executive officers, may or may not also be executive directors.

Corporate Governance in Action 4.3   Lord Caldecote's advice to executive directors

Lord Caldecote, when he was chairman of Delta Metal, called newly appointed executive directors to meet him and reminded them that:[5]

> [e]xecutive directors have two hats—the hat of the executive and the hat of the director. When you come into my boardroom I want you to be wearing your director's hat. Each director is equally responsible with me for directing the company. You are not there to represent your function or your divisional company. Nor are you there to defend your executive performance or bid for resources for your executive activities. You are there to help me govern the company overall.

By contrast, a non-executive director (NED) is a member of the board who does not hold any executive management position in the company. He or she is in the board circle but not the management triangle. In recent years, a further distinction has crystallized between those NEDs who are independent of the company and those who, although not executives of the company, have other connections with it.

The independent non-executive director (INED) is a director with no affiliation or other relationship with the company, other than the directorship, that could affect, or be seen to

[5] Speech at the Oxford Centre for Management Studies, July 1979.

affect, the exercise of objective, independent judgement. The definition of independence in a director is clarified in the codes of good practice in corporate governance. The International Finance Corporation has adopted definitions of independence (see Corporate Governance in Action 4.4), which list criteria reflected in many codes. In reality, however, independence is a state of mind. As well as meeting the independence criteria, the successful INED needs to be capable of thinking independently, making a stand, and, if necessary, being tough-minded in board-level deliberations.

On the other hand, the affiliated or connected non-executive director (CNED) is a director who, although not a member of the management team, does have some relationship with the company. The connection might be that the director is a retired executive of that company, is a close relative of the chair or the CEO, was nominated by a large shareholder, is linked with an important supplier, distributor, or customer, is a representative of a major financial partner, or is even a retired partner of the firm's external audit firm. Of course, there may be good reasons for appointing people with such experience or connections to the board, but they should not be seen as independent. The significance of the distinction between INED and CNED will become clear when we see, in codes of good corporate governance practice, that independent directors are needed to serve on various board committees.

The term outside director is widely used in the United States and jurisdictions influenced by US practices to refer to a non-executive director, as previously noted. Unless there is evidence to the contrary, outside directors are typically perceived to be independent. Under US federal law,[6] independence requires a director not to accept any consulting, advisory, or other compensatory fee from the company or to be a person affiliated to the company or any of its subsidiaries.

Corporate Governance in Action 4.4 An independent director defined by the International Finance Corporation (IFC)

IFC is an international body, which defines an 'independent director' as follows:

The purpose of identifying and appointing independent directors is to ensure that the board includes directors who can effectively exercise their best judgment for the exclusive benefit of the Company, judgment that is not clouded by real or perceived conflicts of interest. IFC expects that in each case where a director is identified as 'independent' the board of directors will affirmatively determine that such director meets the requirements established by the board and is otherwise free of material relations with the Company's management, controllers, or others that might reasonably be expected to interfere with the independent exercise of his/her best judgment for the exclusive interest of the Company.

'Independent Director' means a director who is a person who:

1. has not been employed by the Company or its Related Parties in the past five years;
2. is not, and has not been affiliated with a company that is an advisor or consultant to the Company or its Related Parties;
3. is not affiliated with a significant customer or supplier of the Company or its Related Parties;
4. has no personal service contracts with the Company, its Related Parties, or its senior management;

---

[6] The Sarbanes-Oxley Act of 2002.

5. is not affiliated with a non-profit organization that receives significant funding from the Company or its Related Parties;

6. is not employed as an executive of another company where any of the Company's executives serve on that company's board of directors;

7. is not a member of the immediate family of an individual who is, or has been during the past five years, employed by the Company or its Related Parties as an executive officer;

8. is not, nor in the past five years has been, affiliated with or employed by a present or former auditor of the Company or of a Related Party; or

9. is not a controlling person of the Company (or member of a group of individuals and/or entities that collectively exercise effective control over the Company) or such person's brother, sister, parent, grandparent, child, cousin, aunt, uncle, nephew or niece or a spouse, widow, in-law, heir, legatee and successor of any of the foregoing (or any trust or similar arrangement of which any such persons or a combination thereof are the sole beneficiaries) or the executor, administrator or personal representative of any Person described in this sub-paragraph who is deceased or legally incompetent,

and for the purposes of this definition, a person shall be deemed to be 'affiliated' with a party if such person (i) has a direct or indirect ownership interest in; or (ii) is employed by such party; 'Related Party' shall mean, with respect to the Company, any person or entity that controls, is controlled by, or is under common control with the Company.

Source: www.ifc.org

A *shadow director* is a person who, although not formally a member of a board, is able to exert pressure on the decisions of that board. In many jurisdictions, a shadow director can be held liable as though a legally appointed director of the company.

Corporate Governance in Action 4.5   Shadow directors identified

When the company law in Hong Kong was changed to require the regular publication of individual directors' remuneration, a number of prominent directors resigned. Many of them held major shareholdings in successful family businesses, which had been listed, and wanted to preserve the secrecy of their personal finances. However, where it was apparent that the board continued to be strongly influenced by their thinking, they could be recognized as shadow directors, and held responsible as though they were directors.

The constitutions of some companies allow for the appointment of *alternate directors*, a person who can take the place of another director if that director cannot attend meetings. Alternate directors are often named for directors who live in different countries and cannot attend every board meeting. An alternate is a director in his or her own right, not an agent for the director whom he or she is replacing. When acting as a director, the alternate has all of the rights and duties of any other director under company law.

A *nominee director* is a director who has been nominated to the board by a major share-holder or other contractual stakeholder, such as a significant lender, to represent its interests.

Nominee directors can find themselves in tricky situations because of their inevitable dual loyalties. As directors, they owe a duty to the company—that is, to all of the shareholders equally. In board deliberations, they should be representing the interests of all shareholders and contractual stakeholders equally, not representing one set of interests alone. Moreover, they may not divulge sensitive information to an outside party. Yet that is precisely why the nominator had the director appointed in the first place.

A *governing director* is a title used mainly in Australia to describe a director with dominant powers in a private company. Although the Australian legislation requires such companies to have two directors, the statutes do not prevent companies from framing their articles of association to give virtually all powers to one person: the governing director.

Company law in some jurisdictions permits the appointment of a *corporate director*—that is, another company, not a human being—as a director. Subject to such law, and a company's own constitutions, those exercising control of the corporate director company have the powers of any other director, but it is the corporate director company that is the director, not the individual exercising that power.

A phrase that is sometimes heard, particularly in Europe, is *worker director*, or *employee director*. Proponents of industrial democracy argue that, since governing a major company requires an informal partnership between labour and capital, employees should participate in corporate governance. In the German supervisory board, one-half of the members are chosen under the co-determination laws through the employees' trades union processes. In the 1970s, the Draft Fifth Directive of the European Economic Community (now the European Union) proposed supervisory boards with employee representation for all large companies in all member states. The British Bullock Report, written in response to the EEC Directive, proposed unitary boards, but including some worker directors. Neither proposal became law. Since then, the company law harmonization process in the EU has been overtaken by social legislation, including the requirement that all major firms should have a works council through which employees can participate in significant strategic developments and changes in corporate policy.

Finally and significantly, we come to the person who has the title of director, but who is not legally a member of the board at all. Many companies create titles including the word 'director' for senior executives who are not, in fact, members of either the main board or, indeed, the board of a subsidiary company, for example 'director of operations', 'risk and compliance director', or 'director of customer relations'. Such people are sometimes referred to as *associate directors*.

Why do companies give executives an associate director title? There seem to be three basic reasons—prestige, reward, and status. The title 'director' tends to convey a level of standing and respect that some clients, customers, or other authorities dealing with the company expect. Other companies use the title 'director' as a form of reward: in other words, recognition for success. Finally, in some communities, the title 'director' is a mark of distinction, with important social implications.

Associate directors do not have the rights or responsibilities in law of a formal director, unless those dealing with them reasonably believe they are dealing with a member of the board with the authority to speak for the company, in which case the associate director might be held personally responsible.

While discussing the concept of directorship, we should mention *cross-directorships*, which are directorships held by a set of directors in various companies. In the simplest form, director A of company A is made a director of company B, while director B of company B joins the board of company A. Most cross-directorships form more complex networks. Various studies have plotted cross-directors within a network of companies, identifying the key nodes—the directors who wield real power. In some countries, the network of cross-directorships highlights surprising concentrations of power within a relatively small circle of people. The arguments for cross-directorships are, obviously, that the network of linkages brings economic benefits to the companies concerned, and enables the rare talents of experienced and well-connected directors to be more widely available. The counterargument is that such concentration of power is undesirable because it is not readily transparent and not the focus for accountability. Cross-directorships are typically legal, provided that there is nothing in a company's constitution preventing them and that the companies are not competing, in which case anti-monopoly rules might come into play.

Corporate Governance in Action 4.6 On associate directors

An international insurance broker based in London has a group devoted to writing airline insurance policies. Every member of the senior staff of that group has the title 'executive director'. None of them is a member of the board of directors. The reason for their title is that their airline clients expect to be dealing with a person at director level.

An Australian commodities firm had a long-serving security officer. He began his career as a uniformed guard at the gates. He had been promoted to sergeant, with a smarter uniform, then security officer, with a gold-braided cap, and finally was created 'security director' wearing a suit. Sceptics in the company said that all of this promotion was in lieu of pay increases. The man himself was well pleased. But he was not, legally, a director of the company.

In a major French organization, the title *directeur* was much sought after, even though directors were not members of the board, nor did the title bestow any financial benefit. But *directeurs* were entitled to use the directors' dining room, which boasted superb cuisine, and gave convivial access to members of top management.

Directors' legal duties and rights

Although company law varies in detail from jurisdiction to jurisdiction, the essence of directors' duties are similar. Directors' responsibilities derive from the nature of the joint-stock, limited-liability company and are enshrined in statute law, case law, and stock exchange and other regulations. Essentially, directors' duties are twofold:

- a duty of trust—to exercise a fiduciary responsibility to the shareholders;
- a duty of care—to exercise reasonable care, diligence, and skill.

The duty of trust, or fiduciary duty, requires directors to act with integrity, behaving honestly and fairly for the benefit of the shareholders equally, recognizing the interests of any minority shareholders; they should also promote the aims of the company to ensure its success, and act solely within the powers delegated to them in the company's constitution. Directors of companies incorporated in the United States owe a specific fiduciary duty to any minority shareholders. British Commonwealth-based common law (Australia, Canada, Hong Kong,

India, New Zealand, Singapore, South Africa, and so on) allows directors to determine the best interests of the whole company, subject to the right of appeal to the courts.

In other words, the primary duty of a director is to act honestly in good faith, giving all shareholders equal, sufficient, and accurate information on all issues affecting their interests. The underlying (and universal) principle is that directors should not treat a company as though it exists for their own personal benefit, unless of course they own all of the shares and, even then, they have to recognize the legal rights of creditors and other stakeholders.

In fulfilling their duty of trust, directors should avoid conflicts of interest, declare an interest in any proposed transaction or arrangement, and should not make a secret profit or take any unapproved benefit from their positions as directors.

The duty of care requires directors to exercise independent judgement with care, skill, and diligence. In earlier days, this duty was not particularly onerous, because courts tended to call for a level of care that could be expected of any reasonable person. In many jurisdictions today, however, courts demand a duty of care that is expected of a person capable of serving as a director. Moreover, that duty of care also takes into account the knowledge, skill, and experience that the director should actually have: if a director is an accountant, lawyer, or engineer, he or she is expected to bring those skills to bear as a director. The standard of professionalism now expected of directors around the world is significantly higher than was expected a few years ago.

Broadly, courts recognize that business decisions involve risk and will not second-guess board-level decisions, taken under normal business circumstances, if they subsequently prove to have been ill-judged. This is frequently referred to as the 'business judgement rule'. Courts can act, however, if negligent or fraudulent behaviour is alleged, or where an apparent abuse of power or suppression of minority shareholders' interests has occurred. For example, courts can give a ruling if it is alleged that the directors have negotiated a contract that is detrimental to the interests of minority shareholders.

Every director is a statutory officer of the company and is bound by the requirements of the company law of the state in which the company is incorporated. A company must, of course, also abide by the laws of all other states in which it operates. Directors can face penalties should the company fail in its legal obligations. In some jurisdictions, company directors may also find themselves exposed under other legislation, such as health and safety laws, environmental protection law, or anti-monopoly rules. A recent legal development in the UK raises the possibility of directors being charged with corporate manslaughter.

All directors on a unitary board have the same legal duties and potential liabilities. In most unitary-board jurisdictions, company law does not distinguish between executive and non-executive directors. In a two-tier board structure, on the other hand, the responsibilities of the executive board members to run the enterprise are fundamentally different from those of supervisory board members to monitor and supervise the executive board.

There is widespread misunderstanding about the liability of directors. In a limited-liability company, it is the shareholders' liability for the company debts that is limited, not the directors' liability. Directors are not automatically liable for the debts of their company, provided that they have not acted negligently, nor made it appear that they accepted personal liability. In some jurisdictions, a director can be personally liable for the firm's debts if he or she knew that the company was insolvent and allowed it to continue to trade.

Directors can also be charged if they mislead auditors or fail to file various documents with the companies registry. Most company law jurisdictions provide for the disqualification of directors if they are found unfit to be a director. Causes can include bankruptcy, theft, fraud, and failure to meet the requirements of the companies legislation, or running a company that has traded while insolvent and without a reasonable chance of paying its creditors.

The board leadership role of the chair

Although many commentators refer to the 'chair of the company', the 'company chair' is in fact chair of the board of directors, not of the company. Company law has relatively little to say about the specific role of the chair. It is the company's constitution that determines the way in which the chair of the board is appointed (typically by a simple decision of the board), the duties of the chair, and other aspects of the role.

In the past and in some companies today, the chair does little more than arrange and run directors' meetings. But, in recent years, the chair's role has taken on a much wider responsibility as the leader of the board team. Not only do chairs plan and run directors' and shareholders' meetings, they also need to ensure that the induction of new directors, the training and development of existing directors, and the performance evaluation of the board, its committees, and individual directors are sound, that the structure and membership of the board are appropriate, and that the strategic direction of the company is viable.

In many companies, the chair is an INED, serving on a part-time basis. But occasionally the post is described as 'executive chair' to indicate that the chair is devoting a substantial part of his or her time to the company, even though the role is separate from that of the CEO. In any case, the chair is not a member of management, whereas the CEO (called 'managing director' in some cases) is an employee of the company and, as we saw in Chapter 2, a member of management as well as the board.

The difference between the roles of chair and CEO continues to be one of the contentious and unresolved dilemmas in corporate governance. A key question in contemporary corporate governance is whether the chairship and chief executive roles should be separate or combined in one person. The view of all of the codes of good practice in corporate governance is that the roles should be separate:

> The roles of chairman and chief executive should not be exercised by the same individual. The division of responsibilities between the chairman and chief executive should be clearly established, set out in writing and agreed by the board.

(Principle A2.1, UK Combined Code on Corporate Governance)

The argument is that separation, providing duality at the top of the company, produces a check-and-balance mechanism, avoids the potential for abuse if power is concentrated in a single person, and enables the CEO to concentrate on managing the business while the chair handles the running of the board, relations with shareholders, and other non-contractual stakeholders, such as the government, the regulators, and the media.

Despite the well-honed recommendation around the world that the chair and CEO roles should be separate, in American listed companies the roles are frequently combined. The arguments in favour of combined roles are that a dynamic enterprise needs just one leader, that spreading leadership duties between two people leads to conflict, and that this is the way in which American companies have been run very successfully for generations. In recent years, following a number of dramatic and heavily reported company collapses in the USA, many of them apparently due to the abuse of power by the head of the company, there have been calls from institutional investors for the roles to be separated. Not surprisingly, however, these views have been resisted by many incumbents of the combined position, because separation would erode some of their power. Such views are often supported by their outside directors, because many of them hold similar combined roles in their own companies. Interestingly, however, in the most dramatic collapse of all—Enron—the roles were separated.

There is no doubt that, where the roles of chair and CEO are separated, the relationship between the chair and the CEO is particularly important. Where it works well, as Sir Adrian Cadbury explains in his book on chairship, it can be a subtle, productive, and personally rewarding relationship. Where it fails, it can lead to major corporate problems and considerable personal stress.

This raises a related contentious issue: should a retiring CEO be reappointed as chair of the company's board? Those in favour point out the years of experience, knowledge, and connections that the retiring top executive can bring to the board as its chair—experience that would otherwise be lost. Those questioning the move point out potential difficulties for the new CEO. It is a rare person who, having been a successful CEO, can pass on the executive decision-making reins to a new CEO without interfering in the day-to-day running of the business. Some codes of good practice in corporate governance oppose the retiring CEO becoming chair in that company.

The corporate officers

The officers of a company are defined by the company laws of each jurisdiction. Typically, they include all of the directors and the company secretary, who might also be a director. In some countries, the term embraces officers who may not be on the board, such as the general manager, the treasurer, the comptroller, and the general counsel (Canada Business Corporations Act).

Company law stipulates the duties of the company officers. In the UK, these duties were previously defined by case law, but the Companies Act 2006 confirmed that company directors are responsible for ensuring that their companies are well managed, for promoting their success, and for benefiting the shareholders. The Act further confirmed that directors also have responsibilities to the company's employees, its trading partners, and the state. Company law, too, lays down penalties for failure to carry out these duties.

The company secretary has a formal role in corporate governance. In most jurisdictions, the company secretary is responsible for maintaining the records required by the law, such as the register of members, filing annual returns to the companies registrar, and notifying changes to the company's registered address. Despite the title, the company secretary is a legal office of considerable importance, not a secretarial, clerical function. In the United States, the role is usually referred to as the corporate secretary and filled by the company's general counsel—that is, by the in-house lawyer.

The Cadbury Report (1992) emphasizes the significance of the job:

> The company secretary has a key role to play in ensuring that board procedures are both followed and regularly reviewed. The chairman and the board will look to the company secretary for guidance on what their responsibilities are under the rules and regulations to which they are subject and on how those responsibilities should be discharged. All directors should have access to the advice and services of the company secretary and should recognize that the chairman is entitled to the strong support of the company secretary in ensuring the effective functioning of the board.

Company law in most jurisdictions requires all companies to have a company secretary. In the UK, public companies must have one, who must hold a recognized legal, accountancy, or company secretarial qualification. But unlike most other countries, in the UK private companies need not have a company secretary unless the members so require. In some countries, Australia for example, and public companies in the UK, the company secretary must be a real person, but elsewhere the purely legal function can be delegated to a specialist company or an outside agent such as the company's lawyer, but not auditor. In Hong Kong, for example, under the Companies Ordinance, every company must have a company secretary but the secretary may be an employee of the company or an agent providing services to the company. The company secretary may be a director, but need not be. But under the Listing Rules of the Hong Kong Stock Exchange, a listed company must have a secretary who is a person (not another company) ordinarily resident in Hong Kong. An exception is made in the case of companies listed in Hong Kong but incorporated in the People's Republic of China (PRC).

Case studies

 Case study 4.1 The National Health Service Foundation Trust cases

The five English National Health Service (NHS) Foundation Trust cases, which appear throughout the book, illustrate the reality of interpersonal and political behaviour at board level. To preserve confidentiality, the Trust's name and location are not given and names and descriptions have been changed. However all of the incidents occurred.

The NHS has a code of governance that sets out best practice principles and processes to help NHS Foundation Trust boards of directors:

- maintain good-quality corporate governance;
- contribute to better organizational performance;
- provide safe, effective services for patients.[7]

The NHS also publishes a set of conditions to determine whether a person is 'fit and proper' to serve on its committees.[8] More specifically, the NHS lays down requirements to determine whether a person is fit and proper to be a director.[9]

NHS Foundation Trusts

NHS Foundation Trusts were created in 2013, to govern most services provided by the NHS in local areas around the country.[10] Under the previous system many hospitals had their own governors but policy for the NHS was set and significant decisions approved centrally. Critics complained that this failed to respond to local conditions and needs in different areas, even though they would still have to be ruled by the regulator (NHS Improvement (previously the Trust Development Authority)) and adhere to national policy and finance rules.

---

[7] https://improvement.nhs.uk/resources/nhs-foundation-trusts-code-governance/
[8] https://improvement.nhs.uk/resources/fit-and-proper-persons-requirements/
[9] www.cqc.org.uk/guidance-providers/regulations-enforcement/regulation-5-fit-proper-persons-directors
[10] For more on NHS Foundation Trusts see www.nhshistory.net/foundation.pdf and www.nhs.uk/NHSEngland/thenhs/about/Pages/authoritiesandtrusts.aspx

Trusts have financial freedom and can raise capital from both the public and private sectors within borrowing limits, that are determined by projected cash flows and therefore based on affordability. They can retain financial surpluses to invest in the delivery of new NHS services, although many run deficits. For example, if a magnetic-resonance imaging (MRI) scanner would improve patient care, an NHS Foundation Trust can use existing funds or borrow money to purchase one, without reference to a central hierarchy for approval.

Each NHS foundation trust also has a duty to create, consult, and involve a board of governors—including patients, staff, members of the public, and partner organizations—in the strategic planning of the organization. This case study focuses on board-level behaviour in one trust.

A Foundation Trust has a board of directors and a council of governors. The chair is responsible for leadership of the board of directors and the council of governors. The council of governors has a statutory duty to hold the non-executive directors individually and collectively to account for the performance of the board of directors. This includes ensuring the board of directors acts so that the Foundation Trust does not breach the conditions of its licence. It remains the responsibility of the board of directors to design and then implement agreed priorities, objectives, and the overall strategy of the NHS Foundation Trust. The council of governors is responsible for representing the interests of NHS Foundation Trust members and the public in the governance of the trust. Governors must act in the best interests of the NHS Foundation Trust and should adhere to its values and code of conduct.

The Trust board

The non-executive members of the Trust studied here were:

Lady Audrey Westwood

After a career in senior administration roles in healthcare services in various parts of the world, Lady Westwood retired in 2010, and formed a consultancy service advising hospitals on cost–benefit projects. She was appointed Chair of the Trust in June 2015.

John Brigham-West

Retired from the military with the rank of colonel, he now serves as adviser to the chair of a group of companies in the defence industry.

Robert Evans

Chairman of a multinational company headquartered in the region, and has experience as a non-executive director on boards of other major companies.

Angela Prowess

Professor at a major university, she holds a doctorate in social science.

Marion Mirrlees

On retiring from a career as a senior civil servant, she now advises a local university and other educational establishments on human resource management and governance.

Sally Mudberry

Trained as a social worker, she is now the chief executive officer of a company running care homes.

Charles Windlass

Owner of a large local property development company, he is a chartered accountant. He is also a non-executive director of two listed companies.

The executive members of the Trust were:

Marion Jones CEO

Elizabeth Dogara Deputy CEO

Roy Fosbury Finance director

Peter Gately Medical director

Amy Hardcastle Director for strategy and improvement

Mary Priot Chief nurse

Joan Trend Director of human resources and organizational development

Janet Winslow Director of estates

Four deputy medical directors also attend meetings of the Trust.

The minutes of the last meeting of the Trust included the following items:

Commissioning of MRI scanner

The medical director reported that the new MRI scanner facility had been opened and was working well. Mr Gately said that MRI was the most effective form of diagnosis for many conditions.[11] He reported that, as instructed by the Board, he had ensured that all lay members of the Trust had visited the facility. The cost of the equipment was met from funds raised by the Friends of the Hospital, supplemented by a grant from the Trust's capital budget.

Action: Medical director to report regularly on progress on the MRI department.

Financial report

The finance director outlined the financial reports previously circulated to members. He explained that the budget deficit had continued to increase, partly due to unprecedented demands on A&E (Accident and Emergency Department) leading to more admissions, resulting in higher than expected staff costs. The problem was exacerbated by mainly elderly patients medically fit to leave but unable to be discharged because local authorities could not find suitable beds in care homes or fund home support and care needed. Other Foundation Trusts were facing similar problems and the finance director suggested that the only solution was to apply for more funding from the NHS. Robert Evans strongly disagreed, saying that in his lifetime experience of business there was never a situation in which costs could not be reduced. He called for an independent inquiry into the Trust's control of expenditure. He was supported by Colonel Brigham-West and Mr Windlass.

Action: The chair to discuss the situation with the CEO and the finance director, and to seek the opinion of the chairs of other Foundation Trusts. Report to the next meeting.

---

[11] In Britain surgeons are addressed by the title mister, not doctor.

Health tourism

The finance director reminded members that medical services on the NHS were provided for British residents free of charge, but overseas patients were required to pay. Unfortunately, along with many other Foundation Trusts, this Trust had significant unpaid debts. Attempts to recover the monies due had typically failed because the patients, from all round the world, did not respond or their addresses were found to be false.

Robert Evans said that this situation was totally unacceptable: the British taxpayers were not responsible for the world's medical bills—we have already seen that it cannot afford the cost of its own population. The chief nurse responded that this was not a simple problem: 'patients present at A&E with critical conditions—complex pregnancies, cancer, renal failure—we treat them irrespective of their origins. That is what all medical staff are trained to do.' Colonel Brigham-West disagreed: 'some of these people may be refugees fleeing corrupt and hostile situations. OK we may have a duty to treat them (but I still think the British Government should cover the costs for overseas aid funds). But many of the patients we treat set out to exploit the system. I read of people coming here for a holiday— flying first class, staying at five star hotels, and using our hospitals for free treatment that they cannot receive at home.'
Action: None.

Discussion questions

1. Even with the limited information provided by these extracts from the minutes, what is your opinion of:

   a. the leadership style of Lady Audrey Westwood, the chair of the Trust?
   b. the culture of the board of the Trust?

2. Did the board reach an appropriate decision on each of the three agenda items described?

 Case study 4.2   Sports Direct International PLC

Sports Direct is the UK's largest retailer of sporting goods. Its portfolio includes sports, fitness, fashion, and lifestyle brands, including Slazenger, Everlast, Lonsdale, Karrimor, Kangol, No Fear, and Firetrap. The company operates around 757 sports stores across the UK and internationally, with around 18,000 employees.

The company was established in 1982, by Mike Ashley in Maidenhead as Mike Ashley Sports. Within a decade he had opened 12 stores. In 1996, the name was changed to Sports Soccer and the head office and warehouse relocated to Dunstable. The company now had 50 retail stores, and acquired the Donnay tennis and golf brand. By 2000 there were 80 stores. In 2003, the Lillywhites chain of stores and the Lonsdale brand were bought and there were 150 stores.

Sports Direct is listed

Sports Direct International PLC was floated on the London Stock Exchange. Through an initial public offering (IPO) debuted in February 2007, Ashley maintained control with a significant majority stake. Merrill Lynch advised on the flotation, through their broker Jeff Blue, who appears later in this case.

More merger and acquisition activity followed: a 29.4 per cent stake in the Blacks Leisure Group, a 25 per cent stake in Matalan, in Everlast a £84m stake, and a 12.3 per cent stake in John David Group, parent of JD Sports. The company also traded in the shares of Debenhams, a large UK department store. In December 2016 they sold the remaining rights to their Dunlop brand to Sumitomo Rubber Industries for £112m. Sumitomo already owned rights to the brand in Japan, South Korea, and Taiwan.

The Sports Direct board of directors

The board was reorganized and strengthened when Sports Direct went public.

Mike Ashley

Executive deputy chairman following the listing, appointed CEO in September 2016.

Jon Kemster

CFO appointed in September 2017; a chartered accountant. Previously, finance director: Wincanton, Delta PLC, Low & Bonar PLC, Linden PLC.

Dr Keith Hellawell QPM

Appointed non-executive director November 2009 as chair of the board, chair of nomination committee, member of the remuneration committee. Forty years in public sector management as former Chief Constable of two British police forces, worked directly for Prime Minister Tony Blair from 1998 to 2002. Held non-executive directorships in private companies, and runs his own management and training consultancy.

Simon Bentley

Appointed in March 2007 as senior INED. Member of the remuneration committee. Chair of audit committee. Joined Blacks Leisure Group PLC: chair and CEO for 12 years. Acting chair of Sports Direct International PLC from 31 May–23 November 2007.

David Daly

Appointed non-executive director in October 2017. Member of the audit committee. Thirty-year international career with Nike.

David Brayshaw

Appointed non-executive director in December 2016. Chairman of the remuneration committee. Member of the audit committee. Senior investment and commercial banker: 30 years' experience with Barclays Capital, HSBC, Citigroup, and Pilkington PLC.

A self-made tycoon

Mike Ashley founded Sports Direct and is still its driving force. He has been called a caricature of 'self-made tycoon': '[h]e bats around the country on helicopters ... carries his papers in a plastic bag rather than a briefcase ... at the peak of the scandal over low pay of his warehouse staff, he pulled wads of £50 notes from his pocket in the presence of a photographer from *The Sun*'.[12]

[12] *The Sunday Times*, 2 July 2017.

Employee conditions at Sports Direct have been the subject of adverse media comment. A Channel 4 TV documentary branded Sports Direct a 'sweatshop' with working conditions compared to the Victorian era, and bosses were accused of punishing employees if they talk. In October 2015, the then CEO, David Forsey, was charged with a criminal offence for failing to consult staff, who were made redundant and given only 15 minutes' notice. In December 2015, an investigation by *The Guardian* newspaper found that 'the company fines staff for late clocking on, does not reward overtime for late clocking off, relies on zero hour contracts, and regularly makes staff wait unpaid for a security check at the end of shifts'.[13] A union official suggested that these practices were illegal as they brought workers' earnings below the national minimum wage. In August 2016 the company admitted unlawfully withholding wages.

Ashley is taken to court

In July 2017 Jeff Blue, who had advised on the Sports Direct flotation in 2007, sued Mike Ashley. Between 2012 and 2015, Blue had given Ashley financial advice. He claimed that, during a drinking session at the Horse & Groom pub in 2013, Ashley had offered him a £15m bonus if he could get the Sports Direct shares off the City's blacklist and double the price from £4 to £8. Blue claimed that this had been achieved by February 2014, but he had not been paid. Ashley claimed that the 'deal' was banter. He boasted that he had drunk about five pints of beer within an hour during the meeting.[14]

In May 2014 £1 million had been paid to Blue. Ashley denied it was connected to the alleged agreement: 'It was a discretionary one-off bonus'.[15]

Blue sought £14 million damages, claiming he had an existing services contract with Sports Direct but that the efforts to boost its share price were over and above the terms of that contract.

At the conclusion of the case he commented '[d]espite the judge ruling in favour of the Sports Direct boss, evidence heard by the court painted a stark picture of how Ashley does business.'[16]

Discussion questions

1. What is your opinion of the structure of non-executive membership of the Sports Direct board after listing?

2. How would you describe the culture of the company from the limited information in the case study?

3. What do you think is the likely culture of the board of directors?

Self-test questions

1. What determines shareholder rights?

2. Can shareholders get involved in the day-to-day management of a company or inspect the company financial records?

[13] *The Guardian*, 12 December 2015.
[14] *The Times*, 4 July 2017.
[15] *The Sunday Times*, 2 July 2017.
[16] *Daily Mail*, 14 December 2017.

3. In public companies in the European Union, can members raise questions at the annual general meeting? Do shareholders have a right to put an item on the agenda of the AGM?

4. Under the UK FRC Stewardship Code, should institutional investors have a clear policy on voting and disclose their voting activity? Should they vote all of the shares they hold?

5. Distinguish an independent non-executive director from an affiliated or connected non-executive director.

6. What is an outside director? What is a shadow director?

7. Can people be given the title 'director' without being formally members of a board?

8. Is the chair legally 'chair of the company' or 'chair of the board of directors'?

9. Is it a good idea to appoint a retiring CEO as chair?

10. Does company law in most jurisdictions distinguish the roles of executive and non-executive directors?

 For suggested answers to these self-test questions visit the online resources at: www.oup.com/uk/tricker4e/

Projects and exercises

1. In the 2013 Excellence in Governance Awards, run by the UK Institute of Chartered Secretaries, the award for the Best Sustainability and Stakeholder Disclosure among FTSE 100 companies was won by Unilever PLC. The judges noted that:[17]

   Sustainability is presented from the outset as key to Unilever's strategy, with excellent recognition that value creation for shareholders comes from prioritising the interests of its key stakeholders. From the start, the chairman discusses the integration of the Sustainable Living Plan, and the CEO's introduction actively paints the company's past and future success in the company's sustainability initiatives, with its importance to the strategy clearly laid out. Sustainability KPIs [key performance indicators] are presented alongside financial ones. The overarching strategy and the sustainability goal that underpins it are clearly laid out, with the business model identifying the Sustainable Living Plan as the company's differentiator and driver of success.

   Antofagasta PLC, Aviva PLC, and Johnson Matthey PLC were short-listed. Access their annual reports. Compare their disclosures with that of another listed company of your choice. How do the reports compare?

2. Research the work on worker (or employee) directors. The UK Bullock Report on worker directors (1977) might provide a useful starting point. What are the arguments for and against the concept?

3. You have been retained by the chair/CEO of a company which is about to be floated on the stock market through an IPO. (S)he is opposed to the advice (s)he has received from financial advisers that the roles of the chair and CEO should be separated. Prepare a report or PowerPoint presentation for your client.

[17] *Governance and Compliance*, the journal of the Institute of Chartered Secretaries and Administrators, London, December 2013.

References and further reading

Barker, Roger M. (2010) *Corporate Governance, Competition and Political Parties.* Oxford University Press, Oxford.

Bishop, Matthew and Michael Green (2011) *The Road from Ruin.* A&C Black, Edinburgh.

Cadbury, Adrian Sir (chairman) (1992) The Financial Aspects of Corporate Governance: A Report of the Committee on Corporate Governance. Gee and Co., London.

Cadbury, Adrian Sir (2002) *Corporate Governance and Chairmanship: A Personal View.* Oxford University Press, New York.

Carter, Colin B. (2004) *Back to the Drawing Board: Designing Corporate Boards for a Complex World.* Harvard Business School Press, Boston, MA.

LeBlanc, Richard and James Gillies (2005) *Inside the Boardroom.* Wiley, Canada.

Lorsch, Jay W. and Elizabeth McIver (1989) *Pawns or Potentates: The Reality of America's Corporate Boards.* Harvard Business School Press, Boston, MA.

Mallin, Chris (2006) *International Corporate Governance* (cases). Edward Elgar Publishing, Cheltenham and Northampton, MA.

Useful websites

www.cgfrc.nus.edu.sg

National University of Singapore, Corporate Governance and Financial Reporting Centre—updates on current topics in corporate governance.

www.iwep.org.cn (click on 'English' then 'corporate governance')

Institute of World Economics and Politics, Chinese Academy of Social Sciences.

www.ecgi.org

European Corporate Governance Institute—a forum for dialogue between academics, legislators, and practitioners.

5 The Regulatory Framework

 Learning Objectives

This chapter enables us to:

- Appreciate corporate regulation in the UK, the USA, and other countries.
- Compare corporate governance codes from international agencies, institutional investors, and companies.
- Consider corporate governance codes for the public and voluntary sectors.
- Understand the importance of compliance and corporate governance reports.
- Study the corporate governance debate between principles and prescription.

Legislation, regulation, and corporate governance codes

Being a creation of the law, limited-liability companies depend on company law for their existence, continuity, and winding-up. Company law defines the way in which they are incorporated, how their directors are appointed, and how shareholder relations should be handled, as well as laying down disclosure and filing requirements. Companies must follow the company law of the jurisdiction in which they are incorporated and the laws of other places where they do business. Penalties for failure to obey company law can be heavy on the company, its directors, and its officers, including in many cases both fines and/or prison: in China, the penalty for corruption or other major corporate infractions can be death.

Company laws vary from the highly specific and demanding, as in many US states, the UK, and most other advanced economies, to the quite undemanding, as in some offshore tax havens. In the USA companies are incorporated within a state, not federally, and states' company laws vary, which is why many public companies are incorporated in Delaware with its companies legislation, Court of Chancery, and large body of company-friendly case law.

Companies, their directors, and their officers can also find themselves exposed to other legislation, such as health and safety, consumer protection, and environmental standards. In the UK, a recent development, where lives have been lost, is a potential liability for companies to be charged with manslaughter. Clearly, directors need to ensure that they have the necessary systems and advice to minimize the risk of breaking the law.

Legislation affecting companies, their directors, and managers tends to evolve and expand rapidly: the UK Bribery Act 2010 introduced draconian penalties for acts of bribery, the 2014 Companies Ordinance in Hong Kong brought many new features into company law, the UK Enterprise and Regulatory Reform Act 2013 produced new legislation on intellectual property, European Union directives and regulations have covered human rights and environmental sustainability, and in many jurisdictions new corporate reporting has been required. Boards need to ensure that such legal requirements are integrated effectively into the internal workings of the company. Companies are, of course, also subject to corporate regulations, which extend and amplify the law; for example, taxation regulations, import/export regulations, and requirements on employee working conditions. Directors and their companies can be liable if found guilty of disobeying or not following the regulations, and again boards should ensure that the necessary safeguards are in place.

Accounting standards, another type of company regulation, apply to the specific jurisdiction in which the company is reporting. Generally accepted accounting principles (GAAP) apply in the USA and some other countries, but there is a trend for countries to converge with the International Financial Reporting Standards (IFRS).

For public companies listed on a stock exchange, there are also the stock exchange's rules that must be followed by listed companies. For example, the NYSE Euronext market requires companies to follow an extensive rule book,[1] which was harmonized in 2013. Failure to follow the rules can result in sanctions such as being suspended or ultimately delisted from the exchange.

Company and other relevant law, regulations, accounting standards, and stock exchange listing rules are mandatory: they must be followed if penalties are to be avoided. But in many parts of the world there are also discretionary corporate governance codes, as we will see.

Corporate regulation in the UK

In the UK, companies have to abide by the UK Companies Acts, principally the Companies Act 2006. In 1992, the UK produced the world's first corporate governance report, which contained a formal corporate governance code. Subsequently, the UK has published more corporate governance reports than any other country. In essence the various UK reports have been as follows.

1. The *Cadbury Report* (1992) was produced by a committee chaired by Sir Adrian Cadbury in response to a series of corporate failures in the United Kingdom. It was entitled 'The Financial Aspects of Corporate Governance', and was not intended to be a comprehensive review of the subject, as Sir Adrian subsequently emphasized. It proposed a discretionary code: UK-listed companies being required to report that they had complied with the code or, if they had not, explaining the reasons. The Report called for:

   - the wider use of independent non-executive directors;
   - the introduction of an audit committee of the board with a minimum of three non-executive directors, a majority of whom were to be independent;
   - the division of responsibilities between the chair of the board and the CEO (if the roles were combined in a single person, the board should have a strong independent element);
   - the use of a remuneration committee of the board to oversee executive rewards;
   - the introduction of a nomination committee with independent directors to propose new board members; and

[1] www.euronext.com/regulation/harmonised-rules

- adherence to a detailed code of best practice.

It is interesting to note that, despite being written more than 20 years ago, this report contained many proposals that remain at the heart of today's corporate governance thinking.

2. The *Greenbury Report* (1995) addressed issues of directors' remuneration, then, as now, a matter of concern to directors, the media, and society at large.

The report recommended that:

- the remuneration committees of companies should consist solely of independent non-executive directors;
- the chair of the remuneration committee should respond to shareholders' questions at the AGM;
- annual reports should include details of all director rewards—naming each director;
- directors' contracts should run for no more than a year to avoid excessive golden handshakes;
- share option schemes for directors should be linked to long-term corporate performance.

3. The *Hampel Report* (1998) was a response to a suggestion in the Cadbury and Greenbury Reports that a review should be undertaken after a few years' experience. The report argued that:

- good corporate governance needs broad principles not prescriptive rules;
- compliance with sound governance practices, such as the separation of board chairship from the CEO role, should be flexible and relevant to each company's individual circumstances;
- governance should not be reduced to what the report called a 'box-ticking' exercise;
- the unitary board is totally accepted in the UK—there is no interest in alternative governance structures or processes such as two-tier boards;
- the board is accountable to the company's shareholders—there is no case for redefining directors' responsibilities to other stakeholder groups;
- self-regulation is the preferred approach to corporate governance—there is no need for more company legislation.

The Hampel Committee consisted mainly of directors of major public companies and their professional advisers. Predictably, it did not criticize contemporary corporate governance practices, nor did it advocate any measures that would further limit directors' power to make unfettered decisions, nor widen the scope of their accountability. In fact, it reduced the force of the original Cadbury proposals by suggesting greater 'flexibility'. It was also strident in its insistence that British companies did not want two-tier boards, and rejected calls for broader accountability to stakeholder groups beyond the shareholders. Taking a shareholder value perspective, the report said that '[t]he single overriding objective shared by all listed companies, whatever their size or type of business, is the preservation and the greatest practical enhancement over time of their shareholders' investment'.

The report was also adamant that UK companies did not need any more legislation. Shortly after the report was published, the British government announced a new fundamental review of UK company law.

The Cadbury, Greenbury, and Hampel committees were set up by City of London institutions—that is, by the UK's financial sector. The codes were essentially voluntary and applied principally to listed companies, although it was suggested that many of the recommendations could be applied to private companies.

4. In 1998, the *UK Combined Code* consolidated the Cadbury, Greenbury, and Hampel proposals, and was incorporated into the London Stock Exchange's listing rules. This Combined Code set out standards of good practice on matters such as board composition, director remuneration, accountability, and audit in relation to shareholders. All companies incorporated in the UK and listed on the main market of the London Stock Exchange were now required to report in their annual reports to shareholders on how they had applied the principles in the Combined Code. In these reports, companies had to confirm that they had complied with the Code's provisions or, if they had not, provide explanations of why not. Although the Code had no legislative basis and enforcement, failure to meet its requirements could lead to delisting from the Exchange. Formal delisting, however, would tend to disadvantage the very shareholders whom the corporate governance codes were designed to protect, so delisting was a last resort (and in fact not used). The Stock Exchange rather tends to rely on informal guidance to companies.

5. The *Turnbull Report* (1999, revised 2005) elaborated a call in the Hampel Report for companies to have appropriate internal controls. It set out how directors of UK-listed companies should comply with the Combined Code requirements about internal controls, including financial, operational, compliance, and risk management. The report recognized that risk assessment was vital and recommended that reporting on internal controls become an integral part of the corporate governance process. Thus two new dimensions, enterprise risk management and internal management controls, were added to the field of corporate governance.

6. The *Myners Report* (2001) addressed the responsibilities of institutional investors. The report suggested that:

> Good corporate governance is essential to all forms of business. It provides checks and balances that ensure that firms are run efficiently and meet the objectives of their owners.[2]

7. The *Higgs Report* (January 2003) into the role and effectiveness of non-executive directors, unlike previous reports from the City, was commissioned by the UK Chancellor of the Exchequer and the Secretary of State for Trade and Industry, and published by the Department of Trade and Industry. The Higgs proposals sharpened the requirements in the previous codes, in particular recommending that in listed companies:

[2] HM Treasury press notice (2004), 'Myners Urges All Life Mutuals to Adopt Corporate Governance Best Practice', 20 December. Available at: http://webarchive.nationalarchives.gov.uk/+/http://www.hm-treasury.gov.uk/newsroom_and_speeches/press/2004/press_mynersreview_04.cfm

- at least half the board should be independent non-executive directors;

- all members of the audit and remuneration committees and a majority of the members of the nomination committee should be independent non-executive directors;

- the role of CEO should always be completely separate from that of chair;

- director recruitment should be rigorous, formal, and transparent;

- executive directors should not hold more than one non-executive directorship of a FTSE 100 (Financial Times Stock Exchange) company;

- boards should evaluate the performance of directors and board committees annually, and have a comprehensive induction programme;

- boards should have a senior independent director to liaise with shareholders.

Some of Higgs' initial proposals were contentious. Among the proposals that were *not* accepted were:

- a ban on CEOs moving into the chair of their own company;

- a ban on the chair heading the nomination committee of their own board;

- a ban on anyone being chair of more than one FTSE 100 company;

- a call for regular meetings between the senior independent director and shareholders.

8. The *Smith Report* (2003) looked at the work of the audit committees, a key element in corporate governance concepts. The report called for:

- a strengthening of the role of the audit committee;

- all members of the audit committee to be independent;

- at least one member of the committee to have significant, recent, and relevant financial experience;

- the audit committee should recommend the selection of the external auditor;

- an audit committee report should be included in the annual report to shareholders;

- the chair of the audit committee should attend the AGM to answer shareholders' questions.

9. The *Tyson Report* (June 2003), commissioned by the UK Department of Trade and Industry, was concerned with the recruitment and development of non-executive directors. Laura Tyson, a US White House adviser and then Dean of the London Business School, wrote a report, published by the School, which considered how companies might recruit non-executives from a wider pool of talent following the directive from the Higgs Review for the group to 'describe the profile of relevant skills and experience that make an effective non-executive director with a non-commercial background'.[3] The report called for:

---

[3] London Business School (2003), 'The Tyson Report on the Recruitment and Development of Non-Executive Directors', June. Available at: http://facultyresearch.london.edu/docs/TysonReport.pdf

- more professionalism and transparency in the recruitment of directors;
- the introduction of director induction and training;
- the use of a wider catchment area for outside directors, who could be recruited from what the report called the 'marzipan layer' of senior executives—that is, those just below board level—in unlisted companies, as well as consultancies and organizations in the non-commercial sector.

The UK Combined Code was revised in 2003 and again in 2006. In this later edition, the corporate governance requirements were grouped under four headings:

- independence;
- diligence;
- professional development;
- board performance evaluation.

These editions of the Combined Code were published by the Financial Reporting Council (FRC). The FRC is the UK's independent regulator responsible for promoting high-quality corporate governance and reporting. The FRC, which took over regulatory responsibility from the London Stock Exchange, also oversees the regulatory activities of the actuarial profession and the professional accountancy bodies and operates independent disciplinary arrangements for cases involving accountants and actuaries.

Following the global financial crisis, beginning in 2008, the FRC reviewed the UK Combined Code, and renamed it the *UK Corporate Governance Code* (2010), a name that some commentators felt would have been more appropriate from the start. This Code set out standards of good practice in relation to board leadership and effectiveness, remuneration, accountability, and relations with shareholders. All companies with a listing of shares in the UK were now required under the Stock Exchange Listing Rules to report on how they have applied the Code in their annual report and accounts.[4] Again, the Code was discretionary, with companies required to confirm that they had complied with the Code's main principles or, where they had not, to provide an explanation. The Corporate Governance Code was updated in 2012. The Code contains broad principles, plus some more specific provisions. The main principles are as follows.

Section A: Leadership

- Every company should be headed by an effective board [that] is collectively responsible for the long-term success of the company.
- There should be a clear division of responsibilities at the head of the company between the running of the board and the executive responsibility for the running of the company's business. No one individual should have unfettered powers of decision.
- The chairman is responsible for leadership of the board and ensuring its effectiveness on all aspects of its role.

---

[4] The relevant section of the Listing Rules can be found at: http://fsahandbook.info/FSA/html/handbook/LR/9/8

- As part of their role as members of a unitary board, non-executive directors should constructively challenge and help [to] develop proposals on strategy.

Section B: Effectiveness

- The board and its committees should have the appropriate balance of skills, experience, independence and knowledge of the company to enable them to discharge their respective duties and responsibilities effectively.
- There should be a formal, rigorous, and transparent procedure for the appointment of new directors to the board.
- All directors should be able to allocate sufficient time to the company to discharge their responsibilities effectively.
- All directors should receive induction on joining the board and should regularly update and refresh their skills and knowledge.
- The board should be supplied in a timely manner with information in a form and of a quality appropriate to enable it to discharge its duties.
- The board should undertake a formal and rigorous annual evaluation of its own performance and that of its committees and individual directors.
- All directors should be submitted for re-election at regular intervals, subject to continued satisfactory performance.

Section C: Accountability

- The board should present a balanced and understandable assessment of the company's position and prospects.
- The board is responsible for determining the nature and extent of the significant risks it is willing to take in achieving its strategic objectives. The board should maintain sound risk management and internal control systems.
- The board should establish formal and transparent arrangements for considering how [it] should apply the corporate reporting and risk management and internal control principles, and for maintaining an appropriate relationship with the company's auditor.

Section D: Remuneration

- Levels of remuneration should be sufficient to attract, retain and motivate directors of the quality required to run the company successfully, but a company should avoid paying more than is necessary for this purpose. A significant proportion of executive directors' remuneration should be structured so as to link rewards to corporate and individual performance.
- There should be a formal and transparent procedure for developing policy on executive remuneration and for fixing the remuneration packages of individual directors. No director should be involved in deciding his or her own remuneration.

Section E: Relations with shareholders

- There should be a dialogue with shareholders based on the mutual understanding of objectives. The board as a whole has responsibility for ensuring that a satisfactory dialogue with shareholders takes place.
- The board should use the AGM to communicate with investors and to encourage their participation.[5]

In July 2018, the FRC released the 2018 UK Corporate Governance Code which puts the relationships between companies, shareholders, and stakeholders at the heart of long-term sustainable growth in the UK economy.[6] The new, shorter, sharper Code was the product of extensive consultation.

This revised Code emphasizes businesses building trust by forging strong relationships with key stakeholders. It calls for companies to establish a corporate culture that is aligned with the company purpose and business strategy, promotes integrity, and values diversity. There is a renewed focus on the application of the Principles—the FRC wishes to see clear, meaningful reporting. Investors and proxy advisers must assess explanations carefully and not take a tick-box approach.

The main changes include:

- Workforce and stakeholders: There is a new Provision to enable greater board engagement with the workforce to understand their views. The Code asks boards to describe how they have considered the interests of stakeholders when performing their duty under Section 172 of the 2006 Companies Act.

- Culture: Boards are asked to create a culture which aligns company values with strategy and to assess how they preserve value over the long term.

- Succession and diversity: To ensure that the boards have the right mix of skills and experience, constructive challenge and to promote diversity, the new Code emphasises the need to refresh boards and undertake succession planning. Boards should consider the length of term that chairs remain in post beyond nine years. The new Code strengthens the role of the nomination committee on succession planning and establishing a diverse board. It identifies the importance of external board evaluation for all companies. Nomination committee reports should include details of the contact the external board evaluator has had with the board and individual directors.

- Remuneration: To address public concern over executive remuneration, the new Code emphasises that remuneration committees should take into account workforce remuneration and related policies when setting director remuneration. Importantly formulaic calculations of performance-related pay should be rejected. Remuneration committees should apply discretion when the resulting outcome is not justified.

In December 2016, the UK government published new regulations implementing the European Union Directive on disclosure of non-financial and diversity information (the 'Non-Financial Reporting Directive'). The regulations amend the Companies Act 2006

---

[5] www.frc.org.uk/getattachment/31631a7a-bc5c-4e7b-bc3a-972b7f17d5e2/UK-Corp-Gov-Code-June-2010.pdf

[6] www.frc.org.uk/getattachment/88bd8c45-50ea-4841-95b0-d2f4f48069a2/2018-UK-Corporate-Governance-Code-FINAL.PDF

requirements for the Strategic Report (see next paragraph) and include diversity requirements. The new non-financial reporting regulations only apply to companies with more
than 500 employees.

In 2018, the FRC produced guidance on the Strategic Report required under the UK Corporate Governance Code.[7]

The Hampton-Alexander Review (2016–18)

The review, 'Improving gender balance in FTSE Leadership', is an independent, business-led
report, supported by the British government, which builds on the success of the Davies Review
(in 2011, this called for FTSE 100 boards to increase female membership to at least 25 per cent
by 2015). First reporting in 2016, with subsequent reports in 2017 and 2018, it set a series of
Recommendations aimed at increasing the number of women in leadership positions of FTSE
350 companies.

The Recommendations called for action from all stakeholders and included a target of
33 per cent women on FTSE 350 boards and 33 per cent women in FTSE 100 leadership teams
by 2020. Leadership teams are composed of members of the executive committee and those
senior leaders who are direct reports to executive committee members.

The UK Companies Act 2006

The UK introduced a revised Companies Act in 2006. This was the largest UK Act ever, with
over 1,300 sections. About a third of this was a straightforward restatement of the previous
law in clearer and simpler language. However, some new measures were introduced.

The Act clarified directors' duties for the first time in statute law. Previously, the role and
responsibilities of a director had been determined by case law evolving over the years. The
new law made clear that directors have to act in the interests of shareholders. However,
significantly, the law also added that, in acting in the shareholders' interests, they must pay
regard to the longer-term interests of employees, suppliers, consumers, and the environment.

It also encouraged narrative reporting by companies, calling for them to be forward-looking, identifying risks as well as opportunities. Quoted companies have to provide information
on environmental matters, employees, and social and community issues, including information on any policies relating to these matters and their effectiveness, plus contractual and
other relationships essential to the business, as part of their business review and to the extent
necessary for an understanding of the business.

The Act promoted shareholder involvement in governance by enhancing the powers of
proxies and making it easier for indirect investors to be informed and to exercise governance rights in the company. Shareholders were also able to limit the auditors' liability to the
company to what is fair and reasonable. The Act also provided powers to require institutional
investors to disclose how they used their votes.

[7] See www.frc.org.uk/getattachment/fb05dd7b-c76c-424e-9daf-4293c9fa2d6a/Guidance-on-the-
Strategic-Report-31-7-18.pdf. For more detail see Guidance on Board Effectiveness; Feedback statement:
UK Corporate Governance Code; Feedback statement annex: UK Corporate Governance Code; and Key
Highlights of the Code; all available at: www.frc.org.uk/news/july-2018/a-uk-corporate-governance-code-
that-is-fit-for-the

It included a new offence: recklessly or knowingly including misleading, false, or deceptive matters in an audit report.

It also enabled auditors to agree a limit on their liability with their audit clients, subject to shareholder approval.

The Act also introduced some measures for private companies, including:

- new model articles of association;
- dropping the need for a company secretary unless the members want one;
- dropping the need for an annual general meeting of shareholders if the shareholders agreed.

The UK Financial Reporting Council (FRC)

The FRC has overall responsibility for setting the UK's Corporate Governance Code and the Stewardship Code. It is also the government regulator for the accounting, auditing, and actuarial professions. In February 2017, the FRC announced plans for a comprehensive review of the UK Corporate Governance Code. A public consultation, including a draft revised Code, was issued in December 2017.

The review built on the Code's globally recognized strengths developed over the past 25 years. It also considered the appropriate balance between the Principles and Provisions and the growing demands on the corporate governance framework.

For an example of the work of the FRC see Case study 2.2 'Do boards need diversity?'

The UK Financial Conduct Authority (FCA)

The FCA is an independent entity that regulates the financial services industry in the UK, protecting consumers, ensuring the industry is financially secure, and promoting sound competition between providers of financial services. The FCA has rule-making, investigative, and enforcement powers, and seeks to reduce financial crime. It is funded by the financial institutions it regulates and governed by a board appointed by the UK Treasury, although it receives no government funding.

British standard for delivering effective governance

In response to perceived abuses of authority and societal demands for better organizational governance a British Standard was drawn up, BS 13500 (2013),[8] which clarifies the basic requirements for effective governance in organizations and suggests the fundamentals of good governance.

Corporate regulation in the USA

Each state in the United States has its own companies law, each state jealously guarding its own rights. In addition, federal oversight of companies is provided by the Securities and

---

[8] For details see http://shop.bsigroup.com/ProductDetail/?pid=000000000030228066

Exchange Commission (SEC), which was set up in 1932–3, after the stock market crash of 1929 and the Great Depression that followed. The SEC's mission is to protect investors, to maintain fair, orderly, and efficient markets, and to facilitate capital formation. To achieve this protection for investors, it requires public companies to disclose financial and other information that is then publicly available. The SEC oversees the key participants in the securities world, including securities exchanges, securities brokers and dealers, investment advisers, and mutual funds.

Over the years, the SEC has developed an extensive corporate governance regime for US-listed companies. It was widely believed that US financial regulation would provide a model for the rest of the world. The system seemed to work: companies were well regulated and control was exercised without excessive bureaucracy. The expectation was that the rest of the world would gradually converge with this approach to corporate governance. Indeed, some American institutional investors have proposed changes to corporate governance practices in Germany, Japan, and other countries to encourage this convergence.

Then came the collapse in 2001, of massive companies such as Enron, WorldCom, Tyco, Waste Management, and the 'big five' auditor Arthur Andersen. The response from the US government was the Sarbanes-Oxley Act of 2002, which added the names of Senator Paul Sarbanes and Representative Michael G. Oxley to the lexicon of global corporate governance.

Known colloquially as SOX or Sarbox, this is probably the most influential piece of companies legislation in the world to date, not least because it emphasized the US belief that the regulation of corporate governance should be under the law, not through discretionary codes.

The Sarbanes-Oxley Act

The Sarbanes-Oxley Act (SOX) required certification of internal auditing, increased financial disclosure, and imposed criminal and civil penalties on directors for non-compliance. It applied to all companies listed in the United States, whether resident in the USA or abroad. All publicly traded companies were now required to submit an annual report about their internal accounting controls to the SEC.

Section 302 of the Act mandated a set of internal procedures designed to ensure accurate financial disclosure. Signing officers must certify that they are 'responsible for establishing and maintaining internal controls' and 'have designed such internal controls to ensure that material information relating to the company and its consolidated subsidiaries is made known to such officers by others within those entities, particularly during the period in which the periodic reports are being prepared'. The officers must 'have evaluated the effectiveness of the company's internal controls as of a date within 90 days prior to the report' and 'have presented in the report their conclusions about the effectiveness of their internal controls based on their evaluation as of that date'.[9]

Section 404 required management to produce a report on the company's internal controls as part of the annual report, affirming 'the responsibility of management for establishing and maintaining an adequate internal control structure and procedures for financial reporting'.

---

[9] www.soxlaw.com/introduction.htm

The report must also 'contain an assessment of the effectiveness of the internal control structure and procedures . . . for financial reporting'. Independent external auditors must also attest to management's internal control assessment, pursuant to the new SEC rules. The section has attracted much criticism, particularly on the unexpectedly high cost of compliance to companies listed in the USA and to companies associated with them.

SOX also established:

- new standards for boards and their audit committees;
- new independence standards for external auditors;
- a new Public Company Accounting Oversight Board (PCAOB), to oversee public accounting firms and to issue accounting standards overseen by the SEC.

The SOX legislation was incorporated into the New York Stock Exchange's corporate governance rules in 2003 and 2004. SOX undoubtedly focused attention on corporate governance in the United States. In addition to the costs of compliance, SOX brought significant fees to legal and accounting firms, and spawned a new corporate governance advisory and training industry. Some companies based overseas delisted; others dropped plans to list. More positively, many US companies reported benefits from SOX compliance, including better accountability of individuals, reduced risk of financial fraud, and improved accuracy in financial reports.

Of course, SOX did not prevent the global financial crisis, starting in 2008, in which US companies such as Lehman Brothers failed and American International Group (AIG,) Fannie Mae, Freddie Mac, and others were bailed out by the US government. The result was further federal legislation. The Dodd-Frank Wall Street Reform and Consumer Protection Act of 2010, called by some SOX 2, was enacted to improve American financial regulation and the governance of the US financial services industry. In the words of Mary L. Schapiro, chair of the SEC: 'This law creates a new, more effective regulatory structure, fills a host of regulatory gaps, brings greater public transparency and market accountability to the financial system, and gives investors important protections and greater input into corporate governance.'

Other elements of US corporate governance

Some significant non-governmental organizations also contribute to corporate governance practices in the United States, including the Treadway Commission and COSO, the Business Roundtable, The National Association of Corporate Directors, the American Law Institute, and The Council of Institutional Investors.

1. *The Treadway Commission* was created in 1985, to consider fraudulent corporate financial reporting. Its first report (1987),[10] led to the creation of the Committee of Sponsoring Organizations (COSO) of the Treadway Commission,[11] a private-sector initiative aiming

[10] Report of the National Commission on Fraudulent Financial Reporting (1987).
[11] The Committee of Sponsoring Organizations of the Treadway Commission (COSO), is supported by:
The American Accounting Association;
The Institute of Management Accountants;
The American Institute of Certified Public Accountants;
The Institute of Internal Auditors;
The Financial Executives International.
See www.coso.org

to encourage executive management and boards to improve business activities. COSO is dedicated to guiding executive management and governance entities towards the establishment of more effective, efficient, and ethical business operations on a global basis. It offers frameworks and guidance based on in-depth research, analysis, and best practices, which include:

- Enterprise Risk Management: Integrated Framework (2004);
- Guidance on Monitoring Internal Control Systems (2009).

2. *The Business Roundtable* is an association of CEOs of leading US companies covering nearly one-third of the total value of the US stock markets. In 1997, the Roundtable published a statement on corporate governance, followed by Principles of Corporate Governance in 2002, updated in 2005, and 2010. Other publications include:

- Executive Compensation: Principles and Commentary (2003 and 2007);
- The Nominating Process and Corporate Governance Committees: Principles and Commentary (2004);
- Guidelines for Shareholder–Director Communications (2005).

According to its website, the Business Roundtable believes that the United States has the best corporate governance, financial reporting, and securities markets systems in the world:

These systems work because of the adoption of best practices by public companies within a framework of laws and regulations that establish minimum requirements while affording companies the ability to develop individualized practices that are appropriate for them. However, the Business Roundtable also accepts that no one approach is right for all corporations. Each corporation should look to these principles as a guide in developing structures, practices, and processes that are appropriate for it in light of its needs and circumstances.

The Business Roundtable principles are intended to assist corporate boards of directors and management in their individual efforts to implement best practices of corporate governance. However, the Roundtable recommends that should a company's governance practices diverge from common practice, it should consider disclosing the reasons for this and why its practices are appropriate, consistent with its size, industry, culture, and other relevant factors:

First, the paramount duty of the board of directors of a public corporation is to select a chief executive officer and to oversee the CEO and senior management.

Second, it is the responsibility of management, under the oversight of the board, to operate the corporation in an effective and ethical manner to produce long-term value for shareholders.

Third, it is the responsibility of management, under the oversight of the board, to develop and implement the corporation's strategic plans, and to identify, evaluate and manage the risks inherent in the corporation's strategy.

Fourth, it is the responsibility of management, under the oversight of the audit committee and the board, to produce financial statements that fairly present the financial condition and results of operations of the corporation and to make the timely disclosures investors need to assess the financial and business soundness and risks of the corporation.

Fifth, it is the responsibility of the board, through its audit committee, to engage an independent accounting firm to audit the financial statements prepared by management and issue an opinion that those statements are fairly stated in accordance with Generally Accepted Accounting Principles.

Sixth, it is the responsibility of the board, through its corporate governance committee, to play a leadership role in shaping the corporate governance of the corporation and the composition and leadership of the board.

Seventh, it is the responsibility of the board, through its compensation committee, to adopt and oversee the implementation of compensation policies, establish goals for performance-based compensation, and determine the compensation of the CEO and senior management.

Eighth, it is the responsibility of the corporation to engage with long-term shareholders in a meaningful way on issues and concerns that are of widespread interest to long-term shareholders.

Ninth, it is the responsibility of the corporation to deal with its employees, customers, suppliers and other constituencies in a fair and equitable manner and to exemplify the highest standards of corporate citizenship.[12]

3. *The National Association of Corporate Directors* (NACD), founded in 1977, is a national organization for directors. More than 10,000 directors and key executives from public, private, and non-profit companies form a network for director development, strengthening board practices, and influencing opinion on corporate governance issues.

   In 2001, a NACD Blue Ribbon Commission published 'Director Professionalism'. The report challenged what it believed was the accepted corporate governance paradigm: management is accountable to the board, and the board is accountable to shareholders. In the view of the Commission, 'the board does more than mechanically link those who manage the corporation and those who own it. Rather, as a surrogate for dispersed ownership, the board is at the very centre of corporate governance itself.'

   The Commission emphasized the need for director professionalism and believed that such a culture was evolving in boardrooms not only in the United States, but also gradually elsewhere: 'Professionalism places principal reliance on the actions and attitudes of individual board members'.

4. *The American Law Institute* (ALI), established in 1923, seeks to clarify American common law. In 2002, the ALI published a set of general principles on corporate governance. This was the Institute's first comprehensive review of company law, and examined the duties and responsibilities of directors and officers of corporations.

   Topics covered included the objective and conduct of the business corporation, the structure of the corporation, the duty of care, the duty of fair dealing, the role of directors and shareholders in transactions in control and tender offers, the business judgement rule, and corporate remedies. The business judgement rule is that courts will not intervene even though a board decision is shown to have been wrong, provided

---

[12] www.businessroundtable.org/resources/business-roundtable-principles-of-corporate-governance-2012

that it was made in good faith. Recommendations were also made on sound corporate practices, which are not intended to be legally binding, concerning the composition of the board, the creation, functions, and powers of audit committees, nominating committees, and compensation committees in publicly held corporations.

The review's seven volumes articulated directors' and officers' duty-of-care obligations; the extent to which directors and officers may rely on other persons in formulating decisions on behalf of the corporation. They also cover the duty imposed upon directors, senior executives, and controlling shareholders to deal fairly with the corporation, particularly when their own interests are involved, such as compensation, connected transactions, and competition with the corporation.

5. *The Council of Institutional Investors* (CII) provides the voice for more than 135 United States pension, corporate, and trades union funds, with more than US$4 trillion in assets under management. The founders believed that the companies in which they were investing their members' retirement assets needed more oversight by shareholders. CII has developed a comprehensive body of corporate governance best practices, calling for sound governance standards at public companies and strong shareholder rights. These policies cover for example executive compensation, CEO succession, and board diversity. The CII also provides policies on investment-related issues relevant to institutional investors. It encourages its members to use their proxy votes, propose shareowner resolutions, put pressure on regulators, hold discussions with companies, and, if necessary, launch litigation.[13]

New York Stock Exchange corporate governance listing standards

NYSE Euronext (NYX) sponsored an independent commission on corporate governance chaired by Larry W. Sonsini, which published its report in 2010. The report outlines some core principles, as follows:

- The board's fundamental objective should be to build long-term sustainable growth in shareholder value for the corporation.
- Successful corporate governance depends upon successful management of a company, because management has the primary responsibility for creating a culture of performance with integrity and ethical behaviour.
- Good corporate governance should be integrated with the company's business strategy and not viewed as simply a compliance obligation.
- Shareholders have a responsibility and long-term economic interest to vote their shares in a reasoned and responsible manner, and should engage in a dialogue with companies in a thoughtful manner.
- While legislation and agency rule-making are important to establish the basic tenets of corporate governance, corporate governance issues are generally best solved through collaboration and market-based reforms.

[13] To study the CII corporate governance policies go to: www.cii.org/index.asp

- A critical component of good governance is transparency, because well-governed companies should ensure that they have appropriate disclosure policies and practices, and investors should also be held to appropriate levels of transparency, including disclosure of derivative or other security ownership on a timely basis.

- The Commission supports the NYSE's listing requirements generally providing for a majority of independent directors, but also believes that companies can have additional non-independent directors so that there is an appropriate range and mix of expertise, diversity, and knowledge on the board.

- The Commission recognizes the influence that proxy advisory firms have on the markets, and believes that it is important that such firms be held to appropriate standards of transparency and accountability.

- The SEC should work with exchanges to ease the burden of proxy voting while encouraging greater participation by individual investors in the proxy-voting process.[14]

The NYSE listed company manual lays down the requirements that listed companies must fulfil to be listed. Section 303A includes a set of corporate governance demands, together with some useful explanatory commentary. The specific requirements are that:

- listed companies must have a majority of independent directors;

- to empower non-management directors to serve as a more effective check on management, the non-management directors of each listed company must meet at regularly scheduled executive sessions without management;

- listed companies must have a nominating/corporate governance committee composed entirely of independent directors;

- the nominating/corporate governance committee must have a written charter;

- listed companies must have a compensation committee composed entirely of independent directors;

- the compensation committee must have a written charter;

- listed companies must have an audit committee that satisfies the requirements of rule 10A-3 under the US Exchange Act of 1934, which defines the rules for audit committees and director independence;

- the audit committee must have a minimum of three members who satisfy the requirements for independence;

- the audit committee must have a written charter;

- shareholders must be given the opportunity to vote on all equity-compensation plans;

- listed companies must adopt and disclose corporate governance guidelines;

- listed companies must adopt and disclose a code of business conduct and ethics for directors, officers, and employees;

- listed companies must have and maintain a publicly accessible website.

[14] www.wsgr.com/WSGR/Display.aspx?SectionName=publications/PDFSearch/wsgralert_NYSE_corporate_governance_report.htm

Corporate regulation in other countries

The 1992 UK Cadbury Report on corporate governance was first, but other countries at that time were also facing company collapses and inadequate corporate governance, and followed with their own versions of corporate governance codes. Subsequently, almost all economically significant countries published some form of corporate governance code of principles, recommendations, or good practice.

Appendix 1 summarizes the current state of corporate governance codes around the world. The texts of many of these reports are available on the internet, the majority with an English version. In some countries, ideas on corporate governance can be seen to be evolving. Also notice how the originators of the reports vary, being set up by governments, securities-regulating authorities, stock exchanges, or sometimes by an independent business federation, or the local institute of directors.

In this chapter, we will consider examples of codes from five countries, Australia, Canada, France, Japan, and South Africa, before reviewing worldwide corporate governance codes from the Organisation of Economic Co-operation and Development (OECD) and the Common-wealth, as well as codes from institutional investors and companies themselves. In Chapter 6, we will be contrasting the underlying corporate governance models used in different parts of the world, and in Chapter 12 we will be reviewing approaches to corporate governance in Japan (in more detail), Brazil, Russia, India, mainland China, Hong Kong, and other Southeast Asian countries, as well as the Middle East and North Africa, where Islamic requirements play a part.

Australia

Australia has been a pioneer in corporate governance developments. The first Australian report on corporate governance was written by Fred Hilmer in 1992. He called it *Strictly Boardroom*, after the film *Strictly Ballroom*, in which compliance with the rules (of competitive ballroom dancing) had stifled initiative and creativity. This, Hilmer argued, would happen to companies if corporate governance focused only on compliance. 'The Board's key role is to ensure that the board is continuously and effectively striving for above-average performance, taking account of risk,' he wrote, adding that 'this is not to deny the board's additional role with respect to shareholder protection.'

Following the Hilmer work, Henry Bosch wrote a study on shareholder rights in 1995, and a corporate governance report for the public sector was produced in 1997. Then, in March 2003, the Australian Securities Exchange (ASX) published 'Principles of Good Corporate Governance and Best Practice Recommendations',[15] which provided a non-prescriptive and principles-based framework for corporate governance for listed companies. As the ASX explained, '[w]here a listed company considers that a particular recommendation(s) is not appropriate for its circumstances, it has the flexibility under the "if not, why not?" approach not to adopt the recommendation, provided an explanation is given in their annual reports'. The Principles suggested that a company should take the following actions:

[15] See Corporate Governance in Action 5.1.

1. *Lay solid foundations for management and oversight*—recognize and publish the respective roles and responsibilities of board and management.

2. *Structure the board to add value*—have a board of an effective composition, size, and commitment to adequately discharge its responsibilities and duties.

3. Promote ethical and responsible decision-making.

4. Safeguard integrity in financial reporting.

5. Make timely and balanced disclosure of all material matters concerning the company.

6. Respect the rights of shareholders.

7. Recognize and manage risk.

8. Encourage enhanced board and management performance.

9. *Remunerate fairly and responsibly*—define its relationship to corporate and individual performance.

10. Recognize the legitimate interests of all legitimate stakeholders.

The ASX Council recognized the evolving nature of corporate governance thinking. Accordingly, it has committed to reviewing emerging corporate governance issues to ensure that the principles remain relevant and appropriate to the Australian business community. During 2010, three significant independent reviews were undertaken at the request of the Australian government, leading to further proposed changes to the Principles and Recommendations including: the need to promote board diversity with a gender diversity policy and measurable objectives; new policies on blackout periods during which directors with insider information are not allowed to deal in company shares they own; arranging for widely accessible shareholder briefings with electronic communications, including webcasting and internet and conference calls; and highlighting the potential for conflict of interest if executive directors serve on the remuneration committee.

The Australian Securities and Investments Commission updated its policies in 2014, reflecting legislative changes since 1999, including a policy requiring holders of more than 20 per cent of a listed company to indicate any takeover intentions.

Corporate Governance in Action 5.1   Australian Securities Exchange Principles

Definition of director independence

The 2003 ASX Principles usefully defined director independence in ways that are more detailed than the original notion of 'having no interests that could affect objective judgement'.

An independent director is a non-executive director (i.e. is not a member of management) and:

1. is not a substantial shareholder of the company or an officer of, or otherwise associated directly with, a substantial shareholder of the company;

2. within the last three years has not been employed in an executive capacity by the company or another group member, or been a director after ceasing to hold any such employment;

3. within the last three years has not been a principal of a material professional adviser or a material consultant to the company or another group member, or an employee materially associated with the service provided;

4. is not a material supplier or customer of the company or other group member, or an officer of or otherwise associated directly or indirectly with a material supplier or customer;

5. has no material contractual relationship with the company or another group member other than as a director of the company;

6. has not served on the board for a period which could, or could reasonably be perceived to, materially interfere with the director's ability to act in the best interests of the company;

7. is free from any interest and any business or other relationship which could, or could reasonably be perceived to, materially interfere with the director's ability to act in the best interests of the company.

Source: www.asx.com.au/documents/asx-compliance/principles-and-recommendations-march-2003.pdf

Canada

The Canadian Saucier Report took a performance-orientated view of the nature of corporate governance, arguing that:

The objective of good governance is to promote strong, viable, and competitive corporations.

A committed, cohesive and effective board adds value, first and foremost, by selecting the right CEO for the company. Beyond this, the board contributes to value by

- setting the broad parameters within which the management team operates, including in particular, strategic planning and risk management, and communication policy;
- coaching the CEO and the management team;
- monitoring and assessing performance, setting the CEO's compensation, taking remedial action where warranted, including replacing the CEO; and
- providing assurance to shareholders and stakeholders about the integrity of the corporation's reported financial performance.

France

Employers' organizations in France have published three discretionary corporate governance codes. The Viénot 1 Report (1995) called for the wider use of independent directors and board committees, a reduction in cross-directorships, and a limitation to the number of directorships a person could hold. The Viénot 2 Report (1999) called for the separation of the chairship from the CEO; emphasized the notion of director independence; and suggested more information on director remuneration. The Bouton Report (2002) was written following Enron and financial problems facing the French Vivendi company. The report called for more director independence, formal audit, remuneration, and nomination committees, board evaluation, and better financial information. The three codes are addressed to French-listed companies and are recognized by France's Financial Markets Authority as best practice. Although non-mandatory, listed companies are encouraged to declare whether they have complied with the codes on a 'comply or explain why not' basis.

In the opinion of Gérard Charreaux and Peter Wirtz:[16]

> ... during the last twenty years, the governance of French listed companies has undergone profound transformations, and its formal characteristics appear henceforth close to those of the Anglo-Saxon counterpart. However, even if foreign institutional investors have become its major actors, French capitalism still has a strong family character, and transactions on the market for corporate control are rarely hostile. One may add that minority shareholder activism is modest, even though their rights have been strengthened. The overall evolution of French corporate governance towards Anglo-Saxon standards encounters some resistance, especially due to the characteristics of the market for executives of the main companies, which favour certain elite circles.

Many CEOs of French-listed companies graduated from the same top schools (*grandes écoles*). However, the legal context of corporate governance in France is unlike that of the Anglo-Saxon countries. Being based on civil law, with the judiciary strictly administering statutes enacted by the legislature, there is no room for the evolution of practice through the application of successive cases, as in Anglo-Saxon common law jurisdictions. Consequently, the letter of the law is important in France. The basic company law (1966) was supplemented by new laws on economic regulation (2001), financial market security (2003), and laws to bring confidence and modernization to the economy (2005). Reflecting the French voluntary codes of best corporate governance practice and recognizing European directives, the new laws regulate the financial system including companies, and call for strengthening the power of the board, with more transparency on director remuneration, the separation of chair and CEO, and better protection for minority shareholders.

The legal basis of French corporate governance is composed of three basic laws: the law on new economic regulations (2001—*loi sur les nouvelles régulations économiques*); the law on financial security (2003—*loi de sécurité financière*); and the law on trust and modernization of the economy (2005—*loi pour la confiance et la modernisation de l'économie*).

Japan

The Japanese employers' federation, the *keidanren*, resisted efforts by the Japanese government to introduce Western-style corporate governance procedures. For many years, it was felt that these failed to recognize traditional Japanese ways of running business organizations. However, in March 2015, the Japanese Corporate Governance Code was introduced. We will study the Japanese approach to corporate governance in Chapter 12 'Corporate Governance around the World'.

In launching the Code, the Tokyo Stock Exchange explained that in:

> Japan's Corporate Governance Code, 'corporate governance' means a structure for transparent, fair, timely, and decisive decision-making by companies, with due attention to the needs and perspectives of shareholders and also customers, employees, and local communities.

---

[16] Charreaux, Gérard and Peter Wirtz (2006) *Gouvernance des Entreprises: Nouvelles Perspectives*. Recherche d'enterprise series, Economica Press, Paris.

This Corporate Governance Code establishes fundamental principles for effective corporate governance at listed companies in Japan. It is expected that the Code's appropriate implementation will contribute to the development and success of companies, investors and the Japanese economy as a whole through individual companies' self-motivated actions so as to achieve sustainable growth and increase corporate value over the mid- to long-term.[17]

The Code has five principal components:

1. Securing the rights and equal treatment of shareholders.
2. Appropriate cooperation with stakeholders other than shareholders.
3. Ensuring appropriate information disclosure and transparency.
4. Responsibilities of the board.
5. Dialogue with shareholders.

The reforms to corporate governance thinking in Japan produced results. By 2018, the inclusion of outside, non-executive directors on the boards of public companies, pressures on traditional board-level attitudes, and the promotion of younger executives with wider international experience led to improved performance in some companies. But some shareholder meetings became more contentious and international institutional investors were also more active.

South Africa

Like Australia, South Africa has also been a pioneer in corporate governance. The first report on corporate governance in South Africa was published in 1994. Sponsored by the Institute of Directors in South Africa and written by a committee chaired by Senior Counsel Mervyn King, the report became known as King I, to be followed by three further reports.

King I (1994) took a more integrated approach to corporate governance, looking at social, ethical, and environmental implications, as well as regulatory and financial ones. This was the first report to adopt this participative and inclusive stakeholder approach to corporate governance, recognizing that, in the modern world, companies are part of the society and environment in which they exist, but emphasizing that the company is, nevertheless, accountable to its shareholders. In the words of the report:

Boards have to consider not only the regulatory aspect, but also industry and market standards, industry reputation, the investigative media, and the attitudes of customers, suppliers, consumers, employees, investors, and communities (local, national, and international), ethical pressure groups, public confidence, political opinion. In governance terms, (directors are) *accountable* at common law and by statute to the company, but *responsible* to the stakeholders identified as relevant to the business of the company. The stakeholder concept of being accountable to all legitimate stakeholders must be rejected for the simple reason that to ask boards to be accountable to everyone would result in their being accountable to no one. The modern approach is for a board to identify the company's stakeholders, including

---

[17] Tokyo Stock Exchange (2015), Japan's Corporate Governance Code, June. Available at: www.ijapicap.com/blog/wp-content/uploads/2015/05/TSE-Corporate-Governance-Code.pdf

its shareowners, and to agree policies as to how the relationship with those stakeholders should be advanced and managed in the interests of the company.

King II (2002), the second King report, extended the view that companies need to take an inclusive view of their relationships, not only with shareholders, but also other groups in society affected by their activities. The need was to move, the report said, from the single bottom line, emphasizing economic success, to the triple bottom line, recognizing the economic, environmental, and social aspects of a company's activities simultaneously. The King reports developed seven characteristics of good governance (see Corporate Governance in Action 5.2) and introduced the concept of corporate citizenship.

King III (2008)[18] provided a code for responsible investing by institutional investors in South Africa, guidelines for corporate governance in the public sector, and useful governance guidelines and pro forma reports for companies.

King IV (2016) took the basic corporate governance concepts for listed companies and adapted them for private companies and not-for-profit entities.

Corporate Governance in Action 5.2   King's seven characteristics of good corporate governance

1. Discipline

Corporate discipline is a commitment by a company's senior management to adhere to behaviour that is universally recognized and accepted to be correct and proper.

2. Transparency

Transparency is the ease with which an outsider is able to make meaningful analysis of a company's actions, its economic fundamentals, and the non-financial aspects pertinent to that business.

3. Independence

Independence is the extent to which mechanisms have been put in place to minimize or avoid potential conflicts of interest that may exist, such as dominance by a strong CEO or large shareowner.

4. Accountability

Individuals or groups in a company, who make decisions and take actions on specific issues, need to be accountable for their decisions and actions. Mechanisms must exist and be effective to allow for accountability.

5. Responsibility

With regard to management, responsibility pertains to behaviour that allows for corrective action and for penalizing mismanagement.

[18] See www.iodsa.co.za/books.asp?CatID=277

6.   Fairness

The systems that exist within the company must be balanced in taking into account all those that have an interest in the company and its future. The rights of various groups have to be acknowledged and respected. For example, minority shareowner interests must receive equal consideration to those of the dominant shareowner(s).

7.   Social responsibility

A well-managed company will be aware of, and respond to, social issues, placing a high priority on ethical standards. A good corporate citizen is increasingly seen as one that is non-discriminatory, non-exploitative, and responsible with regard to environmental and human rights issues.

Source: Institute of Directors in Southern Africa (2002) Executive summary of the King Report 2002. Available at: www.ecgi.org/codes/documents/executive_summary.pdf

Codes from international agencies

In addition to the codes developed by specific countries, some international agencies have published principles and guidelines for the guidance of countries. In particular, the Principles from the Organisation for Economic Co-operation and Development (OECD), the Guidelines from the Commonwealth of Nations, and the Statements on Global Corporate Governance Principles from the International Corporate Governance Network (ICGN) have been influential.

1.   *The G20/OECD*[19] *Principles of Corporate Governance* provided the basis for the development of good corporate governance in several countries. Against the backdrop of major corporate scandals around the world, updated principles were launched at the meeting of G20 finance ministers and central bank governors in September 2015, and subsequently endorsed at the G20 leaders summit in November 2015.

   The original OECD principles applied to companies with a large and diverse shareholder base. But most companies around the world are dominated by controlling shareholders—individuals, financial institutions, or other companies. Subsequently, the Principles were revised to apply to such situations and have become the most widely used benchmark for corporate governance around the world, assisting governments in their efforts to evaluate and improve the legal, international, and regulatory framework for corporate governance in their own countries, and providing guidance to stock exchanges, investors, and corporations.

[19] The original member countries of the OECD were Austria, Belgium, Canada, Denmark, France, Germany, Greece, Iceland, Ireland, Italy, Luxembourg, the Netherlands, Norway, Portugal, Spain, Sweden, Switzerland, Turkey, the United Kingdom, and the United States. The following countries became members subsequently, in the years shown: Japan (1964), Finland (1969), Australia (1971), New Zealand (1973), Mexico (1994), the Czech Republic (1995), Hungary (1996), Poland (1996), Korea (1996), and the Slovak Republic (2000). The Commission of the European Communities also takes part in the work of the OECD.

The six OECD Principles cover:

I.   *Ensuring the basis for an effective corporate governance framework*—the corporate governance framework should promote transparent and efficient markets, be consistent with the rule of law, and clearly articulate the division of responsibilities among different supervisory, regulatory, and enforcement authorities.

II.   *The rights of shareholders and key ownership functions*—the corporate governance framework should protect and facilitate the exercise of shareholders' rights.

III.   *The equitable treatment of shareholders*—the corporate governance framework should ensure the equitable treatment of shareholders, including minority and foreign shareholders. All shareholders should have the opportunity to obtain redress for violation of their rights.

IV.   *The role of stakeholders in corporate governance*—the corporate governance framework should recognize the rights of stakeholders established by law or through mutual agreements and encourage active cooperation between the corporations and stakeholders in creating wealth, jobs, and sustainability of financially sound enterprises.

V.   *Disclosure and transparency*—the corporate governance framework should ensure that timely and accurate disclosure is made on all material matters regarding the corporation, including the financial situation, performance, ownership, and governance of the company.

VI.   *The responsibilities of the board*—the corporate governance framework should ensure the strategic guidance of the company, the effective monitoring of management by the board, and the board's accountability to the company and the shareholders.[20]

2.   The *World Bank* and *the International Monetary Fund (IMF),* with the support of the United Nations, are charged with assessing the application of the OECD Principles of Corporate Governance in specific countries and have a programme that *Reports on the Observance of Standards and Codes* (ROSC). The goal of the ROSC initiative is to identify weaknesses that may contribute to a country's economic and financial vulnerability. Each ROSC corporate governance assessment of a country reviews that country's legal and regulatory framework, as well as the practices and compliance of its listed firms, and assesses the framework relative to internationally accepted benchmarks. The OECD produced Guidelines on the Corporate Governance of State-Owned Enterprises in 2005.

Following the global financial crisis of 2007 onwards, the OECD concluded that:

Corporate governance weaknesses in remuneration, risk management, board practices, and the exercise of shareholder rights had played an important role in the development of the financial crisis and that such weaknesses extended to companies more generally. Nevertheless, the Group found that the OECD Principles of Corporate Governance

---

[20] www.oecd-ilibrary.org/governance/g20-oecd-principles-of-corporate-governance-2015_9789264236882-en

provided a good basis on which adequately to address the key concerns that have been raised and that there was no urgent need for them to be revised. A more urgent challenge for the Steering Group was to encourage and support the implementation of already agreed international and national standards, including the OECD Principles of Corporate Governance.[21]

The OECD report recognized that executive remuneration was an important public policy issue and concluded that it is important for boards first to set the strategic goals of the company and its associated risk appetite, establishing and overseeing enterprise-wide risk management systems. They would then be in a position to establish a compensation structure that reflects its strategy and risk profile. The report also argued that tests of the technical and professional competence of board members, including general governance and risk management skills, could be subject to a 'fit and proper person test' by a supervisor.

3. *The Commonwealth Association for Corporate Governance* (CACG) Guidelines—Principles for Corporate Governance in the Commonwealth (1999)[22]—are aimed at the level of individual companies. The executive summary of 15 Principles of Corporate Governance in the Commonwealth Code suggests that a board should:

Principle 1—exercise leadership, enterprise, integrity, and judgement in directing the corporation so as to achieve continuing prosperity for the corporation and to act in the best interests of the business enterprise in a manner based on transparency, accountability, and responsibility;

Principle 2—ensure that through a managed and effective process, board appointments are made that provide a mix of proficient directors, each of whom is able to add value and to bring independent judgement to bear on the decision-making process;

Principle 3—determine the corporation's purpose and values, determine the strategy to achieve its purpose and to implement its values in order to ensure that it survives and thrives, and ensure that procedures and practices are in place that protect the corporation's assets and reputation;

Principle 4—monitor and evaluate the implementation of strategies, policies, management performance criteria, and business plans;

Principle 5—ensure that the corporation complies with all relevant laws, regulations, and codes of best business practice;

Principle 6—ensure that the corporation communicates with shareholders and other stakeholders effectively;

Principle 7—serve the legitimate interest of the shareholders of the corporation and account to them fully;

[21] OECD Guidelines on Corporate Governance of State-Owned Enterprises, 2005. Available at: www.oecd.org/daf/ca/oecd-guidelines-corporate-governance-soes-2005.htm
[22] The Commonwealth, sometimes referred to as the Commonwealth of Nations and formerly as the British Commonwealth, is a network of 54 independent countries, most of which were formerly members of the British Empire.

Principle 8—identify the corporation's internal and external stakeholders and agree a policy, or policies, determining how the corporation should relate to them;

Principle 9—ensure that no person or block of persons has unfettered power and that there is an appropriate balance of power and authority on the board which is, *inter alia*, usually reflected by separating the roles of the CEO and chair, and by having a balance between executive and non-executive directors;

Principle 10—regularly review processes and procedures to ensure the effectiveness of its internal systems of control, so that its decision-making capability and the accuracy of its reporting and financial results are maintained at a high level at all times;

Principle 11—regularly assess its performance and effectiveness as a whole, and that of the individual directors, including the CEO;

Principle 12—appoint the CEO and at least participate in the appointment of senior management, ensure the motivation and protection of intellectual capital intrinsic to the corporation, ensure that there is adequate training in the corporation for management and employees, and a succession plan for senior management;

Principle 13—ensure that all technology and systems used in the corporation are adequate to properly run the business and for it to remain a meaningful competitor;

Principle 14—identify key risk areas and key performance indicators of the business enterprise and monitor these factors;

Principle 15—ensure annually that the corporation will continue as a going concern for its next fiscal year.[23]

4. *The International Corporate Governance Network* is an investor-led organization that represents investors, companies, financial intermediaries, and academics from over 47 countries. Its aim is to encourage international dialogue on global corporate governance. The ICGN emphasizes shareholder responsibilities for good governance and publishes global governance standards and stewardship principles.

For more information go to: www.icgn.org

The ICGN corporate governance principles cover:[24]

1. The board's role and responsibilities.

2. Board leadership and independence.

3. Board composition and director appointment.

4. Corporate culture.

5. Boards' oversight of risk.

6. Director remuneration.

7. Reporting and audit.

8. Shareholder rights.

[23] www.ecseonline.com/PDF/CACG%20Guidelines%20-%20Principles%20for%20Corporate%20Governance%20in%20the%20Commonwealth.pdf

[24] http://icgn.flpbks.com/icgn-global-governance-principles-2017/#p=8

Codes from institutional investors

Some major institutional investors and organizations representing them have also produced corporate governance guidance or codes. The California Public Employees' Retirement System (CalPERS), the largest US public pension fund with assets over US$200 billion and members numbering 1.6 million, was a pioneer. CalPERS published Global Corporate Governance Principles in 1997, and also wrote guidance notes on improvements that it felt were needed in corporate governance in France, Germany, and Japan. In 2010, CalPERS published an important corporate governance code, 'The Global Principles of Accountable Corporate Governance',[25] which forms the basis for its involvement with companies and on which it bases its proxy voting decisions.

Hermes Fund Managers, a UK multispecialist asset manager, produced a set of corporate governance principles,[26] originally in 2002, updated in 2008. Hermes is owned by the BT (British Telecom) Pension Scheme, the UK's largest funded occupational pension scheme, and manages more than £20 billion on behalf of long-term investors, including pension funds, endowments, and charities.

Teachers Insurance and Annuity Association-College Retirement Equities Fund (TIAA-CREF) was one of the first institutional investors to produce a policy on corporate governance for companies in which it invested. TIAA-CREF took a leadership role in opposing abusive anti-takeover provisions during the 1970s and 1980s, when the governance movement focused primarily on the protection of shareholder interests in the context of takeovers and contests for control. During the 1990s, the focus moved towards director independence, board diversity, board committee structure, shareholder rights, accounting for options, and executive compensation. Most recently, TIAA-CREF has led the movement to establish majority voting in director elections.[27]

A limitation to codes produced by institutional investment funds are that they are necessarily investor-orientated, providing corporate governance decision-makers with valuable indications on shareholder expectations, but not necessarily providing them with the guidance they need to improve board-level effectiveness and to produce better long-term corporate performance. A further limitation is that institutional investor codes to date have been Anglo-Saxon, whereas corporate governance is increasingly culturally dependent. Some companies have complained that the proliferation of corporate governance codes and strategic advice from institutional investors has become counterproductive.

Company codes

We have considered corporate governance codes published at the national level, at the international level by international organizations, and from institutional investors. In 2002, the New York Stock Exchange required all listed companies to adopt corporate governance

---

[25] www.calpers-governance.org/docs-sof/principles/2010-5-2-global-principles-of-accountable-corp-gov.pdf
[26] www.acga-asia.org/public/files/(2008)%20Hermes_Principles.pdf
[27] www.tiaa-cref.org/ucm/groups/content/@ap_ucm_p_tcp/documents/document/tiaa01010204.pdf

guidelines and to post them on their websites, so there are now thousands of examples in the public domain.

Among the first of these companies was General Motors in 1994, following a disastrous performance and board restructuring. Today, the company continues this tradition. On its website,[28] General Motors provides investors with details of its corporate governance policies, provides access to various corporate governance documents, and publishes its corporate governance guidelines.

Codes for the non-profit and voluntary sectors

It is now widely recognized that all corporate entities need to be governed, as well as managed. This applies as much to not-for-profit as to profit-orientated entities. Charities, trusts, health authorities, educational institutions, mutual societies, sports associations, cultural organizations, public authorities, non-government organizations, and other entities in the public and voluntary sectors all need sound governance. Moreover, many of the governance concepts developed in the commercial, profit-orientated world are equally applicable to the public and voluntary sectors.

Three differences are often found between the not-for-profit and the profit-orientated sectors—their objectives and their governance structures. First, their governing bodies have a variety of names—council, committee, board of governors, for example, and occasionally the board of directors. Second, organizations in the not-for-profit sector usually have many constituencies to satisfy and, consequently, many objectives and multiple measures of performance, rather than a single bottom line. In a hospital, for example, the governing body needs to satisfy the needs and expectations of patients and their families, the medical staff, administrators, the local community, government, and the health authorities. Third, in many not-for-profit organizations, the governing body is entirely non-executive. In small voluntary organizations, the members of the governing body may also provide the management and run the operations. But in larger voluntary organizations, the governing body is often made up of non-paid volunteer members who oversee the work of the paid employees. Frequently, the CEO attends meetings of the governing body, but is not a voting member.

The governance of voluntary and community organizations in the UK is addressed in the report 'Good Governance: A Code for the Voluntary and Community Sector'.[29] It was launched in 2005, and updated in 2010. Often referred to as 'The Good Governance Code', it is based on the belief that effective boards in the sector provide good governance and leadership by:

- understanding their role;
- ensuring delivery of organizational purpose;
- working effectively both as individuals and as a team;
- exercising effective control;

---

[28] www.gm.com/content/dam/gm/en_us/english/Group4/InvestorsPDFDocuments/Corporate_Governance_Guidelines.pdf

[29] www.goodgovernancecode.org.uk

- behaving with integrity;
- being open and accountable.

The Code recognizes that such principles do not feature separately, but are an integral part of good practice throughout any community or voluntary sector organization.

Local governance

In 2007, the UK's Chartered Institute of Public Finance and Accounting (CIPFA) published a framework[30]—'Delivering Good Governance in Local Government'—updating its 1995 framework of principles and standards of corporate governance for the public services. This framework is intended to be a guide to best practice for public sector authorities in developing their own codes of governance, and for discharging accountability through the publication of an annual governance statement. CIPFA sought to capture the spirit of good governance in such a way that it would enable any public service body to operate in a more open, effective, and publicly acceptable way. Where codes already existed, it was envisaged that the framework would be used as a benchmark against which such codes could be compared and developed further. Where such codes did not exist, it was intended that the framework should encourage their development.

Public services

The UK Independent Commission for Good Governance in Public Services, chaired by Sir Alan Langlands, published a Good Governance Standard for Public Services in 2005.
The Standard had six primary components. 'Good governance', it said, means:

1. Focusing on the organization's purpose and outcomes for citizens.
2. Performing effectively in clearly defined functions and roles.
3. Promoting values for the whole organization and demonstrating the values of good governance through behaviour.
4. Taking informed, transparent decisions and managing risk.
5. Developing the capacity and capability of the governing body to be effective.
6. Engaging stakeholders and making accountability real.

The voluntary and community sector

In 2005, the UK Institute of Chartered Secretaries and Administrators (ICSA) published a code of governance for the voluntary and community sector, which it updated in October 2010. The latest edition recognizes that governance is high on the agenda in all sectors—public, private, and voluntary. As voluntary and community organizations are driven by altruistic values and working for public benefit, they are increasingly expected to demonstrate how well they are governed. Good governance is a vital part of how voluntary and community organizations operate and are held accountable.

[30] http://secure.cipfa.org.uk/cgi-bin/CIPFA.storefront/EN/product/BU012

The report develops six basic principles based on the belief that:

An effective board will provide good governance and leadership by:

1. understanding their role
2. ensuring delivery of organizational purpose
3. working effectively both as individuals and a team
4. exercising effective control
5. behaving with integrity
6. being open and accountable.

In the report, the term 'board' means an organization's governing body, whatever it may be called.[31]

The importance of compliance: corporate governance reports

In the early days, compliance with corporate governance codes was voluntary. Exhortation to follow the spirit of the codes came from financial institutions, the media, directors' professional bodies, and academic commentators. Some institutional investors applied specific pressure. But it was in the boardrooms that decisions were taken on the extent that the relevant code was followed. Then, in many countries, the relevant code was incorporated into the stock exchange listing rules. Conformity with the code became a condition of listing in many countries.

In most countries, compliance remained voluntary, with the company required to explain why, if it chose not to follow the code. In other words, companies conformed to the code either by following its requirements or by explaining why they had not. In a growing number of jurisdictions, companies were now required to make a corporate governance report to their members, confirming that they had complied with the corporate governance requirements.

A few companies produce their corporate governance reports as a chore necessary to maintain their stock market listing, and consequently provide the minimum information necessary to confirm compliance with the code. But increasingly companies are seizing the opportunity to build a reputation for professional and good corporate governance standards with their shareholders and the market, providing far more information than is necessary merely to confirm compliance. Companies have seen that the corporate governance report provides an opportunity to elaborate on the way in which the board and its committees work, how the board approaches the business strategy and handles strategic risk. Some companies also promote the company's ethical standards, and its concern for corporate social responsibility and environmental sustainability to all of the stakeholders, including the shareholders.

The responsibility in listed companies for ensuring compliance with these new listing requirements and laws often fell to the company secretary, but in some companies a new management function appeared—the compliance officer. Moreover, given the importance that was now being placed on the new rules, many boards entrusted the new responsibility to their audit committee. Others created a new board compliance or corporate governance committee.

---

[31] See ICSA, 'Good Governance: A Code for the Voluntary and Community Sector', available online at www.icsa.org.uk/assets/files/pdfs/guidance/NFP.Charities/Code%20of%20governance%20full%20version.pdf

Principles or prescription: the governance debate

Many commentators refer to the 'Anglo-American' approach to corporate governance. They contrast the unitary board, which has both executive and non-executive directors in the Anglo-American common law jurisdictions, with the two-tier, supervisory and executive boards of the continental European and other civil law countries.

But in recent years a schism has emerged within the Anglo-American approach. In the United States, corporate governance has increasingly become enforced by regulation and the rule of law. The US Sarbanes-Oxley Act, which was a response to the collapses of Enron and WorldCom, reinforced federal and state demands for corporate governance conformance by law: obey the law or risk prosecution, subject to significant penalties, including imprisonment. China also has adopted legally enforceable corporate governance, as we will see later.

However, in many other countries, self-regulation and voluntary compliance with corporate governance codes is preferred: comply or explain. In the United Kingdom and many other jurisdictions, particularly Commonwealth countries the company law of which has been influenced over the years by UK common law, including Australia, Canada, New Zealand, South Africa, India, Singapore, and Hong Kong, compliance is discretionary. The clear preference in business communities around the world, other than in the United States, is still for voluntary compliance and the avoidance of legislation, as the UK Hampel Report had indicated.

However, recent revisions of companies law in some jurisdictions, including Australia (2006), and the UK (2006), have clarified directors' duties and thus sharpened legal expectations of corporate governance practices. The 'rule *versus* principle' dilemma has been amplified by the global financial crisis, which has increased calls for more legally enforceable corporate governance, US-style. The intentions of the EU are not clear, but voices have been heard calling for less discretion and more legislation.

This fundamental dichotomy—between the rules-based approach and the principles-based approach—goes to the heart of corporate governance philosophy. Some years ago, there was a widespread belief that corporate governance around the world would gradually converge on the American model, not least because the world needed access to American capital. That is no longer the case. The 'principles *versus* prescription' paradox remains unresolved.

Case studies

 Case study 5.1   Alphabet—Google's approach to corporate governance

Alphabet Inc. is the holding company for Google enterprises, embracing the ubiquitous search engine, which generates advertising revenue around the world, companies in the life sciences, property, technology, and venture capital industries, and research ventures such as driverless cars and delivery drones.

The corporate governance of Alphabet

Alphabet provides a lot of information about its governance. The investor relation site at https://abc.xyz/investor/ includes links to material on:

~ the board of directors;

~ the certificate of incorporation;

~ corporate governance guidelines;

~ the company's code of conduct;

~ sustainability and related information;

~ company bylaws;

~ stockholder meetings;

~ SEC filings;

~ financial information.

The investor relations page also has links to financial information, weekly investor updates, and letters from the founder, Larry Page.

Board of directors

The board has 12 directors:

Larry Page

Sergey Brin

Eric E. Schmidt

L. John Doerr

Roger W. Ferguson, Jr

Diane B. Greene

John L. Hennessy

Ann Mather

Alan R. Mulally

Paul S. Otellini

K. Ram Shriram

Shirley M. Tilghman

Board committees

The board has four standing committees:

Audit Committee

Leadership Development and Compensation Committee

Nominating and Corporate Governance Committee

Board of Directors' Executive Committee

The membership of each committee and considerable detail on their role is given at: https://abc.xyz/investor/other/board.html

Corporate governance guidelines

The guidelines, accessible from https://abc.xyz/investor/, are extensive.

Discussion questions

1. Use the web to identify the executive directors, connected outside directors, and independent outside directors. Do you consider this to be a balanced board?

2. Explore the charter of each committee. Can you identify any board-level responsibility that is not adequately covered?

3. How might the corporate governance guidelines be improved?

4. Should every board have a set of corporate governance guidelines?

 Case study 5.2   The collapse of Northern Rock bank: a classic corporate governance case

A run on a British bank is very rare, but in September 2007 it happened to Northern Rock, the UK's fifth-biggest mortgage lender. Northern Rock had around 1.5 million depositors with savings of £28 billion, and some 800,000 homeowner borrowers. The company, formerly a British building society (savings and loan association), was incorporated as a public company in 1997 and floated on the London Stock Exchange. By 2000, it had grown dramatically to join the FTSE 100 index.

The auditors of the 2006 accounts, the 'Big Four' firm PriceWaterhouseCoopers, expressed no concerns about the financial state of affairs; the company was profitable and had access to funds. Yet a select committee of the House of Lords was subsequently to 'find this complacency disturbing', recognizing that Northern Rock's business model was 'dangerously risky'.

In July 2007, Adam J. Applegarth, the CEO, wrote:[32]

Operationally Northern Rock had a good first half in 2007. Mortgage lending has been particularly strong with a gross market share of 9.7% and a net market share of 18.9%, helped by improvements in retention of home moving customers, keeping customers coming to the end of their product deals, and a strong mortgage market. Credit quality remains robust.

The outlook for the full year is being impacted by sharp increases in money market and swap rates seen in the first half. This has resulted in a negative impact on net interest income as mortgage pricing in the market generally has lagged behind increases in funding costs in the year to date. Action has been taken with changes in our swap transaction policies to minimise exposures in the future to significant changes in interest rates. The medium term outlook for the Company is very positive.

A warning might have been seen in the second paragraph. Northern Rock was hit by the financial world's reluctance to lend short-term, as other institutions hoarded cash to cope with the fallout from

---

[32] Annual report of the Northern Rock Building Society for 2006. The bank de-registered as a UK building society in 2007and was incorporated as a limited-liability company operating as a bank.

defaulting sub-prime mortgage loans in the United States. By mid-September, Northern Rock could not raise enough money to meet its financial obligations.

On Friday 14 September 2007 the Bank of England, acting as 'lender of last resort', provided an emergency facility to prop up Northern Rock. The company urged its savers not to panic, insisting that it was solvent. But its savers did panic. Beleaguered savers, many elderly, queued for hours to withdraw all of their savings. The Northern Rock internet access crashed as online customers tried to log on to access their funds.

The panic had some justification. The compensation scheme run by the Financial Services Authority, the UK financial market watchdog (now the FCA), guaranteed repayments on only £2,000 in full and 90 per cent on the next £33,000. After that, depositors had no recourse to insurance funds. No wonder people queued and withdrew some £3 billion on that day. The British Secretary to the Treasury said that it was not the duty of government to save institutions from the consequences of making risky investments. Northern Rock shares fell by 40 per cent.

On the next day, the queues lengthened. The government feared that financial panic could spread to other banks. So, on Monday 17 September, it took an unprecedented step and gave a cast-iron guarantee to all Northern Rock savers that their savings, £22 billion of personal deposits and £6 billion of business deposits in total, would be underwritten by the government and met in full.

The classical model of mortgage lending is to borrow short from personal savers, who can call on their funds with little or no notice, and lend long to homeowners against mortgages on their properties. The strategy is based on the assumption that the savers trust the bank.

However, the business model of Northern Rock leveraged this classical model by relying on savers' funds for only part of its mortgage financing. It borrowed additional funds from the money market. Some of its loans were securitized and traded on the swap market. This worked well when interest rates were low and funds readily available. As a result, Northern Rock's business grew and its market share far surpassed its competitors with more traditional and cautious strategies. Then came the funds famine and Northern Rock's crisis.

Northern Rock Asset Management (NRAM), formerly Northern Rock PLC, was taken into public ownership on 22 February 2008. The bank came under government control. A new chief executive was appointed. Shareholders were to be recompensed at a level set by an independent panel. The British Chancellor of the Exchequer insisted that the public ownership was temporary, before 'ultimately trying to return it to the private sector'.

Following the completion of a legal and capital restructuring on 1 January 2010, the company no longer operated as a deposit-taking institution (under the FSA's categorization). It was instead regulated by the FSA as a mortgage administration company and the directors believed it had appropriate and adequate levels of capital to support these activities. Further, HM Treasury confirmed its intention then to continue to fund the company so as to maintain it as a going concern and enable it to meet its debts as they fell due, for a period up to at least 1 November 2014. The Treasury also committed to convert up to £1.6 billion of the government loan to meet regulatory capital requirements, if so required.

On 1 October 2010, UK Asset Resolution Limited (UKAR) was established as the holding company for NRAM and Bradford & Bingley PLC (another former building society taken over by the government), bringing together the two brands under shared management and a common board of directors. The overall aim of UKAR was to maximize value for the taxpayer. This would be achieved by focusing on key activities and themes based on the following objectives:

- reduce, protect, and optimize the balance sheet;
- maximize cost-effectiveness via continuous improvement;
- be excellent in customer and debt management.[33]

[33] Further details of the role, structure, and corporate governance of UKAR along with detail of the sale of assets can be found at: www.ukar.co.uk/

Its stated mission was to 'maximise value for the taxpayer while treating customers and stakeholders fairly'.

In late 2011, the sound assets were acquired by Virgin Finance, leaving the toxic debt under government ownership.

In the annual report and accounts for 2012 the new directors explained that 'Northern Rock Asset Management plc and its subsidiary undertakings primarily operate as a servicer of mortgage loans secured on residential properties and of associated services. No new lending is carried out.'

Corporate governance at Northern Rock

The original board of Northern Rock had 12 members: the chair, the CEO, four executive directors, and six non-executive directors. The board had four committees—audit, nominations, remuneration, and risk. The CEO was Adam Applegarth, who had joined the company in 1980 as a graduate trainee. The company had a reputation for making internal appointments.

The chair was Dr the Honourable Matthew White Ridley, the son of a Cabinet Minister under an earlier Conservative government. He was educated at Eton College and Oxford, with a doctorate in zoology. He was not a financier. He joined the board as an INED in 1994 and became chair in 2004. He also chaired the nominations committee. His Northern Rock fee was £300,000 per annum.

The other INEDs were:

Adam Fenwick, 46, the group managing director of Fenwick Ltd and an INED of John Swire and Sons Ltd—Northern Rock annual fee £54,000;

Sir Ian Gibson, 60, the senior INED, who had industrial experience in running Ford Motors and Nissan, and was currently chair of the publishers of the *Daily Mirror* and an INED of GKN PLC and Greggs PLC, and had previously been a member of the Court of the Bank of England—Northern Rock annual fee £80,000;

Nichola Pease, 46, chief executive of JO Hambros Capital Management, previously with Barings, a bank famous for its collapse after a Singapore trader had been allowed to run excessive risks—Northern Rock annual fee £65,000;

Michael Queen, 45, a director of 3i Group PLC—Northern Rock annual fee £54,000;

Rosemary Radcliffe, 62, a leading chartered accountant and a complaints commissioner for the FSA—Northern Rock annual fee £56,000;

Sir Derek Wanless, 59, former CEO of NatWest Bank, who steered it through an acquisition strategy that proved disastrous and left in 1999 with a £3 million pay-off, but was well respected in the City of London and a member of the actuarial committee of the FRC; he carried out a long-term review of the British National Health Service for the government in 2007—Northern Rock annual fee £86,000. He was chair of Northern Rock's audit committee and risk committee.

Discussion questions

1. What role did the original board play in this saga?

2. Did the directors understand the underlying business model and how it differed from the classical banking approach to lending? Did they appreciate their company's exposure if the financial markets changed? Did they know the extent of their business risk?

Self-test questions

1. What were the key recommendations of the first ever code of corporate governance—the Cadbury Code (1992)?

2. What are the requirements of the UK Corporate Governance Code (2018) on professional development and performance evaluation?

3. What is the role of the OECD Principles of Corporate Governance?

4. What do the Hermes Principles have to say about a company's relationships with stakeholders?

5. What does section 404 of the US Sarbanes-Oxley Act require?

6. What do the Hermes Principles have to say about a company's strategy formulation?

7. How does the SOX Act define an INED?

8. What is the minimum number of members of an audit committee under SOX? What qualifications should they have?

9. Is it necessary for companies covered by the SOX Act to adopt and disclose a code of business conduct and ethics for directors, officers, and employees?

10. What are the responsibilities of the board according to the OECD Principles?

 For suggested answers to these self-test questions visit the online resources at: www.oup.com/uk/tricker4e/

Projects and exercises

1. Use the internet to explore some of the corporate governance codes around the world in Appendix 1. Compare and contrast the codes in countries that you find interesting.

2. Prepare an essay/report/presentation on the 'principles or prescription' corporate governance debate. Do you believe that corporate governance codes will converge on one or the other underlying paradigm?

3. Search for the corporate governance reports of some companies with which you are familiar. How do they compare? Do they go beyond the strict requirements of company law and the corporate governance code?

References and further reading

Charreaux, Gérard and Peter Wirtz (2006) *Gouvernance des Entreprises: Nouvelles Perspectives*. Recherche d'enterprise series, Economica Press, Paris.

Chartered Institute of Public Finance and Accountancy (CIPFA) in the United Kingdom (1995) Corporate Governance: A Framework for Public Service Bodies. London.

Cornforth, C. J. (2001) 'What Makes Boards Effective? An Examination of the Relationships between Board Inputs, Structures, Processes and Effectiveness in Non-profit Organizations', *Corporate Governance: An International Review*, 9, 3, pp 217–27.

Cornforth, C. J. and Edwards, C. (1999) 'Board Roles in the Strategic Management of Public Service of Non-profit Organizations: Theory and Practice', *Corporate Governance*, 7, 4, pp 346–62.

FRC (2018) The governance of the UK's Financial Reporting Council: the FRC's own governance www.

frc.org.uk/directors/corporate-governance-and-stewardship/uk-corporate-governance-code

Global Legal Group (2013a) A Practical Cross-border Insight into Corporate Governance, Global Legal Group, London.

Global Legal Group (2013b) The International Comparative Guide to Corporate Governance, Global Legal Group, London

Gordon, Jeffrey N. and Mark J. Roe (2004) *Convergence and Persistence in Corporate Governance*. Cambridge University Press, New York.

Jones, Ian and Michael Pollitt (2004) 'Understanding how Issues in Corporate Governance Develop: Cadbury Report to Higgs Review', *Corporate Governance: An International Review*, 12, 2.

Lee, Thomas A. (2004) *Financial Reporting and Corporate Governance*. John Wiley, Chichester.

Useful websites

www.ecgi.org/organisation/overview.htm

ECGI is an international organization which links academics, legislators, and practitioners, focusing on major corporate governance issues and promoting best practice. It undertakes, commissions, and disseminates research into corporate governance.

www.ecgi.org/codes/all_codes.php

Index of corporate governance codes around the world with access to texts.

www.icgn.org/best-practice

The International Corporate Governance Network.

www.cii.org

Council of Institutional Investors.

http://nysemanual.nyse.com/lcm/help/lcm-rules-map.html

New York Stock Exchange manual.

www.ecgi.org/codes/documents/executive_summary.pdf

South Africa King Reports.

www.soxlaw.com/introduction.htm

The Sarbanes-Oxley Act of 2002 outlined with key sections including section 404.

http://news.findlaw.com/hdocs/docs/gwbush/sarbanesoxley072302.pdf

The Sarbanes-Oxley Act in full.

www.frc.org.uk

UK Financial Reporting Council—for latest on UK codes.

www.fca.org.uk/

UK Financial Conduct Authority.

www.handbook.fca.org.uk/

Financial Conduct Authority handbook.

www.calpers.ca.gov

CalPERS (proactive US pension fund) corporate governance forum.

www.ecgi.org/codes/documents/hermes_principles.pdf

Hermes (proactive UK institutional investor) corporate governance principles.

www.gm.com/corporate/investor_information

General Motors corporate governance guidelines and SEC filings.

www.bus.ualberta.ca/ccgi (go to 'centres')

Canadian Corporate Governance Institute.

www.ccg.uts.edu.au

Centre for Corporate Governance, UTS, Sydney, Australia.

www.oecd.org

The Organisation for Economic Co-operation and Development—corporate governance principles and discussion of corporate governance topics.

www.coso.org

Committee of Sponsoring Organizations of the Treadway Commission.

6 Models of Corporate Governance

 Learning Outcomes

In this chapter we build on the distinction between Western and Eastern approaches to corporate governance mentioned in Chapter 1 and the cultural characteristics of corporate governance discussed in 3hapter 3.

In particular this chapter enables us to:

● Appreciate how context affects corporate governance.

● Compare Western and Eastern approaches to corporate governance.

● Contrast the UK and USA unitary boards with two-tier boards.

● Understand corporate governance models in Asian families, in Japan, and in Korea.

● Consider if corporate governance models are converging.

● Recognize the institutions necessary for successful corporate governance.

How context affects corporate governance

The context in which corporate governance is practised is important because of different patterns of ownership, alternative markets for corporate control, and different ways of financing corporate entities. Consider each of these factors:

Patterns of ownership

Ownership of listed companies around the world varies, from the highly dispersed to the singularly concentrated. Table 6.1 shows, country by country, the proportion of voting shares held by individuals, institutional investors, banks and government, holding companies, and overseas investors.

Notice how, in the United States, individuals and institutional investors together account for 92 per cent of the shareholdings and in the UK 77 per cent, whereas in France it is only 35 per cent. In fact, the dispersed ownership found in UK and US companies is the exception rather than the norm around the world. In Germany, Japan, and the Netherlands, many listed companies are held within corporate groups and their boards find themselves responsible to a holding company. The foreign investors in countries such as the Netherlands (41 per cent) or France (37 per cent) may be an overseas parent company, or the holdings may be dispersed among overseas shareholders.

In a company in which the voting shareholders are highly differentiated—that is, where the shares are held by many dispersed external shareholders as in the USA and the UK—the directors need to respond to their varied expectations, while recognizing that shareholders can, occasionally, act together. On the other hand, where there is a dominant owner, with the other shareholders being in a minority, the directors need to respond to the expectations of that dominant shareholder, whilst protecting the rights of the minority. Examples include a listed company that is nevertheless part of a corporate group, a company with a dominant shareholder such as a government or financial institution, or cases where there is a block of connected shareholders.

Obviously, in the longer term, the pattern of ownership fundamentally affects the ability of a board to exercise power over a company. In a company that has a wide spread of shareholders, a board will have more freedom to act on its own initiative than in one where the shares are dominated by a single or block of investors. Boards need to be acutely aware which parties have the potential to influence their decisions. Unfortunately, some commentators on corporate governance fail to make this distinction.

Markets for corporate control

In countries with a high proportion of external investors, as in the United States and the United Kingdom, a board can be faced with a hostile takeover bid and a consequential loss of control. In other words, the market for corporate control is strong and merger and acquisition activity is likely to be widespread. In countries with a relatively low proportion of external investors, the market for corporate control will be weaker, and merger and acquisition activity less. Hostile takeover bids in British companies have been commonplace for generations but the first contested takeover bid for a German company occurred in the 1990s. In China, there is no market for corporate control at the moment.

Financing corporate entities

In countries where equity markets are relatively large, with high liquidity and significant turnover, shareholdings are often widely spread. This means boards can wield significant power over their companies, even though ultimate power lies with the voting shareholders. In other

Table 6.1 Balance of listed company ownership

Country	Individuals	Institutional investors	Banks and government	Holding company	Foreign
Australia	20%	34%	4%	11%	31%
Canada	15%	38%	8%	14%	25%
France	23%	12%	14%	14%	37%
Germany	17%	15%	17%	39%	12%
Italy	18%	14%	40%	18%	10%
Japan	20%	21%	23%	28%	8%
Sweden	23%	30%	8%	9%	30%
Netherlands	14%	21%	1%	23%	41%
UK	19%	58%	5%	2%	16%
USA	51%	41%	3%	0%	5%

countries, however, where stock markets are relatively small, listed companies may rely on non-equity loan capital. In companies that have leveraged their equity capital, with a high loan to equity gearing ratio, ultimate power over the company may be in the hands of the lender through the terms of the loan agreement.

Western and Eastern approaches to corporate governance

Although the basic intentions of corporate governance around the world are similar, the means of achieving them vary considerably. Evolving history, culture, company legislation, and corporate regulation affect the principles and practices of corporate governance in different countries.

Approaches to corporate governance principles, policies, and practices can be divided between the West and the East. Broadly, the Western models are:

- the UK/Commonwealth principles model;
- the United States rule-based model;
- the continental European two-tier model.

The Eastern models include:

- the Asian family-based model;
- the *keiretsu* model in Japan;
- the *chaebol* model in South Korea.

China has developed a unique approach drawing from both Western and Eastern models. Some of the largest companies floated on the New York, London, and Hong Kong stock markets and fulfilling all the corporate governance listing rules are Chinese; some are state-owned enterprises running under state control; and some are emergent entities run more like family businesses.

Let us now consider the basic models of corporate governance, which have provided the major influences.

The UK/Commonwealth unitary board, principles-based model

The law that recognized the incorporation of the joint-stock shareholder, limited-liability company originated in the United Kingdom in the mid-19th century. Membership of the old British Empire, in the later 19th and early 20th centuries, meant that UK company law influenced the development of company law in Australia, Canada, Hong Kong, India, New Zealand, South Africa, Singapore, and indeed throughout what is now known as the Commonwealth.

Company law in the UK/Commonwealth model is based on common law, rooted in legislation, which is reinforced as the courts decide specific cases. However, in contrast with the United States model, in the United Kingdom and in Commonwealth countries, corporate governance is 'principles-based'. Codes of corporate governance principles or good practice determine board responsibilities, not governance practices. Companies are required to report that they have followed the governance principles laid down in the codes or to explain why they have not. Consequently, this model is often referred to as the 'comply or explain' approach to corporate governance. Self-regulation by each company, not the rule of law, is the underlying theme. Compliance is voluntary, with the sanctions being the exposure of corporate governance failings to the market and, ultimately, delisting from the stock exchange. Stock exchange regulations and company regulators ensure that investors and potential investors have accurate information on which to base their judgements.

Throughout the Commonwealth, corporate governance codes for listed companies, although differing slightly in detail, all call for independent non-executive or outside directors, audit, remuneration, and nomination committees of the board, and high levels of transparency and accountability. The codes also call for a separation between chairman and CEO.

The United States unitary board, rules-based model

Companies in the USA are incorporated in individual states and are subject to those states' company law and corporate regulation. Investor protection, auditing requirements, and financial disclosure of public companies, however, are federal responsibilities, predominantly overseen by the US Securities and Exchange Commission (SEC), which was created in 1934.

The basic governance model for public companies in the United States is the unitary board, with a predominance of independent outside directors. The SEC and stock exchange listing requirements also call for mandatory audit, nomination, and remuneration committees of the main board.

In the United States, governance is regulated by legal statute and mandatory rules, which are inherently inflexible. Litigation levels are high. Directors face legal penalties for non-compliance. The 2002 Sarbanes-Oxley Act strengthened this emphasis on governance under penalty of law, with disclosure requirements that proved more expensive and burdensome than expected. The United States financial markets are still among the best regulated, as well as being the largest and most liquid, in the world; but that lead is being eroded.

The continental European two-tier model

In the two-tier board model a supervisory board, with no management members, sits above the executive board, which is composed entirely of executive (management) members. As the name suggests, the supervisory board oversees the work of the executive board, and can hire and fire its members. Two-tier boards are required in Germany and Holland and are found in France and Italy. In Germany, large companies are seen as a quasi-partnership between capital and labour. Reflecting this idea of social democracy, German co-determination laws require one half of the supervisory board to represent labour, with the employee representative directors elected through the workers' trade unions; the other half, representing capital, is elected by the shareholders.

Typically, members of top management attend and report to their supervisory board to provide information and answer questions, but they do not have a vote and the supervisory board can meet without them. The supervisory board's ultimate power lies in the ability to hire and fire top management.

Critics of the two-tier model of corporate governance argue that the supervisory board is often dominated by top management and lacks the information inputs, advice, and wise counsel that can be provided by outside independent, non-executive directors in unitary boards. Other critics question the effectiveness of supervisory boards, their lack of real power, and their ability to control the management board effectively. Some also argue that the representative character of the supervisory board produces conflicts of interest.

The Asian family-based model

Chinese business people play a fundamental part in the business life of Southeast Asia, as a result of the Chinese diaspora from the mainland over the years.[1] Many companies in the significant Asian economies—Singapore, Taiwan, Malaysia, Thailand, Indonesia, Hong Kong, and the Philippines—are in the hands of Chinese families. For example, nearly half of the share capital invested in Malaysian companies is owned by Chinese residents.

In the governance of overseas Chinese companies, the board tends to play a role supporting the real exercise of power, which is done through relationships between the key players, particularly between the dominant head of the family and other family members in key top management positions. Some of these companies are quite diverse groups with considerable delegation of power to the subsidiary units, but with the owner-manager, or a family-orientated small group, still holding a strategic hand on the tiller.

Research into the management of companies owned by overseas Chinese has suggested some distinguishing characteristics about their management and governance. Such firms tend to be:

- family-centric with close family control;
- entrepreneurial, often with a dominant entrepreneur, so that decision-making is centralized, with close personal links emphasizing trust and control;
- controlled through an equity stake kept within the family;
- paternalistic in management style, within a social fabric dependent on relationships and social harmony, avoiding confrontation and the risk of 'losing face';
- strategically intuitive, with the business seen as more of a succession of contracts or ventures, relying on intuition, superstition, and tough-minded bargaining rather than strategic plans, brand creation, and quantitative analysis.

Where such companies are floated on the stock market, the outside shareholders are often in the minority. Consequently regulatory authorities tend to emphasize the importance of disclosure and the control of related-party transactions. Although many corporate governance codes require independent non-executive directors, the independence of outside directors is less important to the owner than their character, trustworthiness, and overall business ability. Of course, corporate governance problems exist in Chinese and overseas Chinese companies: corruption, insider trading, unfair treatment of minority shareholders, and domination by company leaders, to name a few. But these are unfortunate attributes of corporate governance that reflect human behaviour everywhere.

[1] For more information on the business methods of overseas Chinese, see Redding, S. Gordon (1993) *The Spirit of Chinese Capitalism*, de Gruyter, Berlin.

The *keiretsu* model of corporate governance in Japan

In Japan, the *keiretsu* are networks of companies connected through cross-holdings and interlocking directorships. Member companies tend to inter-trade extensively. Frequently, the network includes a financial institution. The classical model of the *keiretsu* reflects the social cohesion within Japanese society, emphasizing unity throughout the organization, non-adversarial relationships, lifetime employment, enterprise unions, personnel policies that encourage commitment, initiation into the corporate family, decision-making by consensus, cross-functional training, and promotion based on loyalty and social compatibility as well as performance.

In the classical *keiretsu* model, boards of directors tend to be large and are, in effect, the top layers of the management pyramid. People speak of being 'promoted to the board'. The tendency for managers to progress through an organization on tenure rather than performance means that the mediocre can reach board level.

In 2013, the Japanese government introduced a bill calling for audit committees, controlled by independent outside directors, and to ensure the independence of external auditors from boards. Outside directors were not made mandatory because of business resistance.

Japan's 2016 Corporate Governance Code took a pro-investor stance and emphasized that corporate governance should add to the long-term growth of the company. Two governance models were offered—one with a supervisory board, the other with an audit committee of a unitary board, both to have independent outside directors. A nomination committee and a remuneration committee of the main board were also required.

Many Japanese still do not see the need for such intervention. Indeed, they have difficulty in understanding how outside directors operate. How can outsiders possibly know enough about the company to make a contribution, they question, when the other directors have spent their lives working for the company? How can outsiders be sensitive to the corporate culture? They might even damage the harmony of the group.

The *chaebol* model of corporate governance in South Korea

Chaebol groups in South Korea developed following the Second World War, when the government advanced loans on attractive terms to family-based firms in order to stimulate economic revival. Over time, some of these family firms prospered and became large groupings of associated companies. Even *chaebol* companies that are listed are often still controlled by the dominant owner-family interests. Even though companies attracted outside capital, family domination was maintained predominantly through closely connected boards and cross-ownership with subsidiary companies.

Attempts to introduce independent outside directors into South Korean boards have had only limited effect against the entrenched power of the existing block owners. At times, this has led to protests from employees and social unrest. The South Korean government sought to reduce the power of the *chaebol* by requiring them to divest some of their interests. Before the financial and economic crisis of 1997, success was limited. Subsequently, the *chaebol* found it increasingly difficult to compete with other Asian producers, because of their tradition of lifetime employment and militant trade unions, and governance changes were forced on them.

Corporate governance: convergence or differentiation?

Are corporate governance practices around the world converging? This is a question that is often posed by corporate governance practitioners and frequently answered in the affirmative. Certainly, there are many forces that could lead towards convergence, as the following factors show.

Forces for convergence

Corporate governance codes of good practice around the world have a striking similarity, which is not surprising given the way in which they have been influenced by each other. Although different in detail, all emphasize the importance of independence, transparency, and accountability. The codes published by international bodies, such as the World Bank, the Commonwealth of Nations, and the Organisation for Economic Co-operation and Development (OECD), clearly encourage convergence. The corporate governance policies and practices of major corporations operating around the world can also be global influences.

Securities regulations for the world's listed companies are certainly converging. The International Organization of Securities Commissions (IOSCO), which now has the bulk of the world's securities regulatory bodies in membership, encourages convergence. For example, its members have agreed to exchange information on unusual trades, thus making the activities of global insider trading more hazardous.

International accounting standards are also leading towards convergence. The International Accounting Standards Committee (IASC) and the International Auditing Practices Committee (IPAC) have close links with IOSCO, and are further forces working towards international harmonization and standardization of financial reporting and auditing standards. The US general accepted accounting principles (GAAP), although some way from harmonization, are clearly moving in that direction.

In 2007, the SEC announced that US companies could adopt international accounting standards in lieu of US GAAP. However, American accountants and regulators are accustomed to a rules-based regime and international standards are principles-based, requiring judgement rather than adherence to prescriptive regulations.

Global concentration of audit practices into just four firms, since the demise of Arthur Andersen, encourages convergence. Major corporations in most countries, wanting to have the name of one of the four principal firms on their audit reports, are then inevitably locked into that firm's worldwide audit, risk analysis, and other governance practices.

Globalization of companies is also, obviously, a force for convergence. Firms that are truly global in strategic outlook, with production, service provision, added-value chain, markets and customers worldwide, calling on international sources of finance, and the shares of which are held around the world, are moving towards common, effective, transparent, and accountable governance practices.

Unfortunately, the composition of the boards of the parent companies of such groups seldom reflects such globalization, because they are still dominated by nationals of the country of incorporation. However, the proportion of 'foreign' directors—that is, those not nationals of the home country—although small, has been increasing. Companies such as Arcelor incorporated in Belgium, Novartis in Switzerland, Cable and Wireless in the UK, and ABN Amro in the Netherlands do have a significant proportion of directors who are not from the 'home country'. Significantly, no companies incorporated in the United States figure in this list.

Raising capital on overseas stock exchanges, clearly, encourages convergence as listed companies are required to conform to the listing rules of that market. Although the governance requirements of stock exchanges around the world differ in detail, they are moving towards internationally accepted norms through IOSCO.

International institutional investors, such as CalPERS, explicitly demand various corporate governance practices if they are to invest in a specific country or company. Institutional investors with an international portfolio have been an important force for convergence. Of course, as developing and transitional countries grow, generate and plough back their own funds, the call for inward investment will decline, along with the influence of the overseas institutions.

Private equity funding is changing the investment scene. Owners of significant private companies may decide not to list in the first place. Major investors in public companies may find an incentive to privatize. Overall, the existence of private equity funds challenges boards of listed companies by sharpening the market for corporate control. As the power of private equity grows, expect calls for more transparency, accountability, and control.

Cross-border mergers of stock markets could also have an impact on country-centric investment dealing and could influence corporate governance expectations, as could the development of electronic trading in stocks by promoting international securities trading.

Access to the internet with the ability to obtain information globally also leads to harmonization. However, in China this is limited due to government controls.

Research publications, international conferences, and professional journals can also be significant contributors to the convergence of corporate governance thinking and practice.

Forces for differentiation

However, despite all of these forces pushing towards convergence, there are others that, if not direct factors for divergence, at least cause differentiation between countries, jurisdictions, and markets.

Legal differences in company law, contract law, and bankruptcy law between jurisdictions affect corporate governance practices. Differences between the case law traditions of the USA, UK, and Commonwealth countries, and the codified law of continental Europe, Japan, and China distinguish corporate governance outcomes.

Standards in the legal process, too, can differ. Some countries have weak judicial systems. Their courts may have limited powers and be unreliable. Not all judiciaries are separate from the legislature. The state or political activities can be involved in jurisprudence: in China the courts serve the state. In some countries, bringing a company law case can be difficult and, even with a favourable judgment, obtaining satisfaction is not always possible.

Stock market differences in market capitalization, liquidity, and markets for corporate control affect governance practices. Obviously, financial markets vary significantly in their scale and sophistication, affecting their governance influence.

Ownership structures also vary between countries. Some countries have predominantly family-based firms; others have external investors, but the proportion of individual investors compared with institutional investors differs; while some adopt complex networked, chained, or pyramid structures.

History, culture, and ethnic groupings have produced different board structures and governance practices. For example, contrast the governance in Japanese *keiretsu*, continental European two-tier boards with worker co-determination, and family domination in overseas Chinese companies. Moreover, opinions differ on ownership rights and the basis of shareholder power between countries.

The concept of the company was Western, rooted in the notion of shareholder democracy, the stewardship of directors, and trust—the belief that directors recognize a fiduciary duty to their companies. But today's corporate structures have outgrown that simple notion. The corporate concept is now rooted in law, and the legitimacy of the corporate entity rests on regulation and litigation. The Western world has created the most expensive and litigious corporate regulatory regime the world has yet seen. This is not the only approach—and certainly not necessarily the best. The Asian reliance on relationships and trust in governing the enterprise may be closer to the original concept. There is a need to rethink the underlying idea of the corporation, contingent with the reality of power that can (or could) be wielded. Such a concept would need to be built on a pluralistic, rather than an ethnocentric, foundation if it is to be applicable to the corporate groups and strategic alliance networks that are now emerging as the basis of the business world of the future.

Institutions necessary for successful corporate governance

Having seen some of the different ways in which countries and cultures apply corporate governance, we can now identify the institutional arrangements that are needed to support successful governance. These include:

- a reliable legal system including an independent judiciary, courts that are free of bias and corruption, with judgments that are enforceable, free of state and other political involvement;
- a stock market with liquidity, international standing, and institutional investors;
- financial institutions, including brokers, sponsors for new issues, and financial advisers;
- regulatory authorities, covering corporations, stock markets, and futures markets;
- a companies registry that facilitates comprehensive disclosure, with high levels of transparency;
- accounting and legal professions that are internationally respected, and able to discipline their members and to ensure compliance with accounting standards and legal requirements;
- auditing firms that are professional, reliable, and independent of their clients;
- professional organizations, such as director- and company secretary-qualifying and -disciplining bodies;

- educational institutions able to educate and train for relevant qualifications;
- consulting organizations able to advise companies and directors;
- financial and corporate governance training, plus continuous professional development;
- corporate governance research reported in academic and professional publications.

Obviously, in many countries, particularly those with emergent economies, not all of these institutions yet exist and, where they do, they are still in the process of being developed. Moreover, even in those countries recognized as having relatively high standards of corporate governance, there are opportunities for further development and improvement. As we will see later, China has achieved enormous economic success with a judiciary dedicated to serving the people; in fact this means the State. However, taking a longitudinal view, it is interesting to see just how far many countries have come in developing their corporate governance infrastructure in a relatively few years.

Case studies

 Case study 6.1   Lehman Brothers Inc.: a corporate governance classic

Before the global financial crisis began in 2007, Lehman Brothers was a fabled New York-based brokerage firm and investment bank. Founded 157 years earlier, it had survived the American Civil War, the major economic depressions of the 19th and 20th centuries, and two world wars. By 2007, it was the fourth largest investment bank in the United States: only Goldman Sachs, Morgan Stanley, and Merrill Lynch were bigger. But that was not to last much longer.

The Lehman Brothers' board was dominated by Richard S. Fuld, Jr, who served as chairman of the board, chairman of the company's executive committee, and CEO. Early in 2008, the company's stock was trading at US$65. By October 2008, it had sunk to US$3.65, following the company's filing for bankruptcy in September 2008. Faced with the growing international financial crisis, the US Federal Reserve refused to provide funds, as it did with other banks.

Lehman Brothers' problems had begun to appear earlier in the year: dramatic losses on sub-prime mortgages, devaluation of the company's credit rating by the rating agencies, and the loss of clients. In June 2008, the company announced a US$2.8 billion loss for the second quarter, and the stock dropped to its lowest level for eight years. Yet the board seemed unable to grasp the depth of the problems facing the company: there was no investigation by the independent directors, no special study by the board's finance and risk committee, no call for a capital infusion, although it was apparent that one was needed.

The board of Lehman Brothers Inc. had ten independent directors, half aged over 70, with two in their eighties. The executive committee consisted of Fuld, the COO, the CFO, and 80-year-old independent director, John D. Macomber. The board's finance and risk committee was chaired by 80-year-old Henry Kaufman, although this committee met only twice in the financial year 2007–08, despite the growing global financial crisis.

Why were the directors apparently blind to the reality of the risk that the bank was facing? Where were the auditors? Why was the investigative media ignored? Could the culture of the board have encouraged delusions of invincibility? Was this hubris after 158 successful years?

Fuld did change his top management team: president and COO, Joseph Gregory, and CFO, Erin Callan, were 'let go'. In June 2008, Fuld announced that he would decline his bonus for that year. He made no offer to return any of the previous five years' compensation, which in total had been more than a billion dollars.

After the collapse of the company, Fuld was summoned before the Committee on Oversight and Government Reform of the US House of Representatives (Congress). His air of invincibility had gone. Although he accepted personal responsibility, he blamed the circumstances, not himself, claiming that widening credit default swap spreads, naked short-selling attacks, credit agency downgrades, a loss of confidence by clients and counterparties were all part of the explanation. He added that this had been a familiar tale for many other financial institutions at the time, but they had been bailed out by the government.

The company had not been immune from regulatory challenge previously. In 2003, the SEC had settled charges against Lehman Brothers that had arisen when Lehman's research analysts gave supposedly independent investment advice on companies in which Lehman had an interest. Along with nine other brokerage firms, Lehman reached a settlement with the SEC, the New York Stock Exchange, the New York Attorney General, and other state regulators; Lehman agreed to pay US$50 million to settle the conflicts of interest case: one half to state regulators; the other half into a fund for the benefit of customers. In addition, Lehman paid US$25 million over five years to provide the firm's clients with independent research, and US$5 million for investor education.

In March 2010, an examiner appointed by the Bankruptcy Court reported questionable activities in 2007–08, claiming that Lehman had used period-end repurchase agreements, which temporarily removed securities from the balance sheet, showing them as sales to improve its financial standing.

Following the collapse, the British Barclays Bank attempted to buy the company, but was prevented by UK and US regulatory concerns. Eventually, the interests of Lehman Brothers in Japan, Hong Kong, Australia, Asia-Pacific, Europe, and the Middle East were acquired by Nomura Holdings.

Discussion questions

1. The case claims that Lehman Brothers was dominated by Richard S. Fuld, Jr. Was this desirable? What steps could have been taken to avoid it? Who could have initiated these steps?

2. The case highlights Lehman's elderly directors. Does the age of directors matter?

3. Is it possible for the research analysts of a financial institution to give independent investment advice to clients about a company in which the financial institution has an interest?

 Case study 6.2 Tokyo Electric Power and the disaster at Fukushima Daiichi

In an unlikely outburst, Naoto Kan, Japanese Prime Minister, shouted 'What the hell is going on?'[2] to executives of the Tokyo Electric Power Company (TEPCO) following Japan's worst nuclear crisis at the Fukushima Daiichi nuclear power plant, after the tsunami and earthquake on 11 March 2011. Were the directors or the corporate governance systems and procedures at fault?

[2] Bricker, Mindy Kay (2014) *The Fukushima Daiichi Nuclear Power Station Disaster: Investigating the Myth and Reality*, Earthscan, Routledge, New York.

The company appeared to have a commitment to sound corporate governance. As it stated on its website:

> At TEPCO, we have developed corporate governance policies and practices as one of the primary management issues for ensuring sustainable growth in our business and long-term shareholder value. We believe in strengthening mutual trust through interactive communication with our valued stakeholders, including shareholders and investors, customers, local communities, suppliers, employees and the public, so we can move forward toward solid future growth and development. Therefore, TEPCO considers enhancing corporate governance a critical task for management and is working to develop organizational structures and policies for legal and ethical compliance, appropriate and prompt decision-making, effective and efficient business practices, and auditing and supervisory functions.

But behind the reassuring corporate governance explanations on the TEPCO website lay a different reality. The company's opaque handling of the situation at the stricken plant was widely criticized. The extent of the danger was minimized and the full extent of the damage only gradually became apparent, as the risk severity level was gradually increased to rank alongside Chernobyl as a most severe nuclear accident.

The company's handling of the incident exposed failings in its risk management systems. The company had a history of safety violations: in 2002, it had falsified safety test records, and in 2007, following an earthquake, its Niigata nuclear plant experienced a fire and a leak of radioactive water, which were concealed.

In fact, the board was dominated by inside directors, qualified by their seniority within the company. Out of the 20 directors, 18 were insiders, while 1 of the 2 nominally outside directors, Tomijirou Morita, was chairman of Dai-Ichi Life Insurance, which was connected financially with TEPCO. In 2008, Tsunehisa Katsumata, the company president at the time of the 2007 problem, was elevated to chairman, being replaced by Masataka Shimizu, another career-long TEPCO employee. TEPCO had never appointed a head from outside the company.

The company held its AGM on 23 June 2011 and faced withering criticism from shareholders. President Shimizu apologized for the JP¥1.25 trillion (US$15 billion) loss. But a motion to cease generating nuclear power was defeated with the support of institutional investors.

Also in June 2011, the Japanese government appointed a five-man team to look into the company's finances. This committee was forced on the TEPCO board as a condition of financial support from the government to compensate those affected by the crisis at the Fukushima plant.

Three years after the earthquake and tsunami damage to the TEPCO atomic plant the situation had worsened. The company was accused of having been slow to respond to the radiation crisis. Fuel rods from the damaged reactor were cooled in water held in make-shift metal tanks that were bolted rather than welded together. Leaks were sealed with tape. In September 2013, water from the tanks leaked into the sea. Radiation levels 18 times above the safe level were detected, levels that would kill anyone exposed within hours. Neighbouring countries complained at the contamination of their seas.

The Japanese economy was also affected. Following the Fukushima disaster, most other nuclear reactors in Japan were shut down under public pressure. But rising oil prices and the falling value of the yen meant that the alternative energy sources were becoming unsustainable. The government wanted to restart the other reactors, but the public were hostile. Japan is prone to earthquakes and many of these generators were built close to fault lines. But business interests pressed hard for the nuclear plants to reopen and energy costs to be stabilized.

In November 2013, the most hazardous part of the Fukushima shut-down began. The fuel rods had to be moved from their unstable storage tanks to safety. Normally removing spent rods is a routine process. But these rods were not spent. The storage pool could boil dry and without coolant fuel rods could ignite or even explode. Mistrust in TEPCO reached an all-time high. The nuclear power regulatory authority eventually agreed that the Fukushima reactor should be decommissioned.

Discussion questions

1. Did the structure of the board contribute to the failures?

2. How do you account for the discrepancies between the company's alleged concern for corporate governance on its website and the catastrophic failure?

3. What advice would you give to the chairman of TEPCO?

 Case study 6.3   The Huawei Group

Huawei was founded in 1987 by Ren Zhengfei, a former electronics engineer in the People's Liberation Army (PLA). During the 1980s and 1990s, the Chinese government saw the need to modernize telecommunications throughout the country. Telephone exchange equipment needed electronics. Some companies in the industry negotiated joint ventures to link with foreign companies that had the technology, but they proved reluctant to divulge the latest technology. Ren took a different approach: his company obtained foreign equipment and dismantled it (so-called 'reverse engineering') to discover its secrets and replicate them in new equipment.

In 1994, Huawei agreed to build a telecommunication system for the PLA; a relatively small project but crucial in political connections. Ren Zhengfei met Premier Jiang Zemin and convinced him that electronic switching-equipment technology was related to national security and that a nation that did not have its own switching equipment was like one that lacked its own military. Jiang agreed. In 1996, the government decided to support domestic telecommunications manufacturers and restrict access to foreign investors. The Huawei Group thrived and became a leading force in China's creation of 'smart cities', bypassing the personal computer experience of Western nations and adopting smartphone technology as the basis for internet transactions and communication. Huawei became the largest manufacturer of telecommunications equipment in the world, overtaking the US-based Ericsson in 2012.[3]

Huawei was also expanding outside mainland China. In 1997, it signed a contract with Hong Kong's Hutchinson Whampoa to provide a fixed-line network. In 1999, it opened an R&D centre in Bangalore, India, and in 2001 it opened four R&D centres in the USA. By 2005, Huawei's international contracts exceeded domestic sales.

Huawei refers to itself as a private company and calls itself a 'collective', being owned by its employees.[4] The nature of that ownership and the government's continuing relationship with the company remain unclear.

Discussion questions

1. What do you think Huawei means when it calls itself a 'collective'?

2. Are there any governance implications for the Chinese government when a Chinese telecommunications company is the largest in the world?

[3] www.forbes.com/sites/moorinsights/2017/12/04/ericsson-vs-huawei-whos-winning-the-5g-race/#6821 666a8aa5

[4] www.itnews.com.au/news/analysis-who-really-owns-huawei-175946

Self-test questions

1. Distinguish the Anglo-American model of corporate governance from that of continental Europe.

2. Which has the greater proportion of individual, as against institutional, investors: the UK or the USA?

3. Describe the Japanese business network, *keiretsu*, model.

4. Name some characteristics of the overseas Chinese family business.

5. Describe the development of strategy in a Japanese *keiretsu* company.

6. What institutions are necessary for successful corporate governance?

7. Identify some forces for convergence in corporate governance around the world.

8. Identify some forces for differentiation in corporate governance around the world.

9. What value links the original Western concept of the corporation with the contemporary Asian attitude?

 For suggested answers to these self-test questions visit the online resources at: www.oup.com/uk/tricker4e/

Projects and exercises

1. A distinction is drawn in the text between the United States rules-based model and the UK and Commonwealth principles-based model of corporate governance. Which, if either, is likely to prevail in the long term?

2. Research the approaches that were adopted in the privatization of state enterprises in Russia and in China. What were the strengths and weaknesses of each approach? Which has been the more successful?

3. Prepare a report/presentation distinguishing the characteristics of corporate governance around the world.

References and further reading

Accounting Standards Steering Committee (1975) The Corporate Report: A Discussion Paper Published for Comment. Institute of Chartered Accountants in England and Wales, London.

Aoki, Masahiko, Gregory Jackson, and Hideaki Miyajima (2007) *Corporate Governance in Japan: Institutional Change and Organizational Diversity*. Oxford University Press, New York.

Batra, Sumant, Kesar Dass and Associates (2008) India: National Experience with Managing Related-party Transactions. The 2008 Asian Round Table on Corporate Governance , Shanghai Stock

Exchange Research Centre, China, OECD, Hong Kong SAR.

Filatotchev, I. and M. Wright (eds) (2005) *Corporate Governance Life Cycle*. Edward Elgar, London.

Hesterly, William S., Julia Liebeskind, and Todd R. Zenger (1990) 'Organizational Economics: An Impending Revolution in Organization Theory?', *The Academy of Management Review*, 15, 3.

Ho, Kai Leong (ed.) (2005) *Reforming Corporate Governance in South East Asia*. Institute of South East Asia Studies, Singapore, [pubsunit@iseas.edu.sg].

ISI Publications (2004) *The Practitioners' Guide to Corporate Governance in Asia*. www.BooksonBiz.com.

McCarthy, Daniel, Sheila Puffer, and Stanislav Vladimirovich (2004) *Corporate Governance in Russia*. Edward Elgar Publishing, Cheltenham.

Nader, Ralph and Mark Green (1980) The Case for a Corporate Democracy Act of 1980. Public Citizens Congress Watch, et al, Washington.

Nottage, Luke, Leon Wolff, and Kent Anderson (eds) (2008) *Corporate Governance In The 21st Century—Japan's Gradual Transformation*. Edward Elgar, Cheltenham.

Ohmae, Kenichi (1986) *The Mind of the Strategist*. Penguin, London.

Pfeffer, Jeffrey (1992) *Managing with Power: Politics and Influence in Organizations*. Harvard Business School Press, Boston, MA.

Spencer, Anne (1983) *On the Edge of the Organization: The Role of the Outside Director*. Wiley, London.

Steger, Ulrich (2004) *Mastering Global Corporate Governance*. Wiley, Hoboken, NJ.

Watanabee, Shigeru and Isao Yamamoto (1993) 'Corporate Governance in Japan: Ways to Improve Low Profitability', *Corporate Governance: An International Review*, 1, 4.

Whittaker, D. Hugh and Simon Deakin (2010) Corporate Governance and Managerial Reform in Japan, Oxford Scholarship Online.

World Bank and IFC (2002) Corporate Governance in China. World Bank, Washington, DC.

Yu, Guang Hua (2007) *Comparative Corporate Governance in China*. Routledge, Hong Kong.

Zhang, Weidong (2008) Related Transactions: Analysis of China's Listed Companies. The 2008 Asian Round Table on Corporate Governance, Shanghai Stock Exchange Research Centre, China, OECD, Hong Kong SAR.

Useful websites

Worldwide

www.ifc.org/gcgf

Global Corporate Governance Forum of the World Bank.

www.ifc.org/corporategovernance

International Finance Corporation (IFC)—a member of the World Bank.

www.oecd.org

Organisation for Economic Co-operation and Development.

www.iosco.org

International Organization of Securities Commissions (IOSCO).

www.icgn.org

The International Corporate Governance Network.

Australia

www.asic.gov.au

Australian Securities and Investments Commission.

www.governanceinstitute.com.au

Governance Institute of Australia.

www.asx.com.au

Australian Securities Exchange (ASX).

Europe

www.ecgi.org

European Corporate Governance Institute.

Asia

www.acga-asia.org

Asian Corporate Governance Association—working with investors, companies, and regulators for effective corporate governance throughout Asia.

www.clsa.com

CG Watch—corporate governance in Asia.

www.adb.org

Asian Development Bank (for governance, see 'topics').

China

www.csrc.gov.cn

China Securities Regulatory Commission.

www.mof.gov.cn

Ministry of Finance.

www.pbc.gov.cn

People's Bank of China—China's central bank and banking regulator.

www.sse.com.cn

Shanghai Stock Exchange.

www.szse.cn

Shenzhen Stock Exchange.

www.cicpa.org.cn

The Chinese Institute of Certified Public Accountants.

Hong Kong SAR of China

www.sfc.hk

Securities and Futures Commission—the securities regulator.

www.fstb.gov.hk and **www.hkma.gov.hk**

Financial Services and Treasury Bureau and Hong Kong Monetary Authority.

www.icac.org.hk

Hong Kong Independent Commission against Corruption.

www.hkex.com.hk

Hong Kong Stock Exchange.

www.hkgem.com

Hong Kong Growth Enterprises Market.

www.icris.cr.gov.hk

Hong Kong Integrated Companies Registry Information System.

www.info.gov.hk/idt

The Government of the Hong Kong special administrative region of the People's Republic of China—Insider Dealing Tribunal—describes remit and investigations.

www.hkicpa.org.hk

Hong Kong Institute of Certified Public Accountants.

www.hkics.org.hk

Hong Kong Institute of Chartered Secretaries.

www.webb-site.com

Commentary by David Webb on Hong Kong's corporate governance—valuable source of reference to corporate governance in Hong Kong.

India

www.finmin.nic.in

Ministry of Finance India.

www.rbi.org.in

Reserve Bank of India.

www.cvc.nic.in

Central Vigilance Commission.

www.sebi.gov.in

Securities and Exchange Board of India.

www.bseindia.com

Mumbai Stock Exchange.

www.nseindia.com

National Stock Exchange of India.

www.icai.org

Institute of Chartered Accountants of India.

www.icsi.edu

Institute of Company Secretaries of India.

www.iodglobal.com

Institute of Directors in India.

www.academyofcg.org

Indian Academy of Corporate Governance.

Japan

www.rieti.go.jp

Research Institute of Economy, Trade and Industry—Corporate Governance Japan—online governance forum established by government.

www.cg-net.jp

Japan Corporate Governance Network.

www.mof.go.jp

Ministry of Finance in Japan.

www.fsa.go.jp

Financial Services Agency—the Japanese government.

www.jpx.co.jp

Japan Exchange group including Tokyo Stock Exchange.

www.keidanren.or.jp

The Japanese Business Federation with information on governance in Japan.

Middle East

www.hawkamah.org

Hawkamah, The Institute for Corporate Governance.

Russia

www.iclg.ru/english

Institute of Corporate Law and Corporate Governance—Russia.

www.trade.gov/goodgovernance/CorpGovManual.asp

The Russia Corporate Governance Manual—IFC and International Trade Administration (US Department of Commerce).

www.ethicsrussia.org

Centre for Business Ethics and Corporate Governance—Russia.

www.oecd.org/russia/corporategovernanceinrussia.htm

Corporate Governance Roundtable.

www.worldbank.org/publication/rosc

Corporate governance in Russia: Report on the observance of standards and codes.

Singapore

www.bschool.nus.edu.sg/cgio

National University of Singapore's Centre for governance, institutions, and organisations.

www.mas.gov.sg

Monetary Authority of Singapore—central bank and securities regulator (search corporate governance).

www.sgx.com

Singapore Stock Exchange.

www.acra.gov.sg

Accounting and Corporate Regulatory Authority.

www.temasekholdings.com.sg

Singapore government's investment arm.

www.isca.org.sg

Institute of Singapore Chartered Accountants.

UK

www.londonstockexchange.com

London Stock Exchange.

www.companieshouse.gov.uk

Registrar of Companies.

www.fca.org.uk (search on 'corporate governance')

Financial Conduct Authority.

www.icaew.co.uk

Institute of Chartered Accountants in England and Wales.

www.companyspotlight.com/landing/UKHardcopyReports

Annual report service.

(For other corporate governance websites in the UK, see lists at end of chapters.)

USA

www.sec.gov

US Securities and Exchange Commission.

www.aicpa.org

American Institute of Certified Public Accountants.

www.governanceprofessionals.org

Society for Corporate Governance.

www.cii.org

Council of Institutional Investors—the voice of corporate governance.

www.nyse.com

New York Stock Exchange.

www.nasdaq.com

NASDAQ Stock Exchange (National Association of Securities Dealers Automated Quotation System).

www.corp.delaware.gov

State of Delaware.

(For other corporate governance websites in the USA, see lists at the end of chapters.)

Part 2

Policies

7

Functions of the Board

 Learning Outcomes

This chapter enables us to:

- Understand what a board does.
- Compare the board's performance and conformance roles.
- Appreciate the functions and authority of board committees.
- Understand the issue of delegating board functions to management.
- Think about corporate transparency.

What the board does

A simple framework was introduced in Chapter 2 to provide an overview of the functions of the board, showing its responsibility to be looking inwards at the enterprise and outwards to the organization's external situation, focusing on the past, the present, and the strategic future. This is summarized in Figure 7.1.

This model involves a dynamic process: the board's involvement in the formulation of strategy leads to the making of policies and plans, with the board then monitoring and supervising executive performance, before subsequently providing accountability, which forms the basis for reviewing strategy for the future.

Note that the terminology used here—of corporate strategy leading to corporate policy-making—is the usage adopted in the business world. In government circles, at both national and local levels, the terminology tends to be reversed, with policy statements leading to strategic initiatives. Here, we will adopt the business usage.

In fact, some boards delegate part of these activities to management. In many large companies in the United States, for example, the predominant role of the board is seen as appointing and monitoring the chief executive officer (CEO), who works with the top executives to develop corporate strategies that are presented to the board for comment and approval. This is depicted in Figure 7.2. In some smaller companies and many subsidiary companies in corporate groups, directors may be executives, so the distinction between the work of the board and that of top management can become blurred. However, every board of directors has a governance responsibility to ensure that its corporate strategy, risk assessment, and ethical profile are in place and appropriate.

Strategy formulation

Behind every sound corporate strategy is an idea or vision of what those leading the company want it to be and to be seen to be. In formulating corporate strategy the principal purpose of the organization is identified, its core values established, its risk profile determined, and

Figure 7.1 The basic board functions

its longer-term direction set. Directors are so-called because they establish the company's direction. Many companies attempt to encapsulate this sense of purpose and direction in a statement of corporate vision and a mission statement. Some combine the two. Others incorporate a view of the company's values.

Such statements proclaim what the company is trying to achieve and how it intends to achieve it. They provide a mechanism for steering and controlling strategic choices. They also tend to reflect a company's inherent culture: that collection of assumptions, attitudes, and beliefs that all organizations acquire over time. McDonald's has published both its mission and values (see Corporate Governance in Action 7.1).

Figure 7.2 Board functions working through management

Corporate Governance in Action 7.1 McDonald's mission

McDonald's brand mission is to be our customers' favorite place and way to eat and drink. Our worldwide operations are aligned around a global strategy, which center on an exceptional customer experience—People, Products, Place, Price and Promotion. We are committed to continuously improving our operations and enhancing our customers' experience.

McDonald's values

- We place the customer experience at the core of all we do.
- We are committed to our people.
- We believe in the McDonald's System—a business model, depicted by our 'three-legged stool' of owner/operators, suppliers, and company employees.
- We operate our business ethically.
- We give back to our communities.
- We grow our business profitably.
- We strive continually to improve.

Sainsbury's, a UK retailer, has also published a vision and sense of mission (see Corporate Governance in Action 7.2):

Corporate Governance in Action 7.2 Sainsbury's vision and values statement

Our mission is to be the consumer's first choice for food, delivering products of outstanding quality and great service at a competitive cost through working faster, simpler, and together. Our values are critical to achieving this. Our customers trust Sainsbury's to do the right thing, and expect us to maintain high social, ethical and environmental standards. Our values are—being best for food and health, sourcing with integrity, respect for our environment, making a difference to our community, and being a great place to work.

Microsoft's published statement of mission and values is in Corporate Governance in Action 7.3.

Corporate Governance in Action 7.3 Microsoft mission and values

The 2017 mission statement

Our mission is to empower every person and every organization on the planet to achieve more.

> ## Previous statements
>
> At Microsoft, our mission and values are to help people and businesses throughout the world realize their full potential. We consider our mission statement a commitment to our customers. We deliver on that commitment by striving to create technology that is accessible to everyone— of all ages and abilities. Microsoft is one of the industry leaders in accessibility innovation and in building products that are safer and easier to use.
>
> As a company, and as individuals, we value integrity, honesty, openness, personal excellence, constructive self-criticism, continual self-improvement, and mutual respect. We are committed to our customers and partners and have a passion for technology. We take on big challenges, and pride ourselves on seeing them through. We hold ourselves accountable to our customers, shareholders, partners, and employees by honouring our commitments, providing results, and striving for the highest quality.

Some say that Microsoft's mission statement is too bland, and fails to provide a clear vision for its strategy. But others commend the clear statement of corporate values and the company's social emphasis on accessibility through technology. Some directors feel that their mission (or vision) statement provides a concrete description of their company's purpose, values, and direction, which guides strategic decisions, inspires employees, and informs customers and other stakeholders. Such mission statements need to be a clear, but succinct, indication of the core purpose and core values of the enterprise.

Other directors, however, feel that written mission statements can be at best a bland public relations exercise and at worst an exercise in futility. Certainly, unless directors believe in and link their mission with their strategic decisions, a public mission statement becomes little more than a marketing slogan or a sign on the wall for employees.

What does strategy formulation involve? One of the primary duties of every board is to ensure that its enterprise is heading in the right direction. The board that lacks a shared view of the company's purpose and future direction cannot develop an effective corporate strategy. Strategy formulation is the process of generating and reviewing alternative longer-term directions for the firm that lead towards the achievement of its purposes, consistent with the risk profile acceptable to the board.

Who is responsible for formulating strategy? Boards vary in their involvement in the strategy formulation process. In a board with a majority of executive directors, as in many small and family firms, and in some subsidiary companies, the board is likely to be much involved in the strategy formulation process because many of the directors are 'wearing two hats' as both manager and director. Consequently, they can contribute to the strategic discussions directly from their own knowledge and experience of the business. The challenge to boards dominated by executive directors is that they are 'marking their own examination papers', lacking a critical perspective. On such boards, non-executive directors can play a vital role offering alternative insights, raising important questions, for example about risks involved, and by challenging conclusions. Advice from senior managers who are not on the board, external consultants, and other experts can also add important dimensions to strategic reviews.

By contrast, in a board with a majority of independent outside directors, as in most large US and UK companies these days, strategy is inevitably driven by top management—the CEO and the management team. What then *is* the role of the board? Can non-executive directors, who are independent of the company and its business, really know enough about the company and its industry to make a realistic contribution to strategic thinking? Some also question whether they can find sufficient time to make a worthwhile input to strategy, particularly since some of them may be CEOs of companies in their own right. Typically, in such situations, the CEO with the top management team undertakes a strategic review and produces a set of strategic proposals for the board's approval. The independent directors then question, challenge, and maybe refer the strategies back for further work, before giving their approval.

How is strategy formulated? A formal approach to strategic planning, still adopted by a few companies, is the creation of a long-range plan. Essentially, such long-range planning extends the annual budgeting process over a longer strategic time horizon, perhaps three to five years. At least this approach forces boards to focus on the longer term. But the drawbacks are apparent. The planner is, conceptually, inside the organization looking out. The approach fails to take a strategic perspective, perpetuating the existing business, rather than recognizing strategic changes in customer demands, markets, competition, technology, and financing. It also ignores the economic, political, and social context.

A more penetrating approach to strategic analysis is the widely used SWOT analysis (strengths, weaknesses, opportunities, and threats), which seeks to relate the internal situation in the firm to its external strategic context.

An example of a SWOT analysis will show this (see Corporate Governance in Action 7.4). In the analysis that follows, drawn from the experiences of a realtor (estate agent), the ideas were generated during a half-day strategy seminar attended by the directors and top management from the firm's regional offices. The chart represents a synthesis of the ideas produced by small working groups. The strategic situation facing the firm, both internally and externally, is certainly highlighted by this analysis. What emerges is a picture of a long-established, successful, but over-bureaucratic firm in the real-estate business facing vulnerability with an increasingly competitive market, which is being driven by franchised high street chains and a shift towards the internet for property sales. The self-confidence rooted in past success, the difficulty of adapting to change, and the need to develop a sense of urgency for strategic change are apparent.

Corporate Governance in Action 7.4   SWOT analysis for a long-established realtor (estate agent)

Strengths

- A well-known and respected brand name.
- A good market share where we are represented.
- We have been successful for 35 years.
- Both sellers and buyers respect our business methods.
- Our leaflets and adverts for promoting properties are successful.
- A large and experienced staff.
- A reputation as a good employer.
- Effective financial and management control systems.

Weaknesses

- Competition from internet-based agencies with no offices.
- High overheads, particularly rents and salaries.
- Overheads rising.
- Cash flow erratic.
- Slow to respond to new clients—pressure of work.
- Insufficient time with clients.
- Higher management authority required for decisions—slows the contract process and stifles staff initiative.
- Our website is still being improved.
- Telephone inquiries not well handled.
- Staff turnover—experienced staff being poached.
- Organizational inertia—slow to change direction—overconfidence.

Opportunities

- Our business sector is expanding—growth in sales of new house builds and existing properties.
- Commercial property sector sales not yet in portfolio.
- Many opportunities for development of new client services.
- Our competitors may be slow to adopt new technologies.

Threats

- Competition rife—internet agencies, national franchised chains, private sales.
- Vulnerable to internet—developments unpredictable.
- New ways to buy and sell houses erodes our position.
- Developments in technology changes the basics of the business.
- A new strategy by a large competitor ruins our market position.
- More government controls and charges on property transfers.

The SWOT methodology offers the prospect of building on corporate strengths, while working to eliminate or at least mitigate internal weaknesses, exploiting external opportunities faster and better than other firms, and moving to minimize the effect of external threats. A SWOT analysis can provide a penetrating experience for those involved and produce valuable information for board deliberations. But it tends to focus attention on the existing business, looking for threats that it might face and opportunities it could pursue. It does little to identify causes and effects of strategic change and suggest alternatives. Limitations of the methodology can include a failure to identify what is driving change in the market—the technology, or the economic situation—and thus limit the adequate responses. It can also overlook the firm's changing exposure to risk.

In the estate agent case (Corporate Governance in Action 7.4), the SWOT analysis does not generate strategic possibilities such as growth through acquisition, perhaps by franchising the firm's brand, merger (collaborating with, rather than fighting the opposition), buying into another franchise, and/or investing in buying/selling operations through the internet.

To formulate strategy effectively, the strategist needs to be, conceptually, above the enterprise looking down, able to see the enterprise in its strategic context, including the industry, the market, customers and competitors, products and services, wherever the company operates, and to identify the wider political, economic, social, and technological context. Figure 2.1, which shows the scope of corporate governance, can be expanded to depict the scope of strategy formulation. But, as well as understanding the external situation likely to face the company, directors need to be conversant with the internal situation, including the company's finances, labour, markets, products, and processes.

A well-known metaphor, 'helicopter vision', refers to the ability to *perceive* the enterprise in the context of ever-widening circles of influence: when on the ground, the helicopter pilot can see the ground in great detail, but cannot see very far horizontally. As the helicopter rises, the field of vision widens, but the detail lessens. In fact, thinking with helicopter vision is not difficult: the challenge is to determine the appropriate level at which to view the territory.

Surprisingly, many boards fail to devote enough time and attention to strategy formulation. Directors in a professionally led board will have a strategic focus, with relevant, up-to-date knowledge of the internal situation in the company and appropriate information about the firm's external context, covering both the immediate operating situation, including its industry, competitors, customers, products, operations, and financial situation, and the overall political, economic, social, and technological contexts.

Moreover, directors on professionally led boards have to have the ability to think strategically. What is meant by the ability to think strategically? General Sun Tzu, a Chinese leader in the Chou/Zhou dynasty in the first millennium BC, was one of the finest strategic minds the world has ever known. He called for the strategist to 'think with the mind of the enemy'. In business terms, that means identifying existing and potential competitors, understanding their strategic situation, and thinking through the strategies that they might be pursuing. What would directors hear if they were flies on the wall of a competitor's boardroom?

To understand the strategic situation affecting a company, we need to appreciate the forces that determine its competitiveness within that company's industry. These pressures may be harsh because of massive competition; a company in a mature industry, for example, might be facing competition from more advanced or cheaper products, produced in environmentally better circumstances. Alternatively, the pressure to change may be benign because growth of the market leaves all of the players in that sector with unsatisfied demand.

Professor Michael Porter of the Harvard Business School has provided a number of analytical frameworks that provide an understanding of strategic situations.[1] In one, he focuses on the value added by a company to its products and services. In another, often referred to as the 'five forces' model, he challenges the assumptions that a company might make about its immediate strategic environment.

---

[1] Porter, Michael E. (1980) *Competitive Strategy: Techniques for Analyzing Industries and Competitors*, The Free Press, New York, and (1985) *Competitive Advantage: Creating and Sustaining Superior Performance*, The Free Press, New York.

1. Who is currently competing in our market?
   How are they currently competing—price, service, quality, etc?
   How do their costs compare with the value added by this business?

2. What strategic power do our upstream suppliers have over us?
   Are they able to exercise strategic influence on us—by pricing, supply, etc?

3. Who are our customers—by type, location, volume, etc?
   What customer needs do we satisfy?
   What strategic powers do our downstream distributors and ultimate customers have?
   Are they able to exercise strategic influence on us—by price demands, etc?

4. Could our customers' needs be met by substitute goods or services?

5. Could other firms enter the market?
   What is keeping them out—high entry costs, know-how, low margins, etc?

This emphasis on the strategic environment of the company, rather than its internal situation, reflects the advice of General Sun Tzu, mentioned earlier, to 'think with the mind of the enemy'. Directors who are thinking strategically try to understand the strategic situation of their competitors, and to deduce what strategies they are pursuing. This is very different from reacting operationally. Crucial questions include the following.

- Who are the competitors?
- What is their current strategic situation?
- What is their current strategy—how are they currently competing?
- What are their capabilities—both strengths and weaknesses?
- What assumptions do they hold about themselves and their market?
- What beliefs do their directors and top management have about the strategic situation?
- Are they satisfied with their present market or financial position?
- Where might the competitors be vulnerable?
- What strategies could they pursue in the future?
- What is the likelihood?
- How might they react to strategic changes that we might make?

Professional directors understand the importance of such information, and professional boards ensure that they have access to it. Unless directors agree on their firm's strategic situation, they cannot formulate objective strategy.

Critics of Porter's approach to strategy formulation argue that, by focusing on the company's external competitive environment, the strengths of a company's internal resource may be underutilized and its strategies be over-influenced by market conditions. By contrast, a currently popular alternative, often known as 'resource-based theory', sees a firm as a collection of resources and capabilities that need to be utilized to create a winning strategy. The resources could include access to capital, employee skills, unique products or services, managerial talent and experience, equipment, and buildings or goodwill. This resource-based perspective seeks to find a fit between a firm's internal capabilities and its external market situation that will produce a competitive advantage.

Decision modelling has opened up an additional approach to corporate decision-making. Using sophisticated algorithms and the massive amounts of relevant data that are now available on many topics, more accurate predictions and better strategic decisions can be made. The output from such models may help overcome distortions that arise from individual prejudice and bias. Of course, though the output from models may influence decision-makers, the information still has to be acted on to be effective.

Policy-making

Strategies remain nothing more than dreams, statements of intent, until they are turned into actions. To make strategies operational, companies need policies, procedures, plans, and, in some cases, projects. The policies, procedures, and plans provide the criteria against which the board can subsequently monitor management's performance and fulfil their duty to supervise executive management.

Policies can be thought of as the rules, systems, and procedures that are laid down by the board to guide and constrain executive management. Obviously, the details of corporate policies depend on the scale, diversity, and type of operation. Top management may play a large part in the development of policies and in their implementation. In other cases, the board may delegate much policy-making to the CEO and top executive team. Such policies might include policies on customers and marketing, product and service, pricing, technology, innovation and research, employees and labour relations, suppliers and purchasing, downstream distribution and sales, capital projects, accounting and financial controls, risk assessment, and corporate values and ethics. But every board has a duty to ensure that appropriate policies are in place, that they are functioning effectively, and are regularly reviewed in the light of changing circumstances.

The directors may decide that there are some matters that should not be delegated to management, reserving to themselves the power to make such decisions. In such cases, the board creates a policy on reserved powers as in Corporate Governance in Action 7.5.

Corporate Governance in Action 7.5   South American Resources Ltd

Board policy on reserved powers

Matters that must be referred to the board and cannot be delegated

- Approval of overall corporate strategy and direction;
- major business acquisitions or disposals;
- approval of investment projects (over US$1 million);
- board appointments and removals (executive and outside directors);
- directors' remuneration policy;
- terms and appointment of CEO and top executives;
- appointments to board committees.

Financial policies

- Remuneration and selection of auditors;
  - approval of interim and final financial statements;
  - fundamental changes to employee pension scheme rules;
- main treasury policies, e.g. on gearing, borrowing limits;
- currency exposure and risk;
- significant changes to corporate control systems;
- policy on gearing or leverage;
- policy on accounting standards to be adopted in all countries.

Labour relations and employment policies

- Staff terms and conditions policy;
- trades union policy.

IT policies

- Policy on IT security and confidentiality;
- staff use of network.

Merger and acquisition policies

Corporate ethics policies

- Policies on core corporate values;
- code of ethics, creation, training, and enforcement policies;
- whistle-blower policies.

Corporate governance and compliance policies

- Relations with auditors, auditor independence policies;
- internal audit policies;
- internal reporting policies;
- regulatory compliance policies;
- corporate reporting policies.

Enterprise risk management policies

- Business catastrophe recognition and continuity policies;
- strategic risk assessment policy;
- financial exposure policy;
- employment, health and safety risk management policies;
- product risk management and contingency policies.

Risk management policies are of particular importance at board level. The global financial crisis showed that many boards, not just those of financial institutions, had failed to appreciate fully their companies' exposure to risk. Corporate governance codes now expressly recognize directors' responsibility to ensure that risk management policies are in place and that risks are adequately assessed.

Policies need to flow from the company's strategies. Boards have a responsibility to ensure that appropriate policies exist, either by setting these themselves or by approving those proposed by management. Then the board needs to ensure that appropriate management systems are in place to confirm that the policies are working.

Strategy formulation and policy-making together form the board-level performance role. This is a fundamental component of the work of a unitary board. In a two-tier board, the responsibility falls to the executive management board. We now come to the conformance roles—supervising executive activities and accountability. Again, this is a fundamental part of the work of a unitary board. In a two-tier board, the conformance role is the responsibility of the supervisory board.

Supervising executive activities

Almost all corporate entities, large and small, use financial measures and accounting systems as the primary means of monitoring the state of the enterprise and the performance of its managers. At the very least, this is likely to include a balance sheet and profit and loss (or revenue and expenditure) account. To be able to keep a better track of executive activities, many boards also rely on regular reports from a budgetary control system. Budgetary control systems compare actual revenues and expenditures against budgeted revenues and expenditures. The initial development of cost centres and their budgets enable management at all levels to be involved in the budgeting process, with the resultant motivation to achieve the planned performance.

Obviously, budgetary control systems are expressed in terms of costs and revenues. A more sophisticated approach to financially based controls involves the creation of profit centres within a firm. Managers responsible for such profit centres can now be motivated by and held accountable for the profit performance of their unit, possibly including return on investment criteria.

A further refinement is a management control system, which applies multiple performance measures to business units. An example will illustrate this (see Corporate Governance in Action 7.6).

Corporate Governance in Action 7.6   A multiple-measure management control system

The board of a company with profit-responsible divisions required its divisional managers to perform appropriately on ten criteria:

- profitability—return on investment in that division;
- growth in market share, revenue, and profit;
- customer satisfaction;
- capital expenditure project performance;
- management development and succession planning;
- product and service development;

- employee training, labour turnover, and employee attitudes;
- contributing to the group's corporate social responsibility;
- monitoring and management;
- balancing the short term with the long term.

Management control systems that use criteria beyond financial measures may have problems with quantifying some of the criteria. Judgement may be required in the measurement of difficult concepts such as customer satisfaction or employee attitudes. However, such systems do exist and some boards rely on their output.

To reduce the number of reports presented to the board, some firms use exception reporting in which only significant variations from planned performance have occurred and board-level attention is required. We noted, in Chapter 3, the potential agency problem of sub-optimization, where units of an organization are held responsible for the achievement of specific performance measures; in seeking to achieve those goals, each unit takes actions that achieve its own objectives, but that are potentially detrimental to achieving the organization's objectives as a whole. Directors need to be sensitive to such actions when setting and assessing subsidiary company, division, or unit performance measures.

Accountability

To whom is a board accountable? Formally, the answer is 'the members of that corporate entity'. In the case of a joint-stock, limited-liability company, that is the shareholder members with voting rights. In a cooperative society, the members are those with voting rights under the constitution. In a professional body or a trades union the members are those who are paid up and qualified to vote under the rules of that association.

The level and detail of accountability reporting required will be determined by the constitution of the organization, the laws under which it is incorporated, and the demands of any regulating authority. In the case of the limited-liability company in the UK, the required accountability is laid down in the Companies Acts; in the USA, by the company law of the state of incorporation and by the Securities and Exchange Commission. Companies may provide more than this legal requirement: they may not disclose less. Companies in which shares are listed on a stock exchange also have to meet that exchange's requirements for disclosure and the regulatory authorities' rules.

A few companies still take a strictly legal view, arguing that, provided that they obey the laws of the countries in which they operate, they owe no wider duty of disclosure or accountability to stakeholder groups. If a society expects wider accountability, it is up to the legislature to enact laws accordingly, they argue.

However, in recent years, a view has been gaining currency that boards, particularly of significant organizations, which have the potential to affect a lot of people by their behaviour, should recognize some accountability towards a wider range of stakeholders. Many companies recognize this wider responsibility and seek to provide relevant information to a range of connected stakeholders, such as employees, suppliers, and customers. Other companies go further and accept a responsibility to be accountable to society at large.

Balancing the board's performance and conformance roles

Every unitary board faces a challenge to strike a reasonable balance between the performance roles of strategy formulation and policy-making on one hand, and the conformance roles of executive supervision and accountability on the other. Typically, directors' time is under pressure. So the way in which the work of the board and its committees is allocated is crucial. It is also fundamental to the way in which the board approaches corporate governance. The problem is that the more a board concentrates its efforts on the conformance activities—management supervision and accountability—the more that board comes to see its work as ensuring compliance with the corporate governance requirements of respective codes, regulations, and law.

In fact, some directors *do* believe that corporate governance is essentially about compliance. They see their role as the supervision of management and ensuring accountability to legitimate stakeholders. In other words, they emphasize the conformance side of the conformance/performance dichotomy. The formulation of strategy and policy-making is then largely delegated to top management. By focusing on compliance, such boards tend to see corporate governance activities as an expense and wonder whether it is cost-effective.

In a board with a large majority of independent outside directors, the focus on conformance can become inevitable, if directors believe that their ability to contribute to strategy formulation and policy-making is limited.

In a two-tier board, of course, the separation is complete, with the management board running the business, responsible for performance, while the supervisory board oversees that performance and ensures accountability.

An unfortunate effect of the introduction of corporate governance principles and codes, rules and regulations, is the danger that boards, by concentrating on conformance, may overlook their principal mission, which is to direct the enterprise. That means being involved in strategy formulation and policy-making.

Many boards, of course, do recognize that they are responsible for balancing conformance activities with a commitment and contribution to performance. Directors are responsible for directing the company, ensuring that it is heading in the right direction, aware of the risks, and establishing the way ahead. That means sensibly balancing performance with conformance activities.

The responsibility for determining the board's agenda, ensuring that sufficient time is allocated to each of the four functions, and balancing these activities, lies with the board chair. Sensibly, he or she will seek advice from the company secretary and the CEO. Moreover, in a professionally led board, every director will have the opportunity to suggest items that the board should discuss and to express concerns about the balance of the board's deliberations. One chair actually asks each director to write to him/her every year about ways in which (s)he might improve performance as chair and to suggest matters that need more board attention. But not many chairs are that professional.

Board committees: functions and authority

Boards of large or complex organizations often find that there are more issues of board-level concern than can be adequately covered in board meetings. So they create subcommittees of the main board. These may be standing committees, with terms of reference to be responsible for specific matters, or ad hoc committees, formed to cover specific issues such as the progress of a major investment project or the combining of corporate control systems and culture following a merger or acquisition.

Essentially, there are two reasons why unitary boards create subcommittees:

- to enable independent directors to meet separately from the board as a whole, in order to fulfil their oversight roles;
- to delegate board activities to reduce the burden on the board as a whole.

Board committees that oversee management

The first corporate governance code, the UK's Cadbury Report, called for three board subcommittees: an audit committee, a remuneration committee, and a nomination committee, for listed companies. Almost all subsequent codes from countries around the world have adopted a similar governance system. These board committees should have a majority, and today in many cases consist entirely, of independent ONEDs.

Many corporate entities that are not listed, non-governmental organizations (NGOs), and government entities have also adopted similar committees. Board policies should create these committees as standing committees of the board, with formal terms of reference that are regularly reviewed and amended when necessary.

The audit committee

Audit committees existed in the 19th century, with members drawn from shareholders to check directors' reports. But the current notion of the audit committee as a standing committee of the board, composed of independent outside directors, to provide a bridge between the external auditor and the main board, originated in the United States. The New York Stock Exchange endorsed the concept in 1939. Then, in 1972, the SEC recommended that listed companies establish audit committees of non-management directors, which became a listing requirement in 1977. Since being required by corporate governance codes, the audit committee has become a fundamental component of corporate governance.

As a standing committee of the board, the audit committee derives its authority from the formal board policy that created it, and is accountable to the board. In listed companies, the committee derives further authority from listing rules, corporate governance codes, and the law, for example in the United States from the Sarbanes-Oxley Act. Typically, the audit committee has widespread authority to work with the external auditor, senior management (particularly the CEO and CFO), the finance function, and the internal audit function. Ideally, the committee has its own secretariat and can call on external expertise as necessary. The UK Financial Reporting Council produced a guide to boards on audit committees in 2012, which has subsequently been updated.

The remuneration committee

The global financial crisis and the continuing economic problems have thrown a spotlight on top executive and director remuneration. Media attention has been directed particularly at allegedly excessive bankers' bonuses, large awards to retiring directors that have been portrayed as rewards for failure, and the growing differential between the rewards of those at the top of organizations and those at the bottom.

Typically, the remuneration committee has formal responsibility for overseeing the remuneration packages of board members, particularly the executive directors and increasingly members of senior management. As with audit committees, the remuneration committee derives its authority from its formal terms of reference, relevant law, and corporate governance codes.

The nomination committee

There was a time in many countries when boards resembled comfortable clubs of like-minded people, well known to each other, sharing similar interests and often from similar backgrounds. The nominating committee was an attempt to prevent the board becoming a cosy club, in which the incumbent members appointed similar people to join their ranks. In effect, nominating committees offer a check-and-balance mechanism designed to reduce the possibility of dominant directors, particularly chairs or CEOs, pushing through their own favoured candidates. As a subcommittee of the main board, the nominating committee is made up wholly, or mainly, of independent outside directors, to make recommendations on replacement or additional members of the board.

Unfortunately, the creation of a nominating committee does not resolve an underlying dilemma. On one hand, an independent nominating committee can suggest potential directors with appropriate credentials, while avoiding claims of the old boys' club. On the other hand, to be effective a board chair needs to know, respect, and be able to work with the members of the board. To have members imposed on him or her could be divisive. If a board is to work together as a tough-minded, effective team, it is just as well that they know and respect each other. Otherwise board deliberations could become more like a political-adversarial parliament. A further dilemma can arise if supposedly independent outside directors feel a loyalty towards and the need to support the chair or CEO who nominated them.

Of the three committees recommended in the codes of good practice in corporate governance—the audit committee, the remuneration committee, and the nominating committee—it is the nominating committee that has been most resisted by boards in some jurisdictions; nor is that surprising, given that the right to appoint to the board of directors goes to the very heart of corporate power.

Other board committees for the oversight of management

In many companies, board-level responsibility for ensuring compliance with risk assessment and other code requirements is delegated to the audit committee. However, some companies, recognizing the growing complexity of that committee's function, have created a specific board committee to take on such responsibilities. Such committees are typically composed entirely of or have a majority of ONEDs.

Other companies have board standing committees, with significant independent director membership, to recommend policies and to oversee corporate activities on corporate ethics codes, whistle-blowing procedures, and corporate social responsibility (CSR). A few companies add corporate concerns about the sustainability of company activities to this committee's remit.

Board committees that reduce the burden on the board as a whole

Few boards meet more frequently than once a month, unless the company is facing a crisis. Some meet far less often, because the outside directors have other responsibilities and may be geographically distant. However, the scale and complexity of issues facing many boards continue to grow. Consequently, some boards have created subcommittees to handle components of their work.

Executive committees, finance committees, and strategic planning committees are all examples of board subcommittees formed to handle part of the board's overall work. The terms of reference of such board committees need to be clearly identified and bounded to avoid encroaching on issues that should legitimately be the concern of the board as a whole. The minutes of these committees typically form the basis of their reports to the board. A classic danger of such board committees is that directors who are not members abdicate all responsibility for that area of board responsibility, even though in law all directors are equally responsible. The fact that, in the absence of any cause for concern, they might rely on the word of other board colleagues does not absolve them from responsibility. Effective board chairs provide opportunities for the other directors to question subcommittee members and, if necessary, to reopen for discussion matters that have been decided by the subcommittee.

Another reaction to the global financial crisis was a greater focus on boards' responsibility for the assessment and acceptance of risk. Some boards have developed risk management policies and formed a board standing committee with specific responsibility for overseeing the company's exposure to and acceptance of risk. The titles of these committees vary—*enterprise risk management, corporate risk assessment and control, strategic risk governance*, for example—but they are to be found in companies of various sizes and industries, not just in financial institutions. As with other board committees for the oversight of management, such risk committees derive their authority from their terms of reference.

Finally, boards sometimes form ad hoc *committees with delegated responsibilities for specific projects*, such as the oversight of a major investment project, the organizational integration of a recent acquisition, or the launch of a new brand or product line. Such committees will usually include executive directors, and may include relevant managers or outside experts as members. But independent directors may be included to provide objective oversight. The terms of reference of ad hoc board committees should include clear objectives, the scope of their powers, and performance measures, so that they are wound up when they have fulfilled their purpose. Committees have a tendency to perpetuate their own existence.

Figure 7.3 Board functions working through management

Delegating board functions to management

The interplay between the board and management raises a crucial aspect of corporate governance. Subject to the articles and any regulatory demands, boards have considerable freedom to delegate responsibilities to management. In Figure 7.3, the relationship between the work of the board and that of the CEO and his or her management team is at the heart of the four governance functions of the board, as we saw earlier.

The cell in the centre of the quadrant shows management involvement with the board. It may be relatively small and insignificant, with the directors making most of the executive decisions, or it may be large, with the directors expecting top management to make a major contribution to some or all of the four governance functions. Some examples will illustrate this (see Corporate Governance in Action 7.7).

These examples raise an important question: where do boards focus their attention and how do they balance their time between the four basic functions of the board?

Unsurprisingly, research shows that boards vary significantly in the way in which they carry out their functions. In a company with an all-executive board, the directors virtually combine governance with the top management functions and it can be difficult to separate the two. In other cases, particularly in the board of a holding company that has delegated much of the strategy formulation and policy-making in the group to its subsidiary companies, the dominant focus is on setting overall strategies and policies at group level, the internal supervision of the group, and external accountability.

> Corporate Governance in Action 7.7   Examples of the interplay between
> the board and top management
>
> Strategy formulation
>
> The Beaumont Executive Press Ltd was a small publisher based in Oxford, England. There were
> two directors who formulated strategy and made all of the strategic decisions between them. They

decided which materials to publish, where to market, and how the business was financed. There was no delegation to others in the company; indeed, many of the other operational functions were outsourced to specialist firms. The two directors, who were also the owners of the company, determined the corporate strategy and identified the business risks they were prepared to take.

By contrast, the board of General Motors delegates most of the responsibility for formulating strategy to its operational divisions. The operating divisions produce strategies and project proposals that are put to the main board for approval and funding. The largely INED board members are not experts in the automotive industry. Their role is to question the strategic proposals, to raise concerns about level of research and development (R&D), product developments, competitor situation, pricing policy, technological developments, and so on, and to probe the exposure to risk. The main board's strategic decisions are largely about the allocation of resources to fund divisional strategies in the light of overall group strategy.

Policy-making

The Vigilance of Brixham Preservation Co. Ltd is a company incorporated to restore and run a heritage sailing trawler in one of England's few remaining fishing ports. All policies are made by the board. Since only cruise skippers are paid and the company is run by volunteers, there is no management to be involved in policy-making.

By contrast, in conglomerate Jardine Matheson Group (for more information, see Case study 10.1 in Chapter 10), only group financial policy, top management staff policies, and a few broad group management policies are made at main board level. Policy-making follows the formulation of strategy at subsidiary company levels.

Executive monitoring and supervision

The Rainbow Hospice Inc. is a charitable foundation involved in the provision of care in terminal illness. The board consists entirely of independent non-executive volunteers. The chief executive attends board meetings, but is not a director. The board receives a monthly statement on the financial and cash/bank position, reports on projects such as new building works and new equipment, drug use reports, and details of complaints from staff, patients, and their relatives. Directors also study the incidents book, which records health and safety breaches, and receive a written report on patient care and an oral report on staff from the chief executive. Directors then question him on matters that concern them, such as variances from budget plans, and anything else from the other information they have been given. The chief executive complains that the directors are too involved in the day-to-day running of the hospice, and from time to time individual directors even give instructions to the nursing staff.

By contrast, the directors of General Motors also receive detailed reports of the performance of each of the subsidiary companies in the group, supported by briefings from appropriate executives. They seek clarification and raise questions about matters that concern them. They discuss apparent problems with executives attending board meetings and, following discussions between themselves, call for more information, or approve the current executive performance. But they do not give instructions to management and seek the approval of the subsidiary company top management before visiting a plant.

Accountability

The board of a leading boarding school in Canada is composed entirely of independent outside members. The head and the bursar attend board meetings to provide information and advice. The report to the owners of the school comes from the board and it is the board that is held accountable for performance, including the appointment, monitoring, and if necessary removal of the head and senior staff.

By contrast, in General Electric, a large divisionalized company in a number of industries, the chair and directors accept a primary responsibility for the periodic report and accounts to shareholders, and the chairs of the board and of the audit committee address and respond to questions at shareholders' meetings. The senior outside director is also available to respond to shareholder issues. But senior financial management, too, is significantly involved in dealings with shareholders, regulators, and the financial media. Much detailed accountability work is delegated to the finance and the shareholder relations functions.

However, research has also shown that there is a basic difference between what experienced directors believe should happen and what does happen in practice. Asked for their opinion on how a board *should* divide its time and effort at board level, directors in the vast majority of cases suggest that the major focus should be on strategy formulation. A typical allocation of time in these studies is shown in Figure 7.4.

Notice that the respondents believe that most of the emphasis of the board's work should be on the right-hand performance aspects of the board's work (63 per cent). They also see the focus of the board's work being predominantly on the company in its outside context (62 per cent). In this idealized world, directors think that the left-hand conformance should be relegated to a less significant role (37 per cent), with executive supervision taking no more than a quarter of their time and accountability to external stakeholders a relatively insignificant 13 per cent.

However, asked to draw on their own experiences of how boards actually *do* focus their time and effort, directors produce data that resembles the results shown in Figure 7.5. In the real world of business experience, the emphasis of the board's work swings to the left-hand, conformance aspects of the board's work (63 per cent). They also see the focus of the board's work predominantly focusing inside the company (55 per cent).

Figure 7.4 Normative balance of board functions: how directors suggest boards *should* balance their activities

Outward-looking / Inward-looking

	Past- and present-focused	Future-focused	
Outward-looking	Accountability 22%	Strategy formulation 23%	45%
Inward-looking	Monitoring and supervision 41%	Policy-making 14%	55%
	63%	37%	100%

Figure 7.5 Reported balance of board functions: how directors believe boards *do* balance their activities

This exercise, asking directors to give their normative views on board activity, then their actual experience, has been conducted with hundreds of directors around the world. Although, of course, there is a spread of responses reflecting the different situations that can face boards, broadly the results seldom differ from those shown in Figures 7.4 and 7.5. Directors almost always believe the greater emphasis should be on the performance roles, particularly strategy formulation, but report that in practice the emphasis tends to be on conformance, particularly executive monitoring and reacting to internal short-term problems.

Explanations, though varying in detail, have a consistent similarity. Events arise that the board could not have foreseen ('a major discrepancy in the stock position', 'the death of the CFO', 'a massive budget deficit', 'the competitor unexpectedly launched a brand new service that was taking away our clients', 'a potential takeover bid'), so they have to spend more time on executive activities.

In recent years, directors have also reported the need to give a greater emphasis to accountability, partly due to greater regulatory demands and partly due to pressure from society ('shareholder expectations', 'stakeholder demands', 'the media', 'CSR needs').

Of course, these results apply to unitary boards, in which directors have to fulfil both the performance and the conformance roles. In the two-tier board, the roles are separated between the management and the supervisory boards. Nevertheless, directors often do see the need to find more time to concentrate on strategy formulation. In some cases, boards achieve this by actively devoting part of each meeting to strategic issues, by deciding to devote the entire board meeting to strategy, or by holding a strategy seminar—a day or two at which the board can be briefed on the strategic situation, can discuss the implications, can think about alternatives, and can evaluate and move towards a shared strategic vision, which will lead to new strategic plans and action in due course.

Corporate transparency

The call for greater corporate transparency in almost all economically advanced nations was a response to perceived corporate strategic and financial weaknesses, allegedly excess executive remuneration, and, in some cases, corporate corruption such as bribes to obtain contracts. The calls came from institutional investors, the media, and governments. Regulators responded with demands for more disclosure and many companies increased their investor activities and public relations programmes.

Traditionally, boards used the historical audited financial accounts to tell shareholders the story of their stewardship. But today, listed companies are expected to say far more, not only about how the company has been performing, but also to tell the story behind its current performance and to anticipate its future.

Moreover, a whole raft of stakeholders is now likely to be interested, including existing and potential providers of finance, suppliers, customers, employee organizations and unions representing employees, as well as interest groups on issues such as the environment, human rights, gender diversity.

Communication opportunities now include the internet as well as the traditional printed word. Social media has the potential to supersede traditional forms of communication between a company and its stakeholders, including, of course, its shareholders.

The narrative has become as important as the numbers. Some company law jurisdictions and corporate governance codes now call for a statement summarizing the company's mission and main objectives, discussing its performance, its assumptions about the future and its strategies, and its exposures to risk. Indeed, with today's complex financial reporting requirements and standards, the interpretation of accounts and their voluminous footnotes may be well-nigh impossible unless one is a financial expert. Surveys have shown that many readers of annual reports now rely more on the commentary than the accounts.

In the UK in 2014, UK regulations came into effect requiring companies to prepare a strategic report as part of their formal annual company report, with some exemptions for small companies.[2] The need to publish such narrative information can present the chair, the other board members, and the company secretary with some real challenges. What information should be included and in how much detail? Might any of the information raise false hopes or mislead the stock market and therefore be share-price-sensitive? Could any information be useful to existing or prospective competitors?

The typical narrative report, supporting the financial and audit report, includes at least the chair's statement, the directors' report, a corporate governance report, a remuneration report, and, increasingly, a corporate social responsibility and sustainability report. The chair's statement is often the most-read part, because it provides a summary of the company's overall performance, its strategic orientation, and says something about its intentions. The directors' report is likely to contain more detailed management analysis on, for example, products and services, staff, international markets and competition, the corporate mission, values, strategies, and plans. The corporate governance report must contain at least the minimum required by the relevant corporate governance code and listing rules, and may provide a wider discussion of the company's position on governance matters, such as corporate social responsibility and sustainability.

A sound narrative will contain at least:

- a balanced review of the business of the company;
- a comprehensive analysis of key financial and operating performance indicators;

---

[2] The Companies Act (2006) Strategic Reporting and Directors Report Regulations (2013).

- an explanation of the principal risks facing the company;
- details of any significant events that the company has experienced recently (for example, a major acquisition, a damaging fire, or a change of CEO);
- an indication of any planned future developments;
- a statement about the company's relationships with key stakeholders, including employees, customers, and suppliers;
- a report on the company's policies on corporate social responsibility and sustainability.

Integrated reporting, drawing together the required data from various reports into a connected narrative, is becoming more common. The crucial questions that readers of the report want to have answered are:

- what creates value in the company?
- what makes it profitable?
- what is the risk in the business?
- what is affecting the company's prospects?

The answers show how the directors see the situation and describe the real position facing the company. The directors might see the dominant future issue being in products (for example, a car manufacturer's ideas on future models and pollution controls), customers (for example, the thinking a retailer has on the effect of internet trading), patents (for example, a pharmaceutical company's hopes for a new drug), rights (for example, an airline's concerns about landing rights), goodwill (for example, the value of a brand name), or human capital (for example, the significance of skilled staff in an IT company). Such intangible resources, although vital to a company, are seldom on the balance sheet, although international.

Some stock exchanges provide guidelines on what to include in the narrative commentary in a company's report. The International Accounting Standards Board, discussing the basic principles of a good management commentary, calls for 'forward-looking information that focuses on generating value for investors'.

Overall, the aim of the narrative should be to inform the market, both existing and potential shareholders, on the position and trends facing the company. It should be balanced and objective, clear and concise, unbiased and transparent, and should mention all significant possible future changes. The material factors that influence results need to be disclosed. Over- or undue optimism and public relations 'spin' should be avoided. In discussing future expectations, ranges and probabilities can be used instead of absolute predictions. Companies that are seen to have published realistic assessments will become trusted, which in the longer term adds value.

Some stock exchanges have 'safe harbour' provisions in their rules to protect directors from legal actions over statements or omissions in their commentaries, and some Companies Acts limit liability unless statements are untrue, or misleading, in bad faith, reckless, or dishonest.

Auditors do not normally report on narrative statements, but are required to ensure that the commentary is not materially inconsistent with the audited figures. Commentaries are not a substitute for the financial accounts; they should be complementary. The trend towards greater corporate transparency is worldwide, and companies that are seen to be open will be recognized and be valued accordingly.

In the UK, the FRC is responsible for managing the Corporate Governance Code and the Stewardship Code. Consequently, it is intimately involved in corporate reporting and transparency. In its corporate reporting review work the Council's Conduct Committee seeks to ensure that the provision of financial information by public and large private companies complies with relevant reporting requirements. The Conduct Committee reviews the directors' reports and accounts of public and large private companies for compliance with the law. It also keeps under review interim reports of all listed issuers and annual reports of certain other non-corporate listed entities.

In addition to the Code the FRC publishes a series of guidance notes intended to assist companies in addressing specific aspects of governance and accountability. They cover board effectiveness, the role of audit committees and risk management, internal control, and assessing and reporting on whether the business is a going concern. To support the UK Corporate Governance Code investors are encouraged to commit to the principles of the UK Stewardship Code 2012. This sets standards for investors for monitoring and engaging with the companies they own and aims to improve the quality of dialogue between investors and companies to help improve long-term, risk-adjusted returns to shareholders. For more see www.frc.org.uk/publications.

In the United States, the SEC establishes rules for corporate disclosure and transparency. In the words of an official SEC statement:

> A dominant theme in all issues related to corporate governance is the vital importance of disclosure. The more transparent the internal workings of the company and cash flows, the more difficult it will be for management and controlling shareholders to misappropriate company assets or mismanage the company. The most basic and all-encompassing disclosure requirement is that all material information, i.e., anything that could potentially affect share price, should be publicly disclosed. Such information would include earnings results, acquisition or disposal of assets, board changes, related party transactions, shareholdings of directors and changes to ownership. Other information that should always be disclosed includes remuneration (including stock options) of all directors and senior management, corporate strategy, and off balance sheet transactions. All disclosed information should be released via the approved stock exchange procedure for company announcements as well as through the annual report. The Board shall therefore, commit at all times to full disclosure of material information dealings. It shall cause the filing of all required information for the interest of the stakeholders.[3]

Case studies

 Case study 7.1 Educational Services (Europe) Ltd

Educational Services Ltd was incorporated in Hong Kong in the 1980s by Bill Watford, an expatriate Englishman, to provide educational materials to schools, colleges, and the training departments of companies. By 2018, Educational Services had a staff of over 100 and representatives throughout the countries of East Asia, Australia, and in major cities in China. Initially, most of the products were films and videos, but today most content is streamed to the customer over the internet.

[3] www.sec.gov.ph/disclosure-and-transparency/

Merger and acquisition

When the 21st century arrived, Bill Watford recognized that access to customers over the internet offered worldwide strategic opportunities. If he could access potential customers his products could be delivered electronically to every part of the world. The challenge, he felt, was to find the customers in countries where his company lacked representation.

In 2015, Educational Services paid cash for a 60 per cent stake in a London-based private company offering similar products throughout Europe. The company, which had been founded and was still run by Elizabeth Corner and her brother George, changed its name to Educational Services (Europe) Ltd. The directors of ES (Europe) were Bill Watford (chair), Elizabeth Corner (CEO), George Corner (COO), Peter Green (finance director of ES (Hong Kong)), Geoffrey Corner (non-executive director, a retired chartered accountant, and father of Elizabeth and George), and John Chan (non-executive director, a Hong Kong-based lawyer).

For the first year, Bill Watford played no part in the management of ES (Europe). Communication between Hong Kong and London was mainly by email, plus a monthly conference telephone call between all the directors, which they referred to as 'the board meeting'. The entire ES (Europe) board met formally twice a year, once in London to discuss the annual financial accounts and the next year's budget and once in Hong Kong to discuss future strategy.

Board-level problems

At the last board meeting of ES (Europe), held in Hong Kong, three contentious issues appeared on the agenda:

1. Conflict over sales to European customers.

2. Lack of information about ES (Europe) activities.

3. Interference from Hong Kong in ES (Europe) business.

George Corner complained that ES (Europe) was facing competition in Germany and France from its own parent company. 'Customers are telling us,' he said, 'that they already had information about our products and had placed orders with ES (Hong Kong), believing that was us.' Peter Green said that some of their major corporate customers in China had European operations and placed orders for them. Bill Watford said that as long as the sales were made by the group, surely it did not matter. Geoffrey Corner responded that it certainly did matter: 'members of my family own 40 per cent of ES (Europe) and our dividends and the executives' remuneration depend on ES (Europe) profits and they depend on the sales made by that company'.

Bill Watford said he had heard that ES (Europe) had taken on some new products that might be useful for ES (Hong Kong). But he felt the need for more information. 'There's a lack of transparency,' he said. Elizabeth Corner replied that there was no secrecy about their products: 'they're all described on our website'.

George Corner raised the issue of what he called 'meddling from Hong Kong in the affairs of ES (Europe)'. 'Staff from Hong Kong have visited to give us advice on marketing, systems development, and employee contracts,' he said. 'We did not ask for this support. We don't need it; and then they send us a bill for their travel expenses.' Bill Watford pointed out that ES (Europe) was a subsidiary of ES (Hong Kong). 'But not a wholly-owned subsidiary,' replied Geoffrey Corner. Elizabeth Corner said that she was chief executive of ES (Europe) and if she needed help she would ask for it. 'But otherwise staff from ES (Hong Kong) should not attempt to micro-manage my company.'

Discussion questions

1. How would you resolve the problem of prospective clients of ES (Europe) placing orders with ES (Hong Kong)?

2. How might the perceived problem of lack of transparency be overcome?

3. Does ES (Hong Hong) have the right to get involved in the management of ES (Europe)? How might the problem perceived by Elizabeth Corner of 'micro-management' be overcome?

 Case study 7.2   Li & Fung Ltd supply chain code of conduct

Li & Fung is incorporated in Bermuda and listed in Hong Kong. Its turnover in 2013 was over US$9 billion, producing a margin of around 15 per cent. The company partners with international brand owners and retailers around the world to optimize its supply chain management. Li & Fung Ltd is the parent of a group of companies which operate an extensive network offering logistics solutions including warehousing, transport, repacking, customs brokerage, freight forwarding, hubbing, and other value-added services.

The group believes that its:

> reputation capital is built on long-established standards of ethics in conducting business. Guidelines of the Group's core business ethical practices as endorsed by the Board are set out in the Company's Code of Conduct and Business Ethics for all Directors and staff. All the newly joined staff are briefed and requested to acknowledge their understanding of the Code.[4]

Supply chain responsibility

Li & Fung has developed a supplier code of conduct to be observed by its approved suppliers around the globe. The code is a set of standards based on local and national laws and regulations, and International Labour Organization core conventions. A copy of the code is available at its corporate website (www.lifung.com).

The group employs dedicated compliance staff worldwide to conduct supplier evaluations and to monitor compliance with the code among the suppliers that produce its customers' merchandise. The group's vendor compliance (VC) division is organized independently of its sourcing/merchandising divisions and focuses on improving suppliers' labour, health and safety, environmental, and security standards. The VC division conducts evaluations of approved suppliers on a routine and systematic basis in accordance with industry-defined and customers' specific audit standards, protocols, and methodologies. The scope of an evaluation includes an opening meeting, site inspection, employee and management interview, document review, reporting, and closing meeting.

Li & Fung also provides systematic training both internally to its employees and externally to its suppliers to equip them with awareness, knowledge, and the necessary skills and tools to understand and meet compliance requirements. In 2009, the company continued supplier training and education

[4] Li & Fung Limited, Annual Report 2009. Available at: www.lifung.com/wp-content/uploads/2010/03/ar2009_08.pdf.

efforts, expanding the scope to include additional focus areas of energy efficiency, water pollution prevention, and cleaner production.

Environmental protection

Li & Fung has further enhanced its supplier environmental programmes and initiatives aimed at resource conservation, environmental protection, and product stewardship. The group enforced its customers' environmental purchasing policies with respect to eco-friendly materials, package waste minimization, and product stewardship. The company also took an active role in supporting its customers in innovating and developing new tools and systems to support their sustainability programmes. By adopting and promoting environmental considerations as an integral part of its business activities, the group equates the environment with its other critical business considerations such as compliance, quality, and value.

Li & Fung is a component of the Dow Jones Sustainability World Indexes, the world's first global indexes tracking the performance of companies worldwide in the three main dimensions of corporate sustainability: social, economic, and environmental responsibilities. Li & Fung has also been included as a constituent member in the FTSE4Good Index Series from FTSE Group (UK), recognizing Li & Fung's commitment to high corporate social responsibility standards.

Discussion questions

1. Use the company's website to answer the questions:

   What is the structure of the Li & Fung board?

   What board committees does the board have?

   Who are the members and how often do they meet?

   What is the remuneration policy for non-executive directors?

2. What are the key elements of the supplier code of conduct?

3. If you were advising the main directors of Li & Fung, where would you recommend that strategy was formulated and policies made?

Self-test questions

1. Define 'strategy' formulation.
2. What is a mission statement?
3. Why might long-range planning not be a useful tool for strategy formulation?
4. What are the five forces in the 'five forces' model?
5. What is resource-based strategic theory?
6. What are corporate policies?
7. Name some management control systems that can be used by directors to monitor management performance.

8. What is sub-optimization?

9. To whom is a board accountable?

10. What is exception reporting?

 For suggested answers to these self-test questions visit the online resources at: **www.oup.com/uk/tricker4e/**

Projects and exercises

1. Review the mission statements of leading companies, including those listed earlier in this chapter and others found on company websites.

    - Do you think that they really add anything to the strategy formulation process?
    - Is there a danger that they could become merely part of the public relations effort of an organization?
    - If so, how could this be avoided?
    - Do you think that they contribute to corporate culture and the creation of a common approach to management decision-making?

2. Undertake a strategic assessment of an organization to which you have access. Use both SWOT analysis and a review of the competitive strategic environment of the entity. Prepare a report/presentation for the governing body of that organization.

3. Review the management control systems and the reporting to the board for an organization to which you have access.

4. Identify the strategy formulation, policy-making, executive monitoring, and supervision and accountability activities in other organizations with which you are familiar or from which you can obtain information.

References and further reading

Abrahams, Jeffrey (1999) *The Mission Statement Book: 301 Corporate Mission Statements from America's Top Companies*. Ten Speed Press, Berkeley, CA.

Faulkner, David O. (ed.) (2006) *The Oxford Handbook of Strategy*. Oxford University Press, Oxford.

FRC (2011) Guidance on Board Effectiveness, Financial Reporting Council, London.

FRC (2012) Guidance to Audit Committees, Financial Reporting Council, London.

Hartman, Laura P. and Joseph R. Desjardins (2013) *Business Ethics: Decision-Making for Personal Integrity & Social Responsibility*. 2nd edn, McGraw-Hill, New York.

Kakabadse, Andrew and Nada Kakabadse (2007) *Leading the Board*. Palgrave Macmillan, Basingstoke.

Knowdl, Jeremy (2008) *Business Strategy: A Guide to Effective Decision Making*. Economist/Profile Books, London.

McNulty, T. J. and P. Stiles (2003) *Creating Accountability within the Board: The Work of the Non-executive Director*. Department for Trade and Industry, London.

NACD (2006) Role of the Board on Corporate Strategy: Report of a NACD Blue Ribbon Commission, National Association of Corporate Directors, Washington, DC.

Solomon, Jill ([2004] 2013). *Corporate Governance and Accountability*. 4th edn, Wiley, London.

Steinberg, Richard M. (2000) Corporate Governance and the Board: What Works Best. Internal Auditors Research Foundation, Lake Mary, FL.

Tarantino, Anthony (2007) *Manager's Guide to Compliance: Sarbanes-Oxley, COSO, ERM, COBIT, IFRS, BASEL II, OMB's A-123, ASX 10, OECD Principles,* *Turnbull Guidance, Best Practices, and Case Studies.* Wiley, New York.

Useful websites

www.frc.org.uk/

UK corporate reporting regulator.

www.sec.gov/

The US corporate reporting regulator.

On writing a mission statement:

www.bplans.com/dp/missionstatement.cfm

Explaining mission statements:

http://myphliputil.pearsoncmg.com/student/bp_turban_introec_1/MissStmt.html

More on SWOT analysis:

mindtools.com/pages/article/newTMC_05.htm

ICSA on board committees:

www.icsa.org.uk/about-icsa/latest-from-icsa/article/icsa-publishes-new-terms-of-reference?c=1

Chinese General Sun Tzu on the Art of War:

http://acc6.its.brooklyn.cuny.edu/~phalsall/texts/artofwar.html

Examples of board committees:

www.ubm.com/ubm/governance/committees

www.nationalgrid.com/corporate/About+Us/CorporateGovernance

www.hsbc.com/1/2/investor-relations/corporate-governance/board-committees

www.scottishfriendly.co.uk/members/board-committee-terms.html

www.icsa.org.uk/about-icsa/latest-from-icsa/article/icsa-publishes-new-terms-of-reference?c=1

www.huskyenergy.com/abouthusky/corporategovernance/committeecharters/corporategovernancecharter.asp

8

The Governance of Corporate Risk

 Learning Outcomes

This chapter enables us to:

- Appreciate corporate risk.
- Understand enterprise risk management.
- Recognize the board's responsibility for enterprise risk management.
- Consider risk identification, assessment, evaluation, control.
- Review risk management information systems.
- Compare risk strategies.

What is corporate risk?

Many of the early corporate governance codes including the Cadbury Report (1992) had little to say about the board's responsibility for risk. The Cadbury Report mentioned risk only in the context of boards' responsibility for avoiding financial fraud, although, in fairness, Sir Adrian Cadbury always emphasized that his report was about the financial aspects of corporate governance and did not address the entire subject. The global financial crisis in 2008 drew attention to the need for boards to recognize the significance of risk and their responsibility for risk assessment and management. For some boards, this was a new experience.

Corporate risk involves the gain or loss that might be incurred by an uncertain future event. It involves a statistical concept—the probability of an event occurring and its possible effect. A value can often be put on a risk, even though within wide limits in some cases. In a corporate entity, risk can arise at every decision-making level:

- *strategic risk*—for example the risk of an unexpected hostile takeover bid, or the effects of Britain leaving the European Union, or the devaluation of a currency in which the enterprise holds a significant interest;
- *managerial risk* reflects hazards that occur from the organization's activities; for example, product liability, third-party risks, the risk of a fire that destroys production capacity, or the need to recall faulty product, or a cyber-attack that causes the loss of financial data;
- *operational risk*—such as the injury of an employee while at work, a traffic accident involving a company vehicle, or theft of spare parts.

Some events can involve risks at all three levels—for example the loss of the entire electronic support at British Airways (see Case study 8.2) when operationally passengers could not be boarded, managerially flight plans had to be abandoned, and strategically the long-term reputation of the company suffered.

Critical strategic risk, though sometimes difficult to imagine, can be catastrophic. Consider the following examples:

1. At Enron, the board failed to understand that the company had moved beyond being a supplier of energy to become a business trading in financial derivatives (see Case study 1.2). In effect, Enron had become a financial institution with a quite different risk profile. Moreover, the outside directors seemed to be unaware of the high risks that their executive directors were taking.

2. The Toyota Company developed a worldwide reputation for growth based on innovation and quality. The board built up a highly successful company using tight, Japan-centred management oversight and control. Unfortunately, the directors failed to foresee the risks when they expanded the company's supply chains and manufacturing locations around the world. The price they paid was massive product recalls of entire ranges of automobiles with problem brakes, steering, and electronics. The financial cost to the company was heavy; the effect on its reputation was worse.

3. None of the non-executive directors at the British Northern Rock bank were bankers. The chairman was a zoologist. The executive directors, placing more emphasis on revenue generation than risk management, traded in sub-prime mortgage products. The board failed to appreciate the risks involved and the business had to be bailed out by the British government and the company nationalized (see Case study 5.2).

4. The board of BP PLC faced a strategic catastrophe when the collapse of the Deepwater Horizon oil rig led to massive pollution in the Gulf of Mexico. The disaster, which had been treated as operational or managerial risk by the board, had political and economic impacts that more than halved the company's market value and even put its survival at risk (see Case study 8.1).

Some risks, such as accident, theft, or loss of profits following a fire can be insured against; or the organization can decide to carry the risk itself. Other risks can be avoided by deciding not to proceed with that strategy, such as entering a joint venture in China or investing in a particular project. But some risks have to be taken: that is the nature of business enterprise. The vital thing is that the board recognizes the risk, assesses its significance, and decides that the risk fits its risk profile.

Frameworks for enterprise risk management

AON,[1] an international insurance group, suggested that the global financial crisis had significantly increased board-level awareness of the need to manage and leverage risk. The company identified the following hallmarks of advanced enterprise risk management (ERM):

- board-level commitment to ERM as a critical framework for successful decision-making and for driving value;
- the involvement of all stakeholders in the development of risk management strategy and policy-setting;

[1] The author acknowledges the insights into risk management he gained when working with AON as a consultant.

- a move from focusing on risk avoidance and mitigation to leveraging risk and risk management options to extract business value.

In the light of the global financial crisis, the Steering Group on Corporate Governance of the Organisation for Economic Co-operation and Development (OECD) re-examined the adequacy of its corporate governance principles. The Group concluded that the board's responsibility for defining strategy and risk appetite needed to be extended, because in some important cases the risk management system was not compatible with a company's strategy and risk appetite. Building on the OECD Principles, the report proposed that it is good practice for:

- the risk management function to report directly to the board;
- the risk management function to consider any risks arising directly from the compensation and incentive systems in place;
- the effectiveness of the risk assessment and management process to be monitored and the results disclosed, noting that experience with such disclosures up to that point had not been good.

In the United States, the Committee of Sponsoring Organizations (COSO) of the Treadway Commission pioneered the development of ERM, emphasizing the significance of the board's involvement. In 2004 COSO provided an integrated framework for ERM, building on the 2002 Sarbanes-Oxley Act. It explained that:

> [e]nterprise risk management is a process affected by the entity's board of directors, management, and other personnel, applied in strategy setting and across the enterprise, designed to identify potential events that may affect the entity, and manage risk so that it is within the risk appetite, to provide reasonable assurance regarding the achievement of objectives. The challenge facing boards is how to oversee the organization's enterprise-wide risk management effectively in a way that balances managing risks while adding value to the organization. An entity's board of directors plays a critical role in overseeing an enterprise-wide approach to risk management.

COSO's Enterprise Risk Management: Integrated Framework highlights four areas that contribute to board oversight of enterprise risk management:[2]

- understanding the entity's risk philosophy and concurring with the entity's risk appetite;
- knowing the extent to which management has established effective enterprise risk management of the organization;
- reviewing the entity's portfolio of risk and considering it against the entity's risk appetite;
- being apprised of the most significant risks and of whether management is responding appropriately.

The New York Stock Exchange's listing rules require the audit committees of listed corporations to explain their risk assessment and management policies.

In the UK, the 1999 Turnbull Report drew attention to the importance of board-level risk assessment. The UK Corporate Governance Code,[3] previously the UK Combined Code,

[2] An executive summary of COSO's Enterprise Risk Management: Integrated Framework providing an overview of the key principles is available online at www.coso.org

[3] The 2016 Corporate Governance code and the detail of the 2017/18 consultation can be found at www.frc.org.uk/directors/corporate-governance-and-stewardship/uk-corporate-governance-code

includes principles on boards' responsibility for risk management, calling for an integrated approach to ERM. The Financial Review Council (FRC) considered the likely effect of the global financial crisis on the governance of companies, but failed to find evidence of serious failings in the governance of British business, outside the banking sector.

In 2010, the International Corporate Governance Network (ICGN) enhanced its Global Corporate Governance Principles with a set of Corporate Risk Oversight Guidelines.[4] The Guidelines emphasize that:

- the risk oversight process begins with the board;
- corporate management is responsible for developing and executing an enterprise's strategic and routine operational risk programme;
- shareholders, directly or through designated agents, have a responsibility to assess and monitor the effectiveness of boards in overseeing risk at the companies in which they invest:

> Strategy, risk tolerance, and risk are inseparable and should be connected in all discussions in the board or supervisory board. Capital allocation and capital structure should be visibly aligned with strategy and risk tolerance. The board should hold management accountable for developing a strategy that correlates with the risk tolerance of the organization.

In 2012, the FRC required listed companies to disclose in their annual report the company's 'principal risks'. In a guidance note it suggested that 'the principal risks should be disclosed and described irrespective of how they are classified or whether they result from strategic decision, operations, organization or behaviour or from external factors over which the board may have little or no direct control'.

The World Economic Forum risk survey

Each year, 900 members of the World Economic Forum (WEF), drawn from business, academia, civil society, and the public, respond to a Global Risks Perception Survey.

The survey asks respondents to consider 30 global risks categorized as societal, technological, economic, environmental, or geopolitical, over a ten-year time horizon.

The 2018 survey identified environmental and technological risks as likely to rise, and geopolitical and societal risks overall as stable but remaining high, while economic risks were perceived as low in terms both of likelihood and of impact. Extreme weather events were thought to be highly likely. As well as major natural catastrophes, the survey found that large-scale cyber-attacks and data fraud, ranking third in both significance and likelihood, and large-scale involuntary migration were of significant concern.

Although economic risk ranked relatively low in the survey, that does seem somewhat complacent given the trade barriers erected by President Trump in 2018 and the possibility of another global financial crisis sometime in the next decade. However, 93 per cent of respondents expected a worsening of political and economic confrontations/frictions between major powers, and nearly 80 per cent expressed concern about state-on-state military conflict or incursion.

Although companies may feel they can do little to influence such global concerns, they do need to recognize the potential risks as they make their longer-term strategic investment plans.

---

[4] International Corporate Governance Network: ICGN Corporate Risk Oversight Guidelines, ICGN, 16 Park Crescent, London, W1B 1AH, UK, September 2010.

The board's responsibility for enterprise risk management

Running a business, indeed running almost every enterprise, involves risk. Risk can only be avoided by choosing to do nothing—and even then unexpected events can occur. In many business situations, as is well known, the greater the risk, the greater the potential return to the enterprise. The challenge to boards is to balance risk with acceptable reward. In other words, to understand the exposure of their companies to risk, to determine how those risks are faced, and to ensure that they are handled appropriately.

Corporate governance involves creating business value while managing risk. Risk management, not risk minimization, should be the theme. Boards have a specific and vital responsibility to recognize, understand, and accept the risk profile inherent in their corporate strategies, what some people call 'approving the company's risk appetite'.

Every board has a duty to ensure that:

- the corporate risk profile is recognized;
- policies are established throughout the organization that reflect that profile;
- significant risks facing its company are recognized;
- risk assessment systems exist and are effective throughout the organization;
- risk evaluation procedures are developed and operational;
- risk monitoring systems are robust, efficient, and effective;
- business continuity strategies and risk management policies exist, are regularly updated, and are applied in practice.

Some boards include corporate risk assessment in the mandate of the board audit committee. However, audit committees can be orientated towards the past, involved with audit outcomes and approving accountability information for publication, whereas risk assessment needs a proactive, forward-looking orientation.

Consequently, other boards have decided to create a risk assessment or risk management committee as a distinct standing committee of the board. Such a committee might have four or five members, wholly or mainly INEDs with appropriate business experience. Initially, when a company is building its risk management systems, the committee might meet quite frequently, but then two or three times a year, reporting to the board as a whole. Members of senior management and external experts in risk are likely to be invited to attend to advise the committee.

Some corporate governance codes and stock exchanges' listing rules require companies to report on their risk management procedures.

Directors need to understand where value is added within their business, at which points the company is critically exposed to risk, and where the most sensitive areas are in which the very survival of the business could be threatened. Boards need to face up to those risks and to develop relevant risk strategies and policies. Such responsibilities call for a formal system to ensure that risk is properly assessed and considered at board level and then professionally managed throughout the company.

Sophisticated investors around the world focus on the nature and extent of risk in the companies and industries in which they invest. Companies that are recognized as having professional ERM and transparent risk reporting are respected. Their shares can command a premium over those of competitors, and their overall cost of capital is likely to be lower.

An alternative approach is for the board to form a management-based risk management group, perhaps including the CEO, the CFO, profit-responsible division or unit heads, and the responsible risk management executive(s). External experts could also be invited to advise the group. A management-based risk management group needs to take a strategic view of corporate risk and to avoid adopting a purely financial view. In other words, the group needs to see the enterprise in the context of its overall risk profile, not only from a financial perspective. A management-based risk group might typically report to the CEO or CFO, but it is essential that its work is reviewed and approved at board level. Of course, it is possible that a company might decide to have both a board-level risk management committee and a management-based group reporting to it.

Many major companies have specialist risk managers to oversee the company-wide risk assessment systems and procedures, who can advise the board on risk issues. The chief risk officer (CRO) is an increasingly important figure in many companies, just as the global head of risk is in international banks. The risk management committee will typically agree the job description, appoint, and monitor the CRO, who is then secretary to that committee.

The global financial crisis, which resulted in the collapse of financial institutions and the need for government support in a number of countries, also led to the re-evaluation of the governance of risk. In some banks, the power of financial risk-takers was rebalanced in favour of the CRO and the risk assessment function. Goldman Sachs achieves a balance between risk-taking traders and potentially risk-averse risk officers by moving traders into risk management functions as part of their career progression although in other institutions the CRO remains little more than a compliance officer.

The issue of risk management is particularly significant in the case of financial institutions. Indeed in essence, their entire business involves the management of risk. This was confirmed in a report by the Basel Committee on Banking Supervision, widely known as Basel II:[5] '[t]he bank's board of directors has a responsibility for setting the board's tolerance for risks'.

Favourable capital adequacy decisions need to demonstrate that the bank's 'board of directors and senior management, as appropriate, are actively involved in the oversight of the operational risk management framework'. According to the report, a risk policy committee to fulfil this requirement should have its own written charter, board representation with at least three independent directors with the requisite skills and knowledge to oversee risk management, and a chair appointed by the whole board. Basel III has since been developed as an internationally agreed set of measures by the Basel Committee on Banking Supervision in response to the financial crisis of 2007–9. The measures aim to strengthen the regulation, supervision, and risk management of banks.

Unfortunately, in some companies, risk management issues seldom reach board level. The management of risk is piecemeal and undertaken at the business unit level—sometimes known as a 'silo' or 'bucket' approach, with each part of the organization standing on its own base. Responsibility for risk management is then located in middle management, with managers insuring the business against the classic risks of fire, theft, and accident. This orientation is likely to be operational rather than strategic, and to have more to do with cost reduction, searching for the cheapest cover available, than with conscientious risk assessment. Moreover, the middle manager can become a bottleneck, even a block, between the board and its responsibility for overall strategic risk assessment and management.

[5] 'International Convergence of Capital Measurement and Capital Standards: A Revised Framework' (2007). Basel Committee on Banking Supervision (Basel II). www.bis.org/publ/bcbs128.htm

Identifying types of risk

As we have already seen, in every organization risk arises at various levels:

- *corporate strategic risks*—exposure to threats from outside the organization;
- *management-level risks*—exposure to risks arising from the firm's activities;
- *operational risks*—exposure to hazards within the enterprise.

Security of corporate information has emerged as a vital area of risk. Once a technical issue at the operational level, boards need to involve information technology expertise in every major decision at the managerial and strategic levels. Hackers can enter corporate systems through personal information devices that employees use to access corporate systems, through malware in external links such as credit card payment systems and video-conferencing equipment, even external access to printers, thermostat controls, and vending machines. Cyber-attack has become a significant risk. Corporate Governance in Action 8.1 is an extract from the risk management policy handbook of a financial institution, showing the risks recognized at strategic, managerial, and operational levels.

Corporate Governance in Action 8.1   An approach to corporate risk—the Sage Group PLC

Sage is a leading supplier of business management software and services to 6.3 million customers worldwide. Its annual report contains a detailed corporate risk report, with an analysis of each risk, the potential impact, and the factors considered by the company to mitigate that risk.

Principal risks to achieving business objectives and maintaining services to customers need to be managed. Sage's risk management strategy is therefore to support the successful running of the business by identifying and managing risks to an acceptable level, and delivering assurances on this (see Figure 8.1).

Figure 8.1 Risk management responsibilities and processes

For more detail on corporate risk and the Sage Group: www.sage.com/company/about-sage/corporate-governance/corporate-risk. The 2017 annual report includes a section on corporate governance and risk: www.sage.com/corporate/investors/annual-report/

One approach to identifying significant risk is to consider what circumstances or events could affect the key drivers of business value and cause planned performance to fail to meet expected outcomes. A board, having recognized potential catastrophic events that could put the very survival of the firm at risk, needs to have a business continuity strategy to respond to such exposure.

Corporate Governance in Action 8.2   Levels of risk management policy in a London finance house

The main board of a significant financial institution has developed risk management strategies and policies that cover all levels of the organization, from externally generated risks to in-house hazards. The board regularly discusses its risk management policies at each level. The following contents page from its risk management manual lists the areas of responsibility recognized by the risk assessment programme:

External strategic threats

- Competitors' activities;
- customers' activities;
- stock and finance markets hazards;
- government and regulator activities;
- criminal activity;
- loss of electronic communication and hacking of databases;
- terrorism or politically activated actions;
- economic, political, or social events;
- suppliers' activities;
- other external events, hazards, or risks.

Internal strategic and management-level risks

- Board-level strategic failings;
- lack of board-level security;
- management weaknesses;
- shortages of skilled, experienced staff;
- management-level fraud or corruption.

Operational risks and hazards (for each risk management department or unit)

- Fire, explosion, flood;
- loss of power (e.g. inability to carry out trades);
- information technology (IT) systems malfunction, loss or theft of vital data;
- poor cyber-security;
- shortages of staff (e.g. staff turnover, illness, strike, poaching);
- errors in trades (unintentional mistakes);

- deals made by staff beyond their limits, contrary to trading policies;
- fraud and misfeasance (i.e. deliberate actions by traders);
- theft;
- misuse of company information, equipment, systems, or software;
- other events, risks, or hazards.

The extracts from the risk assessment system of a global pharmaceutical company in Corporate Governance in Action 8.3 give an insight into the types of strategic risk that could have catastrophic outcomes. Much of the literature on risk management focuses on risk at the operational level, for example on health and safety hazards to employees, disease risks in hospitals, and waste management hazards in public health. But contemporary thinking about risk recognizes that risk management policies at the operational level are not enough. An enterprise is more likely to fail disastrously from risks at management or strategic levels. Reputational risk, the damage to corporate reputation arising from a strategic event such as a product failure that leads to the loss of life, a massive environmental disaster, or the exposure of a bribery scandal, can be more damaging to profitability and shareholder value in the long term than the immediate direct costs. Even so, a 2013 study, conducted in association with the New York Stock Exchange, found that 25 per cent of board-level respondents felt that risk was given insufficient focus in their board meetings and 26 per cent felt that risk information was received too late for thorough review.

Corporate Governance in Action 8.3   Strategic-level risk assessment policies in an international pharmaceutical company

The main board of this group has agreed a set of risk assessment policies, based on information from a comprehensive and continuous risk management system. The detail runs to many pages, but the following extract indicates the types of risk reviewed at the strategic level.

Strategic-level risks

Marketing area

Competitors

- New entrants into significant products or markets;
- change of ownership of competitors (e.g. mergers);
- change of competitors' distribution strategy;
- new research breakthroughs;
- change of pricing/distribution strategies;
- expansion into new markets (country or type);
- competitors change manufacturing technology.

Customers

- Cost of product recall (financial and reputational);

- adopting substitute products (e.g. generics);

- collapse or bankruptcy of major customer;

- change of ownership of main distributor;

- catastrophic failure of our product in use;

- legal actions for damages;

- alleged patent or copyright infringement.

Governmental

- New pharmacological control laws;

- new environmental or hazard-limitation laws;

- constraints on manufacturing or delivery processes;

- monopoly, anti-trust, or pricing inquiries;

- cost-cutting by government (e.g. UK NHS);

- political threats to operations in overseas countries.

Finance area

Predators

- Hostile takeover approaches;

- acquisition strategies of private equity firms.

Sources of finance

- Recall of debt capital (e.g. bankruptcy of lender);

- change of ownership resulting in new policies.

Shareholders

- Share price collapse following media revelations;

- reputational loss following an adverse law case.

Information technology area

- E-links with customers, suppliers, and shareholders;

- hacking of systems for fraud, spying, or mischief.

Management and operational-level risks are also covered by this risk assessment system.

When one board chair suggested that each director should identify five critical risks that would prove fatal to the achievement of the business plan if they occurred, many of the directors were surprised at the nature and the extent of risks they had not even considered. Such an exercise, of course, leads to the development of strategies and policies to handle the risks. The possibility of the business failing seldom occurs to directors, but business continuity can become a vital issue if a catastrophe occurs.

Disclosures from illegal hacking have heightened awareness in some boardrooms of the importance of IT controls, internal procedures, and a corporate culture that sets strict standards on the use of email, the world-wide-web, and social media to reduce the risk of the loss of trade secrets, the exposure of secret financial negotiations, or the disclosure of confidential market data. The speed of modern media can turn an exposed issue into massive reputational loss unless boards have appropriate policies and plans ready to meet such eventualities.

Controlling risk

The analysis of risk in an organization involves a number of iterative phases:

- risk recognition;
- risk assessment;
- risk evaluation;
- risk management policies;
- risk monitoring.

The basic elements of the risk analysis process are shown in Figure 8.2.

Figure 8.2 The risk analysis and management process

Some countries, including Australia, the United States, and the United Kingdom, have created standards for risk management under the auspices of the International Organization for Standardization (ISO).[6] The Business Continuity Institute also offers benchmarks and evaluation criteria (see www.thebci.org).

The Institute of Chartered Accountants in England and Wales (ICAEW) compiled a list of benefits from the introduction of sound governance and risk management that included:

- greater likelihood of achieving objectives;
- higher share price in the long term;
- greater likelihood of successful change initiatives;
- lower cost of capital;
- early movement into new business areas;
- improved use of insurance;
- reduction in the cost of remedial work;
- achievement of competitive advantage;
- less business interruption;
- achievement of compliance/regulatory targets.

Some commentators suggest that good corporate governance with professional risk management can reduce insurance costs. This is not necessarily true, but good corporate governance can protect against excessive penalties and improve the ability to get cover, even against substantial risks.

In Chapter 2, we introduced the basic quadrant of board performance and conformance activities (see Figure 8.3). The components of the risk analysis process, depicted above, can be mapped onto this quadrant (as in Figure 8.4).

Figure 8.3 Framework for analysing board activities

[6] International Organization for Standardization—Risk management (ISO 31000) www.iso.org/iso-31000-risk-management.html

Figure 8.4 Framework showing board risk analysis and management

Risk recognition and assessment

Although some threats that could significantly harm a business may be obvious and easily guarded against, other risks can be hard to recognize. Unless they have occurred before, there will be no previous experience in the organization. Moreover, other companies tend to hide bad news, thus increasing the underestimation of potential risks.

Threats, such as those caused by critical changes in competitors' strategies, serious loss of business through criminal activity, disgruntled employees' actions or terrorist threats, kidnap or other loss of top executives, or the effects of natural disaster, for example, may be difficult to imagine, yet could prove to be catastrophic. Major business interruption—even challenges to business continuity—can come from unexpected occurrences.

How do firms go about the task of identifying risk at every level? The vital element in corporate risk recognition is the creation of a corporate culture that places risk at the centre of thinking throughout the organization. This can be achieved only with motivation from the top: from the chair and the board. In-house workshops and seminars are used by some to generate insights. External experts may be able to offer experience and an independent view. The advice of INEDs can also be valuable. There are also a number of risk assessment and risk management tools available. Many are qualitative in nature; others seek to add an element of quantification; some involve computerized data collection and analysis. The following approaches show the range of options.

A simple tabular approach

The organization is divided into a series of risk analysis centres, which may well reflect its structure and its management control systems. Executives in each risk analysis centre identify and chart the risks under the following headings:

Nature of risk or hazard	Likely effects and outcome	Likelihood of event occurring	Risk management policy response

The documentation for the risk analysis programme should contain guidance to staff on the range of risks to be covered, including likely effects or outcomes of each occurrence. It is important that the risk analysis is conducted in each part of the organization and at every level. Experience shows that the initial risk assessment report will trigger further ideas and insights, which improve the subsequent risk assessment. The simple narrative table can be turned into a matrix by including estimated costs and an estimated probability of the uncertain risk or hazard occurring. A potential drawback of this approach is that a managerial focus might fail to identify strategic risks.

A questionnaire designed to identify risks and hazards

If this approach is used throughout the organization, insights into risk can be generated in every part of an organization and at every level. A benefit of this approach is standardization of responses throughout the organization. This format can also be used to document compliance and non-compliance with risk management policies. An elaboration of the questionnaire approach is to include multiple-choice responses, as well as to invite a narrative description.

Mind mapping

This involves a visual approach to recognizing risk factors, plotting their interrelationships, and then deriving the possible implications. Users of this method require some training and skill in the methodology. Benefits can include an appreciation of the relationships between risks and the identification of different risk elements from those generated by tabulation or questionnaire.

Risk benchmarking by industry, country, or against other companies

This methodology starts with a list of possible risks or hazards as the basis for developing the risk profile of the subject company. The list can identify risks related to the type of company, its industry, and locations of operation.

Software programs and systems

IT-based solutions to risk analysis and management are used by many organizations. These can provide online access to the identification and reporting of risks. Proprietary programs and systems are available from software houses, consulting firms, and companies in the insurance industry. Some of these programs provide a risk management information system, which link risk recognition and assessment, risk evaluation, and ERM policies, and can also be linked to claims management systems.

Information on strategic-level risks can be generated as part of an on-going strategic review, as discussed in Chapter 7. The firm's strategy formulation process, using tools such as SWOT analysis, Porter's 'five forces' analysis, or some other analytical methodology, can also generate information about potential risk. This can be used to evaluate possible effects, should they happen, estimate the likelihood that they would occur, and decide the suitable policy response. This information can then be incorporated into the strategic-level risk management policies approved by the board.

Experience has shown that a successful risk recognition and assessment programme has a number of critical success factors, including:

- sponsorship and oversight at board level;
- top management commitment;
- involvement throughout all levels of management and in all parts of the enterprise;
- company-wide definition of procedures, documentation, and reporting;
- identification of risk management centres throughout the organization;
- definition of responsibilities for identifying and recommending risk responses;
- risk management centres given appropriate responsibility;
- areas of risk carefully defined and bounded, each one limited in scope;
- involvement of business and technical experts with relevant risk assessment experience;
- documentation at all stages, regularly updated and building on experience;
- defined authentication and approval, confidentiality levels, access control, availability, audit, and overall administration responsibilities;
- creation of a risk-awareness, not risk-avoidance, attitude throughout the organization;
- ensuring participation by identifying the 'ownership' of risks throughout the organization;
- vital board-level leadership and approval of risk management policies.

A risk assessment programme not only enables firms to identify risks and to develop appropriate risk management policies, but it also supports on-going business activities by causing staff to recognize risks and thus avoid them, by enabling directors to appreciate the nature and extent of their risk profiles and to make appropriate judgements, and finally by enabling the firm to report confidently to shareholders and other stakeholders that corporate risks are being well managed.

Risk evaluation

The extent of any risk (R) is a function of the magnitude of the potential cost or loss (L) and the probability (p) that the uncertain future event will occur. Expressed mathematically:

a specific risk $R_i = L_i\, p(L)i$ and the firm's total risk exposure $R\ (\text{total}) = \sum L_i\, p(L_i)$

Unfortunately, both the cost and the probability of some events can often be difficult to assess. Some costs, such as the loss of customer confidence should a product fail, the loss of reputation following a financial or executive scandal, or the effect on the cost of capital following the lowering of a credit rating, can be difficult to estimate. Reliable and current data often preclude an exact estimate, but broad estimates, within ranges, do need to be made.

Similarly, the probability of a risk occurring can be problematical. But a view needs to be taken. The judgement of knowledgeable individuals, including INEDs, can be useful. Careful documentation is important and the resultant policy needs to be well written, so that

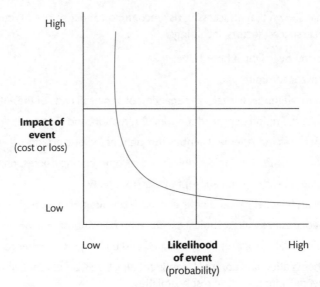

Figure 8.5 **Risk mapping**

subsequent action can be taken to ensure that the policy is being followed and reviewed when necessary.

A risk that would result in a high loss, but with a low chance of occurring, may well be treated differently in a firm's risk management policies from one with a lower cost, but greater probability. There is all the more reason, therefore, to identify the existence of a risk or hazard in the first place, and for management and, ultimately, the board to face up to the reality of the situation. The risk map in Figure 8.5 illustrates the situation, highlighting the importance of board-level involvement in ERM policies.

In the high impact/high likelihood quadrant, the board will want to give a lot of consideration to appropriate policies. For example, the directors might decide to incur considerable expenditure on system redundancy or standby systems, on staff training, on reserves of materials, stock, or finance, or on simulation exercises to test response time and quality. This is the quadrant in which sharing risk through financial instruments or external insurance cover can be of fundamental importance. The board will also want to ensure that it has information systems that monitor such situations and that the company is able to respond quickly to the event.

In the high impact/low likelihood quadrant, the board has the options of taking action to mitigate the impact, assuming the risk, or insuring.

In the low impact/high probability quadrant, the board can take defensive action to limit the impact, but may well decide to carry any further costs itself. Of course, insurance remains an option, but the high probability will produce higher premiums.

In the low impact/low likelihood quadrant, the need for board policies varies from low to insignificant. Control systems to reflect the situation, procedures to respond to it, and some staff training to mitigate adverse effects might be all that are needed.

Risk management information systems

Currently, in some companies, risk management systems are piecemeal and scattered with duplications and errors. Directors in such companies all too often learn of risks once they have become problems. Boards should ensure that they are fully apprised of significant risks so that appropriate business continuity strategies and risk management policies can be put in place ahead of time.

Internationally, the trend is towards centralization of information and risk management responsibility. Such enterprise risk management systems (ERMS) provide information routinely and regularly for management to take executive decisions, and for the board to carry out its monitoring and supervisory function. The ERMS should also generate information to enable the company to communicate externally to auditors, regulators, shareholders, and other legitimate stakeholders, as well as to its insurers and brokers. However, because such systems hold masses of vital information, data protection, confidentiality, and cyber-security are vital. There are a number of so-called 'enterprise governance, risk and compliance platforms' that provide technology-based underpinning for ERMS.

A successful ERM system will provide an information interchange, with links throughout the company to the centre, and also link to brokers and insurers. However, online risk management information systems may contain confidential data on strategic issues. Wrongful access could lead to the loss of valuable corporate information. Security and confidentiality are vital. Rights of access need to be controlled. The right to update information also needs to be secure. Such systems are sometimes built in-house, but increasingly packages are available from specialist firms, for example the Risk Console system from AON Insurance.

Risk strategies

Identifying corporate risk strategies and establishing risk policies are, essentially, board decisions. Board-level strategies that recognize strategic threats to the enterprise are vital, with policies agreed by the board to determine which risk management decisions are reserved to the board. Every board develops a unique risk profile and establishes that board's risk tolerance—that is, the directors' appetite for risks. Detailed work may be delegated to management, but the oversight of risk is a basic element in corporate governance and thus the responsibility of the board. In developing risk policies, a board has to trade off short-term costs against long-term benefits.

In establishing the company's risk policies, every board faces four possible responses to risk:

1. Avoid the risk. Do not commit to the planned action. Abandon the proposed project.

2. Mitigate the risk by making capital investments or incurring on-going expenditure, for example by investing in standby equipment, duplicate/triplicate critical components, staff training, risk policies such as requiring top executives to travel in different cars and planes, or never building on flood plains or in typhoon/hurricane locations.

3. Transfer the risk. Spread the exposure with other parties. Insure against the risk, thereby transferring elements of risk to the insurance company, while recognizing that some risks

may be uninsurable. Create derivative instruments—that is, agreements with financial institutions that transfer risk to third parties. Negotiate forward contracts for the supply of goods and services.

4. Retain the risk. In other words, accept it. Self-insuring is an approach adopted by many governmental organizations. This risk strategy—what some commentators call the firm's 'risk appetite'—needs to be made at board level.

Risk management policies typically involve costs: both capital costs and on-going expenditure, such as the cost of building hardware and software systems into a company's customer order-ing system, to reduce opportunities for a sophisticated hacker to steal information, damage system operations, or perpetrate fraud. Continuing expenditure can include staff and operating expenditure for providing security, on-going training, and updating routines. In determining the overall risk management policy, the board will need to compare the costs of control with the discounted value of the outcome [Li p(L)i] and determine the cost–benefit relationship.

Not only should directors ensure that the firm's risk management policies are in place, but they should also assure themselves that the framework or system for risk management is effective. Induction training and regular updating of directors and senior staff should form part of the firm's risk management programme.

Enterprise risk profiling, risk strategy formulation, and policy-making and risk supervision have now become integral parts of the corporate governance portfolio. Every board has a duty to ensure that risk assessment and management systems are functioning at each level and that appropriate risk management policies are in place. Moreover, regulators increas-ingly require firms to report on the quality of their risk management. Overall, boards that handle risk professionally, as part of their normal corporate governance activities, are able to face increasing risk without making their enterprises riskier.

From relative obscurity in the early days of corporate governance, the board's responsibil-ity for handling risk has come to the fore. It is now recognized as one of the most significant of every board's responsibilities.

Case studies

 Case study 8.1   The BP Deepwater Horizon disaster

On 20 April 2010, the Macondo oil well in the Gulf of Mexico blew out, causing an explosion on its oil rig, Deepwater Horizon. The rig caught fire and sank, killing 11 people, injuring 17, and creating the biggest oil spill in American history, threatening environmental catastrophe. The amount of oil escaping the well was originally estimated by BP to be about 1,000 barrels per day but the US government thought at its peak that it was more than 60,000 barrels per day. The oil slick extended over thousands of square miles and polluted beaches on America's southern coast, destroying fishermen's livelihoods and killing wildlife.

About BP

BP PLC is the UK-based holding company of a group that includes BP Holdings North American Ltd, which has a subsidiary BP North America Inc., the parent company of BP Exploration and Production Inc., which owned the Macondo well.

The Deepwater Horizon oil rig was owned by the Transocean Company, which leased it to BP. The rig had drilled through 18,000 feet of rock below 5,000 feet of water to reach oil. Transocean owned the rig, ran it, and maintained the oil well's blowout preventer, a stack of valves at the well head.

At the time, the board of BP PLC had six British and six American directors,[7] including:

Sir Bill Castell, 63, the senior INED, who was vice chair of the GE Group;

George David, 68, a tycoon who had built up United Technologies Corporation;

Paul Anderson, 65, former chief executive of BHP Billiton;

DeAnne Julius, 61, previously chief economist of Shell and British Airways;

Cynthia Carroll, 53, CEO of the Anglo-American Group.

The disaster and its aftermath

With thousands of barrels of oil pouring uncontrolled out of the well, BP attempted to drill relief wells and put a coffer dam over the well head to pass oil to the surface. Oil washed ashore, where a massive operation was mounted to limit the damage to the shoreline, its industries, and wildlife.

BP blamed Transocean for the failure of the sea-floor blowout preventer, which it alleged was defective. Transocean passed the blame to Halliburton Inc., claiming that the latter was in charge of cement work that was being used to cap the well, sealing it with plugs of cement and drilling mud.

By mid-June, BP PLC's share price had dropped from 655p just before the crisis to 300p. Fitch, a credit-rating agency, downgraded the company to BBB, close to junk bonds. At these prices, commentators raised the spectre of a takeover bid from a foreign competitor.

Anti-BP rage in the United States

A third of America's oil comes from offshore sources, and BP is the biggest operator, with licences to drill auctioned by the US Minerals Management Service (MMS). MMS is not only the licensor, but also the regulator of the industry.

By mid-June, with the well still spewing oil, the crisis took on a political dimension. US President Barack Obama condemned BP, calling it *British* Petroleum, even though the company had changed its name to BP a decade earlier to reflect its global, rather than British, ownership and operations. Obama was facing difficult times politically with his healthcare reforms and forthcoming elections, and used angry rhetoric, saying that he was 'looking for ass to kick ...' and that he would have sacked BP's CEO. UK Prime Minister David Cameron spoke with him, calling for less anti-British rhetoric.

President Obama visited the Gulf four times in six weeks to show his support. Forty-four US senators published a letter demanding that BP suspend its dividend, using the funds to support disaster relief in the Gulf. That would have adversely affected many British pension funds, because the BP dividend contributes £1 in every £7 that pension funds receive from the top 100 British companies. Lord Oakeshott, chairman of the Economic Policy Unit in the UK Department of Business, said it was 'contemptible and illegal to try to bully British savers out of their savings income'. In fact, 40 per cent of BP shareholders were in the USA, and of BP's 83,000 employees, 22,000 were in America, twice as many as worked in Britain.

On 11 June 2010, BP decided to defer payment of its planned dividend to shareholders. The US government further demanded that BP divert funds to pay for the clean-up operation and provide compensation to those whose livelihoods had been affected. BP agreed to set up such a fund. Furious senators questioned the company's executives about the oil-well explosion. There were suggestions

---

[7] For details of the current board members, go to: www.bp.com/managedlistingsection.do?categoryId=9021801&contentId=7040608

that BP's American operations should be put into receivership by the US government so that the government could run the relief operations.

Reputational loss: the second disaster

Immediately after the disaster, the BP board decided that a single person was needed to head the disaster relief efforts, and that would be the Group Chief Executive, Tony Hayward (53). The board felt that having both the chairman and the CEO involved might confuse Americans, who were used to having major companies led by a single chair/CEO.

After earning a PhD in geology, Hayward had worked for BP all his life. In 2007 he had taken over as Group CEO from Lord Browne, whose tenure had been dominated by a strategic widening through acquisition, a financial approach to management control, and some safety lapses. At an early stage, Hayward introduced a new system to evaluate corporate risk.

Hayward's handling of the Gulf disaster was strewn with public relations gaffes. A few days after the explosion he was photographed in cap and sunglasses sailing his yacht off Britain's south coast. He further inflamed public opinion against the company by his flippant remarks and responses in media interviews.

His initial reaction was 'I think the environmental impact of this disaster is likely to be very, very modest'. During a visit to the oil-strewn Gulf coast, he moaned 'I want my life back'. After the event, he commented 'I became the public face (of the disaster) and was demonised and vilified. BP cannot move on in the US with me as its leader ... life isn't fair. Sometimes you step off the pavement and get hit by a bus.'[8]

Where was the chairman?

The board chairman, Carl-Henric Svanberg, Swedish, 58, had only joined BP in January 2010. Just after the Gulf disaster, he went yachting in Thailand with his new partner, Louise Julian. He visited the BP disaster centre in Houston on the way back from his holiday. Faced by TV reporters on his return, he ignored their questions. Shareholders and critics within the company complained at his lack of public profile. They suggested that Svanberg should have camped out in Washington to deal with the political flak, leaving Hayward to handle the practical issues of stopping the leak. Some felt that he should resign. He stated firmly: 'I have no intention of resigning'.

The outcome

On 28 July 2010, Hayward stepped down as CEO, with a golden parachute of his annual £1 million salary and a £10 million pension pot built up during his 28 years with BP. Bob Dudley, born in Mississippi, took over as CEO. One of Hayward's early projects had been the creation of a new safety division for the group with sweeping powers. Staff bonuses would also reflect compliance with safety rules.

On 25 September 2010, BP claimed officially that the well was sealed. Nearly 5 million barrels of oil had been released. BP had incurred huge costs, with more impending from court actions and the possibility of corporate manslaughter charges. But the reputational loss had probably been greater.

In November 2010, a US Presidential Commission cleared BP of cutting corners to boost profits.[9] It found no evidence, its report said, that BP had made conscious decisions to put dollars above safety at the Macondo well. However, it did suggest that there were 'systemic problems in the industry'.

---

[8] www.scotsman.com/news/tony-hayward-pay-off-fury-after-bp-posts-163–11bn-loss-1–818995
[9] Deepwater Horizon BP Gulf of Mexico oil spill, United States Environmental Protection Agency, 2010, www.epa.gov/enforcement/deepwater-horizon-bp-gulf-mexico-oil-spill

Moreover, it identified a failure of management: '[w]ith better management by BP, Halliburton and Transocean would almost certainly have prevented the blowout'.

Transocean, which owned the rig, was charged with negligence and Halliburton, which provided support services, was fined US$200,000, the maximum penalty under the law, for destroying evidence about the spill. Halliburton did offer US$55 million to the National Fish and Wildlife Foundation as a contribution to the damage the spill had caused.

BP's legal battles continued throughout 2013 and 2014. The company's initial response to the catastrophe had been conciliatory, setting up a US$20 billion fund for damages, penalties, and legal costs. But the company seemed unfamiliar with America's litigious culture.

At BP's suggestion, the court in Louisiana had appointed an independent investigator to arbitrate the claims. But when he appeared to see BP as a cash cow, BP called for his claims to be frozen until new controls were imposed. Many of the claims are 'absurd and fictitious', BP told the court, citing a US$357,000 award to a shrimp farmer whose tax returns showed he was unemployed at the time of the oil spill. The court agreed.

BP also sought the court's rejection of a US$7.8 billion deal it had made to compensate individuals and businesses who claimed to have been harmed by the spill, calling for 'proper interpretation of the settlement agreement'. But the court rejected that request. By 2014, BP estimated that the US$7.8 billion had grown to US$9.2 billion. BP's profits for 2013 were 22 per cent down.

BP also filed a fraud suit against a Texan lawyer, representing 40,000 fishermen who claimed to have suffered losses. Many of these claims were 'phantom,' BP said, and included people with social security numbers belonging to dead people and others with no involvement in fishing.

Following the disaster, the US government banned BP from winning federal contracts in the USA, including the supply of fuel to the military. BP took court action to overturn the ban, a decision that was supported officially by the British government.

In April 2014, BP refused to pay the US government £88 million (US$130 million) for studies into the effects of the oil spill on dolphins, oysters, and shrimp. The company complained that they had not been given access to the data and that these studies apparently duplicated earlier work. Facing legal challenges, BP needed information on the revival of wildlife to support their case for lower penalties for environmental damage.

In April 2014, BP took out a full page advertisement in the *New York Times* stating that they had reached an agreement with the federal government that allowed the company once again to bid on new deep-water exploration leases;[10] and that within days they had bid on and won 24 new leases in the Gulf of Mexico. The advert claimed that BP was the largest investor in the Gulf; that they operated four of the largest production hubs in the Gulf—more than any other company—and that BP employed more than 2,300 people in the Gulf as well as supporting tens of thousands of other jobs in the region.

In July 2015, BP agreed to pay an environmental fine of US$18.7 billion to settle legal actions brought by the US Justice Department and the states of Louisiana, Mississippi, Alabama, Texas, and Florida, over the oil spill. The settlement ended all litigation between BP, the states, and the US government, and BP's share price rose after the announcement.

The total cost to BP of the disaster, in fines and claims, was estimated at US$36 billion and BP had to sell assets to meet this cost. Reflecting America's litigious culture, BP faced massive claims for alleged damages and other losses. Many of these were class actions brought by lawyers grouping claims they had sought. Some claims proved fallacious, including a demand for US$5 million from a restaurant worker for loss of earnings. Another claim for US$45,000 was made by Lucy Lu, apparently a deckhand on a fishing trawler,

---

[10] www.bp.com/en_us/bp-us/community/commitment-to-the-gulf-of-mexico.html

but who turned out to be the ship's dog. However, the principal losers were the investors, American and British citizens, and the pension funds and the millions of pensioners they represented.

A narrative of the event and BP's continuing commitment to the Gulf of Mexico can be found on the BP website at: www.bp.com/en_us/bp-us/community/commitment-to-the-gulf-of-mexico.html

Discussion questions

1. BP had a group-wide corporate system to evaluate risk, introduced by Hayward. Why did this not predict the Deepwater Horizon disaster?

2. How might BP have managed the Deepwater Horizon disaster differently to reduce its loss of reputation in the United States?

3. Would the outcome have been different if the roles of board chair and CEO in BP had been combined, as in many large American public companies?

 Case study 8.2   British Airways loses IT

British Airways (BA) used to be called 'the world's favourite airline'. Not any more. On 27 May 2017, a worldwide systems failure grounded all BA flights. Check-in desks at London's Heathrow and Gatwick and other airports around the world were unable to access passenger details. In London 470 flights were cancelled on 27 May and a further 183 the following day, with many more flights stranded around the world. Tens of thousands of passengers were left standing around for hours with no information, until being told to 'come back tomorrow'. BA airport staff seemed unprepared for the huge numbers of stranded passengers. BA websites and inquiry operators had little information, other than that all flights had been cancelled. Passenger baggage piled up and did not reach the owners for days. Compensation claims for delays and lost baggage were estimated at over £100 million. The reputational loss to BA was immeasurable.

Although some immediately thought this must be a cyber-attack, it was not. BA's initial explanation for the systems breakdown was loss of power to servers on the central reservation system. Other systems reliant on access to passenger data, including the flight loading system and the baggage handling system, then shut down.

IT experts suggested that, with such sophisticated systems, BA must have included back-up power supplies. Indeed they had, but it emerged that the power had failed totally because a maintenance worker had turned it off. The back-up systems, a generator, and batteries were working perfectly. Then, once power was restored, efforts to re-boot the systems were bungled.

Some BA ex-employees, who had been laid off as a result of a head office cost-cutting drive, suggested that the heart of the problem was a decision to outsource IT work to an Indian company. 'The BA system is a legacy system that has evolved over generations of equipment and software changes,' they said. 'The inter-relatedness of the systems and the complexity of the data is immense. BA needed people who had grown up with the system. This is not the first time the system has failed this year.'[11] BA denied this suggestion.

[11] *The Economist*, 3 June 2017.

British Airways, once the country's flag-carrier, is now a subsidiary of the International Airline Group (IAG), a Spanish company which also owns Iberia, the Spanish airline. IAG's shares had risen significantly in the previous year and suffered only a small fall following the BA systems saga.

The CEO of IAG, Willie Walsh (who had previously headed BA), did not appear during the crisis, leaving the situation to be handled by BA's CEO, Alex Cruz. They were both criticized for delays in offering explanations or apologies. An official raised a storm by suggesting that passengers would receive full refunds on their tickets, but BA would not pay for the cost of missed connecting flights, alternative travel arrangements, or accommodation.

Subsequently, BA apologized to its customers and commissioned an independent inquiry. The British airlines' regulator, the Civil Aviation Authority, was also called on to examine the case.

At the previous AGM of IAG, shareholders had received a letter from a corporate governance advisory group that 'the board should consider bolstering the IT experience of its non-executive cohort: only one of the serving non-executive directors has IT experience'.

Discussion questions

1. Who was responsible for this debacle?

2. How might such a situation have been avoided?

 Case study 8.3 NHS Foundation Trust—second case study

This is the second in a set of five case studies.

The most significant event since the situation described in the first study (Chapter 4, Case study 4.1) was the unexpected resignation of the chair, Lady Audrey Westwood, owing to her husband's serious illness. On receiving the news, the board met in an emergency session and appointed Roger Evans as chair. The minutes of the first meeting of the Trust that he chaired included the following items:

Appointment of Mr Roger Evans to the chair

Mr Evans had served as a non-executive director of the Trust for four years. The other directors agreed that his life-long experience in business would be valuable to the board given the current problems the Trust faced. Mr Evans was chair of a multinational company head-quartered in the region and had served as a non-executive director on other major companies.
Action: The Board unanimously approved the appointment.

Appointment of new directors

The chairman commented: 'the resignation of Lady Westwood has created a vacancy that we need to fill. I also think we could do with some new talent. People are saying that the Trust needs more people with experience of running large organizations in a cost-effective manner.' He said that he had two people in mind whose CVs had been included in the board papers for this meeting. He had already had preliminary discussions with them, and confirmed that, if appointed, both were prepared to undertake the duties involved.

He proposed the names of:

Justin Belvedere, qualified as a chartered accountant, eight years' experience as a management consultant with one of the Big Four accountancy firms, subsequently financial controller of a listed company, and now CEO of a listed group with interests in haulage, agriculture, and food distribution.

Rupert Hargreaves, engineer, with experience as CEO of a number of manufacturing companies and now chairman of a listed manufacturing company in the defence industry.

The recommendations were strongly supported by Colonel Brigham-West, who knew Hargreaves, and by Mr Windlass, who said that Belvedere was a first-class man, with a wealth of valuable experience. Professor Prowess expressed concern that such appointments were not in line with NHS diversity policies. She felt that a nomination committee of the board should have been formed to consider possible candidates. Ms Mirrlees felt that it was a pity that there were no women candidates.

Action: The board agreed that invitations be given to Messrs Belvedere and Hargreaves, subject to the necessary prior checks and approvals required under NHS policies.

Independent inquiry into efficiency and cost saving

Introducing this agenda item the chairman said that, as he had said at previous meetings, there were many opportunities for cost savings and improved efficiency throughout the services provided by the Trust hospitals. He proposed the appointment of independent consultants to examine and report on cost–benefit opportunities in every department.

The chief executive raised concerns that the way the Trust services were run was an executive matter and his responsibility, working closely with the finance director. He suggested that the role of the board was setting strategic direction for the Trust and overseeing the work of the executive directors. This investigation, he felt, would involve the board directly in management matters.

After a long discussion about the content of such an investigation and possible suitable consultants, the board decided to pursue the chairman's proposal.

Action: The chairman, in consultation with the chief executive and finance director, would draft a detailed proposal for consideration by the board at its next meeting.

Involvement of medical staff in research projects

Ms Mirrlees had asked for this item to be put on the agenda. She explained that junior doctors had spoken with her about the need for them to be able to write research papers to further their career, but the demands of their work did not allow sufficient time. Colonel Brigham-West suggested that medical research was the responsibility of Trusts associated with a university medical school. 'This Trust is not a teaching hospital; we do not have professors to oversee such work; junior doctors need to do what they were hired for.' The medical director disagreed: 'junior doctors need to show some published work if they want to get an appointment at a teaching hospital to further their careers'.

Action: Medical director to report to the next meeting on the extent of research work and make a policy proposal.

Discussion questions

1. Even with the limited information provided by these extracts from the minutes, what is your opinion of:

    a. the leadership style of the new chair of the Trust, Roger Evans?

    b. the culture of the board of the Trust?

2. Did the board reach an appropriate decision on each of the agenda items described?

3. What is your opinion of the style of the minute? Is it too/insufficiently informative? How might it be improved?

Self-test questions

1. Name three regulatory instruments that call for risk management responsibility at board level.

2. Some boards include corporate risk assessment in the mandate of the board audit committee. Why might this have limitations?

3. What alternatives do other companies adopt to bring risk issues to the board?

4. Who might be involved in a risk management subcommittee, and how does it operate?

5. Where else might responsibility for risk assessment and management be placed in a company?

6. Identify the levels of risk in a business.

7. What should an enterprise risk management system (ERMS) provide and to whom?

8. Name the iterative phases involved in the analysis of risk in an organization.

9. Identify some risk assessment and risk management tools that are available.

10. What policy options does a board have when deciding its approach to enterprise risk management?

 For suggested answers to these self-test questions visit the online resources at: www.oup.com/uk/tricker4e/

Projects and exercises

1. Focus on an organization with which you are familiar (perhaps a company, a university, or a sports club). Identify areas of possible risk. Consider risk at strategic, managerial, and operational levels.

2. What consequences might arise should these risks occur?

3. In each situation, make a recommendation to management on what the organization's risk response should be.

References and further reading

Barton, Thomas L., William G. Shenkir, and Paul L. Walker (2002) *Making Enterprise Risk Management Pay Off: How Leading Companies Implement Risk Management.* Financial Times and Prentice Hall, New York.

Conference Board (2005) From Risk Management to Risk Strategy, Report 1363, New York.

Cornelius, Peter K. and Bruce Kogan (eds) (2007) *Global Issues in Corporate Governance: Risk and International Investment.* Oxford University Press, New York.

Lam, James (2003) *Enterprise Risk Management: From Incentives to Controls.* Wiley, New York.

Moeller, Robert (2007) *COSO Enterprise Risk Management: Understanding the New Integrated ERM Framework.* COSO Committee of Sponsoring Organizations of the Treadway Commission, Wiley, New York.

NACD (2005a) Myths, Realities and Prevention: A Report of the NACD Blue Ribbon Commission on Director Liability, National Association of Corporate Directors, Washington, DC.

NACD (2005b) Risk Oversight: Board Lessons for Turbulent Times—A Report of a NACD Blue Ribbon Commission, National Association of Corporate Directors, Washington, DC.

NACD (2005c) Risk Governance: Balancing Risk and Reward—A Report of a NACD Blue Ribbon Commission, National Association of Corporate Directors, Washington, DC.

Tonello, Matteo (2006) Emerging Governance Practices in Enterprise Risk Management: The Conference Board Research Report R-1398–07, New York.

Treadway Commission (2004) Enterprise Risk Management: An Integrated Approach, The Committee of Sponsoring Organizations of the Treadway Commission, USA.

Van Daelen, Marijn and Christoph Van Der Elst (eds) (2011) *Risk Management and Corporate Governance: Interconnections in Law, Accounting and Tax.* Lexis Nexis, London.

Whitlery, Sherry (2004) 'Leadership through Progressive Enterprise Risk Management', *Institute of Internal Auditors, FSA Times*, 3, 4th quarter.

Useful websites

www.iso.org/standard/65694.html

International Organization for Standardization (ISO)—risk management guidelines, 31000:2018.

www.oceg.org

The Open Compliance and Ethics Group.

www.theirm.org

The Institute of Risk Management.

www.msci.com/risk-performance

MSCI—financial risk management expertise.

www.dnv.com

Det Norske Veritas—a foundation safeguarding life, property, and the environment.

www.symbiant.co.uk

Risk management software (ERMS).

www.paisley.thomsonreuters.com/

Software for governance, risk, and compliance.

www.riskhive.com

Risk and scenario modelling—risk management software.

www.ifpo.org/resource-links/articles-and-reports/crime-pre-vention-physical-security-training-and-risk-management/risk-assessment-guidelines/

Risk assessment guidelines—International Foundation for Protection Officers.

The Board and Business Ethics

Learning Outcomes

This chapter enables us to:

- Recognize what business ethics are.
- Review changing expectations in the governance of organizations.
- Understand the concept of corporate social responsibility (CSR).
- Appreciate CSR strategies, policies, and the CSR competency framework.
- Understand enlightened shareholder value (ESV), sustainability, and the triple bottom line.
- Study communication with stakeholders and integrated reporting.
- Be aware of the United Nations Global Reporting Initiative.

What are business ethics?

All organizations develop their own culture, determined by their context, significant events that have affected them, and the influence of dominant individuals in the organization. The culture reflects the way people in that organization are expected to behave; in other words it reflects the ethos and the ethics of the enterprise. In many cases business ethics are implicit, undeclared but evident to all who deal with that enterprise. The following examples suggest some of the elements that might create the weft and warp of a company's ethical tapestry:

1. A professional practice in mid-town Manhattan had 7 partners and about 50 staff members. The partners emphasized the firm's work ethic, encouraging people to work long hours in the evening without extra pay. As a result some staff members slacked during the day to impress their bosses with their out-of-hours dedication, while staff members who had to leave on time for family reasons were undervalued.

2. In the same New York firm, the senior partner had a long-standing and well-known affair with his secretary. Liaisons between other staff members were consequently accepted even though they could adversely affect the staff members' work.

3. The managing director of an electronics company in the UK encouraged senior staff to incur and inflate large bills for meals because he said this was his 'way of rewarding good efforts'. The practice of inflating personal expenses was widespread.

4. The founder and chief executive of a listed company in Hong Kong was a devout Buddhist. Because of his convictions, there were certain companies and countries with whom he

would not trade. His colleagues knew his beliefs, and contracts were lost to competition as a result.

5. A company in Texas had a reputation locally for its 'hire and fire' policies. Its director of human relations was known as 'Hatchet Jonson'. The company had difficulty in attracting the high-tech staff it needed.

6. The chair and CEO of the same Texan company, although very successful in business, was known as a tyrant to his staff. In the boardroom he was known for shouting at senior executives and dominating discussions and as a result, he did have difficulty in attracting outside directors with the calibre and experience to challenge his beliefs.

7. The Chinese founder and owner of a company in Singapore claimed that the company was 'run like one big family'. However, employees who were not members of the founder's real family soon learned that promotions and financial rewards tended to go to the founder's relations.

8. The chief executive of a Latin American subsidiary of an American company was accused by head office of bribing government officials to obtain contracts. The response was that 'this has always been the way things are done here. No handouts = no contracts.'

Although the business ethics of many companies are implicit, part of 'the way things are done here', other companies publish explicit codes of conduct, which form part of that company's culture. Typically, such statements address the relationships between the company, its staff, and the firm's stakeholders, including the customers, suppliers and other business partners, shareholders and other sources of finance, local communities, society, and the state.

Such statements obviously reflect the views of the board. The directors and senior executives of every enterprise create the moral tone of their organization; what some call 'setting the moral compass'.

For example, the John Lewis Partnership, which operates 32 John Lewis department stores and 256 Waitrose supermarkets across the UK, has a history of success with annual sales of over £8.2 billion, although the group is currently facing serious competition from internet sales. Significantly, the group is the UK's largest example of worker co-ownership: all 76,500 staff are called partners in the business. The Group publishes its Principles (see Corporate Governance in Action 9.1) and a detailed Code of Practice.[1]

As can be seen from the Principles, the governance of the John Lewis Partnership lies with three governing authorities: the Partnership Council, the Partnership Board, and the chair. In other words, the Partnership is not subject to UK partnership law, which would give partners rights to ownership of a share of the partnership assets and a vote in partners' meetings. But channels are provided for employee partners to communicate with the governing authorities.

[1] www.johnlewispartnership.co.uk/content/dam/cws/pdfs/our-responsibilities/2017files/John-Lewis-Partnership-Responsible-Sourcing-Code-of-Practice-Jan2017.pdf

Corporate Governance in Action 9.1   The John Lewis Partnership

Our principles

The John Lewis Partnership's principles define how we run our business. They are as relevant today as they were when they were set out by our founder, John Spedan Lewis, in our constitution.

Purpose

The Partnership's ultimate purpose is the happiness of all its members, through their worthwhile and satisfying employment in a successful business. Because the Partnership is owned in trust for its members, they share the responsibilities of ownership as well as its rewards profit, knowledge and power.

The video 'Employee Ownership, A Shared Passion', explains how our employee-owned business model operates in practice, and offers insight and advice to anyone wanting to learn more about this sort of model and its benefits.

Power

Power in the Partnership is shared between three governing authorities: the Partnership Council, the Partnership Board and the Chairman.

Profit

The Partnership aims to make sufficient profit from its trading operations to sustain its commercial vitality and finance its continued development, to distribute a share of those profits each year to its members and to enable it to undertake other activities consistent with its ultimate purpose.

Members

The Partnership aims to employ and retain as its members people of ability and integrity who are committed to working together and to supporting its Principles. Relationships are based on mutual respect and courtesy, with as much equality between its members as differences of responsibility permit. The Partnership aims to recognise their individual contributions and reward them fairly.

Customers

The Partnership aims to deal honestly with its customers and secure their loyalty and trust by providing outstanding choice, value and service.

Business relationships

The Partnership aims to conduct all its business relationships with integrity and courtesy and to honour scrupulously every business agreement.

The community

The Partnership aims to obey the spirit as well as the letter of the law and to contribute to the wellbeing of the communities where it operates.

The John Lewis Partnership is a member of the Ethical Trading Initiative www.ethicaltrade.org/blog/john-lewis-partnership-joins-ethical-trading-initiative.

Source: http://www.johnlewispartnership.co.uk/about/our-principles.html

A company does not have morals; directors do. The board has to be the conscience of the company. In fulfilling its role, the board is responsible for considering the potential effect of the strategies it formulates, for identifying the likely impact of policies it approves (both short- and long-term), for recognizing possible outcomes for people, and for accepting its duty to be accountable.

Every board has a duty to formulate the company's strategy, recognizing the risks involved, and part of that process involves determining how the company will behave—in other words, establishing how social responsibility will be exercised throughout the organization. Balancing competing claims of different stakeholders, while meeting shareholders' expectations, can be quite a challenge. In non-profit entities, broader societal responsibilities also have to be balanced, while meeting the primary duty to the entity's members. Boards need to make choices. Inertia inevitably leads to unresolved dilemmas.

Changing expectations in the governance of organizations

The original corporate governance codes, dating from the early 1990s, were voluntary. At the time, they were derided by some company chairs as being no more than expensive, mindless exercises. But since then three significant changes have taken place:

- first, corporate governance compliance has increasingly become mandatory, enshrined in regulation, law, and stock exchange listing requirements—complaints from companies now tend to be about the cost of compliance rather than the need for corporate governance principles;

- second, risk governance and enterprise risk management have become an integral part of the corporate governance process;

- third, and of relevance to this chapter, corporate social responsibility and sustainability have been added to the corporate governance portfolio.

Questioning the societal legitimacy of corporate entities has a long history. In the original mid-19th century concept of the company, if the liability of the owners for the debts of the company was to be limited, society demanded that the company's activities should be strictly prescribed. Companies could only carry out those functions described in their memorandum of association. In effect, society gave the corporate entity a licence to operate with limited liability provided that it restricted its specified activities and in some cases for a limited time.

Subsequently, lawyers began to draft the memorandum of association and other constitutional documents so widely that the activities of companies were no longer bounded. So the behaviour of corporate entities has had to be constrained by law. Around the world, laws to control monopolies and markets, to protect customers, to regulate employee relations, to safeguard health and safety, to preserve the environment, and much more are now used to regulate and restrain corporate activities.

This raises the vital question, neatly posed by Milton Friedman: *'What responsibilities does a business have?'* His view was that the only legitimate purpose for a company was to create wealth, pursuing its business effectively for the benefit of its customers, while providing a profitable reward to its investors. It was the role of the state, he believed, to provide the legal framework that regulated companies' behaviour in relation to the rest of the community.

As we saw in the discussion of stakeholder philosophies in Chapter 3, the debate continues about companies' responsibilities to their shareholders and other stakeholders. On one side are those who argue, like Friedman, that a company has one and only one objective: to make long-term sustainable profits by satisfying customers for the benefit of its owners, while acting within the law. If society wishes to limit a company's single-minded pursuit of this goal, for example by constraining monopolies, regulating employment, or preventing pollution, it must pass appropriate laws.

On the other side are those who believe that, because a company can and does affect the interests and even the lives of people, it should take account of societal interests over and above those of the owners and beyond the specific requirements of the law. Moreover, some commentators have added that companies should be accountable, or even responsible, to those affected by their actions. Carroll (1979) attempted to answer Friedman's question by suggesting that corporate responsibility has four levels:[2]

- *economic responsibility*—first and foremost, the social responsibility to be profit-orientated and market-driven;
- *legal responsibility*—to adhere to society's laws and regulations as the price for society's licence to operate;
- *ethical responsibilities*—to honour society's wider social norms and expectations of behaviour over and above the law in line with the local culture;
- *discretionary (or philanthropic) responsibilities*—to undertake voluntary activities and expenditures that exceed society's minimum expectations.

As we saw in Chapter 5, the King Report (King I) on corporate governance in South Africa was the first code to recognize the interests of corporate stakeholders as well as shareholders. In the words of its author, Mervyn King:

> That report revolutionised approaches to corporate governance around the world because it said that in the decision-making process you should take account of the legitimate needs, interests, and expectations of stakeholders linked to the company. That did not mean that directors should be accountable to stakeholders, but that they should take account of stakeholder needs and expectations in their decision-making. [Companies should] still act in the best interests of the company through the maximization of the total economic value.[3]

King I has been translated into many languages but although the King perspective has been widely promoted, the concept has its detractors. Anne Bernstein (2010), head of a South African think tank, pointed out that developing nations need more companies that generate wealth, not demands to pursue social responsibilities. In South Africa, where many are jobless and live in poverty, people need work, Bernstein said, not rules designed to protect those

---

[2] Carroll, A. B. (1979) 'A Three-dimensional Conceptual Model of Corporate Performance', *Academy of Management Review*, 4, pp 497–505.

[3] Interview in *CSJ* (2010), Hong Kong Institute of Chartered Secretaries, December.

already in work, which can reduce the number of available jobs, nor environmental demands, which have delayed projects to replace existing shacks with new houses.

As Kofi Annan said, when Secretary-General of the United Nations:[4]

> We have to choose between a global market driven only by calculation of short-term profit, and one which has a human face; between a world which condemns a quarter of the human race to starvation and squalor, and one which offers everyone at least a chance of prosperity, in a healthy environment; between a selfish free-for-all in which we ignore the fate of the losers, and a future in which the strong and successful accept their responsibilities, showing global vision and leadership.

The concept of corporate social responsibility

Broadly, corporate social responsibility (CSR) is about corporate entities acting as good corporate citizens. But although intuitively obvious, CSR has acquired a range of meanings, which overlap yet focus on different aspects of the topic, as can be seen in the following, alternative points of view.

The societal perspective

This view holds that companies have responsibilities beyond just obeying the law and paying their taxes, because their activities have an overall impact on society. A commitment to CSR recognizes that companies should be accountable not only for their financial performance, but also for their impact on society. The definition used by Business for Social Responsibility, a non-profit organization based in San Francisco, is 'CSR involves operating a business in a manner that meets or exceeds the ethical, legal, commercial, and public expectations that society has of business'. The chairman/CEO of AT&T, C. Michael Armstrong, summarized his company's view: 'AT&T understands the need for a global alliance of business, society and the environment. In the 21st century, the world won't tolerate businesses that don't take that partnership seriously, but it will eventually reward companies that do.'

But such thinking is not universally accepted. Robert Reich, who was previously a CSR advocate, argued that consumers today have a world of choice and businesses face more competition than ever before. In pursuit of corporate performance, he believes, a CEO's incentives become aligned with shareholders' interests so they 'slash payrolls, outsource abroad, and drain our main streets of shops'. Reich concluded that if states want to avoid adverse social consequences, they need to pass laws.[5]

The strategy-driven perspective

This perspective starts from the proposition that business social responsibility is an integral part of the wealth-creation process. A company runs in a socially responsible way because its

---

[4] At the World Economic Forum, Davos on 31 January 1999.

[5] Reich, Robert B. (2006) *Super-capitalism: The Transformation of Business, Democracy, and Everyday Life*, Borzoi Books, Random House.

CSR strategies and policies are business-driven, in both the short and long terms. Such companies make a solid business case for their CSR policies based on cost-effective criteria. All corporate strategies—research, exploration, product development, production, marketing, human resources, and financial—are contingent on the CSR objectives. The business case for taking a stakeholder approach to corporate governance is that it enhances competitiveness, increases customer satisfaction, improves employee relations, reduces the cost of capital, and enhances shareholder value, while also investing in communities and increasing wealth creation in society. CSR that is strategy-driven and rooted in a solid business case also produces a more sustainable result long-term. This approach to CSR is now found in many European boardrooms and, increasingly, in the United States. Critics have argued that CSR distracts from the fundamental economic role of business, although studies have actually shown a positive correlation with improved shareholder returns, albeit a small one.

The stakeholder perspective

Companies with this perception see CSR as the alignment of corporate values and actions with the expectations and needs of their stakeholders—shareholders, customers, employees, suppliers, communities, regulators, other interest groups, and society as a whole. Their CSR policies describe the company's commitment and responsibility to its stakeholders. Adopting this perspective, the European Commission has defined CSR as 'a concept whereby companies integrate social and environmental concerns in their business operations and in their interaction with their stakeholders on a voluntary basis'.[6]

If companies fail to achieve acceptable CSR standards, costs can be incurred such as legal damages, restitution costs, legal fees, or product recalls. The loss of reputation can be even higher, affecting sales, costs, and employee turnover. Investigative media increasingly report cases of firms transgressing accepted CSR behaviour, for example, in the employment of children in developing countries in manufacturing and other industries, the alleged ill-treatment of animals in pharmaceutical product-testing, and pollution in the oil drilling and transport industries, even though such practices may be perfectly legal in the places where they occur.

The ethical perspective

The ethical viewpoint sees that corporate entities, like individuals, have an obligation to act for the benefit of society as a whole, contributing to society while doing no harm to others. A wide range of laws and guidelines that steer and control corporate behaviour already exist at state, national, and global levels on health and safety, human rights, environmental issues, and sustainability. But ethical CSR activity needs to go well beyond what is required by such basic standards. The board needs to be the conscience of the company—responsible for establishing its corporate values. Ethical codes, understood throughout the organization, reflect the directors' own behaviour. An ethical standpoint is likely to produce voluntary CSR policies that go well beyond the requirements of laws and guidelines.

[6] Brussels, 18 July 2001 GREEN PAPER Promoting a European framework for Corporate Social Responsibility.

The political perspective

Interest groups, some with an anti-business agenda, argue that CSR is no more than vested self-interest at best and a public relations window-dressing exercise at worst. Some have called for legislation to impose standards of CSR on companies, particularly multinationals. The response from the Confederation of British Industry (CBI) was that CSR should remain market-driven and voluntary. Attempts to raise standards, the CBI believes, would remove the competitive incentive that drives CSR activity and would place an unmanageable burden on companies, particularly small and medium-sized firms. CSR policies should reflect companies' activities and the context in which they operate, while legislation in this area would constrain business activity and reduce CSR to a lowest common denominator, the CBI said. Other political commentators have argued that companies which pursue broader, social goals have no legitimacy. Such roles should be pursued by governments acting for their citizens. Some business leaders concur with this opinion, feeling that their companies do not have a mandate, nor are they equipped, to pursue broader social goals.

The philanthropic perspective

For many years, some companies have sought to 'put something back' into the society that provided them with customers, employees, and success. Such corporate philanthropy may involve charitable giving to support communities, charities, or other causes, in money or corporate services, such as employees' time. Donating to charitable causes without anticipating any reward, save perhaps a reputational benefit, has long been practised in the United States, some European countries, and by Chinese entrepreneurs in places such as Hong Kong. The European Commission has defined such an approach to CSR as 'a concept whereby companies decide voluntarily to contribute to a better society and a cleaner environment'. But a philanthropic approach to CSR is essentially peripheral to the main business. When times get hard, it is also one of the easiest expenditures to cut.

Discussions about these alternative perspectives continue. Many companies in the economically advanced world now accept that their responsibilities go beyond the generation of wealth, while staying within the laws of the states in which they operate. CSR is widely recognized as part of companies' corporate governance responsibilities. But CSR practices vary between countries and cultures. Different value systems, different economic conditions, and different social priorities mean that no 'one size' can 'fit all'.

CSR strategies and policies

A primary duty of the board is to identify the aims of the company, to establish its mission, and to set its values. If the directors are not clear about the firm's purpose and what it stands for, the rest of the organization will be like a boat without a rudder.

To be effective, a company's CSR efforts need to be led by the directors and embedded in its corporate strategy. This will lead to CSR policies, for approval by the board. Basically, a CSR policy determines how the company engages with its shareholders and the other stakeholders, including its employees, customers, and suppliers, the communities in which it operates, and the world generally. A clear CSR policy can also influence potential investors looking for socially responsible, ethical, or environmentally friendly enterprises in which to invest. Successful CSR policies influence management decisions at all levels, and penetrate all aspects and every level of the firm's activities.

Obviously, every company is different and must develop its CSR policies in the context of its corporate strategies, policies, and procedures, including its systems of management supervision and accountability. If they are to be effective, CSR policies should be understood, accepted, and applied throughout the organization. They also need to be reviewed regularly to reflect changing business, economic, and social situations.

A CSR consultant, who was retained by a manufacturing company to advise on its CSR policies, proposed the policy statement in Corporate Governance in Action 9.2.

Corporate Governance in Action 9.2 Extract from the CSR policy of a manufacturing company

For continuing economic success, all company strategies, policies and management decisions should take account of their long-term effects and impact on the following.

1. *All stakeholders including:*
   - original suppliers and others in the upstream supply chain;
   - agents, distributors, and others in the downstream supply chain;
   - customers of the end product or service;
   - creditors;
   - bankers and non-equity sources of finance;
   - employees including part-time employees and managers;
   - self-employed contractors to the company.

2. *All of the communities in which the company operates including:*
   - local communities;
   - regional communities;
   - national communities;
   - international communities.

Consider the economic implications, socially responsible activities that the company undertakes, and our philanthropic efforts.

3. *The environment*

Consider all of the relevant communities, regions, and countries affected by the company's manufacturing and distribution chain, including possible effects of:
   - our production activities, such as:
     - energy use;
     - depletion of resources;
     - exploitation of labour;
     - pollution;

- our products and services, including:
    - the effect of the product in use;
    - energy use;
    - health or other risks;
    - pollution;
- the final disposal of the product, including:
    - energy use;
    - pollution.

Each of these broad policy statements is further amplified in the CSR handbook.

The CSR competency framework

To encourage commitment to CSR practices, the British government created a CSR competency framework—a flexible tool, which is offered as a 'way of thinking' for companies of all sizes.[7] The framework offers six core characteristics, with five levels of attainment for each:

- *understanding society*—a knowledge of how the business operates in the broader societal context and a knowledge of the impact that the business has on society, plus a recognition that the business is an important player in society, seeking to make that impact as positive as possible;
- *building capacity*—working with others to build the capability to manage the business effectively, helping suppliers and employees to understand your environment and to apply social and environmental concerns in their day-to-day roles;
- *questioning 'business as usual'*—constantly questioning your business in relation to a more sustainable future and being open to improving people's quality of life and the environment, acting as an advocate, engaging with bodies outside the business who share this concern for the future;
- *stakeholder relations*—recognizing that stakeholders include all those who have an impact on, or are impacted by, your business, understanding the opportunities and risks they present, and working with them through consultation, taking their views into account;
- *strategic view*—ensuring that social and environmental concerns are included in the overall business strategy so that CSR becomes 'business as usual', with leadership coming from the top and resulting in everyone in the business having an awareness of the social and environmental impacts in their day-to-day roles;
- *harnessing diversity*—recognizing that people differ and harnessing this diversity, reflected in fair and transparent employment practices, promoting the health, well-being, and views of staff with everyone in the business feeling valued.

[7] www.nmiconsulting.co.uk/docs/Competency_Framework_FINAL.pdf

The five levels of attainment are:

- *awareness*—the broad application of the core CSR characteristics and how they might impinge on business decisions;
- *understanding*—a basic knowledge of some of the issues, with the competence to apply them to specific activities;
- *application*—the ability to supplement this basic knowledge of the issues, with the competence to apply it to specific activities;
- *integration*—an in-depth understanding of the issues and an expertise in embedding CSR into the business decision-making process;
- *leadership*—the ability to help managers across the organization in a way that fully integrates CSR in the decision-making process.

Overall, the intention of the CSR framework is to change employees' mindsets and to promote an appropriate CSR strategy throughout the organization and between the company and its stakeholders. Creating a strong CSR culture throughout an organization needs to be part of an on-going performance assessment of both organizational units and individuals, and should not be allowed to become a form-filling exercise.

An organization's response to its social and environmental impacts, recognized through CSR awareness, can provide a cost-effective, yet comprehensive, way of managing social and environmental risk across an organization. However, corporate groups operating in different parts of the world may find it difficult to achieve homogeneous CSR policies throughout the group. The experiences of Exxon in the USA and in Europe, described in Corporate Governance in Action 9.3 and 9.4, are cases in point.

Enlightened shareholder value (ESV)

Boards adopting an investor-driven, ESV approach believe that the satisfaction of the needs of all stakeholders is crucial to corporate success, that it is essential to creating value for shareholders. The ESV concept of corporate governance attempts to overcome apparent conflicts between a shareholder-focused and a stakeholder-focused approach that we saw in corporate governance theory, in Chapter 3. An ESV perspective suggests that profits are generated, shareholder value created, and society's wealth increased by satisfying stakeholder interests, rather than through the classical attempts of shareholder theory to maximize shareholder wealth.

Emphasizing the needs and interests of all corporate stakeholders obviously swings a spotlight onto corporate social responsibility, argues The World Business Council for Sustainable Development:[8]

> For many companies, managing corporate social responsibility well is no longer seen as an extra cost or burden on hard-pressed management. Rather, CSR is increasingly

[8] Holme, Richard and Phil Watts (2000) 'Corporate Social Responsibility: Making Good Business Sense', World Council for Sustainable Development, Geneva, Switzerland.

viewed, not only as making good business sense but also contributing to the long-term prosperity of companies and ultimately its survival. Being a good neighbour and showing that you care on the one hand and being a successful business on the other, are flip sides of the same coin.

Prior to 2006, company law in the UK required directors to act in the best interests of the company, which effectively meant in the long-term interest of the shareholders—in other words, by attempting to maximize shareholder value. But the Companies Act 2006 specifically spelled out a statutory duty to recognize the effect of board decisions on a wider public. For the first time in UK company law, CSR responsibilities were included among the formal duties of company directors:

> A director of a company must act in the way he considers, in good faith, would be most likely to promote the success of the company for the benefit of its members as a whole, and in doing so have regard to:
>
> (a) The likely consequences of any decision in the long term
> (b) The interests of the company's employees
> (c) The need to foster the company's business relations with suppliers, customers and others
> (d) The impact of the company's operations on the community and the environment
> (e) The desirability of the company maintaining a reputation for high standards of business conduct, and
> (f) The need to act fairly as between members of the company

Thus UK company law now requires companies to consider employees, suppliers, customers, and other business partners, as well as the community and the environment, in their decisions.

The UN Principles for Responsible Investment also call for companies to consider environmental, social, and governance (ESG) issues and risks in their strategic decision-making and to report their participation on a 'comply or explain' basis.[9] These Principles were developed by an international group of institutional investors from 12 countries convened by the United Nations Secretary-General and reflect the increasing relevance of environmental, social, and corporate governance issues to investment practices.

Other examples of calls for companies to adopt CSR policies include the European Union's demand for statements of CSR policies when companies tender for contracts (2005), the UK Department for Environment, Food and Rural Affairs (DEFRA) requirement for occupational pension funds to 'report whether environmental, social, and ethical criteria are taken into account in their investment strategy' (2001), and the Australian Securities Exchange listing rule that requires companies to report their performance under environmental legislation (1998). Some institutional investors have also mounted initiatives for companies to take a broader stakeholder perspective, including CalPERS and other US state pension funds.

---

[9] The Principles can be found online at www.unpri.org/about/

Sustainable development

The World Business Council for Sustainable Development (WBCSD) concluded in its first report on CSR, 'Meeting Changing Expectations' (1999), that:

- CSR priorities today are human rights, employee rights, environmental protection, community involvement, and supplier relations;
- a coherent CSR strategy, based on integrity, sound values, and a long-term approach, offers clear business benefits;
- companies should articulate their own core values and codes of conduct, or failing that, endorse and implement codes produced by others;
- it is important to be responsive to local and cultural differences when implementing global policies.

The report added that:

- a coherent CSR strategy, based on integrity, sound values and a long-term approach, offers clear business benefits to companies and a positive contribution to the well-being of society;
- a CSR strategy provides the opportunity to demonstrate the human face of business;
- such a strategy requires engagement in open dialogue and constructive partnerships with government at various levels, intergovernmental organizations (IGOs), non-governmental organizations (NGOs), other elements of civil society, and, in particular, local communities;
- in implementing their CSR strategies, companies should recognize and respect local and cultural differences, while maintaining high and consistent global standards and policies; and
- being responsive to local differences means taking specific initiatives.

A recent report from the WBCSD, 'Vision 2050',[10] called for 'a new agenda for business laying out a pathway to a world in which nine billion people can live well, and within the planet's resources, by mid-century'. The report was compiled following an 18-month long combined effort between CEOs and experts, and dialogues with more than 200 companies and external stakeholders in some 20 countries. The report featured a set of agreed 'must haves', representing vital developments that the WBCSD hopes organizations will consider putting in place within the next decade, to help ensure a steady course towards global sustainability is set. These 'must haves' include:

- incorporating the costs of externalities, starting with carbon, ecosystem services, and water, into the structure of the marketplace;
- doubling agricultural output without increasing the amount of land or water used;
- halting deforestation and increasing yields from planted forests;

[10] www.wbcsd.org/Overview/About-us/Vision2050

- halving carbon emissions worldwide (based on 2005 levels) by 2050 through a shift to low-carbon energy systems;
- improved demand-side energy efficiency, and providing universal access to low-carbon mobility.

A crucial question is whether there is a link between CSR and economic performance. Although research studies have been conducted, a basic problem has been how to measure CSR. Some studies have also been marred by an ideological bias or limited methodology. Although a few studies have shown some correlation between firms' CSR and their financial performance, current research does not point to a decisive link. However, the longer-term effects of a sound CSR reputation in both the consumer market and the stock market may well persuade boards of the importance of CSR efforts.

Some firms have claimed that their CSR policies and reports have:

- improved brand recognition and reputation;
- made the firm more attractive to existing and potential employees;
- improved top management and board-level strategic thinking and decisions;
- produced innovations in the way in which the firm operates;
- responded to customers' demands;
- met stakeholders' and society's changing expectations.

For such reasons, many firms approach CSR as enlightened self-interest. But few claim a demonstrable positive correlation between good CSR practices and corporate financial performance. The growing number of investment funds now focusing on 'socially responsible investing' also suggests that there may be a share-price premium in due course. In addition, CSR reports can build new links between companies and their stakeholders as relationships between companies and their contractual partners, such as suppliers, distributors, and customers, are enhanced. Employees and their trades unions are also provided with an additional focus in their relations with the employer.

A 2011 ISO standard on social responsibility marked a significant development in the international recognition of the importance of CSR and sustainable development. ISO26000 calls on companies to govern and manage their affairs with equity, honesty, and integrity, respecting the interests of all stakeholders affected by the company's activities. The standard seeks to promote ethical behaviour by requiring the:

- development of governance structures that promote ethical conduct;
- identification, adoption, and application of these standards of ethical behaviour;
- encouragement and promotion of such standards throughout the organization and in its activities;
- establishment of appropriate oversight and control systems;
- identification and reporting of deviations from such company policies with appropriate action.

Corporate Governance in Action 9.3   CSR resisted in Exxon Mobil, USA

John D. Rockefeller founded the Standard Oil Corporation, which became Exxon Mobil, the world's largest publicly owned energy company. At the 2008 AGM, some of his descendants brought shareholder motions calling for the company to curb greenhouse gas emissions, to increase renewable energy research, and to develop sources of alternative fuel.

Three resolutions asked Exxon to study the impact of global warming on poor countries, to reduce company emissions of greenhouse gases, and to do more research on renewable energy sources such as wind turbines and solar panels. Neva Rockefeller Goodwin, an economist and great-granddaughter of John D. Rockefeller, told shareholders:[11]

> These increased concentrations of CO_2 in the atmosphere will cause weather disasters that will work against everyone's best hope for robust development in emerging countries, while also increasing the vulnerability of the poor in the rich countries. It will also impact the global economy.

The proposals were opposed by Exxon Mobil's board.

The family also supported resolutions calling for the company to establish an independent chair, separating the role from that of the current chairman and chief executive Rex Tillerson. Shell and BP, they noted, had already separated the positions. The motion to split the roles, which had been raised for the last seven years of shareholder meetings, was supported by a significant number of shareholders. But the final poll showed only 39.5 per cent of the shares were voted in favour.

Commentators suggested that the US$40 billion profit reported by the company in 2007 may have influenced the rest. 'The past year was an outstanding year and a record for our corporation by nearly every measure,' Tillerson said. 'Millions of people have benefited financially by holding Exxon Mobil shares either directly or indirectly through their pension, insurance, and mutual funds,' he added.

Mr Tillerson added that he thought Exxon had to keep focused on its mission of developing more oil and gas reserves, and that oil and gas would remain the primary fuel source for decades to come. Some shareholders disagreed, arguing that the company's emphasis on developing oil and gas as energy sources threatened the global environment and ultimately the company's financial health. One shareholder suggested that the company was 'acting like a dinosaur by not adapting to a changing environment'. Another shareholder, a Dominican nun, said 'We're faced with a profound moral and business challenge'. These shareholders were countered by others who defended the management, saying it had been 'a great engine for profit'.[12]

Corporate Governance in Action 9.4   The CSR policy of Exxon Europe

> We take very seriously our responsibilities to our employees, shareholders, customers, communities, the environment, and society at large.
>
> We strongly believe that the way we achieve results is as important as the results themselves. Therefore, we are working hard to embed CSR into the way we do business.
>
> We have integrated CSR policies and practices into our business, which help us ensure that we meet standards of integrity, safety, health, environment and social responsibility day in and day out and across our worldwide operations. We believe that this approach is essential to achieving superior business results.

[11] www.telegraph.co.uk/business/2017/05/31/exxonmobil-shareholders-defeat-board-climate-rebellion/
[12] As note 11 above.

Our focus is on helping Europe meet energy demand in an economically, socially and environmentally responsible manner. But we cannot be all things to all people. We must balance the needs of a wide variety of stakeholders. To do so sustainably is what the policies, actions and performance improvements behind CSR are all about.

Sustainability and the triple bottom line

The notion of sustainability has become an important part of the study of corporate governance and business ethics. Recognizing that their activities can have a lasting impact on society and the environment, many companies now accept that the essential generation of profits, although vital to reward the providers of capital and provide for future investment, is not enough.

The World Commission on Environment and Development was convened by the United Nations in 1983 and called the Brundtland Commission, after its chairman Gro Harlem Brundtland. The Commission was created to address growing concern 'about the accelerating deterioration of the human environment and natural resources and the consequences of that deterioration for economic and social development'. The Commission defined sustainable development as 'development that meets the needs of the present without compromising the ability of future generations to meet their own needs'.

Some companies, which support sustainability, talk about their *triple bottom line*, striving for sound performance in three areas—economic, social, and environmental. Some add 'in the long term', recognizing that it is possible to achieve acceptable short-term results, but to leave business successors and future generations with inherited problems. Others have called this a 'profits, people, and planet' approach to corporate performance. Some public sector organizations have also adopted this view of their goals.

The Institute for Research and Innovation in Sustainability in Canada has defined sustainability:[13]

as being about living and working in ways that meet and integrate existing environmental, economic, and social needs without compromising the wellbeing of future generations. The transition to sustainable development benefits today's society and builds a more secure future for our children.

Some examples of states' recognition of the need for sustainable development include:

- the European Union's fishing quotas and other fishing limits to sustain fish stocks;
- China's Guangdong Province's requirement that companies that pollute the groundwater table in that region clear up or close down;
- South American and European Union control of forestry products to protect the rainforest and to ensure that woodland is sustained by replanting;

[13] www.sustreport.org

- the Australian government's climate change strategy, the 'three pillars' of mitigation: to reduce gas emissions, to adapt to unavoidable climate change, and global solutions to help to shape an international response;

- attempts to reduce the world's greenhouse gases below 1990 levels to reduce global warming, which produced the Kyoto Protocol to the United Nations Framework Convention on Climate Change (1997), and continuing rounds of negotiations.

Communication with stakeholders: integrated reporting

Calls for companies to report on their non-financial performance are growing. This includes their CSR and sustainability activities, and the effects they have on the societies in which they operate. Such ESG reporting, as it is sometimes known (environmental, social, and governance) has become a significant issue in the business world. The Australian Securities Exchange, and the stock exchanges of Malaysia, Shanghai, and Shenzhen, among others, require ESG reports. According to the UK Ethical Corporation,[14] CSR and sustainability reporting is becoming more strategic for innovative, large corporations, whilst a gap is appearing between these and other, compliance-driven companies, which struggle to compete.

The South African corporate governance code, King III (2008), mentioned in Chapter 3, introduced the phrase 'integrated reporting' in its call for companies to report results of their non-financial performance, in addition to traditional information on financial performance. In South Africa, the listing rules of the Johannesburg Stock Exchange now require listed companies to publish such integrated reports. Denmark requires major companies to report on non-financial aspects of their performance in their annual reports. Other countries, including the UK, have encouraged the publication of a business commentary to support the published financial results. In 2014, Hong Kong required a statutory business review, including an analysis of the company's environmental policies and performance, an account of its key relationships with its employees, customers, and suppliers, and 'others that have a significant impact on the company and on which the company's success depends'.

The International Corporate Governance Network (ICGN) published a statement, and guidance on non-financial business reporting followed in 2009:[15]

> The ICGN believes that reporting of relevant and material non-financial information is an essential part of the disclosure required to enable shareowners and investors to make informed investment decisions. We use the term 'non-financial' to refer to information relevant to the assessment of economic value, but which does not fit easily into the traditional accounting framework. In a fast-changing, globalizing world, information material to investor decision-making is becoming increasingly diverse and dynamic. Long-term success in managing a business in today's complex economic, environmental, and social landscape is increasingly dependent on factors not reflected in financial statements and in some instances thought to be outside the corporation's sphere of concern.

[14] www.ethicalcorp.com
[15] Statement and Guidance on Non-financial Business Reporting (2009), International Corporate Governance Network, London www.icgn.org/sites/default/files/ICGN%20NFBR%20Guidance%20%282008%29_re-print%20May2013_FULL_0.pdf

In preparing an integrated report, a number of issues need to be considered:

- *who the report is intended for*—shareholders and the stock markets (almost certainly), employees, customers, and other contractual stakeholders (very likely), other interest groups including the media, and the general public (possibly);
- *why are you publishing this report*, what story do you want to tell;
- *what material should be included*:

  - business strategic achievements, capacity, and issues, key policies, plans and prospects (almost certainly);
  - governance reporting—board and board committee membership and activities, shareholder matters (almost certainly);
  - remuneration reporting (at least to the mandatory level), human resource information including employee standards, turnover, working conditions, and welfare, policies on diversity and youth recruitment, health and safety records, training improvements (very likely);
  - product, sales, and market information, customer relations (very likely);
  - environmental information such as carbon footprint and other emissions, energy usage, resource scarcity, improvements in waste management, possible effects of climate change, sustainability issues, and corporate social contributions including community involvement and charitable projects (probably);
  - supply chain matters, government or regulatory issues, ethical and anti-corruption policies, media and other societal concerns (possibly);

- *does the information provided meet the minimum requirements for reporting* under the law, by the regulatory authorities, and other mandatory demands such as the stock exchange listing rules;
- *does the report avoid the criticism* of being merely a compliance and 'box-ticking' response to demands for information from various sources;
- *is the level of detail and writing style appropriate* for the intended readership;
- *is the information provided coherent, is it interesting*, does it flow as an integrated dialogue, or is it a disparate set of unconnected commentaries;
- *is it too long*;
- *does the final integrated report really inform the intended readership*—will they read it;
- *how and where should the report be published*—as a hard-copy report (almost certainly); on the company's website (very probably); through social media (quite likely); other forms of publication (possibly);
- *should it be advertised* and made readily available to interested parties?

Predictably, around the world some companies reject the need to tell people any more than is strictly and statutorily required. But such antediluvian thinking is increasingly out of touch with modern governance, CSR, and sustainability beliefs and practice. Companies demonstrating such attitudes are likely to be suspected by the market, attacked by the media, and face reduced investment opportunities.

The United Nations Global Reporting Initiative

The UN Global Compact is a strategic initiative for businesses that commit to aligning their strategies and operations with ten universally accepted principles (the Ten Principles) in the areas of human rights, labour, the environment, and anti-corruption.[16] The Compact calls for participating companies to accept a set of core values in these areas. These values were derived from the Universal Declaration of Human Rights, the International Labour Organization's Declaration of Fundamental Principles and Rights at Work, and the UN Convention against Corruption.

Human Rights

Principle 1: Businesses should support and respect the protection of internationally proclaimed human rights;

Principle 2: make sure that they are not complicit in human rights abuses.

Labour

Principle 3: Businesses should uphold the freedom of association and the effective recognition of the right to collective bargaining;

Principle 4: the elimination of all forms of forced and compulsory labour;

Principle 5: the effective abolition of child labour;

Principle 6: the elimination of discrimination in respect of employment and occupation.

The environment

Principle 7: Businesses should support a precautionary approach to environmental challenges;

Principle 8: undertake initiatives to promote greater environmental responsibility;

Principle 9: encourage the development and diffusion of environmentally friendly technologies.

Anti-corruption

Principle 10: Businesses should work against corruption in all its forms, including extortion and bribery.

The United Nations Environment Programme Finance Initiative (UNEP FI) is a unique global partnership between the UN and the financial sectors around the world.[17] Nearly 200 financial institutions work with UNEP to understand the impacts of environmental and social considerations on financial performance. The programme has developed a set of statements covering the environment and sustainable development that participating organizations accept. By signing up to these statements, the financial institutions recognize the role of the financial sector in making economies and lifestyles sustainable, and commit to the integration of environmental considerations into their operations.

The *Global Reporting Initiative* (GRI), which was sparked by the UN Global Compact, is a worldwide, multistakeholder network aiming to create and develop a sustainability reporting framework, in which business, civil society, labour, investors, accountants, and others

---

[16] www.unglobalcompact.org
[17] www.unepfi.org

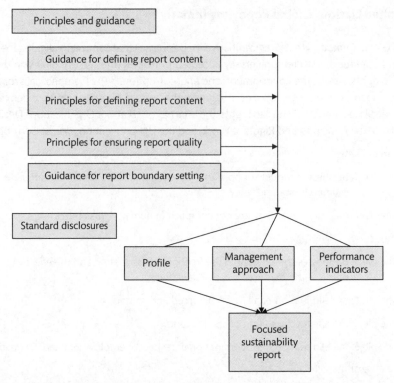

Figure 9.1 Outline of the Sustainability Reporting Guidelines

collaborate.[18] The GRI is based on the underlying belief that reporting on economic, environmental, and social performance by all organizations should be as routine and comparable as financial reporting. The GRI facilitates transparency and accountability by organizations of all sizes and sectors across the world—companies, governmental and other public agencies, and non-profit entities.

The GRI's Sustainability Reporting Guidelines provide the cornerstone for the sustainability reporting framework, which provides organizations with the basis for disclosure about sustainability performance, and stakeholders with a universally recognized comparable framework within which to assess such information. The Guidelines (Figure 9.1) consist of reporting principles and guidance, with standard disclosures and performance indicators.

The principles and guidance section of the framework defines the sustainability report's content, which helps to determine where its boundaries should be drawn. The content principles cover materiality, stakeholder inclusiveness, sustainability context, and completeness, along with a brief set of tests for each principle. The quality principles cover balance, comparability, accuracy, timeliness, reliability, and clarity, along with tests that can be used to help achieve the appropriate quality of the reported information.

[18] www.globalreporting.com

The standard disclosures section of the framework has guidelines that identify the information that is relevant and material to most organizations and of interest to most stakeholders. Three types of standard disclosure are included:

- *the organization's profile*—information that sets the overall context for understanding the organization's performance, including its strategy, profile, and governance;

- *the organization's management approach*—information about the organization that provides the context for understanding its performance;

- *performance indicators*—which provide information on the economic, environmental, and social performance of the organization.

The fourth set of GRI reporting guidelines were published in 2013. These emphasized the importance for companies to report the things that matter, not simply everything they measure; that reports need to be aligned with and shown to be part of companies' strategies; and that assurance is needed on the reliance that can be placed on the data provided. Such reporting needs to be seen by companies as enhancing their performance and their value, not as yet another business expense.

The GRI has been adopted by organizations around the world: hundreds of companies based in many countries now produce sustainability reports using the GRI framework. In addition, many other companies, particularly those operating globally, have developed their own approaches to environmental and sustainability reporting.

As corporate sustainability becomes increasingly important, systems are being developed to manage the masses of data involved in producing regular CSR and sustainability reports. Software has been developed to use companies' existing intranet facilities to collect and collate the necessary information.

Case studies

 Case study 9.1   Foxconn and Apple

When Steve Jobs, the billionaire head of Apple Computers,[19] was shown round the facilities of their supplier Foxconn in Shenzhen, China he was impressed by the movie theatres, swimming pools, and other facilities he saw in this booming city of 17 million people. Thirty years earlier, Shenzhen had been agricultural with rice paddies, water buffalo, duck, fish, and shrimp farms, and a small fishing harbour.

When subsequently Jobs learned that workers at the huge Foxconn factory were attempting suicide, that 14 had taken their own lives in 2010, he said that he found the situation 'troubling' and that he was 'all over it'.

Foxconn International Holdings Ltd, which is part of the Hon Hai group, is one of China's largest exporters, and has around 800,000 employees, half of them in Shenzhen, just across the border from Hong Kong. The Apple iPhone, iPad, and iPod all have Foxconn components.

---

[19] For more information on Apple's policies on supplier responsibility see www.apple.com/supplier-responsibility

The Hon Hai Precision Industry Company Ltd was founded by Terry Gou in 1974. He is alleged to be Taiwan's richest man. A strict disciplinarian and an apparent workaholic, Gou's mantra is 'time is money and efficiency is life'. With over 40 production and R&D centres in Asia, Europe, and the Americas, the group is now the world's largest manufacturer of parts for the computer, communications, and consumer electronics industries, sold under contract to customers such as Apple, Dell, and Sony.

Foxconn's Longhua plant was built as a factory town in the countryside north of Shenzhen when land in China's Pearl River delta was cheap. It attracted tens of thousands of young people (mostly in their late teens or early twenties) looking to leave the poverty of the provinces and believing that a factory job would offer them a 'city life' with friends and plenty of money. Instead they became cheerless human machines who were too exhausted to enjoy what little free time they had. They were hired to work eight-hour shifts but the majority increased their earnings with substantial overtime.

At the start of each shift, thousands of workers in identical uniforms would sing the company song. The public address system broadcast music and propaganda. Posters urged the workers to 'let the company get stronger and stronger', and 'achieve goals unless the sun no longer rises'. They worked standing in one place under constant camera supervision. Pay was docked under a discipline scheme, which handed out points for being late, yawning, talking, or having long fingernails. Although the plant had modern dormitories, workers slept in three-tier bunks with no air-conditioning in summer temperatures that could reach 30°C. Eating facilities were considered good, but the quasi-military atmosphere was dispiriting.

Following the spate of suicides, the company took action. Wire fences were put on roofs and nets were erected below buildings where suicides might occur to catch any who jumped. Social workers were recruited. A suicide prevention hot line was installed and averaged two calls a day. Spotter teams were created to detect employees with possible problems. The Shenzhen Mental Health Centre offered support and monks were brought in to ward off evil spirits. Basic pay was increased significantly but overtime was restricted, so this meant that some employees were no better off financially.

Under Shenzhen law, employers are required to pay a minimum compensation for death at work: as a good employer Foxconn had paid significantly more. It was feared that some employees might have killed themselves to get this generous compensation for their families. Consequently, all employees were required to sign a declaration that their dependants would not sue the company if they killed themselves. There was also a threat to stop paying medical bills following any attempted suicide.

Although the suicide rate was alarming, a visiting psychology professor from Tsinghau University pointed out that the suicide rate was actually lower than the average for young people in the rest of China.

Foxconn had been lauded by the Chinese press for creating jobs in modern surroundings. Now the firm became an object of criticism and undercover investigations. On an impromptu visit to Shenzhen, Terry Gou insisted that he was not running a 'sweatshop'. Clients, including Apple, Dell, and HP, announced their own inquiries to ward off bad press. Tim Cook, who took over Apple following the death of Steve Jobs, went on a highly publicized tour in August 2012. There seemed to be room for improvement.

In 2016, in an apparent attempt to diversify away from dependence on Apple, Gou negotiated to acquire the Japanese Sharp company, a producer of electronic display panels. Gou's management style was strikingly different from the participative Japanese approach, and the Japanese press called him 'a domineering warlord of business'. The connection with China also raised political concerns.

Meanwhile, in Shenzhen Foxconn's robotics group, led by Day Chia Peng, was developing equipment for many manufacturing processes that would reduce the need for manual workers. Day claimed that over 30,000 robots were already working in group companies.

Discussion questions

1. Does Apple have any responsibility for activities undertaken on their behalf at Foxconn?

2. Did Apple do enough in response to the problems they found at Foxconn?

3. Were the problems at Foxconn failures of governance, executive supervision, or of management?

4. Foxconn had raised its basic wages four times in the past three years and in some areas doubled the starting level of pay. Since labour is no longer cheap, should Foxconn invest in automated production lines to keep its competitive edge?

 Case study 9.2   The CLP Group on governance and ethics

CLP is a major generator and supplier of electricity in Australia, China, Hong Kong, India, and Taiwan. CLP's approach to governance and ethics is summarized in Table 9.1.

Table 9.1 CLP's approach to governance and ethics

Vision	What we must do to uphold our values
Mission	What we want to be
Values	What benefits we will bring to our stakeholders
Commitments	What ideals guide us in our mission
Policies and Codes	What we must do to meet our commitments

A set of business principles and ethics define the company's vision, mission, and values, creating its identity and guiding its actions. The concept of sustainable development defines corporate actions, balancing the social, environmental, and economic dimensions of the business, while considering the needs of both current and future generations.

CLP believes that good corporate governance enhances credibility and improves shareholders' and other stakeholders' interests. Maintaining a good, solid, and sensible framework of corporate governance is a top priority. The company is committed to a set of ethics and principles covering every aspect of the business. The code on corporate governance creates the framework and principles for defining company policies and procedures. The code covers every aspect of the business to keep actions consistent with the vision, mission, and values. The company also recognizes that corporate governance is an evolving process, and reviews the principles and practices in light of experience, regulatory changes, and international developments.

CLP recognizes its shareholders as key stakeholders and is committed to creating shareholder value with a sustainable rate of return to shareholders. To earn and maintain shareholder support, the company has adopted the following principles:

● deliver value to them through capital appreciation (expressed in the form of the performance of share price over time) and payment of dividends;

● operate the business in a way that corresponds to their values and expectations;

● communicate honestly, effectively, and frequently with shareholders about the stewardship of their assets by the board and management of CLP;

- manage its investments and business risks in accordance with its principles and code of conduct;
- invest in expanding and preserving the value of its assets, capabilities, and relationships.

(For more information, see www.clpgroup.com/Pages/home.aspx.)

Discussion questions

1. What is your opinion of CLP's corporate governance framework?

2. Would it be suitable for other companies?

3. Could the CLP code on corporate governance be a pro forma code for other companies?

Self-test questions

1. What are business ethics?
2. What different perspectives on CSR are discussed in the chapter?
3. What might a firm's socially responsible activities include?
4. What is enlightened shareholder value?
5. Who should lead a company's CSR efforts?
6. What is a CSR policy?
7. When might a clear CSR policy influence potential investors?
8. How does the Brundtland Report define sustainable development?
9. What is the Global Reporting Initiative and who is involved?
10. What is the basic belief behind the Global Reporting Initiative?

 For suggested answers to these self-test questions visit the online resources at: www.oup.com/uk/tricker4e/

Projects and exercises

1. Develop a CSR policy statement for any organization with which you are familiar. It could, for example, be for a profit-orientated company, an academic institution, or some other not-for-profit enterprise. Develop a set of performance indicators to monitor and measure the organization's achievements.

2. Develop a sustainability report for an organization with which you are familiar.

3. Write an essay on 'What is the real purpose of a business?'

References and further reading

Amao, Olufemi (2013) *Corporate Social Responsibility, Human Rights and the Law: Multinational Corporations in Developing Countries*. Routledge, London.

Andreas, Fred M. et al. (2011) *A Simple Path to Sustainability: Green Business Strategies for Small and Medium-sized Businesses*. ABC-CLIO, Santa Barbara, CA.

Banks, Erik (2004) *Corporate Governance: Financial Responsibility, Controls and Ethics*. Palgrave Macmillan, New York.

Beal, Brent D. (2013) *Corporate Social Responsibility: Definition, Core Issues, and Recent Developments*. Sage, Los Angeles.

Bell, Jeanne, Jan Maaoka, and Steve Zimmerman (2010) *Nonprofit Sustainability: Making Strategic Decisions for Financial Viability*. Jossey-Bass, San Francisco.

Bernstein, Anne (2010) *The Case for Business in Developing Economies*. Penguin Books, Johannesburg.

Blowfield, Mick and Alan Murray (2011) *Corporate Responsibility*. 2nd edn, Oxford University Press, Oxford.

Bolton, Dianne and Suzanne Benn (2012) *Key Concepts in Corporate Social Responsibility*, SAGE Key Concepts series. Sage, Los Angeles.

Carroll, A. B. (1979) 'A Three-dimensional Conceptual Model of Corporate Performance', *Academy of Management Review*, 4, pp 497–505.

Chandler, David and William B. Werther, Jr (2005) *Corporate Social Responsibility: Stakeholders in a Global Environment*. Sage, Los Angeles.

Cramer, Jacqueline (2006) *Corporate Social Responsibility and Globalisation: An Action Plan for Business*. Greenleaf Publishing, Sheffield.

Crane, Andrew et al. (eds) (2009) *The Oxford Handbook of Corporate Social Responsibility*. Oxford University Press, Oxford.

Crane, Andrew, Dirk Matten, and Laura Spence (2013) *Corporate Social Responsibility: Readings and Cases in a Global Context*. 2nd edn, Routledge, Abingdon.

Crowther, David and Lez Rayman-Bacchus (eds) (2004) *Perspectives on Corporate Social Responsibility*. Ashgate Publishing, London.

Department of Education (2017) A Competency Framework for Education—The Knowledge, Skills and Behaviours needed for Effective Governance in Maintained Schools, Academies and Multi-academy Trusts, The Stationery Office, London.

Eccles, Robert G. and Michael P. Krzus (2010) *One Report: Integrated Reporting for a Sustainable Strategy*. Wiley, Hoboken, NJ.

Epstein, Marc J., John Elkington, and Herman B. Leonard (2008) *Making Sustainability Work: Best Practices in Managing and Measuring Corporate Social, Environmental and Economic Impacts*. Greenleaf Publishing, Sheffield.

Fleming, Peter and Marc V. Jones (2013) *The End of Corporate Social Responsibility: Crisis and Critique*. Sage Publications, London.

Habisch, André et al. (eds) (2005) *Corporate Social Responsibility across Europe*. Springer, Heidelberg.

Hamschmidt, Jost (2007) *Cases in Sustainability Management and Strategy: The Oikos Collection*. Greenleaf Publishing, Sheffield.

Hancock, John (2004) *Investing in Corporate Social Responsibility: A Guide to Best Practice, Business Planning and the UK's Leading Companies*. Financial Times, London.

Hitchcock, Darcy and Marsha Willard (2009) *The Business Guide to Sustainability: Practical Strategies and Tools for Organizations*. Earthscan, London.

Holme, Richard and Phil Watts (2000) Corporate Social Responsibility: Making Good Business Sense. World Council for Sustainable Development, Geneva, Switzerland.

Hopwood, A., J. Unerman, and J. Fries (2010) *Accounting for Sustainability: Practical Insights*. Earthscan, London.

ICGN (2009) Statement and Guidance on Non-financial Business Reporting. International Corporate Governance Network, London.

Kotler, Philip and Nancy Lee (2004) *Corporate Social Responsibility: Doing the Most Good for Your Company and Your Cause*. John Wiley and Sons, Chichester.

Laszlo, Chris and Nadya Zhexembayeva (2011) *Embedded Sustainability: The Next Big Competitive Advantage*. Greenleaf Publishing, Sheffield.

Orsato, Renato, J. (2009) *Sustainability Strategies: When Does It Pay To Be Green?* INSEAD Business Press, Fontainebleau, France.

Raynard, Peter (ed.) (2006) *Tomorrow's History: An Anthology of Simon Zadek's Work*. (Academy of Management's 2006 SIM book prize) Greenleaf Publishing, Sheffield.

Reich, Robert B. (2006) *Super-capitalism: The Transformation of Business, Democracy and Everyday Life*. Borzoi Books, Random House, New York.

Rezaee, Zabihollah, Lynn Turner, and Diane L. Swanson (2008) *Corporate Governance and Ethics*. Wiley, Chichester.

Schaltegger, Stephan and Marcus Wagner (eds) (2006) *Managing the Business Case for Sustainability: The Integration of Social, Environmental and Economic Performance*. Greenleaf Publishing, Sheffield.

Tricker, Bob and Gretchen Tricker (2014) *Business Ethics—a Stakeholder, Governance and Risk Approach*. Routledge, Abingdon.

Vogel, David (2006) *The Market for Virtue: The Potential and Limits of CSR*. Brookings Institution Press, Washington, DC.

Waddock, Sandra and Charles Bodwell (2007) *Total Responsibility Management: The Manual*. Greenleaf Publishing, Sheffield.

Werther, William B. and David B. Chandler (2010) *Strategic CSR: Stakeholders in a Global Environment*. Sage, Los Angeles.

Zerk, Jennifer A. (2006) *Multinationals and Corporate Social Responsibility: Limitations and Opportunities in International Law*. Cambridge University Press, Cambridge.

Useful websites

www.business-ethics.com

Business Ethics—the magazine of corporate responsibility.

www.complianceweek.com

Leading information service on corporate governance, risk, and compliance.

www.wbcsd.org

World Business Council for Sustainable Development, 'Corporate Social Responsibility Report: Making Good Business Sense', with CSR questionnaire and tools.

www.csrwire.com

The Corporate Social Responsibility newswire—news items on CSR.

www.sustainability-reports.com

Portal for sustainability reports of multinational companies all over the world.

www.csr.gov.uk

UK government gateway to corporate social responsibility.

www.csracademy.org.uk (search for 'Business in the Community')

CSR Academy.

www.sustreport.org

Canadian Institute for Research and Innovation in Sustainability—'The Sustainability Report'.

www.article13.com

Adviser for business on sustainability.

www.globalreporting.com

Global Reporting Initiative and its guidelines.

www.iso.org

Access to ISO26000 standard on CSR.

www.csr-asia.com

CSR Asia—sustainability pioneer in Asia.

10

The Governance of Listed Companies

 Learning Outcomes

This chapter enables us to:

- Explore the ownership of listed companies.
- Understand shareholder rights.
- Consider shareholder activism and investor relations.
- Review the governance of complex corporate structures.
- Distinguish dual-listed companies and dual-class shares.

Ownership of listed companies

The reality of corporate governance and the way in which power can be wielded over a company reflects the ownership structure. Although some texts treat the owners of listed companies as though they were homogeneous, the actual pattern of ownership can have a major influence on corporate governance.

Contrast the potential differences of shareholder power in the following cases.

1. A listed company in which the shares are widely spread between many individual and institutional shareholders with no one in a dominant position: given a balanced and mixed ownership, no single investor or group of them acting together can exercise undue influence over company affairs.

2. A listed company in which institutional shareholders dominate, particularly one listed in the liquid markets of the United States or the United Kingdom, where a significant proportion of shareholders are institutional investors—banks, insurance companies, pension funds, hedge funds, and sovereign funds. In the United States, institutional investors now account for around two-thirds of the investment in large listed companies. Only three of the world's most valuable listed companies are now American—Exxon Mobil, Walmart, and Microsoft. In the UK in 1963, individuals held 54 per cent of British listed companies with less than a tenth of the market being in the hands of overseas investors; today less than 12 per cent of British shares are held by individuals, while 53 per cent are held by overseas interests.[1]

3. A state-run enterprise, such as Gazprom, run by the Kremlin in Russia, which is really a state bureaucracy masquerading as a company.

[1] UK Office of National Statistics www.ons.gov.uk/.../investmentspensionsandtrusts/.../ownershipofukquotedshares/...

4. A listed company in which a single shareholder owns a major shareholding. Such a controlling shareholder may not need a majority holding to exercise considerable influence, given that no other shareholder has significant voting powers. Such ownership structures are common in Europe and many other countries outside the USA and the UK.

5. A listed company in which some large shareholders form a block and are thus able to influence events, even though none hold a majority of the voting rights. Such block holdings are prevalent in Sweden and some other countries. In Italy, legal agreements can be created that enable shareholders to work and vote together through a voting trust.

6. A family company which is listed with outside shareholders, but in which a significant proportion of the voting shares are still in family hands. Many family companies are in this category. The family do not need to hold as much as 50 per cent to exercise considerable influence; 20 per cent or 30 per cent is often sufficient, if the holdings of the other shares are widely spread. Most of the family companies listed in Hong Kong maintain control, with outside investors holding significantly less than 50 per cent of the voting rights. Some stock exchanges, including Hong Kong, require listed companies to offer a minimum percentage of their shares in a public offering.

7. A company that has been floated on the stock market may still be in the hands of the founder, who dominates because of his/her status and position, even though (s)he now holds less than a controlling share.

8. A Chinese state-owned enterprise with a minority of its shares listed on the London or New York Stock Exchanges.

9. A listed company could be the subsidiary of another major company, if less than 50 per cent of its shares are available to the public. We shall see examples of such companies in group chains and networks later in this chapter.

It is also worth noting at this stage that, although we tend to think of a direct relationship between shareholder and company, in reality there can be a complex chain of intermediaries acting as agents, as we noted earlier. For example, the ultimate owner of a share could be an individual:

- who invests in a private pension fund;
- which invests some of its funds in a hedge fund;
- which in turn invests in a fund of funds to hedge its risk;
- which invests in a commercial property fund;
- which places some of its funds in the hands of a financial institution;
- which invests ultimately in the listed company;
- but lends the shares as collateral for a deal it has made.

In a complex chain, how does the listed company demonstrate its accountability to its ultimate owners? Who is responsible for exercising corporate governance influence on the listed company? These are issues that lie behind some of the challenging questions in contemporary corporate governance.

Public companies, those listed on the stock market, face significantly more demanding governance standards than those applying to private companies, through legislation and regulation, corporate governance codes, and the listing rules of the stock market. Companies planning a stock market listing, probably through an IPO (initial public offering), need to position themselves carefully beforehand. Among the things that need to be considered include:

- position the company beforehand to meet the requirements of the relevant corporate governance codes and listing rules;

- ensure the chair of the board is confident and competent in the role—chairing a board with outside directors, with divergent experiences and views, can be quite different from the close-knit consensus of a private company board;

- seek advice from corporate auditors and lawyers, particularly from compliance and governance specialists, and from the financial institution leading the IPO;

- consider the board structure, ensuring a sufficient number and quality of independent outside directors; consider board diversity; acquiring appropriate independent directors and briefing them takes time;

- ensure that existing directors have the appropriate knowledge, time, and enthusiasm to serve on the board of a quoted company—the time commitment for directors of a listed company is often significantly more demanding than for a private company and the number of board papers much greater;

- create the required board committees, including the audit committee, the remuneration committee, and the nominating committee; and train the members, operating the committees to gain experience;

- agree board-level remuneration and review policies;

- consider board succession, director training and development, and director and board evaluation methods;

- develop the required reporting routines and shareholder interaction processes well ahead of time;

- develop the board reporting systems to ensure they are comprehensive, timely, and accurate for the governance of a listed company.

Shareholder rights

The rights that shareholders acquire with their shares are determined by the Companies Acts or ordinances of the jurisdiction in which the company was incorporated and by its articles of association. Although the details obviously vary between countries, ownership of a share broadly provides the right to:

- have your name, address, and shareholding entered onto the shareholder members' register;

- receive notice of all shareholder meetings within a specific time;

- receive the formal company accounts, directors' and auditors' reports, and other statutory notices;

- attend shareholders' meetings;

- vote, either in person or by proxy, at all shareholder meetings;
- view the company's statutory records, including the register of members, the register of loans charged against the company's assets, the register of directors, officers, and company secretary, and the register of their share interests;
- receive dividends that have been duly declared for that class of share.

Shareholders do not have a right to attend internal meetings of the company, to access management accounts and other corporate information, or to get involved in management. However, shareholder activism is growing and many listed companies now recognize that investor relations are a basic part of sound corporate governance.

In shareholders' annual general meetings (AGMs), ordinary resolutions require a simple majority with over 50 per cent of the members voting in person or by proxy at the meeting. Decisions made by ordinary resolution include the:

- approval of the accounts presented to shareholders by the directors;
- approval of the reappointment of auditors;
- payment of dividends proposed by the directors;
- approval of transactions between the company and connected persons;
- appointment and reappointment of directors.

Longer notice may be required for resolutions to:

- remove a director;
- remove an auditor during their term of office;
- appoint an auditor other than the retiring auditor.

In 2007, the European Union (EU) published a Shareholder Rights Directive, which sought to improve shareholders' rights and solve problems in the exercising of such rights across borders in the member states. The Directive applied only to companies in which shares are traded on stock markets within the European Economic Area (EEA), which encompasses the EU countries plus Iceland, Liechtenstein, and Norway. Switzerland is not a member.

In the UK, the Companies (Shareholder Rights) Regulations were published in 2009 to implement the EU Directive. Shareholders acquired the right to ask questions at shareholder meetings, which companies must answer unless they can show that such disclosure would not be in the company's interest or would be likely to disrupt the meeting. Companies must provide a website, with information relevant to shareholders' interests, including their right to ask questions and how to vote. Holders of at least 5 per cent of the voting shares can now requisition a shareholders' general meeting (previously 10 per cent were required). Also, holders of 5 per cent of the voting shares, or 100 members, can require a company to include an item on the agenda of their company's AGM.

The 2009 Regulations also clarified the way in which companies count proxies when using a 'show of hands' rather than a formal ballot. An electronic address must be provided for the receipt of proxies and electronic voting by shareholders was facilitated. The Regulations also require listed companies to publish information about AGM ballots: the number of votes cast, the percentage of voting shares represented by those votes, and the number of abstentions.

Shareholder activism and the role of institutional investors

In the 19th-century model of the company, shareholders were individuals and met together periodically to receive the report and accounts of their directors, to re-elect them or to propose new ones, and to approve significant changes, such as an alteration in the share capital, as required by company law or the company's articles. Shareholder democracy, with each share having voting rights, was feasible. Ownership was the basis of governance power.

But today, in many listed companies, the shareholders include corporate institutional investors as well as individuals. The shareholders are numerous, geographically spread, and have different expectations of the company. Shareholder democracy ('one share, one vote') no longer provides shareholder power.

In many jurisdictions, it has become difficult for shareholders to ask questions if the chair has no wish to allow them. To get motions onto the agenda of shareholder meetings or to nominate new directors is often near impossible. As Berle and Means showed in the 1930s, in large companies power has moved from shareholders to management.

Dissatisfaction with boards has increased in recent years, with concerns over poor corporate performance, allegedly excessive directors' rewards, loss of investor confidence following downturn in markets, and company collapses. There have been many calls for greater involvement by shareholders in the governance of companies. But the potential for activism by individual shareholders is low, given their large numbers, small individual holdings, and diverse interests, although the internet has provided some small individual shareholders with a platform from which to advance their opinions on corporate issues.

However, institutional investors can wield more power. Even though their shareholding is relatively small, they can have a more significant influence, particularly if they act in concert with their activities coordinated. Many institutional investors now receive voting guidelines from their representative organizations, such as the Council of Institutional Investors or Institutional Shareholders Services in the United States, or the Association of British Insurers, through the Institutional Voting Information Service, and the Pensions and Lifetime Savings Association in the UK.

In the United States the incidence of activist shareholders threatening or initiating proposals for the nomination and election of directors has increased significantly.[2] Moreover, many have been successful. Activist calls for shareholder-sponsored directors to public company boards are also receiving support from financial institutions. Activist shareholders can now be a potential risk for incumbent boards by proposing their own nominees (what some commentators refer to as 'short-slate' elections) and boards need to consider their policies in response to such activism.

However, a distinction needs to be drawn between investors: some seem more like short-term speculators than shareholders who are interested in the long-term prospects and performance of their company.

Private equity investors in listed companies, such as Blackstone, and Wall Street investors such as Carl Icahn, Daniel Loeb, and Nelson Peltz, caused alarm in some American boardrooms when they acquired significant equity stakes that led to them becoming predators, sometimes called 'corporate raiders' or 'greenmailers'. However, some commentators claim that these activist investors research their targets thoroughly, make sound business

---

[2] *Activism Monthly* (2013), 2, 4 and *Activist Annual Review* 2012.

recommendations, and can be a force for good. In recent years, some aggressive American investors have targeted companies in the UK, Europe, and other countries.

A classic example of shareholder activism occurred in 2014, when the Trian Fund Management company, led by Nelson Peltz, published a report they had sent to PepsiCo Inc., the beverages and snacks business. Trian owned US$1.2 billion of Pepsi stock, and in a 57-page report critiqued the board's marketing, manufacturing, and organizational strategies, exposing corporate blunders, and called for a reorganization that would make some brands more independent corporate entities (and, of course, more open to be floated separately for the benefit of investors).[3]

In the UK, shareholders do have the right to have resolutions put on the ballot and, if successful, these are usually binding on the directors. Research from the Harvard Business School has shown how directors' careers can be affected by shareholder activist campaigns.[4] It was found that directors are almost twice as likely to leave over a two-year period if their company had been the subject of a shareholder activist campaign. Directors are also more likely to leave in the year following activism if they receive lower shareholder support on re-election. However, although directors may leave boards following activism, it does not affect their standing on other boards on which they serve.

Shareholder activism can take a number of forms. Usually it involves communication and negotiation directly with management. But activism can involve media campaigns or blogging to change corporate practices, proxy battles advancing shareholder resolutions to force change, calling shareholder meetings, or litigation against companies or their directors. Some shareholder activists use their shareholding to advance their own social, environmental, or other agenda to influence corporate behaviour.

Hedge fund managers can also become active shareholders, acquiring sufficient voting power to nominate a director to the board. They may also be able to afford financial, accounting, and legal advice to protect and promote their interests. In some countries, controlling block-holders of shares, such as founders and their families, are also able to influence decisions in the boardroom over and above the power of the shareholder vote, although the deepening of stock markets in countries such as Sweden, Italy, and Spain is beginning to reduce the significance of such block-holders.

Some have suggested that increasing shareholder activism is irresistible, leading to an inevitable struggle between shareholders and top management. Predictably, not all directors are enthusiastic about shareholder involvement. They would prefer a return to their earlier experiences when shareholders were relatively passive, seldom raised questions, and readily confirmed board recommendations.

Shareholder activism can be controversial. The view is advanced that shareholders, having elected their directors, should allow them freedom to act without having their business decisions second-guessed. Separation between shareholders and top management, it is argued, lies at the heart of the governance system. Boards need freedom to take business decisions in good faith without interference from interventionist institutions. Otherwise, boards might respond to investor pressure by focusing on the short term, failing to make crucial, long-term, strategic decisions. Moreover, some add, institutional investors are in effect intermediaries in the chain between ultimate individual owners and companies. Such institutions have governance problems of their

[3] www.trianwhitepapers.com
[4] Gow, Ian D. Sa-Pyung Sean Shin, and Suraj Srinivasan (2014) Consequences to Directors of Shareholder Activism, Harvard Business School Working Paper 14–071.

own in recognizing and responding to the different aims of their own investors. But most listed companies now recognize the importance of close, positive involvement with their investors.

Investor relations

Proactive shareholder-relation activities provide a two-way channel of information, informing both existing and potential shareholders, securities analysts and the financial community, and the company. Shareholder-relation activities take many forms, including interactive websites, newsletters, shareholder meetings, press conferences, and road-shows, as well as meetings with individual shareholders, to resolve questions and explore issues about the company's strategies, policies, and financial standing. The digital delivery of shareholder services, electronic many-way communication, and social media are tending to accelerate the interaction between companies, their shareholders, and market commentators. Indeed, moves towards paperless relationships between companies and their shareholders, which some call 'dematerialization', is progressing, although some shareholders remain to be convinced.

In the United States, the Sarbanes-Oxley Act of 2002 increased the emphasis on investor relations by demanding greater corporate transparency, compliance, and enhanced financial disclosure, with board-level responsibility for financial reports. In the UK, the Financial Reporting Council requires companies to explain to their AGM how they intend to engage with shareholders when a significant percentage of them have voted against any resolution.

Many publicly traded companies have set up investor or shareholder relations departments. Typically, these departments report to the finance director or chief finance officer (CFO), with the company secretary or corporate attorney closely involved if legal issues arise. However, some companies link their investor-relations activities with their public and media activities. Professional investor relations can improve a company's standing and ultimately its share price, although companies need to be careful to avoid disclosing sensitive information about the share price to only one or a few shareholders.

Investor relations practitioners have achieved a professional status in some countries and have their own professional bodies, for example the National Investor Relations Institute in the United States, the Investor Relations Society in the UK, and the Australian Investor Relations Association. Some professionals in the field now see investor relations as part of broader stakeholder relations and corporate social responsibility, with the need for a coordinated communications programme.

In October 2016, the UK FRC issued guidance to preparers of annual reports of around 1,200 large and smaller listed companies:

> The annual report provides an opportunity to communicate key information to investors about the company's performance, strategy and future prospects. The strategic report should therefore be presented in a user-friendly, clear and concise manner. In particular investors expect:
>
> - The relationship between IFRS or UK GAAP measures and any alternative performance measures used to be clearly explained.
> - Business model reporting to provide clarity of explanations of how the company makes money and what differentiates it from its peers.

- A clear link between the business model and the revenue recognition policies to be disclosed.
- Dividend disclosures to detail how dividend policies operate in practice and how these policies may be impacted by risks and capital management decisions facing the company.

Disclosure of substantial shareholdings and directors' interests

Many jurisdictions, through their company law, and many stock exchanges, through their listing rules, require the disclosure of shareholders with substantial interests in a listed company. Such transparent and timely disclosure of information about the ownership structure allows existing shareholders and potential investors to make informed decisions. In effect, it enables those dealing with the company to appreciate where the balance of power over its governance really lies.

In Singapore, the Companies Act requires a substantial shareholder of a listed company holding 5 per cent or more of the total shareholder votes, whether resident in Singapore or not, to disclose their interests in the voting shares. The shareholder must give written notice to the listed company within two business days of becoming or ceasing to be a substantial shareholder. The company must then inform the Singapore Stock Exchange. In Singapore, failure to obey the Companies Act can incur civil penalties and failure to follow the listing rules could lead to the ultimate sanction of delisting.

In 2013, the UK introduced proposals to enhance the transparency of UK company ownership and increase trust in UK business. These proposals required companies to maintain a registry of companies' beneficial owners, showing who owns and controls them. The proposals also stopped the issue of bearer shares, which do not provide details of the owners. Corporate directors were also prohibited, so that directors would be real people, not other corporations.

A 2017 study of listed companies by the Hong Kong Institute of Chartered Secretaries discovered that over half of the companies responding recognized that their communications

---

Corporate Governance in Action 10.1   Total Oil Company: individual shareholder relations

Total is a leading multinational energy company, based in Paris, France, with over 97,000 employees and operations in more than 130 countries. Together with its subsidiaries and affiliates, Total is the fifth largest, publicly traded, integrated international oil and gas company in the world. Institutional investors hold 87 per cent of its shares. Total engages in all aspects of the petroleum industry, including upstream operations (oil and gas exploration, development, and production) and downstream operations (refining, marketing, and the trading and shipping of crude oil and petroleum products), as well as being a major player in chemicals. Total also has interests in coal mining and power generation, and is developing solar, biomass, and nuclear energy businesses.

Transparency, listening, and dialogue are key to the company's relationship with its shareholders. To strengthen this relationship, the company's individual shareholder relations department provides opportunities to exchange, discuss, and inform, through shareholders' meetings, an annual trade show, meetings with shareholders in a number of cities in France, and the shareholders' newsletter.

with their shareholders needed improving;[5] whilst a few even reported that they were not sure who all their shareholders were.

Public disclosure is also often required of directors' dealings in their company's shares. Such information is intended to deter directors from benefiting from confidential inside knowledge they have of the company's affairs. In Australia, the Corporations Act and the Australian Securities Exchange Listing Rules oblige directors of public companies to notify the exchange of changes to directors' interests in shares.

Insider dealing (or insider trading) is the buying or selling of shares on the basis of information that is not yet available to the stock market. It is now illegal in almost all jurisdictions, although some countries were slow to criminalize the activity. In 2013, SAC Capital, an American hedge fund company, and some of its officers pleaded guilty to federal insider trading charges, and were fined US$1.8 billion, the largest penalty for the offence to date.

The governance of complex corporate structures

Thus far we have looked at governance issues in simple corporate structures in which there is one corporate entity, one governing body, and one set of shareholder members. Certainly, this was the situation in the mid-19th century when joint-stock, limited-liability companies were first developed. Although a few companies did merge during this period, this was achieved by creating a new company, which acquired the assets and liabilities of the merging companies, and then winding up the original companies. Towards the end of the 19th century entrepreneurs realized that a company could legitimately own shares in other companies. These days most listed companies operate through groups of companies, not a single corporate entity. These groups can be quite complex and may include other listed companies. So let us now consider the governance of such companies.

Complex corporate structures can be grouped into three broad categories:

1. pyramids, in which the holding company sits on top of a pyramid of subsidiary and associate companies;

2. chains, in which one company or shareholder group holds an interest in a string of companies;

3. networks, in which a set of companies owns shares in each other.

To be clear on definitions:

- a *holding company* is a company that holds all or a dominant share of the voting rights in another company;

- a *subsidiary company* is a company in which another company (its holding company) holds all of its voting shares (a *wholly owned subsidiary*) or a majority of its voting shares (a *partially owned subsidiary*);

[5] Hong Kong Institute of Chartered Secretaries (2016) Shareholder Communications for Listed Issuers: Five initiatives to break the monologue. Available at: www.hkics.org.hk/media/publication/attachment/PUBLICATION_A_2385_HKICS_Shareholder_Communications_for_Listed_Issuers_(Eng).pdf

- an *associate company* is a company over which another company exercises dominant power, even though it does not hold a majority of the voting rights in that company, for example where the other shareholdings are widely spread.

The governance of pyramid structures

The corporate pyramid is the most straightforward organizational form for a group of companies. It is the structure found most frequently in practice, and is widely used by both private companies and public listed companies. It is also the structure widely used by international groups that own companies incorporated in a number of countries. Figure 10.1 depicts an elementary form of pyramid, showing a holding company with four subsidiaries held at two levels.

Research published over 30 years ago showed that 20 companies at the top of the UK Times 1000 list had 4,600 subsidiaries between them:[6] an average 230 subsidiaries each. The smallest group had 12 subsidiaries, the largest a surprising 800. But more surprising was the number of levels at which the subsidiaries were held (subsidiaries of subsidiaries of subsidiaries, etc.). Most held subsidiaries at two or three levels, but many had subsidiary companies at levels five or six, and one even at level eleven! This had arisen because a company at level five had acquired a company that itself had subsidiaries at five levels. With the growth of globalization and cross-border holdings of companies, the situation today can be even more complex.

Why should a holding company adopt a pyramid structure, rather than operate through a single entity? There are a number of possibilities. First is strategic positioning: a group

Figure 10.1 A simple group pyramid structure

6 Tricker, R. I. (1984) *Corporate Governance: Practices, Procedures, and Powers in British Companies and their Boards of Directors*. Corporate Policy Group and Gower, Aldershot, UK.

structure can be used to set boundaries around identifiable parts of the enterprise in line with the group's corporate strategy (see Case study 10.1: The Jardine Matheson Group).

The second reason to adopt a pyramid structure could be legal: operating through a company incorporated in the country of operation often simplifies legal and regulatory aspects, including business regulation, contracting, employment, taxation, health and safety regulation, and so on. However, incorporating a company in an offshore tax haven can also provide significant financial and legal benefits to the group. As an indication of the importance of offshore companies, a majority of the local companies listed on the Hong Kong stock market are incorporated in the British Virgin Islands, Bermuda, Panama, or other tax havens around the world (see Corporate Governance in Action 10.2).

The third reason to adopt a pyramid structure could be taxation: there can be significant tax benefits in operating through companies registered in countries where the taxation regime is lower than elsewhere. Although the tax laws of most countries seek to ensure that profits are taxed where they are earned, with tough oversight of transfer prices for goods and services passed between group companies in different countries, there are still major benefits to be gained through separate subsidiaries in differently taxed countries.

The fourth reason for a pyramid structure, creating separate limited-liability companies, is an attempt to reduce the group's exposure to the debts of any member company. As we have already seen, the shareholders of a company are not liable for its debts. That applies where the owner is itself a limited company. Consequently, where a group has businesses that could hazard the well-being of the group as a whole if they were to fail, each business can be incorporated as a separate legal entity. For example, some shipping companies operate each of their vessels as a separate limited company. In many jurisdictions, company law protects the owners from liability for the debts of subsidiary companies. Each separate company is shrouded with a veil that cannot be pierced. However, in some other company law jurisdictions, such as Germany, corporate groups are not allowed to protect themselves in this way from the failure of one member of the group. In these countries, creditors of subsidiary companies in a group can pursue their debts with the parent companies up the ownership structure, right to the top.

The fifth reason for creating a pyramid structure could be to provide a legal home for a non-trading activity or to preserve a name. Such companies are sometimes called 'letter box' companies. Some companies in a group could be dormant—that is, they are not trading—but are not wound up in case they are needed in the future.

Finally, many corporate groups have arrived at their complex pyramid structure through mergers and acquisitions. Rather than rationalize their organization structure following acquisitions and mergers into product or regional divisions, these groups continue with a conglomeration of separate companies reporting through the ownership structure to the holding company.

So, what are the corporate governance implications of a group operating with a pyramid structure? Every company in a group must obey the legal requirements of the jurisdiction in which it is incorporated. Moreover, if it is a listed company, it must fulfil the listing requirements of the stock exchanges on which its shares are listed. In most cases, that means each subsidiary and associate company must have its own officers and board of directors, keep its own financial records, file the required company reports, and in some cases have an audit (see Corporate Governance in Action 10.2).

Corporate Governance in Action 10.2   Incorporation in a tax haven: the example of BVI

The British Virgin Islands (BVI) are situated 60 miles east of Puerto Rico in the Eastern Caribbean. Only about 20 islands have permanent residents. BVI is a British Overseas Territory, which uses the US dollar as its legal currency. The capital is Tortola. The BVI Constitution gives executive and legislative power to the Governor, the Executive Council, and the Legislative Council.

BVI is a world leader in offshore company incorporations. These companies are used for a wide range of purposes, including acting as a holding company for multinational and global corporations, as trusts for asset protection, for collective investment, and to hold intellectual property. Such incorporations can offer tax benefits, limited disclosure of financial and ownership information, secrecy of inter-company dealings, and other benefits.

BVI has good communications, political and economic stability, no exchange controls, low taxation with certain classes of business exempt, no capital gains tax, and no wealth tax. Incorporation in BVI offers flexibility, corporate privacy and confidentiality, a pool of professional service providers, sound company law based on British law, and regulation that is reasonable, but not bureaucratic. BVI is also committed to assist the international fight against money laundering.

(For more information, see www.britishvirginislands.com.)

The corporate governance implications for directors of subsidiary or associate companies operating in a pyramid structure are significant. Every director owes a duty to the company on the board of which he or she serves. That board must obey the corporate governance requirements of the relevant company law jurisdiction, the rules of the regulatory regime, and, if a listed company, the listing requirements of the stock exchange. But if the company is controlled through the group management control system, an executive director also has to accept the duties and responsibilities as a member of the group management structure, recognizing that performance appraisal and reward will be determined within that structure. This is particularly important if the subsidiary company on the board of which the director serves has external minority shareholders, in which case the director must ensure that the rights of all shareholders (the external minority shareholders and the group) are recognized. This can be difficult should their interests differ, remembering that the career prospects of a director, who is also a manager in the group, depend on decisions taken in the group. If an independent non-executive director is appointed as a director of a subsidiary company, in order to ensure that the interests of minority shareholders are protected, he or she is a nominee director, with the implications already discussed.

The governance of chain structures

The corporate chain is, as the name suggests, a group of companies in an ownership chain. What distinguishes this structure from a simplified form of pyramid is that the companies in the chain have other outside shareholders, as shown in Figure 10.2. The head of the chain may be another company, a group of investors such as a private equity fund, or an individual. Companies in the chain may be public and listed companies or private companies.

Figure 10.2 A simple chain structure

Why is the chain structure adopted? The answer is simple: those controlling the head of a chain can influence management decisions in the other companies in the chain. With the leveraged power gained from gearing, the head of the chain is able to exercise more influence over the companies in the chain than by investing in each individual company. Figure 10.3 is an example of gearing in a chain of companies.

A successful businessman and his family are the dominant owners in the chain, owning 34 per cent of company A, which owns 40 per cent of company B, which owns 36 per cent of company C. Companies A, B, and C are all public companies listed on a stock exchange. The rest of the shareholdings in each company are held by the public (as in Figure 10.2), with no other dominant holding. In this chain, the financial investment of the head of the chain in company C is actually only 5 per cent (34 per cent of 40 per cent of 36 per cent), yet the

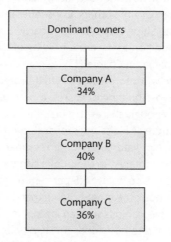

Figure 10.3 Example of gearing in a chain of companies

head of the chain is able to exercise management control over all of the companies in the chain, by being the dominant holder in each company. A chain of companies may also offer a defence against predators, because the companies in the chain have some protection from the gearing.

What are the governance implications for the directors serving on the boards of companies in a chain? Primarily, of course, directors of such companies must fulfil their duties to their company under the company law, the regulatory regime, and, where listed, the stock exchange. But, inevitably, with a dominant shareholder at the head of the chain, the companies in the chain have to respond to the requirements of that shareholder. Indeed, some of the directors may well be their nominees. But, as we have already seen when discussing nominee directors, such directors must also respect the interests of the other shareholders in their company, including any minority shareholders.

Chain structures are found in many countries in Asia, particularly where entrepreneurs and their families leverage their investment with other outside investors through a chain. They are also popular in Europe and other countries where family interests dominate corporate groups. In Italy, for example, the Agnelli family, through family interests held in a limited partnership, were able to exercise considerable influence over Fiat, the automobile firm.

The governance of network structures

The terminology is obvious: a network structure is one in which the member companies form a network of cross-holdings, each company being a node in the network. One or more companies may be dominant or there may be no dominant member.

Why do groups of companies operate in networks? In some cultures, Japan and South Korea for example, the network is the traditional way in which corporate groups operate, working together with mutual operations and cross-holdings of shares. In the rest of the world, there are a number of reasons why groups operate in networks.

First, strategic links can be created between companies that cooperate operationally. For example, a group of companies may agree to work together, with various companies offering research and technological know-how, manufacturing capability, marketing and distribution services, or managerial capability to the others. Consequently, they may agree to exchange shares and accept cross-directorships between their boards. Such linkages can be reinforced by financial relationships, in addition to the cross-holding of shares. We will discuss the governance of joint venture companies in Chapter 11.

Second, companies may network to provide mutual protection, minimizing the chance of hostile predators. With a cross-holding of shares, a potential hostile bidder has a built-in disadvantage in acquiring enough shares to pursue a bid. Case study 10.1 provides an interesting example. Jardine Strategic Holdings is incorporated in Bermuda and listed in London, Singapore, and Bermuda. A private, family-based company, Jardine Matheson Holdings, owns a controlling 82.5 per cent interest in the public company Jardine Strategic Holdings. But Jardine Strategic Holdings in turn holds 55.5 per cent of its parent. The public company is sheltered from predators through the cross-holding that it owns in its parent company. In some jurisdictions, company law prohibits such an arrangement.

Third, networks may be formed to raise funds through equity or loan financing. Pyramids and chains of companies may be buried within the network. In some cases, the apparent complexity of such financing networks can result from the deals made to obtain access to funds. In other cases, however, they can reflect attempts by potential predators to disguise their tracks, where the takeover rules restrict the building of a stake in a target company without notifying the market. Complex ownership networks may conceal the acquisition of dominant positions, at least for a while.

Fourth, networks can be used for taxation avoidance, putting profits in tax havens within the law of their home country, rather than as a means of illegal tax evasion. Networks can also be used to provide anonymity for the ultimate owners of companies.

Fifth, networks can be formed to share risks between companies, part of a strategy to reduce exposure to business risk. For example, companies A, B, and C exchange shares to reinforce an agreement to share risks, profits, and losses from a large construction contract in which they are all involved. An extreme example is shown in the Sincere Group case (see Figure 10.4), in which the companies virtually owned each other. These cross-holdings would also serve to deter a hostile takeover bid for the listed holding company. As mentioned above, such an ownership scheme would not be permitted in some jurisdictions.

Sixth, networks can arise as the unintentional effect of corporate acquisition activity. Companies accept the network structure rather than incurring the costs and organizational stress of redefining the group structure and organizational systems. This can occur particularly if there are outside minority interests in some of the network companies, which interests would have to be valued and redefined in restructuring.

Finally, complex networks can arise as the result of deliberate obfuscation, to reduce a group's visibility, perhaps to confuse competitors, to deter predators, or to avoid the unwanted interest of the authorities. Such network designs may push at the boundaries of legality, for example in taxation, exchange controls, corporate reporting, or money laundering.

Block-holders and universal ownership

Where institutional investors own a significant proportion of the voting shares in a company and could act together, they form a block of shareholders. If they do act as a block, they may be able to influence corporate decisions, for example on corporate strategy, including acquisition policy, on the appointment or dismissal of directors, and on financial strategy, including dividend policy or capital restructuring.

In Sweden, corporate control became concentrated in block holdings in the second half of the 20th century. The Wallenberg Group and Industriväden typify the Swedish model (see

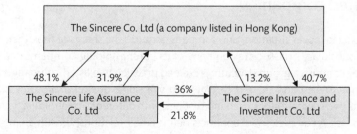

Figure 10.4 The Sincere Co. Ltd

Corporate Governance in Action 10.4), but controlling ownership is being diluted with the growth of firms and the stock market.

Italian voting trusts or voting syndicates (*patti di sindacato*) are groups of large shareholders who sign an explicit legal agreement to vote together. About a third of large Italian companies are dominated by such coalitions of large shareholders. In Italy, information on all such trusts has to be registered and this knowledge is publicly available. Such voting trusts ensure continuity and stability in management strategies and policies, and prevent conflicts of interest between large shareholders. Some proponents of voting trusts argue that concentrated, rather than diverse, ownership produces more monitoring of executive management, better management discipline, and higher returns. The trust agreement typically provides for a management committee to run the trust, arranges its operating procedures and finances, and confirms that no one shareholder can dominate.

Block-holders are also significant in South Korea, Russia, and China (where state-related organizations provide the block) and, following privatization from state ownership, in Spain and Poland. Indeed, listed companies in most economies are not widely held, as they are in the United States and the United Kingdom, but are owned and controlled by families or states.

Although there are no apparent block-holders in listed companies with widely dispersed shareholders, it has been suggested that institutional investors could form such power blocks if they were to act together on governance matters. The recently developed terminology of 'fiduciary capitalism' recognizes the potential power of financial institutions to take collective action reflecting the interests of the 'universal owners'. For example, some of the largest pension funds are those of employees in local and state government, teachers, universities, and other public sector organizations. So employee retirement assets might be used as a power base for action over companies.

Advocates of 'universal ownership' recognize the potential for pension and other funds to improve governance and long-term returns by working together, although each holds only a relatively small percentage of the total shareholding. The idea of universal ownership is most significant where equity holdings are highly diversified and lack a dominant investor. The notion also sees the agency chain of intermediaries that can exist between listed company and ultimate investor/owner. Agents have agents, each acting as the agent for the next principal in the chain, with highly diversified roles, but all bound in law by the fiduciary duty of loyalty and care. But their actions are neither transparent nor accountable. If the idea is to make a contribution, however, a universal holder mindset will be needed to provide the classical governance relationship between corporate body and its owners.

Dual-listed companies

In a traditional takeover situation, one company acquires the shares of the other, which then becomes a subsidiary or associate company of its parent holding company. In a dual-listed company, by contrast, a group structure is created in which two listed companies merge, but both continue to exist and share the ownership of a single operational business. The group maintains its two separate stock exchange listings, with different shareholders typically in different countries. A complex set of contracts defines their relationship with an integrated top management structure and the same directors or some cross-directorships.

The case of the Carnival Corporation (USA) and the Carnival Corporation PLC (see Corporate Governance in Action 10.3) is typical. Other examples include BHP Billiton (Australia and UK), Investec Bank (South Africa and UK), and Unilever (Holland and UK).

The benefits for dual-listing include:

- continuing existing successful businesses;
- protecting brand names;
- taxation benefits;
- sustaining national pride, avoiding claims that one country is losing 'its' company to another.

The disadvantages can be:

- conflict between the two managements, for example on resource allocation;
- disagreements between the boards, unless all directors are common to both;
- legal difficulties in applying the inter-company contracts;
- challenges from shareholders about unfair benefits to the other company;
- taxation difficulties, including transfer prices for inter-group trading;
- problems if the group wants to unravel the dual-listing agreements.

Dual-listed companies need to be distinguished from cases in which a single company is listed on more than one stock exchange, sometimes referred to as 'cross-listed companies'. Many international companies raise funds in this way, usually with a primary listing in their home country and one or more secondary listings elsewhere. For example, many Canadian companies are listed in both Toronto and New York.

Corporate Governance in Action 10.3   Carnival Corporation—a dual-listed group

Carnival Corporation & PLC is a dual-listed company with listings in New York and London. Carnival Corporation Inc., incorporated in Panama, is listed on the New York Stock Exchange. It is the larger of the two holding companies. Carnival PLC is listed on the London Stock Exchange and was formed from the P&O (Peninsular and Oriental Steam Navigation Company) cruise business. This British-American corporation is the only group in the world to be included in both the Standard & Poor's 500 and the FTSE 100 indices.

The combined group is the world's largest cruise operator, including Carnival Cruise Lines, Princess Cruises, Holland America Line, Windstar Cruises, and Seabourn Yachts in North America; P&O Cruises and Cunard Line in the United Kingdom; AIDA in Germany; Costa Cruises in Southern Europe; and P&O Cruises in Australia.

Dual-class shares

Dual-listed corporate groups need to be distinguished from dual-class shares. The corporate constitution of some companies (typically, the articles of association) provides for two or more classes of voting shares in which one class enjoys greater voting rights than the other class, or all of the voting rights. For example, a company might issue 'A' class shares, in which each share has 1 vote, and 'B' class shares, in which each share has 100 votes.

Dual-class shares are often issued to protect the ownership power of a dominant shareholding class, often a family, when a company is floated on the stock market. The founders of Google, Larry Page and Sergey Brin, exercise power through dual-class shares. Although holding only around 20 per cent of the equity, they control around 60 per cent of the votes. The Ford Motor Company has dual-class shares, giving greater power to the Ford family. The Porsche and Piëch families, though owning less than half of the shares in the Porsche company, enjoyed all of the voting rights. In the international media company News Corporation, the Murdoch family held around 13 per cent of the shares, but could exercise over 40 per cent of the voting rights, allowing chair Rupert Murdoch and his son James effectively to control the company's US$60 billion of global assets. Another classic example is the Wallenberg Group in Sweden (see Corporate Governance in Action 10.4).

Some stock exchanges will not list companies with dual-class shares, demanding shareholder democracy in which every voting share carries an equal voting right. Other stock exchanges, however, do list companies with dual-class shares. Predictably, the limited or no-voting class shares typically trade at a discount.

Corporate Governance in Action 10.4   The Wallenberg sphere—dual-class shares

Corporate governance in Sweden has a number of distinctive characteristics—mandatory co-determination, high private share ownership, dual-class shares, shareholders' board nominating committee, and 'spheres' of private owners. The Wallenberg family forms such a sphere, owning a business empire that is more of a dynasty than a company. Now in its fifth generation of family control, and planning for the sixth, this huge empire dominates Swedish business.

The Wallenbergs own some 40 per cent of the value of the Swedish Stock Exchange, but through dual-class shares, which give greater voting rights to their shares than to others, exercise control over many companies. At one time their interests included around 19 per cent by value, but 38 per cent by votes, of carmaker Saab; 5 per cent by value, but 20 per cent by votes, of Ericsson, a leading telecommunications company; around 11 per cent by value, but 28 per cent by votes, of Electrolux, a white goods manufacturer. They also have major interests in Atlas Copco; ABB, a global engineering group; SEB, one of Scandinavia's largest banks; and many other companies.

Wallenberg ownership is exercised through the Wallenberg foundations (assets around US$6 billion), which exercise just under 50 per cent of the votes in Investor, a public company, with over 100,000 other investors sharing in the family fortunes. Companies dominated by Investor are run by professional managers with their own boards of directors. However, the Wallenberg family insist that they are 'not just kingmakers', as some claim, but are closely involved in the companies' corporate strategies. The governance style adopted by the Wallenberg family is based on a network of carefully fostered contacts, a policy to shift investment strategies from the past to the future as industries and technologies change, but then to stick with their companies through thick and thin. The family claim that they deserve their special rights in the multiple-voting, dual-class shares because of the family's role in successfully founding and developing Swedish companies over the years, and their tradition of strong and involved ownership.

Listings on alternative stock markets

Some stock exchanges create a second market, often called a second board, to enable smaller, perhaps riskier, companies to raise capital. The London Stock Exchange established the Alternative Investment Market (AIM) in 1995 to raise capital and to provide a market for companies from all industrial sectors and any country. Some of these companies have subsequently progressed to a listing on the main board. Although many AIM companies are businesses at an early stage of development and may operate in high-risk sectors, the failure rate on AIM has been relatively low.

Unlike the main board, AIM does not stipulate a minimum size or market capitalization—the number of shares in public hands—nor does it require a track record of quality profits and financial history. The regulatory regime for AIM companies is a succinct rule book, which is also less stringent than that of the main board, although regulated under EU and British law.

A crucial element in the corporate governance of AIM companies is the nominated adviser (usually referred to as the 'nomad'), authorized by AIM, which all AIM companies are required to appoint. The nomad's experience provides a quality control mechanism by checking the company's plans and certifying to the Exchange that the company is suitable and ready for listing. The nomad assists the company during the flotation, subsequently ensures that it meets its governance obligations, and handles any on-going market issues. The company deals with AIM through its nomad, who advises AIM on all regulatory matters. The company's broker, lawyers, auditors, and financial institution also provide support services.

In the United States, NYSE Euronext was formed in 2007 by the merger of the New York Stock Exchange, itself a public listed company, and Euronext NV. Then, in 2008, NYSE Euronext acquired the American Stock Exchange, which added a US platform for small-cap companies. The Company's exchanges in Europe and the United States trade equities, futures, options, fixed-income, and exchange-traded products. With approximately 8,000 listed companies from more than 55 countries, NYSE Euronext's equities markets—the New York Stock Exchange, NYSE Euronext, NYSE MKT, NYSE Alternext, and NYSE Arca—represent one-third of the world's equities trading and the highest liquidity of any global exchange group.

The Stock Exchange of Hong Kong also offers a second board—the Growth Enterprise Market (GEM). GEM advertises itself as a 'buyers beware' market for informed investors, emphasizing that emerging companies carry a high investment risk, with potential market volatility and no assurance that there will be a liquid market. Companies listing on GEM are not required to show a track record of profits, or to forecast future profitability. The initial listing document must show the business objectives and activities. Quarterly operating and financial reports are required, with the directors being responsible for disclosure. The GEM is often used by Hong Kong family-based companies to enable family members to capitalize on the wealth in the family business, as well as to provide additional funds for corporate growth.

Singapore Exchange's secondary market, named Catalist, opened in 2008, replacing the previous Sesdaq board. Catalist attracts fast-growing companies from the region, competing with London's AIM for Asian listings. Approved sponsors are responsible for vetting new listings and supervising them thereafter. To be listed, companies should have a healthy financial position and prospects of profitability, but no operating or profit track record is required.

Case studies

Figure 10.5 The corporate structure of the Jardine Matheson Group (simplified)

Jardine Matheson Holdings (JMH) is a private family company, owned by the Keswick family, descendants of the 19th-century founder of the firm. JMH owns 82.5 per cent of Jardine Strategic Holdings Ltd (JSH), while JSH owns 55.5 per cent of JMH, making them subsidiaries of each other. This ownership structure was adopted to prevent hostile takeovers. In 2013 the ownership of JMH included:

Keswick family members and trusts	14.57 per cent
JSH	55.53 per cent
Other (non-family) directors	0.43 per cent
Balance with other shareholders	29.47 per cent

JSH then owns 77.6 per cent of Dairy Farm International Holdings Ltd (DFL), 73.5 per cent of Mandarin Oriental International Ltd (MOL), and 50.01 per cent of Hongkong Land Holdings Ltd (HKL). All of the companies are incorporated in Bermuda, which has company-favourable law, and is a tax haven. JSH is a publicly listed holding company, with a primary (or 'premium') share listing on the London Stock Exchange, and secondary listings on the Bermuda and Singapore stock exchanges. Its shares form part of the Singapore *Straits Times* share index.

Dairy Farm is a leading pan-Asian retailer, with over 5,300 outlets including supermarkets, hypermarkets, health and beauty stores, convenience stores, home furnishings stores, and restaurants, employing over 80,000 people with sales of over US$9 billion. Dairy Farm International Holdings Ltd has its primary share listing on the London Stock Exchange, and secondary listings on the Bermuda and Singapore stock exchanges.

Hongkong Land Holdings is a leading property investment, management, and development group with a major portfolio in Hong Kong, where it owns and manages some 5 million square feet of prime office and retail space in the heart of the central business district. In Singapore, it has interests in a number of major commercial and residential developments. The company has its primary share listing on the London Stock Exchange, and secondary listings on the Bermuda and Singapore stock exchanges.

Mandarin Oriental Hotel Group is a hotel investment and management group operating with over 10,000 rooms in luxury hotels and resorts in 27 countries. The Group has equity interests in many of its properties and net assets of over US$2.3 billion. Like Dairy Farm and Hongkong Land, Mandarin Oriental International Limited has its primary listing in London, with further listings in Bermuda and Singapore.

At one time, all five companies were listed in Hong Kong and were members of the local Hang Seng Index. However, prior to the 1997 change of Hong Kong's sovereignty from Britain to China, in 1994 they de-listed from Hong Kong and moved their primary listing to London.

Under Bermudan company law, subsidiaries can vote shares in their parents. Many other jurisdictions, including the UK and Hong Kong, prohibit companies holding shares in each other in this way. The Bermudan cross-holding allows the boards of JSH and JMH to lock themselves in by voting the cross-shareholdings' pass motions at an AGM. As David Webb, a Hong Kong-based corporate governance commentator, explained:[7]

> Under Bermudan law, subsidiaries can vote shares in their parents. The Bermudan cross-shareholding allows the boards of both companies to lock themselves in by voting the cross-shareholdings to re-elect the directors at any AGM. The cross-shareholding was established in late 1986 at lower levels, and since then, the Jardine group has been gradually swallowing its own tail, each of JSM and JSH increasing its stake in the other, partly by accepting scrip dividends, and JSH increasing its stake in DFL, MOL and HKL.

The Group proposes a downgrade of their London listing

In 2013, the UK Financial Conduct Authority strengthened its listing rules to protect minority shareholders. In March 2014, the Jardine Group proposed downgrading their UK listing status from the primary (or premium) listing to a standard listing. This reduced the rights of minority shareholders and lowered governance standards. Minority shareholders would have very little say in this change, because the controlling shareholders could dominate any vote.

Discussion questions

1. Is the ownership structure depicted in this case a network, a pyramid, or a chain?

2. What is your opinion of this ownership structure?

3. Why do you think the Jardine Group really proposed the downgrading of their London listing?

4. If you were advising Jardine's, how would you suggest they justify their proposal to downgrade their London listing?

 Case study 10.2　Yum China Holdings

Kentucky-based Yum Brands Inc., owners of KFC (Kentucky Fried Chicken, Taco-Bell, and Pizza Hut brands), opened its first restaurant in China in 1987. By the time their Chinese operations were spun off, on 31 October 2016, to Yum China Holdings Inc., it had become China's largest restaurant chain. Yum China owned the franchise for Pizza Hut in China with more than 1,500 restaurants in over 400 cities; and the franchise for KFC, with over 5,000 outlets in nearly 1,000 towns and cities. Taco Bell operations were also starting.

Primavera Capital Group, a China-based global investment firm, made a strategic investment in Yum China and the company was then listed on the New York Stock Exchange (YUMC) in November 2016. Yum China Holdings Inc. is registered in Louisville, Kentucky with headquarters in Shanghai.

[7] http://webb-site.com/articles/jardown.asp

The board of directors of Yum China Holdings

The board has nine members, seven of them independent according to the company.

Fred Hu is chair and founder of Primavera Capital Group, a China-based global investment firm (Dr Hu has served as chair of Primavera since its inception in 2010; prior to Primavera, he served in various roles at Goldman Sachs).

Peter A. Bassi served as president then chair of Yum! International Restaurants. Prior to this, Mr Bassi spent 25 years in a wide range of financial and general management positions at PepsiCo, Inc., Pepsi-Cola International, Pizza Hut (US and international), Frito-Lay, and Taco Bell.

Christian L. Campbell is currently owner of Christian L. Campbell Consulting LLC, specializing in global corporate governance and compliance. Mr Campbell previously served as senior vice-president, general counsel, and secretary of Yum Brands from its formation in 1997 until his retirement in February 2016.

Ed Chan Yiu-Cheong is currently a vice-chair of Charoen Pokphand Group Company Ltd and has been an executive director and vice-chair of CP Lotus Corporation since April 2012. Mr Chan was regional director of North Asia for the Dairy Farm Group.

Edouard Ettedgui currently serves as the non-executive chair of Alliance Française, Hong Kong. Mr Ettedgui also currently serves as a non-executive director of Mandarin Oriental International Ltd, the company for which he was the group chief executive. Prior to that, Mr Ettedgui was the CFO for Dairy Farm International Holdings.

Louis T. Hsieh currently serves as a senior adviser to the CEO and as a director of New Oriental Education & Technology Group.

Jonathan S. Linen is a member of the board of directors of Yum! Brands, a position he has held since 2005, and of Modern Bank, NA. Mr Linen is adviser to the chair of American Express Company after serving as the vice-chair of American Express Company. Mr Linen also served on the board of The Intercontinental Hotels Group.

Micky Pant is the CEO of Yum China. Mr Pant has served as CEO of Yum! Restaurants China since August 2015. Over the past decade, Mr Pant has held a number of leadership positions at Yum! Brands, including CEO of the KFC Division, CEO of Yum! Restaurants International, and president of Global Branding for Yum! Brands and President of Taco Bell International.

Zili Shao has served as co-chair of King & Wood Mallesons, China. Mr Shao held various positions with JP Morgan Chase & Co., including chair and CEO of JP Morgan China, vice-chair of JP Morgan Asia Pacific, and chair of JP Morgan Chase Bank (China) Company Limited.[8]

Yum China announces its chair and CEO succession plans

On 5 October 2017, Yum China announced that its CEO, Mr Micky Pant, would become vice-chair of the board and senior adviser to the company on 1 March 2018. Ms Joey Wat, who served as president and COO, would succeed Mr Pant as CEO.

The company explained that Mr Pant had served as CEO and a member of the board of Yum China since its spin-off from Yum! Brands, Inc. and, prior to that, he served as CEO of Yum! Restaurants (China), when it was a division of Yum! Brands Inc.

'We are exceptionally grateful to Micky for leading the Company through its spin-off and building a solid foundation as an independent company,' said Dr Fred Hu, chair of the board of Yum China Holdings. 'We thank Micky for his many significant contributions and are pleased that he will be vice-chair of the board and will also continue to serve the company as its senior advisor in order to ensure a seamless transition to Joey.'

'Joey is an extraordinarily talented executive and the ideal leader to become our next CEO,' Dr Hu continued. 'Joey has a strong track record of achieving results, and with her unique ability to translate

[8] Source: Yum China press release http://ir.yumchina.com/phoenix.zhtml?c=254434&p=irol-presentations

vision and strategy into future world-class operations, I have no doubt that the Yum China business will continue to grow under her strong leadership.'

Ms Wat spent seven years in management consulting, including time with McKinsey & Company's Hong Kong office. From 2004 to 2014, she served in both management and strategy positions in the Hong Kong-based Hutchison Whampoa group, including time as managing director of their UK company, which operates the pharmacy chain Superdrug. Ms Wat joined Yum China in September 2014, first as president of KFC China and then as CEO of KFC China in August 2015. She has been the president and COO of Yum China since February 2017 and was appointed as a member of the board in July 2017.

Yum China strategy

The company outlines its view of its potential on its website:

Our brands are integrated into popular culture and consumers' daily lives.

We are dedicated to serving our customers' evolving needs by enhancing the in-store experience, improving mobile connectivity, introducing innovative new products, and constantly delivering value. We also remain focused on driving shareholder value by growing sales and profits across our portfolio of brands through increased brand relevance, new store development and enhanced unit economics. With a rapidly growing consumer class and increasing urbanization, Yum China is well positioned for long-term growth.[9]

Discussion questions:

1. What are the strengths and weaknesses of the Yum China board?

2. Why do you think Yum China announced its succession plans well in advance?

3. Should all listed companies be required to declare their chair and CEO succession plans?

Self-test questions

1. Distinguish a holding company, a wholly owned, a partly owned subsidiary company, and an associated company from one another.

2. Why might a company incorporate in an offshore jurisdiction?

3. Can shareholders attend internal meetings of the company or access management accounts and other corporate information?

4. Why do groups adopt a chain structure?

5. What are dual-class shares?

6. What is a nomad?

7. What is a dual-listed company?

8. Why might companies consider entering into a joint venture agreement?

9. What activities might shareholder activism include?

10. Can companies hold shares in themselves? Give examples from the chapter.

[9] http://ir.yumchina.com/phoenix.zhtml?c=254434&p=irol-IRHomepost

For suggested answers to these self-test questions visit the online resources at: www.oup.com/uk/tricker4e/

Projects and exercises

Select three companies listed on different stock exchanges around the world. Prepare a presentation or write a report on:

1. Your opinion on the composition of the board. Are there any weaknesses?

2. The structure of the group. How many subsidiaries are there? Are there any other listed companies in the group? Can you detect any pyramids, chains, or networks?

3. The companies' approach to investor relations. Could they be improved?

4. What impression have you formed of corporate governance in these companies?

References and further reading

Berle, Adolf A. and Gardiner C. Means (1932) *The Modern Corporation and Private Property.* Macmillan, edn revised by Adolf Berle (1967) Columbia University, Harcourt, Brace & World, New York.

Colpan, Asli M., Takashi Hikino, and James R. S. Lincoln (eds) (2010) *The Oxford Handbook of Business Groups.* Oxford University Press, Oxford.

Hong Kong Institute of Chartered Secretaries (2016) Shareholder Communications for Listed Issuers: Five initiatives to break the monologue. Available at: www.hkics.org.hk/media/publication/attachment/PUBLICATION_A_2385_HKICS_Shareholder_Communications_for_Listed_Issuers_(Eng).pdf

Kaen, Fred R. (2003) *A Blueprint for Corporate Governance: Strategy Accountability and the Preservation of Shareholder Value.* American Management Association, New York.

Kane, Yukari Iwatani (2014) *Haunted Empire—Apple after Steve Jobs.* Harper Collins Business, New York.

Lufkin, Joseph C. F. and David Gallagher (1990) *International Corporate Governance.* Euromoney Books, London.

NACD ([2005] 2008) Board: Shareholder Communications—A report of a NACD Blue Ribbon Commission, National Association of Corporate Directors, Washington, DC.

Wright, Robert E. (2004) *History of Corporate Governance: The Importance of Shareholder Activism.* Pickering and Chatto, London.

Useful websites

https://business.nasdaq.com/intel/Boardvantage/index.html

NASDAQ information.

www.nyse.com/regulation/nyse/1147474807344.html

New York Stock Exchange corporate governance listing standards.

www.londonstockexchange.com/companies-and-advisors/main-market/rules/regulations.htm

London Stock Exchange listing rules.

www.microsoft.com/about/companyinformation (click on 'company information' and 'corporate governance')

Microsoft's corporate governance practices.

http://investor.gm.com/corporate-governance/docs/CG%20Guidelines_03%2015%2011%20 (Final).pdf

General Motors corporate governance documents.

www.annualreportandform20f.shell.com/2010/corporategovernance.php

Royal Dutch Shell corporate governance principles.

www.unilever.com/investorrelations/corp_governance/ (follow links to 'corporate governance')

Unilever investors' site.

www.niri.org/FunctionalMenu/About.aspx

National Relations Institute.

www.ir-soc.org.uk

Investor Relations Society.

www.investors.asn.au

The Australian Investors Association.

The Governance of Non-Listed Corporate Entities

 Learning Outcomes

This chapter enables us to:

- Understand the governance of all private companies, including family-owned, employee-owned, subsidiary and associated companies, and joint ventures.
- Explore the governance of not-for-profit organizations, including charities, and cooperative organizations.
- Consider the governance of partnerships.
- Review the governance of hedge and private equity funds, sovereign wealth funds, and state-owned companies.

The original corporate governance codes, following the lead of the UK's Cadbury Report, focused on the governance of public companies listed on the stock exchange, with their shares available to public investors. But of course, there are millions of other corporate entities that are not public companies which need governance as well as management. This chapter focuses on the governance of such organizations.

The governance of private companies

The emphasis in corporate governance principles, policy, and practice to date has been on public, listed companies. The Sarbanes-Oxley Act in the United States, the corporate governance codes in other countries, and most corporate governance research have focused on companies in which shares are available to the general public. Of course, much more information is available about listed companies. Transparency, accountability, and the protection of shareholders' interests, particularly those of minority shareholders, are major concerns.

Yet the number of unlisted, private companies far exceeds those that are listed. These unlisted companies include firms owned by individuals and families, subsidiary and associated companies owned by holding companies, and joint ventures. Many unlisted companies are small or medium-sized enterprises, although a few are large and complex. Together, these companies make an essential contribution to economic growth, employment, and the creation of wealth around the world. Unlisted companies present some unique corporate governance challenges, although many of the basic governance concepts that apply to public companies are also relevant.

In the early days of the joint-stock, limited-liability company, all companies were public companies, incorporated to raise capital from outside investors. Today, most companies around the world are private companies, providing taxation benefits to the proprietors (because corporation tax is often preferable to personal income tax) and giving them the benefit of limited liability.

Companies limited by guarantee

In a few cases private companies are incorporated with guarantors rather than shareholders. Where this is permitted by company law, instead of shareholders, who own a share in the company's value, companies limited by guarantee have guarantors who agree to meet the company debts up to their guarantee. As with a company limited by shares, this limits the liability of those involved for the company's debts. However, the amount of the guarantee is often a nominal sum. Companies limited by guarantee are often used for enterprises with social objectives rather than profit-making.

The governance of family-owned private companies

A large proportion of private companies are owned and controlled by their founders or families. In Asia, India, and Latin America, some 95 per cent of companies are family-owned. The importance of the small and medium-sized enterprise is seen in the Mittelstand—medium-sized companies in Germany. Of course, not all family-owned companies are small: some large companies in Asia, Latin America, and Europe are family-owned. Nor are these family companies always private: in France, one in four of the listed companies on the CAC40 stock market index is family-controlled.

The governance of family-controlled private companies raises some interesting issues. Tracing the evolution of ownership and control in a typical family firm will highlight some of them. Initially, a small company may be incorporated for a business start-up or to take over the existing business of a sole trader, a family firm, or a partnership. The shareholders will be the entrepreneur starting the business, the family members involved in the firm, or the partners in the existing partnership. At this stage, the shareholders are also likely to be directors. In the early years of the family company, management and governance tend to be intertwined, because both are being done by the same people. Distinctions between the two are seldom identified until there is some separation between the owners, the directors, and top management.

Many companies fail within the first two or three years. Thereafter the focus shifts to maintaining success and seeking further growth. The running of the business and its internal management, as well as the governance tasks of strategy formulation, policy-making, periodic supervision, and accountability are all in the heads and hands of the owner/managers. Formal board meetings and meetings of shareholders are likely to be minimal. At this stage, it is important for dominant shareholder-directors to understand that the company is a separate entity and its assets are not their own.

The next stage of governance comes as the company thrives. A need for additional expertise is recognized. Perhaps the existing directors lack the marketing, financial, or international experience, which the company now needs. But the company cannot yet afford to employ a full-time executive in this field. So it invites an outside director with these skills, knowledge, or network contacts to join the board. This is cheaper in the short term than hiring a consultant, although a consultant is much easier to let go when his or her usefulness has ended. Inviting external directors to join the board is likely to change the board culture, not because they fulfil the independent compliance role of the INED in the listed company, but because they are not members of the family and inevitably add a non-family dimension to discussions. The UK's Institute of Directors suggests the creation of an advisory board (see the IoD corporate governance principles for unlisted companies in Corporate Governance in Action 11.1).

Long-serving executives may also be appointed to the board as executive directors, reflecting their contribution to the success of the firm, and tying them more securely to the company. Such appointments can provide reward, recognition, and prestige.

Successful companies often need additional capital, since the plough-back of profits is no longer sufficient to fund growth opportunities. Sometimes the financial institutions providing such facilities call for a nominee director on the board to oversee their interests.

The progression of family members through management to a place on the board can be a reward for success, but can also trigger resentment within the family. Ultimately, a successful family company has to face the challenge of passing governance and management on to the second generation. One solution is for the founder/parent figure to assume the role of chair of the board, while a family member from the second generation becomes chief executive. But experience has shown that such a switch can be difficult to achieve successfully. The new chair often finds it difficult to let go of the executive reins and adopt an advisory role, delegating the executive decision-making to a younger family member.

Throughout the life cycle of the family company, from start-up to the passing of governance power to the next generation, it is vital that the corporate governance framework is appropriate to the stage of development. The corporate governance policies and board-level practices need to reflect the scale and complexity of the company's activities, determining the relationships between shareholders, directors, and management. The structure and composition of the board should reflect the stage of maturity of the company and its business. Similarly, board-level information, board appraisal, and director development need to be appropriate. The UK IoD corporate governance principles for unlisted companies (see Corporate Governance in Action 11.1) emphasize that corporate governance 'is about establishing a framework of company processes and attitudes that add value to the business, help build its reputation, and ensure its long-term continuity and success'.[1]

Corporate Governance in Action 11.1   The UK Institute of Directors Corporate Governance Principles for Unlisted Companies

Phase 1 principles: Corporate governance principles applicable to all unlisted companies

Principle 1: Shareholders should establish an appropriate constitutional and governance framework for the company.

Principle 2: Every company should strive to establish an effective board, which is collectively responsible for the long-term success of the company, including the definition of the corporate strategy. However, an interim step on the road to an effective (and independent) board may be the creation of an advisory board.

---

[1] Institute of Directors (2010) 'Corporate Governance Guidance and Principles for Unlisted Companies in the UK', p. 6. Available at: www.iod.com/Portals/0/PDFs/Campaigns%20and%20Reports/Corporate%20 Governance/Governance%20code%20for%20unlisted%20companies.pdf?ver=2016-11-29-134715-607

Principle 3: The size and composition of the board should reflect the scale and complexity of the company's activities.

Principle 4: The board should meet sufficiently regularly to discharge its duties, and be supplied in a timely manner with appropriate information.

Principle 5: Levels of remuneration should be sufficient to attract, retain, and motivate executives and non-executives of the quality required to run the company successfully.

Principle 6: The board is responsible for risk oversight and should maintain a sound system of internal control to safeguard shareholders' investment and the company's assets.

Principle 7: There should be a dialogue between the board and the shareholders based on a mutual understanding of objectives. The board as a whole has responsibility for ensuring that a satisfactory dialogue with shareholders takes place. The board should not forget that all shareholders have to be treated equally.

Principle 8: All directors should receive induction on joining the board and should regularly update and refresh their skills and knowledge.

Principle 9: Family-controlled companies should establish family governance mechanisms that promote coordination and mutual understanding among family members, as well as organize the relationship between family governance and corporate governance.

Phase 2 principles: Corporate governance principles applicable to *large and/ or more complex* unlisted companies

Principle 10: There should be a clear division of responsibilities at the head of the company between the running of the board and the running of the company's business. No one individual should have unfettered powers of decision.

Principle 11: All boards should contain directors with a sufficient mix of competencies and experiences. No single person (or small group of individuals) should dominate the board's decision-making.

Principle 12: The board should establish appropriate board committees in order to allow a more effective discharge of its duties.

Principle 13: The board should undertake a periodic appraisal of its own performance and that of each individual director.

Principle 14: The board should present a balanced and understandable assessment of the company's position and prospects for external stakeholders, and establish a suitable programme of stakeholder engagement.[2]

Source: Reproduced with the kind permission of the Institute of Directors.

The family council

As ownership of the company passes through the generations of a family company, an inevitable split occurs between shareholders who are involved in management and those who are not. Frequently, one branch of the family runs the company, while another branch is only interested as shareholders. This situation can produce a major headache for families. Those

---

[2] Institute of Directors (2010) 'Corporate Governance Guidance and Principles for Unlisted Companies in the UK', p. 7. Available at: www.iod.com/Portals/0/PDFs/Campaigns%20and%20Reports/Corporate%20 Governance/Governance%20code%20for%20unlisted%20companies.pdf?ver=2016-11-29-134715-607

involved in management want to conserve cash, limit dividends, and plough any surplus into the business while maximizing their own remuneration and benefits (cars, class of travel, pensions, benefits in kind, and so on). But the non-management members of the family want to increase dividends so that they can benefit from their stake in the company or even to sell their shares. If the company wants to change strategy, the interests of the family members in management may well differ from those of the non-management members.

Directors' meetings and shareholders' meetings are not appropriate forums for the discussion of family affairs, because the meetings need to focus on issues affecting the company and its business.

How might this dilemma be overcome? Many experts in the governance of family companies recommend setting up a family council. This consists of all of the family members who own shares, both those who are in management and those who are not, or their representatives. The council enables family members to identify and discuss matters of inheritance, management succession, remuneration, dividend policy, and corporate strategy prior to board or shareholder meetings. In this way, potentially acrimonious issues can be resolved, in the interest of the family as a whole, before formal meetings of directors or shareholders. This becomes particularly important if there are non-family shareholders whose minority interests need to be protected.

A family council can also discuss the employment, development, and career planning of younger family members in the company. In the family-controlled company, the challenge is to incorporate sound corporate governance practices that, on one hand, ensure continuing professional management while, on the other hand, preserve family unity. Of course, some successful family-controlled companies never reach this stage: the company is sold and the capital distributed within the family before the succession issue arises.

As private companies grow, mature, and become more complex, some of the principles adopted in the corporate governance codes for public companies may become applicable. For example, separation between the roles of the chair of the board and the chief executive or managing director may be desirable to avoid domination by one person. The addition of independent directors may also be useful, to protect the interest of any non-family shareholders, to provide additional maturity and experience to board deliberations, and to add some discipline to board-level thinking. The creation of an audit committee and a remuneration committee may also benefit the board as a whole.

The governance of subsidiary and associated companies

The governance of subsidiary and associated companies raises some interesting issues. Essentially, the holding company determines the governance policies and practices of the companies in its group. As we saw in Chapter 10, there are broadly two distinct options in governing and managing a group of companies:

1. Subsidiary company self-governance allows each company in the group to govern itself and to manage its own affairs, subject to overall group-wide policies and resource allocation. Control is exercised through the group's shareholdings, emphasizing the decision-making autonomy of the board of each subsidiary company. Profitability and return on investment in each subsidiary are likely to be the measures of performance. This structure will often be adopted in a conglomerate group in which the subsidiary companies run diverse businesses.

2. *Group-wide governance* treats the group companies as divisions or departments of the holding company with control exercised through the group's management control system—in other words, emphasizing management through the group management organization structure and management control systems, not governance through the boards of each subsidiary. The performance measures set for each subsidiary company will depend on the group control systems.

Subsidiary company self-governance

The first approach, delegating decision-making power to the group's subsidiary company boards, requires each subsidiary in the group to act as an autonomous company, subject to policy requirements and resource allocations determined by its shareholder, the holding company. In other words, the directors of each subsidiary company are expected to run their company as an autonomous entity, within group policies, to meet the performance criteria required by the group. With subsidiary company self-governance, the structure and membership of the subsidiary and associate company boards becomes important. The holding company has the option of drawing the directors of subsidiary companies from:

- the staff of the group holding company, who might or might not be on the main board;
- the management of the subsidiary company;
- the management in other group companies;
- outside the group.

The benefits of drawing subsidiary company directors from other companies in the group include the opportunity for cross-group coordination, the sharing of expertise, training, and development of future main board directors, management development, and the building of group norms and culture. In associate companies and in subsidiaries with outside minority interests, it would be normal to find nominee directors representing the interests of the outside shareholders.

Group-wide governance

In the second approach, the group holding company imposes management control systems and organization structures on the entire group operations, which transcend the operations of the individual subsidiary companies. The control system divides the group into appropriate operating units, which may or may not map onto the subsidiary company structure. Group resources are allocated to these performance units through the management control system, performance criteria are laid down for management of each unit, and outputs are monitored. The power to make decisions throughout the group is delegated along the lines of the management control system not the legal structure of the subsidiaries.

With group-wide governance, the members of subsidiary company boards are typically drawn from the management of group head office and the subsidiary company, because power lies in the management organization structure throughout the group, not in the boardrooms of the subsidiary companies.

For example, in Figure 11.1, the holding company manages its group through a group organization structure with two divisions, A and B. Its management control system, consequently,

Figure 11.1 Control through a group management control system

will monitor the management of the divisions. Managers have their responsibilities delegated down through the levels of management in the organization structure and are accountable back up that structure. Managers owe their primary allegiance to their line manager, not the directors of the subsidiary company of which their business unit may be part.

You might ask why such holding companies controlling through the group management system have subsidiary companies at all. The reasons could be:

- legal (the ability to contract under the laws of the state in which the subsidiary is incorporated and operates);
- fiscal (the opportunity to reduce taxation in high-tax regimes);
- strategic (to protect a brand name or other strategic benefit);
- risk reduction (to obtain the benefit of limited liability).

Because such subsidiaries are legal entities, they must, of course, fulfil their legal reporting and taxation requirements. But power lies in the management organization structure throughout the group, not in the boardrooms of the subsidiary companies.

The governance of employee-owned companies

Some public listed companies offer shares to their employees, either free as part of their remuneration, or for purchase on favourable terms. Such schemes are intended as a reward for service and to motivate and commit employees to the long-term interests of the company. However, other companies are substantially or wholly owned by their employees. The largest employee-owned company in the UK is the John Lewis Partnership, a country-wide chain of retail stores, including the Waitrose food supermarkets. (For more information go to: www.johnlewispartnership.co.uk/csr/our-employees/employee-ownership.html. To watch a video of partners' reactions to the ownership system go to: www.johnlewispartnership.co.uk/media/webcasts-and-videos/being-a-partner.html. See also Corporate Governance in Action 9.1.) In the USA, most employee-owned companies are comparatively small,[3] the largest being Publix supermarkets with around 160,000 employees.

A frequently cited example of employee ownership is the Mondragon Corporation, which is a federation of worker cooperatives in the Basque region of Spain. Founded in 1956, the organization was the idea of a Catholic priest, Father José Arizmendiarrera. He called for attitudes that lead to interpersonal harmony, participation, and technical skills. The Mondragon group is now the seventh largest Spanish company with some 80,000 employees, working in manufacturing, retailing, construction, and insurance. Initially a federation of employee cooperatives, the Mondragon Co-operative Group was established in 1984, to coordinate activities and develop the underlying corporate values—participation, social responsibility, solidarity, and innovation. At Mondragon a Co-operative Congress formulates policies and develops four-year strategy and annual business plans for the component parts of the organization. Ratios of wages between managers and levels of other workers are agreed. Employee-owned businesses can take many forms, but all emphasize the importance of employee commitment and participation in decision-making.

The governance of joint ventures

Joint ventures between companies, or strategic alliances as some call them, have been the preferred way for many companies to enter markets, transfer technology, procure supplies, obtain finance, share management skills, manufacture products around the world, or share risk on an international scale. Sometimes, the partners in a joint venture can be competitors in other fields.

Many joint ventures involve the incorporation of a joint venture company owned by the two or more partners in the joint venture. Top management of such joint venture companies are often drawn from among the senior management of the partners.

Governing joint venture companies can present special challenges. As in Case study 11.1, disagreements can arise between the partners that were not envisaged in the initial joint venture agreement. Directors then face conflicts of interest between their responsibilities to the joint venture company and to the partner company that employs them. Moreover, joint venture companies may be incorporated in foreign jurisdictions, with diverse and different company laws and regulatory regimes, and have overseas partners with different cultural expectations.

A crucial aspect of the governance of joint venture companies is to realize that only matters concerning the joint venture can properly be handled by the joint venture company board. Issues affecting relations between the joint venture partners cannot be resolved at the joint venture company level. They need to be handled at partner-board level, if necessary by revising the joint venture agreement.

The composition of the board of joint venture companies needs to be considered carefully and written into the joint venture agreement, including how many representative directors

[3] www.nceo.org/articles/employee-ownership-100

there will be from each side and whether INEDs are desirable. Although many joint venture companies do appoint the managing director or CEO of the joint venture to the board, others now appoint representative directors from the partner companies, plus INEDs in some cases, with the joint venture project manager attending meetings in a non-voting, non-partisan way.

The governance of not-for-profit organizations

Most of the companies we have considered so far have been set up for the benefit of their shareholders with profit and growth over the long term as the fundamental objectives and measures of success. But there are other forms of corporate entity in modern society that are hugely important to economic, social, and environmental well-being, which are not limited-liability companies. It is now widely recognized that such corporate entities need sound governance as well as good management, just as profit-orientated companies do. The fundamental corporate governance framework of performance (strategy formulation and policy-making) and conformance (management supervision and accountability) applies, although it has to be applied to reflect the unique characteristics of not-for-profit entities.

Examples of not-for-profit entities are legion:

- major organizations created to benefit the community, such as the British Broadcasting Corporation (BBC) or the Smithsonian Institute in the United States;
- organizations providing health services, such as the UK National Health Service (NHS);
- educational institutions including universities, colleges, and schools;
- religious entities such as cathedrals, churches, synagogues, and mosques;
- sports clubs;
- organizations supporting arts and culture;
- charities pursuing objectives to benefit society;
- trades unions;
- housing and loan associations (building societies) set up to link savers with home buyers;
- non-governmental organizations (NGOs);
- other enterprises set for up a social purpose.

Typical distinguishing features of such not-for-profit organizations include:

- they are working for the benefit of society, or of a section of society, rather than the benefit of shareholders;
- they may have multiple objectives, not only long-term profit and growth;
- they may have a 'multiple bottom line' to monitor these objectives;
- such multiple goals are often difficult to measure;
- they may have multiple stakeholders to satisfy;

- their legal status may be rooted in the law of trusts, charities, cooperatives, or legislation or regulation other than company law;

- they can have various legal structures (such as a company limited by guarantee, a private, profit-making company owned by the not-for-profit organization, or an entity without limited liability run under its own constitution);

- their underpinning constitution determines their form and purpose;

- governance is provided by a governing body, which might be known as a council, board of trustees, management committee; or, of course, the governing body could be called a board of directors;

- governing bodies are often large and drawn entirely from outside, non-executive members; consequently, the chief executive is seldom also the chair of the governing body, except in small organizations involving few people;

- objectives can conflict: for example, a hospital might find that it cannot simultaneously deliver the highest performance on patient care and medical standards, financial effectiveness, administrative efficiency, staff welfare, and community approval;

- nomination and election to the governing body may come from members, funding bodies including the state, representative bodies (staff, beneficiaries, funding bodies, the local community, etc.), subject to the constitution; difficult conflicts of interest can arise where governing body members 'represent' interest groups associated with the organization;

- although they are seldom members of the governing body, the top executive and members of the management team are typically invited to attend meetings of the governing body, to make reports, and to answer questions—but they seldom vote on agenda matters;

- membership of the governing body is usually voluntary and unpaid, with no fees, remuneration, or capital gains, subject perhaps to reasonable expenses.

The significance of the constitution

The foundation of governance in a not-for-profit organization is the constitution. This determines its name and purpose, the way those associated with it (often its members) elect the governing body, the rights and meetings of those members, the way the governing body operates, the officers of the organization, the keeping of records, financial reporting and audit, and other matters relevant to sound governance.

Constitutions can take many forms and have many names. Oxford colleges are often created under a Royal charter granted by the UK's Privy Council. Some NGOs, such as the Port of London Authority and the New Jersey Turnpike Authority, are formed under their own legislative acts. However, the governance of many organizations is based on just a rule book. Nevertheless, the constitution is basic to governance.

In earlier days, charities and other public-interest organizations relied on values in society to ensure that their trustees behaved appropriately. Today, given the greater diversity of voluntary and community organizations, their many aims, and changing social norms, in some parts of the world more use is being made of codes and legal sanctions.

The governance of charities

Charitable organizations form a special group of the not-for-profit entities because:

- their primary purpose is to provide a public service, although their roles can be quite different; for example, to promote conservation (e.g. the Woodland Trust), heritage (e.g. the National Trust), safety at sea (the Royal National Lifeboat Institute), animal welfare (the American Society for the Prevention of Cruelty to Animals), or education (scholarship programmes)—although many well-known charities are national or international, many are small and local;
- the source of funds can include membership subscriptions, donations and legacies, charitable events and collections, public appeals, and charges for services provided;
- although executives may be remunerated, much of the activity is supported by unpaid volunteers.

Because of the diversity of charities, both in scale and purpose, many countries recognize the need to regulate them comprehensively. The potential for fraud and misfeasance also calls for careful monitoring. Such regulation often requires charities to be registered, with regular reports on their activities, finances, and governance.

In 2005, and most recently updated in 2017, the UK Charity Commission published a non-mandatory code for good governance of the voluntary and community sector. Working with the National Council for Voluntary Organizations (www.ncvo-vol.org.uk), the following 'hallmarks' of good charity trusteeship were suggested.

UK code for the voluntary and community sectors

1. Board leadership

Organizations should be led and controlled by an effective board of trustees, which collectively ensures delivery of their aims, sets their strategic direction, and upholds their values. The board has ultimate responsibility for ensuring that the organization is well run, solvent, and delivers the desired outcomes. Further, the board should focus on strategic direction and avoid becoming involved in day-to-day operations, unless strategic and operational roles of individuals are separated.

2. Board control

The board is responsible and accountable for monitoring and ensuring that the organization is performing well, including compliance with its constitution, the law, and regulatory requirements. The board should maintain and regularly review the organization's internal controls, policies, and procedures for reporting performance, and organization risk management. Principles of equality and diversity should be upheld and the organization should be fair and open to all sections of the community in its activities.

3. The high-performance board

The board should have and achieve clear responsibilities and functions, with a statement of trustees' duties and responsibilities, which the trustees understand. The board should have a diverse range of skills, experience, and knowledge, and make the most effective use of trustees' time and abilities. Induction, training, and on-going support should be available to trustees, along with appropriate information and advice. The board is responsible for the supervision, support, appraisal, and remuneration of its chief executive (or whatever the head of the organization is called).

4. Board review and renewal

The board should periodically review its own effectiveness, and that of its committees and the organization as a whole.

5. Board delegation

The board should set out the functions of its subcommittees, the chief executive (if any), and other staff in clear, delegated authorities. The terms of reference and roles should be clear and the delegation effective.

6. Board and trustee integrity

Individual trustees and the board as a whole should act according to the highest ethical standards and ensure that any conflicts of interest are properly disclosed and handled. Trustees must not benefit from their position beyond what may be allowed by the constitution and the law.

7. Board openness

The board should be open, responsive, and accountable to the organization's members, beneficiaries, other users, partners, and all those with an interest in its work. Stakeholder communication should be effective, and key stakeholders should be involved in the organization's planning and decision-making.

In the UK public sector, an independent commission for good governance in public services, chaired by Sir Alan Langlands, produced a good governance standard for public services in 2005.[4] The standard argued that good governance means:

---

[4] The Independent Commission on Good Governance in Public Services (2004) 'The Good Governance Standard for Public Services'. Available at: www.jrf.org.uk/report/good-governance-standard-public-services

1. focusing on the organization's purpose and on outcomes for citizens and service users;
2. performing effectively in clearly defined functions and roles;
3. promoting values for the whole organization and demonstrating values of good governance through behaviour;
4. taking informed, transparent decisions and managing risk;
5. developing the capacity and capability of the governing body to be effective;
6. engaging stakeholders and making accountability real.

In the United States, even though the Sarbanes-Oxley Act (SOX) does not formally apply to non-profits, SOX standards are being applied to not-for-profit entities. In California, SOX-like standards have been imposed on all large non-profit organizations.

Some problems that are frequently found in the governance of voluntary and community organizations include:

- founders of the organization become permanent members of the governing body;
- stagnant board membership and poor chairing;
- lack of succession planning for the governing body;
- board members elected by representative groups who have conflicts of interest either as individuals or as representatives of a stakeholder group;
- boards packed with representative members who are well-meaning, but who contribute little;
- lack of board members with necessary skills, knowledge, or experience;
- executive management failing to keep board members informed;
- board members not well briefed on the organization's activities;
- inadequate control systems, performance measures, and monitoring of executive actions;
- failure to meet reporting obligations;
- lack of a strategic focus and failure to rethink strategies as circumstances change;
- interpersonal politics among members of the governing body.

Some community and voluntary sector organizations include limited companies within their organization structure, for example running a profit-making mail order catalogue company to raise funds. Such companies, of course, must abide by company law, regulations, and governance codes as appropriate.

The UK has created two legal forms for such companies—the community interest company (CIC) and the incorporated charitable company (ICC). CICs are regulated by a government-appointed regulator, who determines whether organizations meet the necessary criteria of community interest and ensures compliance with the CIC regulations.

In the United States such entities are called mutual-benefit non-profit corporations. Such corporations are required to file tax returns and are different from public-benefit non-profit corporations, which have objectives for the common good.

The key criteria for board membership of a voluntary or community organization should be merit and contribution, not representation and status. In many communities, the importance of the voluntary sector is growing. In some countries, more governmental funds are being made available to such organizations, with related calls for wider accountability and transparency. Inevitably, there is a growing need to recognize the vital significance of sound corporate governance.

The governance of cooperative organizations

The cooperative movement began in the UK in the 19th century, based on the principle of self-help among the working class. Building societies were formed to funnel the savings of members to provide mortgage funds for others to buy their homes (in the United States these entities were called savings and loan associations). Burial societies were formed to enable poorly paid people to set aside a few pennies each week to pay for their funerals. Subsequently, many building societies gave up their mutual status and reincorporated as profit-orientated financial institutions. Few burial societies still remain. But the cooperative retail movement, with retail stores in almost all towns and cities, prospered.

Customers of the Co-op, as it is frequently called, are invited to join the local cooperative society as members. While members do not actually own the society (their shares have no market value) they are part of the governance mechanism, invited to annual meetings, receive financial information, and appoint directors. Co-op members receive a small dividend based on profits and related to the amount of their purchases. In Cambridge, Massachusetts the Harvard Cooperative Society Store is known affectionately as the 'coop' at Harvard and MIT.

The governance of partnerships

A partnership is a legal organizational form in which two or more people agree to join together to achieve common goals under a partnership agreement that determines the contribution that each partner is required to make to the partnership, the way in which the partnership will be governed and managed, and the way in which profits and losses will be shared. Typically, partners are personally liable for the debts of the partnership. A partnership is not a company and in most jurisdictions operates under specific partnership law. The partnership model has a long tradition and has shown itself to be robust and flexible. Around the world, professional practices, in accountancy and medicine for example, have adopted the partnership form for many years.

Corporate Governance in Action 11.2   The collapse of the Arthur Andersen partnership

Arthur Andersen was one of the Big Five global accounting practices. Operating in many countries in the world, the firm provided audit, accountancy, and consultancy services to its client companies. The firm had developed many pioneering accounting practices and systems. Its reputation, and certainly the partnership's self-image, was as the international leader of the profession.

Then, in the early years of the 21st century, things went badly wrong. Some of Andersen's major US clients—Waste Management, Worldcom, and Enron—became spectacularly insolvent and the auditor was claimed to be less than blameless. The claims for damages from disgruntled creditors and shareholders of the failed companies threatened the financial viability of the Andersen firm. The American firm was also found guilty of destroying evidence, although that verdict was quashed on appeal.

The question was whether the Andersen partnership was based in America, or whether partners in the Andersen practices around the world were also exposed. Some claimed that the partnerships were legally distinct; in the event, the rapid loss of clients in countries around the world and partners leaving for other firms resulted in the failure of the global practice and the end of the Arthur Andersen partnership.

A partnership has fewer constraints and lower requirements for reporting than a limited-liability company. As a result, partners are free to decide how they want to govern their partnership. In a small partnership with relatively few partners, the normal form of governance is through a meeting of all the partners. In larger practices with many partners, and particularly if they are geographically spread, the partnership may decide to appoint a managing partner and a governing body, perhaps called an executive or management committee or board, which meets regularly to manage partnership affairs, with a periodic, perhaps annual meeting of the entire partnership to accept the accounts, transact business reserved to that meeting, and appoint members to the governing body.

In the past, some partnership law put a limit on the maximum number of partners allowed in a partnership. But this law has been relaxed in some jurisdictions, and partnerships in those places can now be large and international. As a result, partners could find themselves personally exposed to the partnership risks of a widely spread and diverse practice, without being personally able to influence partnership decisions, except though periodic voting for members of the governing body. This was the case when the international accountancy partnership Arthur Andersen found itself financially exposed in the collapse of Enron, as seen in Corporate Governance in Action 11.2.

Following the Enron and Andersen debacle, a call to limit the exposure of audit firms to unlimited actions for damages in such cases was widely heard. It was further suggested that many claimants sued the auditors, even though they might have had only a relatively small part in the overall collapse, because accountancy firms have 'deep pockets'—the result of insurance cover—whereas the directors of a failed company, who might have been far more culpable, have only their private resources.

Some countries have now provided for a form of limited-liability partnership (LLP). This governance vehicle gives the benefits of limited liability to the members, but allows the flexibility to organize as a traditional partnership. The governance of an LLP is similar to that of a partnership: members provide the capital, contribute personally, and share profits and losses. To give some protection to those dealing with a limited partnership, however, the disclosure requirements tend to be more stringent than for a traditional partnership, and similar to those of a company. For example, in the UK LLPs are required to have a registered office, to file an annual return with financial accounts, and to notify changes to their membership.

In the United States, the master limited partnership (MLP) has become a significant means of raising capital. An MLP combines the advantages of limited liability for the owners, the tax advantages of a partnership, and the more limited governance of a private business. Commentators have suggested that the growing interest in the MLP, as a means of raising capital and governing entities, has been a response to the regulatory burden on companies under the Sarbanes-Oxley Act and other rules designed to make business safer, but at a cost. Others comment that if the MLP becomes a significant means of raising funds and limiting tax payments, it will change the face of American capitalism.

The governance of hedge funds and private equity funds

Hedge funds

As the name suggests, the essential element of a hedge fund is to provide its investors with a hedge against future uncertainty. For example, the managers of a normal fund might invest in shares in, say, the commercial property sector because they believe that there will be significant growth there. Hedge fund managers might also buy such shares, but will complement the purchase by selling short an equivalent quantity of other stocks (that is, they sell shares they have borrowed for a fee, buying them back later). If the price rises, the purchase of the commercial property shares will show a profit; if the market falls, the shorted shares will compensate for the loss. So whichever way the market moves, the fund is hedged. Of course, the fund is still at risk of losing money if its managers misjudged the prices at which they bought and sold. Moreover, in reality, hedge funds are involved in much more complex trades than these and are typically highly geared, increasing their exposure.

Large sums of money are provided to hedge fund managers by sophisticated rich individuals who have been attracted by the fund's prospectus, the fund managers, and their track record. Institutional investors, including some public and corporate pension funds, also invest in hedge funds to improve their overall performance, subject to the aims of the fund.

Hedge funds may take positions in commodities, buy equity shares, trade in debt, invest in futures, such as energy futures, sugar prices, carbon emission prices, even the weather, or make other exotic contracts, while using all of the tools in the contemporary financial management tool box, such as economic forecasting, statistical analysis, mathematical modelling, gearing, short-selling, securitization, and more. The massive sums often involved in hedge fund investments can result in spectacular profits and, of course, correspondingly devastating losses. But the aim of most hedge funds is to produce consistent returns, recognizing that providing a hedge will tend to damp down major rises or falls in the market. Sensible investors further spread their exposure by investing in a basket of hedge funds.

It is estimated that there are now more than 10,000 hedge funds around the world. The most successful funds are often closed to new investors. The majority trade trying to provide sustained returns and raising new investment as necessary. The least successful fail and lose their investors' money.

Hedge funds typically make heavy use of gearing, thus increasing their potential return and their exposure to risk. If investments are successful, the firm reaches break-even between revenues and costs earlier, and thereafter contributes more rapidly to investors' profit. Conversely, if investments are unsuccessful, the fund reaches break-even more slowly, because it still has to meet the interest costs, and the investors are saddled with a loss.

Some politicians around the world have expressed suspicion of hedge funds. Germany's Deputy Chancellor called hedge funds 'locusts', when blaming them for the hostile takeover of German companies. Others claimed that hedge funds forced Britain out of the European Exchange Rate Mechanism in 1992. Malaysia's Prime Minister blamed hedge funds for the East Asian financial crisis in the late 1990s. In each case, there were other forces at work as well. There is little doubt that most hedge funds take a short-term view of their investments, rather than assuming the role of stewards working with management long-term. Warren Buffet's highly successful Hathaway Fund, however, has proved to be a classic exception to this generalization.

Other criticisms of the governance of hedge funds include their concern for privacy, the lack of disclosure on matters such as their investment strategies and profitability, the extraordinary earnings of successful fund managers both from fees and percentages on gains, and that share traders are not responsible shareholders, but interested only in the short term. At the societal level, there is also the fear that, as we saw with banks around the world during the sub-prime mortgage crisis in 2007–8, things can spiral downwards. The collapse of one fund could affect the others by driving down prices on the market, triggering margin calls, forcing more selling, driving prices still lower, with more margin calls and more losses, until funds collapse and the pension funds providing the capital and/or the banks providing the gearing funds would be hit.

Compared with the heavy regulation of listed companies, the hedge fund industry is relatively unregulated, except for controls on the financial viability and available wealth of those allowed to invest. Of course hedge fund managers have to abide by insider-dealing laws and stock exchange regulations when they trade in equities. There have been calls for regulation or voluntary codes. The International Corporate Governance Network supports the creation of a code of best practice for hedge funds, based on the 'comply or explain' principle. Others call for information on hedge funds' indebtedness and society's exposure to risk, rather than requiring them to disclose their business models, their complex statistical programmes, or their investment strategies.

Private equity firms

Private equity firms operate funds that can invest massively in the acquisition of companies. These can include listed companies, which are taken private, thus avoiding the public company disclosure requirements of the stock market and corporate regulators. These funds may also provide venture capital to grow existing businesses or new start-up ventures, and some also seek special investment opportunities, such as buying a failing company from which value can be realized.

Private equity firms seek capital for their funds mainly from institutional investors, including state and corporate pension funds, banks and other financial institutions, and from rich individuals. Some states restrict investment in such funds to accredited investors who are able to shoulder the risk. Usually, investors subscribe to a specific fund managed by a firm, becoming a limited partner in the fund rather than becoming an investor in the firm itself. Investors in such limited partnerships recognize that their funds can be locked in for a long period and that the risk is high with the potential to lose their entire investment, and they therefore expect high returns. Some private equity funds spread their risk by investing in a range of other private equity funds, sometimes called a fund of funds. The managers of private equity firms may also invest in their own funds, typically providing up to 5 per cent of the overall capital.

Mergers and acquisition activity in the United States and the United Kingdom reached an all-time high prior to the sub-prime lending crisis in 2007–8. Much of this growth in acquisition activity was attributable to private equity institutions acquiring control of previously listed companies.

In the United Kingdom, some well-known companies have come into private equity own-ership, including Boots the Chemist, Hilton Hotels, and the EMI music business. Britain has probably gone further than any country in allowing its core companies to be sold to overseas interests: Thames Water is now owned by a German company; London Electricity by a French company; and the ownership of the British Airports Authority, which runs major UK airports, is Spanish. In the United States, many well-known companies have been helped by private equity investment, including Apple Computers, Avis, FedEx, and Microsoft.

Typically, private equity funds generate returns on their investments by the sale of acquired business to other interests, or by floating the acquired company through an initial public offer-ing. Private equity is a notoriously secretive sector. Firms do not often publish information on their history, their ownership, the senior members of their management and advisory teams, or their investment strategy. Private equity funds also provide little indication of the partners in the fund, or of their capacity to invest. Nor do they disclose the portfolio of companies in the fund, other than to their investors. However, a few private equity firms have been floated as public companies and are listed on stock markets. In these cases, more information is available on the overall funding, but not of individual funds, nor of their investors. The vignette case of Black-stone provides a good example (see Corporate Governance in Action 11.3).

Corporate Governance in Action 11.3   The private equity Blackstone Group

Peter G. Peterson and Stephen A. Schwarzman founded The Blackstone Group with a shared secretary and a balance sheet of US$400,000 in 1985. Today, Blackstone is a leading global alternative asset manager and provider of financial advisory services listed on the New York Stock Exchange, with total assets under management of US$110 billion in 2010. The asset management businesses include the management of:

- corporate private equity funds;

- real estate opportunity funds;

- marketable alternative asset management funds, including:
  - funds of hedge funds;
  - mezzanine funds;
  - senior debt vehicles;
  - proprietary hedge funds;
  - closed-end mutual funds.

The corporate private equity operation, established in 1987, is a global business with offices in New York, London, Mumbai, and Hong Kong, and is a world leader in private equity investing, having managed five general private equity funds as well as one specialized fund focusing on communications-related investments.

From an operation focused in the early years on consummating leveraged buyout acquisitions of US-based companies, the company has grown into a business pursuing transactions throughout the world and executing not only typical leveraged buyout acquisitions of seasoned companies, but also transactions involving start-up businesses in established industries, turnarounds, minority investments, corporate partnerships, and industry consolidations—in all cases, in friendly transactions supported by the subject company's board of directors.

Income for 2010 was US$1.4 billion, and distributable earning was US$702 million. Blackstone acquired, floated, and sold Southern Cross Healthcare.

Source: www.blackstone.com

Some commentators have felt that the acquisition of listed companies by private equity interests would dilute stock markets through 'privatization'. In fact, such developments could be seen as a return to the earlier 19th-century model of joint-stock companies, when a handful of external shareholders invested in a public company, elected the directors, and held them to account for their stewardship.

Typically, private equity firms are unregulated, other than within the company and banking regulations and laws of the relevant jurisdiction. Calls for more transparency and greater disclosure are sometimes heard on the grounds of potential conflicts of interest, finance market stability, or public interest, particularly when a well-known listed company disappears under the veil of private equity. The response of private equity interests is, predictably, that their responsibility is to the owners of their firm and the investors in their funds. Greater exposure of their funding, strategies, or portfolios would inhibit the private deals that enable private equity to generate impressive returns on the back of significant risk.

The strengths of private equity investment also reflect its potential weaknesses. In essence these can be summarized as:

- *high gearing*, which increases volatility and risk (private equity firms are typically highly leveraged, using interest-bearing debt rather than equity capital for growth);
- *a strategic orientation towards financial rather than business strategies*—in other words, private equity investors are more interested in realizing value from underperforming companies and undervalued assets, than in acting in the best long-term interests of the companies in their portfolio;
- *cost-reduction policies*, seen by some as stripping out costs without regard for other stakeholders, particularly staff and customers;
- *the disposal of unnecessary assets*, sometimes described by others as asset-stripping or 'selling the family silver';
- *the use of tax advantages* on the sale of entities in some tax jurisdictions;
- the charging of *high fees and top management remuneration*.

Sir David Walker's voluntary code for private equity firms (summarized in Corporate Governance in Action 11.4) applies only to the UK, although many private equity deals involve cross-border deals.

Corporate Governance in Action 11.4   Sir David Walker's voluntary code for UK private equity firms

A private equity firm should publish an annual review accessible on its website or ensure regular updating of its website to communicate:

- a description of the way in which the FCA-authorised entity fits into the firm of which it is a part with
- an indication of the firm's history and investment approach, including investment holding periods, where possible illustrated with case studies.
- a commitment to conform to the guidelines on a comply or explain basis and to promote conformity on the part of the portfolio companies owned by its fund or funds.

● an indication of the leadership of the UK element of the firm, identifying the most senior members of the management or advisory team and confirmation that arrangements are in place to deal appropriately with conflicts of interest, in particular where it has a corporate advisory capability alongside its fiduciary responsibility for management of the fund or funds.

● a description of UK portfolio companies in the private equity firm's portfolio.

● a categorisation of the limited partners in the funds or funds that invest or have a designated capability to invest in companies that would be UK portfolio companies for the purpose of these guidelines, indicating separately a geographic breakdown between UK and overseas sources and a breakdown by type of investor, typically including pension funds, insurance companies, corporate investors, funds of funds, banks, government agencies, endowments of academic and other institutions, private individuals, and others.

The governance of sovereign wealth funds

Surging Asian exports and high oil prices in the Middle East generated massive surpluses. In some developing Arab and Asian countries state-owned funds have been used to re-cycle some of these surpluses by investing in companies in developed countries. These sovereign wealth funds (SWFs) have invested in telecoms, technology, real estate, ports and transport operations, and significantly in the financial sectors, particularly in the United States and Europe.

The Sovereign Wealth Fund Institute is an organization designed to study SWFs and their impact on global economics, politics, financial markets, trade, and public policy. Table 11.1 lists the larger sovereign funds and gives an indication of the scale involved. According to the Institute, the value of SWFs has now passed US$6 trillion.

Table 11.1 Top ten sovereign wealth funds

Country	Fund name	Assets (US$bn)	Inception	Origin	Linaburg-Maduell transparency index
Norway	Government Pension Fund—Global	1,058.05	1990	Oil	10
China	China Investment Corporation	941.4	2007	Non-commodity	8
UAE—Abu Dhabi	Abu Dhabi Investment Authority	683	1976	Oil	6
Kuwait	Kuwait Investment Authority	592	1953	Oil	6

China–Hong Kong	Hong Kong Monetary Authority Investment Portfolio	522.6	1993	Non-commodity	8
Saudi Arabia	SAMA Foreign Holdings	515.6	1952	Oil	4
China	SAFE Investment Company	441*	1997	Non-commodity	4
Singapore	Government of Singapore Investment Corporation	390	1981	Non-commodity	6
Singapore	Temasek Holdings	375*	1974	Non-commodity	10
Saudi Arabia	Public Investment Fund	360	2008	Oil	5

* This number is a best guess estimation.

Source: The Sovereign Wealth Fund Institute, 2018. For up-to-date data, see www.swfinstitute.org/sovereign-wealth-fund-rankings/

The Linaburg-Maduell transparency index, shown in Table 11.1, is a method of rating transparency in SWFs, developed by the Sovereign Wealth Fund Institute. The index is based on ten essential principles that depict SWF transparency to the public, with 10 as the top score.

Sovereign wealth funds raise two basic corporate governance issues:

- any shortcomings in the fund's governance;
- the strategic potential of the sovereign nation to exert power over its investments.

Criticisms of the governance of SWFs include complaints that they lack transparency and are secretive, neither stating their objectives nor disclosing their portfolios, that they lack accountability except to their government paymasters, and that they are inadequately regulated. Unlike most other corporate entities, they are not accountable to their shareholders, nor to corporate regulators; neither are they accountable directly to the citizens or voters in their sovereign nation.

Concerns about the strategic intentions of sovereign nations include the worries that they might not be driven solely by a financial motive and that financial markets could be manipulated, because with its enormous wealth a fund could affect financial markets detrimentally. Others see a potential abuse of power if SWFs use their investments to exercise strategic, possibly political, power around the world, perhaps by promoting or protecting their own national champions, restricting competition, or using the investment as a pawn in a diplomatic wrangle. For example, they fear that a SWF with a controlling stake in a European or American bank might threaten to withhold bank funds unless the country accedes to its demands, or having acquired an oil or mineral producer, might close it down to protect the industries in the fund's home country, although running a company for political rather than economic reasons could well prove expensive.

An international working group of SWFs produced what have become known as the 'Santiago principles and practices' in 2008. Among the 24 principles are the statements that the policy purpose of the SWF should be clearly defined and publicly disclosed, and that where the SWF's activities have significant, direct, domestic, macroeconomic implications, those activities should be closely coordinated with the domestic fiscal and monetary authorities, so as to ensure consistency with the overall macroeconomic policies.

A predictable nationalistic and protectionist backlash, expressing concerns about 'national treasures' such as energy, airlines, ports, and utilities being owned by foreigners, has been heard in developed nations. The US Congress objected to the proposed Kuwait ownership of US port management and to China owning a US oil firm. President Donald Trump has extended the rhetoric. However, it would be somewhat hypocritical to erect national barriers to inward investment from developing countries when expecting access to their developing markets. On the positive side, Singapore, Kuwait, and South Korea provided a multibillion-dollar lifeline to Citigroup and Merrill Lynch, two banks that had lost massively in America's sub-prime credit crisis in 2008, which helped to stabilize the financial markets.

One of the largest SWFs is Norway's oil fund, which has appointed a board to advise it on corporate governance matters. Some took this as a sign that it intended to take a more active role in managing its portfolio, for example in the appointment of directors, and calling for corporate governance changes. However, investment managers of other SWFs say that their strategy limits them to minority stakes, so that they do not get locked into a massive investment, which could involve them in governance responsibilities and which they might have difficulty selling.

The governance of SWFs is likely to remain in focus for some time. As corporate governance guru Bob Monks has commented, 'sovereign wealth investors raise all the questions of ownership power and responsibilities'. In the longer term, some international agreement may be reached, with a code of conduct for sovereign funds, perhaps regulated by an international body such as the International Monetary Fund.

The state as shareholder

A political feature around the world during the 20th century was the nationalization by governments of enterprises in the private sector. Typically, these operations were then run under strong government supervision. In state-owned public enterprises, sometimes called 'political' companies, political processes can affect corporate decisions. On nationalization, the government established the governing body, nominating and appointing its members. Government determined corporate objectives, provided funding, and decided performance criteria. Government intervened in management, influencing operations, appointing managers, and in some cases fixing market prices. Incentives for managers to meet corporate objectives came to be determined politically. Concerns about security of managerial employment arose.

Companies were used to pursue political objectives. Managers of the company might then find themselves following different strategies from those of the controlling governmental body. In democratic countries, a change of political party could also mean a change of corporate objectives, sometimes causing confusion. In nationalized companies, longer-term corporate strategic objectives could be sacrificed to shorter-term political expediency.

Towards the end of the 20th century and into the 21st century, the privatization of nationalized firms became politically desirable in some countries; for example, electricity in New

Zealand; energy, water supply, communications, and rail transport in the UK (see Case study 3.1 on Network Rail); and many state-owned enterprises (SOEs) in Russia and China.

In China, the SOEs were first turned into corporations, creating an ownership balance sheet and an equity structure, and then privatized by offering their shares on the stock markets in China and sometimes abroad. However, in many cases the Chinese state still maintains the dominant voting shareholding.

In response to the global financial crisis, which started in 2007, the governments of the United States, the United Kingdom, and some other countries became the unwilling share-holders of some of their countries' financial institutions, being forced to bail them out to protect the rest of their economies. The UK government, for example, acquired all the shares of the Northern Rock bank (see Case study 5.2) and a substantial portion of the much larger Lloyds Bank, creating a special organization, United Kingdom Financial Investments, for the purpose. In the United States, it was Bear Stearns, Fannie Mae, and Freddie Mac (which pro-vided funds for American homeowners), and AIG, which provided hedging cover for the US insurance industry. Special governance arrangements had to be made to handle the govern-ments' new corporate responsibilities.

The governance of state-owned companies, whether they are wholly owned as nationalized entities, or partially owned with outside minority shareholders, needs to have clear and inde-pendent lines of responsibility. The relationship between the company and the government, through the overseeing state department or regulatory body, needs to be crystal clear. The com-pany's constitution, whether that is a parliamentary act or ordinance creating the entity, or a more typical memorandum and articles of association, needs to determine how the governing body is to be nominated and elected, the directors' terms of service, and their role.

The responsibility for establishing strategies, laying down policies, and setting prices, par-ticularly in monopoly markets, needs to be predetermined. Appropriate financial incentives for top management also need to be agreed—sufficient to secure, hold, and motivate key personnel, while being justifiable politically. Precise criteria of corporate transparency and accountability are essential. There needs to be an appropriate balance between freedom of corporate decision and state bureaucratic control.

Case studies

 Case study 11.1   Teletronic Riches Ltd—governance of a joint venture

Teletronic Riches Ltd was a joint venture company set up between Lichfield Teletronics Ltd [Lichfield], a UK company, and Great Riches Ltd [Riches], a company based in Hong Kong, although incorporated in Bermuda. Riches was quoted on the Hong Kong Stock Exchange, although 66 per cent of the voting stock was owned by Albert Li Cheuk Yan and his family. Lichfield was the wholly owned subsidiary of a US-based public company, listed on the Nasdaq stock exchange.

The joint venture had been set up to manufacture the Teletronic range of integrated iPhones and recording machines in Shenzhen, China. In the joint venture agreement, Lichfield would provide technological know-how, specialist manufacturing equipment, and the top management; Riches would introduce the manufacturing site, labour, and local management. Both sides put up an equal amount of working capital and would share equally in profits. The entire output was to be supplied to Lichfield for distribution through its worldwide marketing organization, except for sales to the market in China, for which Riches was given the rights.

Lichfield and Riches had equal shareholdings and voting rights, and each appointed three members to the board. Teletronic's managing director, Bill Torrington, was also made a member of the board. He had run a very successful division of Lichfield in the UK and in 1997 was seconded to Teletronics on a five-year contract. He expected, when the joint venture was successful, to become a director of the Lichfield main board on his return to England.

Initially, all went well, but after three years tensions emerged. Relations between the two sets of directors on the Teletronic board were frosty. The Riches-nominated directors complained that the venture was not being given the latest products or technology. The Lichfield directors claimed that their company's products, made in Shenzhen, were being sold throughout Asia, in contravention of the joint venture agreement.

Bill Torrington found himself in an impossible position. He wanted what was good for Teletronics, but his Lichfield colleagues expected him to side with them. His career prospects were on the line.

Discussion question

1. What should Bill Torrington do?

 Case study 11.2   The governance of the Co-op

The first co-operative society in England was formed in 1844 in Rochdale, a northern mill town. The Co-op, as it was soon called, sold food and other goods to its members and the profits were shared between them according to their purchases. Similar co-operative societies soon sprang up in other towns and cities around the country, reflecting the self-help attitudes of newly industrializing, mid-Victorian society.

But the Co-op was more than a business: it was a movement based on ethical trading, a belief in democracy among its members, and a mission to improve the local community. Anyone over 16 could join, as long as they shared the values of the society, working together for everyone's benefit.

The Co-op movement in Britain thrived and is now one of the main food retailers, with over 4,000 outlets, runs a major chain of pharmacies, provides a country-wide funeral service, and offers insurance, legal, and travel services, with around 90,000 employees. It also has a bank.

Nevertheless, the underlying principles to build a better society still influence its community-led programmes, social goals, and political ambitions. The Co-op regularly funds charities and local community groups. The movement spread around the world, with the International Co-operative Alliance describing a co-operative as 'an autonomous association of persons united voluntarily to meet their common economic, social and cultural needs and aspirations through a jointly-owned and democratically controlled enterprise'.[5]

The original governance of the Co-op

Despite the size of the modern movement in Britain, the Co-op tried to maintain its local orientation by linking local co-op societies, initially through an association, and then forming a group, which now represents the interests of the 80 independent local co-operative societies and over 6 million individual members.

---

[5] www.ica.coop/en/whats-co-op/co-operative-identity-values-principles

The Co-operative Group had three levels of governance:[6]

- *Area Committees*—any member could stand for election to their local area committee. All members in each area had one vote, irrespective of how much money they had in their share account, reflecting a democratic principle developed by the co-op movement. Area committees represented their members' interests—from how the businesses might be improved, to how to help their local communities.

- *Regional Boards*—the seven regional boards were made up of representatives nominated by the area committees. Each regional board helped manage the businesses in their region, for example, by approving spending on new and improved stores, and supervising the strategy for assisting that region's local communities.

- *The Co-operative Group Board of Directors*—the Group Board was entirely non-executive, consisting of 21 directors: 5 nominated by the independent co-operative societies, 15 nominated by the Regional Boards, plus 1 INED. Each year one-third of Group Board members retired and could seek re-election.

The Group Board was responsible for the long-term success of the Co-op Group by:

- ensuring that the Group's affairs were conducted and managed in accordance with its objectives, in the best interests of the independent co-operative societies and the individual members;

- determining the vision and strategy of the Group in consultation with the Group Chief Executive and executive management;

- monitoring performance against key financial and non-financial indicators;

- supervising the Group's risk management systems;

- overseeing the Group chief executive and executive management in the day-to-day management of the Group;

- setting standards in governance matters.

A chair of the Group Board was chosen by the Board's members. The Group Board also appointed the chief executive to implement the agreed strategic objectives, who was accountable to the Board for the financial and operational performance of the Group.

Recent troubles

The return on capital employed of the trading group for 2013 was 6.9 per cent—down from 8.6 per cent in 2012. The fall in profitability was largely due to the decline in the food business profits from £383 million in 2010 to £247 million in 2013, and the rise in central overheads from £98 million in 2010 to £192 million in 2013.

As newly appointed Group chair, Ursula Lidbetter wrote in her 2013 annual report:[7]

> This report will make painful reading for our members, customers, colleagues ... [w]hat follows lays bare some fundamental failings of management and governance ... During a most difficult period, our (over) 87,000 colleagues stuck resolutely to the task of serving our members and customers throughout our diverse businesses. I am hugely grateful to them for their loyalty and for sticking with us in adversity. We owe it to all of them to recover the fortunes of this great organisation, an obligation that I and the executive team are determined to fulfil.

---

[6] Extracted from www.co-operative.coop/corporate/Investors/Governance/
[7] www.co-operative.coop/corporate/Investors/Annual-Results-2013/

She continued:

We entered 2013 focused on the future development of the organisation. Our food business was developing a new strategy and underlying performance from our trading businesses was encouraging. In May 2013, we welcomed our new Chief Executive, Euan Sutherland, recruited from outside the organisation, to revitalise the Group for the next generation.

Within days of his joining, an unfolding crisis in our Bank emerged that risked not only its future but that of the entire Group. There followed a six notch downgrade by Moody's in the credit rating of the Bank, as the extent of a significant capital shortfall became apparent. In order to meet regulatory capital requirements as laid-down by the Prudential Regulation Authority (PRA) the Bank was required to raise a further £1.5 bn. of new capital. Although this reduced the Group's ownership in the Bank to a 30% stake, this action was essential in order to safeguard the Bank for customers, colleagues and members. The battle to save the Bank dominated our activity for the remainder of the year, only concluding in December 2013.

The near-collapse of the Bank led to a wholesale change of leadership at both the Group and Bank. Euan moved decisively to recruit a new team well equipped to deal with the crisis. We were particularly fortunate that Richard Pym agreed to take the role of Chair at the Bank during such a crucial period.

His experience and authoritative leadership have helped steer the Bank through this difficult phase.

Additionally, we could not have succeeded without the support of our syndicate banks and the considered response of our pension trustees, and I thank them too for their contribution. Finally, I would like to acknowledge the contribution of Andrew Bailey and his team at the PRA for their calm guidance through a difficult time.

It was at this point that I was appointed by the Board as Chair of the Group, with a determination to resolve the weaknesses of our governance structure which had been made plain by the events of the year.

The unprecedented nature of our crisis inevitably led to the establishment of a number of inquiries by official bodies, including the Financial Conduct Authority, the Treasury, the Prudential Regulation Authority, a Treasury Select Committee, and the police. We co-operated fully with each of these. We also commissioned our own reviews. The first, by Sir Christopher Kelly, examined the circumstances that led to the Bank crisis.

Later in the year, Lord Myners agreed to undertake an independent governance review on behalf of the Board, whilst also agreeing to join the Group Board as Senior Independent Non-Executive Director.[8] His recommendations are covered later. Lord Myners stood down from our Board at the AGM in May 2014. We are indebted to him for being so generous with his time and expertise.

The near-failure of our Bank also highlighted wider financial weaknesses across the Group. In particular, our overall indebtedness is too high for an organisation of our nature. When the recent problems arose, we had limited resources with which to cover losses. Consequently, and regrettably, we have had to take some difficult decisions to sell some of our businesses. This will change the shape of our Group significantly as we adapt our strategy and cost base accordingly.

It is a matter of great regret that Euan Sutherland felt compelled to resign subsequent to the year-end.[9] Without question his leadership saved our Bank, and he built a top-flight team capable of redefining the purpose and relevance of our Co-op.

As Group Chair, I recognise the scale of the change required to our governance. This essential and urgent work is critical to our future and will enable us to build a more effective organisation which can deliver for all our members, customers and colleagues.

---

[8] Lord Myners, an experienced City of London financier, whose corporate governance report was mentioned in Chapter 5.

[9] Sutherland is reported to have said that 'the Co-op is ungovernable'.

What went wrong?

Facing enormous competition

In recent years, the Co-op retail stores have faced massive and increasing competition. In addition to national competitors, Tesco, Sainsbury, Asda, and Morrisons, two German firms, Aldi and Lidl, recently entered the British market, taking market share with lower prices for high-quality goods. The Co-op stores no longer rate highly in customers' opinion.

A dubious supermarket acquisition

In 2009 following an expansionist strategy, the Co-op acquired the Somerfield chain of small to medium-sized food stores in a £1.6 billion deal. Other supermarket chains were not interested. The Somerfield name was replaced and supply chains changed. But a rolling programme of refurbishment meant that in many towns there are now two Co-ops within a few hundred yards of each other, each offering a stock of similar goods.

A poor banking merger

Also in 2009, the Co-operative Bank took over the ailing Britannia Building Society (savings and loans association) in a merger that put considerable debt on the bank's balance sheet, significantly increasing its risk profile. Due diligence studies were 'extremely cursory', it was reported. Claims were made of the extent of the dubious loans being covered up.

The Co-op bank is in trouble

In April 2013, following a protracted period of due diligence, the Co-operative Bank withdrew from the acquisition of branches and accounts from Lloyds Banking Group, which had been hit by a disastrous bail-out during the global financial crisis.

In May 2013, the Co-op bank reported losses of £600 million. Moody's downgraded its credit rating by six notches to junk level (Ba3). A bail-out by other financial institutions and hedge funds reduced the co-op organization's holding in the bank to around 30 per cent. The bank's chief executive, Barry Tootell, resigned.

The bank's dubious chairman

For three years, from April 2010 to June 2013, the chairman of the Co-operative Bank was the Reverend Paul Flowers, a minister in the Methodist Church and a former Labour Party councillor. Under his chairship the bank reported substantial losses and had its credit rating downgraded. Flowers' lack of knowledge about the bank's balance sheet was highlighted by a Parliamentary select committee. Apparently, he had been appointed to the chair after an hour-and-a-half interview without references.

In November 2013, Flowers was exposed by a Sunday newspaper buying crack cocaine and methamphetamine. He was suspended by the Labour Party, the Methodist Church, and the Co-op. In November 2013, the Co-op Group chair, Len Wardle, who had led the board that appointed Flowers, resigned.

Labyrinthine voting structure and board domination

Despite the Co-op's oft-repeated claim to be a democratic organization, the grass-roots members had little opportunity to influence significant decisions. Governance power lay with the 100, or so, regional board members, who controlled the majority of votes in members' meetings, and each of whom received between £30,000 and £80,000 a year in fees. As the press pointed out, the future of the Co-op lay with a handful of members, most without business experience, including an engineer, a retired deputy head teacher, a computer technician, and a plasterer. In March 2014, private investigators were hired to discover which director had leaked information about executive salaries.

In April 2014, it was reported that another director had been suspended for claiming that he was a chartered accountant when he had been struck off by the professional body for being bankrupt.

Lord Myners' governance recommendations

Following a comprehensive review of the Group's governance, Lord Myners, the Co-operative Group's senior INED, published his detailed report in May 2014.[10] The report described 'deplorable governance failures' that have been exposed over the past year which had led to the 'near-collapse of the Group'. Myners warned that, without change, the Group's level of debt would see its 'autonomy and independence being strictly curtailed'. He described the present governance architecture and allocation of responsibilities as 'not fit for purpose' and called for radical change.

Despite the repeated claims that the Co-op was democratic, the Myners report identified a 'significant democratic deficit', in which the vast bulk of ordinary members had limited ability to influence the group. Lord Myners urged the current members of the Group Board and regional boards to 'put their self-interest to one side for the greater good', and vote through far-reaching reforms.

In his report Lord Myners stated:

> The co-operative ownership model can—and often does—deliver powerful economic advantages. But its superiority over other forms of ownership is not inevitable and guaranteed. For a consumer co-operative, such as the Group, its advantages have to be earned, day by day, through delivering outstanding service and value for money to customers who, especially in food retailing, have plenty of choice where to spend their money ... There is no short cut to recovery from the present weakened state. It will require retrenchment and some painful choices. Financial health can only be restored through steady, step by step, re-building of the Group's profitability and repayment of its excessive debt.
>
> Because of the losses exposed last year and their severe impact on the Group's balance sheet, the high level of debt now being carried by the Group has made it inevitable that the bank syndicates providing this funding will, for quite obvious reasons, continue to take the closest interest in the Group making rapid progress to strengthen its governance. Elected members need to understand that while autonomy and independence are cherished principles of co-operation, the harsh truth is that bad governance results directly in such autonomy being strictly curtailed.
>
> The reforms I have set out are fully compatible with the core values and principles of co-operative ownership. I have no interest in advocating the adoption of a PLC model, as some of my critics have claimed. But I do want to see a governance structure that works; the present one has lamentably failed.

The Myners report contained three specific reform objectives:

- to produce a highly competent and qualified Group Board with independent non-executive directors who possess the skills and experience needed to exercise leadership and effective oversight of executive management running a business of massive scale and complexity, quite unlike any other co-operative business in the UK;

- to ensure that, without compromising the effectiveness of the Group Board, genuine co-operative values and principles are protected and securely embedded in the future governance architecture;

- to ensure that as a customer-owned organization, the tangible benefits of membership are not deliberately restricted to a tiny and potentially quite unrepresentative body of elected members, but are extended so that the interests of the entire membership are properly understood and promoted and their fundamental rights are respected.

[10] www.co-operative.coop/MynersReview

The report then set out four key reforms to the governance structure:

Reform the Group Board

Create a new Group Board with six to seven independent non-executive directors and two executive directors and an independent chair having no previous association or involvement with the Group. The non-executive directors should have the skills and experience of the non-executive directors that sit on the boards of the Co-operative Group's primary competitors.

Establish an influential National Membership Council

Establish an elected National Membership Council ('NMC') of around 50 individuals, including provision for representation of around 10 employees. The NMC would elect from its membership a steering committee of 12 which would include corporate representation from independent co-op societies.

Create a Nominations Committee

Create a Nominations Committee to screen and propose candidates for Group Board approval and for election/re-election by members at each AGM. The Committee would comprise five non-executive members, including up to two representatives designated by the NMC and the balance from the Group Board.

Extend constitutional rights

Extend constitutional rights to the entire membership of the Group, consistent with the fundamental co-operative principle of 'one member one vote'.

The Co-op Group's response to Lord Myners

Myners faced bitter in-fighting to his turnaround plans. Indeed, his was a case of the messenger being shot at before he even delivered his message. The principal complaint was the potential loss of 'co-operative values', but for some the Co-op's original support for working people in their local communities had been replaced by a central support for socialism and the Labour Party. Others pointed out that the existing regional and group board members would lose their power over the organization and the privileges that went with it. Faced with such opposition, Myners resigned his independent non-executive directorship after four months.

Some of the current leaders of the Co-op, calling themselves 'the apex body for the co-operatives', proposed some amendments to the Myners proposals,[11] addressing what they saw as potential risks to the co-operative ideals:

> A strong alignment with co-operative values is essential for every board director [they wrote] as the Myners Review recognizes. There can also be a form of expertise that may be needed, alongside professional business and retail strategy, financial and innovation skills, which is the ability to re-represent the interests of everyday members.

The apex body accepted the real need for change, and appointing professional non-executive directors to the main board, but added that these should be 'member-representatives' rather than independent. To achieve this they proposed that the appointment of these directors would be made by members of the NMC that Myners had proposed, rather than the new nominations committee of the main board that Myners had proposed.

---

[11] www.thenews.coop/85555/news/democracy/sector-body-proposes-additional-changes-co-operative-group-governance/#.U3XaQilOUdU

In addressing what they meant by 'member representatives', the authors said that

it is a misunderstanding of governance practice to say how many expert or lay members should be on a board, since ultimately all directors are accountable to the members ... When people say (we) want to ensure that 'co-operators' are on the board, it is easy then for sceptics to read this as saying that they want to keep existing representatives in place rather than to disband. In truth, they ought to be saying something very different.

The apex body called for a single chair for both the Group Board and the NMC. Two chairs would lead to cost and potential conflict, they suggested. They also called for the social goals programme to be overseen by the Group Board, rather than being a separate activity run by the NMC. 'Activity on social goals needs to be embedded in core operations, and become a source of commercial innovation,' said the authors, 'rather than sitting as a separate exercise, as if it was a semi-detached corporate charitable trust.'

At a meeting of the members on 17 May 2014, dominated by the regional members, a watered-down version of the Myners Report was accepted.

Discussion questions

1. Are Lord Myners' recommendations on the future governance of the Co-op consistent with the culture of Britain's largest mutual company?

2. If you were advising the board of the Co-op what would you propose?

3. Is the concept of a business enterprise 'owned' by its customers a viable alternative to one owned by its shareholders (including individual investors, institutional investors such as pension funds and insurance companies, and hedge funds)?

 Case study 11.3   NHS Foundation Trust—third case study

Extracts from the minutes of a Board meeting of the Trust.

As decided at the previous Board meeting (Case study 8.3) the Chairman, in consultation with the Chief Executive and Finance Director, had produced a detailed proposal for an Independent inquiry into efficiency and cost saving throughout the Trust. The report, which had been circulated to all Directors, was discussed at length. Reservations about the need for such an inquiry and concerns about possible adverse effects on staff morale were voiced by some Executive Directors. However, the Chairman suggested that the consultants would be sensitive to the culture of the Trust and that the results of the inquiry would show the rest of the NHS how a professionally led organization could run effectively within budget. He was supported by . . . Belvedere, Brigham-West . . . and Windlass . . . Various suggestions were made for possible consultants.

Action: It was agreed to put the proposal for the inquiry out to tender.

Resignation of the Chief Executive

The Board received the resignation of the Chief Executive. She indicated that she had been considering a move in recent months and had received an informal approach from another

Trust, which she had accepted. The Board expressed their regret and thanked her for her considerable contribution to the Trust over many years.

Action: The Board accepted the resignation of the Chief Executive with regret and wished to minute their recognition and thanks for many years' service. The Deputy Chief Executive would work with the Chief Executive until she left and then resume her duties until another appointment was confirmed. An executive search exercise was authorised.

Special meeting of the Board

A Special Meeting of the Board of the Trust was called to consider the outcome of the tendering process for the independent inquiry into efficiency and cost saving.

Independent inquiry into efficiency and cost saving

The tendering process had been conducted according to Trust policies, with sealed tenders opened simultaneously. Seven proposals had been received. The Chief Executive had recommended that four of them be rejected because the consultants lacked experience of health service management. The Board ranked the remaining three tenders by cost and after discussion added their assessment.

Consultant A—The cheapest. A well-presented proposal. Similar assignments had been undertaken for other clients, although none had been in the health service. Some health sector experience in human relations management and in financial planning. Some Executive Directors liked this proposal and were supported by three Non-executive Directors (Mirrlees, Prowess, and Mudberry). The Chairman and the other Non-executive Directors felt that the lack of relevant health service experience was a failing.

Consultant B—Fifteen percent more expensive than Consultant A and with a two month longer project timetable. Provided a published report on a cost savings project in a Singapore hospital. The Chairman suggested that the Singapore experience was irrelevant because this was for a hospital in the private sector with profit-orientated goals. Other Non-executive Directors agreed. This consultancy firm had also worked with Lady Audrey Westwood, which could raise media comments about favourable treatment, even though she had resigned from the Trust.

Consultant C—The most expensive end of list although the time table was acceptable. An international consultancy with considerable experience in hospital management around the world particularly in the United States. The Chairman felt that this project was most likely to deliver the outcomes he wanted. He was supported by . . . Belvedere, Brigham-West . . . and Windlass . . . none of the Executive Directors raised an objection.

Action: Decided to appoint Consultant C.

Discussion question

1. Within the limited information of the minutes, what internal, board-level, behavioural processes were apparent?

Self-test questions

1. Should the managing director/CEO of a joint venture company, who is also employed by one of the joint venture partners, be a member of the joint venture company board?

2. How are partnerships governed?

3. What is a limited-liability partnership?

4. Explain the differences between a holding, a subsidiary, and an associated company.

5. Explain the two distinct options in governing and managing a group of companies.

6. What are the benefits of drawing subsidiary company directors from other companies in the group?

7. Explain what a family council is and does in a family company.

8. What are some of the typical characteristics of the governance of charities?

9. Explain what a sovereign wealth fund is and which countries have been particularly involved.

 For suggested answers to these self-test questions visit the online resources at:
www.oup.com/uk/tricker4e/

Projects and exercises

1. Choose a well-known charity and explore the information it provides about its governance. Write a critique of its objectives, its governance, including the nomination and appointment of its governing body, its finances, and the information provided for stakeholders.

2. Draft an explanatory paper and presentation for the chair of a voluntary or community organization explaining what is needed for successful corporate governance in his or her organization.

3. Draft an explanatory paper or presentation for the head of a family-based company on the pros and cons of a family council.

References and further reading

Burrough, Bryan and John Helyar (1990) *Barbarians at the Gate: The Fall of RJR Nabisco*. (The story of two private equity firms—Forstmann Little and Kohlberg Kravis Roberts—and their aggressive US$25 billion takeover of RJR Nabisco.) Random House/Jonathan Cape, London.

Cogan, Philip (2009) *Guide to Hedge Funds*. The Economist/Profile Books, London.

Cornforth, C. (2003) *The Governance of Public and Non-profit Organisations: What Do Boards Do?* Routledge, New York, London.

McCahery, Joseph A. and Erik P. M. Vermeulen (2010)

Corporate Governance of Non-Listed Companies. Oxford University Press, Oxford.

PERG (2016) Private Equity Reporting Group, Ninth Report, December. Available at: http://privateequityreportinggroup.co.uk/wp-content/uploads/2016/12/Private-Equity-Reporting-Group-Ninth-Report-December-2016.pdf

Solomon, Jill ([2004] 2007) *Corporate Governance and Accountability*. 3rd edn, Wiley, Chichester, UK.

Wright, Robert E. (2014) *Corporate Nation*. University of Pennsylvania Press, Philadelphia.

Useful websites

www.londonstockexchange.com
Listing rules including the Alternative Investment Market (AIM).

www.hkgem.com
Hong Kong Stock Exchange Growth Enterprise Market (GEM).
www.gcgf.org
The World Bank and OECD corporate governance forum.
www.ifc.org/ifcext/corporategovernance.nsf/Content/CG_Tools
The IFC/World Bank offer a number of corporate governance tools for family and founder-owned unlisted companies, listed companies, financial institutions, privatized transition economy companies, and state-owned enterprises.
www.swd.gov.hk/doc/ngo/corp-gov-eng.pdf
Leading your NGO board (Canada)—a reference guide.
www.mapnp.org/library/boards/boards.htm
Free Management Library guidelines for profit and not-for-profit organizations.
www.iod.com/MainWebsite/Resources/Document/corp_gov_guidance_and_principles_for_unlisted_companies_in_the_uk_final_1011.pdf
Corporate governance guidance and principles for unlisted companies, Institute of Directors, London, 2010.
www.ncvo-vol.org.uk
National Council for Voluntary Organisations.
www.charity-commission.gov.uk
Information on governance in voluntary and community organizations.
www.guidestar.org/nonprofit-directory/public-societal-benefit.aspx
List of US charities and non-profit organizations.

12

Corporate Governance around the World

 Learning Outcomes

This chapter enables us to:

- Study the different approaches to corporate governance in the East: in China, Hong Kong SAR, India, Singapore, South Korea and Japan.
- Review the approaches to corporate governance in the Middle East, North Africa, Brazil, and Russia.

Corporate governance in China

The development of corporate governance in China

Twenty years ago the Chinese economy was emergent: today it is the second largest in the world after the United States.[1] Twenty years ago business in China was dominated by state-owned enterprises (SOE): now many of these state-owned firms have been corporatized and their shares listed on stock exchanges in China and abroad. China now also has a massive private sector. One of these independent companies tops the board of the New York Stock Exchange.

The People's Republic of China (PRC) was established in 1949 by Mao Tse Tung, following the defeat of the Nationalist Army under Chiang Kai Shek and its retreat to Taiwan after the civil war of 1946 to 1949. Mao founded the PRC and remained chairman of the Chinese Communist Party from 1949 until his death in 1976. Over that period, the state proclaimed ownership of the means of production, prohibited private property, and banned incorporated companies. In 1958, Chairman Mao initiated the Great Leap Forward, relocating millions of farmers, peasants, and city workers. Massive economic dislocation and famine resulted. The Cultural Revolution began in 1966, and lasted a decade. Communes were reorganized and SOEs were created, most relying on state subsidies.

In the 1970s, Mao's successor as paramount leader, Deng Xiao Ping, introduced a type of market economy, whilst maintaining control by the centralized communist state. The industrial SOEs, which were large bureaucracies, continued to receive their production and distribution orders from state planners. Employees of the SOEs received housing, medical care, and schooling for their children. Some foreign investment in China was now permitted.

---

[1] For a more detailed discussion of corporate governance in China see Tricker, Bob and Gregg Li (2019) *Understanding Corporate Governance in China*, Hong Kong University Press, Hong Kong.

Deng stood down in 1989, and is now recognized as the initiator of the changes that led to the subsequent, incredible, economic growth. His successor, Jiang Ze Min, assumed power following the Tiananmen Square protests and continued until 2002, overseeing the return of Hong Kong and Macau to mainland control. Jiang continued the economic reforms. Between 1984 and 1993, the SOEs were given more autonomy, with a transitional model of governance to improve their productivity and profitability.

In 1994 a new corporate law, revised in 2006, provided for the restructuring of traditional large and medium-sized SOEs as legal entities. Four years later, in 1998, the State Council of the PRC, advised by Organisation for Economic Co-operation and Development (OECD) experts, produced a set of corporate governance directives for SOE reform.

In September 1999, the Fourth Plenary Session of the 15th Chinese Communist Party's Central Committee took a vital decision on enterprise reform, in what was termed a 'strategic adjustment' of the state sector, agreeing that the state should be 'withdrawing from what should be withdrawn'.[2] Interestingly, corporate governance was recognized as being at the core of the modern enterprise system.

The 16th Congress of the Party called for a joint-stock system with the state controlling critical enterprises, while other SOEs continued their corporate reforms. Many small and medium-sized firms were transformed into non-SOEs, and some SOEs were restructured prior to stock market listing. Some of the reformed corporate entities were listed on the Hong Kong market, others on the two China stock markets in Shanghai and Shenzhen, which had been set up in 1991 and 1992 respectively.

In a country with strong central control, in which the Communist Party, the State Council, the National People's Congress, the Politburo Standing Committee, and the Central Military Commission (the People's Liberation Army) play significant roles, share ownership is not the obvious basis for exercising governance power over state-owned companies, even if they had been listed on a stock exchange. The governance of newly emerging private companies in China presented a different range of challenges. Even so, the PRC developed an innovative corporate governance regime, to become one of the world's leading economies.

Governance of SOEs in China

The China Securities Regulatory Commission of the State Council (CSRC) is the Chinese government's corporate regulator. The CSRC issues the Corporate Governance Code and other corporate governance regulations, and publishes regular reports on corporate governance reform and performance in China. The CSRC also liaises closely with the management of the stock exchanges in Shanghai and Shenzhen, and subsequently Hong Kong, as well as with exchanges overseas that list Chinese stock.

In 2001, the CSRC formulated some basic norms of corporate governance, promoting the separation of listed companies from controlling shareholders. At least one-third of the board should consist of independent directors, and include at least one accounting professional, although initially there was a lack of suitable people. Independent directors could be

---

[2] Chinese Communist Party, 15th Central Committee meeting, Plenary Session 4, September 1999.

nominated by the board of directors, the board of supervisors, or any shareholders holding 5 per cent of the shares. China became a member of the World Trade Organization in 2001.

In 2002, a Code of Corporate Governance for listed companies was formulated, which included basic principles for the protection of investors' rights, basic behaviour rules, and standards for directors, supervisors, and senior management. Significantly, the corporate governance code called for the appointment of independent directors to boards, even though the concept of director independence was not well understood in China at the time.

The State-owned Assets Supervision and Administration Commission of the State Council (SASAC) holds the Chinese government's shareholding in all China's listed companies (other than those in the finance sector). SASAC is the largest institutional shareholder in the world, with eight in the *Fortune* list of the world's top 500 companies. SASAC ensures that the state's interests are represented in the activities of China's listed companies, including the appointment of directors and top executives to state majority-owned companies. In 2013, the head of SASAC, Jiang Jiemin, was investigated for 'serious disciplinary violations', which usually refers to corruption-related issues.

China has thus created a unique form of corporate governance structure for listed companies—a board of directors, with some independent outside directors, and a board of supervisors, with both employee and shareholder representatives—thus combining elements of both the German-style two-tier board model and the unitary board model's use of outside directors, as well as recognizing China's political concept of employees being masters of enterprises. However, some commentators have suggested that China's model is more closely aligned to the Japanese model, which is essentially a unitary board system, and provides for the independent outside directors on the board to form a separate committee outside the board.

However, in one respect the governance of SOEs differed fundamentally from Western practice: CEOs were appointed by state regulators, not by the board of each SOE. State regulators monitor the performance of CEOs of the SOEs under their control, moving them frequently. This helps to reduce the possibility of corruption through over-familiarity with a single situation. It also means that CEOs are treated more like civil servants, employees of the state, than as heads of independent organizations. Moreover, it ties their remuneration to that of equivalent level civil servants, not to international levels of top executive remuneration. Another effect of this approach is that chief executives of SOEs are in a powerful position when dealing with members of their own management and supervisory boards. Moreover, the board of Chinese SOEs has no need to plan succession or use corporate executives.

Officially, the board of supervisors oversees finances, ensures the due diligence of directors and senior management personnel, safeguards company assets, reduces the company's risks, and protects shareholders' interests. In practice, leaders of companies' political party committees have often taken the chair and vice chair of their companies' boards of supervisors. Some commentators have criticized the effectiveness of some supervisory boards, because their members have less professional experience and education than the directors and managers they supervise.

Governance of independent companies in China

Supplementing the state-owned enterprises, China has developed a significant independent sector, including collectively owned enterprises such as urban collectives and rural township

organizations; privately owned organizations, defined as firms with more than seven employees; and small, individually owned enterprises with no more than seven employees.

The dawning of the market economy in China produced many private enterprises (PEs)
and foreign-invested enterprises (FIEs), many of them joint ventures with Chinese partners.
On PE boards, a study found that 'like Chinese society, patriarchy prevails, similar to the cultural context of the Asian family-based model' (as discussed in Chapter 6). 'The tendency of
a weak board and strong chairman is common, and boards tend to be tight-knit groups built
on business or personal networks. Independent directors tend to be brought in to fulfil legal
requirements and are limited to advisory roles.'[3]

Many of the privately owned firms are family-based businesses that are relatively small, often
with only a handful of employees. The predecessors of many of these company founders were
business people in mainland China who left the country in successive waves of the diaspora.[4]

Many of the larger private companies have governance issues. A lack of transparency is a
significant problem, which can be particularly challenging for foreign investors. Another challenge can be the lack of a moral compass in making business decisions. This lack of ethical
standards reflects the fact that many of these companies are led by first-time entrepreneurs,
with no experience of business, no moral training, and little guidance. A few business leaders,
however, do seem to be taking a professional approach to governance, particularly where
some of their directors or senior executives have relevant training or experience, although, it
has to be said, that for others corporate governance is more for show than substance.

However, some private companies are significantly larger than most family firms. Some of
these large private companies have been floated on a stock exchange through an initial public
offer. In such cases the sponsoring financial institution, advising on the float, is more likely
to pay attention to the record and motivation of the company's founders, than to written
longer-term plans. Consistency of performance is more important than rapid growth, which
might not be sustainable. Again, trust at the personal level is crucial. Mutual trust, rather than
financial analysis, is the key to good long-term relations between a company's founders and
potential investors in China.

In a few cases, significant private companies have been listed abroad in New York or London. In these circumstances the company must meet the demands of the regulators—the
USA's SEC rules or the UK's corporate governance code, which is part of the London Stock
Exchange's listing requirements. Consequently, Chinese companies listed overseas typically
provide a showcase for sound corporate governance. But they can still have governance
issues—for example, see Case study 12.3 on Alibaba Group Holding Ltd.

The future of corporate governance in China

Three decades ago, Chinese corporate governance did not exist. Initially, learning from the
West, China developed law, rules, and regulation, and created attitudes that produced dramatic and sustained economic growth. China is also bringing its accounting and auditing

---

[3] Leng Jing (2009) *Corporate Governance and Financial Reform in China's Transition Economy*, Hong Kong
University Press, Hong Kong.
[4] For more information on the business methods of overseas Chinese see Redding, S. G. (1993) *The Spirit
of Chinese Capitalism*, de Gruyter, Berlin.

rules into line with international standards. The Chinese are intelligent and astute learners, have studied foreign corporate governance methods, and chosen those that are relevant.[5] Of course, corporate governance in China remains a work in progress; challenges still exist. The CSRC suffers from being both the promoter of the investment market and its regulator. Other problems include: the identification, training, and development of independent directors; the potential influence of Party members on boards, particularly where directors are also members of a company's Party Committee; and changing attitudes from the previous centralized, state-directed decision-making to a market-orientated perspective.

Corporate governance in the Western world did not evolve from a desire to facilitate corporate success but as a regulatory response to perceived corporate failings. In the United States, the SEC was formed as a reaction to concerns about the securities industry. The genesis of the UK's Cadbury Code was a series of high-profile company failures. Corporate governance codes in other countries followed the Cadbury lead. Consequently, corporate governance in the West tends to be seen as regulatory; a set of laws, regulations, or voluntary codes designed to regulate corporate behaviour, prevent excesses, and protect the interests of legitimate stakeholders.

By contrast, China has developed its own form of corporate governance, appropriate to a country in which the law, the judiciary, and the courts serve the state, and are not an independent check on the legislature. The Chinese recognize corporate governance as a fluid learning-system, dedicated to encouraging corporate success, building economic wealth, and improving society in the interests of the people, the Party, and the state. To understand the purpose and processes of corporate governance in China requires a different perspective from the Western viewpoint.

Corporate governance in Hong Kong (SAR)

Quite unlike mainland China, corporate governance in Hong Kong evolved under the influence of British law and corporate regulation, reflecting the British oversight of the territory up to 1997, when Hong Kong became a Special Administrative Region (SAR) of China.

In Hong Kong, corporate governance is a fascinating melange of Anglo-American and Asian ideas. The corporate governance system is an outgrowth of British company law and regulation. When Hong Kong became a SAR of China in 1997, it kept its currency (tied to the US dollar), legal system, and institutions including the Securities and Futures Commission, the Institute of Certified Public Accountants, and the Law Society. On the Hong Kong stock market most listed companies are either family firms, with control kept firmly within the family, or mainland China-based corporations, plus a handful of large trading companies.

Although the Hong Kong regulatory authorities require a minimum of three INEDs, the heads of some family companies see little value in them. Their secretive, authoritarian, and family-centric approach to business does not lend itself to outside directors who might disagree with their decisions. Furthermore, evidence of abnormal dealing prior to acquisition or merger activity has suggested insider dealing. Incidentally, most Hong Kong-listed Chinese

---

[5] Li, Gregg, in Tricker and Li (2019).

family companies are incorporated in Bermuda or the Cayman Islands, so that, while Hong Kong's listing rules and takeover codes apply, Hong Kong companies ordinances do not (other than those applying to overseas companies).

In 2014, after many years of deliberation, Hong Kong introduced a new Companies Ordinance designed to simplify and rationalize company law. Among many other provisions, the new law extended the exposure of directors and 'other responsible persons' to prosecution for failing to exercise 'due care, skill, and diligence'.[6] The law also introduced a new solvency test that companies need to meet.

The Hong Kong corporate governance code is based on the 'comply or explain' approach, and was much influenced by the UK's Cadbury Report.[7] It calls for the board of listed companies to have a majority of independent directors; audit, remuneration, and nomination committees; director and board evaluation; and director induction and training. Compliance levels are relatively high.

When China began its market-orientated reforms in the 1980s, no mainland-owned companies were incorporated abroad. SOEs responded to demands from the state. Private companies were not allowed in mainland China. In Hong Kong things were different. Many of the companies listed on the Hong Kong stock market were incorporated in overseas tax havens. The major trading houses, such as Jardine's, Swire, and Hong Kong Land had interests abroad, as did other local companies. These subsidiaries offered products or services in the same line as their parent company, or were entrepreneurial attempts to make money, often in property. Two of the tallest skyscrapers in London, for instance, are owned by Hong Kong companies.[8]

Many of these subsidiaries operated in Singapore, Australia, or the UK, where English was spoken and company law was similar to Hong Kong's British-influenced law; many others were in countries in the Far East. None of them had a global brand, nor could they really be classified as multinational.

Corporate governance in India

As with China, history has played a part in the development of corporate governance in India. Originally a member of the British Empire ('the jewel in the crown'), India benefited from the early creation of government administrative processes, with the rule of law, including a body of company law backed by a reliable judiciary, as did Hong Kong and Singapore. A drawback was the accompanying bureaucracy.

Following independence, the country took a socialist road, with large state-owned enterprises and the public sector dominating the economy. Bureaucracy grew and inefficiency, corruption, and nepotism flourished. By the 1990s, the need for India to develop its business

[6] Hong Kong SAR Government, Cap. 622 Companies Ordinance, 2014. www.elegislation.gov.hk/hk/cap622?tab=m&xpid=ID_1438403540072_001

[7] The writer was a member of the committee of the Hong Kong Society of Accountants (as it was then called) which drafted the original Hong Kong code.

[8] Nicknamed the 'Cheese grater' and the 'Walkie talkie'.

infrastructure and attract capital was recognized. Better corporate governance of companies and improved regulation of its stock markets was needed. In 1992, Parliament created the Securities and Exchange Board of India (SEBI).

The first corporate governance code was published in 1998, by the Confederation of Indian Industry (CII), titled 'Desirable Corporate Governance'. Unlike codes in some other countries, the CII code did not make statements of principle, but addressed specific business issues in India. Focused on the governance of listed companies, the code called for 'professionally competent, independent non-executive directors' to constitute at least 30 per cent of the board if the chair is a non-executive director and at least 50 per cent where the chair and the CEO were the same person. Non-executive directors should 'play a material role in corporate decision-making and maximizing long-term shareholder value(, becoming) active participants in boards, not passive advisers'. No one should hold directorships in more than ten listed companies. The code also called for audit committees. But the code was exhortatory and was not endorsed by the regulatory body, nor incorporated into the listing rules.

A year later, in 1999, a government committee chaired by Shri Kumar Manalam Biria, a businessman, released India's National Code on Corporate Governance. Reflecting international standards, the Code was approved by the SEBI and incorporated into stock exchange listing rules.

Corporate governance standards in India's top-tier listed companies, such as Infosys and the major banks, are high. But such commitment is not general. Small- and medium-capital companies are largely unconvinced of the value of corporate governance activities and expenditures.

As in other parts of the world, interest in corporate governance in India was a reaction to corporate scandals, often involving stock price manipulation: for example the Harshad Mehta scam, the UTI case, and the so-called 'vanishing company scam'. As the Central Vigilance Commissioner, N. Vittal, said in the Tata Memorial Lecture in 2002:[9]

> I find that the legal and administrative environment in India provides excellent scope for corrupt practices in business. As a result, unless a management is committed to be honest and observe the principles of propriety, the atmosphere is too tempting to observe good corporate governance in practice.
>
>   Many feel that the situation is no better nearly two decades later. In 2002, reflecting international concern at the fallout from the US Enron debacle, the government set up a high-level committee chaired by Shri Naresh Chandra to examine corporate auditing and independent directors. The report called for independent directors to represent at least 50% of the board of listed companies, strengthened the definition of independence, and called for the rotation of audit partners (but not audit firms).

A further committee, chaired by Shri Narayana Murthy, chairman of Infosys, was set up in 2003 by SEBI to 'evaluate the adequacy of existing corporate governance practices'. Audit committees, risk management, director remuneration, codes of conduct, and the role of independent directors were all addressed.

The Indian Companies Act of 1956 was amended in 1999 to improve shareholder rights, and in 2000 to require audit committees. In 2002, a committee reported on a revision of the

---

[9] Vittal, Nagarajan, Tata Memorial Lecture, Mumbai, 2002.

1956 Act. In 2005, an expert committee on company law chaired by Dr J. J. Irani of Tata Indus-tries, reported, but this has not yet led to a new Act.

In 2007, the government issued guidelines on corporate governance in central public sector enterprises covering the composition of boards, audit committees, management of group companies, accounting standards, and risk management.

In many organizations in India, including public sector organizations, multinationals, and private sector companies, boards find themselves dominated by majority shareholders. Pre-emption rights for minority shareholders are frequently ignored. Competent regulators and capital market action are needed to protect minority investors.

In 2013, India introduced a revised Companies Act, sharpening controls, and SEBI improved the corporate governance disclosure norms required of listed companies. Stock exchanges were required to ensure compliance with these disclosure norms. But corruption remains entrenched, not least in government administration. India ranked 81st out of 180 countries in Transparency International's 2017 Index of Corruption Perceptions.[10] Distrust of government is high, with bureaucracy and red tape sometimes stifling entrepreneurial flair. The Indian Ministry of Com-pany Affairs and SEBI need more competent staff experienced in corporate governance matters.

The chair of SEBI, U.K. Sinha, commented in 2013 that 'nearly one-fifth of listed companies in India do not comply with basic shareholding reporting norms set by the regulator'.[11] He expressed concern at the quality of filings companies make, and stressed the need for stock exchanges to hire more people to monitor whether companies were complying with the let-ter and spirit of listing agreements. Poor corporate governance remains a concern for both Indian and international investors, particularly the stock exchanges' failure to take action against companies that fail to meet SEBI standards.

Corporate governance in Russia

Some of the Eastern European transitional economies, including Hungary, Poland, and the previous East Germany, took a similar approach to China in privatizing their state enterprises, creating companies in which shares were sold to external strategic investors, often foreign investment institutions.

Russia, however, along with Bulgaria and the Czech Republic, took a different approach. Many Russian citizens were dubious about privatization, holding old Soviet beliefs that indus-try should be run by the state, that everyone should be guaranteed a job, and that incomes should be controlled. Recognizing the need to overcome such resistance and to make chang-es irreversible, during the 1990s the state attempted to transfer ownership to the people through three forms of privatization:

1. The free distribution to all Russian citizens of vouchers, which could be exchanged for company shares or invested in voucher investment funds. Although all citizens were supposed to have equal shares, insiders often benefited, particularly incumbent management, who were given bonus shares to overcome resistance.

[10] www.transparency.org/news/feature/corruption_perceptions_index_2017
[11] www.livemint.com/Opinion/hxFqnfbyCG5fRWD6PuiGfP/The-fight-for-corporate-governance-in-India.html

2. Investment tenders, in which investors had to make substantial investments to redevelop companies. There was little or no state monitoring or control, which led to deception, with investment proposals that were not undertaken or else were fictitious.

3. Loan-for-shares auctions—the government provided finance from the federal budget for the purchase of shares in public companies that were put up for auction, such as Yukos, Sibneft, and Lukoil. Fraudulent practices, violence, and social injustice were rife, and many of the major businesses that emerged were dominated by relatively few people, many of them now very rich. Small banks evolved into major financial institutions and industrial groups.

Ownership concentration was high, typically involving the previous managers. The minority shareholders, who typically included members of the public and foreign investment institutions, saw their rights violated by these dominant interests.

Some Russian companies were floated on foreign stock exchanges, mainly London and New York. Of course, these companies had to comply with the listing agreements reflecting the corporate governance requirements of the countries concerned, including independent directors, board committees, and corporate governance compliance reports.

The first federal law on joint-stock companies in Russia was enacted in 1995, followed by securities laws in 1996, and laws on the protection of rights and legal interests of investors in the securities market three years later in 1999. Shareholders with at least 2 per cent of the voting rights gained the right to introduce items to the agenda of shareholders' meetings and to nominate candidates for the board. Shareholders with 1 per cent could file a complaint against the board or specific directors for damage to the company caused by their actions. In 1998, a new bankruptcy law was enacted.

But there were problems with implementation, not least because many directors felt that they owed their allegiance not to the shareholders as a whole, but to the controlling shareholders who had nominated and, in effect, appointed them. Although the law called for directors to act reasonably and in good faith towards the company, neither directors nor the courts had relevant experience. Moreover, state interests could take precedence. The need for director training and board development was apparent.

In the early stages of privatization, the state was inevitably involved in the process, but companies tended to adopt the unitary board structure with some independent outside directors, reflecting the US and UK/Commonwealth models based on the rule of law and regulation by the stock market. Unfortunately, the company and securities law that was enacted did not reflect the way in which companies were typically run.

But, in 1998, Russia faced a major financial crisis: the state defaulted on government bonds, the currency was devalued, and rising oil prices provided the opportunity for the existing owners to consolidate their control.

Faced with the domination of many boards by insider and controlling shareholder interests, and widespread corruption, there was a call for better understanding of corporate governance. In 2000, a Centre for Business Ethics and Corporate Governance was founded to encourage corporate governance reform in Russia. The OECD, through its Centre for Co-operation with Non-members, offered advice and created the Russian Corporate Governance Roundtable, which brought together an influential network of Russian and international policy-makers. The Roundtable produced a White Paper for reform in corporate governance in Russia in

2002 and a report on improving the transparency of related party transactions in 2005. The International Finance Corporation, working with the World Bank, also produced a corporate governance manual for Russia, including drafts for a corporate charter, director contracts, and bylaws on shareholder meetings, the corporate secretary, proxy voting, and the board of directors. Russia also formed an Independent Directors Association.

Under the company law and corporate governance code recommendations, companies are governed by the general shareholders' meeting, which elects the members of the board through cumulative voting, a board of directors (sometimes confusingly called the supervisory board) with both independent directors and management directors, and an executive (or management) committee. The audit committee reports to the board, the chair of which is not allowed to be the head of the executive committee.

The need for sound corporate governance is recognized in Russia. There is more transparency, standards for corporate governance are more widely understood, and losses through unfair practices have been reduced. A new Russian Code of Corporate Conduct was published in 2013.[12]

But under Vladimir Putin, President of Russia, the role of the state has expanded, the substance of democracy has disappeared, the press has been muzzled, and opponents imprisoned. Government influence over companies has increased. In some cases ownership has been transferred back to the state by expropriation or by acquisition in the market.

Corporate governance in Brazil

Brazil's economy boomed until around 2012. Then it faltered disastrously. Rising costs, lack of improvement in business efficiency, and failure to re-invest the profits of the boom years were cited. So were a Byzantine tax system, endemic poverty, and corruption. With tax rates and state pension costs dramatically high, economic growth in Brazil stalled.

In Brazil, many companies are either state-owned or family-dominated. The Brazilian Institute of Corporate Governance was founded in 1995. The Brazilian Code of Best Practice of Corporate Governance was published by the Institute in 1999. Now in its fourth edition (2009), it serves as the primary reference for corporate governance in Brazil. Brazilian company law and the Brazilian Code have three unusual corporate governance features—the fiscal council, the family council, and the advisory board.

A *fiscal council* can be provided by the company's constitution or established at the request of shareholders. The role of the fiscal council is to inspect the work of the board, to review the activities of the company, to ensure compliance with legal and statutory duties, and to provide an opinion on the annual management report and on board proposals for investment projects, changes to capital, and dividend payouts. The fiscal council is required, at least quarterly, to analyse and comment on the balance sheet and other financial statements, and to provide an opinion to the shareholders' general meeting on board proposals. Fiscal councils have the right to consult with outside professionals, and are typically recognized as adding value to the company's owners by providing independent control.

[12] www.ecgi.org/codes/documents/final_code_english.pdf

The Brazilian Code encourages the creation of a *family council* in family-dominated companies. Its role is to discuss family issues and the alignment of its members' expectations with those of the other shareholders. Family councils enable boundaries to be set between family and company interests, preserve longer-term family values, and formalize succession planning for family members in both management and on the board. Family councils can also consider issues of inheritance and the transfer of property, which are inappropriate in shareholders' meetings.

The constitutions of some Brazilian companies also provide for an *advisory board*. The Code suggests that:

> [t]he existence of an advisory board, preferably made up of independent members, is good practice, particularly for organizations taking the first steps in the adoption of good practices of corporate governance. It allows independent members to contribute to the organization and gradually improve its corporate governance.

The Code calls for the advisory board's performance to be guided by the same principles that govern the board of directors. The ideas of the fiscal board, the family council, and the advisory board might provide approaches to corporate governance for other developing countries.

Corporate governance in Singapore

The Singapore corporate governance code, like those of Hong Kong and most Asian countries, is based on a 'comply or explain' approach, and calls for independent directors, audit committees, director training, and so on. Compliance is high, although companies listed on the SESDAQ market (Stock Exchange of Singapore Dealing and Automated Quotation System)—now called the Catalist market—tend to meet only the minimum requirements, unlike companies listed on the Singapore main board. In Singapore, the government is a significant player in the market, using government funds and those of the state pension fund to own and control significant companies incorporated there.

Corporate governance in South Korea

As described in Chapter 6, *chaebol* groups in South Korea developed following the Second World War, when the government advanced loans on attractive terms to family-based firms to stimulate economic revival. Over time, some of these family firms prospered and became large groupings of associated companies. Even *chaebol* companies that are listed are often still controlled by the dominant owner-family interests. Even though companies attracted outside capital, family domination was maintained predominantly through insider boards and cross-ownership with subsidiary companies.

Attempts to introduce independent outside directors onto South Korean boards have had only limited effect against the entrenched power of the existing block owners. At times, this has led to protests from employees and social unrest. In recent years, the South Korean government has sought to reduce the power of the *chaebol* by requiring them to divest some of their interests. But before the financial and economic crisis of 1997, success was limited. Subsequently, the *chaebol* found it increasingly difficult to compete with other Asian producers, because of their traditions of lifetime employment and militant trade unions, and governance changes were forced on them.

Corporate governance in Japan

In the 1970/80s, Japanese business methods were applauded by Western business schools, with 'just-in-time' manufacturing procurement systems, worker participation methods, and *ringi* decision-making throughout organizations. Then Japan hit more than two decades of deflation, poor economic growth, and poor corporate performance.

Corporate governance in Japanese companies had not evolved from the hierarchical, insider culture of the networked *keiretsu* groups, as described in Chapter 6. The result was highlighted by the case of Olympus, the optical equipment maker, in 2012 (Case study 17.1), in which the British president/CEO was unceremoniously dumped by his Japanese board for exposing fraud, without any comment from Japanese shareholders.

But, at last, Japanese companies are coming under more outside governance scrutiny. Among a number of reforms designed to restart the sluggish economy, the government of prime minister Shinzo Abe launched a new corporate governance code, which was introduced in 2016. The code called for independent, outside directors on company boards. Like corporate governance codes in the West, adherence to the code would be voluntary, but companies would report whether they had complied with the code or explain why if they had not. The government also introduced a new stewardship code giving shareholders more powers to monitor the boards of companies in which they invest. Together, the new corporate governance code and the stewardship code promise to change corporate governance in Japan.

Moreover, with around a third of investment in major firms now coming from abroad, companies are under more pressure to conform to international norms.

However, corporate governance cultures take time to evolve. The existence of outside directors does not, of itself, guarantee that the dominating power of executives at the top of companies will be broken. Independent directors could be little more than token members of ceremonial boards, while the real power, for example over succession, remains with the chair and his or her collaborators.

Japan's Corporate Governance Code, published in 2016, overcame decades of resistance to the inclusion of independent outside directors on Japanese boards. The Code took a pro-investor stance and emphasized that corporate governance should add to the long-term growth of the company. Two governance models were offered—one with a supervisory board, the other a unitary board with a board-level audit committee. In both models, new directors should be proposed by a nomination committee of non-executive directors.

Corporate governance in the Middle East and North Africa

The states that are typically grouped together as the Middle East and North Africa (MENA) are:

- Algeria;
- Bahrain;
- Egypt;
- Jordan;
- Kuwait;
- Lebanon;
- Morocco;
- Oman;
- Qatar;
- Tunisia;
- United Arab Emirates (UAE) (Abu Dhabi, Dubai, and five other states);
- Saudi Arabia.

Some of these countries are, of course, oil-rich, while others have relatively low GDPs with slow industrial growth. In recent years, the oil-producing countries, benefiting from rising oil prices, have generated large surpluses, which have been deposited abroad. Banking reforms have attempted to channel some of these savings into local growth, but domestic financial markets are emergent. States also appreciate the need to attract inward investment and therefore recognize the importance of sound corporate governance. The capital markets are small and illiquid, but slowly evolving. Consequently, the market for corporate control is poor.

Of course, there are exceptions to such general observations: for example, Dubai has made massive investments in tourism and property, while attempting to become an international financial centre, although subsequently running into financial difficulty.

Businesses in the region can be typified as having:

- concentrated ownership, with strong family ownership of both private and listed companies or state ownership;
- dominant family oversight and control, with leadership from the head of the family, entrepreneurial decision-making, opaque communications, and relationship-based trading;
- debt financing in which bank financing is often more than shareholders' equity;
- banking sector equity investment, with banks holding significant shares in companies.

The legal underpinnings around the region vary interestingly. In the Gulf states, Egypt, and Jordan, jurisdictions are orientated towards common law, reflecting earlier UK/Commonwealth influences. Elsewhere, jurisdictions have adopted European-style civil law. Throughout the region, company and securities laws exist, but are evolving to meet changing circumstances.

However, the most significant legal influence is the overarching Islamic Sharia law introducing religious rules and interpretations, which can affect attitudes towards contracts, property rights, and borrowing. Essentially, finance is based on the principle that charging interest is forbidden and that both sides of a deal must share risks.

The framework for corporate governance is broadly in place, although development is at an early stage and implementation and enforcement varied. Government securities commissions have also created different sets of rules. The Organisation for Economic Co-operation and Development, through the MENA/OECD Investment Programme, has sponsored an important study of corporate governance in the region, analysing the position in each country and recommending developments. Essentially, the OECD has recommended the adoption of rules-based corporate governance because of the state of financial markets, the lack of experience, and poor corporate discipline. In other words, it calls for legal and regulatory control not self-control by management, shareholders, and creditors.

So, in retrospect, we see around the world how corporate governance is conditioned by local cultures: heritage and expectations about the way business should be done; the legal system and the reliability of the judiciary; and the standing of the governance infrastructure; and the economic, social, and, in some cases, religious circumstances.

Case studies

 Case study 12.1   Yukos and Mikhail Khodorkovsky

The Yukos Oil Company, founded by Mikhail B. Khodorkovsky in 1993, acquired vast assets from the privatization of Russia's state enterprises. Yukos owned and operated oil and gas fields, oil refineries, and pipelines across Russia and Central Europe, and was the largest non-state oil company in Russia, producing around 20 per cent of Russian oil.

Khodorkovsky was keen to introduce Western-style corporate governance to his vast Yukos group. In 2000, he had the *Economist Pocket Director,* an ABC of corporate governance and effective board-level direction, translated into Russian, adding a personal foreword and a discussion of governance in Yukos.

At its peak in mid-2003, Yukos was vastly rich. But within two years the company had been seized by the state, with the company claiming 'an unprecedented campaign of illegal, discriminatory, and disproportionate tax claims escalating into raids and confiscation, culminating in intimidation and arrests ...' and Mikhail Khodorkovsky was in jail in Siberia.[13] The Yukos story is long, complex, and still controversial. In this case, we see the need for the state's approval in Russia for the exercise of corporate governance power.

The Yeltsin years

Following the dissolution of the Soviet Union, Boris Yeltsin became President of Russia in 1991, with a mission to turn a Communist, centrally planned economy into a capitalist market economy. The 1990s proved to be a turbulent period in Russian history. The economic reforms came too slowly and the living standards of many people were devastated, especially those dependent on Soviet-era state subsidies.

In 1998, Russia's economy collapsed, bringing economic chaos, humiliation, and suffering. The state was unable to pay its workers. With their personal savings destroyed, millions of Russians

[13] http://news.bbc.co.uk/1/hi/business/4097551.stm

were plunged into poverty. The currency fell 70 per cent, Russia defaulted on its foreign debt, and the International Monetary Fund (IMF) bailed the country out with loans of US$40 billion, but with demanding conditions.

However, a few people were able to enrich themselves during the decade. Called oligarchs, or the *'novi Russki'*, they benefited from the privatization of Russian state assets. They became super-rich, lived extravagantly, imported expensive cars, and travelled the world. The era also saw the rise of a middle class, unthinkable in Soviet days. Unexpectedly, Yeltsin resigned at the end of 1999, passing the presidency to Vladimir Putin, a former secret service chief.

The Putin era

Putin's first term of office was a significant success. He was able to end the chaotic excesses of the Yeltsin years and brought millions out of poverty. Under the watchful eye of the IMF, Russia repaid her international loans. The people developed a new confidence and, in 2004, Putin was re-elected with a huge majority. Although he accepted that the previous Soviet system had failed, he has made clear his preference for authoritarian leadership. Actions in the Crimea and the Ukraine backed by Putin in 2014 support this thesis.

The Yukos Oil Company

Inevitably, Putin saw the privatized entities as a problem and thought that the oligarchs were a potential threat to his plans. Khodorkovsky was arrested at gun-point in October 2003 on charges of fraud and tax evasion. Commentators suggested, however, that the real reason was Khodorkovsky's support for political opposition parties and championing of an anti-corruption campaign. He was held in a gulag, where Russia's once richest man worked in the prison sewing shop. Tried and found guilty on further charges at the end of his first sentence, he was finally released in December 2013. Now outside Russia, he wrote a short book on his prison experiences.[14] He concluded that Russia is 'a society where goodness and empathy are seen as synonymous with madness'.

The UK *Economist* (16 April 2016) reported that:

> [a] decade on from Vladimir Putin's expropriation and dismemberment of Yukos, things are not going according to plan. The Russian oil company was seized from its owners, then bankrupted and broken up, after being accused on flimsy evidence of tax evasion. Its boss, Mikhail Khodorkovsky, was jailed. Yukos's livid shareholders sued the government, and after years of legal wrangling, began to score victories. The biggest came in 2014: a $50 billion award against Russia by a court in The Hague, a record for international arbitration ... Russia refused to pay, sending Yukos's well-resourced former owners in a hunt to seize Russian assets (outside Russia).

However, in 2016 in a landmark ruling, the Hague District Court agreed with the Russian government that the Court had no jurisdiction to hear the case.

Discussion question

1. What lessons might be learned from the Yukos case about corporate governance in Russia?

---

[14] Khodorkovsky, Mikhail (2014) *My Fellow Prisoners*, Penguin Books, London.

Case study 12.2   The Tata Group

The Tata Group is an international conglomerate based in Mumbai, India. Since Jamsetji Nusserwanji Tata started the business in 1888, the Group has grown, often by acquisition, into a massive worldwide enterprise. It consists of over 1,000 companies on six continents. Among the principal operations are companies in the iron and steel industry (including some of the largest heavy steel works in India and Europe), the automotive industry (including Rover and Land Rover vehicles in the UK), defence, aerospace, chemicals, food and drink, consumer services and retail, hotels, financial services, consultancy services, IT and communications, and real estate. In 2017, the Group employed nearly 700,000 people and its revenues were equivalent to more than US$100 billion.[15]

Governance of the Tata Group

The investment holding company of the Tata Group is Tata Sons Ltd. The chair of Tata Sons is also chair of the Tata Group. A third of the equity of Tata Sons is held by Tata family members and associates: the balance is held by philanthropic trusts endowed by members of the Tata family, which support education, health, livelihood generation, and art and culture. The largest of these trusts are the Sir Dorabji Tata Trust and the Sir Ratan Tata Trust, created by the sons of the founder.

Within the Tata Group are 29 public listed companies, with a market capitalization of around US$130 billion in 2017. Listed companies in the Group have their own boards of directors responsible to their shareholders and meeting the listing requirements of the relevant stock exchange.

The mission and purpose of the Tata Group

The stated mission of the Tata Group is 'to improve the quality of life of the communities we serve globally through long-term stakeholder value creation based on Leadership with Trust'.[16] The Group also claims to be

> committed to improving the quality of life of the communities we serve . . . by striving for leadership and global competitiveness in the business sectors in which we operate. Our practice of returning to society what we earn evokes trust among consumers, employees, shareholders and the community. We are committed to protecting this heritage of leadership with trust through the manner in which we conduct our business . . . We do this by striving for leadership and global competitiveness in the business sectors in which we operate.[17]

The Tata core values

The five core values underpinning the way Tata do business are:

- *Integrity:* We will be fair, honest, transparent and ethical in our conduct; everything we do must stand the test of public scrutiny.

---

[15] For more on Tata Group activities see www.tata.com/. See also: www.tata.com/ebook/tata_brochure/mobile/index.html#p=1

[16] www.tata.com/aboutus/articlesinside/Values-and-purpose

[17] www.tata.com/aboutus/articlesinside/Values-and-purpose

- *Excellence:* We will be passionate about achieving the highest standards of quality, always promoting meritocracy.
- *Unity:* We will invest in our people and partners, enable continuous learning, and build caring and collaborative relationships based on trust and mutual respect.
- *Responsibility:* We will integrate environmental and social principles in our businesses, ensuring that what comes from the people goes back to the people many times over.
- *Pioneering:* We will be bold and agile, courageously taking on challenges, using deep customer insight to develop innovative solutions.[18]

The Tata Code of Conduct

Tata's code of conduct serves as an ethical road map for Tata employees and companies, as well as providing guidelines by which the group should conduct its businesses.

Tata companies have consistently adhered to the values and ideals articulated by the Founder for over 150 years. The Tata Code of Conduct was first formalized by Mr Ratan Tata. It articulates the Group's values and ideals that guide and govern the conduct of our companies as well as our colleagues in all matters relating to business. Today, the Code is a bed-rock on which we base our individual, as well as leadership commitments to core Tata values.

The Tata Code of Conduct outlines our commitment to each of our stakeholders, including the communities in which we operate, and is our guiding light when we are sometimes faced with business dilemmas that leave us at ethical crossroads. The Code is also dynamic in that it has been periodically refreshed in order to remain contemporary and contextual to the changes in law and regulations. However it remains unaltered at its core.

Our stellar reputation and success as a business entity has been defined by the powerful commitment and adherence to the core values and principles expressed in this Code, by all our employees, directors and partners. I trust every Tata colleague and Tata company will continue to not only comply with the laws and regulations that govern our business interests around the world, but will continue to set new standards of ethical conduct that will generate deep respect and inspire emulation by others.

N. Chandrasekaran, Chairman, Tata Sons
February 21, 2017[19]

Discussion questions

1. The public can invest in Tata through the listed companies in the Tata Group, ultimate governance of which lies with the Tata Trusts and members of the Tata family and associates. What are the pros and cons of this approach to governance?

2. In its governance, the Tata Group emphasizes the importance of core values throughout the Group. But the Group is an international conglomerate. Given the diversity of the business activities and the many countries in which it does business, is this realistic?

3. How can the directors of the overall holding company of the Tata Group ensure that the Group's mission and core values are being met?

[18] www.tata.com/aboutus/articlesinside/Values-and-purpose
[19] www.tata.com/aboutus/articlesinside/Values-and-purpose

Case study 12.3   Alibaba Group Holding Ltd

The Alibaba Group Holding Ltd is China's largest e-commerce group and processes more transactions each year than Amazon and eBay combined. Alibaba is a global leader in internet-based businesses, offering advertising and marketing services, electronic payment systems, cloud-based computing, network services, and mobile communications. The Group also provides wholesale and retail online markets. Gross revenues (excluding investment income) for the year to 31 March 2016 were RMB10,143 million (US$15,686 million).

The Alibaba Group was listed in New York in 2014, raising US$22 billion, the largest initial public offering on record, with bankers handling the float claiming they had orders for more than ten times that amount.

Alibaba has a strategic alliance with Ant Financial Services Group, to provide MYbank, one of China's first privately owned online banks; Sesame Credit, a credit-scoring service; and Koubei, which provides financial services to the China market. Alibaba Group also has a strategic alliance with Suning to build on synergies in e-commerce, logistics, and online-to-offline (O2O) commerce, which draws potential customers from online channels to physical stores. Alibaba also runs DingTalk, a mobile group messaging tool for small to medium-sized enterprises (SMEs), and owns the Hong Kong English-language newspaper the *South China Morning Post*.

The hub of the Group's European operations is in London. The international headquarters of Alibaba Cloud is in Singapore. Cainiao is the Alibaba Group's logistics company, formed in 2013. It provides a China-wide parcel-delivery system, and offers next-day delivery in 50 cities for goods ordered from Alibaba's online marketplaces.[20]

The origins of Alibaba

Alibaba was founded in 1999, by Jack Yun Ma, a teacher of English from Hangzhou, the capital of Zhejiang Province on China's east coast. Ma created a website for the rapidly growing number of entrepreneurial, but relatively small, Chinese manufacturers, retailers, and exporters to sell their goods around the world. At the time Alibaba had 18 employees.

The founders saw that the internet could be used by smaller enterprises to compete in the global as well as the Chinese market against larger companies with well-established supply chains, distribution networks, and marketing outlets. Users of the Alibaba internet services could apply their innovation, technology, and entrepreneurial skills more effectively.

In 2005, Alibaba acquired the China operations of US-based IT company Yahoo! for a 43 per cent stake in Alibaba. Prior to the New York listing in 2014, 43 per cent of Alibaba shares were held by Yahoo!, 28 per cent by Japanese IT company Softbank, and 29 per cent by Jack Ma and colleagues in top management.

At the time, Yahoo! was losing market share in its American and other worldwide operations, so Alibaba became a jewel in its crown.

The AliPay saga

A significant component of the Alibaba Group was a business called AliPay, which was launched in 2004 to provide the online payment portal for transactions on Alibaba.com. It became the world's largest online payment system.

---

[20] For more detailed information on the businesses of the Alibaba Group see www.alibaba.com/.

But in 2010 the Chinese government ruled that all internet payment systems should be wholly owned by Chinese interests. AliPay did not qualify, because Alibaba was 71 per cent foreign-owned. AliPay risked losing its licence to operate, which would destroy its business. Jack Ma then made a unilateral decision to transfer ownership of AliPay to a new entity—Zhejiang Alibaba e-commerce Ltd—which he and Shihuang Xie, his co-founder, controlled. Apparently, neither the Alibaba board nor Yahoo! were informed at the time.

In March 2011, Yahoo! and Softbank were told officially that AliPay had been spun off from Alibaba. Yahoo! shareholders found out in May 2011 from an SEC filing, and the share price fell 10 per cent.

When asked why he had bypassed the board, Ma apparently said that the Alibaba board seldom met formally and taking the matter to the board might have meant a delay, the loss of the licence, and the end of AliPay. AliPay did obtain a licence to operate as a Chinese-owned company in May 2011.

A formal agreement was ultimately signed between Alibaba, Yahoo!, and Softbank for the transfer out of the AliPay business, involving a capital sum, an agreement on sharing profits, and licensing agreements.

The Alibaba Group's mission, vision, and value

Today the company has a clear mission statement:

To make it easy to do business anywhere [which it achieves by providing] the fundamental technology infrastructure and marketing reach to help merchants, brands and other businesses that provide products, services and digital content to leverage the power of the Internet to engage with their users and customers. Our businesses are comprised of core commerce, cloud computing, digital media and entertainment, innovation initiatives and others. Through investee affiliates, we also participate in the logistics and local services sectors. [The company reinforces its mission statement with its vision that] [w]e aim to build the future infrastructure of commerce. We envision that our customers will meet, work and live at Alibaba, and that we will be a company that lasts at least 102 years [thus covering three centuries since its creation in 1999]. We enable hundreds of millions of commercial and social interactions among our users, between consumers and merchants, and among businesses every day. We empower our customers with the fundamental infrastructure for commerce and data technology, so that they can build businesses and create value that can be shared among our ecosystem participants. We strive to expand our products and services to become central to the everyday lives of our customers.[21]

The Group emphasizes the importance of its values and publishes a code of ethics, stating that 'the conduct of all employees should reflect Alibaba Group's values and promote a work environment that upholds and improves Alibaba Group's reputation for integrity and trust'.[22]

Corporate governance of the Alibaba Group

Today, Alibaba is a leader in its approach to corporate governance, not least because it has to meet the demands of the US SEC and the listing rules of the NYSE.[23]

The board has established corporate governance guidelines describing the principles and practices that it follows in carrying out its responsibilities. The corporate governance guidelines cover:

---

[21] www.alibabagroup.com/en/about/overview
[22] For details of the code of ethics go to: http://alibabagroup.com/en/ir/governance_4
[23] For the latest SEC filing go to: www.alibabagroup.com/en/ir/pdf/agm160524_ar.pdf

- the role and responsibility of the board;
- board composition, structure, and policies;
- board meetings;
- committees of the board;
- expectations of directors;
- management succession-planning;
- evaluation of board performance;
- board remuneration;
- approval of related party transactions;
- equity incentive plans;
- communications with shareholders.[24]

The board of directors currently has 11 members. Six are executive or connected directors:

Jack Yun Ma, executive chair

Joseph C. Tsai, executive vice chair

Daniel Yong Zhang, director and CEO

J. Michael Evans, director and president

Masayoshi Son, director

Eric Xiandong Jing, director

And there are five independent directors:

Chee Hwa Tung

Walter Teh Ming Kwauk

Jerry Yang

Börje E. Ekholm

Wan Ling Martello.[25]

The board has three standing committees:

- audit committee;
- compensation committee;
- nominating and corporate governance committee.[26]

The corporate governance guidelines are reviewed periodically by the nominating and corporate governance committee to ensure that they continue to promote the best interests of the company and its shareholders; and that they comply with all relevant laws, regulations, and stock exchange requirements, and are in line with the company's memorandum and articles of association.

[24] http://alibabagroup.com/en/ir/governance_1

[25] Detailed biographies of each of the directors can be read at: http://alibabagroup.com/en/ir/governance_6

[26] Each committee has a published charter, which can be read together with details of the committee membership at: http://alibabagroup.com/en/ir/governance_7

Exercising governance power over the Alibaba Group

Shareholders do not own shares in the Alibaba company itself, but in a company incorporated in the Cayman Islands, tied to the company by complicated legal agreements. Power over that company is exercised by a somewhat opaque entity called the Alibaba Partnership.

Shareholders in Alibaba Group Holding Ltd have few powers over the governance of their company. Their interests are side-lined: in the words of the *Economist* 'Alibaba's legal structure is controversial'.[27] The Hong Kong Stock Exchange, which was approached first to list Alibaba, turned down the opportunity because of its listing rules, which require all shares to carry equal voting rights. Dual-class shares, with one class able to maintain control even though they represent a minority of the equity, are not allowed.

New York has no such restriction. Indeed, many prominent US public companies, including some in Silicon Valley, have dual-class shares, with the founders owning shares that have enhanced voting rights to maintain their control.

The Alibaba Group justifies the use of the Alibaba Partnership as the vehicle for exercising governance power over the company as follows:

> Our partnership is a dynamic body that rejuvenates itself through admission of new partners each year, which we believe enhances our excellence, innovation and sustainability.
>
> Unlike dual-class ownership structures that employ a high-vote class of shares to concentrate control in a few founders, our approach is designed to embody the vision of a large group of management partners. This structure is our solution for preserving the culture shaped by our founders, while at the same time accounting for the fact that founders will inevitably retire from the company.[28]

The company further explained that, in the early days of Alibaba, the directors realized that their new business, built on innovation, technology, and harnessing the internet, had also created a distinct culture. As the company grew larger, more complex, and was moving into new businesses, the directors wanted to maintain this distinctive culture, because they felt it was fundamental to the Group's success.

From the outset, the company explains, directors and management had acted in a spirit of partnership, to serve their customers, develop their employees, and deliver long-term value to their shareholders. To preserve this spirit of partnership and to ensure the sustainability of the Group's mission, vision, and values, the founders formalized the Alibaba Partnership.

The Alibaba Partnership currently has 32 members comprising 24 members of senior management, 7 members of management from Ant Financial Services, and 1 member of management from Cainiao Network. The number of partners is not fixed and can change from time to time. All partnership decisions are made on a one-partner-one-vote basis. The Partnership is governed by a partnership agreement and operates under principles, policies, and procedures that have evolved with the business.

The Group believes that the peer nature of the Partnership enables senior managers to collaborate and override bureaucracy and hierarchy.

In September 2018, Jack Ma announced his intention to step aside from his role as executive chair by the end of 2019. He was 54. He wanted, he said, to devote himself to philanthropic works, in particular his interest in education. 'Teachers always want their students to exceed them, so the responsible thing for me and the company to do is to let younger, more talented people take

[27] *The Economist*, 9 August 2018.
[28] www.alibabagroup.com/en/ir/governance_9

over in leadership roles,' Mr Ma said. Daniel Yong Zhang, director and CEO, will become executive chair on 10 September 2019, according to a company statement.

Discussion questions:

1. The Alibaba Group appears to meet the norms of good corporate governance, with one exception: shareholder rights. Is the Alibaba arrangement using the Alibaba Partnership to exercise governance control acceptable?

2. Do you believe that 'one share one vote' should apply to investment in all companies listed on stock markets?

3. The Hong Kong Stock Exchange does not allow companies with dual-class, different voting rights to list. Discussions continue on whether allowing companies with dual-class shares to list would encourage founders of successful start-up companies to make an IPO (*Initial Public Offering*). Should the Exchange change its rules?

Self-test questions

1. What is the name of the corporate regulator in China and what are its principal duties?

2. What aspects of Hong Kong's Western-orientated corporate governance regime had to change when Hong Kong became a Special Administrative Region of China in 1997?

3. What is a major problem facing boards in many Indian companies? How does the Asian Corporate Governance Association rate Indian corporate governance?

4. In Russia, what have been the significant changes in corporate governance under the presidency of Vladimir Putin?

5. What did the International Finance Corporation, working with the World Bank, provide for Russia?

6. What are the unusual corporate governance features in Brazilian company law and corporate governance codes?

7. Hong Kong is a Special Administrative Region of China. Do Hong Kong-listed companies have to follow the Chinese corporate governance rules laid down by the CSRC?

8. Who often controls listed *chaebol* companies in South Korea? How is that control maintained?

9. What typifies the governance of businesses in the MENA region?

10. What is the most significant legal influence on corporate governance in the MENA countries?

 For suggested answers to these self-test questions visit the online resources at:
www.oup.com/uk/tricker4e/

Projects and exercises

1. Choose three Chinese companies listed on the London or New York Stock Exchanges. Prepare a presentation or write a report comparing their corporate governance reporting. Rank your opinion of their investor relations.

2. A foreign company is reviewing its strategy to develop trade with China. The board is considering setting up a company in Hong Kong or mainland China. Draft a report advising them of the corporate governance implications.

3. Identify some major companies listed in South Korea. Choose one and research its approach to corporate governance.

References and further reading

Chen, Jian (2005) *Corporate Governance in China*. RoutledgeCurzon, New York and Abingdon.

China–United States Exchange Foundation (2011) US–China Economic Relations in the next ten years, Hong Kong http://www.cusef.org.hk/wp-ontent/uploads/2016/10/Part-01_and_Part-02_Book-1.pdf

Clarke, Thomas (2007) *International Corporate Governance: A Comparative Approach*. Routledge, New York and Abingdon.

Clarke, Thomas and Jean-François Chanlat (eds) (2009) *European Corporate Governance*. Routledge, New York and Abingdon.

De Groot, Cornelis (2009) *Corporate Governance as a Limited Legal Concept (European Company Law)*. Kluwer Law, The Netherlands.

Gul, F. A. and J. S. L. Tsui (2004) *The Governance of East Asian Corporations: Post Asian Financial Crisis*. Palgrave Macmillan, London.

Hadjiemmanuil, Christos and Joseph Jude Norton

(eds) (2009) *Corporate Governance Post-Enron: Comparative and International Perspectives (Studies in International Financial, Economic and Technology Law)*. British Institute of International and Comparative Law, London.

Morris, Ian (2011) *Why the West Rules—For Now: Patterns of History and What They Reveal About the Future*. Profile Books, London.

Schipani, Cindy and Junhai Liu (2002) *Corporate Governance in China: Then and Now*. Columbia Business Law Review, New York.

Tenev, Stoyan and Zhang Chunlan (2002) Corporate Governance and Enterprise Reform in China: Building the Institutions of Modern Markets, The World Bank and the International Finance Corporation, Washington, DC.

Tricker, Bob and Gregg Li (2019) *Understanding Corporate Governance in China*. Hong Kong University Press, Hong Kong.

Useful websites

Access to corporate governance codes in many countries is found in Appendix 1.

www.virtusinterpress.org/-Open-Access-Book-Corporate-Governance-in-a-Transition-Economy-.html

Corporate Governance in a Transitional Economy.

www.ecgi.org/codes

Full texts of corporate governance codes, principles of corporate governance, and corporate governance reforms both in Europe and elsewhere.

www.acga-asia.org

Asia Corporate Governance Association.

China

www.csrc.gov.cn/pub/csrc_en/
Access to CSRC site.
www.sasac.gov.cn/n1180/index.htm
Access to SASAC site.

India

www.in.kpmg.com/tl_files/pictures/cg_survey_report.pdf
The state of corporate governance in India.
www.nfcgindia.org/home.html
National Foundation for Corporate Governance.

Russia

www.imf.org/external/pubs/ft/seminar/2000/invest/pdf/vasil2.pdf
Corporate governance in Russia—any chance of improvement?

Brazil

www.estandardsforum.org/brazil/standards/principles-of-corporate-governance
Corporate Governance in Brazil, Financial Standards Institute.

Hong Kong

www.adb.org/documents/books/rising_to_the_challenge/sound_practices/hkcg.pdf

Singapore

www.iclg.co.uk/khadmin/Publications/pdf/4558.pdf
International comparative legal guide—Singapore 2011.

South Korea

www.lawnet.lk/docs/articles/international/HTML/A43.html
Corporate governance in Asia—a survey.

Middle East and North Africa

www.oecd.org/mena/investment
OECD initiative on the Middle East and North Africa (MENA).

Part 3

Practices

13

Board Membership: Directors' Appointment, Roles, and Remuneration

 Learning Outcomes

This chapter enables us to:

- Understand the appointment of directors.
- Appreciate desirable attributes and core competencies in a director.
- Consider roles directors play.
- Recognize directors' duties, rights, powers, and conflicts of interest.
- Grasp insider information and. service contracts.
- Discuss directors' remuneration.

The appointment of directors

How directors are appointed

In the original 19th-century model of the limited-liability company, the founder of the business, the existing directors, and perhaps the shareholders suggested names for new directors. The shareholders then met, and a decision was reached. This is still the case in many private companies: decisions are taken by dominant shareholders, such as family members in a family firm, or the directors of the holding company in a corporate group.

But as listed companies became larger, more diverse and geographically spread, so did their shareholders. With a large number of shareholders located around the world, with varying interests in the company, it was no longer feasible for them to influence decisions on the choice of directors. Power had shifted from shareholders to directors, as Berle and Means had shown in 1932.[1] Directors of major listed companies were now nominated by the chair and the existing directors, and then routinely approved by shareholders in their annual general meeting. Critics complained that boards became self-perpetuating clubs of like-minded people, routinely chosen from small networks of influence, typically those who came from similar backgrounds to themselves. In the United States recommendations from business contacts, fellow members of the country club, or business school fraternity held sway. In England, director appointments were influenced by 'the old school tie' and social standing such as a knighthood. In France, those educated in the elite *grandes écoles* dominated both boardroom and government.

[1] Berle, Adolf and Gardiner Means, *The Modern Corporation and Private Property*, 1932, 1967.

The introduction of a board-level nomination committee was an attempt to resolve this dilemma. The nomination committee is a standing subcommittee of the main board, made up wholly, or mainly, of independent non-executive directors, called on to recommend new directors. Relying on independent directors is intended to avoid a dominant director, such as the chair or CEO, pushing through his or her own preferred candidates.

Unfortunately, the supposed independence of outside directors on the nomination committee can be illusory. If the committee's members have themselves been selected by the chair, and have worked with him or her for years, they are likely to feel an allegiance towards him or her and support his or her candidates. On the other hand, it can be argued that newly appointed directors need to be acceptable to the chair if they are to work in harmony as part of an effective board team. Calls for more diversity on boards, particularly gender diversity, have to be heeded by nomination committees.

In the United Kingdom, Hong Kong, and some other countries, although listed companies have adopted most of the requirements of the corporate governance codes, the requirement to have a nominating committee has been resisted by some. This is not surprising, since the right to influence appointments to the board goes to the very heart of corporate power.

Shareholders in public listed companies still have little opportunity to influence the nomination of new directors, unless they hold a significant proportion of the voting shares. Various proposals have been put forward to enable shareholders to nominate directors. Some would have the institutional investors play a larger role; others would allow shareholders to create and vote on a 'slate' of directors, including those they had proposed. Another idea, from Shann Turnbull, is for shareholders to form a shareholders' committee, which would represent all of the shareholders in dealings with the company, including the nomination of new directors.

Director appointments can arise:

- on re-appointment at the expiry of a director's term of office;
- to fill a vacancy;
- on the creation of an additional directorship;
- on the initial incorporation of a company.

To summarize, legally the right to appoint directors lies with the shareholder members of a company: that is one of the rights of ownership provided by the concept of the joint-stock, limited-liability company. In practice, the names of potential directors are often proposed (nominated) by incumbent board members and put to the shareholders for confirmation. In companies required to follow corporate governance codes, the board-level nomination committee is expected to propose the list of candidates for board and subsequently shareholder approval. In recent years, however, shareholder resistance to board nominees has grown, particularly from institutional investors. Where allowed by the law and listing rules, alternative names can be added to the 'slate' of nominees and proxy votes of other shareholders sought to support them. In many non-listed and family companies, however, the power to nominate directors still lies with incumbent board.

The rotation of directors

Companies' articles of association typically lay down the terms of service for directors, including how long they will act before coming up for re-election and when that should occur. In the past, many companies' articles called for a fixed proportion of the directors to retire each year. For example, if directors' appointments were for three years, one-third would stand down each year, offering themselves for re-election if eligible. It was felt that this practice provided stability, since there would always be a proportion of directors on the board with experience of the company's business, enabling a longer-term strategic perspective to be taken. Critics of these so-called 'staggered' or 'classified' boards complain that, in an under-performing company, directors become entrenched. Further, because the entire board cannot be replaced at a single election, staggered boards effectively block hostile takeover bids, and can be used as a takeover defence. Annual election of all directors allows a change of control through a single successful proxy contest.

The size of boards

Many articles of association put upper and lower limits on board size. Some company law jurisdictions also have rules on board size, particularly the minimum number of directors; some prohibit single director boards. Others do not allow companies to act as directors (corporate directors), insisting that directors are real persons. Where corporate directors are allowed, the directors of the corporate director take on the responsibilities of the directorship.

In practice, the case is often made for additional directors to join a board to remedy perceived weaknesses, to add necessary skills and experience, or to bring new knowledge or contacts. The case is seldom heard for a reduction in numbers. The ideal number, obviously, depends on the circumstances in each case, but boards can become too large. Beyond a certain number, psychologists say between eight and ten, a board ceases to be a cohesive, decision-making body. The time each director has to contribute to discussion is limited. Directors are more likely to form cliques or cabals. Chairship then becomes challenging and bringing the board to a consensus is more difficult.

Retirement, disqualification, and removal of directors

Many articles of association also have rules on directors' ages, calling for shareholder approval. Company law often imposes a minimum age on appointments to the board, frequently 16 or 18. Company law in some jurisdictions puts an upper age limit on directors, often 70.

Elsewhere, the view is taken that this is ageist and that many older people have the wisdom, experience, and abilities to make significant contributions to companies. The important factor is to ensure that older directors are making that contribution and not being re-elected out of a misplaced sense of respect or loyalty.

Company law can also disqualify certain people from serving as directors, including those who are bankrupt, mentally ill, or disqualified by the courts from being a director. Disqualification by the courts usually follows a guilty verdict of an offence in running a company or persistently defaulting in the filing of official returns.

In principle, the shareholders of a company have the right to appoint and to remove their directors. In practice, this can be difficult. Subject to company law and the company's articles, members can propose a resolution calling for the removal of directors, and seek a shareholders' meeting to consider this resolution. Much depends on the voting power of the recalcitrant shareholders. The incumbent board may resist, adopt delaying tactics, and circulate contrary information at the company's expense, while requiring the challenging shareholders to cover the costs of their campaign.

Desirable attributes in a director

In the first part of this book, we focused on corporate governance principles; in the second, on corporate governance policies. But behind the corporate constitutions, board structures, and corporate governance codes are people—people who bring a wide range of prejudices, political behaviours, and power plays to board affairs. So what personal attributes are needed to be a successful, professional director?

The primary prerequisite for every director is *integrity*. Directors are stewards of the interests of the company (that is, of the entire body of shareholders). The enterprise does not belong to the directors. They hold it in trust for the owners to whom they owe a fiduciary duty to act with care, openly and honestly in their interests. This applies whether the company is a family business, with a few shareholders, or a vast, listed company.

What does integrity mean? It means being ethically aware, able to distinguish right from wrong, and able to judge corporate behaviour accordingly. It implies honesty, fairness, and sound moral principles. It means acting in the company interest, not self-interest, resisting the temptation to make a personal gain to the detriment of the company. Integrity also means being able to recognize and declare a conflict of interest. Essentially, integrity means acting honestly for the benefit of the company. A director with integrity is trusted, which is basic because the very concept of the company is based on trust.

In law, a company is a legal entity and enjoys many of the rights of an individual person. But, unlike a real person, a company does not have a conscience. The board has to act as the corporate conscience. Clearly, that means ensuring that the company obeys the laws of the jurisdictions in which it operates. Further, the board creates the company's value system, its corporate culture and character establishing the way the whole organization operates, over and above just staying within the law (see Corporate Governance in Action 13.1).

In practice, many boards publish a formal statement of their corporate mission and the core values to which they aspire. In some cases, these statements are no more than pious aspirations, which do little to affect the way in which the company is run. In other cases, however, such mission statements can lead to rigorous policies, approved and monitored by the board on, for example, how the company treats its customers, its relations with employees, and its commitment to corporate social responsibility.

In addition to integrity, high-calibre directors demonstrate other personal qualities. These can be summarized as intellect, character, and personality.

Intellect is what, in Oxford colleges, they call having 'a good mind'. It combines an appropriate level of intelligence, the ability to think at different levels of abstraction, and the imagination to see situations from different perspectives, rather than always seeing things from a fixed viewpoint. A sound intellect is able to exercise independent judgement, to think originally, and to act creatively.

Character traits, what some call 'strength of character', include being independently minded, objective, and impartial. A director needs to be capable of moving towards consensus. Yet, from time to time, a director needs to be tough-minded, tenacious, and resilient, with the courage to make a stand. Further, a director needs to be results-orientated, with a balanced approach to risk—neither risk-averse nor rash. Finally, some might add wisdom or just plain common sense to useful director character traits (even though common sense is not all that common).

Desirable *personality* traits in a director include the ability to interact positively with others, which from time to time may call for openness, flexibility, sensitivity, diplomacy, persuasiveness, the ability to motivate, and a sense of humour. Such interpersonal abilities are particularly important in interactions with the chair and boardroom peers. Other desirable personality traits include being a sound listener and a good communicator, as well as being politically astute.

Corporate Governance in Action 13.1   Microsoft 2017 vision statement

Microsoft is a technology company whose mission is to empower every person and every organization on the planet to achieve more. We strive to create local opportunity, growth, and impact in every country around the world. Our strategy is to build best-in-class platforms and productivity services for an intelligent cloud and an intelligent edge infused with artificial intelligence ('AI').

The way individuals and organizations use and interact with technology continues to evolve. A person's experience with technology increasingly spans a multitude of devices and becomes more natural and multi-sensory with voice, ink, and gaze interactions. We believe a new technology paradigm is emerging that manifests itself through an intelligent cloud and an intelligent edge where computing is more distributed, AI drives insights and acts on the user's behalf, and user experiences span devices with a user's available data and information. We continue to transform our business to lead this new era of digital transformation and enable our customers and partners to thrive in this evolving world.

The previous mission statement was:

Microsoft is a technology company whose mission is to empower every person and every organization on the planet to achieve more. Our strategy is to build best-in-class platforms and productivity services for a mobile-first, cloud-first world.

The mobile-first, cloud-first world is transforming the way individuals and organizations use and interact with technology. Mobility is not focused on any one device; it is centered on the mobility of experiences that, in turn, are orchestrated by the cloud. Cloud computing and storage solutions provide people and enterprises with various capabilities to store and process their data in third-party data centers. Mobility encompasses the rich collection of data, applications, and services that accompany our customers as they move from setting to setting in their lives. We are transforming our businesses to enable Microsoft to lead the direction of this digital transformation, and enable our customers and partners to thrive in this evolving world.[2]

Microsoft published values

Microsoft's Code outlines six values to guide employee conduct:[3]

- integrity and honesty;
- passion for customers, partners, and technology;

[2] www.geekwire.com/2017/microsofts-new-corporate-vision-artificial-intelligence-mobile/
[3] https://bizfluent.com/facts-6155106-microsoft-company-code-ethics.html

- being open and respectful with others and dedicated to making them better;
- a willingness to take on big challenges and see them through;
- being self-critical, questioning, and committed to personal excellence and self-improvement;
- accountable for commitments, results, and quality to customers, shareholders, partners, and employees.

Compliance officer

Microsoft's General Counsel Brad Smith also serves as the company's chief compliance officer. He is responsible for enforcing the Code of Ethics.

Reporting

Microsoft has established a Business Conduct Line to enable employees and the public to report any breach of ethics. The Business Conduct Line can be reached at 877-320-MSFT (6738). Microsoft also allows for direct contact with its Office of Legal Compliance.

Partner conduct

Microsoft has released a separate Code of Conduct for its International Association of Microsoft Certified Partners. The code tasks Microsoft partners with protecting Microsoft intellectual property, with social responsibility to the public, as well as competence, personal conduct, and being knowledgeable in representing Microsoft worldwide.

Consumer sentiment

Whatever the criticism of Microsoft ethics, and its past legal troubles (such as anti-trust lawsuits in Europe), a survey by the Boston College Center for Corporate Citizenship in 2009 named Microsoft as the second most admired company by US consumers. The Walt Disney Co. was first and Google third. Social responsibility is only one element of Microsoft's Code of Conduct.

Further attributes of a successful director

Successful directors look ahead, anticipate problems, and can articulate possible solutions. They are open, welcome questioning, and seek feedback. But they also listen, try to understand others' points of view, and seek consensus. Overall, they are reliable and trusted by their chair and peers. On the other hand, poor directors tend to adopt a negative attitude, offer platitudes, and fail to face up to serious issues. Strategic thinking is replaced by reliance on past successes and rigorous risk analysis by hope. Obviously, an independent outside director needs to be genuinely independent. As the Cadbury Report put it, 'independent of management and free from any business or other relationships which could materially interfere with the exercise of their independent judgement'.

These attributes tend to be inherent in people by the time they are nominated for a board appointment, having been culturally determined and acquired over a lifetime. By contrast, there are certain core competencies that a director needs, which can be developed or acquired through director induction programmes, director training, and director development and updating.

A committee, chaired by Lord Nolan in the United Kingdom, produced a set of principles to guide the holders of public office in the United Kingdom. These principles can be readily applied to company directors in fulfilling their fiduciary duty.

Corporate Governance in Action 13.2   Lord Nolan's Seven Principles of Public Life

1. *Selflessness*—Holders of public office should serve the public interest, and not seek gains for their friends.

2. *Integrity*—They should not place themselves under financial obligation to outsiders who might influence their duties.

3. *Objectivity*—They should award public appointments and contracts on merit.

4. *Accountability*—They should submit themselves to the appropriate scrutiny.

5. *Openness*—They should give reasons for their decisions.

6. *Honesty*—They should declare conflicts of interest.

7. *Leadership*—They should support these principles by personal example.

Core competencies of a director

Every corporate entity and every governing body is different, and each director brings a different set of experience, skills, and knowledge to the board. But, in the aggregate, every board needs to have a mix of capabilities that provide a balanced and well-qualified team relevant to that board and that company. So every director needs to have some basic core competencies appropriate to the type, location, and scale of the enterprise. What experience, skills, and knowledge should a director have?

The *experience* of outside directors should be used to supplement the knowledge available to the board, not to second-guess the executives in the company. For example, a director could bring experience about corporate governance, board procedures, or strategy formulation and policy-making from other (non-competing) companies. Or a director might have experience of overseas markets, frontier technologies, international finance, or other areas that supplement the experience of the existing board.

The essential director-level *skills* include:

- strategic reasoning, perception, and vision;
- a critical faculty capable of quantitative and qualitative analysis and financial interpretation;
- planning and decision-making capabilities;
- communication and interpersonal skills;
- networking and political abilities.

Directors also need appropriate *knowledge* of the enterprise, its business, and board-level activities, as well as relevant information about the company's political, economic, social, and technological contexts. If directors are to make sense of board information and contribute meaningfully to board discussions, they must have basic knowledge about the company itself, its business, and the company's financials.

Knowledge of the company includes:

- a clear understanding of the basis of power (who the shareholders are and where the power lies to change membership of the governing body);
- the basis of law under which the company operates and what the governance rules and regulations are (for a limited company, these are company law and the company's memorandum and articles of association, plus the listing regulations for a listed company);
- the board structure, membership, and directors' personalities;
- the board processes, including the use of board committees, the focus of board and committee activities, and the nature of board information.

An awareness of the history of the entity can also be helpful in understanding the board culture, interpreting the current situation, and appreciating the perspectives of the chair and other board members.

Knowledge of the business embraces an understanding of the basic business activities and processes: its purpose and aims; its strengths and weaknesses, and how it measures success; the field of its operations (including markets, competitors, and its current operating context); the strategies being pursued; the structure of the organization; its culture, management, and people; and the form of management control and management control systems. Risk assessment is an important aspect of the board's role and all directors need to know where the enterprise is exposed to risk and its nature. Increasingly, knowledge of the company's stakeholders and its approach to corporate social responsibility and sustainability should form part of directors' knowledge base.

Knowledge of the financials includes knowing how the company is financed, a sound appreciation of its annual accounts and directors' reports, knowledge of emerging trends in key financial ratios, the criteria used in investment appraisals, the calibre of financial control and risk management, and who the auditors are. Many board-level reports are presented in financial terms and the ability both to interpret them and to appreciate their strengths and weaknesses is important. It is not necessary to be an accountant to be a good director; indeed, some might argue the reverse! But an ability to appreciate the financial aspects of the company is vital.

Roles directors play

Given their various personal attributes and different competencies, directors inevitably make a variety of contributions to their boards and can play a number of roles. Some of these roles contribute to the performance aspects of the board's work (strategy formulation and policy-making); others contribute to the conformance aspects (executive supervision and accountability).

The following are examples of some performance-orientated roles that directors play.

1. *Bringing wider business and board experience* to the identification, discussion, and decision-making—identifying issues that the board, not management, should be handling. Directors

tend to respect the wisdom of the director who brings to bear accumulated knowledge and experience in business and elsewhere on issues facing the board. As the Cadbury Report put it, 'the board should include non-executive directors of sufficient calibre and number for their views to carry significant weight in the board's decisions'. Long-serving directors may well find themselves cast in this role by newer board colleagues. Accumulated wisdom can, of course, have limitations in rapidly changing situations.

2. *Adding specialist knowledge, skills, and know-how* to board deliberations. Here, a director relies on his or her particular professional training, skills, and knowledge to make a contribution. For example, the specialism might be in the realm of accountancy, banking, engineering, finance, or law, or it could stem from specialist knowledge of a particular market, technology, or functional area, such as marketing, manufacturing, or personnel. In some newer, growing companies, outside directors are appointed to the board specifically to provide such specialist inputs until such time as the company can afford to acquire such skills in-house at the executive level. When a board is relying on such expertise, it is important to ensure that the director remains up to date in the subject, which can sometimes prove difficult for those operating at board level.

3. *Being the source of external information* for board discussions—a window on the world for other directors. The director is used as a source of information on issues relevant to board discussions. Usually, this will be on matters external to the company, such as insights into market opportunities, new technologies, industry developments, financial and economic concerns, or international matters. Obviously, it is essential that the information is relevant, accurate, and current. This is often a role specifically sought from outside directors, who are in a position to obtain such information through their other day-to-day activities. A danger is that directors, chosen because of their access to specific information, lose touch with it.

4. *Being a figurehead or an ambassador for the company*, being able to represent the company in the outside world. The director represents the company in the external arena: for example, in meetings with fund managers and financial analysts, or in trade and industry gatherings. The chair of the board often takes on this responsibility, perhaps being invited to join public committees, commissions, and the governing bodies of important public institutions, as well as joining the boards of other, non-competing companies. These days, this role can be taken by the director identified as the senior INED. For many companies, a figurehead is increasingly important in dealing with the media.

5. *Connecting the board to networks of useful people* not otherwise available to the board. This can be an important role for outside directors, who are able through their personal contacts to connect the board and top management to networks of potentially useful people and organizations. For example, the director might be well placed to forge contacts in the world of politics and government, to link the company with relevant banking, finance, or stock exchange connections, or to make introductions within industry or international trade. Retiring politicians are sometimes offered directorships on the assumption that they have useful contacts and influence in the corridors of power. Such a role may also provide advice on succession in the board and in top management.

6. *Providing status to the board and the company, adding capability, reputation, and position.* This role is not as significant today as it was a few years ago. In the past, eminent public figures

were often invited to join boards just to add status, rather than any specific contribution they could make to board deliberations. Previous service as a US Senator or a knighthood in the United Kingdom almost guaranteed an invitation to join the board of a public company in the past. But these days boards need professionalism ahead of prestige. However, the status role can be useful at times; for example when a particular listed company faced a financial crisis, the market was reassured when a well-known financier joined the board. Exposure to litigation may now deter some public figures from accepting directorships. However, even today, if a company has been experiencing problems, confidence may be restored if a high-profile, well-respected figure joins the board.

The following are examples of some conformance-orientated roles that directors play.

A. *Providing independent judgement*, the ability to see issues in their totality and from various perspectives, leading to objective judgement—in other words, 'helicopter vision'. This can be a vital contribution of the outside director, who, obviously, has the opportunity to see board matters from an external and independent point of view. As the Cadbury Report suggested, 'non-executive directors should bring an independent judgement to bear on issues of strategy, performance, resources, including key appointments and standards of conduct'. Such an objective evaluation of top management performance can overcome the tunnel vision sometimes found in those too closely involved with the situation, or the myopia brought on by being personally affected by the outcome. Overall, providing independent judgement brings wise counsel that leads to better decisions.

B. *Being a catalyst for change*, questioning existing assumptions, introducing new ideas and approaches, and stimulating developments. This role can be played by a director who questions the board's assumptions, and makes others rethink situations. Catalysts point out that what appears to be an incontrovertible truth to some board members is, in fact, rooted in some questionable beliefs about the company, its markets, or its competitors. They highlight inferences that are masquerading as facts. They show when value judgements, rather than rigorous analysis, are being used in board deliberations. Most valuably, catalysts stimulate the board discussions with new, alternative insights and ideas.

C. *Being a monitor of executive activities*, offering objective criticism and comments on management performance and issues such as the hiring and firing of top management. The entire board is responsible for the monitoring and supervision of executive management, but INEDs can bring a particular focus to this role.

D. *Playing the role of watchdog*, able to provide an independent voice and protect the interests of minority shareholders or lending bankers. Directors cast in this role are seen as protectors of the interests of other parties, such as the shareholders or, more often, a specific interest group. Nominee directors inevitably find themselves in this position, as they look out for the interests of the party who nominated them to the board. This might be a representative of a major investor in the case of a director on the board of an American or British listed company, a representative of the employees for a director on a German supervisory board, or a representative of the *keiretsu* group interests for a director on the board of a major Japanese company. Every director has a duty to be concerned with the interests of the company as a whole (that is, with the interests of *all* of the shareholders without discrimination), so the watchdog role has to be applied with care.

E. *Being a confidant(e) or sounding board for the chair*, the CEO or other directors; a trusted and respected counsellor in times of uncertainty and stress; someone to share concerns about issues (often interpersonal problems) outside the boardroom. Political processes at board level inevitably involve the use, and sometimes abuse, of power, and the confidant(e) can sometimes make a valuable contribution. But it is vital that he or she commands the trust of all of the directors, otherwise the problem can be reinforced rather than resolved.

F. *Acting as a safety valve*, able to act in a crisis in order to release the pressure, prevent further damage, and save the situation. A classic example would be when a company has run into financial problems, management performance has deteriorated, or the CEO has to be replaced. Another example might be if the company faces an unexpected catastrophe. The sensible and steadying counsel of a wise member of the board could overcome an otherwise disastrous situation.

Directors' duties, rights, and powers

Duties

Directors around the world have two fundamental duties: a duty of trust and a duty of care—a duty of trust to exercise a fiduciary responsibility to the shareholders, and a duty of care to exercise reasonable care, diligence, and skill. Beyond those two broad duties, directors' responsibilities are often enshrined in laws designed to protect consumers, employees, the environment, and so on.

Directors' duties in case law countries have not been specifically laid down by statute, but developed through cases. In Australia, for example, directors' duties are designed to promote good governance and to ensure that directors act in the interests of the company, which means putting the interests of the shareholders ahead of their own. In particular, a director in Australia has a statutory duty:

- to act bona fide (in good faith) in the interests of the company as a whole;
- not to act for an improper purpose;
- to avoid conflicts of interest;
- not to make improper use of position;
- not to make improper use of information;
- not to trade while insolvent;
- as well as duties of care and diligence.

The US Sarbanes-Oxley Act of 2002 added some directors' duties to statute, including the need to confirm the effectiveness of the company's reporting and management control systems, and the handling of strategic risk. The United Kingdom is an exception to the general rule that directors' duties are not specifically defined by statute law. The UK Companies Act 2006 attempted to consolidate the common law duties of directors in a definitive statement. In the United Kingdom, directors must act in the way they consider, in good faith, would be most likely to promote the success of the company for the benefit of its shareholder members as a whole and in doing so have regard to:

- the likely consequences of any decision in the long term;
- the interests of the company's employees;
- the need to foster the company's business relationships with suppliers, customers, and others;
- the impact of the company's operations on the community and the environment;
- the desirability of the company to maintain a reputation for high standards of business conduct;
- the need to act fairly, as between members of the company.

Notice that, for the first time, statute law explicitly required directors to recognize their corporate social responsibility to employees, other stakeholders, the community, and the environment. The Act links responsible business behaviour with business success.

In civil law countries such as Germany, the managing director is given the responsibility for managing the company and acts as its legal representative. He or she must employ the diligence of an orderly businessman, specifically to:

- pursue the business purpose;
- manage the company properly;
- be loyal to the company;
- not disclose confidential information or company secrets;
- not take advantage of his or her position.

Rights

Companies' articles of association determine the power of the directors. They typically grant a wide degree of freedom, but could, for example, restrict corporate activities by defining the purpose for which the business was created, or limit borrowing powers. The website of the UK Companies Registry has a model set of articles (go to www.companieshouse.gov.uk and use the search facility).

All directors have the right to information about the company, its business, and its financial and operating situation. This right to information goes beyond routine board papers and reports, to receiving answers to any question a director wants to ask about the company's affairs. All directors have a right to attend and take part in board meetings and meetings of the shareholders.

Powers

In general, boards have a wide discretion to take business decisions, provided that they act within the law and the company's constitution, respecting their duties of trust and care. The directors run the company for the benefit of its shareholders—to contract, invest, pledge its assets, buy and sell, hire and fire, set its strategies and corporate policies, and supervise management. Directors must act within powers granted by the company's articles and only exercise powers for the purposes for which they were conferred. It is the board's role to take risks in pursuit of business. Should the company run into trouble as a result, the courts will not usually question decisions taken by the directors in the normal pursuit of business. Provided that the directors have acted within the company's constitution and not failed in their duties of trust and care, they will not normally be held liable for any resulting loss suffered by the company.

The detail of the law surrounding directors' duties, rights, and powers varies between jurisdictions and can be complicated. Obviously only a general indication of basic practice can be given here. If a director is in any doubt, he or she should raise the matter with the company secretary, who might well be in a position to explain the situation, discuss the matter with the board chair, and if necessary seek legal advice.

Conflicts of interest

A *corporate conflict of interest* occurs if a company (and therefore its shareholders) takes advantage of its unique position of trust. An example occurred in the UK in 2018 when it was revealed that companies supplying drugs, prescribed by National Health Service doctors, were owned by some of those doctors.

A *personal conflict of interest* arises if a director could benefit personally from a situation involving the company or from a decision taken by the board. A conflict can arise directly from a director's own interests or indirectly if a family member or close associate is involved. For example, a conflict of interest would arise if a director:

- owned a business that supplied the company or was a major customer, sometimes called 'connected transactions';
- served on the board of another company that had business dealings with the company;
- had a significant personal shareholding in another company that the board was considering as an acquisition target;
- interviewed a relative or close friend in a recruitment exercise;
- had the personal use of property belonging to the company;
- used company information for his or her personal benefit.

Every director has a fiduciary duty to recognize and disclose any conflict of interest they perceive to the company, typically through the company secretary to the chair of the board. As commentators have pointed out, if someone perceives a conflict of interest, they have one. Recognizing potential conflicts is sometimes glaringly obvious to everyone involved. But in other cases the conflict may only be known to the person involved, so making the decision to declare the conflict and lose the personal benefit is an ethical choice based on that person's own moral compass; although the risk to personal finances and reputation can be significant if a failure to disclose is found out.

In some jurisdictions reporting conflicts of interest to the company is required by company law. Many companies have policies on the handling of conflicts of interest and include rules on their identification and disclosure in their code of conduct. Conflicts can also exist with other employees and professional advisers to the company, such as lawyers and accountants. Of course, the obligation to disclose conflicts of interest also applies to those involved in other, non-commercial, public sector organizations.

Having disclosed the interest to the chair of the board, typically before the board meeting through the company secretary, the director with the conflict should not take part in any board decision-making on the matter, until the chair and fellow directors have decided on the appropriate action. The director might be asked to leave the meeting while that matter is discussed or to listen but not participate in the discussion and abstain from voting. Having noted the declaration of a personal interest, the chair and fellow directors may decide that it is not material and allow the director to participate in the decision-making. Should the chair of the board be the one declaring the conflict of interest, someone else should chair the meeting for the discussion of that agenda item.

Directors should ensure that any conflict of interest they have declared is clearly recorded in the minutes with the board's ruling in response. This provides written evidence should there be a subsequent challenge.

In some cases shareholder approval may be needed on a board decision involving a conflict of interest. For example, in a listed company with dominant shareholders, such as the founding family, the approval of the minority public shareholders might be required. The company's articles, the listing rules of the stock exchange, and company law would be relevant.

A conflict of interest sometimes called a *conflict of roles* can arise if an executive director holds more than one position in the company: for example, as chief executive and chair of the board. As chief executive, the role is that of the head of the management team; as chair, the role involves ensuring a full discussion of issues including dissenting views, and leading the board towards consensus. Most corporate governance codes, of course, consequently call for these two posts to be held by different people.

In fact, a similar challenge faces all executive directors during board deliberations, if the responsibilities and interests of the executive post conflict with what appears to be best for the company as a whole. Role conflict can then arise, particularly if the individual concerned is a dominant personality—as such people often are. Members of the management team report to the chief executive; but as directors their responsibility is to the company, which may mean disagreeing with the chief executive. In some smaller companies the role of company secretary may be held by the finance director, again introducing potential conflicts of interest. In larger companies the work of the company secretary is usually sufficiently demanding to require a separate person.

Using insider information

Directors of listed companies have to be particularly careful not to benefit personally from confidential corporate information they receive. The confidentiality of the boardroom must be respected and not passed to third parties, whatever the circumstances. Situations can arise when information, such as a significant strategic issue or an acquisition approach, need to be disclosed to the relevant stock market. In the UK, it might also be prudent to notify the event to the Financial Conduct Authority, and in the USA to the SEC.

Not trading in their company's shares when in possession of inside, privileged information, such as the company results just prior to publication and before the stock market has that information, is particularly important. The listing rules of many stock exchanges lay down a 'blackout' period, just prior to the announcement of a company's results, during which time directors may not trade in shares in that company. The company secretary will often inform directors when the window of opportunity for trading in the company's shares is open and, more importantly, when it is closed.

Insider dealing, sometimes called insider trading, involves the buying or selling of shares in a listed company on the basis of privileged, share-price-sensitive, insider information. Insider dealing may involve making a secret profit by buying shares in the privileged knowledge of events that would drive the price up, or avoiding a loss by selling shares on the basis of privileged intelligence that would cause the price to fall. Insider dealing laws apply to directors, but also to officers and senior executives. Indeed, anyone with access to privileged information, however obtained, can be held liable for committing an offence.

Some people find it difficult to see why insider trading is wrong: 'no one really loses,' they say. The argument against the practice is not so much that it is morally wrong or unfair, or that it involves a misuse of information, but that insider dealing destroys the credibility and the integrity of the stock market. Insider dealing is a breach of a director's fiduciary duty: it is illegal in almost all countries.

Japan, Hong Kong, and Germany were among the last jurisdictions to make insider trading a criminal offence.

It can be difficult to obtain convincing information to support a prosecution, which is why some jurisdictions waited so long to introduce anti-insider trading legislation. The United States has the most severe penalties for insider dealing. China added more recently. Listed companies often include statements about insider dealing in their corporate ethics or values codes, using compliance officers to ensure that directors and employees do not trade on privileged, insider information.

A *related-party transaction* is one between a company and another person or company closely related to it, such as a director or a major shareholder. For example, the purchase by a company of a property from one of its directors would be a related-party transaction and would need to be disclosed by that director to the board.

The listing rules of most stock exchanges and the rules of securities regulators require related-party transactions to be disclosed and, in some cases, to be approved by the shareholders.

Related-party transactions are frequently found in family firms where there are close links between family members and companies connected with the family. Related-party transactions proved to be a significant problem in the early days of privatization of state companies in both China and Russia, as existing senior managers arranged transfers of assets for their own benefit.

Directors' service contracts and agreements

An executive director is both an employee and a director of the company. The employment is regulated by employment law; the directorship by company law. An executive director's employment agreement is a contract between the director and the company, which regulates the employment relationship, and will include terms required by employment law, such as remuneration, holidays, and pension arrangements. It may also include entitlements to a company car, the right to acquire shares, and the need for confidentiality.

However, all directors, executive and non-executive alike, may have a service contract as a director, which lays down the terms of the directorship. In some jurisdictions, shareholder approval is required before a company enters into long-term service contract with its directors. In the United Kingdom, a long-term service contract is defined as a contract for a guaranteed term of more than two years which cannot be terminated by notice within that period. A company can terminate a director's contract having given reasonable notice, without requiring shareholder approval, although it may face costs, depending on the terms of the contract. UK law also gives shareholders a right to inspect such service contracts and to request copies.

Directors' remuneration

In many countries, directors' remuneration has become contentious. Investors, particularly in the United States and the United Kingdom, encouraged by investigative media, have been challenging allegedly excessive levels of directors' remuneration, suggesting that they are out of line with the market, unrelated to performance, and sometimes even a 'reward for failure'.

The remuneration committee

In 1995, a group of City of London institutions commissioned Sir Richard Greenbury, then chairman of Marks and Spencer PLC, to look into board-level pay. The Greenbury Report provided a code of conduct, which has now been incorporated in the UK Corporate Governance Code. This report recommended that companies should have remuneration committees consisting solely of INEDs. Most corporate governance codes now call for remuneration committees. The remuneration committee's remit is sometimes broadened to include other highly paid senior executives.

The remuneration committee needs to establish a formal and transparent procedure for developing policy on executive director remuneration. The challenge is to provide sufficient incentive to attract and retain top management in a competitive market for talent, rewarding success, while avoiding excesses and apparently rewarding failure.

Independent directors form the committee because the principle is that directors should not be involved in fixing their own remuneration. However, a committee composed entirely of independent directors may not be completely independent in its judgement. Members may feel a loyalty towards the top executives because they were nominated by them to the board. Further, they may be executive directors of other companies themselves, so recommending high rewards may tend to inflate their own market rates. Of course, there remains an unanswered question: who should fix the remuneration of the members of the remuneration committee? For an example of the terms of reference for a remuneration committee, see Corporate Governance in Action 13.3.

Determining directors' remuneration

So, how are the appropriate rewards for executive directors to be determined? Clearly, they need to be sufficient to attract the necessary top executives, to provide an incentive for better than average performance, to reward success, and to retain the vital executives' commitment to the company. The challenge is to balance the interests of the directors with those of the shareholders both in the short and the long term.

The focus on board-level remuneration has created a market for remuneration consultants to advise remuneration committees. Comparative information about similar companies can clearly be useful, but consultants' recommendations can mislead. One problem has been called 'remuneration ratcheting'. Various arguments are sometimes advanced to justify high board-level rewards, including the following:

- *international comparison is essential:* 'to ensure that our company attracts and holds executive directors of the calibre we need against international competition, it is essential that we give our directors rewards that are broadly comparable to those they could obtain in our industry anywhere in the world'—such an argument may be advanced even if the directors concerned have no prospects of being headhunted and whether or not they have any possibility of working anywhere else in the world;

- *the headhunter argument:* 'we have just recruited a new executive director and the headhunters assured us that he had to receive a package that is 30 per cent more than that of the highest-paid director; of course, we all had to have an increase to maintain differentials'—this argument conveniently overlooks the fact that the fee of the headhunter may be based on 30–35 per cent of the first year's total package of the new appointee;

- *the better than average argument:* 'we cannot pay our directors below the median for firms our size in this industry'—an argument that has a built-in escalation effect;

- *the 'top of the industry' claim:* 'our firm prides itself on being one of the leaders in the industry, even though at the moment we are not among the most profitable; we expect to pay our directors in the upper quartile of the industry range as shown by the comparator pay research'—this argument ignores the performance of the firm or its directors;

- *the transparency effect:* 'greater transparency in directors' pay leads to higher remuneration as companies play "catch-up"';

- *the fear of loss of people:* 'the best people receive offers from elsewhere; we could lose our directors and top management to the competition unless we pay competitive rates'—this argument is sometimes advanced even though the directors concerned are within a year or two of retirement and would be of absolutely no interest to competitors;

- *doubling up the bonus:* 'we believe that it is important for directors' rewards to be performance-related; moreover, we expect excellent performance in both the short and the long term; so we calculate bonuses on the annual profits, then we have a parallel three-year scheme that rewards directors if earnings per share grow by 30 per cent over that period'—this way, directors get rewarded twice for the same performance, inflation is ignored, and there is no upside cap should there be exceptional circumstances; moreover, directors do not get penalized for poor performance.

As an indication of the escalation in top executive pay, in 1980 executives at the top of US organizations earned around 20 times the pay of those at the bottom of their organizations; today, those at the top are receiving over 200 times the pay of those at the bottom. Interestingly, the remuneration of senior executives in the John Lewis Partnership, a retail group in the United Kingdom owned by its employees, is actually determined as a ratio of the pay of the lowest-paid workers.

What are appropriate fees for non-executive directors? In the past, these have often been relatively low. But it is now widely recognized that sufficient rewards are necessary to persuade people of the required calibre to afford the time and, increasingly important, to shoulder the risk of being an independent director. In the United States, share options are often issued to outside directors. Hermes, one of the United Kingdom's largest fund managers, has suggested that non-executive directors should receive some of their remuneration in shares. But the counterargument is that share options should be linked to outstanding performance and given only to those top executives whose actions directly determine the results.

Share options

Ideally, the component parts of executive directors' remuneration should be structured to link rewards to both corporate and individual performance over time. The hope is that incentives rewarding exceptional performance will align managers' interests with those of the shareholders. But rather than encouraging exceptional performance, such schemes can encourage exceptional deception, if directors manipulate share prices, revenues, or profits to meet the target criteria of the incentive scheme.

Share options have been used as a way of rewarding and motivating top executives for many years. Options give the right to buy shares at a predetermined price at some time in the future, thus enabling the recipient to benefit by exercising the right once the share price has risen. The exercise price is typically that at the time the option is given. Obviously, the belief is that options provide a strong incentive to directors to raise the share price by improving corporate performance and the market's expectations.

Following the global financial crisis in 2008/9, the European Union called for bankers' remuneration to be linked to risks taken. Reflecting this policy, the Financial Conduct Authority (FCA) in the United Kingdom required financial institutions to apply 'remuneration policies, practices, and procedures that are consistent with and promote effective risk management'.[4] The FCA Remuneration Code calls for at least 50 per cent of variable remuneration (bonuses) to be in shares that must be retained for a given period.

Some argue that such incentives reward exceptional performance and align directors' interests with those of the shareholders. Unfortunately, that is not always the case. In fact, the interests of shareholders are not the same as those of the holders of share options. Shareholders have to invest their funds and run the risk of loss; option holders have no downside, having invested nothing, and are not at risk of a financial loss.

Moreover, on a rising stock market, all prices rise, so option holders reap a reward that is not linked to performance. Some schemes attempt to overcome this problem by building in a market index, so that only performance better than the market is rewarded. Such indexation

---

[4] www.fca.org.uk/about/supervision/attestations

will also work on a falling market, benefiting executives if their company value falls less than the market.

Other disadvantages of options include the possibility of unscrupulous directors attempting to bolster the firm's share price with short-term manoeuvres that do not really reflect improved performance—a classic agency dilemma. If a company gives new options, whenever they are exercised (reloading), executives may be able to play the market, irrespective of their performance. Share options are obviously unattractive on a falling market, so some companies lower the bid price of their directors' options (resetting). Clearly, this fails to reward outstanding performance.

In the past, firms were not required to account for share options, merely issuing more shares. Boards tended to act as though they were free of cost to the company. But, obviously, although not a cash charge on the company, when an option is exercised there is a cost, because the interests of the other shareholders are diluted. Today, accounting standards require options to be valued at their net present values using appropriate valuation models, and a charge to be shown.

The use of share options tends to be falling and attention has turned to bonuses and other incentive schemes to reward performance. But, unfortunately, unless carefully handled, such schemes can also encourage sub-optimization as directors manipulate the target criteria of the incentive scheme.

Reporting and voting on director remuneration

In many jurisdictions, a company's annual report needs to contain a statement of remuneration policy and details of the remuneration of each director. Transparency is vital in corporate governance. Legislation enacted in the United Kingdom in 2003 required quoted companies to publish a directors' remuneration report and put this to shareholder vote at the annual general meeting (AGM). The report has to contain details of the members of the remuneration committee and anyone who advised that committee, a statement of the company's policy on directors' remuneration, details of individual directors' remuneration, giving details of the performance criteria in incentive schemes, pensions and retirement benefits, their service contracts, and a line graph for the past five years showing how the company's performance has compared with that of competitors.

In the United States, Securities and Exchange Commission rules since 2007 have required full disclosure of pay packages of top management. The US Corporate and Financial Institution Compensation Fairness Act, passed in 2009 in response to perceived excessive rewards in financial institutions following the global financial crisis, did not impose pay limits, but passed the responsibility to shareholders. In the United Kingdom, shareholders have had the opportunity to vote on directors' pay since 2002. Admittedly, the result is then only advisory: the board does not have to take any notice, but in practice shareholders' opinions, plus private conversations with institutional investors, resolve many issues and avoid confrontation. An interesting initiative by the UK Institute of Management Accountants, PriceWaterhouse-Coopers, and Radley Yaldar has produced a model remuneration report, which shows the principles of a company's remuneration policy, the link between performance and reward, and the alignment with shareholder interests.[5]

[5] www.reportleadership.com

The Commission of the European Union announced a cap on bankers' bonuses which came into force in January 2014, limiting them to 100 per cent of annual salaries, or 200 per cent with shareholder approval. The EU ruling was, predictably, opposed by many banks but also by the UK government. In their annual reports, both Barclays Bank and Lloyds Banking Group said they would pay their chief executives in shares, on top of their salaries and bonuses, thus sidestepping the EU rules. Other European banks just increased their CEO's base salary.

In 2013, the US SEC decided to implement the section of the Dodd-Frank Wall Street Reform and Consumer Protection Act that called for public companies to disclose the median of the total annual compensation of the employees and the ratio of that median to the CEO's annual remuneration; in other words, how many times more than the average worker the CEO was paid.

In 2018, the UK's FRC introduced an updated Corporate Governance Code.[6] To address public concern over executive remuneration, the new Code emphasized that remuneration committees should take into account workforce remuneration and related policies when setting director remuneration. Complaints had been heard that some top executive remuneration packages had become so complex that even the recipients did not fully understand them, so they could not be an incentive to better performance. In response the FRC proposed that too formulaic calculations of performance-related pay should be rejected. 'Remuneration committees should apply discretion when the resulting outcome is not justified,' the FRC commented when introducing the new Code.

Some commentators felt that blandishments to 'take into account workforce remuneration and related policies when setting director remuneration' or to 'apply discretion' lacked teeth and set no boundaries for director remuneration. Others pointed out the difficulties facing the FRC when the very concept of the corporation gave the directors power to make all executive decisions, including those on their own remuneration. Shareholders' power was limited to electing the directors.

Shareholder reactions to remuneration reports seldom bind a board, but can indicate shareholder dissatisfaction and, hence, stock market standing, which can lead to board action.

Director remuneration remains a provocative corporate governance issue.

Corporate Governance in Action 13.3   J. Sainsbury PLC

The following are drawn from Sainsbury's statement of corporate governance.[7]

J. Sainsbury PLC—corporate governance

We're committed to high standards of corporate governance, and apply the main and supporting principles of the UK Corporate Governance Code. This Code emphasises the need for well-balanced, effective boards, strong overseeing of risk management, alignment of remuneration policies with shareholder interests, and sound shareholder relations.

Further information is available in our Annual Report, which includes our Corporate governance statement and Remuneration report.

[6] UK Corporate Governance Code—July 2018; Guidance on Board Effectiveness—July 2018.
[7] www.about.sainsburys.co.uk/about-us/corporate-governance

Our Board and committees

The Board

The Board is responsible for the long-term success of the Company, setting the Company's strategy, financial objectives and risk appetite, providing leadership to the business including on culture, values and ethics, monitoring the Company's overall financial performance and ensuring effective corporate governance and succession planning.

Our Chairman is responsible for leading the Board, setting its agenda and monitoring its effectiveness. Our Chief Executive is responsible for executing the strategy once it's been agreed by the Board.

Audit Committee

The Audit Committee reviews the integrity of the financial information provided to shareholders, oversees the Company's system of internal controls and risk management, approves the internal and external audit process, and monitors the process for compliance with relevant laws, regulations and policies.

Remuneration Committee

The Remuneration Committee recommends and reviews the remuneration policy, ensuring it is aligned to the long-term success of the Company. It also approves the remuneration and benefits of Executive and Operating Board Directors.

Nomination Committee

The Nomination Committee reviews the balance of skills, knowledge, experience, independence and diversity of the Board and its Committees, and succession planning at Board and senior management levels.

Corporate Responsibility and Sustainability Committee

The Corporate Responsibility and Sustainability (CR&S) Committee reviews the broad CR&S strategy and the Company's progress on the key corporate responsibility initiatives including diversity, values and colleague and customer insights.

J Sainsbury plc Remuneration Committee–Terms of Reference

Approved by the Board on 2 November 2017[8]

1. Purpose

   1.1 The primary function of the Committee is to recommend to the Board the remuneration strategy for the Executive Directors, Chairman and senior management and to determine within that framework a remuneration policy aligned to the long-term success of the Company.

2. Membership

   2.1 The Board is responsible for the appointment of members to the Remuneration Committee, for setting the term of members' appointments and for the revocation of any such appointments.

---

[8] www.about.sainsburys.co.uk/~/media/Files/S/Sainsburys/documents/about-us/remuneration-terms-of -reference-nov-17.pdf

2.2 Appointments to the Committee shall be for a period of up to three years, extendable by no more than two additional three-year periods, so as long members continue to be independent.

2.3 The Remuneration Committee shall comprise not less than three members, all of whom shall be independent Non-Executive Directors. The Chairman of the Board may also be a member of the Remuneration Committee if he or she was considered independent on appointment as Chairman, but may not chair it.

2.4 The Board shall appoint the Chairman of the Committee, who shall be a Non-Executive Director. The Chairman of the Committee will normally have been a member of the Committee for at least a year prior to being appointed Chairman. In the absence of the Committee Chairman, the other members shall elect one of themselves to chair the meeting.

2.5 No one other than members of the Committee is entitled to be present at Committee meetings. The Company Chairman, Chief Executive Officer and Group HR Director shall normally be in attendance, and other individuals may be invited to attend, except when issues regarding their own remuneration are discussed. The Committee's remuneration consultants shall attend meetings as requested by the Committee Chairman.

3. Secretary

3.1 The Company Secretary shall act as secretary to the Committee and shall produce such papers and minutes of the Committee's meetings as are appropriate, in a timely manner.

4. Quorum

4.1 The quorum shall be two Committee members, one of whom should be the Committee Chairman unless he/she is unable to attend.

5. Meetings

5.1 Meetings of the Remuneration Committee shall be held as necessary but not less than three times a year and at such other times as the Chairman of the Committee shall require.

5.2 All members of the Committee shall be advised of the business to be transacted at any meeting even if they are unable to be present.

6. Minutes

6.1 The minutes of the meetings shall be circulated to all members of the Committee, the Company Chairman and Chief Executive Officer and Group HR Director and, if not members of the Committee, the other Non-Executive Directors of the Company, unless in the opinion of the Chairman of the Committee it would be inappropriate to do so.

7. Duties

7.1 The Committee shall:

(a) set a remuneration policy which promotes the long-term success of the Company;

(b) determine and agree with the Board the broad policy for the remuneration of the Board Executive Directors, the Chairman and other members of the senior management referred to below;

(c) have delegated authority to set individual remuneration arrangements for the Company's Chairman, the Chief Executive Officer and other Board Executive

Directors. No individual will be involved in any decision relating to their own remuneration;

(d) approve, monitor and note the level and structure of remuneration for members of the Operating Board and the Company Secretary;

(e) monitor and note the level and structure of remuneration for any executive whose salary exceeds that of any Operating Board Director;

(f) in determining remuneration for those referred to above, review and agree:

—overall market positioning of the remuneration package;

—individual base salaries and increases;

—the design and operation of any performance related/variable pay schemes (including annual, medium and long-term incentive/bonus arrangements), set the relevant performance targets and determine the payouts under the arrangements; and

—pension arrangements, benefits and any other remuneration.

(g) be responsible for authorising all remuneration arrangements that involve the use of shares, including all-employee share plans. For any such plans, determine each year whether awards will be made, and if so, the overall amount of such awards, the individual awards to Board Executive Directors and the performance targets to be used. The Committee will monitor compliance with the recognized Institutional Investor limits on the issue of the Company's shares under employee share plans;

(h) note any major change to the terms of the Company's all-employee share plans;

(i) approve the service contracts of Board Executive Directors, including termination arrangements;

(j) review the terms and operation of the Share Ownership Guidelines;

(k) review and note annually the remuneration trends across the Company and be aware of and consider any major changes in employee pay and benefit structures when determining executive remuneration;

(l) be responsible for establishing the selection criteria, selecting, appointing and setting the terms of reference for any remuneration consultant who advises the Committee;

(m) in determining remuneration policy and packages, have regard to the UK Corporate Governance Code, the UKLA Listing Rules and all other relevant codes, laws and regulations;

(n) agree the policy for authorising claims for expenses from the directors;

(o) ratify the appointment of the Group HR Director; and

(p) determine any remuneration related matters affecting Sainsbury's Bank as delegated by the Board under its Reserved Powers and note any other material remuneration matters affecting the Bank.

7.2 The fees and other payment arrangements for Non-Executive Directors are matters for consideration by a sub-committee of the Board, consisting of the Chairman and one or more Executive Directors, which shall make recommendations to the Board as a whole.

8. Reporting responsibilities

8.1 The Chairman of the Committee shall report to the Board after each meeting.

9. Other matters

9.1 The Committee should consult the Chairman and/or the Chief Executive Officer about their proposals relating to the remuneration of other Executive Directors. The Committee shall be supported by the Group HR Director.

9.2 The Committee will consider and recommend to the Board the content of the Directors' Remuneration Report which will have regard to and reflect all relevant legislation and regulations.

9.3 The Chairman of the Committee shall be available to answer questions at the Annual General Meeting on remuneration issues with regard to the Board and senior management and generally on remuneration principles and practice.

9.4 The Committee Chairman shall undertake to liaise as necessary with institutional investors on policy or any other aspect of senior remuneration. Where appropriate such engagement may also be through the Company Chairman or such other individual deemed appropriate by the Committee.

9.5 The Committee shall undertake any other duties as directed by the Board.

9.6 Where considered appropriate, Committee members should have access to suitable training, in the form of an induction programme for new members and/or on an ongoing basis for all members.

9.7 Once a year the Committee should consider its own performance and review its membership and terms of reference to ensure it is operating effectively and recommend any changes it considers necessary to the Board for approval

10. Authority

10.1 The Remuneration Committee is authorized by the Board to obtain legal, remuneration or other professional advice from both inside and outside the Group as and when required, at the Company's expense, and to appoint and secure the attendance of external consultants and advisors if it considers it necessary.

Case studies

 Case study 13.1   RBS and Fred the Shred

The Royal Bank of Scotland (RBS) was founded in 1727 by royal charter from King George I. This case study describes its incredible growth and acquisition strategy under entrepreneurial chief executive, Sir Fred Goodwin, until its collapse in 2008 and nationalization by the British government.

The RBS Group, which is headquartered in Edinburgh, has branches throughout Scotland and the rest of the British Isles with banking operations elsewhere in the world. Its subsidiaries include the Royal Bank of Scotland, the London-based Westminster Bank, the Citizens Financial Group (the eighth-largest bank in the United States), Ulster Bank, and Her Majesty the Queen's bankers Coutts and Co. It also owns insurance companies including Churchill Insurance, Direct Line, and Privilege. RBS is listed on the London Stock Exchange and the New York Stock Exchange. Before its collapse in 2008, RBS was briefly the largest bank in the world by both assets (£1.9 trillion) and liabilities (£1.8 trillion).

Growth and death by acquisition

Chief executive Sir Fred Goodwin's strategy was to grow by acquisition. In 2000, in a campaign to reduce costs and improve efficiency, Sir Fred cut around 18,000 jobs from the RBS Group, earning himself the moniker 'Fred the Shred', a nickname that was to stick.

Sir Fred was conscious of risk: in his 2006 annual corporate review, he had written that 'sound control of risk is fundamental to business ... central to this is our longstanding aversion to sub-prime lending, wherever we do business'. But the acquisition of the Dutch bank ABN Amro, in 2007, was to prove his undoing, because it was full of toxic sub-prime debt.

In February 2009, RBS reported a loss of £24 billion, the highest loss ever recorded for a UK company. In October 2008, the British government arranged a £37 billion bail-out and guaranteed £325 billion against the toxic sub-prime loans. In return it took a 58 per cent stake in RBS voting shares, which was to increase to 82 per cent. Sir Fred Goodwin resigned in November 2008, and was subsequently stripped of his knighthood.

Concerns over Goodwin's compensation package

Despite being credited with destroying the bank, Sir Fred left with a pension of £703,000 a year for life, estimated to be worth £17 million (US$25 million) including an initial tax-free lump-sum of £3 million (US$4.5 million). Even though Sir Fred was only 50, his pension became payable immediately.

The UK Chancellor of the Exchequer challenged him to return all, or at least some, of his gains; but he replied that he did not intend to return a penny. A leader in *The Times* newspaper (18 March 2009) wrote:

> it is a public scandal that, while his business decisions have incurred immense social costs, his compensation packages confer huge personal benefits ... The behaviour of the RBS board was beyond generous and worse than ludicrous. It was craven. It deemed that Sir Fred had joined the pension scheme at the age of 20, although he was in fact 40. It allowed him to choose his 12-month earnings figure from the best year in the previous decade. It even gave him the choice of taking his full pension at the age of 60 or at 50.

Lord Myners, a financial expert, had approved Sir Fred's remuneration package on behalf of the government. Many asked how such a huge figure had been negotiated. Myners replied that the deal had been done while trying to avoid the collapse of RBS, and he had relied on Sir Tom McKillop, then RBS chair, Bob Scott, the senior non-executive director, and the RBS board's remuneration committee.

The UK financial regulator, the FSA (now the FCA), was criticized for its failure during the 2008 financial crisis and for its apparent inability to withstand pressure from the financial industry. A UK Treasury Select Committee concluded in 2012 that the ABN Amro acquisition should have been subjected to regulatory control in what amounted to 'a serious indictment' of the FSA's senior management. A 'failed culture of box-ticking' at the FSA had contributed to the collapse of RBS and the huge costs to the taxpayer. The FSA should have stopped this toxic takeover.

RBS subsequently

Even though RBS reported losses of £1.1 billion in 2010, staff bonuses amounted to nearly £1 billion. More than 100 senior bank executives received at least £1 million, causing some criticism. Fred Goodwin's successor as CEO, Stephen Hester, renounced a £1 million bonus after complaints about the bank's subsequent performance. Sir Philip Hampton, chair of the board, admitted that the level at which the bonus scheme would pay out, based on a rise in the share price, was too low and pledged to start stricter criteria for the CEO's bonus.

In 2012, Hester wrote:

RBS has completed the first three years of its recovery plan. Over that period the Bank's results across our key goals—customers, risk and value—have exceeded the plan targets we put together in 2009. This is pleasing and puts the bank in a vastly better position than before to serve our different constituencies.

The RBS board chair, Sir Philip Hampton, added:

When I became chairman in 2009, our urgent task was to stabilise RBS and then to begin the job of rebuilding the company. We have made good progress in three years. The balance sheet has been reduced by over £700 billion from its peak. Our reliance on short-term wholesale funding, which stood at £297 billion at the end of 2008 has been cut to £102 billion. We repaid more than £20 billion of government guaranteed debt in 2011.

But in November 2012, Hester faced an uncomfortable two hours in front of the UK Banking Commission. Justin Welby, the future Archbishop of Canterbury, head of the Anglican Church, and a member of the Commission, asked 'what is the duty of an enormous bank like yours, approaching 100 per cent of GDP, well into the hundreds of billions of pounds, what is your duty to society, and why didn't you mention it (in earlier comments)?' Hester responded by suggesting that RBS fulfilled a role in society by providing saving accounts, paying taxes, and employing people responsibly. The Archbishop replied: 'That is motherhood and apple pie. I am really looking for a bit more penetrating analysis of what your duty is to society—other than just saying obeying the law and paying taxes.'

In 2013, an RBS Shareholder Action Group launched a £4 billion (US$6 billion) lawsuit against RBS, its former CEO Fred Goodwin, and former chair Sir Tom McKillop. The action group claimed that investors had thought RBS was a solid, well-funded business when they responded to a £12 billion (US$18 billion) rights issue in 2008, although financial collapse loomed. Goodwin claimed that he was being 'unfairly and wrongly' chased for compensation. 'I did no wrong,' he said, 'you're wasting your time and money.' Repercussions from involvement in toxic sub-prime loans continued. The RBS Group was fined £26 million (US$39 million) by the state of Nevada in 2012 for selling such loans, potentially triggering claims from other states. With the UK government still owning 84 per cent of RBS, such charges effectively hit the UK taxpayer. The US Federal Housing Finance Agency, which controls government-sponsored lenders Freddie Mac and Fannie Mae, also threatened action on US$32 billion of securities they had bought from RBS Group companies.

In February 2013, RBS CEO Stephen Hester launched an impassioned plea to keep his bonus of £780,000 (US$1,250,000) in shares. RBS chair, Sir Philip Hampton, backed his plea, describing Hester's basic pay of more than £1.6 million (US$2.5 million) as 'modest'. Sir Philip's comment was described by campaigners as an insult to ordinary British taxpayers who had bailed out RBS during the financial crisis.

Stephen Hester joined RBS as CEO in 2008, after it had been bailed out by the British government. His annual salary was £1.1 million (US$1.7 million), plus an annual bonus and pension fund contributions. The bonus was £1.5 million in 2010. For 2011 Hester was offered a bonus of £963,000 in shares, but under pressure from politicians and the media he declined it for both that year and the next. For 2013, Hester, along with 76 other senior staff, expected bonuses of more than £1 million, in many cases doubling their salaries, despite the bank posting an £8 million loss. But the British Chancellor of the Exchequer intervened to stop the payments,[9] because RBS was still 81 per cent owned by the government.

In June 2013, RBS announced that Hester would stand down as CEO in December 2013 after five years with the bank. He received a pay-off of £1.65 million plus £23,000 to cover legal costs

[9] *Daily Mail*, 26 April 2014.

negotiating his termination agreement. His successor, Ross McEwan, was alleged to have been offered annual remuneration of £2.75 million, rising to £4.75 million.

In May 2014, the bank revealed a profit for the first three months of the year of £1.2 billion and immediately planned to give senior staff the maximum bonus allowed under the European Union's bonus cap of the equivalent of one year's salary. McEwan, the new CEO, said that less than 0.5 per cent of staff were involved and that he would 'do whatever it takes to hold on to higher-paid bankers'. But the annual report also stated that executive directors will no longer receive bonuses related to performance but will be given an allowance, paid in RBS shares, which is not part of basic pay and not tied to performance.

Following the government bail-out, RBS shut down many of its overseas operations and continued to close branches in the UK. In 2018 the UK government sold a major tranche of its RBS shares, making a loss of just over £2 billion. The shares were sold at 271p each, almost half the 502p a share paid in the government's bailout of RBS a decade earlier when it had rescued the bank at the height of the financial crisis.

The return was 'based on the reality of the situation that RBS is now in', said Treasury Economic Secretary John Glen. The taxpayers' holding in RBS will fall to 62.4 per cent from 70.1 per cent due to the sale. Mr Glen told the BBC's *Today* programme that the bank was in a 'much healthier position ... and the taxpayer needs to receive some of that money back'. He said RBS was 'a completely different institution to where it was ten years ago. They've gone from operating in 38 countries to 9, their total assets have fallen significantly.'

Discussion questions

1. What do the comments of interviewers on the Select Committee, appointed by the UK Treasury, tell you about the culture at the top of RBS?

2. In your opinion, how should Goodwin's compensation have been calculated following his resignation? Who should have been involved in the decision?

3. Was the remuneration paid to Hester appropriate?

 Case study 13.2 NHS Foundation Trust—fourth case study

Emergency meeting of the board

The acting CEO had convened an emergency meeting of the board following an investigation by a local newspaper into the activities of the chair of the Trust, Mr Roger Evans. The newspaper report had led to a frenzy of media attention, including the national press and television; the NHS legal team had also become involved. Mr Evans did not attend the emergency board meeting.

The report alleged that Mr Evans had received benefits from PFL International Ltd, a company based in Hong Kong, which was the parent company of PFL (UK) Ltd, the consultancy firm contracted to carry out the investigation into the Trust's cost-efficiency. Investigative journalists had discovered that Mr Evans and his wife had been given first-class air tickets to attend a PFL conference in Dubai. They had stayed at a six-star hotel, all expenses paid, for an eight-day holiday after the PFL event.

The newspaper claimed that Mr Evans had not disclosed the link with PFL when the tenders for the contract were being discussed. The newspaper reports, which ran for a number of days, implied that the benefits in kind were in recognition of the lucrative Trust contract. They implied, but did not state, that the Dubai trip might not have been the only benefit that Mr Evans received.

An extract from the minutes of the emergency meeting of the Board reads:

Emergency meeting of the Board

The Board appointed Professor Angela Prowess to chair the meeting. The Acting Chief Executive summarized the extent of the media coverage and noted the concerns expressed by NHS authorities.

The Chair said that the Board should avoid over-reacting until a full investigation had discovered all the facts, and Mr Evans had been given a chance to explain. However, if it was shown that Mr Evans had failed to disclose a relationship with PFL when the tenders were being discussed, and had received benefits from that relationship, this was a very serious matter and would require his resignation and possible legal action. Ms Mirrlees took a harder line, demanding the police be informed and Mr Evans to be sacked immediately for bringing the Trust into disrepute.

Mr Windlass said: 'Before we go overboard about all this, we need to hear from Mr Evans. This trip PFL apparently paid for is hardly a big deal. International companies hold conferences all the time. I think the paper is muck-raking to sell copies.' Ms Mudberry felt that Mr Evans should have disclosed any link with PFL: not to do so was against the Trust's rules.

Mr Brigham-West supported the position taken by the Chair. 'We only have newspaper gossip so far. I think Mr Evans should be asked to stand down from the Chairmanship until we have all the facts. I propose a small sub-committee of three Non-executive directors be formed to go into the matter and report back to us.'

In concluding, the Chair said that should Mr Evans resign or have to stand down, she had heard that Lady Audrey might be available. Her husband had died and she had mentioned that she would like to serve the Trust again as a non-executive director.

Action: Sub-committee of the Board to interview Mr Evans, collect all the facts, and report to the Board with recommendations.

Discussion questions

1. Of the various arguments advanced by Board members, which do you support?

2. Did the Board take appropriate action?

Self-test questions

1. What is a remuneration committee?

2. What does integrity mean?

3. Name some of the corporate values declared by Microsoft.

4. In addition to integrity, what other personal qualities are found in high-calibre directors?

5. Name some essential director-level skills.

6. What character traits are desirable in a director?

7. What are the essential legal duties of a director?

8. How does a related-party transaction affect a director?

9. What are the essential duties of a remuneration committee? To whom does it report?

10. Some believe that share options reward exceptional performance and align directors' interests with those of the shareholders. Do they always?

 For suggested answers to these self-test questions visit the online resources at: **www.oup.com/uk/tricker4e/**

Projects and exercises

1. Design a pro forma checklist for the appointment of a director, identifying the core competencies needed and outlining personal attributes that would be desirable for the appointment.

2. Lord Nolan produced a set of principles (see Corporate Governance in Action 13.2) to guide the holders of public office in the United Kingdom. Do you believe that these are equally appropriate for directors of a listed public company? If not, why not? Would your answer be different if the company were a private, family firm?

3. Draft a briefing paper for a newly appointed director of a listed company explaining the legal duties as a director. Do you think that most directors are aware of this information?

4. Major companies in some European countries adopt a two-tier board structure, with supervisory and executive boards. Advise the directors of a company incorporated in Delaware, USA, which is considering the acquisition of a German subsidiary, on two-tier boards.

References and further reading

Berle, Adolf A. and Gardiner C. Means (1932) *The Modern Corporation and Private Property*. Macmillan, edn revised by Adolf Berle (1967) Columbia University, Harcourt, Brace & World, New York.

Bower, Tom (2006) *Conrad and Lady Black—Dancing on the Edge*. Harper Press, London.

Dorff, Michael (2014) *Indispensable and other Myths: Why the CEO Pay Experiment Failed and How to Fix it*. University of California Press, Oakland, CA.

ICSA (2013a), *The Non-executive Directors' Handbook*. 3rd edn, ICSA for the Non-executive Directors Association, London.

ICSA (2013b) *Corporate Governance Handbook*. 3rd edn, ICSA, London.

McNish, Jacquie and Sinclair Stewart (2004) *The Fall of Conrad Black*. Allen Lane, London.

NACD (2006) Director communications—purpose, principles and best practice. Report of a NACD Blue Ribbon Commission, National Association of Corporate Directors, Washington, DC.

NACD (2010) Audit Committees—a practical guide. Report of a NACD Blue Ribbon Commission, National Association of Corporate Directors, Washington, DC.

Spira, Laura F. (2002) *The Audit Committee—Performing Corporate Governance*. Kluwer, Boston, MA.

Turnbull, Shann (1975) *Democratising the Wealth of Nations*. Company Directors' Association, Sydney, Australia.

Wearing, Robert T. (2005) *Cases in Corporate Governance*. Sage, London.

14 Board Leadership: The Reality of the Boardroom

 Learning Outcomes

This chapter enables us to:

- Appreciate how people, power, and politics affect practice.
- Recognize the chair's leadership role.
- Understand the sources of governance power.
- Enjoy considering games directors play.
- Review board styles, culture, and ethics.
- Think about whistle blowing.

How people, power, and politics affect practice

Unless they have served on a board, people may imagine that directors behave rationally, that board-level discussions are analytical, and that decisions are reached after a careful consideration of alternatives. Sometimes, but not often, experience of board meetings, or the activities of any governing body for that matter, shows that reality can be quite different. Directors' behaviour is influenced by interpersonal relationships, by perceptions of position and prestige, and by the processes of power. In fact, corporate governance is more about human behaviour than about structures and strictures, rules and regulations. Corporate governance involves the use of power. It is a political process.

The experience and prestige of board members does not guarantee a successful board. Members of Enron's audit committee (Case study 1.2) had some eminent and experienced people, including one of America's best-known accounting academics, and a member of the British House of Lords who was chair of the UK Press Complaints Council. In board activities, so much depends on board leadership and the way in which the directors work together. Good leaders create successful teams. Sound boards have sound leaders.

It has been said that 'outside directors never know enough about the business to be useful and inside directors always know too much to be independent'. Successful boards avoid this claim, because all of the directors, executive and non-executive alike, form a cohesive team in which independent, tough-minded individuals work together with trust and mutual understanding towards a common goal. To achieve that needs leadership.

By contrast, poorly performing boards probably have weak leadership and members with little commitment, focus, or time. Some directors may lack interest or, worse, be motivated by self-interest; others may be complacent, arrogant, or dominating; some may be easily led or weak-willed, failing to speak out when in disagreement; and a few may be just incompetent.

The chair's leadership role

Many people speak broadly of the chair of the company, whereas the role is strictly chair of the company's board of directors. Shareholders do not vote to elect someone chair, although the chair will usually chair meetings of the shareholders. Unless there is anything to the contrary in the company's articles, the directors elect one of themselves to be chair. There are few statutory requirements for the role, so chairs vary considerably in the way they carry out the responsibilities. At one extreme is the powerful chair, who acts as a leader of the company, influences its strategic direction, interacts strongly with the chief executive, and provides wide-ranging leadership of the board. Of course, that is almost inevitable where the roles of chair and chief executive are combined. At the other extreme, the weak chair does little more than run board meetings.

Before proceeding, there are some other issues of nomenclature to settle. Although the chairs of most major companies are men, many women occupy the position in quangos and not-for-profit organizations. To avoid the use of the inelegant terms 'chairperson' or 'chairwoman', some boards refer to their board leader as 'Lady Chair' or 'Madam Chair'. Others have adopted the genderless title of 'chair', as in 'the chair announced the results'. Here, we will avoid confusion and controversy by using the genderless word 'chair'.

Another confusion can arise with the term 'executive chair', which is typically used to indicate either that the holder has a full-time commitment to the office of chair, rather than being part-time as is frequently the case, or that the chair and chief executive roles are combined, as in the boards of some US companies. Some companies use the title vice-chair to spread the work of the chair; others use the title to indicate a chair-elect; and it is used by a few boards to confer prestige without necessarily giving additional responsibilities or powers.

An effective board operates as a team, not just a legal necessity calling for an occasional meeting. A successful board depends on the personality, commitment, and leadership qualities of the chair. The chair is the keystone of every board. Even a board composed of brilliant and highly experienced individuals is unlikely to be effective unless it is well led. A successful chair does not lead by being at the top of a power hierarchy, but by being 'first among equals', exercising leadership through the trust and respect of fellow directors.

So what should a chair do? In the opinion of the Cadbury Report (1992):

> The chairman's role in securing good corporate governance is crucial. Chairmen are primarily responsible for the working of the board, for its balance of membership subject to board and shareholders' approval, for ensuring that all relevant issues are on the agenda, and for ensuring that all directors, executive and non-executive alike, are enabled and encouraged to play their full part in its activities. (It is important for chairmen to ensure that executive directors look beyond their executive duties and accept their full share of their responsibilities for the governance of the company as a whole.) Chairmen should be able to stand sufficiently well back from the day-to-day running of the business to ensure that their boards are in full control of the company's affairs and alert to their obligations to shareholders and all other stake holders.

The following six functions for a board chair elaborate the above perspective.

Leadership of the board

Leadership of the board team is the chair's primary duty. This provides the foundations of the board's culture and style of operation. The chair sets the tone for board activities.

The chair should play a pivotal role in determining the size, structure, and membership of the board, along with the nominating committee and subject to the articles. This involves determining the balance between executive, independent, and connected non-executive directors. The chair will normally want to be involved with the nominating committee, in the identification, selection, and nomination of directors. He or she will want to ensure that they have the necessary qualifications and experience, that they will fit into the existing board culture, that they have the time to devote to board activities, and that they have no conflicting interests. After all, these will be members of the team that the chair is responsible for leading. Succession issues can call for the guiding hand of the chair, sometimes with the support of the independent directors, particularly the senior independent director.

Following the appointment of a new director, the chair will often brief him or her on the corporate situation and board practices and will want to ensure that the director's induction programme is adequate. The chair also has a vital role in reviewing the performance of each director: a responsibility that in the past was often informal and casual, but is now formally expected under some of the corporate governance codes. Similarly, the chair needs to ensure that director training, updating, and development, both for individuals and the board as a whole, are appropriate: again, an expectation of some governance codes. The duties, membership, and chairing of board committees also need to be managed by the chair. Finally, the chair needs to initiate the project that evaluates the effectiveness of the board and board committees, and to follow through on necessary changes within the board and its policies, procedures, and practices. To achieve success as a leader of the board, the chair needs to be a skilful communicator sensitive to human relations, a good listener, and politically astute.

Management of meetings

This is the conventional view of the role of chair and, for most directors, the most visible. In the management of board meetings, the board's culture and the chair's style become apparent. A sound chair:

- encourages independence of thought in the boardroom;
- ensures that the views of all present are heard, controlling the garrulous, while encouraging others;
- handles in an adult way discussions that can be tough and testing;
- encourages an atmosphere in which all directors feel able to ask questions and to probe issues;
- ensures that discussions stay focused;
- keeps the climate of discussion open, with challenges to the point, rather than aggressive;
- avoids boardroom cosiness;
- does not make a stand on issues, forcing them through, but leads the board towards a consensus;

- is not a cheerleader for management, discouraging mutual self-congratulation;
- ensures that directors are not playing games (a section on games that directors play appears later in this chapter).

Some chairs cannot handle challenges, discouraging disagreements and branding directors who ask too many questions as members of the awkward squad. Others interpret their leadership role as an opportunity to impose their own will on the meeting, instead of ensuring that all points of view are considered and leading towards agreement.

Meetings need planning as well as running. Prior to the meeting, the chair needs to consider the time, location, duration of the meeting, and who should attend, whether as statutory members, or to provide information, or to observe. The chair has to agree the topics on the agenda; not just the conventional ones, but any issue that he or she feels the board should be aware of and discuss. The chair should ensure that each director is adequately and appropriately informed, not only through routine board reports, but also with individual material and briefings if necessary. In conducting the meeting, the chair needs to ensure that each director has the opportunity to contribute, that different points of view are succinctly summarized, and that the board, as far as possible, is led to a consensus on the outcome. Getting directors involved, restraining the dominant, while focusing attention where needed and balancing the available time appropriately between topics, is the essence of good meeting management. The diffident director may seldom speak, but when he or she does that insight can be worth more than many tedious moments from the garrulous. The chair should beware of the pitfalls of 'group-think', political game-playing, and anchoring discussions in past experiences. We will explore some of these matters further in Chapter 16 on board effectiveness.

Most of the above comments about sound chairing and the running of meetings apply to the chairing of board subcommittees. Although many board committees are made up wholly of independent directors, the chief executive officer (CEO), other executives, or indeed anyone who can provide information and contribute to deliberations could be invited to attend. But they will be non-voting members and could be asked to leave committee deliberations at some stage.

Strategic leadership

Although some boards delegate a lot of the responsibility for developing the corporate strategy to the CEO and top executive team, the directors still have overall responsibility for setting the company's strategic direction. So the chair needs to ensure that the board pays appropriate attention to strategy formulation and policy-making. All of the directors should understand the company's mission and its strategic context, and share a common view of the strategic direction being followed.

Linking the board with management

Where the chairship is separate from the CEO, the chair provides the link between the board and management, working through the CEO and any other executive directors on the board. Where the CEO and the executive team are strong, the chair and independent directors need to be able to interact. Likewise, the CEO and the top management team must engage with the board.

The relationship between the chair and the CEO is one of the most crucial, most sensitive, and most subtle relationships in the company. The relationship is crucial because these are the two most important roles in the entire organization. It is sensitive because these are often people of significance with high public profiles, and big stakes can be involved. And it is subtle because it involves close liaison between two people who each have the power to affect the other. At its best, the CEO perceives the chair as a wise counsellor, someone with wide and relevant experience, and a person to be trusted implicitly; the chair sees the CEO as the most successful appointment the board has made.

At times, of course, the relationship can prove difficult. Typical problems arise through a clash of personalities, interference by the chair in the executive running of the business, or when disciplining or ultimately replacing the CEO. The 'promotion' of a retiring CEO to the chair (discouraged or prohibited in some governance codes) is also a potential disaster, unless the new chair can adapt to the duties of the chair and leave the running of the business to the new CEO.

Arbitration between board members and others

Occasionally, some chairs find themselves playing the role of safety valve, arbitrating between feuding members of the board, responding to aggrieved shareholders, or negotiating with other parties in disagreement with management. In some cases, the best advice may be for the parties to see their lawyers. But a respected chair can, at times, provide wise counsel and conciliation to the benefit of the parties, the board, and the company.

Being the public face of the company

Finally, we come to a role that chairs of major corporations are increasingly expected to fulfil: being a representative for the board and the company. Where the chair takes on this role, the CEO can focus more specifically on running the business, which can be useful given a climate of corporate complexity and change. As the public face for the company, the chair might be called on to interact with shareholders, particularly institutional investors, financial institutions, and analysts, to meet with customers or clients for the company's products, and to represent the company in the external world of public inquiries, media investigations, and public relations exercises.

Although some corporate governance codes now give the role of interacting with institutional investors and financial analysts to the independent director nominated under the code as the senior INED, in other cases this can fall to the chair. Occasionally, the chair will represent the company, providing a shareholder perspective to the workforce and management. But treading on the chief executive's legitimate territory needs to be avoided. As the public face of the company, the chair could be called on to make public statements, to appear at inquiries, and to represent the company. The UK Corporate Governance Code now includes an emphasis on the leadership role of the chair, and a suggestion for the annual re-election of the chair or the whole board.

Sir Adrian Cadbury identified three principles that,[1] he believed, chairs should apply:

Openness is one of them—the need to be open to ideas and open in explaining the company's actions and intentions. Openness is particularly important in dealing with people.

Balance is another—the duty to weigh up the consequences of decisions on all those who will be affected by them, and to hold the scales between the demands of today and the needs of tomorrow.

A third principle is the well-established one that *rights and responsibilities* go together. Chairmen, therefore, have responsibilities to their boards, as do boards to their chairmen.

Dean Jay Light of the Harvard Business School wrote in 2009 about leadership:[2]

The need for leaders who know how to make a difference in the world has never been greater than it is today ... qualities that are fundamental to good leadership (include) judgment that leads to sound decision-making, an entrepreneurial point of view, the ability to listen and communicate effectively, a deep sense of one's values and ethics, and the courage to act, based on those values and ethics. The need extends beyond business to the social, government, and non-profit sectors as well.

Obviously, each chair brings a different style to the leadership of the board. Some have a light touch full of humour and charm, others bring a decisive, no-nonsense approach, and a few are downright Napoleonic. Chairing a board or board committee can be challenging. Successful chairs often claim that the success is due to their team. But that team needs good leadership.

The UK Financial Reporting Council (FRC) provides useful guidance on the role of chair based on good practice suggestions from the Higgs Report (2003). The Council points out that good boards are created by good chairs. The chair creates the conditions for overall board and individual director effectiveness. Moreover, the chair should demonstrate the highest standards of integrity and probity, and set clear expectations concerning the company's culture, values, and behaviours, and the style and tone of board discussions.

The FRC suggests that the chair's role includes:[3]

- demonstrating ethical leadership;
- setting a board agenda that is primarily focused on strategy, performance, value creation, and accountability, and ensuring that issues relevant to these areas are reserved for board decision;
- ensuring a timely flow of high-quality supporting information;
- making certain that the board determines the nature, and extent, of the significant risks that the company is willing to embrace in the implementation of its strategy, and that there are no 'no go' areas, which prevent directors from operating effective oversight in this area;
- regularly considering succession planning and the composition of the board;
- making certain that the board has effective decision-making processes and applies sufficient challenge to major proposals;

[1] Sir Adrian Cadbury (2002) *Corporate Governance and Chairmanship: A Personal View.* Oxford University Press, Oxford, p. 242.
[2] Dean Jay Light (2009) 'Harvard Business School Annual Report'. Available online at www.hbs.edu/about/annualreport/2009
[3] Financial Reporting Council (2011) *Guidance on Board Effectiveness,* March.

- ensuring the board's committees are properly structured with appropriate terms of reference;

- encouraging all board members to engage in board and committee meetings by drawing on their skills, experience, knowledge, and, where appropriate, independence;

- fostering relationships founded on mutual respect and open communication—both in and outside the boardroom—between the non-executive directors and the executive team;

- developing productive working relationships with all executive directors, and the CEO in particular, providing support and advice, while respecting executive responsibility;

- consulting the senior independent director on board matters in accordance with the Code;

- taking the lead on issues of director development, including through induction programmes for new directors and regular reviews with all directors;

- acting on the results of board evaluation;

- being aware of, and responding to, his or her own development needs, including people and other skills, especially when taking on the role for the first time;

- ensuring effective communication with shareholders and other stakeholders and, in particular, ensuring that all directors are made aware of the views of those who provide the company's capital.

Sources of governance power

As we have seen, corporate governance can be thought of as the way in which power is exercised over corporate entities. The issue now is how that power is derived, who wields it, and how it is used. What is power? Mary Parker Follet's definition will serve us well: 'power is the ability to make things happen'.

The fundamental legal power of the board derives from the shareholder members who have delegated the running of the company to their directors. This power is reinforced by authority derived from the company's constitution, backed up by company law. However, a board can also find itself influenced in a number of ways, such as:

- by a dominant shareholder or group of shareholders putting pressure on the board— for example, the board of a wholly owned subsidiary company must conform to the business policies, plans, and investment decisions made by the group holding company;

- from the threat of a potential takeover—in a public company quoted on a liquid financial market, the ambitions of predators through the market for corporate control can be a constant source of power over a board's behaviour;

- by the prospect of litigation—in a litigious climate, the threat of significant lawsuits from customers (e.g. claiming damages for a faulty product or service), from employees (e.g. suing for damages from health hazards), or competitors (e.g. alleging infringement of patents or copyright) can concentrate a board's collective mind;

- through the influence of the auditors—an independent external auditor's threat to qualify the audit report, unless significant changes are made to the declared profit, perhaps because of disputed asset valuations, backdated share options, or unrecorded exposure to risk, is likely to affect a board's deliberations;

- from the effects of legislation and regulation—the prospect of new rules regulating the way the company does its business (immigration controls on employees, tariff barriers, corporation tax changes, for example) are bound to influence a board's deliberations and, for example, the effects of Britain leaving the European Union concerned many boards of companies trading across UK borders;

- from media pressure and other external exhortation—recent years have seen a significant increase in the interest an investigative media has in companies, and external lobbyists, interest groups, and institutional investors may all seek to exert power over a board's thinking;

- from the risk of damage to personal reputations—directors' decisions can be affected by individual directors' concerns about their exposure to risk, both financial and reputational;

- by a dominant or charismatic leader—as we will see later, the effect of the chair, chief executive, or other board member exerting leadership can have dramatic effects on other members and on the way the board acts;

- through changing business circumstances.

How a board handles these potential influences is a mark of its professionalism. But in addition to external sources of power over a company and the decisions of its board, individual directors can also wield personal power over board matters.

The power of individual directors also derives from a variety of sources, for example:

- *personality power*—in other words, the power wielded by a charismatic or a dominant individual over other members of the board;

- *knowledge power*—that is, the power derived from access to information, skills, or experiences not available to the other directors, such as the influence that an independent director, who is also a director of an international bank, has when the board is discussing the effect changes in currency or interest rates might have on the company's finances;

- *sanction power*, which is the power that exists if a director can apply some sanction to the company or to other directors, such as, in a joint venture company the possibility of one partner removing access to an essential source of supply, or in a family company the threat of the father to cut his son out of his will;

- *political power*—that is, the ability of directors to play board-level games, which we will briefly consider in the next section of this chapter;

- *interpersonal power* that one person might have over another because of their relationship, such as where a father and son serve on the same board, or where one director has private knowledge about another;

- *organizational power* derived from position in the organizational hierarchy—for example, a CEO inevitably has potential power over other executive directors because managerially they work for him and their prospects depend on that relationship;

- *networking power* derived from contacts and acquaintances of value to the company and useful in board decisions, as captured in the well-known phrase 'it's not what you know but who you know that matters in this world';

- *societal power* derived from a position of influence in society—a well-respected and connected member of society may be able to influence decisions to the company's benefit and public opinion about company activities, which is why retiring politicians are offered board positions, and why 'cooling-off' periods are written into their contracts;

- *ownership power* and the ability to determine board membership—a director who is also either the majority shareholder in a company or that person's nominee has undoubted influence on board deliberations, even though the right to hire or fire other directors may seldom be mentioned;

- *representative or nominee power* delegated from an external power source such as an institutional investor, a joint venture partner, or, in a not-for-profit entity, the members.

Games directors play

Board-level processes, the conduct of meetings, and interactions between directors above all involve communication. Deconstructing directors' comments—mainly spoken, but sometimes written—can identify many layers of underlying meaning. What a director says, and even more significantly what he or she chooses not to say, can demonstrate their understanding of and involvement in a topic under discussion. At a higher level of abstraction, it can illustrate their views on that subject. But it may also illuminate their personal beliefs and values, their opinions of other members of the board, and their sensitivity to what other people are feeling.

In board-level dialogue, the manner and form of communication are significant. Many board members are powerful people, with high self-esteem and big egos. Some are arrogant, self-opinionated, or boastful; a few may be bullies. But others can be diffident, insecure, and shy. Being a good listener is a hallmark of an effective director. Sensitivity to the views of colleagues, not only hearing what they say, but also deducing why they are saying it, creates a climate of mutual trust.

Of course, being a good advocate for an issue under discussion, being able to advance a case clearly, concisely, and with conviction, is also an important attribute. So is the ability to debate contentious issues, in which others hold contrary views. The effective director is aware that if people's proposals are rudely attacked, they are more likely to counterattack than change their position. Politeness has its place in the boardroom.

In badly led boards, personalities and political manoeuvring can prevail and directors will play games. An awareness of some of these games can help to create a board culture in which they become apparent and stop. In a light-hearted review, the following are a few of the games that directors can play.

Alliances

Two or more members of the board conspire together to influence a board decision. For example, two executive directors, each responsible for an operating division in a group, work together to prevent the introduction of a proposed management control system that would result in greater transparency of their divisional activities; however, they both agree to argue their case on the grounds that the system would prove expensive and that cost would outweigh any benefit.

Coalitions and cabals

Groups of directors work together, inside and outside the boardroom, to bring about a specific outcome to a board decision. Coalition building involves the canvassing of support for an issue informally outside the boardroom so that there is a sufficient consensus when the matter is discussed formally in the boardroom. For example, a group of directors in a not-for-profit company incorporated to run a sports facility opposed plans to build a new swimming pool. The members of this clique were tennis players not swimmers, and refused to sanction other expenditure unless the swimming pool plan was dropped.

Conspiracy of silence

In some boardrooms, there are issues that everyone recognizes are not discussed: the classic 'elephant in the room', seen but never mentioned. For some, this is a coping strategy, to avoid facing up to an unpleasant reality. Other directors can feign a selective deafness, by refusing to accept a situation. In such circumstances, the chair needs to make the board face the truth.

Cronyism

Personal relationships between directors can influence decisions rather than the rational merits of the case. Cronyism can produce decisions that are not in the best interests of the company. For example, three directors on the board of a listed company were all members of the same country club. They tended to support each other in board discussions, all favouring the same outcome, and opposing the same alternatives. Cronyism can affect an entire board. For example, a director declared a personal interest in a tender for a project being discussed by the board. He was asked to leave the room during the discussion of that contract. But the board decided to support this bid because of their personal relationships with that director, even though his bid was not the most worthy.

Deal-making

Agreements made outside the boardroom between two or more directors to achieve a specific outcome on a board issue. Deal-making is a classic game, usually involving compromise. The medical members of a hospital board agreed, during a private dinner, to put pressure on the board to acquire some new sophisticated medical equipment that they wanted. They were successful, even though there were more pressing needs for the available funds, including cleaning equipment for the wards.

Dereliction of duty

On a board, all directors have equal responsibility. But some directors fail to accept that responsibility. They concur with the thinking of the chair or CEO, and thereby are transferring their power and forgoing their duty as directors.

Disparaging

In an attempt to bolster his own position, one director might belittle opinions expressed, or information provided by another director, suggesting lack of knowledge or experience of that matter.

Divide and rule

When a contentious issue is being discussed, the outcome wanted by one faction is more likely to be achieved if the other directors can be divided into a number of disagreeing factions. This is a ploy adopted from the chair in some boards. Divide and rule can be a dirty game, in which the player sees the chance to set one director against another, or groups of directors against each other. An issue in the financial accounts might be used, for example, to divide the executive directors, the non-executive directors, and the auditors from each other, in order to achieve an entirely different personal aim. For example, a senior outside director serving on the board of a Canadian cooperative advanced arguments that divided the board into three groups reflecting the views of the various representative groups—suppliers, customers, and the administration—this way, he could push through the strategy he wanted.

Electronic device manipulations

The advent of smart devices has added new dimensions to director-level game playing. At the simplest level, the use of a smartphone during a board discussion shows lack of attention and can distract others: a sound chair will not allow it. More subtle is the introduction of information apparently relevant to the matter under discussion by one director using a tablet. Without careful chairing, that director can effectively dominate the discussion, accessing sites and reciting information that (s)he has already researched, which supports his or her position on the issue. For example, (s)he might quote comments from the social media about the company, quotes from critical analysts' reports, or competitors' material. If relevant, such information should have been collated before the meeting and provided to every director. The director with the tablet should not be allowed to lead the discussion.

Empire-building

Usually adopted by executive directors, empire-building involves the misuse of privileged access to information, people, or other resources to acquire power over organizational territory. The process can involve intrigue, battles, and conquests. Consider the example of a company in the IT consulting business, which acquired a marketing company to promote its business. The operations director of the IT company moved her staff to the more palatial offices of the marketing company, took over its fleet of cars, and argued in the board meeting that her deputy should also become a director because of his enlarged portfolio of responsibilities.

Group-think

Some boards, particularly if the members have served together for a long time, can tend to think the same way, interpreting situations and reaching conclusions without debate or dissension. Group-think is not so much a game as a board-wide attitude of mind. Sound chairing will avoid the danger, prompting constructive challenge. The probability of group-think is reduced with a diverse board of directors holding different perspectives and able to speak their minds.

Half-truths

By presenting only part of the information on an issue before the board, an unscrupulous director can bias the discussion in favour of his or her own preferred outcome. While the director does not actually lie, the half-truth obscures the full story. For example, an executive director argued strongly in favour of his own project, presenting impressive cost–benefit information in support, but failing totally to mention that the risk of stoppage to the firm's entire operation would be significantly increased. Email is a potential vehicle for spreading half-truths.

Hidden agendas

An individual director offers a convincing argument in support of a particular line in a board discussion without adding that additional outcomes to her advantage would then arise—this is the hidden agenda. Hidden agendas usually involve the pursuit of secret goals that benefit a director's own interests or further their own career. In other words, the ploy is another example of the agency dilemma. For example, in advocating a contract to acquire services for a joint venture, a director on the joint venture company board failed to mention that this contract would bring significant sales discounts on products bought by one of the joint venture partners—his employer.

Lobbying

Lobbying involves attempts to influence directors, or those in a position to influence directors, made outside the boardroom. For some boards, and some chairs, this is the normal way of behaving: directors are individually briefed on others' ideas and are influenced. Consequently, the outcome of decisions is usually already known. Some people call this decision-making in the corridor. One chair was so adept at 'lobbying in the corridor' that she is said to be able to write the minutes of each meeting when she writes the agenda! Nor is lobbying limited to directors: a partner of a consulting practice sought out the wife of a client's CEO during a cocktail party and encouraged her to persuade her husband to accept a quotation.

Log-rolling

Two or more directors colluding, to their mutual benefit, is a classic board-level game. For example, two executive directors in a manufacturing company came to an agreement before the board meeting: the first would enthusiastically support an investment proposal benefiting the second; while the other would offer mitigating arguments during the review of the poor budgetary performance of the first.

Machiavellian emails

If some directors have information about an issue under discussion, those who do not are under a disadvantage. On this game the protagonist sends an email with the information only to those directors she thinks would be supportive. Individual emails are used so no circulation list appears. Those lacking the data are at a disadvantage in the boardroom discussion.

Personal agendas

Without strong chairing, a lot of board time and effort can be wasted on directors who hijack board meetings by promoting matters in which they have a personal interest, but which are not on the agenda. The agenda item 'any other business' offers a prime opportunity.

Propaganda

Propaganda is the dissemination of information to support a cause, without attempting to show the complete picture. The chief executive of a finance institution made a PowerPoint presentation to his board, advocating the introduction of a new derivative-based product, without once mentioning the word 'risk'. Unfortunately, none of the non-executive directors raised the question, the board approved the proposal, and a year later the company had to issue a profit warning following losses on the new product.

Rival camps

Rival camps occur where there are opposing factions on a board in an extreme case of coalitions and cabals. Hostilities, spies, and double agents can be involved. The board of a *Fortune* 500 company were totally split on a proposal led by the chair/CEO to bid for a rival company. Leaders of each faction emerged and the two groups began to hold separate meetings, to brief the press independently, and to talk with institutional investors about their own perspectives on the bid.

Scaremongering

Scaremongering is used by some directors to emphasize the downside risks in a board decision, casting doubts on the situation without presenting a balanced perspective, thus attempting to have the proposal turned down. As a director in a multinational manufacturing group argued convincingly, when the board was considering building a new manufacturing facility in another country, 'we shall have nothing but labour troubles and high taxes, if we locate there, and possibly government interference ... and who knows what might happen if the present government falls? We could find all our assets nationalized without recompense.' A risk assessment would have shown the probability of those uncertain future events to be low.

Snowing

Snowing involves deluging any director who asks for more information on a topic with masses of data, thus confusing the situation and hiding any cracks. This game is usually played by executive directors on unsuspecting outside directors. A refinement of the practice has occurred with the advent of massive corporate databases and access to 'big data'. Directors asking for more information are given links to mass data which may, or may not, contain the information they need.

Spinning

Spinning, a form of gaming developed at governmental level, intentionally presents a distorted view of a person or a situation, in a way that favours the spinner's interests. In corporate governance, spinning can be carried out at the level of board committees, the board as a whole, the shareholders, or the media.

Sponsorship

Sponsorship is support by a powerful director for another director, often a newly elected director, usually for their joint benefit. For example, the long-serving director of the Australian subsidiary of an American global group commented during a board meeting: 'Madam Chair, I'll have a word with Robert (a new director) after the meeting to explain how we handle these things. As you know I've a lot of experience of this type of situation and what we've done in the past.' In the ensuing discussion, the experienced director relayed a lot of gossip about the ways of the board and its chair to his own future benefit.

Sub-optimization

Sub-optimization occurs when a director supports a part of the organization to the detriment of the company as a whole. We have explored this situation already, both when considering the agency dilemma in Chapter 3 and in discussing group management control systems in Chapter 10.

Some executive directors suffer from tunnel vision, because they are too closely involved with a functional department, division, or subsidiary company. Others may have a myopic view of the situation because they would be personally affected by the outcome. An independent evaluation of the overall strategic situation and top management performance by outside directors can help to overcome such problems.

Window-dressing

Window-dressing includes making a fine external show of sound corporate governance principles and practice, while minimizing failures. Some companies' mission statements, social responsibility, and sustainability reports, as well as core principles, suffer from window-dressing. The practice can also involve showing financial results in the best possible light, while hiding weaknesses, although this runs the risk of an adverse audit report or worse.

One of the problems facing companies publishing non-financial statements to shareholders, such as those increasingly required in operating reports, is that they can give rise to concerns about window-dressing. Information about strategic intentions is open to optimistic presentation and is not amenable to conventional financial audit. On the other hand, few boards are likely to expose their shareholders to information about potential risks facing the company from competitors, or other uncertain future events.

Notice that most of the 'games' described involve the subtleties of communication and interpersonal relations. Most of the tactics are not illegal, do not amount to fraud, nor are they inherently unethical or dishonest. They are a means to achieving directors' personal preferences. Notice, too, that many of these 'games' are commonplace in the world of government, where they are considered legitimate. Indeed, in some boards, too, game playing becomes an art form and board meetings more like the deliberations of an adversarial parliament. Strong chairing can reduce the disadvantages of game playing, unless of course the chair is also playing games! The ideal is a well-led professional board team working together with integrity, in which directors understand and trust each other, and do not need to resort to game playing. In such situations, directors can take tough-minded positions and defend their point of view strongly, but are also flexible enough to see other points of view and seek consensus through compromise.

Before leaving the topic of board-level politics, here are a few more light-hearted thoughts on the board-level game of manipulating meetings.

Meeting manipulation

There are a number of devices that directors have been known to use to achieve the results they want in meetings:

- *management of the agenda* determines what is and is not discussed—influencing the agenda is a powerful weapon and experienced chairs will ensure that they remain in control;

- *challenging the minutes* of the last meeting at the start of the next meeting can be used to re-open discussion of an item that was resolved, against the manipulator's interests, previously—strong chairing again prevents such activities;

- *hijacking the chair*—in other words, taking over the running of the meeting—can only work if the chair is new or ineffective;

- *refocusing the debate* when the tenor of the meeting is running against the manipulator's interests can involve a number of devices. Talking around the subject, while shifting the discussion onto favourable ground, is a particular skill of the meeting manipulator. Profound irrelevance is their stock-in-trade. But filibustering to run the discussion out of time will seldom work in the boardroom, although labouring a point until the meeting agrees can;

- *the 'put-down'* involves the skilful introduction of doubt when responding to a proposal before the board, as in 'the bank would never agree with anything like that'—good put-downs often adopt an air of superiority, as in 'we discussed this matter before you joined the board and decided against it';

- *presenting ideas in the context of other people's comments* can be powerful: 'I was inclined to believe ... until I heard X, now I am sure we should ...'—the fact that X was advocating something quite different is irrelevant;

- *summarizing* the discussion thus far can be used to emphasize favourable points and to downplay others: 'Mr Chair, what the meeting seems to be saying is ...';

- *predetermining the outcome* is an extension of the summarizing device used to foreclose discussion by stating the outcome of a decision, preferably in Latin, as in 'Madam Chair, we seem to have reached the decision *nem con*' (without contradiction: 'no one against or without objection'), whether anyone is against or not;

- *a challenge*, when a discussion seems to be flowing against the manipulator's interests, can be persuasive: 'on a point of order, Mr Chair' is a call that, if offered with sufficient challenge and conviction, will stop an orator in full flight. Strictly, points of order are only relevant if there are standing orders covering the running of the meeting—but that will not deter a skilful meeting manipulator;

- *a call to the chair* that the discussion has strayed from the point of the agenda item, that irrelevant issues are being raised, or that the discussion would be more appropriate under another item can be used to deflect an on-going discussion that is moving against the manipulator's interests;

- *'any other business'* on the agenda can also be used to re-open debate or introduce new items. However, the chair may insist that only items previously notified can be discussed and that no papers can be tabled. No matter: the manipulator will use the agendum 'date of the next meeting' to introduce a new topic, to explain the issue, to hand out the papers, to express an opinion, to suggest further discussion or the formation of a subcommittee with him or her in the chair: 'we need to look into this issue with the care and attention it deserves', ensuring that the subcommittee has a majority of those who favour the idea;

- *calling for a postponement of discussion* until the next meeting, on the grounds of the lack of information, the need for more reflection, or until an absent member is present, can also be used to postpone a decision that seems likely to be decided against the manipulator's interests;

- *calling for an adjournment of the meeting* is a heavier version of the postponement device;

- *lack of a quorum* can be used to stymie a decision if the articles of association or the rulebook specify a quorum: that is, the minimum numbers of members required to be present for the meeting to be formal. The lack of a quorum will prevent further decision-making. The chances are that few present will know whether the rules require a quorum or what it is;

- finally, the *management of the minutes* can provide a crucial opportunity to manipulate the conclusions reached by a meeting.

Some will say that this section on game playing and meeting manipulation takes a cynical view of board-level interaction. Others will believe that it more closely mirrors their own experience of boardroom life than explorations of board structures and codes of good governance practice. What is undoubtedly true is that the reality of boardroom life involves people, power, and politics as much as rigorous analysis and rational debate.

Board styles and the culture of the board

It is apparent that the dynamics of the boardroom vary considerably. Boards differ in their cultures and their styles. Some boards are highly professional in their operations, with experienced, well-informed, and collaborative directors, often holding strong views and engaging in tough-minded, but amicable, discussion. Outside directors are closely involved in decision-making and share a common view of the corporate strategy. Deliberations in such boards tend to seek consensus and votes are rarely taken. The boards of many listed companies in Western cultures fall into this category.

However, even in Western cultures, the behaviour of boards is not always professional. For example, board culture can evolve into a comfortable, convivial relationship between the directors. Outside directors may ask questions and offer suggestions, but not probe in depth; some never challenge the executive directors. In board deliberations, such directors tend to support each other and do not have tough-minded exchanges. In such companies, the climate in the boardroom is cosy—in fact, more like that of a privileged old country club.

Then there is a category of company in which the board provides little more than a legalizing rubber stamp for decisions taken elsewhere. As we shall see, there are some situations in which this can be legitimate.

Finally, there is a fourth category of board, which has members representing different interests. A hospital board, with members representing the hospital administration, the medical team, the patients, and funding bodies, would be an example. In such boards, members tend to take positions that reflect the interests of the groups they represent. Debates can be lively and votes are often called for on issues. The governance style, in fact, is more like that of opposing political parties in a local or national government.

What determines these board styles? Board style is a function of a number of variables. First and foremost is the board leadership and the role played by the board chair. The size of the board also affects its style: too many members, and the opportunity for individuals to contribute become limited, and the board may divide into factions; too few and there may be insufficient diversity of view. The balance of the board between independent and connected executive directors will clearly affect the tenor of board deliberations, as will the balance of experience and background among the board members as well. The actual set of attributes among all the directors—their combined experience, knowledge, and skills—is also a major causal factor in determining board style.

The culture of the board, including its history, its past leadership, and previous events affecting the business, will also influence its style. The following set of cultural criteria lists various attributes affecting board style and shows some of the likely effects. Notice the range of differences that can exist between different boards.

Board traditions

In some boards, rituals and customs mean a lot. Corporate stories and traditions are frequently mentioned. Board procedures and precedents are well established. Many members of the board are likely to be long-serving. There is probably a formal boardroom and there may be pictures of past chairs on the wall. At the other extreme are boards with no time for tradition, in which board practices evolve readily. The average length of directors' service is relatively short. Informality is the keynote of their meetings, which are held wherever and whenever it is convenient.

Corporate vision

This attribute of style indicates the extent to which directors share the same strategic vision about the company's present position and its future direction and prospects. In some companies, all of the directors can readily articulate the company's mission and strategic situation; in others, directors either do not understand the company's strategic context or, worse, disagree on what should be.

Innovation

Some boards expect all innovation to be driven by the CEO and the top management team.

In others each director is expected to contribute new ideas. In some boards, all ideas are welcomed, even if controversial. In others, new thinking is discouraged, developments are expected to fit established norms, change is resisted, and past successes influence views on the future.

Control

This reflects the way in which the board accepts responsibility for exerting overall control over the enterprise, if necessary becoming involved in responding to business problems, or delegating that responsibility to management through the chief executive.

Decision-taking

Decision-taking may be strongly influenced by one person or a small group of directors, in which case there may be little analysis and many dogmatic statements. In such situations the chair may play a dominant role. Alternatively, decisions may be reached after much discussion, leading eventually to a consensus among all directors.

Leadership

In some boards, authority is jealously guarded by one or a few of the directors, with other board members expected to give advice only when called on. In other boards, the leadership style encourages all directors to contribute to board deliberations, with people respected for their experience, knowledge, and wisdom.

Commitment

At one extreme are those boards whose members show a low commitment to the board, with high levels of self-interest; at the other extreme, all directors are highly committed to the company, the board, and their fellow directors.

Adaptability

Some boards are slow to adapt to changing circumstances. Consequently, board meetings tend to be predictable. Other boards are highly adaptive, with flexible responses to changing situations, even though their meetings can sometimes be turbulent.

Collaboration

In some boards, the directors support each other, ensuring that everyone is informed, involved, and committed. At the other extreme are boards whose members tend to compete with each other, showing distrust, poor interpersonal relationships, and even hostility towards one another.

Conflict

Board-level conflict can be either desirable or destructive. Conflict that is creative, with tough-minded, but courteous, interactions between members who say what they believe, but try to understand conflicting points of view, is found in successful boards. In others, overt conflict may be discouraged, but then there may be behind-the-scenes political activity.

Relationships

In some boards, directors see themselves as part of the board team, and treat each other with frankness, respect, and trust. In others, directors act as individuals, distrusting or disliking some colleagues. In such cases, image-building, posturing, and boardroom games may be prevalent.

Communication

Access to information is a source of potential board-level power. Consequently, in some boards, directors guard the information they have, protecting their sources, and encouraging secrecy. Gossip and grapevine communication are likely to be prevalent. Other boards, however, seem to encourage open communication, with a ready exchange of data, information, and knowledge.

Status

Directors' perceptions of their status can be important, with visible signs of the directors' prestige being of value, formal even ritual meetings, and probably ornate boardrooms and elaborate meals. Conversely, in other boards, status is relatively unimportant, directors not needing ego-reinforcing signals to be sent to the rest of the organization or the outside world.

Conformity

Some board chairs, believing that a board has to be united, expect their directors to conform to group norms. Non-conformists are not tolerated; indeed, they are unlikely to be appointed in the first place. By contrast, other chairs welcome non-conformists, recognizing that they can bring fresh insights and enliven board thinking.

Trust

Trust is the underpinning of the concept of the corporation. Typically, this refers to the fiduciary duty owed by directors to their shareholders. But the relationship *between* directors also plays an important part. In some boards, directors trust each other implicitly. But it has to be noted that in others trust can be low and directors suspicious of each other's ability or motives. Much hinges on the ability and leadership style of the board chair.

Some of these characteristics of board style reflect relationships at board level and the way in which the board members work together. Others affect how well the board does its work and achieves its goals. The challenge is to balance concern for relationships with concern for achieving board success. The simple matrix in Figure 14.1 contrasts a board's concern for the relationships between its members with its concern for getting the job done.

Boards that show a high concern for board relationships and have a high regard for the achievement of the board's task can be considered to have a professional style. Concentrating on the board task, but less on relationships, is a feature of the representative board. The board of the hospital discussed earlier, in which board members represented various stakeholder groups, is an example. Conversely, a board that focuses more on personal relationships than on the task in hand is the hallmark of the country-club board style. Those scoring low on each

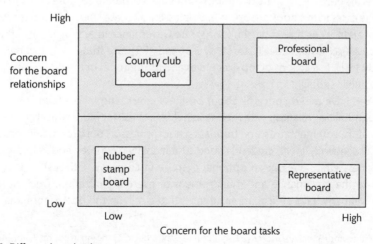

Figure 14.1 Different board styles

count are effectively acting as rubber stamps to decisions taken elsewhere. This can be appropriate in subsidiary companies that are managed through a group management structure, or in 'letter box' companies incorporated to protect a name, to limit liability on an exposed risk, or for tax-planning purposes.

The characteristics listed above can be used as the basis for a board-level exercise to plot a board's style. Obviously, the results reflect the perceptions of those making assessment on the range between the extremes for each criterion. The exercise can be used in both director development and the assessment of board performance.

Business ethics begin in the boardroom

Each country, society, or company has its own unique culture. Each culture incorporates a value system, which reflects the attitudes, beliefs, and expected behaviour in that culture. Corporate values influence the way the people in the organization behave towards each other and towards those with whom they come into contact outside the organization. Corporate values are involved in every activity, from board-level decisions of strategic significance, such as switching production to a developing country, to everyday interactions between managers and employees, staff and customers.[4]

Corporate values reflect the values of the corporate leaders. Ruthless leaders produce ruthless followers. Weak leaders create weak organizations. Leaders who display a short-term, bottom-line orientation will produce organizations in which these characteristics dominate: some financial institutions prior to the global financial crisis provide perfect examples. Leaders who are tough-minded yet fair create organizations that encourage these attributes. The respected leader has to earn that respect both in personal actions and behaviour towards others.

Corporate values are often implicit, part of people's perceptions about what sort of behaviour is expected, how people relate to each other, 'what you do and don't do around here'. However, increasingly companies are trying to make corporate values explicit, articulating what the board aspires to and wants to encourage.

Recent years have seen a spate of business crises and corporate collapses around the world. Many of the cases in this book are prime examples: Enron (Case study 1.2) and the worldwide collapse of auditors Arthur Andersen (Corporate Governance in Action 11.2), in the UK BHS (Case study 2.1), Northern Rock (Case study 5.2), and RBS (Case study 13.1), in Japan Olympus (Case study 17.1). The actions of top executives and the attitudes of their directors have come under the public spotlight.

Such cases have raised concerns about business ethics. The media focus on companies' social responsibilities, relations with their stakeholders, or call for more ethical business behaviour. Regulators, commentators, and business school professors push for better corporate citizenship. Subsequently, green credentials and sustainability have been added to the agenda.

But business ethics are not an optional exercise in corporate citizenship, they are fundamental to the governance and management of every organization. Decisions at every level in a company have ethical implications—strategically in the boardroom, managerially

---

[4] Tricker, Bob and Gretchen Tricker (2014) 'Business ethics begin in the boardroom', *European Financial Review*, 23 April.

throughout the organization, and operationally in every one of its activities. Ethics reflect behaviour *in* business and the behaviour *of* business. In business, ethics include the recognition and management of risk.

With risks that arise from moral hazards, that is ethical risk, mitigation—for example by duplicating systems, or transferring the risk, such as through insurance—is seldom a viable option. Recognizing and accepting a risk may be the only alternative to abandoning that opportunity. Consequently, the consideration of exposure to ethical risk needs to be part of every board's strategy formulation, and enshrined in corporate policy and enterprise risk management. With moral dilemmas in business it is seldom a matter that actions are good or bad, right or wrong, but of what is the best choice, the most appropriate decision, for the company and those affected by its actions.

Most boards insist that their company should not break the laws of any jurisdiction in which they operate. Unfortunately such an attitude does not address ethical questions that can arise in other countries. Major companies, including Google, Amazon, and Microsoft, have been criticized for 'aggressive tax avoidance' when they manoeuvred funds through tax havens to reduce global taxation, even though their actions were perfectly legal. Alleged excessive top-management remuneration has also been a source of concern, particularly to increasingly vocal shareholder activists.

Business ethics have not traditionally been thought of as part of corporate governance. They have been seen (and researched and taught) as separate subjects. Corporate governance is concerned with the way companies use their power and the way power is exercised over them. The use, and sometimes the abuse, of that power often raises ethical issues.

Enron, the giant American energy business, failed dramatically. Some of its directors went to jail. Yet that company appeared to meet the tenets of good corporate governance: the board had distinguished independent directors; there were audit, nomination, and remuneration committees; and the role of board chair was separate from that of chief executive, not always the case in American corporations at the time. What the board failed to realize was that the company's risk profile had changed dramatically when it moved beyond generating energy to trading in energy futures. It had moved from being a producer of energy to a financial institution. Moreover, the directors failed to see the moral hazard in some of the accounting methods that management had adopted.

Despite written policies on corporate social responsibility and sustainability, the oil company BP faced a disaster in the Gulf of Mexico when its Deepwater Horizon oil-rig exploded and sank. The board had failed to recognize this exposure to risk in their operations, or had accepted it. Further, following the disaster top management were slow to respond to public and political concerns, failing to realize the company's exposure to reputational damage. The company lost over half its share value.

Critics of business behaviour point to fraud, bribery, and corruption. They allege price-rigging, pollution, and counterfeiting. They claim arrogance, greed, and abuse of power by those at the top of companies. Trust in business has been eroded. For some, business ethics has become an oxymoron, as they cite corporate avarice, disparity of wealth, and director rewards that are not reflected in corporate performance.

Yet business exists by satisfying customers, creating employment, and generating wealth. Business provides the taxes that society needs to function. Many companies accept a social responsibility to be sound corporate citizens. They recognize that they have a duty to respect the interests of all the stakeholders who might be affected by their actions. Many also seek a sustainable, environmentally friendly approach to their operations. To those who doubt whether modern business can be trusted, they point out that business dealings and the very concept of the limited-liability company are based on trust. Trust in business will not be rebuilt by more rules, regulations, or corporate governance codes, but as directors create cultures that recognize and handle ethical risk.

Ultimately, the board of directors and top management are responsible for the ethical behaviour of their enterprise. Directors set the standards for their organization, provide the corporate conscience, fashion its culture, determine the risks to be taken, and set the ethical climate. They generate the value system for the organization. Business ethics begin in the boardroom. Not every board or board chair recognizes that reality.

Some boards delegate to their audit committee the responsibility for developing ethics policies by creating and enforcing codes of conduct or ethics. Others form a corporate governance or compliance committee that includes such duties, although the use of the word 'compliance' could suggest a conformist approach to corporate governance, overlooking the performance aspects. Yet other boards believe that the corporate culture, corporate values, and ethical issues are properly the responsibility of the board as a whole.

Corporate codes of ethics and their enforcement

Corporate values can be influenced from within an organization, but predominantly corporate values are derived from the top. A successful ethics policy reflects a company's core values, stems from its corporate mission, and is consistent with its corporate strategies. Without board and top management involvement and commitment, ethics policies are unlikely to succeed.

Some companies develop ethics policies that set standards for employee behaviour and require employee compliance with those norms. The codes of ethics that flow from such policies set standards of expected behaviour, seek to enforce discipline, and are inevitably employee-centred. Other companies set ethical policies to encourage commitment to good relations with all stakeholders. A successful ethics policy probably embraces both of these perspectives: describing the expected relationships between the organization and each of its stakeholders, while outlining the behaviour expected from employees.

A sound ethics policy is likely to:

- be orientated towards corporate values, rather than organizational discipline;
- seek genuine commitment rather than being a cosmetic exercise;
- recognize the cultural context of the company and its stakeholders;
- avoid credibility gaps between ethical codes and actual behaviour;
- link with corporate governance policies and practices;
- have associated ethics management systems, including information and control systems, whistle-blowing procedures, regular audit, policy review procedures, and social accounting systems;
- demonstrate accountability with regular reports.

Codes of ethics

A corporate ethics policy is usually supported by a corporate code of ethics or code of conduct. This is an explicit statement setting out the ethical standards expected of everyone in that organization. Typically, it will be approved and issued by the board of directors. Ethical codes can be found at various organizational levels:

- corporate codes that relate to a single corporate entity;
- professional codes that apply to the members of a particular profession;
- industry codes that are developed for use throughout a specific industry;
- group codes that are used within a given set of members, for example companies that are part of a marketing standards programme.

Codes of ethics can be used to:

- define and create the value system required for the organization;
- define and set standards of expected behaviour;
- improve individuals' ethical awareness, attitudes, and judgement;
- promote high standards of practice;
- set benchmarks for self-evaluation and monitoring by peers and others;
- inform external stakeholders of the values of the organization.

In some cases, companies require every employee formally to accept the code and to confirm that he or she has followed it. Companies with a global supply chain sometimes also create supply chain codes of conduct, typically a set of standards based on local and national laws and regulations, which reflect the International Labour Organization core conventions, including, for example, standards on underage labour, forced/prison labour, wages and compensation, working hours, discrimination, disciplinary practices, freedom of association, health and safety, and the environment. For an example, see the supplier code of Li & Fung Ltd (at www.lifung.com; see also Case study 7.2).

Since sound business ethics involve being seen to be 'doing the right thing' by all those likely to be affected by a company's activities, involving stakeholders in the ethical management process can be important. This may be little more than occasional dialogue to obtain feedback on past performance and future plans. Or it could take the form of more formal consultations on specific issues, for example noise-reduction plans with local communities affected by corporate activities. It might even involve a more formal partnership relationship, in which representatives of stakeholder groups, such as suppliers, customers, or local interest groups, become involved in an on-going relationship that directly influences corporate behaviour.

Information is fundamental to successful ethics management. Information about ethical codes, policies, and procedures needs to be promulgated to all those concerned. Standards, goals, and performance criteria need to be set and accepted. Achievement of these criteria needs to be monitored and relevant, timely information reported so that managers can monitor situations within their area of responsibility and take appropriate action when necessary. Some organizations create reporting channels for all employees, including ethics hotlines that can be used to report ethical concerns, sometimes anonymously, sometimes providing feedback advice.

On whistle blowing and whistle blowers

'Blowing the whistle' means informing on a person or an organization believed to be acting improperly. The whistle blower provides the information to someone with the authority to take appropriate action. The alleged wrongdoer could be a colleague, a manager, or an entire organization. The issue might be the breaking of laws or regulations, contravention of an ethical code, or offending in some other way.

Whistle blowing can have many implications and should not be undertaken lightly. What action should a potential whistle blower take? The first, most obvious step is to convey the concern to a person in authority. Should that resolve the problem, there is no call for whistle blowing. But if the person in authority assumes responsibility for the issue yet takes no action to put it right, the whistle blower has to decide whether to take the next step: to go to a higher authority, perhaps the chair of the audit committee, the chair of the board, or the auditors.

Clearly, whistle blowing can have serious ramifications for informers. They may be seen as trouble-makers and victimized. Their career prospects could be damaged. They might be fired. They could be 'black-listed', unable to get a reference for another job.

An Enron accountant sent an email to her boss saying that the company's financial policies were suspect and could lead to a collapse. She was fired. The boss knew that the company was in financial trouble, but he publicly encouraged other employees to invest in the company's shares, while he sold his own.

Studies have suggested that retaliation against whistle blowers has increased, including acts of physical violence; others have experienced some form of retaliation.

How far should a whistle blower go? Of course, if a whistle blower leaves the organization, a number of channels may be open to pursue the problem further: contact the company's auditors, the company regulator, or the media, for example, although the laws of libel, slander, and defamation need to be considered. These days, whistle blowers might use the internet to write a blog; although again they need to be aware of laws designed to protect privacy and wrongful allegation. Sometimes, companies offer whistle blowers a payment if they resign from the company, provided that they sign an agreement not to disclose the issue to anyone else. Obviously, such an action creates a further ethical dilemma.

In recent years, some governments have recognized the value of whistle blowers in drawing attention to wrongs in society, and realized that whistle blowers need some protection from the potential reaction to their whistle blowing. Following the Enron case, the Sarbanes-Oxley Act of 2002 specifically requires US-listed companies to provide systems for reporting unethical behaviour and other wrongdoing anonymously to an audit committee made up of independent outside directors.

The US Securities and Exchange Commission (SEC) introduced new rules in 2011 to encourage corporate whistle-blowing. Whistle blowers can receive between 10 and 30 per cent of fines levied by the regulator over US$1 million. The US Chamber of Commerce has deprecated such payments, calling them 'a bounty program that will reward amateur sleuths in search of a big pay-day'. Keith Edwards, a junior vice-president in JP Morgan Chase, was sacked in 2008 for whistle blowing on alleged false payments made under government contracts. The bank was fined US$614 million under the US False Claims Act and Edwards received US$63 million for blowing the whistle. The US Internal Revenue Service paid a whistle blower US$104 million in 2012 for information about the Swiss Bank UBS, which had encouraged over 4,000 wealthy Americans to place funds with them in Switzerland to avoid US tax. UBS was fined US$780 million. There have been calls for similar cash payments to whistle blowers in the United Kingdom, noting that many companies are now multinationals and rules on whistle blowing should converge.

In the United Kingdom, the Public Interest Disclosures at Work Act 1998 provided some protection for potential whistle blowers. In 2013, a whistle-blowing commission, formed by the charity Public Concern at Work, published a report on the Act and concluded that it was not fit for purpose. It called for a whistle blowers code. In 2014, it emerged that UK public sector bodies, including the National Health Service, had paid large sums to staff who had drawn attention to failings, provided they signed 'gagging clauses' not to publicize the issues.

Both the European Union and the Organisation for Economic Co-operation and Development (OECD), an international organization formed to help governments tackle economic, social, and governance problems, have indicated the importance of member states having legislation to protect whistle blowers.

Anti-corruption and bribery laws

Integrity in business life and anti-corruption policies have been long-standing traditions in the United States, enshrined in the laws of the various states and federally in the act that set up the SEC in 1934. The anti-bribery provisions of the Foreign Corrupt Practices Act of 1977 prohibit companies incorporated in the United States or having their principal place of business in the United States, and any individual who is a citizen, national, or resident of the United States, from offering anything of value to a foreign party to obtain business. The Act also has provisions that require companies to keep records that reflect the transactions of the corporation, to maintain an adequate system of internal accounting controls, and to report to the SEC. The Act does allow so-called 'grease payments' to facilitate the operation of a contract once the agreement has been made. More recently, the United States and over 30 other countries agreed to work together to reduce corruption and money laundering throughout the global financial system, acting together against bribery of government officials.

The UK Bribery Act 2010 made it a criminal offence to offer, ask for, or accept an inducement for acting improperly. Moreover, companies commit an offence if they fail to prevent bribery by an employee. The Act applies to UK organizations, whether the alleged offence was committed in the United Kingdom or abroad.

Hong Kong has extensive and tight regulations against bribery and other forms of business corruption. An organization separate from government, the Independent Commission against Corruption, has police-like powers of investigation, arrest, and prosecution. Similarly, Singapore has the Corrupt Practices Investigation Bureau. Consequently, these two places rank highly on indices of sound places in which to do business. In recent years China has also enacted laws against bribery and corruption and applied them rigorously, particularly pursuing government officials and managers of state-owned enterprises.

Around the world, many business people still protest that, in some countries and cultures, the only way to do business is by accepting local attitudes to 'commissions', 'discounts', 'fees', and other personal favours, which are expected, indeed demanded, by those able to influence the outcome of business negotiations. They complain that the restrictions imposed on them by their own country's anti-bribery legislation puts them at a negotiating disadvantage. Such attitudes emphasize the importance of board-level policies on corporate values, the creation of corporate codes of ethics, and their enforcement.

Implementing corporate governance below board level

Although the need for sound corporate governance is widely accepted, and despite the basics of corporate governance being clearly articulated in principles and codes, many directors and particularly board chairs still question how it applies in their own case. They ask, for example:

- what is the *real* role of the board?
- how should a board relate to top management?
- how should the board balance collaboration with management control?
- what should a board delegate to management?
- how much freedom of action should the CEO have in practice?
- how can a unitary board contribute to performance while ensuring conformance?

In Chapter 7, the recommendation was made that boards should establish a policy on decisions that are retained to the board—that is, those that cannot be delegated to management. But the concerns listed above go far beyond the establishment of a formal checklist of retained decisions. They go to the heart of the board's role, the directors' work, and the way in which corporate governance links with management. In particular, the leadership role of the chair comes under the spotlight.

Surprisingly perhaps, answers to the questions posed above vary significantly between companies and between cultures. Much depends on how corporate governance is perceived and, particularly, on the attitude and competence of the chair.

In the UK/Commonwealth model, the principles-based 'comply or explain' approach to corporate governance gives boards freedom to interpret the relevant corporate governance code and allows directors considerable freedom to determine their relationship with management. In these circumstances, boards face a range of options. These are reinforced by the separation of board chair from chief executive. At one extreme, the directors can delegate power over the business of the company to CEOs and their management teams, in effect discussing and eventually approving strategies, policies, and plans proposed by management, then ensuring that the proposals are followed and the expected results achieved. At the other extreme, the directors can retain power over much of the strategic direction and planning of the business, requiring the CEO and top management to carry out those plans and be accountable for results. In between the extremes, the delegation of power from the board to management can vary considerably and may change as chairs, directors, senior managers, or business circumstances change.

In the American model, the rules-based approach to corporate governance gives boards fewer degrees of freedom. Combining the roles of board chair and CEO concentrates power in that person. The top management team, which reports to the chair/CEO, runs the business operations whatever and wherever they are. The chair/CEO is then accountable to the board, and in effect becomes the linchpin between the board and the management. The presence of one or two other executive directors on the board—say the COO and the CFO—typically serves only to reinforce the chair/CEO's position. In these circumstances, a board consisting predominantly of independent outside directors is likely to perceive its role as advising the chair/CEO—perhaps questioning the strategies, risks, and resources, ensuring conformance to plans, and confirming compliance with legal requirements.

Although the board is responsible for the CEO's remuneration and contract, disciplining a successful and strong-minded CEO can be difficult. Some critics have suggested that, given the abundance of independent directors, this form of board is closer to the European two-tier supervisory board model than the UK/Commonwealth model. The primary differences are, of course, that the American board *does* have some executive directors, probably the CEO and perhaps the COO and CFO, whereas in the European board no common membership is allowed between the supervisory board members and the executive management board.

The powerful chair/CEO is at the apex of the American model of corporate governance. This fundamentally differentiates the perception of the board's role and its relationship with management from the UK/Commonwealth model. The American model tends to see the board as a group of independent outside directors, with the stature to satisfy the market, and whose experience and knowledge provide advice and oversight. Primarily, the power lies in their duty to appoint, to assess, and ultimately, if necessary, to sack the chair/CEO. But overall responsibility for the company then lies with that powerful CEO/chair. Indeed, this has caused shareholder activist Bob Monks to question whether boards of some American corporations have ever really understood corporate governance.

In the continental European model, the two-tier board structure attempts to overcome the fundamental problem of the unitary board by separating the performance role of the management board from the conformance responsibility of the supervisory board. Thus, unlike the unitary board, no single body is responsible for both performance and conformance. Consequently, the relationship between the board and management has quite different dimensions from the unitary board model. In the two-tier model, the relationships between the members of the supervisory board and the top executives on the management board are fundamental. Experience shows that, although the separation of performance and conformance functions between the two boards is conceptually appealing, in practice significant problems can arise between top management and the supervisory board, particularly where representatives of labour and capital sit on that board.

In the family-centric model of Asian corporate governance, the head of the family is typically the head of management as well as the leader of the board. In the *keiretsu* and *chaebol* models of Japanese and South Korean corporate governance, power to determine what decisions are delegated from board to management is often heavily centralized. In the state-owned or state-dominated models of Asian corporate governance, the state often retains the power to appoint directors and influence the work of the board, which in turn determines what is decided at board level and what is delegated to management.

Case studies

 Case study 14.1   Should Terry blow the whistle?

Many companies listed on the Hong Kong Stock Exchange are family firms with a minority of the voting shares available to the public.[5] Under the Listing Rules of the Stock Exchange, public companies must have a minimum of three INEDs on the board, at least one of whom must have professional qualifications in accounting or financial management expertise.

[5] Other than companies based in mainland China that have listed in Hong Kong in recent years.

LTN Manufacturing was a typical case. Founded by K. L. Lee in the 1970s, the company started as a furniture maker in the Wan Chai district of Hong Kong, but over the years had developed into a significant shop-fitting business and supplier of stands for exhibitions. Mr Lee, who was the major shareholder and chair/managing director, had a paternalistic management style and continued to play a hands-on role in the day-to-day management. The Lee family held 59 per cent of the voting shares, the balance being held by international and local institutional investors and Hong Kong people.

Terry, Tam Tat Sing, joined the company in 2002 as internal auditor, reporting to Mr Lee. Terry had trained with one of the Big Five accounting firms and was a member of the Hong Kong Institute of Certified Public Accountants (HKICPA).

To his surprise, Terry received an anonymous letter, alleging that the head of the purchasing department had incorporated a company, which was invoicing LTN with goods that were not being supplied. The head of the purchasing department, K. K. Poon, was an executive director of the company. He was also married to Mr Lee's sister. However, Terry knew that if these allegations were true, this was a serious situation, and as internal auditor he needed to investigate.

With the help of his staff, Terry began checking the goods-inwards records with invoices. After a while it became clear a company was being paid for goods that had not been delivered. All the invoices from this company had been approved by Mr Poon but entries in the goods-inwards records were missing. Terry traced the fraudulent payments for the past two years and had a colleague double-check his figures. Now what should he do?

He wrote a confidential report to Mr Lee, explaining the situation, suggesting that it was serious and should be referred to the board of directors, including the INEDs, for a decision on the appropriate action to be taken. Alternatively, he proposed that the independent external auditors or the firm's lawyers should be notified.

Terry was surprised at his managing director's reaction. Lee defended Poon, accused Terry of acting without proper authority, and said he had been over-zealous. Lee said:

> You should have referred the anonymous letter to me immediately. I would then have decided how to react. Remember this is a family business. My family and I own most of the shares and we decide how to treat issues like this. Personally, I ignore people who write anonymously. Clearly they lack the courage of their convictions. It must have been somebody in the company. I want you to find out who it is, tell me, and I'll make sure they don't cause any more trouble.

Lee went on to say that he did not want the matter taken any further and certainly not referred to the board. He said:

> Mr Poon has worked for this company for many years and is a respected member of staff, and of my family. I have studied your report in detail and, in fact, the amounts involved are not significant. There is no need to involve the board at all in any of this.

As a trusted employee, Terry did as he was told: he did not involve the board, he did not inform the auditors or the lawyers, neither did he seek the advice of his professional organization, the HKICPA. Instead, as instructed, he began an inquiry into all the employees who could possibly have known about the alleged fraud. And he found the whistle blower. Under cross-examination she admitted writing the letter. Now what should Terry do?

He gave the details to Mr Lee, who said that the company wanted to keep the matter private and that the whistle blower should be offered a substantial payment if she resigned from the company, having signed an agreement not to disclose the matter to anyone.

Discussion questions

1. Why did the whistle blower make the original claim?

2. Did Terry do the right thing in just informing Mr Lee?

3. What should Terry do, if anything, about Mr Lee's decision to pay off the whistle blower?

 Case study 14.2   The LIBOR rate rigging scandal

'Dude, I owe you big time. Come over one day after work and I'm opening a bottle of Bollinger,' emailed a bank trader to his opposite number at Barclays Bank in London, who had manipulated the LIBOR inter-bank interest rate, making a lot of money for his bank and himself. The Barclays trader replied 'please keep all this to yourself, otherwise it won't work ... this is the way you pull off deals like this chicken, don't talk about it too much'. In June 2012, Barclays Bank was fined £291 million (US$440 million) for its part in manipulating the interest rates.

What is LIBOR? How is it set? Who benefits if it is rigged?

The London Interbank Offer Rate (LIBOR) is the interest rate, set daily, that all participating banks charge on short-term loans between each other. LIBOR rates provide the benchmark for trillions of pounds and dollars in complex financial derivative transactions. They also influence the rates that banks charge their own customers. The rate is set by a panel of bankers from participating banks, who submit details of the interest rates their own bank is paying on the international money market for overnight money and on loans for up to 12 months. In principle, the bank officials submitting the daily rates to LIBOR should have no connection with the traders in their bank who are making the deals. The system was overseen by the British Bankers' Association (BBA).[6]

If the LIBOR rates were manipulated, bankers in the know could make dramatic profits for their banks and significantly improve their own bonuses.

A further incentive to rig the rates was provided by the international financial crisis which began in 2007, with the failure of the Northern Rock bank.[7] The supply of funds in financial markets dried up and interest rates rose. If a bank reported a high rate to LIBOR, this would suggest that the money market thought that the liquidity and credit quality of that bank was doubtful. If it reported a relatively low rate, this would imply that the market thought that bank was sound.

In June 2008, Timothy Geithner, then President of the New York Federal Reserve, sent a note to the Governor of the Bank of England warning him of the 'incentive to misreport' interest rates to LIBOR. He proposed a raft of reforms,[8] including increasing the number of reporting banks, a plan to overhaul the LIBOR process, and better governance. The suggestions were not pursued.

The Barclays Bank story

Evidence emerged that Barclays Bank had tried to manipulate the LIBOR interest rates at the suggestion of its own derivatives traders in London, New York, and Tokyo, as well as at the request of

---

[6] www.bba.org.uk
[7] See Case study 5.2.
[8] In a report 'Recommendations for enhancing the credibility of LIBOR'.

traders in other banks. The UK Financial Services Authority (FSA—now the FCA) reported that the rate had been manipulated on 257 occasions between 2005 and mid-2009.

During the 2007–9 financial crisis Barclays was one of the few major British banks that did not have to appeal to the government for financial support. This was partly attributable to its ability to raise funds in a very tight money market. It was also due to contentious fund-raising in Abu Dhabi and Qatar, and a financing scheme that shifted billions of pounds of toxic debt from Barclays' balance sheet to a company in the Cayman Islands called Protium. The scheme had been developed by Bob Diamond, an American-trained investment banker and CEO of Barclays Capital, the investment banking arm of Barclays.

On 28 October 2008, the Deputy Governor of the Bank of England, Paul Tucker, telephoned Diamond. The financial crisis was at its height. Fear, distrust, and confusion reigned in the money markets. Bank shares were collapsing. Barclays did not want to fail as RBS had done (see Case study 13.1). The Deputy Governor said that 'some senior figures in the government' were fearful that Barclays' high LIBOR rates suggested that Barclays was under financial pressure, and would need support.

Diamond believed that the Bank of England was complicit in manipulating Barclays' LIBOR rates. The Bank of England subsequently denied that it had intervened in an attempt to lower rates during the financial crisis. Not everyone believed them.

In December 2007, the US Commodity Futures Trading Commission (CFTC)[9] was contacted by a Barclays' employee in New York responsible for submitting that bank's dollar LIBOR rates. He said that the rates the bank had been reporting were not honest, but patently false. By early 2008, the suspicion that LIBOR was being fixed grew, and the CFTC, the US Department of Justice, the UK FSA, the BBA, and the Bank of England cooperated in investigating.

Barclays did not set up an impenetrable firewall (a so-called 'Chinese Wall') between its derivatives traders and the officers reporting the bank's rates to LIBOR until December 2009. In June 2010, new rules at Barclays prohibited any communication with traders that could 'be seen as an attempt to agree on or impact LIBOR levels'. The rules required LIBOR rate submitters to report to the company's compliance department if any attempts were made to influence them.

On 1 January 2011, Bob Diamond took over as CEO of Barclays Bank. The FSA, concerned that a major bank was now led by a risk-taking investment banker, questioned his lack of experience in retail banking.

In the United Kingdom, investigations by the regulators into rate-fixing continued at Lloyds Bank, HSBC, and Royal Bank of Scotland. In late 2011, four bankers were dismissed by the Royal Bank of Scotland for their part in LIBOR rate manipulation.

Barclays admits wrongdoing and the fall-out

It took until 2012 for the investigations into Barclays' part in the LIBOR scandal to come to a head. In April 2012, the FSA raised concerns about the culture of the bank, questioning 'the tone from the top'.[10] In June 2012, the bank admitted wrongdoing and was fined a total of £291 million (US$440 million) by the CFTC, the US Department of Justice, and the FSA for manipulating the LIBOR rate. Commentators pointed out that this was a charge on the shareholders, not on the perpetrators of the scandal. Shares in Barclays fell from £1.96 to £1.65. Shareholders threatened legal action.

In July 2012, Marcus Agius, Barclays' Chairman; Bob Diamond, the CEO; and Jerry del Missier, the COO of Barclays Capital, all resigned. Alison Carnwath, a Barclays' independent director and chair of the board remuneration committee, also resigned. She had only been a Barclays' director since August 2010, and was untainted by the LIBOR scandal. Allegedly she had been overruled by Agius when she called for Diamond's £2.7 million bonus to be cut. It also emerged that del Missier had

[9] www.cftc.gov
[10] www.fsa.gov.uk/static/pubs/final/barclays-jun12.pdf

received a cash payout of around £9 million (US$13.5 million) even though some commentators said he had 'resigned in disgrace'. Agius also resigned his chair of the BBA, which ran the LIBOR system.

Also in July, the US Federal Reserve chair, Ben Bernanke, told a Senate hearing that the LIBOR system was 'structurally flawed'. The senior independent director on Barclays' board was Sir Michael Rake, a former senior partner of the Big Four accountant KPMG, and also chair of the board of BT, Britain's largest telephone company, and of EasyJet, an airline. Subsequently, the founder of EasyJet, Stelios Haji-Ioannou, questioned why Sir Michael, who had been chair of Barclays' audit committee and a member of its risk committee, had failed to detect and expose the wrongdoings. He was 'the dog who didn't bark,' said Haji-Ioannou.

A UK Independent Commission on Banking, chaired by Sir John Vickers, called for the 'casino', risk-taking investment banking to be ring-fenced from retail banking. The two arms of banking had been legally separated until the mid-1990s, when the then UK Labour government, seeking to enhance the international competitiveness of the City of London, introduced 'light-touch' financial regulation, and allowed banking conglomerates to be built.

Anthony Jenkins, previously head of Barclaycard, the bank's credit card arm, was appointed chief executive of Barclays on an £8.6 million (US$13 million) pay package. He promised that Barclays would become a 'more honourable bank'. But that claim was challenged when the bank then announced a pay-out of £40 million to nine top executives, including Jenkins, while all the media attention was on reporting the details of the British budget.

In August 2012, the Commons Select Treasury Committee reported that Diamond had misled Parliament, failing to 'act with candour and frankness' and giving 'highly selective evidence' about the LIBOR scandal. The report said that Diamond had presided over a culture at the bank where there was 'something deeply wrong'.

A new financial regulatory regime

In September 2012, the BBA members voted to withdraw from its responsibility to manage the LIBOR system. The British government accepted that the existing financial regulatory system was discredited: 'failing to sound the alarm as the financial system went wrong', in the words of the British Chancellor of the Exchequer. The FSA, the regulator throughout the financial crisis, was disbanded. Regulatory power was passed to the Bank of England and two new regulatory bodies were created:

- the Prudential Regulation Authority (PRA)[11] became responsible for the regulation and supervision of banks, building societies (savings and loan associations), credit unions, insurance and major investment firms—a total of some 1,700 financial firms;
- the Financial Conduct Authority (FCA),[12] a quasi-governmental agency incorporated as a company limited by guarantee, and not part of the Bank of England, in effect was set up to succeed the FSA: the FCA is responsible for promoting effective competition in the financial markets, ensuring that they function well, and for regulating the conduct of all financial services firms.

Subsequent developments in the Barclays' LIBOR scandal

In January 2013, the former head of the FSA, Sir Hector Sants, joined Barclays as head of compliance. In April 2013, Barclays published a report about deficiencies at the bank, which it had commissioned from well-known lawyer Anthony Salz (at a cost of £14.8 million). Salz commented that, although the bank had originally been founded on prudent Quaker religious principles, it had 'become aggressive, too clever by half, and looked to the letter, rather than the spirit of the law'. Increasingly dominated

[11] www.bankofengland.co.uk./pra
[12] www.fca.org.uk

by the investment bank's culture, the report suggested that 'winning at all costs comes at a price: collateral issues of rivalry, arrogance, selfishness, and a lack of humility and generosity'.

Three months after he had said that he expected to stay in his job 'for years to come', Rick Ricci 'retired' on 30 June 2013. This American-born investment banker, known for his flamboyant lifestyle including racehorses and private jets, was reputed to have earned £44 million (US$66 million) in 2010.

Court actions against Barclays multiplied, from customers alleging that they had lost money from loan products based on the rigged LIBOR rates. Calls to bring the LIBOR manipulators to trial, to obtain a judicial view on bankers' morals, also grew. Other banks around the world were hit with large fines over LIBOR-rate rigging.

Calls were heard from shareholders, the media, and others for those responsible for the LIBOR scandal to be prosecuted. Six UK bankers *were* prosecuted but cleared in 2016. However, in August 2015, a British bank trader, Tim Hayes (35), was found guilty of conspiracy to defraud, while working for Swiss bank UBS and Citigroup between 2008 and 2010 and jailed for 14 tears. Hayes' evidence exposed an acceptance of rate rigging among some of the world's largest financial institutions prior to the financial crisis. Hayes said that others above him had encouraged and helped him to rig rates. 'Everything I did,' he said, 'my management knew about ... sometimes going all the way up to the CEO.' Citigroup fired Hayes but allowed him to keep a £2.2 million bonus and provided legal aid to his appeal.

Discussion questions

1. Why did this situation occur?

2. Who failed: Barclays' external auditors, the outside directors, its chair, its CEO and top executives, its traders, the bank officers who submitted the bank's interest rates to LIBOR, Barclays' compliance systems, the BBA which operated LIBOR, the British government which introduced light-touch banking regulation, the Bank of England, the FSA, anyone else?

3. Should investment banking be ring-fenced from retail banking?

Self-test questions

1. What is the fundamental basis of board power?
2. Name some other ways in which a board can find itself influenced.
3. What is the knowledge power that a director might have?
4. Name five other sources of director power.
5. Name four different board styles.
6. What criteria affect board style?
7. What is a chair's primary duty?
8. Name six functions of a chair.
9. Explain the chair's role in strategic leadership.
10. In what ways might a chair be the public face for the company?

For suggested answers to these self-test questions visit the online resources at: www.oup.com/uk/tricker4e/

Projects and exercises

1. Review the section on board-level games and meeting manipulation. Develop other examples in each case that might be used to illustrate the idea.
2. Use recent examples of corporate problems, discussed in the financial press, to identify examples of the effect of power on board-level situations.
3. Prepare a set of guidelines for chairs of listed companies, outlining their duties.
4. In groups of eight or ten, simulate a board meeting.

References and further reading

Brountas, Paul P. (2004) *Boardroom Excellence: A Commonsense Perspective on Corporate Governance.* Jossey-Bass, San Francisco, CA.

Cadbury, Sir Adrian (1992) The Financial Aspects of Corporate Governance: A Report of the Committee on Corporate Governance. Gee & Co., London.

Cornford, F. M. (1908) *Microcosmographia Academia: A Guide to the Young Academic Politician.* Bowes & Bowes, London.

Conger, Jay A. and Ronal Riggio (2007) *The Practice of Leadership: Developing the Next Generation of Leaders.* John Wiley & Sons, San Francisco, CA.

Lipman, Frederick D. and L. Keith Lipman (2006) *Corporate Governance Best Practices: Strategies for Public, Private and Not-for-Profit Organizations.* John Wiley, Hoboken, NJ.

Low, Chee Keong (ed.) (2002) *Corporate Governance: An Asia-Pacific Critique.* Sweet and Maxwell (Asia), Hong Kong.

NACD ([2004] 2005) Board Leadership: A Report of a NACD Blue Ribbon Commission. National Association of Corporate Directors, Washington, DC.

Roe, Mark J. (2003) *Political Determinants of Corporate Governance.* Oxford University Press, Oxford.

Salter, Malcolm (2008) *Innovation Corrupted: The Origins and Legacy of Enron's Collapse.* Harvard University Press, Cambridge, MA.

15

Board Activities: Corporate Governance in Practice

 Learning Outcomes

This chapter enables us to:

- Understand the importance of board committees.
- Appreciate the role and influence of the audit committee.
- Recognize the role of internal audit and the external auditor.
- Consider the significance of the company secretary.

Committees of the board

Thus far, our study of corporate governance practice has focused on the membership and leadership of the board of directors as a whole. We now turn to some other contributors to sound governance practice: committees of the board—in particular the audit committee, independent external auditors, and company secretaries.

An important development in corporate governance was the formalization of board subcommittees. A principal requirement now under almost all corporate governance codes is for at least three board committees—the remuneration committee, the nomination committee, and the audit committee. These standing subcommittees of the main board are established for specific purposes, usually with a charter or formal terms of reference. These board subcommittees are composed entirely (or in some jurisdictions mainly) of independent ONEDs: that is, directors who are not part of executive management, nor connected non-executive directors (those with some connections to executive members or other business connections) but directors with no links to the company other than their directorship. Consequently, these committees can provide independent and objective performance and conformance oversight, avoiding executive domination of board deliberations.

The remuneration (or compensation) committee is responsible for recommending to the board the remuneration packages of executive directors, and sometimes other top management, including their salary, fees, pension arrangements, options to acquire shares in the company, and other benefits. The role of the nomination committee is to suggest names for board membership, in an attempt to introduce different experience, personalities, and diversity to the board, and to avoid domination of the nomination process by the chair, chief executive officer (CEO), or any other dominant directors. The audit committee plays a fundamental role in corporate governance practice and will be discussed at length later in this chapter.

Some boards also create other standing board committees to handle specific areas of board responsibility, such as risk governance (or management) committees, corporate governance and compliance committees, and corporate social responsibility and ethics committees. Microsoft (see Corporate Governance in Action 15.1) has created four subcommittees: an audit committee; a compensation committee; a governance and nominating committee; and a regulatory and public policy committee.

Given the heavy workload facing many boards and the demands on the time of directors, particularly the ONEDs, some chairs decide to delegate other aspects of the board's work to subcommittees. Some boards appoint a risk committee, to ensure that the company's activities conform to the risk profile accepted by the board in its strategy. For example, as businesses become increasingly dependent on the internet for their activities, the risk of cyber-crime has become increasingly significant.

Other boards have an executive committee or general purposes committee to cover aspects of the board's role in supervising executive activities, a finance committee able to devote more time to financial issues, or a strategic committee to address longer-term strategic matters. Such arrangements can contribute to board effectiveness, provided that the deliberations and decisions of any subcommittee are carefully minuted and reported to the main board, with opportunity for the other directors to be informed, to question, and, if necessary, for the board to amend the subcommittee's decisions.

The challenge to board subcommittees can be keeping the other directors informed and involved in their activities and decisions. Since all directors are equally responsible for the overall actions and performance of the company, delegation to a subcommittee must not result in abdication of the responsibility of the other directors. Certainly, they may rely on the work of subcommittees, unless they have any cause for doubt, in which case their duty is to pursue the issue at main board meetings until the issue is resolved.

Boards also form ad hoc committees to be responsible for handling specific, one-off issues: for example, a committee to provide board-level oversight of a major investment project, to respond to the threat of a hostile takeover bid, or to handle the merger of two organizations. In setting up an ad hoc committee, it is important that the objectives of the committee, the scope of its powers, and the form of its output are carefully described in the board's policy document that creates it. Even more important is establishing how and when an ad hoc committee is to be wound up once its mission has been completed: committees have a tendency to find other matters to pursue and perpetuate their existence.

To be effective, board subcommittees require clear terms of reference, which need to cover:

- details of membership—committee size and quorum, qualifications for membership (e.g. independent directors or those with financial expertise), the nomination process, terms of appointment, rotation and removal of members, and remuneration (if any);

- chair's appointment and responsibilities;

- committee purpose and duties—with authority delegated by the main board;

- relations between the committee and top executives;

- frequency of meetings;

- secretary to the committee, notice for meetings, agenda, minutes;

- staff support, access to legal and other professional advice;

- accountability, transparency, reporting requirements, circulation of committee minutes to all directors;

- opportunity for other directors to raise questions and discuss subcommittee issues at main board meetings;
- regular review of the committee's performance and purpose;
- amendments to constitution and terms of reference where appropriate.

The influence of the audit committee

Inevitably, questions arise during an audit, such as the valuation of assets, whether certain expenditures should be capitalized or written off to the profit and loss account, or concerns about the financial control systems. Every director should be aware of significant matters that have been raised during the audit by the independent, external auditor. However, since the chief finance officer (CFO) and, perhaps, the CEO tend to be closely involved with the auditors, such issues are often resolved before the auditor writes the detailed report on the audit. Consequently, other directors could be left ignorant of matters that they might well have wanted to explore. The concept of the audit committee, which originated in the United States in the 1970s, was developed to provide a solution.

The audit committee, a standing committee of the main board, composed entirely or predominantly of independent, outside directors, provides a bridge between the external auditor and the board. Its charter aims to avoid any domination of the audit process by senior executives. Typically, the audit committee meets four or five times a year, more if needed, to discuss the details of the audit, to consider any contentious points that had arisen on the accounts, and to receive the auditor's recommendations on audit-related matters such as financial controls. The audit committee will often negotiate the audit fee and, if appropriate, recommend to the board if a change of auditor is needed.

Today, all codes of good practice in corporate governance and stock exchange listing rules require listed companies to have audit committees. In most cases, the members must all be INEDs, at least one of whom should have current financial expertise. Over the years, the role and responsibilities of the audit committee have expanded. In many cases, they now include:

- advising the board on the company's systems of internal management control;
- oversight of internal audit;
- liaising with the external auditors and reporting to the board on the audit process and on any audit issues;
- reviewing financial information to be provided to shareholders, the stock market, and the media;
- advising the board on matters of board accountability;
- the oversight of enterprise risk management; and corporate governance compliance.

The role and responsibilities of the audit committee should be established in writing in a charter or constitution agreed by the board and should be regularly reviewed. The specific duties of an audit committee might include:

- liaising between the board and the independent external auditors, including:

- making recommendations to the board on their appointment, reappointment, or removal and replacement;

- reviewing and approving their terms of engagement;

- ensuring their objectivity and independence from the company, confirming that no conflicts of interest exist that could affect the auditor's ability to issue an unbiased opinion on the company's financial statements;

- developing and implementing a policy for their engagement on non-audit work;

- approving their remuneration;

- working with them on audit procedures and plans, receiving the auditors' report and management letter about issues that have arisen during the audit, and reviewing and acting on these issues;

- liaising between the external auditor, the internal auditor, and the board as a whole;

- ensuring the independence of the external auditors, reviewing the extent of non-audit work undertaken by the external auditors, and the fees involved (in the United States, since the Sarbanes-Oxley (SOX) Act, and elsewhere given the review of many codes of best practice, ensuring the external auditor's independence has become an important responsibility);

- reviewing the audit fees and advising the board accordingly;

- considering the scope and process of the audit by the external auditors;

- agreeing to the scope of the work and plans of the internal audit;

- supervising the work of the head of the internal audit function, including the setting of policies, procedures, and plans, the budgeting of resources, the remuneration and performance of staff, the regular monitoring of results, and the overall effectiveness of the function;

- ensuring that the activities of the external and internal auditors are coordinated, avoiding either duplication or incomplete coverage;

- reviewing the appointment, performance, remuneration, and replacement, or dismissal, of the head of the internal audit function, and ensuring continuing independence of the internal audit function from undue managerial influence;

- reviewing with the external and internal auditors, and advising the board on, the adequacy of the company's internal control systems, security of physical assets, and protection of information;

- reviewing with the external and internal auditors, and advising the board on, the conduct of the external audit, particularly on any important findings or matters raised, usually contained in the auditor's 'management letter', with the management's response, and reporting any significant changes to the reporting of financial results or to procedures and management controls that resulted;

- reviewing with the external and internal auditors, and advising the board on, the company's financial statements (interim and annual) prior to publication, the auditor's report to the shareholders, any changes to accounting policies, material issues arising in or from the financial statements, and compliance with accounting standards, company law, stock exchange reporting requirements, and corporate governance codes of good practice;

- reviewing and approving all financial reports and disclosure to shareholders and the market, ensuring the integrity of any judgements made in them before publication;

- reviewing other published information, such as the directors' report, and operating statement, and ensuring that they are consistent with the audited financial statements;

- reviewing the exposure of the company to risk and any issues that might have a material effect on the company's financial position, including any matters raised by company regulators or stock exchange listing committees;

- reviewing annually the charter of the audit committee itself and advising the chair of the board if changes are necessary;

- approving the company's internal risk assessment and management policies, and assessing and monitoring related control systems, unless this responsibility has been delegated to another board committee;

- monitoring and reporting to the board on the company's internal audit function—in some organizations, the internal audit function reports directly to the audit committee, rather than to the finance function, to ensure independence and objectivity;

- ensuring compliance with all legal, regulatory, and corporate governance code requirements, unless this responsibility has been delegated to another board committee;

- recommending policies on corporate code of ethics, whistle blowing, and corporate social responsibility, and ensuring compliance, unless this responsibility has been delegated to another board committee;

- reviewing regularly the committee's terms of reference, membership, and performance, and recommending changes for board approval.

In practice, audit committees frequently have between three and five members, with at least one, often the chair, experienced in the world of accounting and finance.

Formal audit committee meetings tend to follow the audit cycle, typically at least four times a year. But ad hoc meetings may be more frequent, particularly where the committee's responsibilities have multiplied. The meetings held by the audit committee of Microsoft and their purpose are shown in Corporate Governance in Action 15.1.

Corporate Governance in Action 15.1   Microsoft Corporation Audit Committee Charter

Microsoft's board of directors has four committees to assist it in discharging its oversight responsibilities:

- an audit committee;
- a compensation committee;
- a governance and nominating committee;
- a regulatory and public policy committee.

The directors who serve on each of the four committees are independent. In determining the independence of a director, the board has adopted director independence guidelines to assist in affirmatively determining that a director has no relationship that would interfere with the exercise of independent judgement in carrying out the responsibilities of a director. The guidelines include, and either meet or are more restrictive than, the independence requirements of Nasdaq listing standards and SEC rules.

Microsoft's board has ten members who serve on the following board committees.

C = Chair M = Member

Director	Audit	Compensation	Governance and Nominating	Regulatory and Public Policy
Independent				
Ms Dublon	M	C		
Dr Klawe		M		M
Mr Marquardt			M	
Mr Morfit	M			
Mr Noski	C		M	
Dr Panke	M	M		C
Mr Stanton		M		
Mr Thompson			C	M
Non-Independent				
Mr Gates				
Mr Nadella				

Source: www.microsoft.com/investor/CorporateGovernance/BoardOfDirectors/committees/audit.aspx
Charters for other Microsoft board committees can be found online at www.microsoft.com/investor/CorporateGovernance/BoardOfDirectors/committees.aspx

The audit committee reports to the main board, which has delegated to it a vital part of the financial oversight of the business and financial reporting to the shareholders, the stock market, and the financial media; also the filings required by the Securities and Exchange Commission (SEC) in the United States, the Financial Reporting Council (FRC) in the United Kingdom, and other regulatory bodies. The increasing expectation of detailed narrative discussions of the company's strategy, business model, and prospects also add to the audit committee's work. All directors have fiduciary responsibilities to ensure that the company is financially sound and that the internal and external audit have been satisfactory, so they need to be able to trust the chair and their fellow directors on the audit committee. Many audit committees now publish a public report of their activities, which has become an increasingly important document.

Role of the Microsoft audit committee

The Audit Committee assists the Board of Directors in fulfilling its responsibility for oversight of the quality and integrity of the accounting, auditing, and reporting practices of the Company, and such other duties as directed by the Board. The Committee's purpose is to oversee the accounting and financial reporting processes of the Company, the audits of the Company's financial statements, the qualifications of the public accounting firm engaged as the Company's independent auditor to prepare or issue an audit report on the financial statements of the Company and internal control over financial reporting, and the performance of the Company's internal audit function and independent auditor. The Committee reviews and assesses the qualitative aspects of financial reporting to shareholders, the Company's financial risk assessment and management, and the Company's ethics and compliance programs. The Committee is directly responsible for the appointment (subject to shareholder ratification), compensation, retention, and oversight of the independent auditor. The Committee also reviews and assesses the Company's processes to manage and control risk, except for risks assigned to other committees of the Board or retained by the Board.

Membership of the Microsoft audit committee

The membership of the Committee consists of at least three directors, each of whom shall meet the independence requirements established by the Board and applicable laws, regulations, and listing requirements. Each member shall in the judgment of the Board have the ability to read and understand fundamental financial statements and otherwise meet the financial sophistication standard established by the requirements of the NASDAQ Stock Market, LLC. At least one member of the Committee shall in the judgment of the Board be an 'audit committee financial expert' as defined by the rules and regulations of the Securities and Exchange Commission. The Board appoints the members of the Committee and the chairperson. The Board may remove any member from the Committee at any time with or without cause.

Generally, no member of the Committee may serve on more than three audit committees of publicly traded companies (including the Audit Committee of the Company) at the same time. For this purpose, service on the audit committees of a parent and its substantially owned subsidiaries counts as service on a single audit committee.

Operations of the Microsoft audit committee

The Committee meets at least eight times a year. Additional meetings may occur as the Committee or its chair deems advisable. The Committee will meet periodically in executive session without Company management present. The Committee will cause to be kept adequate minutes of its proceedings, and will report on its actions and activities at the next quarterly meeting of the Board. Committee members will be furnished with copies of the minutes of each meeting and any action taken by unanimous consent. The Committee is governed by the same rules regarding meetings (including meetings by conference telephone or similar communications equipment), action without meetings, notice, waiver of notice, and quorum and voting requirements as are applicable to the Board. The Committee is authorized and empowered to adopt its own rules of procedure not inconsistent with (a) this Charter, (b) the Bylaws of the Company, or (c) the laws of the state of Washington.

Microsoft audit committee communications

The independent auditor reports directly to the Committee. The Committee is expected to maintain free and open communication with the independent auditor, the internal auditors, and management. This communication will include periodic private executive sessions with each of these parties.

Education of Microsoft audit committee members

The Company is responsible for providing new members with appropriate orientation briefings and educational opportunities, and the full Committee with educational resources related to accounting principles and procedures, current accounting topics pertinent to the Company, and other matters as may be requested by the Committee. The Company will assist the Committee in maintaining appropriate financial literacy.

Authority of the Microsoft audit committee

The Committee will have the resources and authority necessary to discharge its duties and responsibilities. The Committee has complete authority to retain and terminate outside counsel or other experts or consultants, as it deems appropriate, including complete authority to approve their fees and other retention terms. The Company will provide the Committee with appropriate funding, as the Committee determines, for the payment of compensation to the Company's independent auditor, outside counsel, and other advisors as it deems appropriate, and administrative expenses of the Committee that are necessary or appropriate in carrying out its duties. In discharging its oversight role, the Committee is empowered to investigate any matter brought to its attention. The Committee will have access to the Company's books, records, facilities, and personnel. Any communications between the Committee and legal counsel while obtaining legal advice will be privileged communications of the Company, and the Committee will take all necessary steps to preserve the privileged nature of those communications.

The Committee may form and delegate authority to subcommittees and may delegate authority to one or more designated members of the Committee.

Responsibilities of the Microsoft audit committee

The Committee's specific responsibilities in carrying out its oversight role are delineated in the Audit Committee Responsibilities Calendar. The Responsibilities Calendar will be updated annually as necessary to reflect changes in regulatory requirements, authoritative guidance, and evolving oversight practices. The most recently updated Responsibilities Calendar will be considered to be an addendum to this Charter.

The Committee relies on the expertise and knowledge of management, the internal auditors, and the independent auditor in carrying out its oversight responsibilities. Management of the Company is responsible for determining the Company's financial statements are complete, accurate, and in accordance with generally accepted accounting principles, and establishing satisfactory internal control over financial reporting. The independent auditor is responsible for auditing the Company's financial statements and the effectiveness of the Company's internal control over financial reporting. It is not the duty of the Committee to plan or conduct audits, to determine that the financial statements are complete and accurate and in accordance with generally accepted accounting principles, to conduct investigations, or to assure compliance with laws and regulations or the Company's standards of business conduct, codes of ethics, internal policies, procedures, and controls, or to manage and control risks to which the Company may be exposed.

For more detail on the Microsoft board committees go to:
www.microsoft.com/en-us/Investor/corporate-governance/policies.aspx

The role of the audit committee

Audit committees manage their own agenda and produce minutes of the meetings they hold. But they do need to work closely with senior officers, particularly the CFO, and with the finance function, internal audit, and, obviously, the independent auditors, particularly the audit firm's partner leading the audit. Private meetings with key members of management or the external auditors are often scheduled to obtain information about financial issues, risk, or management control, and to receive feedback about the progress of the audit. The minutes of audit committee meetings are often circulated to all board members, with an opportunity given at board meetings for questions to be raised.

An audit committee should have the power to hold whatever meetings, interviews, or investigations it deems necessary, seeking information directly from any company employee, although normally this should be done with the knowledge of the CEO or CFO. The head of the internal audit function often reports directly to the chair of the audit committee, thus providing a degree of independence from the finance function. An audit committee may also be able to obtain independent professional advice in pursuit of its responsibilities.

The chair of the audit committee is typically appointed by the board. Frequently, the CFO or members of the finance function, the internal auditor, and a representative of the external auditors are invited to attend meetings of the audit committee. Other executive directors or members of management may be asked to attend if necessary. The audit committee may meet separately with the external auditor, the internal auditor, other directors, or members of management, should they have matters they wish to raise directly with them. At least once a year, the audit committee should meet formally with the external auditor without any members of management being present. The external auditors should also meet with the entire board at least once a year and be available to answer questions at meetings of the shareholders.

Chairing an audit committee in any company and particularly a listed company can be an onerous responsibility, as the chair of Enron's audit committee discovered. Indeed, some directors may be hesitant to take on the duty. Nevertheless, the role of the audit committee and the leadership of its chair should be a fundamental plank in every company's corporate governance platform.

A board will rely on its audit committee to ensure that a balanced and understandable assessment of the company's position and prospects is presented to shareholders and other legitimate stakeholders, such as the taxation authorities. The board may also expect the audit committee to ensure that the systems of internal control in the organization are sound, to safeguard shareholders' investment and the company's assets. Further, the audit committee may be expected to have formal and transparent arrangements applying financial reporting and internal control principles, and for maintaining an appropriate relationship with the company's auditors.

The audit committee should set itself clear and measurable objectives (unless they are already covered in a charter), and review performance against them. If they fail to meet their objectives the reasons should be diagnosed and remedied, reporting accordingly to the board. Some corporate governance codes now call for a regular evaluation of the performance of the audit committee. Experience of this process varies from a simple discussion among the members about the process and progress of the committee, through an evaluation carried out by an independent director who is not a member of the committee, often the board chair, to commissioning a detailed performance evaluation and formal report from an experienced, independent, external professional.

In the United States, the SOX Act (2002) introduced new and strict requirements on independent external auditors and increased audit committees' responsibilities and authority. In the United Kingdom, the Smith Report (2003) focused on the audit committee with requirements that have subsequently been enhanced by the UK Corporate Governance Code.

Criticisms of audit committees include the concern that members can get too involved in executive management matters and interfere in management's legitimate responsibilities. Others complain that an audit committee can become bureaucratic and process-driven rather than exercising sound commercial judgement. Concerns have also been expressed that the creation of a subset of the board with specific responsibility for ensuring compliance represents a move towards the European-style two-tier supervisory board, which proponents of the unitary board distrust.

Many companies that are not listed have adopted the concept of the audit committee to improve their own governance, as have some not-for-profit entities, NGOs, and government bodies. The Internal Control Standards for the Public Sector published by the International Organization of Supreme Audit Institutions define the audit committee for central and local government corporate entities as:[1]

> [a] committee of the board of directors whose role typically focuses on aspects of financial reporting and on the entity's processes to manage business and financial risk, and for compliance with significant applicable legal, ethical, and regulatory requirements. The audit committee typically assists the board with the oversight of (a) the integrity of the entity's financial statements, (b) the entity's compliance with legal and regulatory requirements, (c) the independent auditors' qualifications and independence, (d) the performance of the entity's internal audit function and that of the independent auditors and (e) compensation of company executives (in the absence of a remuneration committee).

Although the modern concept of the audit committee stems from the later years of the 20th century, in fact the notion of an audit committee, drawn from the shareholders rather than independent directors, dates back to the late 19th century. See Corporate Governance in Action 15.2 for the report of the audit committee to the shareholders of the Great Western Railway Company in England in 1872.

Corporate Governance in Action 15.2   Great Western Railway Company—the report of the original Audit Committee in 1872

The auditors and Mr Deloitte attended the committee and explained the various matters concerned with the Finances and other departments of the railway, which explanations were highly satisfactory.[2]

The Committee considered the auditors had performed their arduous duties with great care and intelligence and therefore confidently recommends that they be continued in office.

Paddington Station   Benjamin Lancaster—Chairman
22 February 1872

---

[1] www.issai.org/media/13329/intosai_gov_9100_e.pdf
[2] Tricker, R. I. (1978) *The Independent Director—a study of the non-executive director and the audit committee*, Tolley and Deloittes, London.

The role of internal audit

Recent developments in corporate governance around the world have highlighted boards' responsibility for the oversight of internal controls and for ensuring the effectiveness of their companies' management and financial control systems. An internal audit function can make a major contribution if it is efficient and effective. Yet, while the potential value of an internal audit function is widely recognized, the US SOX Act makes no mention of internal audit. However, the rules of the New York Stock Exchange state that each listed company must have an internal audit function.

The Institute of Internal Audit explains the role of this function:[3]

> The role of internal audit is to provide independent assurance that an organisation's risk management, governance, and internal control processes are operating effectively . . . Internal auditors deal with issues that are fundamentally important to the survival and prosperity of any organisation. Unlike external auditors, they look beyond financial risks and statements to consider wider issues such as the organisation's reputation, growth, its impact on the environment, and the way it treats its employees . . . Internal auditors have to be independent people who are willing to stand up and be counted. Their employers value them because they provide an independent, objective, and constructive view. To do this, they need a remarkably varied mix of skills and knowledge.

In many cases, boards, and in particular their audit committees, look to the internal audit function to provide them with:

- an on-going analysis of business processes and the associated control systems;
- an evaluation of the extent and effectiveness of these control systems;
- regular reviews of operational and financial performance;
- assessments of whether the corporate mission, policies, and objectives are being achieved;
- identification of areas for more efficient use of resources;
- confirmation of the existence and value of the company's assets;
- ad hoc inquiries into possible irregularities and frauds;
- reviews of the compliance framework;
- identification of compliance issues and confirmation of compliance;
- reviews of the organization's values and code of conduct or ethics.

The board-level risk committee, where there is one, or otherwise the audit committee, may call on the internal audit function to provide:

- an evaluation of the risk assessment and review systems;
- regular evaluation of risk at all levels in the organization;
- ad hoc reviews of unacceptable levels of risk.

[3] www.iia.org.uk/about-us/what-is-internal-audit

However, there is an ambiguity surrounding the internal audit function in some companies: to whom is it responsible and where does it fit in the organization's structure? Should internal audit be treated as part of the management organization and report to senior management such as the CFO, as is frequently the case, or to the board, probably through the audit committee, as some authorities recommend?

The UK Smith Report (2003), reflected in subsequent UK Corporate Governance Codes, is ambiguous. Its guidance to audit committees suggests that management has the responsibility for 'the identification, assessment, management, and monitoring of risk, for developing, operating, and monitoring the system of internal control, and for providing assurance to the board that it has done so', but then adds 'except where the board is expressly responsible for reviewing the effectiveness of the internal control and risk management systems'.

In Australia, the ASX Principles of Good Corporate Governance (2003, 3rd edition 2014) also recommend that internal audit 'should report to management and should have all necessary access to management and the right to seek information and explanations'. But then the Principles add that 'companies should consider a second reporting line from the internal audit function to the board or relevant committee'. The Principles also suggest that the audit committee has access to internal audit without the presence of management, and that 'the audit committee should recommend to the board the appointment and dismissal of a chief internal audit executive'.

According to a study by KPMG,[4] the international accounting firm, 'the only satisfactory solution to this problem is for internal audit to report primarily and directly to the board and its audit committee rather than to senior management'. This report provides an interesting summary of the pros and cons of the reporting relationship. The benefits of the audit function being responsible to and reporting directly to the audit committee, it suggests, are:

- the ability to bypass all departments without fear of limitation of scope by being tied to, for example, the finance department;
- the board and audit committee know that the information they are receiving on the internal controls and risk management systems reflects a true description and has not been 'watered down' or filtered by management beforehand;
- the independence of the internal audit function is absolute;
- the funding of the internal audit function is outside the normal process of budgeting, thereby allowing resources to be allocated by the assurance needs of the organization as assessed by the board or the audit committee;
- it enables the board/audit committee to directly and critically analyse and evaluate the internal audit function in its contribution to the fulfilment of the board's responsibility for internal control;
- it reinforces the board/audit committee's knowledge of the business and its risk profile when dealing with management and stakeholders.

---

[4] www.kpmg.com.cn/en/virtual_library/Risk_advisory_services/Internal_audit_role.pdf

On the other hand, the downside of the internal audit function being responsible to and reporting directly to the audit committee, the report suggests, includes the following:

- internal audit may not be privy to all sources of information throughout the company if seen as 'outside' the management structure;

- the chair of the audit committee may not have allocated sufficient time, or have adequate resources/capacity, to oversee the internal audit function;

- it would be necessary to set up a specific charter outlining the roles and responsibilities of the board in relation to internal audit, as separate from management: for example, who would look after human resources issues, such as personnel evaluations, compensation, and career planning? could the head of internal audit have a career elsewhere in the organization?

- the audit committee would be assuming more responsibility and therefore, perhaps, more liability in relation to the adequacy of the internal control and risk systems of the organization;

- potentially, it restricts the ability of the CEO to use internal audit as a tool to reinforce control principles, or in special projects.

The Institute of Internal Auditors suggests that whoever the internal audit function is responsible to there are some key measures to ensure that the reporting lines enable effectiveness and independence.[5] These key measures are as follows:

- the head of internal audit should meet privately with the board/audit committee without the presence of management, thus reinforcing the independence and direct nature of the reporting relationship;

- the board or audit committee should have the final authority to review and approve the annual audit plan and all major changes to the plan;

- the board or audit committee should review the performance of the head of internal audit and the overall internal audit function at least once a year, as well as approve the compensation levels for the head of internal audit;

- the charter for the internal audit function should clearly articulate both the functional and administrative reporting lines for the function, as well as its principal activities;

- the reporting line should be to someone with sufficient authority to provide internal audit with enough support to accomplish its day-to-day activities;

- the reporting line should facilitate open and direct communications with the CEO, the senior executive group, and line management;

- the reporting line should enable adequate communications and information flows, so that internal audit receives adequate and timely information concerning the activities, plans, and business initiatives of the organization;

- budgetary controls and considerations imposed by the administrative reporting line should not impede internal audit in accomplishing its brief.

[5] Institute of Internal Auditors, 'Practice Advisory 1110–2: Chief Audit Executive Reporting Lines', December 2002.

Given the ever-increasing expectations of directors' knowledge and experience, and demands on their time, it seems likely that the contribution of internal audit to corporate governance can only be enhanced and grow.

The importance of the external auditor

The external, independent auditor is a fundamental component of the corporate governance system. Traditionally, the independent auditor had access to all of the books and records of the company, and reported to the shareholders that the financial statements provided to it by the directors gave a true and fair view of the state of the company's financial affairs. However, the auditor's role has evolved, as the need for professional risk management and the assessment of internal control became apparent, following the collapse of Enron and other companies around the world in the early years of the 21st century, and the effects of the global financial crisis from 2007 onwards.

In the United States, the Public Company Accounting Oversight Board (PCAOB), set up by the SOX Act 2002, has enhanced the external auditor's role in companies listed in the United States and their subsidiaries around the world. The PCAOB standards require auditors to:

- obtain reasonable assurance that effective internal control over financial reporting has been maintained;
- assess the risk that a material weakness exists, testing and evaluating the design and operating effectiveness of internal control based on the assessed risk;
- perform such other procedures as are considered necessary in the circumstances.

These standards have been incorporated into the traditional approaches to financial audit. The report of the external auditors to General Motors (see Corporate Governance in Action 15.3) provides some useful insights into the audit standards that are now being followed and the processes involved.

The appointment, remuneration, and removal of auditors

In most jurisdictions, the auditor of publicly listed companies is formally appointed and reappointed by the shareholders in general meeting on the advice of the board, typically working through its audit committee. In private companies, the auditor is typically chosen by the board. Indeed, some jurisdictions, including the United Kingdom, do not require private companies to have a formal audit unless the shareholders so wish.

Auditors' remuneration and their removal, should it become necessary, are also generally agreed by the board on the advice of the audit committee. In most jurisdictions, the external auditor has to be a member of a recognized accounting profession, such as the American Institute of Certified Public Accountants (AICPA) in the United States, or the Institute of Chartered Accountants and various other recognized bodies in the United Kingdom, Canada, and other Commonwealth countries.

But who does the auditor work for and report to: the management, the directors, or the shareholders? Historically, in the USA the external auditor reported to management. That was changed by the SOX Act and the creation of PCAOB. In the USA the external auditor now works for and is accountable to the independent outside directors forming the audit committee, and through them to the board of directors, as the representatives of the shareholders. This is now enshrined in PCAOB and securities regulation in the USA and Canadian Instrument 52–110. In other jurisdictions, including the United Kingdom, the external auditors work for and report to the shareholders, although *de facto* they work with management and report to the directors through the independent directors on the audit committee.

Corporate Governance in Action 15.3   General Motors Company

REPORT OF INDEPENDENT REGISTERED PUBLIC ACCOUNTING FIRM

General Motors Company, its Directors, and Stockholders:

We have audited the accompanying Consolidated Balance Sheets of General Motors Company and subsidiaries (the Company) as of December 31, 2015 and 2014, and the related Consolidated Statements of Income, Comprehensive Income, Cash Flows and Equity for each of the three years in the period ended December 31, 2015.

These financial statements are the responsibility of the Company's management. Our responsibility is to express an opinion on the financial statements based on our audits. We conducted our audits in accordance with the standards of the Public Company Accounting Oversight Board (United States). Those standards require that we plan and perform the audit to obtain reasonable assurance about whether the financial statements are free of material misstatement. An audit includes examining, on a test basis, evidence supporting the amounts and disclosures in the financial statements. An audit also includes assessing the accounting principles used and significant estimates made by management, as well as evaluating the overall financial statement presentation. We believe that our audits provide a reasonable basis for our opinion. In our opinion, such consolidated financial statements present fairly, in all material respects, the financial position of General Motors Company and subsidiaries at December 31, 2015 and 2014, and the results of their operations and their cash flows for each of the three years in the period ended December 31, 2015, in conformity with accounting principles generally accepted in the United States of America. We have also audited, in accordance with the standards of Public Company Accounting Oversight Board (United States), the Company's internal control over financial reporting as of December 31, 2015, based on the criteria established in Internal Control—Integrated Framework (2013) issued by the Committee of Sponsoring Organizations of the Treadway Commission and our report dated February 3, 2016 expressed an unqualified opinion on the Company's internal control over financial reporting.

Deloitte & Touche LLP Detroit, Michigan February 3, 2016

Corporate Governance in Action 15.4   Auditors' relations with client companies—more on Arthur Andersen

Arthur Andersen, one of the world's top five accounting firms, prided itself on the quality and originality of its work. But it went dramatically out of business following a number of audit failures, including Waste Management, Worldcom, and Enron.

Andersen's audit and consultancy fees from Enron were running at about US$52 million a year, more on consultancy than audit. Enron also employed several former Andersen partners as senior financial executives. Partners of Andersen discussed dropping Enron because of their client's accounting policies, but decided not to give up the audit. Memorably, after Enron collapsed, Andersen was accused of shredding Enron papers sought by an SEC investigation, and appeared before a grand jury on charges of obstructing justice, although it was subsequently exonerated.

Clients quickly distanced themselves and many Andersen partners around the world smartly joined one of the remaining Big Four global audit firms. The confidence of the accounting profession, which traditionally had relied on professional self-regulation, was threatened when it realized that the market was really in control.

Subsequent concerns have been expressed about the loss of competitiveness in the audit market with a potential oligopoly of just four firms competing for the business of the major global corporations. In the United States, the SOX Act of 2002 introduced new controls on the audit profession.

The independence of external auditors

The standing of independent external auditors clearly hinges on the definition and confirmation of independence. In the past, some audit firms developed a close relationship with their audit clients, earning significant fees from consultancy advice, taxation services, and other non-audit work. Questions have been asked about whether this violated their independence as auditors. It has even been suggested that some firms used the audit as a 'loss-leader' to attract consultancy income.

In the United States, communications between external auditors and audit committees concerning independence are covered by PCAOB rule 3526.[6] The rule requires that a registered public accounting firm take the following steps, prior to accepting an initial engagement:

- describe, in writing, to the audit committee of the listed company all relationships between the registered public accounting firm or any affiliates of the firm and the potential audit client or persons in financial reporting oversight roles at the potential audit client that, as of the date of the communication, may reasonably be thought to bear on independence;
- discuss with the audit committee of the listed company the potential effects of the relationships should it be appointed the listed company's auditor;
- document the substance of its discussion with the audit committee of the issuer.

At least annually with respect to each of its listed company audit clients:

- describe, in writing, to the audit committee of the issue listed company, all relationships between the registered public accounting firm or any affiliates of the firm and the audit client or persons in financial reporting oversight roles at the audit client that, as of the date of the communication, may reasonably be thought to bear on independence;
- discuss with the audit committee of the listed company the potential effects of the relationships;
- affirm to the audit committee of the listed company, in writing, that, as of the date of the communication, the registered public accounting firm is independent in compliance with Rule 3520; and

[6] http://pcaobus.org/Rules/PCAOBRules/Pages/Section_3.aspx#Rule3526

- document the substance of its discussion with the audit committee of the listed company.

These PCAOB requirements, though only relevant to US companies, provide a valuable guide to the determination of external auditor independence worldwide.

Independent assessment of audit practitioners

In the past, the accounting profession was self-regulating, relying on peer assessment to maintain standards. More recently, demands have been made for independent assessment of audit quality. In 2008, the European Commission issued a recommendation on external quality assurance for firms auditing public companies in member states. It provided guidance to member states to establish an independent and effective system of inspections on the basis of the Directive on Statutory Audit. In essence, this recommendation gave more responsibilities to the public oversight bodies, strengthened the independence of inspection teams, and enhanced transparency of the results of inspections of individual audit firms. In 2014, after four years of deliberation, the European Parliament introduced changes to prevent the relationship between auditor and company becoming too close. In addition to measures restricting the services that an audit firm could provide, other than the audit, the new rules required companies to put their audit out to tender at least every ten years and to change to a new auditor every twenty years.

The significance of the company secretary

Many company law jurisdictions require the appointment of a company secretary with statutory duties. Like directors, the company secretary is an officer of the company and, like them, has a duty to act in good faith in the best interest of the company and to avoid conflicts of interest. Some listing rules require that all directors should have access to the advice and services of the company secretary, with a view to ensuring that board procedures, and all applicable rules and regulations, are followed.

The duties of the company secretary might typically include:

- advising the chair on legal rules and regulations affecting the company;
- convening board, board committee, and company (shareholder) meetings;
- advising on and guiding board and board committee procedures.

In some companies, the company secretary plays a part in shareholder communications; in others that is the responsibility of the CFO or the senior manager responsible for investor relations.

In the United States, the role of company secretary, typically known as the corporate secretary, is frequently carried out by the corporate lawyer. The American Society of Corporate Secretaries suggests that the duties and responsibilities include organizing meetings of the board, board committees, and shareholders, maintaining the corporate records and stock (shareholder) records, and liaising with the securities markets. It further states that the corporate secretary should be 'the primary liaison between the corporation's directors and management'. The company secretary need not be an employee of the company; he or she may work for an outside agency or partnership.

In the United Kingdom, the Companies Act (2006) required public companies to have a company secretary; and gave private companies the option to have a company secretary only if the shareholders wanted one. In some jurisdictions, the company secretary can be a 'legal person'—that is, a limited company—and smaller companies may appoint a firm of accountants, lawyers, or a specialist company registrar firm to act as company secretary. In other jurisdictions, including Australia, the company secretary must be an actual person.

The UK Cadbury Report (1992) felt that:

> [t]he company secretary has a key role to play in ensuring that the board procedures are both followed and regularly reviewed. The chairman and the board should look to the company secretary for guidance on what their responsibilities are under the rules and regulations to which they are subject and on how these responsibilities should be discharged. All directors should have access to the advice and services of the company secretary and should recognize that the chairman is entitled to strong support from the company secretary in ensuring the effective functioning of the board.

The UK Corporate Governance Code (2012) requires that 'the company secretary should be responsible for advising the board through the chair on all governance matters', and under direction of the chair, the company secretary's responsibilities include ensuring good information flows within the board and its committees and between senior executive and non-executive directors, as well as facilitating induction and assisting with professional development as required. The Code adds that the removal of a company secretary should be a matter for the whole board.

The evolution of the company secretary's role highlights its current significance. In Britain in the mid-19th century, when the joint-stock, limited-liability company was developed, directors needed someone to keep their records. This was the job of the secretary to the board. The function was largely clerical, with the directors holding the power. The above list of duties, however, shows just how far the function has moved, not least in line with the growing complexity of modern organizations, the globalization of business, and the vast array of modern regulation, legislation, and exhortation about company affairs. For views on the role of the company secretary from a prominent British businessman see Corporate Governance in Action 15.5, and on the development of that role by a prominent British judge see Corporate Governance in Action 15.6.

Corporate Governance in Action 15.5   Sir John Harvey-Jones on the role of the company secretary

Sir John Harvey-Jones, previously the CEO of the British company ICI, wrote:[7]

> a company secretary should have considerable personal integrity and be seen to stand for probity and right within the company. The secretary should be seen to 'side with the angels' and be prepared to state when the occasion demands that 'I fear that while what we are doing is within the letter of the law we are not within the spirit'. They have to be trusted by everyone. It is a bloody tough job.

[7] Harvey-Jones, John (1993) *Managing To Survive*, Heinemann, London.

Corporate Governance in Action 15.6   Lord Denning on the evolution of the company secretary's role

Changing attitudes to company secretaries can be seen in the contrasting comments of two senior British judges.

In 1887, Lord Esher, Master of the Rolls (the head of the judiciary), said:

> A secretary is a mere servant. His position is that he is to do what he is told and no person can assume that he has the authority to represent anything at all, nor can anyone assume that statements made by him are necessarily accepted as trustworthy without further enquiry.

A century later, things had changed. Corporate life had become complicated. Many companies ran diverse enterprises through complex groups of subsidiary and associated companies. Legislation affecting companies had become substantial. The role of the company secretary called for professional knowledge and skill. In 1971, Lord Denning, Master of the Rolls, said:

> Times have changed. A company secretary is a much more important person nowadays than he was in 1887. He is an officer of the company with extensive duties and responsibilities. This appears not only in modern Companies Acts but also by the role, which he plays in the day-to-day business of companies. He is no longer merely a clerk. He regularly makes representations on behalf of the company and enters into contracts on its behalf . . . so much so that he may be regarded as (doing) such things on behalf of the company. He is certainly entitled to sign contracts connected with the administrative side of the company's affairs, such as employing staff, ordering cars, and so forth. All such matters come within the ostensible authority of a company secretary.

Case studies

 ## Case study 15.1   The Wells Fargo fraud

The fraud is revealed

The first sign that something was seriously wrong in the Wells Fargo Bank was complaints from customers that they had been charged unexplained and unnecessary fees. An initial investigation found that about 130,000 accounts had been charged. A subsequent study raised the number to 190,000. But that was only the beginning.

Another investigation found that between 2011 and mid-2015 no less than 1 million fake accounts had been opened in customers' names without their knowledge. But when the inquiry was expanded to cover accounts opened between 2009 and 2016, 4 million additional fake accounts were revealed.

Furthermore, over half a million customers were enrolled in the Bank's online bill payment system, again without their knowledge.

Why did it happen?

The Chairman and Chief Executive of Wells Fargo Bank was John G. Stumpf, born in 1953 on a dairy farm in Pierz, Minnesota. Stumpf, one of 11 children, graduated from St Cloud State University, Minnesota, and received an MBA with an emphasis in finance from the Carlson School of Management.

As chair/CEO, Stumpf encouraged a growth culture throughout Wells Fargo Bank. The directors accepted this strategy for some years and were pleased with the results presented to them.

Unlike many prudent retail banks, Wells Fargo adopted a growth-orientated marketing strategy, which produced aggressive sales policies. Interest rates, higher than those of competitors, were offered for new online savings accounts. Wells Fargo credit cards were offered with 0% interest APR until 2019, and their Premier card gave 60,000 bonus points for qualifying purchases.

The Bank's employees were set aggressive sales targets, with bonuses for success and the threat of redundancy for failure. To meet their targets, thousands of employees created bogus accounts in customers' names.

The outcome

John G. Stumpf, who had encouraged the growth-orientated culture and allowed the fraud to continue for some years, resigned but only under pressure from the board. He was replaced by Timothy J. Sloan.

The US Government brought three lawsuits alleging the creation of sham accounts, which cost the Bank US$185 million. The Bank also paid US$480 million to settle class-action securities fraud lawsuits, brought by shareholders, which claimed that the Bank had misled them in reporting the scandal and reduced the value of their holdings.

The damage to the reputation of Wells Fargo Bank was significant. Shareholders and customers suffered (and sued). Many employees lost their jobs. Further investigations by government lawmakers, regulators, the US Justice Department, and state attorneys general were continuing when this case study was written.

Timothy J. Sloan, Wells Fargo's new chief executive, said: 'We are working hard to ensure this never happens again and to build a better bank for the future ... We apologize to everyone who was harmed.'[8]

Discussion questions

1. Should the external auditors have detected the scandal in the early years of the fraud?

2. Should the outside directors, in particular the audit committee, have questioned the company's growth rate brought about by the marketing strategy and growth culture?

 Case study 15.2   Tax avoidance strategies

A case study in the third edition of this book featured an edited discussion between experts in the field of corporate taxation in Britain. Their insights and opinions were reported on the understanding of anonymity. The group included the CFO of an international business, an academic economist, a lawyer, an accountant with one of the Big Four firms, a business school professor, and a researcher working for a doctorate in corporate governance. Since that case study, some of the participants in the original discussion have offered additional comments on subsequent developments in companies' aggressive taxation strategies around the world.

Extracts from the original discussion follow:

Professor: Welcome. There has recently been a lot of criticism of international companies apparently avoiding tax in the countries where they generated profits, using accounting dodges to move

[8] Herbert, J. (2018) 'Wells Fargo makes transformation changes', *The Chief Executive*, 22 July.

those profits offshore to low-tax regimes. Media commentators and politicians have been vocal in condemning such manoeuvres.

Lawyer: Before we start rehearsing experiences, let's be clear on the law. In almost all jurisdictions, there is nothing illegal in tax avoidance, in other words arranging your affairs so that the tax man takes the minimum possible from you. Indeed, in some countries, the courts have actually confirmed that doctrine.[9] What is illegal, totally unacceptable, and unethical, is breaking the law to evade paying tax that is legitimately due. We need to distinguish tax avoidance from tax evasion at the outset.

Economist: With respect, that's not really the issue here. Everyone accepts that tax evasion is illegal and morally corrupt. The issue is about the ethical boundaries of tax avoidance. What may be within the law may not be morally, socially, or politically acceptable. For some companies, paying corporation tax has become a matter of taste.

CFO: That's exactly the problem we face. My company has been criticized in the press, backed-up by considerable heckling on the internet, for doing what every international company does. We try to minimize tax within the boundaries of the law. The board has a duty to maximize the value of the company for the benefit of the shareholders.

Professor: But what exactly do you do to reduce taxation?

CFO: We use transfer pricing to shift profits from high-tax regimes to low ones. Let me give you an example. An international company in the coffee business has a subsidiary company in Jamaica that grows coffee beans. The coffee is shipped and sold through other group companies in France, Germany, the UK, and elsewhere. But the coffee is not sold directly to those companies. It is all sold to another group company in Jersey, which is an offshore, low-tax regime. The Jamaican group company sells the coffee to its Jersey sister-company at low prices; the Jersey company then sells it on to its European affiliates at high prices. The profits are then left in Jersey where they attract low tax. Totally legal.

Economist: Totally legal. But is it ethical? That coffee has been sold throughout Northern Europe where corporate taxation is high. That's where the revenue is generated and profits really made. And that's where tax on those profits should be paid. But by artificially trading the coffee through Jersey, the profit has ended up there. As a result, Jersey, which doesn't grow a single coffee bean, shows up in the statistics as a major exporter of coffee!

Accountant: The transfer price mechanism you have described we call 'the plain vanilla option'—simple and much liked. In fact, tax authorities try to force companies to use arm's-length prices for inter-group transfers. But of course if the transactions go through a third country they can't do that. But companies use far more sophisticated devices to move profits offshore to low-tax regimes. The tax department in my firm has a whole section devoted to advising clients on such schemes. They work with the lawyers. It's a game of keeping a step ahead of the revenue authorities: you find a loophole, and exploit it before it's closed.

Professor: Give us an example of such schemes.

Accountant: Well, you could incorporate a company in a tax haven to hold the group's intellectual property rights—its brand name, its patents, its trade secrets—and charge the group companies making profits in high-tax countries for the use of them. Nothing to stop charging really high fees for what, after all, is the reason for the profits in the first place.

Economist: Isn't another way to move profits around to create inter-group loans and charge high rates of interest?

---

[9] 'The legal right of a taxpayer to decrease the amount of what otherwise would be his taxes, or altogether avoid them, by means which the law permits, cannot be doubted.' Chief Justice Charles E. Hughes in *Gregory v Helvering (US Commissioner of Internal Revenue)* 293 US 465 (1935).

CFO: Yes. Incidentally, my coffee-importing example can work in the other direction. A subsidiary in a high-tax country can sell its output to one in a low-tax country at a price way below its true value, thus moving potential profits to the buying company. And it's not only corporation tax: some big companies avoid UK value-added tax by exporting goods to Britain from Luxembourg.

Researcher: It seems to me that the high-tax countries need to sharpen up their regulations and their compliance efforts.

Lawyer: For corporate tax dodging to be stopped, all the major economically advanced countries would need to cooperate. They would all have to introduce the same controls.

Accountant: I think it's hypocritical of governments and the media to go on about tax dodging being immoral. If a company pays the tax that is legally due, that's it. If a government wants to change things, change the law.

CFO: I agree. Tax planning is legitimate and necessary. I feel sorry for the small and medium domestic companies that can't exploit the tax planning opportunities open to the big multinationals. It's the firms that get hit.

Researcher: You said 'exploit': that's just the right word.

Economist: Frankly, I think all this talk about the immorality of tax planning is bunk. Company directors have a legal duty not to pay more tax than is legally necessary. I believe that is their moral obligation too. Minimizing costs and using the factors of production as well as possible creates more wealth. Competition, in an open economy, lowers the cost of production, reduces excess profits, and the benefits are passed on to consumers.

Professor: I wonder if it's really a matter of fairness. If companies generate revenues in a country, they should pay their fair share of tax in that country. It shouldn't be optional or voluntary.

Accountant: But most countries tax profits not sales, except for sales taxes, which are relatively small, and paid by purchasers anyway.

CFO: Your suggestion that it's not fair has another side. Fair to whom? You are thinking of the taxpayer. But if companies paid higher taxes what about the effects on employees, customers, and, of course, shareholders? Remember, the shareholders are not just rich individuals and financial institutions. They include millions of pensioners whose pension funds are invested in those companies.

Lawyer: For me it's not a matter of fairness, or morality. It's a matter of law, full disclosure, and compliance, with proper regulation. Companies don't have morals.

Recently, the Professor asked the Researcher (who had received his doctorate), the Accountant, and the CFO for their recent experiences.

Researcher: The controversy over alleged tax avoidance by international corporations continues. According to the *Guardian* newspaper multinational Amazon paid just €16.5 million (£15 million) in tax on revenues from their European online retail business of €21.6 billion (£19.5 billion) in 2016,[10] according to figures from their Luxembourg European subsidiary. Apparently a surge in the Amazon share price at the time made Amazon founder Jeff Bezos the world's richest man.

Accountant: I saw those figures. They will reignite the debate about companies using complex cross-border devices to minimize tax.[11] Apparently, the Amazon Luxembourg headquarters aggregates

---

[10] *The Guardian*, 10 August 2017.

[11] In October 2018, Phillip Hammond, the British Chancellor of the Exchequer, announced in his budget statement that a new tax would be introduced on the revenues (not the profits) of international companies reporting large turnover but small profits. Companies with smaller total revenues would be exempt, so as not to penalize high-tech start-up companies. Critics argued that without multilateral agreement between countries, such a tax was an open invitation to tax accountants and lawyers to devise schemes to lower reported revenues.

the massive sales revenues from each of its European operations. But although it is very successful, its margins are quite low and it even reports a loss some quarters.

CFO: We also have to remember that Amazon pays all the taxes that are required in every country where it operates. It also gives its customers a great service, provides an outlet for countless suppliers, and employs tens of thousands in Britain.

Researcher: From what I hear those workers are not well paid.

Professor: I'm inclined to agree with Ana Arendar, the head of inequality at Oxfam, who said: 'Despite some action by ministers and companies, widespread corporate tax avoidance continues to cost both rich and poor countries billions every year that could pay for schools and lifesaving healthcare.'

Discussion questions

1. Is it ethically wrong for companies to avoid tax through legal schemes? Is it moral for accounting firms and financial institutions to advise them how to do it?

2. What would be the best way to require companies with substantial sales in a country to contribute a fair share to that country in tax?

3. In the case, the lawyer says 'companies don't have morals'. Do you agree?

Self-test questions

1. What is the principal role of the remuneration committee of the board?

2. What is the principal role of the nomination committee of the board?

3. What is the primary role of the audit committee?

4. What might that primary role include?

5. What other duties might a modern audit committee undertake?

6. What might boards, and in particular their audit committees, look to the internal audit function to provide?

7. Who is responsible for the financial accounts of a listed company—the auditors or the directors?

8. In the United States, what do the PCAOB standards require auditors to do?

9. In the United States, what is the company secretary typically known as, and who carries out that role?

10. What might the duties of a company secretary typically include?

 For suggested answers to these self-test questions visit the online resources at: www.oup.com/uk/tricker4e/

Projects and exercises

1. The governing body of a not-for-profit organization is composed entirely of outside directors, with the chief executive and other senior officials attending meetings. Write a report to the chair explaining why an audit committee of the governing body might be a good idea. The organization could be, for example, a hospital, a charity, or an educational body, or a private company.

2. Use the internet to compare the annual accounts of a variety of companies in different countries and different industries. Do they all include a report from their independent external auditor, and one from the board audit committee? If you find any significant differences, explain why this might be.

3. Draft a briefing note for the chair of the audit committee of a listed company outlining other questions that should be asked during a meeting with the external auditors on the completion of their audit.

4. What is your opinion of the following ideas offered to preserve the independence of audit firms:

   - prohibiting audit staff from joining a client company (at least until after a given period of time)?
   - requiring the staff leading the audit of a client company to rotate periodically?

References and further reading

Armour, Douglas (2013) *The Company Secretary's Handbook*. 8th edn, ICSA, London.

Ashton, Helen (2008) *The Company Secretary's Handbook: A Guide to Statutory Duties and Responsibilities*. 5th edn, Kogan Page and Sunday Times (Business Development Series), London.

Bowman, Brenda and Alison Dillon Kibirige (2014) CSIA Corporate Secretaries Toolkit—a modular training programme. Corporate Secretaries International Association, Hong Kong.

Braiotta, Louis, Jr, et al. (2010) *The Audit Committee Handbook*. 5th edn, Institute of Internal Auditors, Wiley, Hoboken, NJ.

Bromilow, Catherine L. and Barbara L. Berlin (2005) *Audit Committee Effectiveness: What Works Best*. 3rd edn, PriceWaterhouseCoopers, The Institute of Internal Auditors Research Foundation, New York.

Carver, John (2002) *Corporate Boards that Create Value—Governing Company Performance from the Boardroom*. Jossey-Bass, San Francisco, CA.

Charan, Ra (2005) *Boards that Deliver: Advancing Corporate Governance from Compliance to Competitive Advantage*. Jossey-Bass, San Francisco, CA.

Cosserat, Graham W. and Neil Rodda (2009) *Modern Auditing*. 3rd edn, John Wiley, Chichester.

Cutler, Sally F. (2009) *Audit Committee Reporting: A Guide for Internal Auditing*. The Institute of Internal Auditors, New York.

Gray, Ian and Stuart Manson (2008) *The Audit Process: Principles, Practice, and Cases*. 3rd edn, Thomson Learning, London.

Lai, Gerry P. L. (2010) *Tolley's Company Secretary's Handbook 2010–2011*. LexisNexis, London.

NACD ([2005] 2010) The Audit Committee: A Report of a NACD Blue Ribbon Commission. National Association of Corporate Directors, Washington, DC.

Pickett, K. H. Spencer (2010) *The Internal Auditing Handbook*. 3rd edn, John Wiley, Chichester.

Porter, Brenda, Jon Simon, and David Hatherly (2008) *Principles of External Auditing*. 3rd edn, John Wiley, Chichester.

Ridley, Jeffrey (2008) *Cutting Edge Internal Auditing*. John Wiley, Chichester.

Scholes, Myron (2016) *Tax Strategy*. 5th edn, Pearson, London.

Swanson, D. (2010) *Swanson on Internal Auditing: Raising the Bar*. IT Governance Publishing, Ely.

Trautmann, Ted and James Hamilton (2005) *Guide for Audit Committees*. 3rd edn, Perfect Paperback CCH Inc., New York.

Verschoor, Curtis C. (2008) *Audit Committee Essentials*. Institute of Internal Auditors, Wiley, Hoboken, NJ.

Weiss, Renee (2009) *Audit Committee Characteristics and Monitoring Effectiveness: An Evaluation of Independence, Financial Expertise, Firm Support, and Oversight Activities*. VDM Verlag, Saarbrücken, Germany.

16

Board Effectiveness: Building Better Boards

 Learning Outcomes

This chapter enables us to:

- Consider what makes a board effective.
- Study director induction, development, training, and updating.
- Understand directors' liabilities and indemnity.
- Improve board information and meeting management, agenda, and minutes.
- Think about communications with shareholders and other stakeholders.

Making a board effective

In the past, many board meetings tended to be relatively cosy affairs—but no longer, as economic pressures, competitive forces, and investors' demands for performance have created a tough environment. Decisions that used to be straightforward have become complex. Comfortable meetings between friends have been replaced by tough-minded discussion and difficult decisions.

The principal attributes of an effective board are sound leadership with an appropriate leadership style, supported by a well-balanced board team, as discussed in Chapter 14. The 'six Cs' of board behaviour provide an insight into the characteristics that an effective board needs:

1. *Commitment*

   A commitment by every member of the board to the company's mission, values, and strategy is essential. Without a shared vision of the company's future, there can be no real commitment to success.

2. *Culture*

   Each board has its own culture. Effective boards depend on the integrity of each director. Their personal values reflect in the standing of the board and permeate the organization as a whole. Companies have a character too. Strong companies have strong characters.

3. *Collaboration*

   Boards work as a team, each member playing a part. Effective team-play calls for communication based on trust, reliance on others, and mutual respect. Balance in deliberations means being prepared to question, to challenge with tough-minded discussion not group-think, but always to be open to others' points of view.

Perseverance is sometimes needed. So is enthusiasm, which can be reinforced by lightness of touch and occasional humour to hold the board together.

4. *Competence*

A well-balanced board has the appropriate experience, skills, and knowledge, which it draws on to ensure confidence, reliability, and excellence.

5. *Creativity*

Creativity means challenging conventional wisdom, encouraging unconventional ideas rather than resisting them, and facilitating change. Yet creativity is probably the least appreciated hallmark of an effective board.

6. *Contribution*

An achievement-orientated board strives to achieve the company's full potential.

The UK Financial Reporting Council (FRC) guidance on board effectiveness,[1] written to assist companies to apply the principles of the UK Corporate Governance Code, suggests that:

> [t]he FRC's mission is to promote transparency and integrity in business. The FRC sets the UK Corporate Governance and Stewardship Codes and UK standards for accounting and actuarial work; monitors and takes action to promote the quality of corporate reporting; and operates independent enforcement arrangements for accountants and actuaries. As the Competent Authority for audit in the UK the FRC sets auditing and ethical standards and monitors and enforces audit quality.

The FRC guidance notes (referenced below) provide boards with a comprehensive insight into board effectiveness, posing a useful series of questions which boards might address to their own effectiveness. The FRC guidance is worth studying; in essence it suggests that:

1. An effective board defines the company's purpose and then sets a strategy to deliver it, underpinned by the values and behaviours that shape its culture and the way it conducts its business. It will be able to explain the main trends and factors affecting the long-term success and future viability of the company—for example, technological change or environmental impacts—and how these and the company's principal risks and uncertainties have been addressed.

2. A company's purpose is the reason for which it exists. The board is responsible for setting and reconfirming the company's purpose. A well-defined purpose will help companies to articulate their business model, and develop their strategy, operating practices, and approach to risk. Companies with a clear purpose often find it easier to engage with their workforce, customers, and the wider public.

3. A sound understanding at board level of how value is created over time is key in steering strategies and business models towards a sustainable future. This is not limited to value that is found in the financial statements. An understanding of how intangible sources of value are developed, managed, and sustained—for example, a highly trained workforce, intellectual property, or brand recognition—is increasingly relevant to an understanding of the company's performance and the impact of its activity. These are important considerations for boards when setting corporate strategy.

[1] Guidance on Board Effectiveness (2018) Financial Reporting Council, London, March. Available online at www.frc.org.uk/getattachment/61232f60-a338-471b-ba5a-bfed25219147/2018-Guidance-on-Board-Effectiveness-FINAL.PDF

4. Boards have a responsibility for the health of the company and need to take a long-term view. This is in contrast to the priorities of some investors, not all of whom will be aligned with the pursuit of success over the long term. An effective board will manage the conflict between short-term interests and the long-term impacts of its decisions; it will assess shareholder and stakeholder interests from the perspective of the long-term sustainable success of the company.

To be effective, all board members need to bring a tough-minded independence to board deliberations. The range of alternative views needs to be declared, the various positions probed, challenged, and debated, without unnecessary provocation or obstruction. Board relationships are vital, with members respecting and trusting each other. A complacent, 'group-think' culture needs to be avoided. The chair is responsible for creating the climate in which this can happen.

> ## Corporate Governance in Action 16.1   FRC questions for boards
>
> The following questions are taken from the FRC's Guidance on Board Effectiveness:[2]
>
> 1. How do we know that management is identifying and addressing future challenges and opportunities, for example, changes in technology, environmental issues, or changing stakeholder expectations?
>
> 2. What proportion of board time is spent on financial performance management *versus* other matters of strategic importance?
>
> 3. Is the balance between the focus on immediate issues and long-term success appropriate?
>
> 4. Are we playing an active role in shaping long-term investment plans to underpin delivery of strategy and value creation?
>
> 5. Is sufficient board time allocated to idea generation, opportunity identification, and innovation?
>
> 6. Are we using scenario analysis to help us assess the strategic importance and potential impact of our challenges and opportunities?
>
> 7. Are we securing the benefits of 'big data' to give us a competitive edge?
>
> 8. How will we assess and measure the impact of our decisions on financial performance, the value for shareholders, and the impact on key stakeholders?
>
> 9. Are shareholders driving the company to act in a way that is out of line with its purpose, values, and wider responsibilities?

Director orientation and director induction

Director orientation

A newly appointed director needs orientation on the company, its business, and the company's financials before joining the board. Some companies use a director mentoring programme, in which an experienced member of the board accepts a responsibility, usually quite

---

[2] For more questions for Boards see: www.frc.org.uk/getattachment/61232f60-a338-471b-ba5a-bfed25219147/2018-Guidance-on-Board-Effectiveness-FINAL.PDF

informally, to orient and guide a new member into the ways of the board and the company. This relationship can help a new director to contribute more quickly and effectively.

Director induction

Many companies use an induction programme for new directors to provide the necessary orientation. An independent director, because of that independence, is unlikely to have much knowledge of the company, its business, and probably its industry. Consequently, an induction programme can provide vital information and knowledge. Otherwise, new independent directors can learn only from their experiences in the boardroom. Interestingly, however, newly appointed executive directors may also need a suitable induction programme, since they were 'promoted' to the board for their successful performance as executives in a particular function or division. They then need information on their duties as directors, on the company's board-level processes, and probably about the way in which the company as a whole runs. A well-planned induction programme can reduce the learning time before a new director begins to contribute meaningfully to board deliberations.

It is the duty of the board chair to recognize the needs of new directors for orientation and to ensure that a suitable induction programme is provided. The chair may undertake the responsibility of providing the induction experience himself or herself, but is more likely to delegate the task to the company secretary or another director, such as the senior independent director. Induction programmes may be built on a standard foundation, but different directors have different needs for briefing. Induction programmes should be tailored to the specific needs of individuals.

The three fundamental areas in which the new director needs to be fully informed are knowledge of the company, of its business, and of its financial situation.

Director development, training, and updating

Until quite recently, many directors saw no call for director-level training and development. They felt that the business knowledge and management experience that had led them to a seat in the boardroom demonstrated their capacity to be a director. Few hold that view today. Most corporate governance codes now call for director training. A professional approach is needed. With the rapid acceleration of new regulations, codes, and legal requirements, with the ever-changing aspects of global business, and given the litigious society that exists in many parts of the world, continuous updating and professional education and training for directors has become vital.

The interest in corporate governance in general, and director training in particular, has increased dramatically, in many parts of the world. The various alternative approaches to director training and development include:

1. *Formal, external training courses.*

   Many organizations around the world—institutes of directors; legal, accounting, and managerial professional bodies; and specialist consulting and research organizations—now run programmes for director training and updating. The NYSE Euronext announced in 2011 a board education programme designed to provide voluntary education for public and private board members. An advantage of such programmes is that they enable directors to be given relevant theoretical frameworks, principles, and practice updates that reflect the latest situation. Such experience can be enhanced by having directors from different types of entity, different industries, and various styles and scales of operation in the programme to exchange experiences.

2. *In-house board development programmes* designed specifically for the entire board.

   It is vital that all directors understand the current and emerging issues of strategic significance to the company and the possible risks involved. Such activities may involve board-level evaluation, with discussions that lead to learning in the context of that board. We will discuss director and board evaluation in Chapter 17.

3. *Updating and briefing sessions for the board, or individual directors.*

   Workshops with experts to lead and provide relevant knowledge, for example on recent developments in relevant company law or employee legislation, new developments in financial instruments, or the implication of private-equity-funded acquisitions of previously listed companies, can be valuable learning experiences.

4. *Relevant higher degree courses and focused professional courses* in corporate governance, corporate strategy, and other board-related topics are now offered by some business schools around the world.

5. *Experiential sponsorship programmes* can provide individual directors with relevant experience and knowledge.

   An executive director might be encouraged to become an independent director of a non-competing company to gain experience of board, governance, and managerial topics. Another director might be encouraged to chair an in-house inquiry, to join the board of a subsidiary in the group, or to lead an in-house project team. Such activities, however, may lack depth and relevance to the needs of the sponsoring company.

6. *Mentoring* provides another learning opportunity with a one-to-one personal trainer. Although it should be mentioned that such relationships are not value-free, particularly if the mentor is a fellow director, when hidden agendas may affect the relationship.

7. *Self-directed learning and continuous self-development* is, probably, the most prevalent learning experience adopted by directors. Participating in conferences, networking with peers, following distance learning courses, and reading books, journals, and professional articles can all provide learning experiences. As the old saying goes, 'if you want a helping hand, look at the end of your arm'.

8. *Site visits to different company locations* can be a useful source of knowledge.

   Some chairmen decide to hold an occasional board meeting in the offices of a division or subsidiary company, which can be motivating to the local staff as well as informative to the directors.

9. *Board experience* itself can be one of the best learning opportunities, provided that the learning experience is recognized. A professional chair will sometimes raise the question with his or her board: 'What have we learned from this experience?'

A challenge to every director is to remain up to date. That means continuous learning. Executive directors may need to delegate some day-to-day managerial work to focus on their director responsibilities. In addition to director evaluation programmes discussed in Chapter 17, directors can recognize their own development needs. They can question whether they are sufficiently knowledgeable to contribute fully and responsibly to board-level discussions and decision-making. Professional directors understand their strengths and their weaknesses, and create an informal self-development plan to remedy the gaps in their knowledge and their competencies. By reinforcing their strengths and remedying weaknesses, directors can increase their self-confidence and increase their contributions to their boards.

Listed companies in the United States[3] and the United Kingdom[4] are required to provide information to their shareholders and the public about their induction and continuing education policies.

Corporate Governance in Action 16.2   Vancouver Coastal Health Board Guidelines (abbreviated)

1. Introduction

The terms of reference for the Board of directors (the 'Board') defines the role and responsibilities of the Board. These Guidelines govern how the Board operates to carry out its duties of stewardship and accountability.[5]

2. Best Interests of the Authority

The Board is responsible for managing, or supervising the management of, the affairs and business of the Vancouver Coastal Health Authority (the 'Authority'). The Board oversees the conduct of business of the Authority and supervises management, which is responsible for the day-to-day conduct of business.

3. Principal Stakeholders

The Board's primary accountability is to the Government of British Columbia through the Ministry of Health. It is recognized that there are other key stakeholders whose interests must be considered. These stakeholders include: a) patients; b) the medical staff; c) healthcare professionals and other staff members; d) hospital and health foundations; and e) the public.

4. Accountability to the Ministry of Health

a) Each year the Ministry issues a Mandate Letter which confirms the health authority's mandated priorities, strategic direction from Government and establishes key performance expectations.

b) The Ministry requires the Board to submit a Service Plan that outlines, at a high level, health authority objectives and strategic initiatives for the three-year planning period in alignment with the Ministry's goals for the health system.

[3] NYSE Listed Company Manual 303A.09.
[4] UK Combined Corporate Governance Code, Principle A5.
[5] http://oasis.vch.ca/media/BoardOfDirectorsGuidelinesBoardPoliciesGuidelines.pdf

c) In addition, the taxpayer accountability principles will form the basis of an orientation for board members to promote understanding of the government strategic mandate and standards of conduct and fiscal responsibility.

5. The Medical Staff

a) Medical staff plays a unique role in BC's [British Columbia's] health systems. As clinical leaders, they exert a major influence on Regional Health Authorities. However, since they usually work on a fee-for-service basis, and are not employees of the Authorities, they maintain a great deal of independence.

b) Since the Board has the ultimate responsibility for the provision of medical care, it is important for the Board to ensure that the Authority is receiving appropriate service from these independent practitioners, and that these services provide the highest possible quality of care.

c) The Board is committed to maintaining open and clear communication with the medical staff in the interests of optimal patient care and service.

d) Medical Staff Bylaws identify the organization of the medical staff, and describe the roles and responsibilities of the medical staff, individually and collectively, within the region.

e) In general it is the Board's understanding that the responsibilities of the Medical Advisory Committee(s) include the following:

   i)   recommend to the Board proposed medical staff bylaws, rules and regulations;

   ii) ensure compliance with these as well as the Authority's policies and codes of ethics;

   iii) conduct peer appraisal and review of performance;

   iv) review physicians' credentials;

   v)   assist with appraising physician utilization and impact analysis;

   vi) organize clinical quality assurance;

   vii) provide for continuing medical education; and

   viii) provide advice on ethics, policy and procedural matters, and planning for new programs or service.

6. Terms of Reference

a) The Governance and Human Resources Committee reviews annually all of the Board's terms of reference.

b) The Governance and Human Resources Committee proposes changes to the Board for approval as required.

7. Strategic and Business Plans

a) Strategic and annual operating plans must be developed within the context of the Service Plan as it may be amended from time to time.

b) Management is responsible for the development of the 'draft' strategic plan and the subsequent development of the annual operating plan, supporting health human resource plan, and capital and operating budgets.

c) The Board's role is to ensure there is a strategic planning process in place, and then to participate in the planning process by reviewing, questioning, validating, and ultimately approving the strategic plan for the Authority and monitoring its implementation.

8. Principal Risks

a) The Board should have a continuing understanding of the principal risks associated with the Authority's objectives. It is management's responsibility to ensure the Board and its committees are kept well informed of changing risks.

b) The principal mechanisms through which the Board reviews risks are the strategic planning and monitoring process, an annual review of the Risk Register, the Audit and other committees and ongoing reports from the CEO.

9. Management Succession Planning and Development

a) The Board considers succession planning and management development ongoing processes that include annual reports to the Board by the CEO.

b) The CEO's views as to a successor in the event of unexpected incapacity and ongoing management development plans should be discussed regularly with the Governance and Human Resources Committee.

10. The Board Chair

The Board Chair's role is to manage and provide leadership to the Board. The separation of the roles of Board Chair and CEO allow the Board to act independently of management when necessary.

11. Communications

a) The Board ensures there is a comprehensive communication program in place which recognizes the Authority's accountability to the Government and the needs of other stakeholders.

b) Together, and in consultation with one another, the CEO and from time-to-time the Board Chair act as spokespeople for the Authority.

c) Individual directors do not act as spokespeople for the Authority unless specifically requested to do so by the CEO or the Board Chair.

d) It is expected that, from time to time, stakeholders will communicate their concerns and questions to directors rather than to management. It is important that directors inform management of such communications, so proper action can be taken and the appropriate representative of the Authority can make accurate responses.

12. Guiding Principles for Performance Reporting to the Board

The Board has adopted the following guiding principles regarding performance reporting to the Board. Performance reporting should:

a) be reliable—accurate enough to support intended uses, capable of being replicated, and sensitive enough to reflect changes in underlying performance;

b) be fair—presenting all relevant information without undue bias;

c) be timely—presented in time to be useful and relevant to the Board's decisions;

d) be consistent—presenting information consistently from period to period;

e) focus on the critical aspects of performance;

f) identify and explain goals and expectations; and relate results achieved to stated goals and expectations;

g) integrate financial and non-financial information to show how resources were allocated and how adopted strategies influenced results.

13. Board Committees

a) The function of committees is to help the Board with a task that belongs to the Board. It is a mechanism that permits deeper examination to be given to issues than could reasonably be given by the full Board in consideration of the many items with which it must deal at any one point in time. The role of committees is to support, not supplant, Board responsibility.

b) The Board has developed a set of guidelines for Board committees that apply to all committees established by the Board.

14. Committee Chairs and Committee Members

a) The Board Chair is responsible to the Board for annually proposing the leadership and membership of each committee.

b) In preparing recommendations the Board Chair will consult with the CEO, and take into account the preferences, skills and experience of each director.

c) Committee Chairs and members are appointed at the first Board meeting of the new fiscal year, or as needed to fill vacancies during the year.

d) The Board favours a periodic rotation in committee leadership and membership in a way that recognizes and balances the needs for new ideas, continuity and maintenance of functional expertise.

15. Task Forces

a) Task forces are Board committees, but differ from other committees in that each task force is established for a specific period of time to undertake a specific task, and is then disbanded.

b) Each task force operates according to a Board approved mandate outlining its duties and responsibilities.

16. Participation on Other Boards, Committees and Agencies

a) The Board may be called upon to appoint or elect representatives to related boards and committees, committees of management or other agencies such as the Clinical and Systems Transformation Health Organization Board Liaison Committee. The Chair will make all appointments and the Board will elect representatives where applicable.

b) Participation on such other boards, committees and agencies will be considered as part of the responsibilities of the participating director and that director will be permitted to claim compensation and re-imbursement for related expenses in accordance with the Director Compensation and Expenses Guidelines.

17. Board Meetings and Agendas

a) The Board meets at least five times within the calendar year.

b) The Board may also meet at the call of the Board Chair and/or the CEO.

c) The Board Chair and the CEO, in consultation with the Board Secretary, will develop the agenda for each Board meeting.

d) Under normal circumstances, the agenda and the material will be distributed to directors at least one week before the meeting.

e) All directors are free to suggest additions to the agenda and, whenever possible, adequate notice should be given to the Chair or Secretary to afford management, when appropriate, the time to develop background information to support the discussion.

18. Secretarial Duties

a) The Board delegates the administrative responsibilities of the Secretary to the Board Support Lead who will also serve as recording secretary at all meetings of the Board.

b) The Board Support Lead will provide within reason, such other assistance as may be requested by the Chair or the individual directors to facilitate the operation of the Board and its committees.

19. Special Meetings of the Directors

a) The directors may, on a regular or random basis, choose to meet in a seminar format for educational or informational activities or to deal with issues such as the evaluation processes relating to the Board, its Committees, and the CEO, or the Strategic Planning Process, which would be considered *in-camera* agenda items and involve time commitments that cannot be reasonably met in a scheduled meeting of the Board.

b) Any such meeting will fall within the provisions of the Director Compensation and Expense Guidelines.

20. Public Board Meetings

a) At the discretion of the Board, part or all, of the Board meeting may be open to the public in accordance with section 8(3) of the Health Authorities Act.

b) The Board may exclude the public from a meeting or a portion of a meeting, if the Board considers that, in order to protect the interest of a person or the public interest, the desirability of avoiding disclosure of information to [be] presented outweighs the desirability of public disclosure of that information.

21. Board Meetings Without Management

a) Practices that provide opportunity to build relationships, confidence and cohesion among directors are essential to allow the board to help develop an understanding of its role. One such practice is a regular meeting of directors without management present.

b) Such meetings can be used to provide feedback about Board processes, including the adequacy and timeliness of information being provided to the board. At times, such meetings might also focus on substantive issues that may be more difficult for some board members to discuss with management present. They can also provide opportunities for the Board Chair to discuss areas where the performance of the directors could be strengthened.

c) It is important that these opportunities occur regularly, even if the meetings are short, so that they become a recognized and accepted governance practice. The Board Chair should communicate quickly and directly to the CEO any issues arising in these sessions that bear on the relationship between the Board and management.

22. Information for Board Meetings

a) Material distributed to directors in advance of Board meetings should be concise, yet complete, and prepared in a way that focuses attention on critical issues to be considered.

b) Reports may be presented during Board meetings by directors, management or staff, or by invited outside advisors.

c) Presentations at Board meetings should briefly summarize the material sent to directors, so as to maximize the time available for discussion on questions regarding the material.

23. Non-Directors at Board Meetings

a) The Board appreciates the value of having management team members and other advisors attend Board meetings to provide information and opinions to assist the directors in their deliberations.

b) Other visitors, with the approval of the Board Chair, may be invited to attend Board meetings.

24. Board/Management Relations

a) Directors may direct questions or concerns on management performance to the Board Chair, to the CEO, or through Board and committee meetings.

b) Directors must respect the organizational structure of management. A director has no authority to direct any staff member.

25. Size of the Board

a) Although the Government determines the size of the Board, the current Board has considered its size relative to its mandate and is satisfied that a Board size of nine is appropriate for the Authority.

b) Board size has been established balancing two important governance effectiveness considerations. On the one hand, there is the need to ensure a proper diversity of perspectives, backgrounds, expertise and experience within a Board. On the other hand, there is the need to keep Board size sufficiently small to facilitate open and effective dialogue and the full participation and contribution of each director.

26. New Director Orientation and Continuing Director Development

a) The Governance and Human Resources Committee and the CEO share the responsibility to ensure that there is a new director orientation program and that directors receive continuing education/development as required.

b) New directors will be provided with an orientation and education program, which will include written information about the duties and obligations of directors and the business and operations of the Authority, documents from recent Board meetings and opportunities for meetings and discussion with the senior management of the Authority.

c) The orientation program for each new director will be tailored to that director's needs and areas of interest.

d) The issue of continuing development or education is important because the health care issues are complex and the operating environment is changing.

e) Continuing development should be focused on critical issues. Periodic presentations from staff and outside experts give directors a better sense of how the environment in which the Authority operates is changing.

f) Management tries to include an educational component in every Board meeting.

27. Assessing Board Performance

a) The Governance and Human Resources Committee is responsible for ensuring there is a process for annually assessing the performance of the Board, the Board Chair and the Board committees.

b) The objective of this review is to contribute to a process of continuous improvement in the Board's execution of its responsibilities.

c) The review should identify any areas where the directors or management believe that the Board could be working more effectively.

d) The Board evaluation process may change from year to year on the recommendation of the Governance and Human Resources Committee. It may not be appropriate to do a 'stem to stern' Board evaluation every year. Some years it may be appropriate to focus attention on some aspect of the governance process that the Board feels requires particular attention.

e) The Board evaluation methodology may also vary from year to year. Some years a questionnaire may be appropriate, other years it may be more effective to undertake interviews with each director.

28. Term of Service

a) Directors are appointed by the Minister of Health for a one, two or three year term.

b) Directors will normally be appointed for a maximum of six years. In order to achieve staggering of appointments, terms may be for other than three years.

c) The Government may rescind Director appointments, generally on the recommendation of the Board Chair.

29. Evaluation of the CEO

The Governance and Human Resources Committee will conduct an annual evaluation of the CEO's performance, measured against objectives and other relevant criteria established in the previous year by the Board and the CEO.

30. Outside Advisors for Committees and Directors

Occasionally, a committee or a director may need the services of a consultant or an advisor to assist with matters involving their responsibilities. A committee or director who wishes to engage an outside advisor at the expense of the Authority must first obtain the authorization of the Board Chair or the Chair of the Governance and Human Resources Committee, in either case in consultation with the CEO.

31. Board Guidelines Review

The Governance and Human Resources Committee reviews these Board Guidelines annually and any changes are recommended to the Board for approval.
  Board Guidelines approved 12 July 2016.

Directors' liabilities and indemnity

Many years ago, a member of the British royal family, who was being trained as a potential independent non-executive director, said to the author: 'You speak of the limited-liability company: does that mean the liability of the directors is limited?' He was obviously hopeful; but the answer was a resounding 'no'.

When serving as a company director, exposure to personal liability is real. In some countries, including the United States and the United Kingdom, the threat of litigation is significant. Contingency or conditional fee arrangements, the so-called 'no win, no fee' arrangements, are available in some jurisdictions. Lawyers accept a share of the risk in exchange for larger fees or, in some jurisdictions, a share of any damages awarded on a successful outcome. In some jurisdictions, class actions enable groups of litigants to combine their claims and bring a consolidated action against a company, its board, or a named director. Such hostile litigation, long accepted in the United States, is now growing in other jurisdictions, including the United Kingdom.

Who might bring such actions? Suits against directors can be brought by shareholders, employees, creditors, customers, suppliers, government and regulatory bodies, auditors, and liquidators. For directors of significant listed companies, investor-led proceedings are most likely. Directors of small or medium-sized enterprises are more likely to face proceedings from customers, clients, or employees. Should the company become insolvent, a liquidator or administrator could bring an action against a board or a director. The extent of the risk will depend on the jurisdiction in which the action is brought. Most significantly, the propensity to sue the company, its auditors, the board, or specific directors is increasing in many countries.

Directors can be held legally accountable in their personal capacity for actions that they are alleged to have taken or failed to take, but also for the actions of other members of the board or top management. Claims may be for unlimited amounts. Even if an action is successfully defended, legal costs can be incurred and directors' personal reputation damaged. Directors' personal assets can be at risk, which is why some people think twice before accepting a directorship. The need for sound legal advice in such circumstances is paramount.

In addition to the duties that directors may owe to third parties under corporate contracts, in many jurisdictions statute laws now impose statutory duties on directors. This legislation may include company law, and laws protecting health and safety, the environment, the consumer, employees and creditors, as well as anti-corruption legislation and laws designed for specific industries, such as financial services. In many countries, the criminal and regulatory authorities have strong investigative powers, and are able to bring prosecutions or levy penalties themselves. The need for all directors to have access to clear legal advice and for director orientation and induction programmes to cover such matters is vital. Contravening some Acts can lead to a criminal conviction with fines, prison, and in China even death. Disqualification from service as a director and personal liability for the company's debts can also occur.

Further, directors are responsible for ensuring that company accounts, reports, and other statutory documents are prepared and filed with the relevant regulatory body under the local companies legislation. If in doubt, take professional advice. Failure to do so can incur serious penalties.

Directors' and officers' insurance

Directors might legitimately expect their companies to provide them with some protection from the risks of litigation, but there are no formal standards. In most jurisdictions, directors can take some steps to protect themselves. Most jurisdictions allow a company to take out directors' and officers' liability (D&O) insurance on behalf of its directors.[6] In the United Kingdom, for example, as a result of legal changes in 2005, companies are now permitted to indemnify their directors against a broad range of liabilities and defaults. It is even possible for a company to fund the cost of the defence of any civil, regulatory, or criminal proceedings, provided that any loan to a director for such purpose is repaid immediately if the director is found liable.

However, directors cannot be indemnified by their company or by insurance against acts that are shown to be illegal, contrary to companies legislation, or other kinds of misfeasance. D&O insurance provides some protection to directors, company officers (such as the company secretary), and senior managers, if they are sued as the result of decisions taken while governing or managing the business. Some investors, such as venture capitalists, insist on D&O insurance before providing funds to a company. D&O insurance should not be confused with E&O (errors and omissions) cover, which is concerned with performance failures affecting products and services.

D&O insurance policies pay for actually or allegedly wrong decisions, which policies call 'wrongful acts'. Each insurer defines coverage in its own way, but typically covers 'any actual or alleged act or omission, error, misstatement, misleading statement, neglect or breach of duty by an insured person in the discharge of his/her duties'. For example, a D&O policy might cover claims of mismanagement of assets, claims by the shareholders of an acquired company that they had been misled by former directors, claims under health and safety legislation (although many D&O policies exclude bodily injury or property damage), actions under employment legislation including harassment, discrimination, and wrongful termination, and environmental legislation (although pollution damage is often excluded in D&O policies).

---

[6] The author acknowledges helpful advice from the Corporate Governance Practice of Aon Asia.

D&O insurance cover is not available for all who seek it. Successful, long-established companies are more likely to be able to obtain cover than companies in riskier situations, such as start-ups or those with financial problems. Some companies have found that they obtain lower D&O premiums when they are recognized as having high corporate governance standards. What is almost always true, however, is that a reputation for poor corporate governance will result in higher premiums, a reduction in cover, or even a failure to find insurance.

A 2004 report from the Australian Corporations and Markets Advisory Committee noted that:[7]

> there is an increasing trend to impose personal liability on directors and other officers for the shortcomings of companies. In considering the practical consequences of this liability regime, it cannot be assumed that all those exposed to personal liability are able to obtain protection through insurance. The availability of insurance cover reflects the market's appreciation of relevant risks. D&O insurance does not serve as an across-the-board mitigation of the personal financial liabilities to which corporate directors and officers are increasingly exposed. It cannot provide a complete cushion.

Just as all boards need a strategy for assessing and handling risk, they need a related policy on D&O insurance. The hope that misfortune will be avoided is neither a strategy nor a policy.

Board information

As we saw earlier, directors have a right to the information that they feel is necessary to fulfil their responsibilities as directors. Obviously, different directors are likely to have different information needs. Executive directors usually know more about the internal operations of the firm than the independent directors. Conversely, some outside directors are likely to have a wider knowledge of fields such as finance, international markets, or the economy than the executive directors. Each may need additional briefing on specific items on the agenda.

The UK Cadbury Report (2002) suggested that 'it is for chairmen to make certain that their non-executive directors receive timely, relevant information tailored to their needs, that they are properly briefed on the issues arising at board meetings, and that they make an effective contribution as board members in practice'. The same applies to executive directors.

Types of information

The information that directors acquire can come from both formal and informal sources on both a routine and non-routine basis. Table 16.1 illustrates this quadrant, indicating some of the likely sources for such information. Each of the quadrants can highlight different types and sources of information.

[7] www.camac.gov.au/camac/camac.nsf/byHeadline/PDFFinal+Reports+2004/$file/Large_Enterprises_report_Oct04.pdf

Table 16.1 How directors get their information: sources and provision of board-level information

	Provision on a regular and routine basis	Provision on an occasional and non-routine basis
Unofficial and informal sources	Briefings to the board Contacts within the company Questioning in meetings Discussions with staff 'Grapevine' gossip	Contacts outside the company 'Off the record' comments Casual reading/TV reports, etc. Unofficial probing and inquiry Visits, presentations, conferences
Official and formal sources	Regular board operating reports Regular board financial reports Statutory and regulatory reports Use of the company seal report Minutes of board committees Presentations to the board	Ad hoc reports and presentations: – in-house studies – consultants' reports – investment proposals – merger & acquisition proposals – market reports – technology reports – financial studies Details of legal actions

Official and regular information

Most boards develop a routine set of board papers, which go to all of the directors with the agenda for each meeting. These papers might include, for example, the latest financial accounts, a cash flow report, a report on business activity levels, the current order situation, a market report, and a routine report from the chief executive officer (CEO). Increasingly these 'papers' are provided electronically.

A good report with high-quality information will be all of the following:

- *understandable*—at a level of detail, language, and content appropriate to the likely readers. It would be counterproductive to produce a document assuming technological or financial knowledge that the readers lacked; but conversely, an expert might find a lay-person's guide patronizing and irritating;

- *reliable*—of fundamental importance, the reader must be able to trust that any facts given are accurate and any opinions advanced clearly shown as such;

- *relevant*—reports need to refer to the matter in hand—however interesting, significant, or worthy the information, unless it refers directly to the issue under consideration, the material is not useful;

- *comprehensive*—half of a story, like half-truths, can mislead; reports need to be complete and cover all relevant aspects of the situation;

- *concise*—directors are inevitably under time constraints; verbose reports may not be given the attention they deserve, being merely scanned and some of the salient information missed; good report writing involves a skill that can be learned and developed with practice;

- *timely*—directors need reports in sufficient time for them to study the contents, but with material that is up to date—the frequency of provision needs to be appropriate to the decisions that are being faced;

- *cost-effective*—an aspect of report writing that is often overlooked; report writing involves a cost, sometimes a substantial one. Chairmen need to ensure that unnecessary expense is not incurred producing reports with little value. With formal board reports a periodic review is sound policy: there can be a tendency to go on producing standard reports long after the need for them has disappeared.

The entire board or committee can also be informed by presentations made to them, for example by a senior executive, a consultant, or other expert in a relevant field. Such information may be supplemented by visits made by the board as a whole to various locations.

Occasional and non-routine sources of information

Some agenda items may call for special reports with information that is required by all of the directors. Ad hoc papers can then be developed for these items. For example, a proposal for a major capital investment, a report on an on-going project such as a reorganization, or an acquisition proposal would all require one or more specific non-routine reports.

A professional chair will not assume that the information needs of all directors can be met by a standard set of routine board papers, however comprehensive. Some directors need information that others already have. A good chair, as the Cadbury Report recommended, should ensure that each director is adequately briefed on every item on the agenda to contribute to the board's deliberations. Such briefings might be with the chair, the CEO, chief finance officer (CFO), or a divisional, regional, or departmental head, the company's auditors, its lawyers, management consultants working with the firm, or other relevant professional advisers. If independent non-executive directors are allowed to approach company staff below board level for information, a clear policy is needed to ensure that managerial authority is not compromised. Courses, tutorials, and mentoring can also provide sources of information for directors.

Director information systems

Many formal board and board committee reports are still provided on paper, particularly in smaller companies. However, in the ten years since the first edition of this book, there have been significant developments in the electronic provision of board information. Portable electronic communication devices are changing the way in which directors are informed. The IT industry has produced some useful tools to facilitate board support, including the compilation and distribution of board papers. Board portals, combined with advanced spreadsheets, word-processing, and database software, can now provide directors with online information that replicates hard-copy board papers. The internet is emerging as the foremost vehicle for handling corporate information.

Devices such as smartphones and tablets are providing the ability to access director-level data anytime, anywhere, at less cost, and often with the facility to annotate the screen with personal notes.

A number of programs have been written that present board papers on the screen. The applications now available include BoardPacks,[8] BoardPad,[9] BoardVantage,[10] and Diligent Boardbooks.[11]

In considering an electronic solution as an alternative to traditional board papers, a number of issues need to be considered.

1. *Confidentiality*—corporate information at board level needs to be sacrosanct, being commercially valuable and share-price-sensitive. Organizational, physical, and technological security measures need to be in place, effective, and regularly tested. Directors' passwords need to be seen as extremely valuable keys to strategic data and not noted down on post-it notes on the iPad. Information transmitted as email attachments carries too high a security risk for board-level strategic information.

2. *Security*—service providers need to demonstrate that they operate to the highest security standards at all times and in all locations. To be trusted to host sensitive board materials, suppliers' systems need to be designed to meet the stringent security requirements in industries such as banking, defence, and health. Where client databases are hosted on service providers' systems and transmitted over publicly accessible channels, particular reassurance is needed. The WikiLeaks and other disclosures show that hackers can breach the most stringent security walls. But even where dedicated corporate intranet systems are used, special care is needed when board-level data is involved. Controls at the corporate level need to be in place against the loss of data, for example from hacking, system failure, error, or theft. Right of access to the information needs to be rigorously defined and policed through access controls such as PINs, passwords, and codes, which should be changed frequently.

3. *Integrity*—the accuracy, robustness, and stability of corporate information, at the level of both the internet server and the local communication devices, needs to be ensured.

4. *Availability*—access to all files of data needs to be assured at all times and everywhere in the world that access might be needed. With communication systems reliant on satellite or ocean cable links, this can prove to be quite a challenge.

5. *Assurance*—compatibility with the US auditing standards (Statement SAS No. 70) confirms that service providers' control activities, servers, and processes have been audited to meet the standard as this reassurance is disclosed to their customers and their customers' auditors.

6. *Cost-effectiveness*—detailed cost–benefit studies need to be undertaken before dropping hard-copy paper delivery of board papers. For example, the costs of mobile communications across international borders can be high.

7. *Flexibility, simplicity, and ease of use* of the paperless system should be at least as good as that of the printed page.

The significant advantages of online access to board information are that it is timely, easy to update, and usually costs less. Some older directors, and perhaps a few not so old, will still

[8] www.boardpacks.com
[9] www.boardpad.com
[10] www.boardvantage.com
[11] www.boardbooks.com

prefer paper reports. In introducing a paperless system, training, experience, and patience will be required. In the early stages, information could be provided in tandem with both hard-copy and electronic access. When the paperless system is operational, companies should seek feedback, review regularly, and update as necessary.

Director-level information systems, which enable individual directors to access company files from remote locations and to seek answers to questions about the business situation, are in the relatively early stages of development. Such facilities go far beyond providing directors with corporate reports online. They provide access to the company databases. At issue, how-ever, is how to provide access to the material that the director needs in order to be appropri-ately informed, while preventing the tendency to 'drill down' into the data to obtain material that is far too detailed and irrelevant to a director's needs. But, in a world of increasingly sophisticated hacking of information systems, ensuring that confidentiality is maintained and that security is protected is vital.

Such systems have the potential to change the nature of director information. Routine reports, in which management (the company secretary, the CEO, CFO, etc.) decide what directors need to know and produce reports accordingly, are essentially one-way—company to director. Face-to-face communication and question-and-answer opportunities provide a two-way link. When directors can search for the information they feel they need, the direction becomes director to company.

Board information audit

A board information audit is a useful exercise. The framework that was introduced in Chap-ter 2 (see Figure 2.6), when applied as in Table 16.1, can be used as a checklist for analysing the extent and quality of board information. The audit would review the extent and nature of information made available at board level in each segment of the quadrant. What is the source? Is it adequate? What is its quality? How might it be improved in content, presenta-tion, or availability? Can all directors readily access any information they might need, given the extent of their knowledge of the company, its business, and its strategic context?

In strategy formulation, for example, is each director adequately briefed on the firm's stra-tegic situation—its markets, distribution, customers, competitors, its suppliers and sources of finance, the labour market, the political, economic, social, and technological environment in all of the countries in which the firm operates? Is that knowledge current?

In policy-making, is every director familiar with the firm's policies and able to contribute fully to discussions when they are reviewed? Do directors have the background knowledge, for example, about labour relations, trades unions, product safety, or credit control, to take an informed view of corporate policies?

In most organizations, the management information and control systems, rooted in the on-going transactions of the business, report on the performance and the state of internal resourc-es. Board-level reporting of recent performance for monitoring and management supervision is most fully developed. As we saw in Chapter 14, boards too readily concentrate on manage-ment supervision and control, because that highlights issues that need immediate board action. Nevertheless, it is also frequently an area in which reporting systems can be improved.

Accountability, reporting to the outside world, has tended to be the least well-developed segment of board-level information. Of course, companies must satisfy the minimum disclosure requirements of company laws and stock market listing rules. But for many companies, reporting in a narrative beyond financial matters, including detailed strategic plans and projections, corporate social responsibility and sustainability reporting, and risk analysis, is still evolving.

The review of the current director-level information should be documented and discussed with those involved, looking for improvements. Consider the sensitivity of each piece of information and confirm that existing confidentiality controls are adequate. Also review the cost of providing access. The documentation produced by a board information audit can provide the start of an exercise to put board data online. A danger in director-level reporting is that reports produce more data, but not more information. In fact, what is needed is not even more information, but better-informed directors, better able to contribute to the board's activities, and to produce better-quality discussion, and more successful decisions.

Managing meetings, agenda, and minutes

Meetings need planning as well as running. Meetings also need management and leadership. Meetings of the board and its committees should be learning experiences for all involved. The basic considerations in planning a meeting involve the questions: why, what, when, where, and who? The first questions—'why?' and 'what?'—are not often asked by the chair when calling a meeting. Why is it being called? Clarify its purpose and, also, what it is intended to achieve. Sometimes a meeting may not be necessary at all. At other times, consideration of the purpose can avoid repetitive and time-wasting issues being brought up and discussed.

The question 'when?' highlights the need to give adequate notice of the meeting. Some meetings, such as the annual general meeting of shareholders, have the minimum period of notice determined by statute, corporate constitution, or standing orders. Notice may also have to be in writing. Whether notice by email will suffice is a matter for the law of the jurisdiction.

The question 'where?' emphasizes that not all meetings need to be held in the conventional location, typically the boardroom. Holding an occasional company board meeting in one of the other locations of the company—a divisional headquarters, or a regional location—can provide an opportunity for directors to learn from first-hand experience and meet the personnel, for whom the arrival and interest of the directors can be motivating. Meetings are increasingly held by teleconference. Provided that proper attention is given to notice, agenda, and chairing, and given that the technical facilities are appropriate, such meetings can bring together members from different locations, saving travel time and expense.

Finally, the question 'who?' makes the point that other people, in addition to the board members, can be invited to attend meetings, either for specific items or for the whole meeting on a non-voting basis. Such people could include those who have relevant information to present to the board and whom directors might question, those who can relay board discussion and decisions to others, and also potential future directors as part of their learning experience and development. In some public organizations, members of the public have the right to attend meetings of the council, governing body, or committee. Of course, subject to the constitution, parts of such meetings may be held in private (*in camera*).

An agenda is a list of the items of business to be covered in a meeting. The decision regarding what matters get on the agenda can be a crucial issue in boards playing political games. So who should decide each item on the agenda? The final decision should rest with the chair, but in many cases the company secretary and/or the CEO make suggestions. Professional chairs give all members of the board the opportunity to ask for matters to be discussed and arrange a periodic review of matters covered. For the comments of experienced chairs on building an agenda, see Corporate Governance in Action 16.3 and 16.4.

Corporate Governance in Action 16.3   Lord Caldecote on building an agenda

Lord Caldecote, when chair of the Delta Group, wrote to each of his directors periodically to ask whether there were matters they felt that the board should be discussing for the future benefit of the firm. 'In the past year, what have we not discussed that we should have discussed?' he would ask, 'and how could I improve my chairing of our meetings?'

Corporate Governance in Action 16.4   Another opinion on drafting agenda and minutes

The head of an Oxford college, after a career in the British civil service, believed that good chairs, among whom he counted himself, should put much effort into designing an agenda. Care should be taken in choosing the items to be discussed; attention given to the time allocated to each, and in their positioning on the agenda. Matters likely to be controversial should come towards the end, he recommended, when members were expecting the meeting to end, or had already left, thus increasing the chair's chances of getting the decision he or she wanted. This chair also drafted the minutes along with the agenda, because he believed that a good chair always has a preferred outcome. He knew that those who draft the minutes wield the power. His colleagues had to agree.

Three approaches to agenda design can be distinguished:

- the routine approach, in which each meeting follows the pattern of the previous (apologies, approval of the minutes of the last meeting, matters arising from those minutes, the usual substantive items—such as the financial and operating reports—and any other business);
- the chair-led approach, in which the chair determines the agenda and probably dominates the meeting;
- the professional approach, in which the chair seeks advice from relevant people about the agenda, and takes great care in balancing the items and ensuring that adequate time is available for a competent discussion and sound resolution of each issue.

Another important role for the chair prior to the meeting is to ensure that all directors have adequate information and are properly briefed, if necessary, on each item on the agenda. Directors cannot opt out of certain items because they lack appropriate knowledge, although they may rely on information received and the opinions of fellow directors, given in good faith, unless they have any reason to doubt—in which case, they must pursue the issue to its root. Similarly, a director may rely on information from a board subcommittee, unless unsure, in which case again the director has a duty to pursue the issue until satisfied.

The minutes are the formal record of a meeting. Although, subject to the articles, there are no specific rules governing the content or format of minutes of board or board subcommittee meetings, they should provide a competent and complete record of what transpired, what was decided, and what actions are to be taken by whom and when. Should there be any future challenge, the minutes, which have been duly approved as a true and fair report at a subsequent meeting, can be used as strong evidence of what was intended.

Companies tend to develop their own style in minute-keeping. Some boards note the names of the key contributors to the discussion; others do not. In some cases, it has to be admitted, the minutes are no more than a staccato record of who attended and what was decided. At the other extreme, there are minutes that are almost a verbatim report of the proceedings, complete with stage directions. The ideal lies between the two. Minutes should contain sufficient information to capture the key threads of the discussion, any disclosures of personal interest, the alternatives considered, the agreement reached, and plans and responsibilities for action. The person responsible for writing the minutes potentially wields considerable power, although typically minutes of the last meeting are approved and can be challenged at the following meeting.

A few boards video-record their meetings. This can help in writing the minutes, but, if used as a record of proceedings, may inhibit discussion. In a few companies, minutes are occasionally created for meetings that did not take place, in order to meet statutory requirements. This is bad practice, as is the backdating of minutes, which could be considered fraudulent.

Communications with shareholders and other stakeholders

Demonstrating accountability is one of the four principal elements of the board's role, the way in which it proves its performance. Corporate transparency is increasingly demanded by investors, other stakeholders, and society generally. But companies' approach to their interaction with their shareholders and the wider world vary considerably among:

- the minimum disclosure necessary to satisfy statutory requirements, including companies' legislation, auditing and accounting standards, and, for listed companies, the demands of the stock exchange's rules;
- a directors' report and financial accounts that go beyond the minimum statutory requirements by reporting corporate activities and major developments, but make no attempt to comment on the company's strategic situation, its risk profile, or its prospects—for listed companies, this approach would not meet the demands of corporate governance codes or stock exchange rules, but there are still a few markets where this is feasible; for private companies, such an attitude is feasible if all shareholders are compliant;

- a recognition that the annual report and accounts, together with other periodic shareholder communications, provide a way of presenting the company, its products, policies, and processes as part of an on-going public relations and advertising policy;

- a board-level communications policy, which identifies and differentiates audiences for the company's communications, establishes the purpose and the appropriate content of communications to each, and uses a wide range of different media. (Such a policy enables the success of board-level communications to be assessed and developed where appropriate.)

Poor corporate reporting, to be avoided, includes:

- making statements of the obvious, including 'boilerplate' statements that the board supports sound corporate governance;

- mixing compliance statements that are 'required' with the 'story' of the report—the statements can be put in boxes, so that the report flows;

- referring back to the last report to show changes.

Some countries now require major companies to include a commentary on the company's situation, strategies, prospects, and perceived risks.

Where a company has a board-level communications policy, it is likely to identify a range of potential audiences for corporate communications, including:

- existing and potential shareholders, perhaps recognizing that the interests, knowledge, and skills of small retail investors are likely to be different from those of institutional investors, and attempts to produce material that will satisfy both may satisfy neither;

- for listed companies, the stock market, financial analysts, the financial press, and other media; for companies in a group, the interests of the holding company; for other private companies, the expectations and needs of minority shareholders, family members, and potential acquirers;

- regulators, including those appointed under companies legislation, mergers and acquisition law, competition and monopoly law; for listed companies, the requirements of the listing rules, tax authorities, and national and international financial regulators, including money laundering controls;

- for other stakeholders, the interests of customers and the marketplace for the company's products and services, those of middle management, employees and their trades unions, of suppliers and others in the company's added-value chain, and of providers of non-equity funds. (Such a policy projects a coherent corporate image and supports the corporate culture.)

Having identified a wide range of those who might be interested in corporate communications, it is a small step to accepting that different content and means of delivery might be required. Companies with a professional board-level communications policy recognize that a traditional directors' report and financial accounts will not suffice: the inevitable and increasing complexity of financial reporting may satisfy the financially sophisticated, but is too complex for many others.

Consequently, some companies attempt to produce summaries or separate documents to satisfy the needs of different audiences. Where this is done, it is vital, of course, for the various documents to correspond and to conform to regulatory requirements. Other companies adopt a range of communication media including:

- the delivery of statutory information to shareholders electronically, which company law in some jurisdictions now permits—this option has opened a range of new opportunities for communicating with shareholders and, if necessary, receiving responses, such as proxy votes; information available might include the periodic financial statements, stock exchange announcements, newsletters and factsheets, and messages from the chair, CEO, or other corporate officials;

- corporate websites giving access to a wide range of information about the company;

- CD-ROMs, telecasts, and video distribution of shareholder meetings, briefings, and other presentations;

- use of Twitter, Facebook, and other social media for pages of company information and commentary;

- access to company directors and officers by email and the company's website.

While printed documents distributed through the mail are likely to remain a significant vehicle for board-level communication, companies with a professional communications policy will be continuously looking for new opportunities to improve their communications and to reduce their costs.

Case studies

 Case study 16.1 Explaining the structure and membership of the board

In 1998, after a successful career as a researcher at the Massachusetts Institute of Technology (MIT), Dr Jeremy Cunniford decided to branch out on his own to research, develop, and test batteries based on lithium ion technology, in which he had acquired an international reputation.[12] He negotiated funding from a well-known manufacturer of electronic equipment for an initial five years, on the understanding that patents derived from his work would belong to the sponsor, while Cunniford would receive funding for his research, a generous salary, a commission on related sales, and the promise of shares if the project succeeded and a business was floated on the stock market or sold.

Cunniford took a lease on a small research facility near Mountain View, in Silicon Valley, and recruited a few staff, including one of his former MIT colleagues, Bruce Lamb. Initially, the research group was funded through a subsidiary of the sponsor based in Switzerland. In 2003, after the initial five years, the project was reviewed. A number of patents had been obtained, at least one thought to have considerable potential. The sponsor seemed content with progress and what it described as 'the rate of burn' of project funding: as far as they were concerned this was research and development

[12] The names and some of the details in this case have been disguised.

expenditure done on their behalf by an independent contractor in whom they had a lot of faith. Looking ahead for the next decade, the sponsor decided that the project should now be launched as a private company, Cunniford Batteries Inc., with 10 per cent of the shares going to Cunniford, 5 per cent to Lamb, and the balance to the sponsoring group.

Around 2008, it became apparent that a range of batteries, based on new technology developed by Cunniford Batteries, had made a breakthrough. Lithium ion batteries had become important in aviation electronics and the Cunniford design was more efficient, lighter, and less of a fire hazard than its competitors. The company now entered a manufacturing cycle, as well as continuing its research and development activities.

In 2013, the parent company decided that the time had come to launch their subsidiary, Cunniford Batteries, on the stock market, through an initial public offering. This generated additional funds to support the continuing growth of the company and provide a reward for over 15 years of investment support. The sponsoring group would take 45 per cent of the equity, Cunniford 10 per cent, and Lamb 5 per cent, with three significant institutional investors taking the remaining 40 per cent. The sponsor group formalized an agreement to use Cunniford products and to continue to have access to Cunniford research.

The challenge

In 2017, the company received a proxy request from one of the institutional investors calling for 'an explanation of the structure and membership of the board and whether it was representative'. Jeremy Cunniford asked the corporate secretary to draft a paper for discussion at the next board meeting. What follows is that paper.

Cunniford Batteries Inc.

Board meeting 10 December 2017

Agendum 17. *To discuss the future structure and membership of the board*

The company has received a formal request from a shareholder for 'an explanation of the structure and membership of the board and whether it was representative'. Jeremy has asked me to draft this paper to provide the basis for a board discussion prior to our response.

Reasonably, our major shareholders want to ensure that our governance structure is consistent with the planned growth of the company. Our corporate strategy looks to significant growth over the next five years, followed by accelerating expansion in the next five, despite the inevitable uncertainties and risks in our industry. We are also required by the Securities and Exchange Commission to explain our policies on nominating directors, including our attitudes towards diversity. Currently, we have no formal policy on such matters.

Current structure and membership of the board

Inevitably, our board reflects the evolution of the company, and currently consists of:

Executive directors

Jeremy Cunniford III (1966–) Chairman and CEO, PhD MIT 1996, senior researcher MIT 1996–1998, formed independent research team 1998.
Bruce Lamb (1970–) Chief Research Officer, PhD MIT 1998, joined Cunniford's research team 1998.
Peter Bennett (1964–) CPA, Chief Finance Officer.

Independent outside directors

Robert T. Jones (1944–) CPA, retired senior partner from the sponsoring company's audit firm.
Henry G. George (1950–) lawyer, nominated by the sponsoring company.
Anthony P. Parker (1945–) financier, prominent in the IPO flotation, nominated by one of the institutional investors.

Size and structure of the board

Role and size of the board

The real challenge we face is deciding what we expect the board to do, and whether we have the appropriate mix of experience and skills. We have the statutory board committees in place—audit, remuneration, and nomination—and they fulfil their compliance and reporting duties. Main board meetings have tended to be opportunities for the chair/CEO to report progress on research projects, and for the CFO to explain the financial situation. Annually, prior to the AGM we have a longer meeting to receive the auditor's report, to approve the published accounts, and to discuss and agree the budgets for the following year.

There are no legal restrictions on the number of directors on our board. We could add further members if that was felt appropriate, but a larger board would inevitably change the interpersonal dynamics. Large boards, with lots of independent directors, can be difficult to handle, with diverse views and potential domination by strong characters.

The shareholder's request for an explanation of the structure and membership of the board does not, necessarily, mean that they are looking for significant changes at board level. They may be seeking assurance that we have policies in place to review board membership that are consistent with our business strategy.

Executive directors

As our organization grows, it might be appropriate to identify potential main board directors from within top management. The nomination committee could propose a short-list reflecting the structure of the organization planned for the future. We might feel the need for board-level representation from our growing product division. We could ensure that those selected are given appropriate responsibilities, experience, and training for directorship. They could be invited to attend board meetings as observers, for example.

Independent outside directors

If we add more executive directors, we would need to increase the number of outside directors to maintain the proportion of independent directors required by the listing rules. The nomination committee could also be asked to produce a short-list of candidates. At the moment, our outside directors are heavy on the financial and legal side. We might consider whether a technical expert in our field of research would be useful: perhaps from one of the universities we have contracted out research. Of course, we could continue to rely on the advice of consultants and other experts, as we do now; this means we can dispense with their services when no longer needed—not so easy with elected directors.

Chairman and CEO

Since the company was first incorporated, we have combined the roles of chairman of the board and chief executive of the company. This has worked well, with a single leader as its figurehead, directing the company's efforts. However, we may need to consider whether this is the best model for the longer term. Companies are coming under some pressure to split the roles, perhaps with a non-executive chairman. This issue may be concerning the shareholder who asked for information on board *structure and membership*.

On board diversity

The challenge to show that the board is 'representative' raises some interesting issues. Board diversity can have a number of meanings.

Diversity of skills, experience, and knowledge

If a board is to work well together it needs to have a balance of skills, experience, and knowledge relevant to the company's business. Our leading executive directors are both research-orientated, reflecting the company's origins. The nomination committee may want to consider whether this will be appropriate in the future. Similarly, the balance of skills among the outside directors is strongly in the financial and legal fields.

Age diversity

Our present executive directors are aged 44, 48, and 50; and continue to serve the company well. The outside directors are older being 64, 69, and 70. We may want to establish a policy for board renewal over time, bringing in younger people with fresh ideas and experiences, both as executive and non-executive directors.

Gender diversity

Gender diversity is a goal being pursued by many governments, institutions, and interest groups to achieve better representation of women at board level. Some board members and investors have been unenthusiastic, calling for the best candidates irrespective of gender, despite the obvious missed talent and benefits of a female perspective. Overall, however, North American companies have appointed women to their boards in recent years: the Federal Reserve, the International Monetary Fund, and General Motors are now all led by women.

Our problem is that although there are women in middle management, we have no one in senior management who might be earmarked for executive directorship. Of course, there are experienced women we could consider as outside directors. We may want to include in our policy a statement about our commitment to appointing suitable women to the board.

Representative diversity

On a higher plane, some commentators suggest that boards should reflect the interests of all stakeholders affected by companies' actions—employees, suppliers, customers, for example—not just the shareholders. Some have even called for corporate boards to mirror the diversity of society. Our company is probably too small to consider such matters. However, we are already committed to being good corporate citizens and might consider creating a corporate social responsibility, sustainability, and environmental committee of representative employees, led by a director, to make recommendations to the board on these matters.

Proposal

That the nomination committee be asked to develop a policy on the structure and characteristics of the board and board members for further discussion.

Discussion questions

1. What are your reactions to the paper presented to the board?

2. Draft a policy statement that the nomination committee might propose to the main board.

Case study 16.2   The corporate culture at Goldman Sachs

Founded in 1869, the Goldman Sachs Group is headquartered in New York and maintains offices in all major financial centres around the world, including London. The firm provides investment banking, institutional client services, financing, and investment management to a substantial client base of companies, financial institutions, and high-net-worth individuals. The Group has over 30,000 employees worldwide and produces around US$30 billion in revenue and US$2.5 billion in profit.

The corporate website describes the firm's activities:[13]

- advising companies on buying and selling businesses, raising capital, and managing risks, which enables them to grow;
- helping local, state, and national governments finance their operations so they can invest in infrastructure, like schools, hospitals, and roads;
- transacting in all key financial markets for clients, including equities, bonds, currencies, and commodities, so that capital flows, jobs are created and economies can grow;
- helping markets remain efficient and liquid, so investors and companies can meet their needs, whether to invest, raise money, or manage risk;
- preserving and growing assets for institutions, including mutual funds, pension funds, and foundations, as well as individuals;
- investing our capital alongside our clients' capital to help businesses grow;
- developing ideas and analysis that drive new perspectives, new products, and new paths to growth.

The firm was a partnership until 1999, when the partners decided to go public.

Initially, only a small portion of the shares were listed, but after further stock offerings Goldman Sachs is now owned around 70 per cent by institutional investors. The first chair and CEO of the company was Henry Paulson, who left in 2006 to become US Treasury Secretary. Lloyd C. Blankfein replaced him, receiving a bonus of US$67.9 million in his first year, some of which he took in cash, unlike Paulson who had taken his bonus entirely in company stock.

Goldman Sachs is one of the most prestigious investment banks in the world, but since the global financial crisis began in 2007, its business practices, ethics, and culture have been questioned.

Goldman Sachs profits from the sub-prime mortgage crisis

In the sub-prime mortgage market, banks provided loans to high-risk customers against their property, sometimes at over 100 per cent of the property's current value, in the belief that it would increase. The banks then bundled their mortgages together and sold them on as bonds to investors. Many believed that they were spreading and thus reducing their exposure to risk. A few commentators, however, warned that rather than reducing risk, derivatives merely spread the risk and made tracing the underlying assets more difficult.

Goldman Sachs created structured products called collateralized debt obligations (CDOs), which it sold to investors around the world. CDOs were pools of bonds backed by bundles of mortgages. CDO volume grew dramatically between 2000 and 2006. As long as global investors had the confidence to buy them, all was well.

---

[13] For more on Goldman Sachs, see www.goldmansachs.com. Financial accounts are at www.goldmansachs.com/investor-relations/financials/index.html

Then in 2007 the property market began to collapse. Starting in the United States, property prices fell, and borrowers found themselves in negative equity, their properties now worth less than their loans. Doubts about the worth of sub-prime mortgages grew. Uncertainty about the bonds and CDOs derived from them spread. Global investors were no longer prepared to risk their funds. The source of financial liquidity had dried up. The sub-prime market crisis had arrived and spread quickly around the world as banks were unable to raise funds.

Some Goldman Sachs traders foresaw the potential worsening position in the sub-prime market and began to sell CDOs short: that is they contracted to sell them at a lower price on a future date. The firm claims that this was prudent hedging to protect their position. Others criticized them for 'betting' against their own clients, gambling that the price would fall as the derivative market collapsed. As that happened Goldman Sachs was able to write down its losses from sub-prime securitized loans it held by offsetting gains on its shorted market position.

Goldman Sachs made substantial profits from the sub-prime mortgage crisis, rather than being caught out like many other financial institutions. The *New York Times* lauded its financial prowess. But in 2009 the paper also told the story of how the firm had created CDOs, sold them to investors, and then bet short against them. Goldman Sachs claimed that its investors knew it was betting against the products it was selling to them.

The Goldman Sachs culture

William D. Cohan, who won the 2007 FT/Goldman Sachs Business Book of the year award, subsequently wrote a penetrating book about Goldman Sachs.[14] In it he quotes a Goldman banker: 'The people who are going to be successful at Goldman are the folks who are prepared to sacrifice all. All. Everything. To the greater glory.' Cohan explained: 'Goldman takes only the brightest and the best . . . academic success is not enough. Each job applicant has to be thoroughly investigated by the reputational risk department. The hours are famously punishing. Cars collect senior executives at 5.30 a.m. Breakfast, lunch, and dinner are taken at desks. Breaks are unheard of. Brokers routinely work past midnight. Bosses expect you to be available nothing less than 24-7. The answer to why so many staff keep going is money ... huge bonuses that will set them up financially for life.' The success of such experience can be seen as former Goldman employees went on to head the New York Stock Exchange, the World Bank, the US Treasury Department, the White House staff, as well as major banks and financial institutions.

But this demanding culture had its downside. In March 2012, the *New York Times* published, as an opinion piece, a resignation letter from Greg Smith,[15] the former head of Goldman Sachs' equity derivatives business in the firm's Europe, Middle East, and Africa Division. Smith claimed that the firm was 'morally bankrupt'. 'The decline in the firm's moral fibre,' he wrote, 'was due to Chairman/Chief Executive Officer Lloyd Blankfein and President Gary Cohn.' They had changed the company's culture from 'the secret sauce that made this place great and allowed us to earn our clients' trust' to a 'toxic culture' in which 'the interests of the client continue to be sidelined'. Colleagues talked about 'ripping their clients off', and senior management described clients as 'muppets'—a reference to amusingly stupid puppets created for TV's *The Muppet Show* in the United Kingdom and Sesame Street in the United States. A friend of Smith's said that, by resigning, Smith had thrown away his career for his principles. 'I admire the man and I admire his courage. But there's no way I'd do that myself.'

[14] Cohan, William D. (2011) *Money and Power: How Goldman Sachs Came to Rule the World*, Anchor Books, Random House, New York.
[15] Smith, Greg (2012) 'Why I am leaving Goldman Sachs', *New York Times*, 14 March.

Goldman Sachs responded to the letter by saying 'we don't think [the letter] reflects the way we run our business. We will only be successful if our clients are successful.'

Discussion questions

1. What is your opinion of the board-level culture and its effect on the bankers at Goldman Sachs?

2. His friend said that by resigning, Greg Smith had thrown away his career for his principles. 'I admire the man and I admire his courage. But there's no way I'd do that myself.' What would you have done in Smith's place?

Self-test questions

1. What are the 'six Cs' for an effective board?

2. Name eight matters that new directors should know about if they have followed a properly planned orientation programme.

3. Name some issues that need to be considered before adopting an electronic paperless system for board reports.

4. What are the key questions that should be posed before calling a meeting?

5. If a director lacks appropriate knowledge on a subject before the board, can he or she, legitimately, opt out of discussions on that item?

6. Are there any specific rules governing the content or format of minutes of board or board subcommittee meetings?

7. Name five qualities of a good report with high-quality information.

8. Why should companies have a director induction programme?

9. What is D&O?

10. In a limited-liability company, are the liabilities of the directors limited?

 For suggested answers to these self-test questions visit the online resources at:
www.oup.com/uk/tricker4e/

Projects and exercises

1. Use the internet to study the websites of five companies, the names of which you know. What is your opinion of their communications? Do they seem to have a board-level communications policy? How do their communications with shareholders and other stakeholders compare?

2. Draft a set of briefing notes for directors on the following topics:
   - director orientation and director induction programmes;
   - director development, training, and updating;
   - directors' and officers' insurance.

3. Knowing that you have been studying corporate governance, the chair of an organization has asked your advice on how (s)he might improve the effectiveness of her/his governing body. Draft a letter giving some advice.

References and further reading

Brenkert, George G. and Tom L. Beauchamp (eds) (2009) *The Oxford Handbook of Business Ethics*. Oxford University Press, Oxford.

FRC (2011) Guidance on Board Effectiveness. Financial Reporting Council, London.

NACD (2005a) Board Leadership: A Report of a NACD Blue Ribbon Commission. National Association of Corporate Directors, Washington, DC.

NACD (2005b) Director Liability: Myths, Realities, and Prevention—A Report of a NACD Blue Ribbon Commission. National Association of Corporate Directors, Washington, DC.

NACD (2005c) Governance Committee: Driving Board Performance—A Report of a NACD Blue Ribbon Commission. National Association of Corporate Directors, Washington, DC.

Steger, Ulrich and Wolfgang Amann (2008) *Corporate Governance: Cases in Adding Value*. Wiley, Chichester.

Stiles, P. and B. Taylor (2001) *Boards at Work: How Directors View Their Roles and Responsibilities*. Oxford University Press, New York.

Wallace, Peter and John Zinken (2003) *Corporate Governance*. Mastering Business in Asia series, John Wiley, Singapore.

Board Evaluation: Reviewing Directors and Boards

 Learning Outcomes

This chapter enables us to:

- Understand the assessment of boards and board committees.
- Appreciate what a board assessment involves.
- Assess individual directors' performance.
- Study corporate governance rating systems for companies.
- Compare corporate governance assessment systems.

Assessing boards and board committees

The corporate governance rules of the New York Stock Exchange require boards of listed companies to conduct a self-evaluation at least annually to determine whether the board and its committees are functioning effectively. The US National Association of Corporate Directors has recommended that all boards introduce formal procedures to assess both their own collective performance and that of individual directors.

Two main principles of the UK Corporate Governance Code are that the board:

- should undertake a formal and rigorous annual evaluation of its own performance and that of its committees and individual directors;
- should state in the annual report how the performance evaluation of the board, its committees, and its individual directors has been conducted.

Supporting principles encourage the chair to act on the results of the performance evaluation by recognizing the strengths and addressing the weaknesses of the board, and, where appropriate, proposing new members be appointed to the board or seeking the resignation of directors. Further, individual evaluation should aim to show whether each director continues to contribute effectively and to demonstrate commitment to the role (including commitment of time for board and committee meetings and any other duties).

Corporate governance codes in many other countries now have similar requirements. An extension to the UK Corporate Governance Code required the evaluation of the board of FTSE 350 companies to be *externally* facilitated at least every three years. A statement is also required explaining whether the external facilitator has any other connection with the company.

Of course, companies in countries with voluntary corporate governance codes can refuse to follow the code principles, explaining why they have not done so in their corporate governance report. A continuing challenge is how to ensure compliance with the spirit, as well as the letter, of corporate governance codes.

The UK Stewardship Code (2010) published by the Financial Reporting Council (FRC) states that:

> institutional investors should monitor investee companies to determine when it is necessary to enter into an active dialogue with their boards. This monitoring should be regular and the process clearly communicable and checked periodically for its effectiveness. As part of this monitoring, institutional investors should:
>
> - seek to satisfy themselves ... that the investee company's board and committee structures are effective, and that independent directors provide adequate oversight, including by meeting the chairman and, where appropriate, other board members;
> - maintain a clear audit trail, for example, records of private meetings held with companies, of votes cast, and of reasons for voting against the investee company's management, for abstaining, or for voting with management in a contentious situation; and
> - attend the General Meetings of companies in which they have a major holding, where appropriate and practicable.

Institutional investors should consider carefully explanations given if companies in which they invest depart from the UK Corporate Governance Code and make reasoned judgements in each case. They should give a timely explanation to the company, in writing where appropriate, and be prepared to enter a dialogue if they do not accept the company's position. In effect, the FRC was calling on institutional investors to support it in applying the stewardship code and to take a proactive role in their relations with companies.

When board assessment was first introduced, some directors faced the prospect with trepidation. But experience has shown that a board with strong and respected leadership, with directors who trust each other, and which is directing a successful enterprise, finds the exercise worthwhile and the experience rewarding. Unfortunately, on the other hand, experience also suggests that a poorly led board, with directors in disagreement, leading an organization that is failing to meet its goals, finds the process antagonistic and the outcome potentially catastrophic.

Interestingly, research has shown that the typical corporate governance indicators, such as board structure, the independence of directors, and the use of board committees, are not the best predictors of board effectiveness. Rather, less specific indicators, sometimes called 'soft' governance, such as the working relationships between directors, the standard of chairing, or directors' knowledge of the company, were found to be more significant.

Why undertake a board review? The worst response is 'because we are required to by the regulations'. A more positive response would be that 'we see the review as a fundamental part of our corporate governance strategy, which forms part of our overall corporate strategy'.

Sir Bryan Nicholson, when he was chair of the FRC,[1] commented:

> ... the evaluation process is particularly important. It provides the opportunity for companies to create a virtuous circle of sustained improvement in board effectiveness based on

---

[1] Between 2001 and 2005. Sir Win Bischoff was appointed Chairman of the FRC in May 2014. He was previously Chairman of Lloyds Banking Group from 2009.

regular objective assessment of past performance and the company's changing needs and circumstances. It introduces a new dynamic which companies can use to improve the quality of their corporate governance and secure competitive advantage.

A competent and regular board performance review can:

- check whether directors' knowledge of the business and its strategic situation is up to date;
- review the board structure, including board diversity and the balance between independent outside directors and executive directors;
- assess the balance of skills, knowledge, and experience on the board and its committees;
- identify director weaknesses to be remedied by director training and development, or by additional or replacement board members;
- review current board and board committee practices, including directors' access to information and opportunities to improve efficiency;
- review the effectiveness of the board's strategic thinking, risk management, and decision-making;
- provide an on-going challenge to attitudes in boards with long-serving directors;
- confirm the succession plan for the board is current and create the climate for change particularly if a change of chair is needed;
- review the quality of reporting and announcements to the market, for listed companies;
- confirm that the company is compliant with all relevant law, regulations and, where appropriate, listing rules, including the disclosure of directors' interests and controls on insider dealing;
- provide information for the board's corporate governance report and respond to questions from shareholders and other legitimate stakeholders.

A board review holds up a mirror to the board, its behaviour, and its performance. It is as important for well-performing boards as for those that are not performing well. A board review should take a strategic perspective, considering the directors' ability to handle long-term issues as well as reflecting on recent experience in the short term. Otherwise the board may not be adapting to the company's changing strategic situation. The board review process to be explored later in this chapter takes just such a strategic perspective. The entire review process is set in the context of the overall corporate strategy and leads to a corporate governance strategy. The outcome can lead to changes in corporate governance policies and plans for board-level development.

Who should initiate the board assessment?

The board as a whole is responsible for ensuring that its company is complying with the corporate governance laws, rules, and regulations, and any other related policies that the board has agreed. The board chair should ensure that appropriate time and attention are given to such matters, which can easily be overshadowed by other claims on the board's time from pressing business issues, as we have already seen. Detailed work on the board review may be delegated to the company secretary or other officer, but the board's overall responsibility and accountability cannot be delegated. A regular corporate governance and board review ensures that all directors periodically pay attention to this area.

Who should carry out the board assessment?

In some companies, the chair assumes the role. But experience has shown that this approach lacks the independence and objectivity that a serious review really needs. Such chairs are effectively marking their own examination paper. An experienced independent director, perhaps the senior INED, could be asked to lead the work. Some boards form a special board committee, typically nominating independent directors, to undertake the review; others give the responsibility to the audit committee supported by the internal audit function. While an executive director such as the chief executive officer (CEO) or chief finance officer (CFO) will have appropriate knowledge of the business and the board, his or her perspective is unlikely to be seen as objective by other board members. Self-evaluation by boards needs initial agreement on goals, and openness and honesty from every director, including the chair. A thorough board review demands a lot of time and effort, in marshalling written material, interviewing directors and support staff, talking with auditors, institutional investors, and so on. Staff support will be needed if a board member or a committee undertakes the review.

The real concern is whether an internally driven evaluation process (particularly where it is limited to the use of questionnaires) has been objective and rigorous in every case. Adherence to an internally driven process carries with it the danger over time of the evaluation becoming devalued. This is where shareholders should be taking a closer interest.

Externally facilitated independent assessment

An alternative approach is for the board to seek an independent perspective, inviting someone outside the board to lead the review process and report. A past chair might be a possibility: he or she would have knowledge of the business, but might lack objectivity on board politics. Another possibility might be a respected chair or director from the board of another, non-competitor company.

The requirement of the UK Corporate Governance Code for the evaluation of the board to be externally facilitated at least every three years has led to the creation of specialist units in consultancy firms, executive search firms, and the formation of board assessment advisers and firms. Some professional bodies and other independent organizations also undertake board assessment projects.[2] Two caveats: executive search firms may not be entirely independent, and management consultancy projects often call for a different mindset from those dealing with board-level interactions and political processes.

[2] For a code of practice for independent external board evaluation, see www.abexcellence.com. See also National Association of Corporate Directors at www.nacdonline.org

Corporate Governance in Action 17.1   General Motors Company

Corporate governance guidelines (extracts)[3]

Paragraph 6. *Director Orientation and Continuing Education*

All new Directors must participate in the Company's director orientation program, which generally commences promptly after the meeting at which a new director is elected. The Governance Committee oversees an orientation process developed by management to familiarize new directors with the Company's business and strategic plans, significant financial matters, core values including ethics, compliance programs, corporate governance practices, and other key policies and practices through a review of background material, meetings with senior management, and visits to GM facilities. The Board also recognizes the importance of continuing education for its directors and is committed to provide such education in order to improve both Board and committee performance. Director continuing education may be provided in a variety of different forms including: external or internal education programs, presentations or briefings on particular topics, educational materials, meetings with key management and visits to GM facilities, dealers and auto shows. It is the responsibility of the Governance Committee to advise the directors about their continuing education on subjects that would assist them in discharging their duties, including leading corporate governance and automotive industry issues. Directors are encouraged to attend, at GM's expense, continuing education programs sponsored by educational and other institutions.

Paragraph 20. *Assessing the Board's Performance*

The Board conducts a self-evaluation on an annual basis, generally in the fall, to determine whether the Board and its committees are functioning effectively. The Governance Committee, working with the Chairman (or the Lead Director if the Chairman is not independent), oversees the self-evaluation process of the Board and its committees and reports an assessment of the Board's performance annually to the Board. As part of the evaluation, the Governance Committee invites director input on the contributions and performance of individual directors, including the Chairman or Lead Director. The Governance Committee usually reviews the evaluation structure prior to the meeting when the full Board conducts its evaluation during the executive session. The assessment will focus on the Board's contribution to the Company and specifically focus on areas in which the Board or management believes that the Board or any of its committees could improve. In addition, the Governance Committee utilizes the results of this evaluation process to determine whether the individuals sitting on the Board bring the skills and expertise appropriate for the Company and how they work as a group. The qualifications and performance of all Board members are considered in connection with re-nomination.

Paragraph 21. *Ethics and Conflicts of Interest*

The Board is committed to upholding the highest legal and ethical conduct in fulfilling its responsibilities. The Board expects all directors, as well as officers and employees, to act ethically at all times and to adhere to the policies set forth in 'Winning With Integrity: Our Values and Guidelines for Employee Conduct' (available on the Internet at https://investor.gm.com, under 'Corporate Governance'). The Board will not permit any waiver of any ethics policy for any director or executive officer. If an actual or potential conflict of interest arises for a director, the director will promptly inform the Chairman of the Board, Lead Director or Chair of the Governance Committee. If a significant conflict exists and cannot be resolved, the director should resign. All directors must recuse themselves from any discussion or decision affecting their business or personal interests.

[3] www.gm.com/content/dam/gm/en_us/english/Group4/InvestorsPDFDocuments/Corporate_Governance_Guidelines.pdf

What does a board assessment involve?

Some boards and their consultants take an external perspective of the corporate governance activities of the company. The review checks whether the accountability reporting demands of company legislation, codes, and stock exchange regulation are being met, and whether the reporting by the company of financial, operational, and corporate social responsibility matters to shareholders and other legitimate stakeholders is appropriate. The opinions of major shareholders, regulators, financial commentators, and others are sought. The resultant report can then be used by the board to confirm that their corporate governance conformance and reporting responsibilities are being met. However, such an approach does not address the company's corporate governance process itself.

The more thorough approach described here, in addition to ensuring that appropriate disclosure and accountability are being provided, analyses the board and committee structures, studies the strengths and weaknesses of the board, and reviews the processes of the board and its committee. The resultant report leads to a new strategy for board development and corporate governance improvement. This might include proposals to increase directors' competencies and to improve board-level performance.

Just as an enterprise may have longer-term strategies for market development, technological development, or management development, so too the board review project should lead towards an agreed strategy for board and corporate governance development. Because the review will affect all of the members of the board, it is vital for all directors to understand fully the project's objectives, the processes, and the intended outputs. Moreover, it is essential that every director is committed to the project. Lack of commitment by a director can easily lead to poor cooperation in the project, unwelcome political manoeuvres, and unhelpful criticism of the proposals.

A real danger in long-serving boards is that members all grow older together and become increasingly out of touch with the dynamics of the organization and the strategic situation of the underlying business. A successful company over the long term may well have long-standing retainers whose focus is on the past. A rigorous board review will highlight any such possibility.

The process now to be described establishes the board review in the context of the overall corporate strategy. See the flowchart (Figure 17.1), which we will consider section by section. This schema depicts the elements of a board review and assessment. We can now work through the stages to see what is involved.

The chair has an important role in establishing an enthusiastic climate for the study and the report's conclusions. The strategic focus of the study should be emphasized: it is not only reviewing existing corporate governance and board activities, but also looking forward to developing strategies and policies for the future. A strategic time horizon should be established, which links the corporate governance and board development strategy with the other elements of the company's overall corporate strategy. In this way, the board development strategy will be consistent with the overall corporate strategy. For example, if the corporate strategy calls for strategic developments in new technologies, new markets, new territories, or new forms of finance during the life of that strategy, the board development strategy will ask whether the board's composition and processes will be adequate to these challenges.

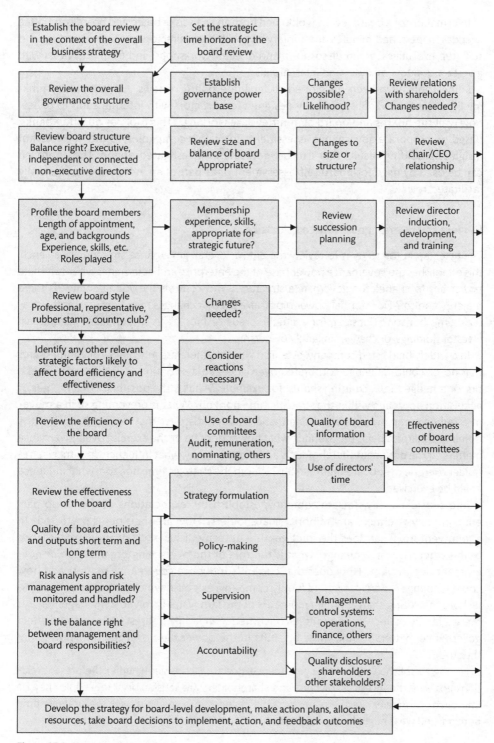

Figure 17.1 Elements of a board review

Information for a board review is obtained from an analysis of board and board committee agendas, papers, and minutes, from interviews with each director, company secretary, and staff, top executives, group discussions, and director workshops, and from interviews with investors, auditors, analysts, and internal staff.

Some tools have been developed to facilitate board reviews. For example, 'Thinking Board' is a web tool specifically designed for directors with internal audit to review how well the boards and board committees are working.[4] This tool has question banks, based on corporate governance assessments for major companies, to provide relevant insights, providing results that can be viewed and investigated online. The approach can be used by itself for board self-assessment or as part of an independent, externally facilitated review.

Review the overall governance structure

The first step in the study is to review the entity's overall governance structure. In essence, this establishes the governance power base of the enterprise and determines where ultimate power lies to change the governance structure. Who controls the voting equity? Is there majority control? Do informal power blocks exist? What changes might occur over the strategic time horizon? Consider, for example, predator bids, shifts in dominant institutional investor holdings, or changes in family ownership.

In a widely held listed company, establish whether there are any blocks of voting shares that do or could influence corporate governance: an association of institutional investors, or a hedge fund acquiring shares, for example. What is the possibility of a merger or acquisition approach within the strategic time horizon? What is preventing such a move? In a public company with a dominant shareholder, discover that investor's aims. If the dominant shareholder is the founder, what power does he or she exercise over governance matters? If the dominant shareholder is a parent company, what influence does that shareholder exercise over board membership? Within the strategic time horizon, what influence could be exercised?

In a subsidiary or associate company, establish the expectations of the group parent company. Are there any minority shareholders? How are their rights protected? In a joint venture, what does the joint venture agreement have to say about governance of the enterprise? In a quango, what is the role of the overseeing organization or government department? How does that currently influence governance matters and how could it change? In a closely held family company, establish which branches of the family hold the voting shares. Which members of the family are involved in management? Is there a family council or committee concerned with family interests, which could affect governance matters? Could there be shifts in the power base over the time horizon of the study?

Having established the existing governance structure, consider whether the present relationships with the investors, owners, and shareholders are satisfactory. How could they be improved? Moreover, are there any possible changes in ownership over the strategic time horizon, and what might be the implications?

[4] www.independentaudit.com

Review the board structure

The next step is to review the board structure. Is the balance between executive directors, independent directors, and connected non-executive directors appropriate, now and for the strategic future? Consider the size of the board. The corporate constitution, such as the articles of association, may put limits on board size. Boards tend to grow in size. The case tends to be made for additional people to meet specific needs. One seldom hears the case being argued for a reduction in board size. Yet, as has already been noted, boards with a large number of members tend to inhibit directors' contributions and are in danger of splitting into cliques. Identify any changes necessary. This stage also provides the opportunity to review the relationship between the chair and the CEO.

Profile board members

Now the contributions of each individual director should be reviewed. Profile each director, noting the length of service on the board, the terms of appointment, the age, education, and professional background, relevant experience and skills, and the roles played and contributions made to the board and board committees, including personality characteristics and interpersonal abilities. In the context of the corporate strategy, what experience, skills, and roles will be needed? Identify gaps and develop succession planning for the board.

The profiling and reviewing of the contributions made by individual directors can be linked with each director's performance assessment.

This can then lead directly to a review of director induction, education, and training, whether there is continual development and if this is a learning board. Alternatives and improvements can be identified.

Given the international focus on director remuneration, with claims of excess and lack of linkage between bonuses and performance, some boards are using the review of the board to take a strategic view of executive director and top management remuneration. Others continue to rely on their board remuneration committee.

Review board style, efficiency, and effectiveness

The next stage involves a review of board style. Consider how the board and board committees spend their time, the issues on the agenda, the quality of leadership, and how meetings are planned and run. The board style (see Chapter 14) can then be identified and the need for any changes clarified.

Now board efficiency and effectiveness can be considered. It is worthwhile to reflect, at this stage, whether there are any other relevant, strategic factors that could affect the governance of the company over the strategic time horizon. For example, are any changes likely to company law, corporate regulation, or stock exchange listing requirements that would affect corporate governance activities? For companies in a group or network, are there any feasible shifts of power and influence over the strategic time horizon? What might be an appropriate reaction?

Next, the review process turns to the efficiency of the board. Does the board have audit, remuneration, and nominating committees? Are there other board standing committees—such as an executive committee, a strategy committee, or a compliance committee? How effective are each of these committees?

Assess the quality of board information: formal and informal reports, opportunities for directors to obtain information and answers to their questions, access to corporate data, as considered in Chapter 16.

How do directors spend their time: on main board meetings, board committee meetings, and in other board-related activities, including visits and preparation time? Is this efficient? What improvements might be made?

We next turn to the effectiveness of the board and its committees. Essentially, here the concern is with the quality of board processes and outputs, both in the short and the longer term. The four functions of the board—strategy formulation, policy-making, executive supervision, and accountability—need to be considered separately.

Strategy formulation, as we have seen, is a prime function for the board. This stage of the review considers the time and effort, the depth and quality of analysis that go into the board's strategic thinking. Could a new competitor unexpectedly intervene in the firm's markets? Could a new technology significantly change the cost structure? Would a different way of delivering the firm's service dramatically affect the market share, or might an alternative product meet customer needs better? This part of the review also considers whether external risks are adequately recognized. As we saw in Chapter 7, the significance of strategy formulation to the board's work might call for a special effort—perhaps a board strategy seminar or workshop to explore the firm's strategic situation and review the overall corporate strategy.

Moving from strategy to policy, the review asks whether the board's policies are still appropriate to the company's situation. This is the place to explore the delegation of board responsibilities to board committees and the work of those committees. Are the terms of reference of the audit committee, the remuneration committee, the nomination committee, and any other board committees still relevant? If not, what changes are needed?

In considering the performance functions—strategy formulation and policy-making—is the balance right between those activities delegated to management and those retained by the board? Will this be appropriate through the changing situations envisaged over the company's strategic time horizon?

Reviewing the third function of the board—executive supervision—provides an opportunity to review management controls and management reporting systems. Can the board monitor management in an active, accurate, and timely manner? Enterprise risk assessment and management systems, which are now seen as fundamental to corporate governance, should be reviewed at this stage.

The fourth function of the board—ensuring adequate accountability—has, in recent years, been under the corporate governance spotlight. Is the company conforming to the requirements of the corporate governance codes, company law requirements, and, where appropriate, stock exchange listing requirements? Are the company's public statements to the shareholders, the media, and other legitimate stakeholders meeting the legal requirements and, ideally, projecting the company as the board expect? In addition to the required audited financial statements, are operating statements, corporate social responsibility and sustainability reports, and other narrative reports at the level and in the form that the board want?

Determine a strategy for board development

Finally, after all of the data collection and analysis has been done and the results collated, comes report writing and the determination of a strategy for board development, consistent with and part of the overall corporate strategy.

Directors tend to spend relatively little time together and board-level assessment should provide information for valuable board discussion. In successful companies, particularly those with long-standing boards, inertia and complacency can be a danger. Once the directors have discussed and accepted the report, they should develop a strategy for board development, and create related policies and plans that lead to action. The chair's leadership role is vital at this stage.

Unlike the directors mentioned earlier in this chapter, who reported that corporate governance was a matter of complying with corporate governance codes, an informed professional director might reply that:

> ... in our company we have a set of board-level policies which lay down how the board and its committees operate; then a periodic board-level review enables us to check on whether these policies are being followed, that we are meeting all the accountability criteria the board has set for the organization, and whether our corporate governance strategy is still appropriate.

Experience has shown that board assessments often identify a similar set of issues, including the need to spend more board time and effort on:

- corporate strategy and risk assessment;
- executive succession;
- executive remuneration;
- the tenure of outside directors;
- problems in the link between board and management;
- concern about directors' abilities and the need for more training and briefing;
- corporate social responsibility policies and links with stakeholders.

In summary, the approach to board assessment advocated here analyses the board and committee structures and processes, studies the strengths and weaknesses of the directors, reviews the processes of the board and its committees, and ensures that appropriate disclosure and accountability are being provided. The outcome is a strategy for board development and corporate governance improvement. Just as an enterprise has longer-term strategies for developing its operations, technologies, markets, finances, and people, the board review project leads towards an agreed strategy for board and governance development. In other words, the strategy for board development becomes part of the overall corporate strategy. The assessment of boards and board committees is at the core of professional corporate governance.

Once the assessment exercise has been completed, a review of the results can provide a valuable learning experience and provide some useful insights for the future. The review questions might include the following:

- Is the company's corporate governance compliant with company law, corporate governance codes, and listing rules?

- How does the company's corporate governance performance compare with the industry average and the industry leaders? Are benchmarks available?
- Did the appraisal identify critical issues? Has anything been done about them?
- Did the appraisal deal with 'elephants in the room'—that is, things that everyone knows, but about which no one will speak?
- Have the objectives of the assessment been met?
- Has the assessment led to improved board effectiveness?
- Was the assessment well done, did it conform with best practice, and how might it be improved?

Assess individual directors' performance

Not many years ago, many directors would have baulked at the idea of having their own performance assessed. Appointment to the board, they would have argued, proved that they had the requisite knowledge, experience, and skills, as we saw earlier. Moreover, how can director-level performance *be* assessed when boardroom activity is a collective team effort? Inevitably, directors make different contributions, they would claim, which have to change as the circumstances facing the company change, so assessment is pointless.

Today, few directors hold these opinions. Attitudes have changed. Corporate governance codes and stock exchange listing rules now recommend, or require, an annual assessment of the performance of individual directors. Further, listed companies in many jurisdictions now have to report on their corporate governance practices. Most directors now recognize the importance of an effective, director-level, appraisal programme, just as they accept the need for management-level appraisal systems.

Currently, many director appraisals are informal, with the chair personally assessing each director's performance and commenting privately to the director involved. The UK Corporate Governance Code calls on chairs to hold regular development meetings with every director. But the pressure is on for director appraisals to be more formalized. A board policy decision, with the full support of all the directors, is needed to set up such a process. Given that directors often have considerable experience, strong personalities, and high self-esteem, the need to obtain everyone's support for the process at the outset is vital. Without that support, an appraisal exercise can become threatening, adversarial, and dysfunctional.

First, the contribution that is expected of each director needs to be known, to provide the basis for the assessment. Ideally, when a director is nominated to the board, the chair will provide a clear explanation of what is expected. A welcome letter from the board chair can be used to elaborate these expectations. The chair should explain what time commitment will be needed, what board-level skills are required, and why the director has been chosen, including any specific expertise, knowledge, experience, or contacts that the director is expected to bring to the board. As we saw in Chapter 16, an induction briefing can provide an opportunity for the incoming director to explore the way in which the board and its committees work, to have appropriate briefings, visits, and discussions with key people. Once a director's contribution has been agreed, the foundations for director performance appraisal have been laid.

Next, the criteria to be used for the evaluation need to be clarified. The chair needs to play a key role, outlining the purpose and the process of the assessment, and leading his or her board to recognize the value of a rigorous and regular appraisal system. The director attributes and core competencies, discussed in detail in Chapter 13, can provide a pro forma for the individual appraisal. The experience, skills, and knowledge expected of the director when he or she first joined the board need to be reviewed in the light of subsequent changes in the company's strategic situation. Directors particularly need to be aware of the critical success factors in the business and where it is significantly exposed to risk.

Review management evaluation and succession

One company explains in a confidential briefing document for new board members:

> The Compensation Committee conducts an annual review of the performance of the corporation, the CEO, and senior management. Neither the CEO nor senior management is present when the Committee meets to evaluate their individual performance. The Chairman of the Board presents the CEO's annual performance review for the Committee's approval. The CEO's annual performance review is based, in large part, upon an annual performance report prepared by the Chairman of the Board and upon ratings and commentary provided by individual Board members. The senior management performance reviews include the Compensation Committee's own assessment and reflect discussions with other Board members. The Board's independent directors approve the compensation of the CEO, and the full Board approves the compensation of the corporation's executive vice presidents, both approvals subject to the consent of the conservator.
>
> On an annual basis, the Compensation Committee reviews management succession planning with the CEO in preparation for discussion by the entire Board. The Board discussion on management succession occurs during executive session, and focuses on succession planning for the CEO and other key members of senior management.

The next stage in the appraisal is to determine who is to lead the exercise. Typically, the board chair will take the initiative, instigating the review—but the chair need not necessarily carry it out personally. The chair of the board nomination committee could be asked to play a significant role. A past chair, the senior independent director, an experienced independent consultant, or a firm specializing in board appraisal could also be considered. Some company secretary organizations, institutes of directors, and consultancies offer professional services for the assessment of individual directors and boards.

In a formalized director performance review, the data collection stage follows. Typically, this involves interviewing each director to discuss his or her experience as a member of both board and board committees. Information is also obtained by analysing attendance records, and board and board committee minutes, looking for innovative inputs and contributions to discussions and decisions. Sometimes, peer-review techniques are used in board reviews. So-called '360 degree' inputs seek comments from 'above', such as from auditors, institutional investors, and others outside the company dealing with a director, from the 'same level', including the chair and other board members, and from 'below', involving staff who come in contact with a director.

Typically, following the data gathering, a confidential report is drafted to the chair. Given the personal nature of the report, most chairs will not table it at a board meeting, but will discuss the relevant portion with each director. During that discussion, a strategy for further personal development should be discussed, resulting in an action plan including any training or development activities, such as committee leadership, or service on other boards. The intention, of course, is that each director will be able to make a greater contribution to board effectiveness in the future. Records of the discussion can be used to check progress at the next appraisal.

There could be opportunities for accelerating the contribution of outside directors by asking them to lead various board projects, to chair board committees, and to lead board discussions on specific topics. But even without a formal review, for example in subsidiary companies or family firms, self-evaluation that leads to the recognition of needs and a drive for continuous personal improvement can be valuable.

Finally, in considering individual director performance appraisal, we come to the ultimate question: who evaluates the chair and against what criteria? As the Roman poet Juvenal asked: *'Quis custodiet ipsos custodes?'* (Who will guard the guards?) Although, it has to be admitted, he was worried about who would watch his wife while he was away from home. Professor Fred Neubauer, when at IMD Business School in Lausanne, Switzerland, recommended that the performance of board chairs should be evaluated. In some cases, an appraisal of the chair is carried out by a senior independent outside director, or the chair of the audit or nomination committees. The UK Corporate Governance Code calls on the non-executive directors, led by the senior independent director, to be responsible for performance evaluation of the chair, taking into account the views of executive directors. But, in the end, a chair's performance is reflected in the performance of the company as a whole. Continued poor performance will bring calls for a change of chair from major investors, the media, or occasionally from dissatisfied board colleagues.

Corporate Governance in Action 17.2   Board evaluation—advice from the ICSA

The UK Institute of Chartered Secretaries and Administrators (ICSA) notes that a well-conducted evaluation helps the board, committees, and individual directors perform to their maximum capabilities, and:

- assess the balance of skills within the board;
- identify attributes required for new appointments;
- review practices and procedures to improve efficiency and effectiveness;
- review practices and procedures of the board's decision-making processes;
- recognize the board's outputs and achievements.

Corporate governance rating systems for companies

The financial climate changed significantly after Enron and the US Sarbanes-Oxley Act, not only in the United States, but around the world. The quality of a company's corporate governance was now seen as vital to its longer-term performance. Investors, particularly institutional investors, focus on corporate governance in valuing companies. The standard of corporate governance became an important element in the risk evaluation of a company. A reliable corporate governance rating from an independent and respected organization can reduce a company's cost of capital, reflecting the premium that investors are now prepared to pay for sound governance.

Consequently, there is a need to measure, evaluate, and rate standards of corporate governance. Various systems have been developed: some by rating agencies, some by financial institutions, and others by organizations providing consultancy services. However, it is important to recognize that they use different criteria, and that the scores are not necessarily compatible. Further, their conclusions sometimes differ. Let us review some of the more popular rating schemes.

Standard and Poor's (S&P), an organization better known for its credit ratings, offers a corporate governance rating service to companies. Unlike some other providers of corporate governance ratings, S&P is independent and does not also offer company advisory or training services. It acts with the cooperation of the company, interviewing senior executives and directors, and reviewing both information in the public domain and confidential data. S&P's GAMMA governance metric reflects S&P's opinion of the relative strength of a company's corporate governance practices. Designed for equity investors, the score provides some protection against governance-related losses or failure to create value. The GAMMA rating also provides companies with a comparative rating and a means of identifying opportunities for improvement in governance practices. The proprietary methodology produces a score based on a synthesis of best practices and codes around the world. The final score is numeric and based on four sectors:

- ownership structure and external influences, which considers the transparency of ownership structure, the concentration and the influence of ownership, and other external stakeholders;

- shareholder rights and relations, including shareholder meetings and voting procedures, ownership rights and takeover defences, and other stakeholder relations;

- transparency, disclosure, and audit, such as the content of public disclosure, the timing of and access to public disclosure, and the audit process;

- board structure and effectiveness, including director independence, the role and effectiveness of the board, and director and senior executive compensation.

Institutional Shareholder Services (ISS) offers a proprietary analytical tool called Governance Risk Indicators™ (GRId) to help listed companies to improve their corporate governance practices, and investors to assess the governance quality of their investments. The GRId indicators rank companies' governance standing (low, medium, high) across five independent dimensions of governance:

- compensation schemes for executive and non-executive directors, including the remuneration structure and schemes that are used to reward directors;

- executive and non-executive director stock ownership, such as the alignment of director equity ownership with shareholder interests;

- equity structure, including the protection of shareholder rights and the existence of any anti-takeover devices;

- structure of the board, independence of directors, and processes of the board and board committees;

- independence and integrity of the audit process, including the process itself, audit fees, services provided, and members of the audit committee.

Each company is assessed using between 60 and 80 variables depending on its local market, and the GRId indicators are based on that assessment. ISS also offers subscribers a benchmark proxy-voting policy service aligned with the GRId indicators, and access to a range of corporate governance services, including webcasts, White Papers, surveys, and expert analysis and advice. Online discussion forums facilitate dialogue on corporate governance issues between corporate executives, institutional investors, and board directors.

As part of their well-known credit rating service, *Moody's* offers an 'Enhanced Analysis Initiative' which reviews the corporate governance reviews of large debt issuers in North America, including financial institutions. In their experience, corporate governance is a key driver in good credit ratings. *Fitch Ratings* also offers a corporate governance rating service, as do some financial institutions including:

- *Deutsche Bank*, with a corporate governance scoring system based on four 'pillars'—board independence, shareholder treatment, information disclosure, and best practices;
- *Prudential Securities*, a US-based brokerage, based on three key corporate governance categories for banks—board independence, board accountability, and external audit.

Governance Metrics International (GMI) offers a rating system to monitor corporate governance. Subscribers to its service receive an independent evaluation of the governance characteristics of each company across a large universe of companies. GMI ratings cover over 4,000 companies, including companies in all significant markets. The GMI rating criteria are based on securities regulations, stock exchange listing requirements, and various corporate governance codes and principles, which produce a set of metrics structured to produce 'yes', 'no', or 'not disclosed' answers, to eliminate a large degree of subjectivity. The GMI research process starts with a review of a company's relevant public data, including regulatory filings, company websites, news services, and other specialized websites. Once the research template answers have been compiled and have been subjected to various quality control checks, data entry reports are sent to each company for an accuracy check. The GMI scoring model calculates ratings for each company on a scale of one (lowest) to ten (highest).

The *Investor Responsibility Research Center (IRRC)* is a source of impartial information on corporate governance and social responsibility research and proxy voting services. Founded in 1972, the IRRC also provides a corporate benchmarking service on governance issues to more than 500 institutional investors, corporations, law firms, foundations, academics, and other organizations.

The *International Finance Corporation (IFC)* works with countries that have an important potential for growth, but weak corporate governance practices. It engages at various levels:

- the firm—corporate governance assessments, advisory services to improve governance practices;
- the sector—building capacity of local consulting firms, institutes of directors, educational institutions, and stock exchanges;
- the market—alignment of standards and practices, development of corporate governance codes, and listing requirements;

- public policy and awareness—media training, conferences and roundtables, and sharing best practices.

IFC offers a corporate governance methodology and assessment service to client companies. The methodology uses assessment tools tailored to the different governance priorities of publicly listed companies, founder and family-owned firms, financial institutions, newly privatized enterprises, and state-owned enterprises. IFC staff review the client's governance practices and use that review for risk analysis, investment decision-making, and, where necessary, to develop a corporate governance improvement programme with the client.

In the IFC's experience:[5]

> [s]ound corporate governance makes companies stronger, more efficient and more accountable. With good corporate governance structures and practices in place, businesses mitigate risk, safeguard against mismanagement and are able to attract investment and capital—giving them the fuel for growth.

CoreRatings is a European-based rating agency, providing independent investment analysis of corporate responsibility risks. CoreRatings takes an investor's view on corporate governance, environmental, and social performance, and provides services to asset managers, pension funds, and companies worldwide. CoreRatings benchmarks the standing of companies' corporate governance and corporate responsibility against comparable companies. The methodology works with the company for answers to detailed questions derived from the international codes, best practice experience, and the writings of corporate governance experts. The resultant rating assesses the company's risk profile in seven areas:

- governance policy and business ethics;
- risk management processes;
- ownership structure and control;
- financial reporting, audit, and verification;
- board structure and management;
- board executive compensation;
- investor rights and relations.

Corporate governance assessment systems for countries

Attempts have also been made to monitor and assess the overall level of corporate governance country by country. This reflects the growing recognition that corporate governance is important to national financial markets and, ultimately, to national economic success.

In the wake of various financial crises, the *World Bank* and the *International Monetary Fund* (IMF) launched a joint initiative to assess corporate governance country by country, recognizing the major role that the observance of international standards and codes of best practice can play

---

[5] 'IFC Corporate Governance Advisory Services: Helping Companies to Operate More Profitably and Grow', International Finance Corporation, Washington, DC.

in strengthening national and international financial systems. The executive boards of the World Bank and the IMF identified a group of 12 areas that they deem to be important for the institutional underpinning of macroeconomic stability and central to the operational work of the two institutions. The Reports on the Observance of Standards and Codes (ROSC) programme considers each country's legal and regulatory framework, as well as the practices and compliance of listed firms, against the OECD Principles of Corporate Governance. The diagnostic work is intended to strengthen international financial systems. A ROSC study leads to an assessment of the degree to which a country observes internationally recognized standards and codes.

The *European Bank for Reconstruction and Development* (EBRD) is one of the largest lenders and investors in Central and Eastern Europe, and other transitional economies. As an investor, EBRD is interested in promoting better standards of corporate governance, because it is limited to a minority shareholder position in its investments or co-invests with minority shareholders. The bank is, therefore, particularly concerned with how its investee companies treat their shareholders and whether the legal rights of minority shareholders are capable of being protected. As a law reformer, the EBRD is also actively engaged in promoting better corporate governance rules at the country level. The bank believes that:

> [g]ood corporate governance is essential for companies wishing to access external capital and for countries aiming to stimulate private sector investments. If companies are well run, they will prosper. Poor corporate governance weakens the company's potential and paves the way for financial difficulties and even fraud.

The EBRD tries to encourage, influence, and provide guidance to governments, policymakers, and all those in charge of promoting new legislation for the development of corporate governance-related legal reform. To study corporate governance in a country, the EBRD devised a checklist with lists of questions covering key corporate governance issues.

The financial institution *Société Generale Global Equities* also addresses the corporate governance of countries, identifying five key corporate governance categories—shareholder rights, the enforcement of shareholder rights, disclosure, analysts' access to management, and board independence.

The most comprehensive country-level corporate governance rating to date is the FTSE ISS corporate governance index.[6] FTSE and ISS joined in a global corporate governance ratings and index project in 2004. With over US$2.5 trillion benchmarked against its indices, the FTSE had proven international index experience. The initiative was rooted in the belief that international investors need a reliable, cost-effective standard to measure governance practice across a range of international companies, with tools to evaluate companies' corporate governance risk. The partners believed that investors would tend to reward companies with sound governance practices and possibly underweight companies with poor governance practices to reduce portfolio risk. After reviewing a wide range of accepted standards and codes, the project identified a set of common principles—independence, accountability, and transparency.

The index was then based on five major areas:

- structure and independence of the board (44 per cent);
- equity structure (21 per cent);

---

[6] www.bolagsstyrning.se/UserFiles/Archive/462/2005-12-15_corporate_governance_rating_bilaga_1.pdf

- compensation system, for executive and non-executive directors (17 per cent);
- executive and non-executive stock ownership (9 per cent);
- independence and integrity of the audit process (9 per cent).

The index allows comparisons to be made across countries, across industrial sectors, and across financial markets. For example, it was discovered that Canada and the United Kingdom had the highest average corporate governance scores by country, that the oil and gas industry scores highest by sector, and that the FTSE 100 had the highest score by stock market sector. Research findings from the project showed that 88 per cent of respondents expected interest in corporate governance to increase over the next two years, and 75 per cent expected consideration of corporate governance factors in their day-to-day operations to increase.

Case studies

 Case study 17.1   Board failings at Olympus Japan

When British-born Michael Woodford (51) was promoted in 2011 to the top executive position of Olympus, the Japanese camera firm,[7] he did not expect that within weeks he would be dismissed, stripped of his house and company car, and told to take a bus to the airport. Following a 30-year career with Olympus, Woodford had become the company president; the first non-Japanese to lead the company in its 93-year history. Olympus, better known for its cameras, actually made more money from medical equipment such as endoscopes.

Soon after arriving in his new job, Woodford was alerted to an article in a journal called *Facta*, which made some wild allegations that Olympus had massively over-paid nearly US$1 billion to buy three small companies. This led Woodford to uncover accounting irregularities and suspicious deals involving the recent acquisition of UK medical equipment manufacturer Gyrus. He called in the company's auditors, PriceWaterhouseCoopers, to examine payments of £460 million (US$687 million) for financial advice made to an unknown and now defunct firm incorporated in the Cayman Islands with a New York address. A fraud of £1.1 billion (US$1.7 billion) emerged, including an accounting scandal to disguise losses. Woodford spoke to the chair, Tsuyoshi Kikukawa, expecting immediate action. But Kikukawa refused to discuss the matter.

So Woodford confronted the board of directors, raising embarrassing questions. The other directors were hostile. Blowing the whistle offended their corporate culture. In October 2011, Woodford was summarily sacked and told to leave the company and take a bus to the airport. He disobeyed these orders, went public with the information, informed the Japanese serious fraud office, and sought police protection while he stayed in hotels under pseudonyms.

The board initially claimed that Woodford had left because of 'differences in management style'. Employees were warned not to support Woodford or 'their careers might be damaged'. But by November 2011, the company admitted a cover-up of losses going back to the 1990s. Tsuyoshi Kikukawa resigned the chair but stayed on the board. In December, Tokyo prosecutors raided the Olympus offices, and in February 2012 the former chair and other top officials were arrested.

In March 2012 Olympus declared a loss of £383 million (US$575 million). During this saga the share price fell by 80 per cent. In April 2012, Japanese prosecutors charged Olympus and six of its directors with a £1.1 billion (US$1.7 billion) fraud. The company's ex-chair and other executives were accused of

---

[7] For a personal account of the Olympus case, see Woodford, Michael (2012) *Exposure: Inside the Olympus Scandal—How I went from CEO to whistleblower*, Portfolio Penguin, London.

inflating the company's net worth by hiding huge investment losses in a complex web of acquisitions and buy-backs. Woodford was also questioned by the FBI over the Cayman Islands transactions.

Following the prosecution a company spokesman said 'we take these charges very seriously and will continue to strengthen our corporate governance. We again express our deep apologies to shareholders, investors, business partners, and customers.'[8]

The Japanese business network model

Traditionally, investors play a relatively small part in Japanese corporate affairs. There is no significant market for corporate control since hostile takeover bids are virtually unknown. The classical model of Japanese corporate governance has a stakeholder, not a shareholder, orientation. Power lies within a network of companies, the *keiretsu*, which are connected through cross-holdings, interlocking directorships, and inter-trading. Frequently the network includes a financial institution.

The classical model of the *keiretsu* reflects the social cohesion within Japanese society, emphasizing unity throughout the organization, non-adversarial relationships, lifetime employment, enterprise unions, personnel policies encouraging commitment, initiation into the corporate family, decision-making by consensus, cross-functional training, with promotion based on loyalty and social compatibility as well as performance. Boards of directors tend to be large and are, in effect, the top layers of the management pyramid. People speak of being 'promoted to the board'.

Independent non-executive directors, in the Western sense, are unusual in Japan, although the proportion is increasing. Many Japanese do not see the need for such intervention 'from the outside'. Indeed, they have difficulty in understanding how outside directors operate. 'How can outsiders possibly know enough about the company to make a contribution,' they question, 'when the other directors have spent their lives working for the company? How can an outsider be sensitive to the corporate culture? They could even damage the harmony of the group.'

Chairs and senior directors of companies in a *keiretsu* meet regularly and have close, informal relationships. Meetings of the CEOs with the directors in their teams are also crucial, as are the informal relationships between the top echelons of the board. Ultimate power lies with the top managers, particularly the president and the chair.

Woodford offer to run the company is rebuffed

At an Olympus shareholders' meeting, Woodford offered to return to run the company. He was supported by international investors. But the largest shareholders—Japanese institutional investors and members of the Olympus *keiretsu*—did not. The chair of that meeting was asked if 'anti-social forces' had been involved in any of these transactions, a code meaning the Japanese *yakuza* or mafia. 'I am absolutely not aware of such a thing,' the chair replied.

Woodford claimed damages for unfair dismissal in the London courts, demanding ten years' salary, totalling £35 million (US$52 million), because he said that the debacle had made him unemployable. His claim was settled by the company out of court for an undisclosed sum, widely reported as around £10 million (US$15 million).

Subsequently, under new leadership, Olympus laid off workers, closed 12 of its 30 factories, sold off the 3 divisions implicated in the fraud case, raising capital and acquiring a strategic partner by selling a 10 per cent stake in the company to Japanese company Sony.

The Japanese authorities proposed some changes to company law to strengthen corporate governance, including a requirement for at least one INED. But that proposal was dropped when the employers' lobby, the *keidanren*, objected.

---

[8] *The JIL Labor Flash*, Shinjuku Monolith, 2–3–1 Nishi-Shinjuku, Shinjuku-ku, Tokyo 163–0914, Japan.

In 2010 and 2011, the British Serious Fraud Office (SFO) launched an investigation into a British subsidiary of Olympus called Gyrus. The SFO examined the possibility of fraud by concealing losses over a long period from its auditors. In November 2015, the SFO dropped the inquiry after a ruling by the British Court of Appeal that it did not consider a company misleading its auditors to be a crime. The SFO did not prosecute any senior officers in the parent company, Olympus, because Japan does not extradite its own citizens to countries abroad.

Michael Woodford had exposed the greatest scandal in Japanese corporate history and badly damaged the reputation and prospects of medical instrument and camera maker, Olympus. But the company made a comeback: in 2016 it launched a multi-million dollar lawsuit against Woodford, alleging fraud on his part by manipulating profits to benefit his own pension.

Discussion questions

1. Having discovered the accounting irregularities and suspicious deals, did Woodford take the most appropriate action? What would you have done?

2. Do those Japanese critics of the concept of the independent non-executive director have a point?

3. What can we learn about Japanese corporate governance and management from this case? Do you think it might change? Why?

 Case study 17.2   The collapse of Halifax Bank of Scotland (HBOS)

The Halifax Mutual Building Society (savings and loan association) was corporatized and floated on the London Stock Exchange. In 2001, Halifax merged with the Bank of Scotland, a long-established Scottish bank, to form the HBOS Group. During the bull market of 2000 to 2008, under chief executive Sir James Crosby, HBOS became the world's fifth-largest bank, by pursuing a culture which emphasized sales and profit growth led by salesmen, rather than prudent, risk-orientated banking led by bankers.

As early as 2004, Mike Ellis, the finance director, alerted the board to a concern expressed by the UK regulator, the Financial Services Authority (FSA), that HBOS was growing too fast. He said subsequently that 'the conclusion being drawn by the FSA and the shift in internal capital ratios were significant warning shots'.[9] Neither the chief executive nor the board acted on this advice.

In the same year, Paul Moore, the head of regulatory risk at HBOS, who had previously been a partner in the accounting firm KPMG, warned the board that HBOS was over-exposed to risk. He was also ignored. In December 2004, Moore felt that he should contact the FSA. The FSA mounted an investigation, but called on the HBOS auditors, KPMG, to undertake the study. Moore said their report merely gave the answer HBOS wanted. In 2005, Moore accepted a six-figure pay-off and left the bank.

HBOS in serious financial trouble is bailed out by Lloyds

In 2008, the global financial crisis and the resultant shortage of funds left HBOS in serious financial trouble. The British government became involved. Chancellor of the Exchequer Gordon Brown spoke to the chair of Lloyds TSB Bank, Sir Victor Blank, over dinner to the following effect.[10] 'If Lloyds would

[9] In evidence subsequently given to a UK Parliamentary Commission on Banking Standards.
[10] *The Times* and *Financial Times* reports during October 2008.

take on the ailing HBOS,' Brown suggested, 'normal competition rules (which would have referred such a merger to the Monopolies Commission) will be waived.'

Intuitively, the idea seemed to make strategic sense to Sir Victor. So Lloyds rode to the rescue of HBOS, taking over its assets and liabilities for £7.7 billion (US$11.5 billion). Sir Victor assured his shareholders that the deal would 'create great value for both sets of shareholders'. What he did not know was that HBOS had around £200 billion (US$300 billion) of toxic assets in doubtful loans.

Traditionally, Lloyds had been a robust and conservative lender, recognized as one of the more cautious British banks. Now it, too, needed support from the government, which offered a £260 billion (US$390 billion) loan guarantee, in exchange for equity capital. With an initial 43 per cent of its equity in government hands and more promised, Lloyds had lost its independence and its conservative reputation, whilst its shareholders' capital had been seriously diluted. The chief executive of Lloyds, Eric Daniels, admitted that they had done much less due diligence on this deal than would be normal because of the urgency of the negotiations.[11] 'We would have liked more time to examine HBOS accounts. If we had not taken HBOS over, we would not have needed government money,' he said. Lloyds' share price plunged.

Lloyds' chair, Sir Victor Blank, stepped down in 2009, and there was pressure on chief executive, Eric Daniels, to follow suit. US-based shareholders sued both Sir Victor and Daniels, alleging that they had shown 'a reckless disregard to the truth during the HBOS merger'. A group of UK shareholders, Lloyds Action Now, also threatened legal action. In 2013, however, Daniels was reported to have said that 'I think we did a very good job in due diligence of HBOS. We understood the nature of loans, but I don't think anyone would have called the financial crisis.'[12]

Toxic loans in Bank of Scotland part of HBOS

The commercial lending division of the Bank of Scotland, led by Peter Cummings, who had been with the bank since the age of 16, had made huge loans to property companies: a cyclical industry which would be exposed in a market downturn. The commercial lending division accounted for about 40 per cent of the bank's profits. Asked about his approach to risk, Cummings had said that 'I just make sure I don't lend to idiots'.

Cummings was criticized in a FSA report for making increasingly risky loans, even as it became clear the credit bubble was about to burst. Cummings had 'failed to exercise due skill, care and diligence by pursuing an aggressive expansion strategy ... without suitable controls in place to manage the associated risks', the report said. Denying these failings, Cummings claimed he had done nothing wrong, and had followed the bank's guidelines. Subsequently Cummings was fined £500,000 and barred from the City of London financial sector.

The FSA report also found that the auditors, KPMG, had been unable to see the full extent of the problems, and their attempts to persuade the bank to take a more prudent attitude to provisions for bad debts had been ignored.

In 2006, the chief executive of HBOS, Sir James Crosby, handed over to Andy Hornby, who had been top of his MBA class at the Harvard Business School. The FSA brought no disciplinary proceedings against either Crosby or Hornby, even though insiders allege that Hornby had put pressure on Cummings to increase lending and profits to make up a shortfall that had arisen when the bank adopted more prudent policies on home loans.

In 2012, the report of an inquiry into events at HBOS by the FSA found that when Halifax had taken over Bank of Scotland to form HBOS, it had failed to control its affairs responsibly. The report suggested that staff had been given incentives to build revenue, not monitor risk. The culture was all about getting business. The report said that corporate culture believed that 'risk management was for wimps'.

[11] BBC News Report, 30 January 2017.
[12] *Daily Mail*, 15 February 2013.

The findings of the Parliamentary Commission on Banking Standards

In late 2012, the British Parliamentary Commission on Banking Standards cross-examined leading players in the collapse of HBOS.[13]

Moore, the HBOS head of regulatory risk until 2005, when he resigned, told the Commission:

There was an 'us and them' culture at the bank in which risk officers had told him: 'People hid papers. They wouldn't turn up for meetings. They were rude and would swear at us. The culture was resistant to any sort of challenge.'

Peter Cummings, the former head of the corporate lending division of HBOS, complained that he had been singled out for punishment.[14] 'Sir James Crosby and Andy Hornby were behind disastrous decisions to ratchet up lending targets,' he said, 'putting pressure on me to boost profits.'

Sir James Crosby admitted under hostile questioning that incompetence had brought down the bank, and apologized. He agreed that he had sold two-thirds of his holding in HBOS in advance of the bank's collapse. But he rejected suggestions that he should forgo his knighthood or pay back any of the rewards he had received, including a pension of £572,000 a year. Sir James had resigned from HBOS in 2006 just before the bank's collapse, was knighted for his services to the banking industry, and became the deputy chair of the financial industry's watchdog, the FSA.

Lord Stevenson, the former chair of HBOS, was shown a letter he had written to the FSA six months before the bank collapsed,[15] saying 'HBOS is "boringly boring"' and a 'highly conservative organization'. That, said the Commission chair, was a travesty of the truth. 'The bank was by then dangerously exposed because of its reliance on wholesale funding and in the wake of a prolonged and reckless lending binge.' Stevenson explained that he had been a non-executive chair and could not remember details. In his letter to the FSA he had written that he was 'part-time (but not non-executive)'. He had assured the regulator that he was not the type of chair who took an interest in 'only Olympian matters'. He agreed with Commission members that 'there was a lot of mistaken lending', but added 'I wasn't there in the trenches with the people making the decisions. I was only there at the most part-time.' Stevenson was paid £815,000 (US$1.2 million) a year in fees and benefits. As the *Daily Mail*'s financial commentator wrote:

No one expects a bank chairman to sign off on every loan. But it is inconceivable that Stevenson was not made aware of the multi-billion pound loans, many to the property sector, handed out by the Bank of Scotland.

Members of the Commission accused Stevenson of being 'either delusional or dishonest', one commenting that 'you are living in Cloud Cuckoo Land. You were responsible for a strategy of reckless growth and that is what led you into difficulties.' The chair of the Commission concluded that his evidence had been 'evasive, repetitive, and unrealistic'. Despite his role in the collapse of HBOS, Stevenson continued to serve on the boards of Western Union, the *Economist* magazine, and a number of private equity and venture capital firms.

Sir Charles Dunstone, a former non-executive director of HBOS, said that 'while the bank modelled a variety of threats in its stress tests, it never hypothesized the collapse of the wholesale market'.

Sir Ronald Garrick, former deputy chair of HBOS, said in evidence:

I did not recognize the depiction of the doomed bank set out by the Financial Services Authority [report] ... that did not chime with what was going on at the time ... I have no doubt that the HBOS board was by far and away the best board I have ever sat on.

---

[13] https://publications.parliament.uk/pa/jt201213/jtselect/jtpcbs/144/121123.htm
[14] In evidence given in December 2012 to a member of the Parliamentary Commission.
[15] https://publications.parliament.uk/pa/jt201213/jtselect/jtpcbs/144/121123.htm

Pressed on why HBOS relied so heavily on wholesale funding, and reminded that a senior manager had warned that this reliance was 'untenable and unsustainable', Sir Ronald admitted that the words were 'quite strong', but added 'but I wouldn't be sure they went to the board'.

Parliamentary Banking Commission report: a 'manual for bad banking'

In April 2013, the Parliamentary Commission reported on the HBOS collapse. In what it described as 'a manual for bad banking', the report concluded that the collapse had been caused by 'a colossal failure of senior management and the board'. The report named the successive chief executives Sir James Crosby and Andy Hornby and the chair Lord Stevenson as having 'primary responsibility for these failures'. All three men left HBOS to take up lucrative top posts in other companies.

The report also expressed surprise that the FSA had chosen to criticize Peter Cummings, a more junior HBOS employee, instead of the CEOs and chair. The report concluded: 'The commission was very disappointed by the attempts of those who led HBOS into the abyss to acknowledge even now either the nature of the problems that eventually consumed the bank or the extent to which they flowed from their own decisions rather than unforeseeable events.' The Commission rejected the reason for the bank's collapse given by all three: that it had been caused by wholesale funds drying up following the international financial crisis.

Following the publication of the Commission's report, Sir James Crosby agreed to take a 30 per cent reduction in his inflation-proofed pension, worth £240,000 (US$360,000) a year. He also offered to hand back his knighthood. Lord Stevenson and Andy Hornby came under pressure in the press to react likewise to the Commission's criticism.

Another fall-out from the Commission's report was growing criticism of the HBOS auditors, KPMG, for failing to notice the extent of the toxic loans when they signed clear audit reports between 2001 and 2009. It was suggested that KPMG could now be sued by Lloyds Bank, which had taken over HBOS. KPMG denied any liability. Pensions & Investment Research Consultants Ltd (PIRC) called for an independent investigation.[16] The chair of KPMG at the time of the HBOS implosion was John Griffith-Jones.

Regulators in the spotlight

By 2013, the regulators were also coming under the spotlight for not investigating the apparent audit failure by KPMG more fully. The FRC, which is responsible for investigation of alleged audit failures, said it was monitoring the situation. But an insider said that the FRC had not investigated KPMG at the time of the HBOS collapse because 'it lacked the necessary resources. It was reluctant to get into it, as it would be just too disrupting and damaging. It had left the HBOS investigation to the Financial Services Authority (FSA).'

The FSA had been created by the previous Labour government to provide deliberately 'light touch' regulation of the finance industry. There were close links between banks, the Big Four auditors, the regulators, and the Treasury. In 2003, James Crosby, then CEO of HBOS, was appointed to the board of the FSA. He was knighted in 2006. In 2008, he was promoted to deputy chair of the FSA at a salary of £63,000 a year (part-time). He resigned in 2009, several months after the HBOS debacle.

The weaknesses of the FSA were recognized by the new Coalition government, and in April 2013 the FSA was replaced by the Financial Conduct Authority (FCA), with John Griffith-Jones of KPMG as its chair.

---

[16] PIRC is a leading UK independent research and advisory consultancy providing services to institutional investors on corporate governance and corporate social responsibility. See www.pirc.co.uk

In 2015, the Prudential Regulation Authority (PRA—regulator of the banking sector) and the FCA published a review into the failure of HBOS Group. The FRC has also published reports of their investigations of KPMG's 2007 and 2008 audits of HBOS.

This review was originally started by the FSA before that body was reformed. Its purpose is to analyse the causes of the firm's failure, and to draw out lessons for the future, for both the industry and the regulatory system as a whole. The report suggests that:

[o]n 1 October 2008 HBOS was approaching a point at which it was no longer able to meet its liabilities as they fell due and so sought Emergency Liquidity Assistance from the Bank of England. This report seeks to explain why HBOS failed, the role that HBOS Board and senior management played in the failure and the FSA's supervision of HBOS. [The review concludes that] ultimate responsibility for the failure of HBOS rests with the Board and senior management. They failed to set an appropriate strategy for the firm's business and failed to challenge a flawed business model which placed inappropriate reliance on continuous growth without due regard to risks involved. In addition, flaws in the FSA's supervisory approach meant it did not appreciate the full extent of the risks HBOS was running and was not in a position to intervene before it was too late.

In July 2016, the House of Commons Treasury Committee published a paper on the reports into the failure of HBOS.[17] It suggested that:

Why HBOS failed

In 2007 there was a sharp deterioration in credit conditions and an increasing number of UK financial institutions began to run into difficulty. Initially HBOS, as one of the UK's larger banks, was viewed by some as a safe harbour in challenging times. However, beginning in the spring of 2008, investors and depositors began to question its ability to weather the storm facing the UK and global economies.

These concerns were validated later in the year when HBOS was forced, along with RBS, to seek emergency liquidity assistance (ELA) from the Bank of England. In 2012, the Financial Conduct Authority (FCA) and Prudential Regulation Authority (PRA) began work on a review intended to examine the causes behind the collapse of HBOS. This review culminated in a report—'The failure of HBOS plc (HBOS)'—published in November 2015, which identified a number of reasons why HBOS failed.

The cost of both HBOS's and the regulator's failings was high. Although HBOS was acquired by Lloyds TSB in 2009, a number of government-led financial interventions were needed to stabilise its balance sheet, eventually totalling over £20 billion.

The role of HBOS's Board

While the PRA/FCA report into the failure of HBOS makes clear that broader macroeconomic conditions both before and during the crisis had a role to play, there were also a number of factors specific to HBOS that made the firm particularly vulnerable to a change in external conditions

First, the PRA/FCA report attributes ultimate responsibility for HBOS's failure to its Board. In particular, the report argues that the Board failed to instill an appropriate culture at HBOS or to set out a clearly defined risk appetite for the firm, both of which had significant consequences for HBOS's business strategy.

---

[17] https://publications.parliament.uk/pa/cm201617/cmselect/cmtreasy/582/582.pdf

The report also finds that the Board did not provide effective challenge to the HBOS executive during the review period. For instance, there was little evidence of the Board debating the firm's reliance on wholesale funding or the risks associated with high levels of asset growth. The outcome of this was that the risks facing HBOS at a Group level were never fully articulated or addressed.

Discussion questions

1. Where do *you* think the blame lies for this debacle?

2. Why did the HBOS board act as they did?

3. Why do you think the chief executive and the board ignored comments from the CFO and the head of regulatory risk as early in the affair as 2004?

4. What is the role of the chair of the board?

5. Should the auditors or the regulators take any share of the blame?

Self-test questions

1. How does one go about assessing a director's performance?

2. How are many director appraisals done at the moment?

3. Is there pressure for director appraisals to be more formalized? What is needed to set up such a process?

4. What is the usual output of an individual director performance assessment? How is it used?

5. How is the performance of a chair assessed?

6. Do many corporate governance codes and stock exchange listing rules now call for an annual assessment of the performance of individual directors, and of the performance of the board and board committees?

7. Who might be asked to undertake a board review?

8. Describe the stages in a board review project.

9. What are the principal elements in the Standard and Poor's GAMMA corporate governance ratings?

10. Name some of the systems for evaluating corporate governance at the country level.

 For suggested answers to these self-test questions visit the online resources at: www.oup.com/uk/tricker4e/

Projects and exercises

1. Draft a note in response to a director who has told you that assessing the performance of individual directors is unnecessary and unrealistic, because directors bring different skills, experience, and knowledge to the board table.

2. Study and compare the corporate governance rating systems noted in the text. Which would you recommend?

3. What problems might be encountered in using the board review process described in Figure 17.1?

References and further reading

Anand, Sanjay (2007) *Essentials of Corporate Governance.* Wiley, Hoboken, NJ.

Garratt, Bob (2003) *Thin on Top—Why Corporate Governance Matters and How to Measure and Improve Board Performance.* Brealy Publishing, London.

NACD ([2005] 2010a) Board Evaluation: Improving Director Effectiveness—A Report of a NACD Blue Ribbon Commission. National Association of Corporate Directors, Washington, DC.

NACD ([2005] 2010b) Performance Metrics: Understanding the Board's Role—A Report of a NACD Blue Ribbon Commission. National Association of Corporate Directors, Washington, DC.

Solomon, Jill (2004) *Corporate Governance and Accountability.* Wiley, Hoboken, NJ.

Sonnenfeld, Jeffrey (2012) 'What Makes Great Boards Great', *Harvard Business Review,* September.

Useful websites

www.frc.org.uk/directors/corporate-governance-and-stewardship/uk-corporate-governance-code/frc-guidance-for-boards-and-board-committees
Financial Reporting Council Guide to Board Effectiveness.

https://hbr.org/2002/09/what-makes-great-boards-great

Corporate Governance: The Next 30 Years

 Learning Outcomes

This chapter enables us to:

- Study the present frontiers of corporate governance.
- Consider some possible drivers of change.
- Discuss likely frontiers of corporate governance in the future.
- Study the future of strategic reporting.
- Recognize the need for a philosophy of corporate governance.

On living in interesting times

In China, many years ago, a man could curse another by wishing 'may you live in interesting times'. In the ancient Confucian culture, stability, hierarchy, and respect for tradition were paramount: 'interesting times' were unknown, frightening, and foreshadowed havoc. Today we are living in interesting times. Around the world corporate entities in their economic, political, and societal contexts face more instability, confusion, and riskier situations than existed when the first edition of this book was published a decade ago. The world's economic order is changing: the future for economies around the world is volatile. The United States (facing the 'America first' policies of President Trump), the United Kingdom (meeting the ambiguities of leaving the European Union), China, Latin American countries, the countries remaining in the European Union (some facing growing nationalism), Russia, India—all present companies with management and governance challenges, particularly those with supply chains or marketing strategies that cross international borders. Such developments might cause companies to review their corporate structures and, hence, their approach to corporate governance. Changes to financial controls and tax laws around the world could also cause companies to rethink their governance. But such risks also bring opportunities—new technologies, new markets, and different business models, for example.

Significant changes could also occur in the way countries and their governments view relationships with companies domiciled or operating in their jurisdictions, to enhance economic well-being, increase tax revenues, protect financial stability, or respond to societal interests, such as protecting the environment. Such developments would affect the way power is exercised over corporate entities; in other words, influence their corporate governance.

Meanwhile, the business world is becoming ever more electronically networked and digitally dependent. New block-chained sources of finance may be available. Data has become the basis of new business models and needs managing appropriately. Directors must now have appropriate knowledge, which may not have been gained from their previous business experience. The significance of political and psychological behaviour at board level may also need more attention.

Earlier, we traced the evolution of the limited-liability company from the elegantly simple concept of the 19th century to the variety and complexity of today's corporate scene. Many of the companies listed on the world's stock markets are complex and massive groups with a wide diversity of investors having differing objectives. Yet some of the most successful listed companies, in both the United States and China, are still majority-owned and dominated by their founders. Moreover, other types of corporate enterprise have multiplied: family companies, joint ventures, public-interest companies, not-for-profit enterprises, non-government organizations, and many more. All need sound governance as well as good management.

Around the world, in large and small enterprises, in both public and private sectors, governance has come under the spotlight. The effectiveness of their governing bodies, their responsibilities, and their accountability are now recognized as vital. The legitimacy of corporate entities, their transparency, and their role in society are also being questioned. Ultimately, nothing less than a rebalancing of the interests of the individual, the enterprise, and the state is needed. The field of corporate governance is changing and expanding rapidly.

To consider such developments, we will first review the topics currently on the frontiers of corporate governance; then consider what might bring about change; and, finally, examine what the frontiers might be in the future.

Frontiers of corporate governance today

First, we consider topics on the minds of directors, regulators, and those who advise them at the moment; issues that feature in professional journals and the proceedings of conferences.

Shareholder activism

Over the years, many commentators have called for investors to 'exercise the power of the proxy' and to vote the shares they hold. They argue that by focusing on corporate performance shareholders can provide checks on excesses, such as executive remuneration, rein in inefficiencies, and challenge strategies and capital investments. There have been pressures for board renewal, less director entrenchment, and limits to tenure: predictably resisted by some boards. Classified boards, in which only a proportion of the directors are elected each year, have also come in for criticism, because they can be used as a defence against predators.

But despite these calls, many fund managers show relatively little interest in the governance of companies in which they invest, preferring to 'do the Wall Street walk' by trading their shares, rather than incurring the costs of involvement in governance, and risking getting locked in with a falling share price. Moreover, if institutional investors do become proactive in governance and the stock price falls, might they themselves be held accountable for losses?

In many markets, particularly the highly liquid US and UK markets, rapid, high-frequency trading driven by computer models has increased. Such traders seek opportunities for short-term advantage, and have no inclination to do detailed analysis of the long-term prospects of the companies in which they invest, let alone become involved in their corporate governance.

The primary responsibility of institutional investors, including investment trusts, mutual funds, pension funds, unit trusts, life assurance companies, banks, and brokers running portfolios for clients, is to their members or investors. If they do vote their shares, it must be in the interests of those remote beneficial owners, whose objectives may well differ from one another. Some regulations now require institutional investors to declare whether and how they have voted their shares.

Tracker investment funds, which invest in all of the companies in the market or index they track, sometimes get involved in the governance of those companies; talking to executives, attending meetings, and voting their shares. Significant listed companies, particularly in the United States, may also face lobbying from various interest groups, such as those representing environmental, climate-change, human rights, or anti-alcohol and tobacco interests.

Chair of the board and CEO

It is now widely accepted around the world that, in major companies, the role of chair of the board should be separated from that of the chief executive officer (CEO) to avoid domination of decision-making and overenthusiastic risk-taking by a single, all-powerful individual. Most codes of corporate governance principles and practice call for this separation. A few codes do recognize that, in some circumstances, a single leader may be appropriate, but in that case a strong group of independent non-executive directors (INEDs) is needed, with their own appointed leader.

Nevertheless, in the United States and a few other countries, the roles of CEO and chair of the board, sometimes with the added title of 'president', are combined in a single, powerful individual who leads the company in both management and governance. In such cases, the independent outside directors should provide a check-and-balance mechanism, supported by independent external auditors and the requirements of the law, the regulators, and stock exchange rules.

Most recently, the issue has arisen in the continuing leadership of some highly successful new companies, particularly in the high-tech, information-based sectors where the founder and colleagues keep dominant voting rights, even though the company is listed. Some stock exchanges, including Hong Kong, will not list companies having dual-class shares with different voting rights, insisting on the classical 'one share, one vote' principle.

The question is which is preferable: a dominant leader, providing single-minded leadership and thereby enhancing performance, or shared responsibility, which reduces risk? This duality issue is unresolved.

Where the roles are separated, another issue can arise: should a retiring CEO step up to become chair? Retiring CEOs have experience of the company, the business, and the board. Their personal qualities—integrity, leadership, and communication skills—are well known. Moreover, the retiring CEO has well-connected networks and is trusted by investors, customers, employees, and others dealing with the company. So risks associated with introducing a new chair would be reduced.

However, arguments against allowing a retiring CEO to become chair are also formidable. Chairing the board, it can be argued, is a quite different role from that of CEO. Strong performance at one does not guarantee success at the other. Moreover, some retiring CEOs find it hard to pass on the responsibilities of top management to their successors and continue to interfere in management matters that are the responsibility of the CEO.

Director information

In the first edition of this book (2009), we predicted that technology would allow directors to receive information electronically on personal devices, wherever and whenever needed. That has now happened. Such access enables directors to be updated immediately on relevant aspects of the company, to be kept informed about the financial situation, on the competitive market position, and with relevant information about the firm's political, economic, technological, and societal context. But that is a one-way information process—from company to director.

More sophisticated board-level information systems allow directors to search for the information they feel they need, applying other tools such as simulations to explore possible outcomes, while communicating their ideas to other board colleagues online in a networked information process.

Predictably, some directors still prefer the old one-way, hard-copy set of monthly board papers. Nevertheless, the development of director-level information and communication systems remains on the frontier.

Levels of director and senior management remuneration

In the United States, the UK, and some other advanced economies, the gap between those at the top of companies and the average pay of workers has widened dramatically. Consequently, social inequality is increasing. In the past, in major British companies, for example, chief executives received around 70 times the average pay of shop-floor workers; within ten years the ratio has doubled.

Some institutional investors have called for restraint and links to long-term performance. Some commentators, particularly in the popular media, have criticized the overall packages enjoyed by some directors, suggesting that in some cases these seemed to be rewards for failure. Prompted by the investigative media, often referring to 'fat cats', the issue has attracted public and political attention.

Although the justification for most director bonus remuneration schemes is the maximization of long-term shareholder value, the bias of power on many boards in favour of incumbent executive directors can mean that remuneration schemes are structured to benefit top executives at the expense of the shareholders. The practical question is: how should directors' remuneration be determined? The preferred solution in the corporate governance literature is for a board remuneration committee, comprised entirely of independent outside directors, to determine executive director remuneration. One problem with that is whether such directors can be seen to be genuinely independent, since often they are themselves in receipt of high rewards as directors of other companies.

Proposals for monitoring directors' rewards have included mandatory shareholder voting on director rewards, as now occurs in the United Kingdom, or legislation that would impose statutory limits. In the United States shareholders can now vote on proposed director remuneration, but the outcome is advisory, potentially capable of influencing board decisions, but not capable of overriding them. The European Union sought a cap on executive bonuses of twice the annual salary, but this invited the raising of basic salaries and other forms of game-playing. Remuneration packages need to be sufficiently generous to attract and hold people of high calibre, but end the transfer of shareholder wealth to those directors whose overriding motivation is personal greed. The issue remains on the frontier.

Gender diversity

Diversity in board membership has become of major interest around the world in recent years, particularly gender diversity, driven by a concern for greater equality at the top of organizations. A UK government-commissioned report by Lord Davies, 'Women on Boards', recognized the benefits of different skills and perspectives and called for listed companies to explain their board nomination policies.

To redress the gender balance, some countries have adopted quotas for women on boards. Norway introduced a quota in 2005 and the percentage of women has increased significantly. Eleven EU member states now have laws to promote gender equality on company boards and the European Union is considering introducing quotas in all member states. India, Malaysia, and South Africa have adopted quotas. The European Union has also suggested that companies should use clear, gender-neutral criteria when choosing non-executive directors, and that if candidates are found to be equally qualified, preference should be given to women.

Some directors are opposed to quotas, arguing that they do not guarantee that the most appropriate people become directors and, if mandated, the female board members could become 'token directors', with important decisions taken by powerful male elites outside the boardroom. However, a growing body of research has shown improvements in corporate governance and financial performance as gender diversity has improved.[1]

Governance of strategic risk

While there is evidence that boards are taking their company's exposure to risk more seriously, new issues are extending the nature and extent of that exposure. Unfortunately, the risk management systems in some organizations are immature. Some modern approaches to business have increased exposure to strategic, managerial, and operational risk. Cyber-attack or -manipulation have become a significant threat, particularly for companies with interactive, market-based systems that link customers and companies through the internet. Data theft through hacking or employees attaching their own portable IT devices to corporate systems can also prove a challenge; as can the loss of data through inadvertence (executives leaving laptops on trains, say). Overall systems failure poses a potentially catastrophic threat to day-to-day business activities, share price, or even corporate existence. Reports of the loss of customer data have increased the potential for serious reputational risk, even the possibility of lawsuits from customers or investors for alleged losses. Risk expertise is needed at board level, among both individual board members and external advisers. Some companies have expanded the role of the audit committee to include the oversight of risk: others have formed a separate board risk committee.

---

[1] For example, see Littenfeld, Doreen and Nell Beckman (2014) 'The imperative for gender diversity on boards', The Corporate Governance Advisor, May/June.

Regulations on the recognition and reporting of risk have increased, for example data protection regulations. In 2014, the UK Financial Reporting Council published new rules requiring boards to report significant behavioural, organizational, and reputational risks in the annual strategy reports of the companies it regulates. Meanwhile, new approaches to catastrophe cover are emerging; by sharing strategic risk with an investor through bonds that are repaid with interest or drawn on if specified catastrophic loss(es) occur, for example the long-term flooding of an underground railway.

Electronic and integrated reporting

Already many jurisdictions allow companies to communicate electronically with their share-holders and the market. Some jurisdictions permit electronic proxy voting by shareholders. Leading companies link investor relations with their marketing and public relations efforts. More frequent and more informative communication between boards, shareholders (particularly institutional investors), and the market is certainly a critical corporate governance frontier.

Demands for 'integrated reporting', in other words corporate communication that tells a coherent, linked narrative, are frequently heard, and are required by some regulators. An integrated report might, typically, include a discussion of the current business situation and the directors' expectations, with corporate strategies and policies for the future. Strategic reporting, going far beyond classic financial reports, might now include transparency proto-cols, the disclosure of metrics for long-term product cycles, and comments on exposure to risk. The reporting of remuneration, for example, used to be highly summarized, but some remuneration reports now provide detail by employee number, level, type, and location around the world, facilitating useful comparisons of corporate policies.

Regulations in some countries now require reporting on sustainability, pollution indices, carbon emissions, and human rights issues. Demands for access to more information from shareholder proxies have increased significantly, particularly in the United States, sometimes meeting resistance from management and their advisers. De-materialization, that is reliance on electronic links rather than paper-based systems, has increased this trend.

Another trend is an expectation from significant shareholders for personal interaction with board members, not just investment relations officers or more junior members of management. This development can offer a dialogue that is valuable to both parties, provided that topics to be discussed are identified, no price-sensitive, privileged information is given, and all major investors are offered the same rights.

Corporate governance, corporate social responsibility, and sustainability

Most voluntary corporate governance codes require formal reporting that the code has been followed or, if not, explanations given for any divergence. Unfortunately, such reporting can too easily become a recital of the company's conformance to each element of the code: what some authorities refer to as 'boilerplate' reporting. Successive reports begin to look strikingly familiar.

However, a corporate governance report actually provides an opportunity for the board to explain and comment on the way it governs the company, describing how power is exercised over shareholders' funds, how employee, customer, and investor relations are handled, how business ethics, corporate social responsibility (CSR), and sustainability are reflected in corporate policies on, for example on whistle blowing, avoiding human rights abuses, or bribery and corruption.

The growing emphasis on corporate governance, CSR, and sustainability has added another dimension to corporate reporting, acknowledging the rights of stakeholders and society to be informed on corporate issues that could affect them. The disclosure of environmental, social, and governance information (often now called ESG reporting), which was originally voluntary, has increasingly become mandatory.

Moreover, rather than being a self-serving rehearsal of a firm's achievements, mandatory business reviews require companies to quantify non-financial factors using key performance indicators, as well as providing contextual and forward-looking information. Expect more such quantitative metrics to be introduced, allowing comparison of companies' changing performance over time and between companies. ESG reporting is becoming as important to the commercial and community well-being of companies as financial reports have been to investors in the past.

Core principles of corporate governance

In 2013, the Institute of Chartered Accountants in England and Wales published what it suggested were the five overarching principles of corporate governance.[2] These are:

- *leadership:* an effective board should lead the company, steering it to meet the business purpose in both the short and long term;
- *capability:* the board should have an appropriate mix of skills, experience, and independence;
- *accountability:* the board should communicate to the company's shareholders and other stakeholders at regular intervals a fair, balanced, and understandable assessment of how the company is achieving its business purpose and meeting its other responsibilities;
- *sustainability:* the board should guide the business to create value and allocate it fairly and sustainably to reinvestment and distribution to stakeholders including shareholders, directors, employees, and customers;
- *integrity:* the board should lead the company to conduct its business in a fair and transparent manner that can withstand the scrutiny of stakeholders.

In 2010, the New York Stock Exchange (NYSE) published the report of a Commission on Corporate Governance that it had sponsored.[3] Chaired by Larry W. Sonsini, this independent commission represented investors, issuers, broker-dealers, and governance experts, and was established to examine core governance principles that could be widely supported by issuers, investors, directors, and other market participants.

The report affirmed a number of basic beliefs that:

---

[2] www.icaew.com/en/technical/corporate-governance
[3] www.nyse.com/pdfs/CCGReport.pdf

- the board's fundamental objective is to build long-term sustainable growth in shareholder value, and thus corporate policies that encourage excessive risk-taking for the sake of short-term increases in stock price are inconsistent with sound corporate governance;

- corporate management has a critical role in corporate governance, because management has the primary responsibility for creating an environment in which a culture of performance with integrity can flourish;

- while independence is an important attribute for board members, the NYSE's Listing Standards do not limit a board to only one non-independent (outside) director, and boards should seek an appropriate balance between independent and non-independent directors to ensure a proper mix of expertise, diversity, and knowledge;

- while legislation and agency rule-making are important to establish the basic tenets of corporate governance, the Commission believed that over-reliance on legislation and agency rule-making may not be in the best interests of shareholders, companies, or society, and it therefore preferred market-based governance solutions whenever possible.

The Commission predicated ten core principles of corporate governance, which appear in Corporate Governance in Action 18.1.

Corporate Governance in Action 18.1   Ten core principles of corporate governance

These appear in the 2010 Report of the Commission on Corporate Governance of the New York Stock Exchange (2010):

1. The Board's fundamental objective should be to build long-term sustainable growth in shareholder value for the corporation.

2. Successful corporate governance depends upon successful management of the company, as management has the primary responsibility for creating a culture of performance with integrity and ethical behavior.

3. Good corporate governance should be integrated with the company's business strategy and not viewed as simply a compliance obligation.

4. Shareholders have a responsibility and long-term economic interest to vote their shares in a reasoned and responsible manner, and should engage in a dialogue with companies in a thoughtful manner.

5. While legislation and agency rule-making are important to establish the basic tenets of corporate governance, corporate governance issues are generally best solved through collaboration and market-based reforms.

6. A critical component of good governance is transparency, as well-governed companies should ensure that they have appropriate disclosure policies and practices and investors should also be held to appropriate levels of transparency, including disclosure of derivative or other security ownership on a timely basis.

7. The Commission supports the NYSE's listing requirements generally providing for a majority of independent directors, but also believes that companies can have additional non-independent directors so that there is an appropriate range and mix of expertise, diversity, and knowledge on the board.

8. The Commission recognizes the influence that proxy advisory firms have on the markets, and believes that it is important that such firms be held to appropriate standards of transparency and accountability.

9. The SEC should work with exchanges to ease the burden of proxy voting while encouraging greater participation by individual investors in the proxy voting process.

10. The SEC and/or the NYSE should periodically assess the impact of major governance reforms to determine if these reforms are achieving their goals, and in light of the many reforms adopted over the last decade the SEC should consider the expanded use of 'pilot' programs, including the use of 'sunset provisions' to help identify any implementation problems before a program is fully rolled out.

These beliefs characterize the frontier of today's corporate governance thinking and practice in the United Kingdom and the United States. They also suggest some of the issues that might lie beyond that frontier in the future.

Drivers of change

So what determines the development of corporate governance in a country?

Firstly, some fundamental realities in each country and jurisdiction:

1. *The history of the country*

   Its cultural inheritance, the influence of religion on values, beliefs, and behaviour, ethnic make-up, and the development of business in the past.

2. *Government of the country*

   The effects of democracy, one-party state, or autocracy.

3. *The legal system and the rule of law*

   The underpinning of the judiciary—independent or state-led—the development of company law and regulation.

4. *Economic development*

   National resource—natural resources, technology, labour and skill levels, wealth.

5. *Calibre of professional services and institutions*

   Legal, accountancy, auditing, company secretarial institutions, and training support for corporate governance practices, including education and training.

Secondly, some specific drivers of change, which are discussed below.

Responses to corruption, corporate collapse, and economic catastrophe

The original driving forces in corporate governance thinking and practice came from the United States. Federal protection for investors and the regulation of listed companies dates back to the 1930s, with the creation of the SEC. America's historical pre-eminence in corporate governance reflects the vast amounts of capital provided through reliable and liquid markets, the availability of sophisticated legal and accountancy services, and the existence of well-developed investor information systems, with strong and trusted regulation, backed up by a massive and successful economy.

However, the collapses of Enron, WorldCom, and other companies in the United States were rooted in excessive risk-taking by management and in fraud. The Sarbanes-Oxley Act (2002) was the regulatory response and increased the influence of US governance practices on governance thinking worldwide. Most significantly, it reinforced and emphasized the rules-based underpinning of American corporate governance: a mandatory 'obey or face the consequences' regime.

But the focus has changed. In recent years, corporate governance initiatives have originated in other countries, starting with the influential 1992 Cadbury Report on the financial aspects of corporate governance in the United Kingdom. Subsequently, many other countries produced their own governance codes, followed by international codes from organizations such as the OECD and the World Bank. The underpinning philosophy of these codes has been principles-based, not rules-based; in other words, based on a voluntary 'conform or explain' regime.

The need to access investment capital from the United States was, at one time, thought likely to lead to the adoption of US corporate governance practices. But this has become less important as other economies, including the Middle East and China, have generated surpluses on the back of oil prices or economic growth. That said, major Chinese companies that have listed in the United States, consequently, have to meet SEC requirements.

Meanwhile, other financial markets are growing in scale, sophistication, and reputation, particularly in Asia. Moreover, the expensive regulatory demands and, as some perceive them, challenging attitudes of the Sarbanes-Oxley Act, SEC regulation, and US listing rules could be a disincentive for non-US companies to list in the United States. The lighter regulatory touch of other jurisdictions and financial markets is seen as more attractive, with their call to comply with corporate governance principles (or explain why not), rather than adhere strictly to legally binding rules or risk prosecution. The costs of compliance in some of these markets may also be lower. Successful capital markets will inevitably be those that are judged effective by their users—both those investing and those raising capital.

Efforts by reformers and interest groups

Over the years, efforts to reform and improve corporate governance have come from many sources. Corporate governance interest groups have encouraged sound corporate governance and contributed to the development and improvement of the subject. The *Organisation for Economic Co-operation and Development* (OECD) has been prominent,[4] advising government bodies seeking to establish norms, and publishing the OECD Principles of Corporate Governance and the OECD Guidelines on Corporate Governance of State-Owned Enterprises.

The *International Corporate Governance Network* links those interested in corporate governance reform and seeks to raise standards of corporate governance worldwide.[5] In the United States, the *Committee of Sponsoring Organizations of the Treadway Commission*

[4] www.oecd.org/about
[5] www.icgn.org

(COSO),[6] a private sector organization, is dedicated to improving the quality of financial reporting through business ethics, effective internal controls, and corporate governance. *International Shareholder Services* (ISS) is based in the United States,[7] though it operates internationally and advises institutional investors on corporate governance issues in companies around the world. ISS has an influential proxy advisory service offering analysis and recommendations. In 2018 it launched an Annual Policy Survey, a key component of ISS' annual global policy development process, looking at potential changes for 2019. Institutional investors, companies, corporate directors, and other market constituents are invited to participate.

The *European Corporate Governance Institute* (ECGI) provides a focal point for academics working on corporate governance.[8] The Global Corporate Governance Forum, run by the *International Finance Corporation* (IFC),[9] offers assistance on corporate governance to developing transition economies. The *Asian Corporate Governance Association* (ACGA) works with investors, companies, and regulators to improve corporate governance practices throughout Asia.[10] ACGA publishes regular reports on corporate governance throughout the region.

Some professional bodies also contribute to the development of ideas on corporate governance. Prominent among them are *The Conference Board* in the United States and other countries,[11] professional accounting and auditing bodies including the *Institute of Chartered Accountants in England and Wales*,[12] the *Institute of Chartered Secretaries and Administrators in London*,[13] and some law societies. A few institutional investors and other organizations developed to support and advise them have also contributed to the development of the subject. The California Public Employees Retirement System (*CalPERS*) has influenced corporate governance practices in countries and companies in which it invests,[14] by demanding US levels of governance, and publishing advisory reports. *PIRC*,[15] an independent research and advisory consultancy based in the UK, which provides services to institutional investors, has also contributed to corporate governance research and development.

It seems likely that corporate governance reformers and interest groups will continue to be drivers of change in the future, perhaps introducing ideas from other cultures, regulatory jurisdictions, and market conditions in addition to those based on Western free-market ideology.

Corporate governance research and development

On a theoretical level, more academic research and publications on corporate governance have come from American scholars than the rest of the world combined, although the extent and quality of published research from around the world continues to grow.

[6] www.coso.org
[7] www.issgovernance.com
[8] www.ecgi.global
[9] www.ifc.org
[10] www.acga-asia.org
[11] www.conference-board.org/
[12] www.icaew.com/
[13] www.icsa.org.uk/
[14] www.calpers.ca.gov
[15] www.pirc.co.uk/

In 2009, Professor Jay Lorsch and colleagues at the Harvard Business School interviewed directors of major US corporations about their reactions to the global financial crisis.[16] Their research paper found that recent corporate governance problems were primarily attributable to the growing complexity of the companies that boards governed.[17]

The Harvard research found a strong consensus among directors that the key to improving boards' performance was not government action, but action by each board. Moreover, the researchers emphasized that companies and boards differ. Each board needs to develop structures, processes, and practices that fit the needs of the company and its business: 'one size fits all' was viewed with scepticism.

The Harvard paper identified six areas for improvement:

- clarifying the board's role;
- acquiring better information and deeper understanding of the company;
- maintaining a sound relationship with management;
- providing oversight of company strategy;
- assuring management development and succession;
- improving risk management.

Unfortunately, much corporate governance research has remained in academe and has not influenced the development of corporate governance law, regulation, or practice. The metamorphosis that will determine an underpinning theory of the subject has yet to occur. Present practice is still rooted in a 19th-century legal concept of the corporation that no longer reflects corporate practices in the global business environment. Present theory is even less capable of explaining coherently the way in which modern organizations are governed.

What is needed is a vibrant alternative that explains how power is exercised over every type and form of corporate entity and strategic alliance around the world, in a way that ensures both effective performance and appropriate social accountability and responsibility. It would be good for such concepts to be rooted in rigorous and replicable research. Unfortunately, the driver of further changes in corporate governance is most likely to be exposure to further board-level excesses, corporate collapses, or the need for economic stimulus.

Social, political, and economic changes

The growing political importance and wealth-generating capacities of emerging economies, particularly China, India, and perhaps Brazil, may give them the leverage to influence international corporate governance requirements and accounting standards. Some of their companies have the potential to become global through cross-border acquisitions, influencing

---

[16] Professor Jay Lorsch is Louis Kirstein Professor of Human Relations at Harvard Business School, a member of the editorial board of *Corporate Governance: An International Review*, and author (with Colin B. Carter) of *Back to the Drawing Board* (2004), Harvard Business School Press, and other books.

[17] www.calpers.ca.gov

the economies of the host nations, although some host nations have challenged acquisitions by foreign companies, when economic performance or national interests seem threatened. Growing nationalism and economic patriotism could lead to attempts by nation states to protect domestic employment, wealth creation, or their tax base.

The governance of sovereign wealth funds, particularly their transparency, will have to be addressed at an international level. The outcome could be a code of conduct for sovereign funds requiring disclosure of their strategic aims, and details of their main holdings, perhaps regulated by an international body such as the International Monetary Fund. Unfortunately, there seems to be little enthusiasm for such controls among the countries with massive sovereign wealth.

Classical audited annual accounts are being replaced by more frequent financial reviews, strategic reports, risk analyses, corporate resource reviews, operating statements, and corporate governance reports, some responding to events as they occur. Statements of directors' expectations of the likelihood of future events may include estimates of probability ranges.

As the complexities, challenges, and risks of taking on a directorship grow, more clarification and better definition will be required of the skills, experience, and knowledge that directors need. Going beyond the structures and strictures of the compliance codes, more attention is likely to be paid to board dynamics and the chair's leadership role to achieve corporate success. The vital importance of the chair's leadership responsibility is likely to be reinforced. Forms of network governance structures, based on responsibility centres and information flows, might emerge to replace the static governing body, as a response to growing complexity, which could improve performance, and provide easier adaptation to change.

The importance of corporate governance systems that relate to the home country's political, social, and economic situation is becoming apparent. Developing nations may have as much to learn from each other as from Western experience. The future of corporate governance is unlikely to look like its past.

Society's changing expectations

The limited-liability company was a child of mid-19th century Victorian England. This was an era of institutional invention. Britain was at the height of Empire-led self-confidence. Other corporate entities—trades unions, building societies (savings and loan associations), cooperative societies, missionary societies, and professional bodies including law societies and accountants' associations—were all formed in the latter half of the 19th century. Religion, individualism, and self-help flourished. This was a society in which the concepts of duty, trust, and self-reliance were basic.

These qualities were reflected in the brilliant idea of the joint-stock company. The state passed legislation that permitted the incorporation of corporate entities separate from those managing and investing in them, while limiting the liability of those shareholders for their companies' debts. In effect, the state licensed corporate entities, and regulated their behaviour, while the directors, appointed by the investors, were trusted to act on their behalf.

As Daniel Bell has commented, capitalism developed and drew its strength from an ethic of sobriety, saving, and deferred gratification—although he also noted that free-market capitalism actually worked to undermine these qualities, stimulating hedonism and instant gratification.[18]

Every subsequent development—the formation of millions of private companies; power over companies shifting from shareholders to directors; the creation of regulatory bodies; the formation of complex corporate groups with pyramids, chains, and networks; the growth and concentration of the auditing profession; corporate governance codes; the Sarbanes-Oxley Act; calls for CSR and sustainability; indeed, everything that has happened since—is still rooted in that 19th-century creation: the virtual reality of an autonomous corporate entity.

But a company is a concept. It is a fiction, albeit a legal one. The directors and officers, managers and employees, individual shareholders, customers and suppliers, competitors, government and tax authorities, auditors and regulators are the reality. All corporate governance to date has been based on the old legal-entity paradigm. The corporate governance literature has uncritically embraced this virtual reality. As we have seen throughout this book, the corporate form has its limitations—corporate collapses, environmental hazards, corruption and abuse of power, with personal greed, rather than a fiduciary concern for members' interests, as the driving force.

But society today is not satisfied with corporate behaviour. Evidence is widespread. Scepticism abounds about business which is seen to lead to greed, excessive remuneration that erodes shareholder wealth, retirement awards and performance bonuses not linked to performance, and growing disparity of wealth in society. Around the world corruption seems rife at every level. Too many cases are reported of top management domination, arrogance, and abuse of power.

Just as economic and political forces around the world are driving change in corporate governance, society's changing expectations, particularly in the developed world, are also prompting change. Society is expecting more of corporate entities operating in its midst. Demands for CSR, sustainability, and business ethics are increasingly commonplace in the advanced world. Eventually, they are likely to be written into regulations and law. Current initiatives in this area by the United Nations are diffuse, but are being taken up at national level. The inevitable differences between cultures, jurisdictions, and stages of economic development need to be recognized more specifically in defining governance requirements, and appropriate risk profiles created, avoiding the process of merely applying advanced-country norms where they may be inappropriate.

It is apparent that there is no single ideal structure for the governance of all corporate entities. Many alternative structures and systems can work in the appropriate context. In fact, despite all of the commentary on governance structures—unitary and two-tier boards, the proportion of outside directors with lead independent director, defining director independence, the separation of chair and CEO, board committees, and the rest—the issue of effective governance is not really about structure, but about process; not about procedures, but about people.

Governance involves a political process. Governing bodies need to ensure that the entity fulfils its mission, whether this is providing goods or services to satisfy markets, offering a service to meet society's needs, or fulfilling some other purpose. In the process, the entity may

---

[18] Bell, Daniel (1962) *The End of Ideology*, Harvard University Press, Cambridge, MA.

create wealth, provide employment, facilitate innovation, and contribute to society, not least by paying taxes, at the local and national levels.

A successful governing body needs a cadre of the competent. Respected leadership is a crucial driving force. Professionalism, with continuous personal development and learning, is fundamental. In future, governing bodies may have to be less rigid, less bounded, and more adaptable. That might mean board styles that are transient, more flexible, and certainly less formal. Eventually, the place of companies in society will need to be rethought, moving beyond shareholder primacy towards a form of capitalism that embraces and links the interests of individuals, enterprises, and states.

The originators of the limited-liability company in the 19th century created a corporate governance system in which society required them to meet specific roles and responsibilities, and bounded their activities. Subsequently, the growing diversity of corporate objectives, complex ownership structures, and intricate corporate groups, led to abuse. Society lost the control that it originally demanded for the right to incorporate companies in which shareholders had no liability for corporate debts beyond their equity stake. Companies again need to be held responsible for meeting society's expectations. Incorporating a company, in which shareholders are not responsible for their company's debts, should require them to meet society's expectations. Limited liability is a privilege, not a right. What society grants, it can take away.

In the 19th century, trust was at the heart of business; it underpinned the original concept of the limited-liability company. Trust was at the heart of the capitalist system. Agreements were sealed with a handshake. Directors were recognized as reliable stewards of the interests of others. But, with the passage of time, trust has been replaced by contract and litigation.

The first edition of this book called for governing bodies with people who could be trusted, people who understood their fiduciary responsibilities, people who could put the rights and needs of others ahead of their own. Critics argued that, desirable though this might be, such altruism is not feasible: successful organizations are run by people who are primarily acting in their own best interests. However, the best interests of people need not be solely power, personal aggrandizement, or greed. In the not-for-profit sector, and indeed in the corporate sector too, some people do act responsibly in the interests of others, showing integrity, treating employees and other stakeholders fairly, and contributing to their community's and society's needs, being reliable stewards for the benefit of others. Trust remains the foundation of corporate governance.

The frontiers of corporate governance in the future

Finally, we look beyond the frontiers of corporate governance today and possible drivers of change to consider what might become dominant issues in the future.

Principles or rules?

Should the regulation and practice of corporate governance be based on principles or rules? In other words, should companies have discretion in the way in which they run their affairs or should they be constrained by the rule of law? Voluntary or mandatory: this is a fundamental issue that goes to the heart of corporate governance.

Some commentators still refer to the 'Anglo-American' approach to corporate governance, contrasting the unitary board of the Anglo-American common law jurisdictions with the two-tier supervisory and executive boards of the continental European and other civil law countries. But, in reality, a schism has appeared between American and British concepts of corporate governance.

In the United States, corporate governance is increasingly enforced by the rule of law and mandatory regulation. The US Sarbanes-Oxley Act of 2002, which was a response to the collapses of Enron, WorldCom, and the Big Five auditor Arthur Andersen, is backed up by federal and state laws, and reinforced by SEC requirements. 'Obey the law and the rules or risk the consequences' is the mantra.

By contrast, the basis of corporate governance in the United Kingdom and other countries whose company law has been influenced over the years by UK common law,[19] as well as countries with codes based on the OECD Principles, adopts a discretionary approach. Listed companies need to recognize voluntary codes of principle and best practice then report that they have complied, or explain why they have not.

Some years ago, the belief that corporate governance around the world would converge on the American model was widespread, not least because the world then needed access to American capital. That is no longer the case. So this dilemma remains unresolved. Countries that rely on the 'principles' model stoutly defend the discretion allowed by this approach, arguing that this gives companies the flexibility they need in today's business world.

In recent years, financial accounting standards in most economically advanced countries have tended to converge. International Financial Reporting Standards (IFRS), which began as an attempt to harmonize financial reporting in Europe, were originally called International Accounting Standards. The standards are published by the International Accounting Standards Board (IASB), the standard-setting arm of the IFRS Foundation, an independent, not-for-profit, private sector organization.

The objectives of the Foundation are:

- to develop a single set of high-quality, understandable, enforceable, and globally accepted IFRSs;
- to promote the use and rigorous application of those standards;
- to take account of the financial reporting needs of emerging economies and small and medium-sized enterprises (SMEs);
- to promote and facilitate the adoption of IFRSs, being the standards and interpretations issued by the IASB, through the convergence of national accounting standards and IFRSs.

In fulfilling its standard-setting duties, the IASB follows a transparent process, with the publication of consultative documents, discussion papers, and exposure drafts for public comment. All meetings of the IASB are held in public and webcast.

In the United States, companies must follow the US generally accepted accounting principles (GAAP), although the SEC has indicated that it is moving towards IFRS. In the United Kingdom, work on financial reporting policy is carried out by the Accounting Council (AC),

---

[19] Including Australia, Canada, Hong Kong, India, Malaysia, New Zealand, Singapore, and South Africa.

including financial standards, often called the UK GAAP. From January 2015, a new set of standards replaced almost all existing accounting standards with three Financial Reporting Standards (FRS 100, 101, and 102). French GAAP are called Plan Comptable Général (PCG), and are published by the French Committee of Accountancy Regulation, and validated by the French government. All of these financial reporting standards around the world are rule-based.

Trends in corporate governance around the world seem to be towards a law- and rules-based approach. To attract investors, countries need to move towards the corporate governance expectations of economically advanced nations. In the European Union, the search to harmonize company law is leading towards some standardization; although such moves meet opposition from those who prefer a country-by-country, discretionary approach.

The Corporate Secretaries International Association (CSIA) is an international federation of professional bodies promoting good governance and corporate secretaryship. CSIA asked corporate governance experts from around the world for their opinions on the corporate governance implications of the global financial crisis and subsequent economic hiatus. Their responses were condensed into 20 practical steps to better corporate governance (see Corporate Governance in Action 18.2):[20]

Corporate Governance in Action 18.2   Twenty practical steps to better corporate governance

1. Recognize that good corporate governance is about the effectiveness of the governing body—not about compliance with codes.

2. Confirm the leadership role of the board chairman.

3. Check that the non-executive directors have the necessary skills, experience, and courage.

4. Consider the calibre of the non-executive directors.

5. Review the role and contribution of non-executive directors.

6. Ensure that all directors have a sound understanding of the company.

7. Confirm that the board's relationship with executive management is sound.

8. Check that directors can access all the information they need.

9. Consider whether the board is responsible for formulating strategy.

10. Recognize that the governance of risk is a board responsibility.

11. Monitor board performance and pursue opportunities for improvement.

12. Review relations with shareholders—particularly institutional investors.

13. Emphasize that the company does not belong to the directors.

14. Ensure that directors' remuneration packages are justifiable and justified.

[20] www.corporategovernanceoup.wordpress.com/2010/05/31/twenty-steps-to-better-corporate-governance

15. Review relations between external auditors and the company.

16. Consider relations with the corporate regulators.

17. Develop written board-level policies covering relations between the company and the societies it affects.

18. Review the company's attitudes to ethical behavior.

19. Ensure that [the] company secretary's function is providing value.

20. Consider how [the] corporate secretary's function might be developed.

Shareholders or stakeholders?

In profit-orientated companies there are typically four principal groups of stakeholders—the customers, the providers of goods and services (suppliers), employees, and of course the providers of finance (typically the shareholders). Obviously, to be successful a board must ensure that over time the company satisfies each of them. However, the classical model of the joint-stock, limited-liability company gives pre-eminent power to the shareholders: ownership is recognized as the basis of that power to elect the directors and require them to report to shareholders on their stewardship. This concept applies to both public companies, owned by investors through a stock market, and private companies, owned by another company (a subsidiary or associated company) or by individuals, such as members of a family. The primacy of shareholders is still recognized by many authorities, as we saw in Corporate Governance in Action 18.1:

> The Board's fundamental objective should be to build long-term sustainable growth in shareholder value for the corporation.

However, in recent years, a new emphasis has emerged: the company as a member of society, with a duty to recognize the interests of all the stakeholders who could be affected by its actions. The entire thrust of the call for CSR recognizes responsibilities to all stakeholders as well as to shareholders. Many corporate governance codes, including the latest UK code, identify boards' responsibilities to these other stakeholders. The UK 2006 Companies Act even writes the requirement into company law.

Not-for-profit entities, many of them incorporated as companies limited by guarantee, and including the governing bodies of some medical facilities, education establishments, and trades unions, also have their groups of stakeholders. In a hospital, for example, there are the patients, the doctors, the nurses and other medical staff, other employees, suppliers, sub-contractors, suppliers of goods and services, and the funding authorities, as well as various regulators.

The advantage of the pursuit of long-term profit as the primary goal (the 'single bottom line') is its simplicity. The problem with pursuing a variety of goals ('multiple bottom lines') is difficulty in reliably measuring the achievement of some stakeholders' goals, but more significantly that the goals of different stakeholders may conflict with each other. Inevitably, the interests of different stakeholders in a company are in tension.

It is clear that the 19th-century model of limited-liability companies no longer reflects reality; nor does it meet society's present expectations, which will continue to evolve.

Board culture and dynamics

Corporate governance codes (and in the United States SEC regulations), which tend to reflect accepted best practice, tend to emphasize board structures, board audit, remuneration, and nomination committees, the importance of independent outside directors, and corporate governance reporting. In other words, the emphasis to date has been on board structure and compliance. Such guidance sets boundaries, which can prevent board-level abuse and excess; but may also restrain imaginative, original, and entrepreneurial thinking and practice. Corporate governance codes and regulation have not found the universal corporate governance principles they have searched for. Despite their compliance, many boards fail to fulfil their potential.

More penetrating insights are now needed. Boards are not just legal entities or compliers with codes. They are human artefacts; living, changing organisms. Each team of directors has its own dynamic. Over time, every board develops its own culture—that set of shared experiences, perceptions, and beliefs which determines how it sees and responds to corporate situations.

The behaviour of boards varies significantly. Some boards reach agreement easily; others are more like debating societies, even adversarial parliaments. Interpersonal relations between directors can be significant; so can the role of dominant members. The personalities of the board chair, the CEO, and perhaps the lead independent director can differ dramatically. Relationships between the CEO and other executive directors—and between the executive directors and the outside directors—are fundamental to board culture. The leadership style of the board chair crucially affects board culture, as anyone experiencing a change of chair will testify.

Independence in outside directors is rigorously defined in most codes, but only personality, knowledge, and experience can determine the real contribution that an independent director makes. Character, interpersonal skills, and toughness of mind determine independence, not code definitions.

Critical insights into a board's culture can sometimes be found in its approach to corporate strategy, how it responds to crises, and the way it deals with disagreements. Changes in the membership of the board can affect its culture as new expectations are introduced and old beliefs challenged. In the future, expect more emphasis on board dynamics, culture, and leadership, than on structure and compliance with codes. The focus of corporate governance development is unlikely to come from more work on structure, reporting, or regulation, but on understanding board dynamics and directors' behaviour. That said, it has to be admitted that another dramatic collapse, like Enron, or another international financial catastrophe, will bring calls for more corporate regulation, structure, and reporting.

More effective boards and board chairs

As the focus in corporate governance swings from structure and routines towards board culture and dynamics, more attention will inevitably be paid to the effectiveness of the board and its subcommittees, the contribution of each board member, and, in particular, the calibre and the ability of the board chair. Independent, external assessment of board activities and directors' behaviour, seeking opportunities for improvement, could become a regular feature of board assessment. Every meeting of the board and board committee provides a potential learning opportunity. Indeed, a professional chair might ask 'what have we learned from this meeting—both in content and process?'

More attention is likely to be focused on the board chair as the leader of the board team, rather than the facilitator of board meetings. The same could also apply to the chairs of board committees. Most chairs acquire their chairing abilities by serving under other chairs and experience in the role themselves. Once the responsibility of board chair as leader of the board is recognized, opportunities for training and personal development will occur.

Every director should realize that however much knowledge, experience, and training they have, continual technological, market, and competitive change is happening, which calls for constant learning. Similarly, developments in the company's economic, political, legal, and societal situation need to be updated regularly.

The future of strategic reporting

The intention of regular strategic reports, now required by many corporate governance codes, is to give existing and potential investors and the market an insight into the board's expectations and beliefs about their company's future. Some strategic reports have become little more than a recital of the company's lines of business and the market they serve. But others provide valuable information about planned developments, research and development activities, as well as intimating the implications of uncertain economic, political, and social changes around the world.

However, none can provide information on unforeseen strategic events, such as a hostile takeover bid, the effects of currency devaluation, or the imposition of massive tariff barriers abroad. Moreover, there is an inevitable tension between the stock markets' search for information about potential corporate value and risk exposure, and companies' need not to give vital information to their competitors or predators' acquisition teams.

Nevertheless, pressure on companies in the world's advanced stock markets is likely to continue to grow. Companies may respond by providing more details of the assumptions underlying forecasts with probability estimates. For example: rather than 'our sales in China are likely to grow', a company might report that 'sales in China are expected to increase by between 25 and 45 per cent over the next five years with the most likely forecast being 30 per cent, subject to the continuation of existing import controls by the Chinese government'. Such statistical techniques provide a wider range of information but also serve to indicate the uncertainties facing a company. More use might also be made of scenarios about uncertain future events. For example, a car manufacturer might suggest possible effects on its sales from the development of driverless cars and the strategic reactions being planned.

Other developments in strategic reporting might include more discussion of companies' competitive markets, including possible actions by competitors, responses to investment analysts' 'buy, sell, keep' reports, and top management succession plans. The notion that strategic reporting is an annual event is also likely to be replaced by a fluid approach more in keeping with modern social media and information technology.

(See also FRC Guidance on Strategic Reporting (2018), available at www.frc.org.uk/getattachment/fb05dd7b-c76c-424e-9daf-4293c9fa2d6a/Guidance-on-the-Strategic-Report-31-7-18.pdf)

In October 2018, the UK Financial Reporting Council (FRC) launched a major initiative to challenge existing thinking about corporate reporting and consider how companies could better meet the information needs of shareholders and other stakeholders.[21] Paul George, executive director of corporate governance and reporting at the FRC, said:

> Accounting and reporting plays an important role in building trust in business and providing information for investment decisions, and the Annual Report is one of the cornerstones of reporting. However, corporate reporting is wider than this. We are seeing developments in the responsible business agenda and the need for businesses to be accountable to a wider group of stakeholders. Reporting is evolving in response to these developments and so the project will examine the extent to which the annual report or other communication channels best serve all stakeholder needs.

Investor and societal involvement

Many listed companies now recognize the value of social media to connect with their stakeholders, particularly their customers and potential customers, employees and future employees, and their investors and potential investors. The investor relations endeavours of many quoted companies are now substantial, often using investor relations websites to provide director reports, corporate governance reports, financial and other performance information, and, in the case of companies listed in the United States, access to SEC-filed reports. Many websites provide not only one-way information from the company to investors, but also an opportunity to communicate with the company to seek information or provide comment.

This use of electronic media to provide continuous updates to the stock market and investment community is a far cry from the traditional, periodic, printed shareholder report, published long after the end of a financial period.

However, despite the efforts of many companies to improve and increase their investor relations, a recent study of companies on the Hong Kong stock market showed that a minority of listed companies there still paid little attention to their shareholders; indeed, a few did not know (or seem to care) who their shareholders were.

Nevertheless, improving investor relations is likely to remain on the corporate governance frontier, seeking ever more innovative ways, including webcasts, online forums, and new forms of interaction, to improve the company's reputation and its share price in the long term. Investor relations are likely to be recognized as an increasingly important part of the board's work and a responsibility of every director.

New organizational forms

The original corporate concept did not envisage the complexity of today's organizational structures, with interwoven supply chains, networks of subsidiary and associated companies, companies with off-balance-sheet financing vehicles, chains of companies giving leveraged power to companies at the top of the chain, limited partnerships controlling listed companies, groups with cross-holdings of shares and cross-directorships, and other networks with joint ventures and strategic alliances. Frequently, these networks of corporate interests operate in multiple jurisdictions, cultures, and currencies. They may have voracious appetites for growth, with the attendant risks. These new organizational forms may use other forms of financing than the stock market.

[21] www.frc.org.uk/news/october-2018/frc-to-examine-the-future-of-corporate-reporting

Such organizational forms can raise significant questions for corporate governance and financial reporting. New forms of networked, digitally based organization could emerge that link entities created as classical joint-stock, limited-liability companies with government and non-government organizations and community groupings. Moreover, such entities could be dynamic and evolve rapidly. Corporate-regulation and financial-disclosure rules may struggle to keep pace. How such organizations are governed in the future will provide a major challenge.

The implications of globalization have been well recognized for years. Multinational groups operate in many countries and in different jurisdictions, sometimes generating more wealth than the GDP of host countries. But multinational companies have tended to have a specific 'home' country, often defined by the nationality of their directors, where they are incorporated, where the head office is located, where they are listed, and where most of their investors live. Now a new phenomenon is emerging: 'meta-national corporate entities' which operate not only *in* many nation states but exist *above* them. Such groups can be defined by the many nationalities of their main board directors, the diversity of their markets and customers, the international spread of their facilities and where their employees are located, where they have headquarters, and probably most significantly, where they have decided to be domiciled for tax purposes. Nestlé, AstraZeneca, and some of the international oil companies fit this model, which may become more prevalent, but raises corporate governance issues for country-based regulators and stock markets.

Moreover, the economic and political world in which international companies operate is itself in a state of flux. Changes to border tariffs and corporate taxes promoted by President Trump have already caused some US-based companies, which operate supply chains and customer delivery systems across national frontiers, to repatriate funds to the USA and review their international corporate structures. Britain's exit from the European Union has also caused some British-based companies to reorganize their European corporate operations. Other countries have seen growing nationalism, which could affect international companies' strategic plans and, thus, their organizational and corporate governance arrangements.

The independence of external auditors and board advisers

Independent external auditors play a fundamental role in corporate governance systems throughout the world. Their principal role is to reassure investors, regulators, tax authorities, and others that the financial and other public reports produced by the directors truly and fairly reflect the state of the company's affairs. Clearly, to fulfil this duty objectively, auditors need to be completely independent of their client company and its directors.

Auditors to the world's major companies are now themselves major businesses. However, the formal audit can provide a platform to offer non-audit work, such as tax services, management consultancy, information technology, and more. Partners of the major audit firms are judged by fee generation, growth, and profit performance.

Serious questions have been asked about the auditors' position. Does the auditors' economic dependency infringe their independence? Who are their *real* clients: the directors or the shareholders? The *de jure* response is that the client is the company, which means the shareholders. The *de facto* reality is that the client is the board, particularly the board's audit committee and the chief financial officer.

The dilemma is that, in effect, external auditors serve two masters—the financial market, for whom they provide an independent external check, and the directors with whom the audit firm must work closely. Moreover, the directors approve the fees, and reappointment.

The audits of most major companies around the world are in the hands of an oligopoly of just four international accounting firms. Some now feel that domination of the market for audit is unhealthy and suggest breaking up the firms or opening the audit market to second-tier firms. Some competition authorities have also questioned the situation. But financial markets like the assurance they believe they get from an audit opinion signed by one of the Big Four. Periodic tendering for audits has been suggested to reduce over-familiarity and introduced in some countries. Occasional mandatory rotation of audit firms and audit partners have also been suggested. Others have proposed further rules to regulate auditors' activities, like the US Sarbanes-Oxley Act (2002). But this approach has proved more expensive and less effective than expected, as seen in the subsequent collapse and bail-out of financial institutions, particularly in the USA and UK.

Another proposal has been made that auditors be appointed by and report to company regulators, as well as the directors.[22] In this way, close relationships between directors and auditors would be avoided. Under the proposal, the client company would still pay for their audit. If auditors reported to the regulator rather than the directors, a new mindset about audit would be needed.

Furthermore, there are other professions and firms that advise boards and their directors, such as lawyers, recruitment agencies, and compensation consultants, who need to provide independent advice, but whose independence has sometimes been questioned. The independence of external auditors and others who work with and for boards is likely to remain a frontier topic.

Corporate governance lessons from China

Forty years ago, before China's modernization drive, there was no corporate governance in the country, because there were no corporate entities: everything belonged to and was run by the State. When state-owned enterprises (SOEs) were corporatized and, in some cases, listed on a stock exchange in 1994, corporate governance systems were needed. Subsequently, when independent private companies were created, the need was amplified. Western experience was drawn on, with the help of the OECD and the World Bank, to create an infrastructure of company regulation and law, a corporate governance code, and listing rules for China's two stock exchanges in Shanghai and Shenzhen (a city just across the border from Hong Kong).

But they were not particularly effective. Systems of checks and balances proved cumbersome or non-existent. Lack of integrity and corruption were rife. Some ventures failed. Yet today a few of the largest and most successful companies in the world are Chinese. Key companies on the stock exchange boards in New York, London, Hong Kong, as well as on Nasdaq, are Chinese. Meanwhile the state-owned sector has been reorganized, reinvigorated, and is also investing abroad. In recent years, corporate governance in China has taken a different direction from the West. Are there lessons that might benefit the rest of the world?

The Chinese are intelligent and astute learners and have studied foreign corporate governance codes and regulations, keeping parts that would be relevant. Of course, corporate

---

[22] Tricker, Bob (2011) 'Re-engineering the limited liability company', *Corporate Governance: An International Review*, 19 (4), July.

governance in China remains a work in progress; just as leader Xi Jinping sees the governance of the country as an evolving activity.

Around the world, sound corporate governance is recognized as important. But China has developed a unique approach. Although initially building on Western experience, the Chinese see corporate governance as a means of improving the economy and building society in the interests of the people, the Party, and the State. Clearly, there is more than one approach to corporate governance. Maybe, the Western, OECD-led mechanisms are not the only way to sound governance.

The economic success of the Chinese socialist model does raise questions about the universality of market-led capitalism and democratic norms. A new insight into corporate governance in China is needed. China is different. Consider some of its unique characteristics:[23]

- The Chinese retail market is vast and has created a crucial opportunity for companies. The Chinese middle class now has a massive disposable income. The size of the Chinese market in many sectors provides overwhelming opportunities.

- Broadly, the State sets the basic parameters for business development, with local government and businesses competing among themselves. Unlike Western democracies, one party—the Chinese Communist Party—sets the tone for business.

- Crucially, China has focused on results rather than regulation in its corporate governance. In the early stages development included discussion of a wide range of alternatives. A system has evolved that incorporates supervisory boards, often with party members in evidence, as well as an executive board but with experienced independent members.

- Explore, experiment, and innovate have become the watchwords of advancing Chinese companies. Experimentation in their basic business model has been a contributor to the success of many Chinese firms. The same 'experiment and innovate' approach can be seen in corporate governance. Facing the challenge to catch up with the advanced world, Chinese companies were willing to explore ideas, and experiment in pursuing them.

- Fortuitously, the digital revolution offered opportunities and many Chinese companies were prepared to explore the opportunities. Both the Chinese government and Chinese companies are practical. If a corporate governance idea does not work, it is instantly replaced. The Chinese authorities were bold in experimenting with governance practices, focusing on the real purpose of such and the desired outcome. Perhaps this sense of uncertainty and freshness gave rise to the variety of options.

- Basically, the State sees corporate governance as a means of developing the economy and society in the service of the people, rather than a means of regulation and control.

- In China optimism is pervasive. There is a yearning to catch up quickly, to jump at opportunities, and sometimes unfortunately to trade off on detail and quality. Contracts are kept simple, then negotiated and adjusted along the way. The need to keep agreements simple reflects the Chinese culture and the way companies make decisions. Decision-making in Chinese companies is by consensus. This means that by the time an action is executed, support is already there. Everyone knows about the decision

---

[23] Tricker, Bob and Gregg Li (2019) *Understanding Corporate Governance in China*, Hong Kong University Press.

and people are committed. Shared accountability for the outcome of decisions is encouraged. Lines of responsibility are often blurred and demarcation is difficult.

- Successful corporate governance needs competent directors. Chinese authorities have made major efforts to find excellent directors for SOEs. Good directors are pampered and protected. The CEOs of SOEs are government employees. CEOs are paid on civil service scales. Consequently, remuneration costs are lower than competitors in the rest of the world. CEOs are assessed by government authorities and moved between enterprises according to their performance and the needs of the State. Top management of independent private companies in China are often the founders and their close associates. Their rewards are reflected in the rising worth of their companies and the value of their shareholdings, if the company is listed.

New theories of corporate governance

At the moment, there is no universally accepted theory of corporate governance. Relationships between corporate governance practices and the performance of companies, their boards, and directors are still unclear, although evidence is growing that sound corporate governance leads to better, sustainable performance, higher share prices, and lower cost of capital. Developments in corporate governance policies and practices have often been more responses to corporate collapses and malaise in the finance markets than the results of rigorous research.

New insights from such research could lead to future developments in the subject. Fundamental rethinking may follow the recognition that the statistically significant conclusions from agency theoretical studies are based on a bounded model of reality. New fields for research could include academic perspectives other than those of financial economics, including interpersonal, behavioural, or political concepts. New models, frameworks, and concepts are needed and are likely to emerge. Systems theory offers the potential of a better understanding of boundaries, levels, and input/output relationships. Corporate governance could be studied as an information process. Other insights could come from studies of the socio-politics of boards, studying boards as teams, or as communication networks.

New thinking and better understanding might also emerge from studies of board leadership and the style of the chair. The concept of power in corporate governance might repay further exploration. The psychology of boards and the individual motivations of key players could also offer insights. A real problem with corporate governance research has been getting access to the boardroom. But that is being overcome and further rigorous studies are likely to be reported.

Reinventing the corporation

But before such thinking can be developed, a dilemma has to be resolved. The classification of corporate entities has not changed for over 100 years. Around the world, limited companies are still divided into just two categories: public and private. This simple distinction between public companies, which permit the raising of outside investment, and private companies, which do not, is naive, and a totally inadequate categorization of corporations. Nor is there a comprehensive classification of the myriad other corporate entities that need governing.

A classification scheme, or taxonomy, is needed that distinguishes different species and subspecies of corporate entity. One approach might be to differentiate corporate types by the way in which power is, or could be, exercised over them. Such a categorization would need to cover all types of corporate entity in every jurisdiction, including, for example, South Korean *chaebols*, Japanese *keiretsu*, and Italian chained companies. It would need to include entities in different cultures, with different legal systems, institutions, and regulatory bodies. There seems little justification for excluding other corporate types such as non-government organizations (NGOs), trade unions, charities, professional bodies, and not-for-profit organizations.

Clearly, investment is not the only basis for the exercise of power over corporate entities. Classically, monarchs, dictators, or the church wielded power over valuable resources, and these leaders were subsequently replaced in some places by the federal state. Elsewhere, community organizations at the state, regional, or local level manage resources, provide local facilities, and run utilities, with power exercised through members of that community. Members of organizations provide the basis for corporate governance, in membership organizations such as trades unions, consumer and supplier cooperatives, savings and loan associations (building societies), mutual insurance associations, the accountancy, legal, and medical professions, universities, and some charities. Governance by employees can be through employee shareholdings—as in United Airlines in the United States—through partnership—as in the John Lewis Partnership in the United Kingdom—or through worker cooperatives—as in the Mondragon worker cooperative in Spain.

Tighter definition is also needed for listed companies to differentiate those with widely held shareholdings, those dominated by one or a block of shareholders, those owned by another listed company, state-chartered companies with a minority of shares listed, and public companies that are not listed on a stock exchange.

Private companies also need to be differentiated between parent companies of groups, wholly owned subsidiaries in a group, partly owned subsidiaries, and associated companies dominated by another company. Other categories could include private equity firms, sovereign wealth funds, hedge funds, joint venture companies, and private companies dominated by family interests. Partnerships, both with and without limited liability, could form other classes; as could government departments, organizations mandated by government, NGOs, not-for-profit entities with guarantors not shareholders, self-governing social organizations, unincorporated family firms, and sole traders.

Each of these arrangements could provide the base for wielding power over corporate resources—in other words, for corporate governance. So far, a great deal of corporate governance thinking has been focused on the governance of quoted companies. The list above suggests that there is considerable scope for further work. The opportunity exists to create a new paradigm of corporate governance which would rethink the relationship between individual, enterprise, and state in a way appropriate to the 21st century rather than the 19th or 20th.

In all ecosystems, diversity is essential for survival. The rich variety of organizational forms and potential governance mechanisms above suggests that the frontiers of corporate diversity, far from converging, are evolving and multiplying. Indeed, it has been suggested that the era of the listed, public company has passed its zenith.

Taxonomy of different types of corporate entity could lead to new theoretical insights and developments. Corporate entities are at once legal beings, economic artefacts, and social organizations. They can be studied as any of them. As a legal entity, the corporation is an artificial being created, bounded, and controlled by the laws of the country in which it was incorporated and operates. As an economic artefact, it strives to respond to market forces and to meet the economic goals of its owners and directors, keeping within the law. But corporate bodies could also be seen as self-governing social institutions. Their boundaries, connections, and functions could be defined by cybernetic communication and control linkages with the nodes defined with requisite variety, rather than legal rules and governance regulations.

Information boundaries and linkages to stakeholders, rather than ownership boundaries, could be used to define an entity. Dynamic and rapidly evolving groupings of networked or chained entities could be represented as organic systems rather than through the mechanistic, legal model.

Some companies operating globally are now larger than the states in which they operate. Nevertheless, they have to act in the legal, economic, and cultural shadows of these host countries. Not since the days of the East India Company have they been permitted to operate their own armies. Companies do not acquire power from their global scale. States give corporate entities the licence to operate. What states give, they can take away. Governance power can be redefined by the state.

The governance agenda

Finally, in considering the frontiers of corporate governance around the world, we need to recognize legitimate differences between countries' economic, social, and political levels of development. Countries with advanced economies are likely to have the instruments and institutions necessary for successful corporate governance: well-developed company law and regulation, corporate governance codes, reliable legal systems, liquid stock markets, trustworthy financial institutions including brokers, sponsors, and financial advisers, comprehensive disclosure with high transparency, respected accounting and legal professions, reliable auditing firms, director-related professional organizations and educational institutions, and reputable corporate governance research.

While many nations with developing and transitional economies properly aspire to such situations, allowances have to be made for the evolution of, for example, company law, the legitimacy of the courts, the prevention of corruption, or state involvement in corporate affairs. The frontiers of corporate governance vary and are constantly on the move.

Towards a philosophy of corporate governance

The initial focus on corporate governance, once the subject acquired a name, was on structure and reporting—the structure of boards and board committees with INEDs, reflecting the guidelines of corporate governance codes and reporting in line with them, as well as compliance with regulatory requirements and company law. Subsequently, the significance of culture was recognized; the culture in the board itself and throughout the company.

A significant body of knowledge has now been accumulated within the subject; but thus far, little attempt has been made to relate it to its societal, political, or economic context. The evolution of limited-liability companies, their directors, shareholders, and other stakeholders owes more to a series of historical accidents than developments rooted in logical reasoning. Nor have the values and expected behaviours inherent in corporate governance practices been adequately recognized. Much of the corporate governance literature takes as a given the place of corporate entities in society: yet in reality alternatives are feasible. For example, the development of successful corporate governance in China, a one-party state, has shown that democratic institutions are not an essential ingredient.

A focus on the knowledge, values, relationships, and reality of corporate governance around the world suggests that, given logical reasoning, a philosophy of the subject could be developed that would integrate corporate governance with its societal, economic, and political context. Such theory would embrace every corporate entity, whatever its size, purpose, or domicile, distinguish governance from management, and clarify its relationships with its societal, economic, and political reality.

So we come to the end of this book, but not to the end of the story of corporate governance. Forty years ago the phrase 'corporate governance' was not used.[24] Today, Google had nearly 2,000 million references to the term. The way power is exercised over corporate entities around the world continues to fascinate. The importance of the subject can only grow. The value of those who have mastered the subject seems assured.

Case studies

 Case study 18.1   Amazon: president, CEO, and chair

Amazon was started by Jeff Bezos as an online bookseller from his home in Seattle, Washington State. He had previously been vice-president of a Wall Street firm. In July 1994, Bezos incorporated a company in the US state of Washington called Cadabra (from the conjuring phrase 'abracadabra'). A year later, he incorporated Amazon in the state of Delaware, a state with friendlier companies legislation and company courts. The Cadabra business was backed into the new company.

 Amazon then diversified with CDs, videos, and software, adding the downloading and streaming of film, and Kindles and other e-readers when the technology became available. But Amazon's great strength lay in its mastery of cloud computing, allowing it to offer infrastructure worldwide with merchandising platforms for its own and other companies' products. Amazon provides several websites in the USA, and others in Australia, Brazil, France, Germany, Holland, India, Japan, and elsewhere. Amazon is the largest retailer in the United States, by market capitalization, having overtaken Walmart in 2015.

Corporate governance at Amazon

Amazon's website has a lot of corporate governance information on its investor relations home page including:

- financial reports;
- SEC filings;
- shareholder letters (including the founder's comments on corporate philosophy and policies);
- press releases on investor matters;

---

[24] The first book with the title *Corporate Governance* was published in 1984—Tricker, R. I. (1984) *Corporate Governance—practices. procedures and powers: British companies and their boards of directors*, Gower Publishing Company and the Corporate Policy Group, Nuffield College, Oxford.

- shareholder webcasts and a webcast archive.[25]

The founder and other owners connected with him maintain their control over the company with a class of shares that have dominant voting rights.

The board has twelve members and three standing committees:

- audit committee;
- nominating and corporate governance committees;
- leadership development and compensation committee.

Directors and their membership of board committees

Jeffrey P. Bezos	President, Chief Executive Officer, and Chairman of the Board
Tom Alberg	Managing Partner, Madrona Venture Group Audit Committee
John Seeley Brown	Visiting Scholar and Adviser to the Provost of the University of Southern California Nominating Committee
Bing Gordon	Partner, Kliener, Pweekins, Caulfield, and Byers
Jamie Groelick	Partner, Wilmer, Cutter, Pickering, Hale, and Dorr LLP Chair, Nominating Committee
Dania. P. Huttenlocher	Compensation Committee
Judith A. McGrath	Former CEO, MTV Networks Compensation Committee
Alain Monié	CEO, Ingram Micro
Jonathan J. Rubenstein	Former Chair and CEO, Palm Inc. Chair, Compensation Committee
Thomas O. Ryder	Former Chair and CEO, Readers' Digest Association Chair, Audit Committee
Patricia O. (Patty) Stonesifer	President and CEO, Martha's Table Nominating Committee
Wendell P. Weeks	Chair, President, and CEO, Corning Inc.

Officers of the Company

Jeffrey P. Bezos	President, Chief Executive Officer, and Chair of the Board
Brian T. Olsavsky	Senior Vice-President and Chief Financial Officer
Jeffrey M. Blackburn	Senior Vice-President, Business Development
Andrew R. Jassy	CEO, Amazon Web Services
Shelley L. Reynolds	Vice-President, Worldwide Controller, and Principal Accounting Officer
Jeffrey A. Wilke	CEO, Worldwide Consumer
David A. Zapolsky	Senior Vice-President, General Counsel, and Secretary

[25] The investor relations home page is at: http://phx.corporate-ir.net/phoenix.zhtml%3Fc%3D97664%26p%3Dirol-irhome

Discussion Questions

1. Does Amazon have a well-balanced board?

2. Jeff Bezos has the title of president, chief executive officer, and chair of the board. Some of the members of his board also carry multiple titles such as chair, president, and CEO. Is such centralization of authority and power in one person a good idea?

3. Should the roles of CEO and chair of the board be separated?

4. Should Jeff Bezos' succession be planned? If so, how?

 Case study 18.2   NHS Foundation Trust—fifth case study

After the board meeting described in Case study 13.2, Mr Evans had resigned. The board subcommittees and other NHS authorities had interviewed Mr Evans and established a *prima facie* case that he did have a long-standing business relationship with PGL International, which he had not disclosed at the time of the OFK tender. Consideration was being given to a prosecution for misconduct in public office, which would need to establish that Mr Evans held a public office and had wilfully misconducted himself to such a degree as to amount to an abuse of the public's trust in the office holder.

Lady Beechwood had been invited to rejoin the board as a non-executive director and had accepted. The following extracts are from the next meeting.

Appointment of Board Chair

Lady Beechwood was invited to resume her chairmanship of the Board, with the unanimous approval of all members. Lady Beechwood accepted on the understanding that she would only serve for two years—the remaining duration of her previous chairmanship.

Action: Lady Beechwood takes the Chair.

Formation of a standing Board Nomination Committee

The Chair emphasized the need for succession planning for non-executive Directors and senior administrative and medical staff. She proposed formation of a Nomination Committee as a standing committee of the Board, responsible for recommending suitable candidates. The Nomination Committee would have three non-executive members and be supported by the Chief Executive, the Finance Director and other executives as needed. As the Chair explained, this would be preferable to the present ad hoc formation of a committee whenever a vacancy arose.

Action: Form Board Nomination Committee.

Succession planning

The Chair proposed that the first task of the Nomination Committee would be to develop a succession plan for Non-executive Directors, identifying suitable candidates and, where appropriate, discussing the Board's world with them, giving corporate governance training if necessary, and assessing their willingness to serve. The Board agreed.

Action: Nomination Committee to produce a succession plan.

Strategic thinking

The Chair said that looking back over her experience with the Board, too much time had been spent responding to short-term crises and not enough to a long-term strategic view. She suggested that the Board should convene for a whole day, perhaps in a different location than the board room, to talk about the Trust's work in five and ten years' time. Position papers could be prepared on the likely local demographics, the population size, and age distribution, and possible medical and technological changes, for example the increasing use by patients of self-diagnosis through the internet.

The Medical Director said that a view would have to be taken of political changes and whether there would be more privatisation of health services. It would also mean taking a view on possible moves towards private medicine. The Chief Nurse said that the real difficulty with long-term planning was staff availability, particularly whether overseas staff could get visas. Mr Belvedere commented that he was amazed longer-term planning was not the norm; you can't run a successful business without long-term thinking. The Acting Chief Executive said that longer-term plans had been prepared before but unexpected events always upset them.

Action: The Board agreed to pursue the Chair's proposal for a one-day session to consider longer-term issues.

Discussion questions

1. Has the newly appointed chair begun to change the board culture?

2. Is it a sound idea to identify possible future non-executive directors before there is a vacancy?

3. Is five- and ten-year planning feasible for a NHS Foundation Trust?

 Case study 18.3   Unilever rethinks its corporate governance structure

In September 2018, the board of Unilever announced plans to abandon its 88-year-old Anglo-Dutch dual governance structure.[26] Immediately some of the largest institutional investors in the UK Unilever company said they would vote against the proposals, which included moving the Unilever headquarters and its UK domicile from London to the Netherlands. The downsides for UK funds included the forced sale of Unilever (UK) shares and exposure to additional tax risks in the Netherlands.

[26] Reuters and *The Times*, London, 15 and 19 September 2018.

The Unilever Group

Unilever is one of the largest producers of consumer goods in the world. It operates through subsidiary companies and associated enterprises in over 150 countries. Unilever markets over 500 brands including soaps, detergents, dish- and clothes-washing products, soups, sauces, salad dressings, pasta, cooking fats, spreads, ice cream, tea, and kitchen equipment.

The governance of Unilever

The Unilever Group is owned by two public, listed companies—Unilever NV (NV) based in the Netherlands and Unilever PLC (PLC) based in the UK. The shares are listed in Amsterdam, London, and New York. Dutch investors hold about 55 per cent of the combined share capital of the Group.

The Unilever Group recognizes the importance of good corporate governance. It ranked second in the UK Institute of Directors' survey of the ten best companies' corporate governance. Group companies have to meet the corporate governance requirements in the Netherlands, the UK, and as a foreign private issuer in the United States. For a detailed description of the governance of Unilever under this structure see www.unilever.com/Images/ir-governance-of-unilever-1-jan-2015-final_tcm244-485172_en.pdf.

In its document 'The Governance of Unilever',[27] the company says

> we conduct our operations in accordance with internationally accepted principles of good governance and best practice, whilst ensuring compliance with the corporate governance requirements applicable in the countries in which we operate.
>
> NV and PLC, together with their group companies, operate effectively as a single economic entity. This is achieved by a series of agreements between NV and PLC, together with special provisions in the articles of association of both NV and PLC. NV and PLC have the same directors, adopt the same accounting principles, and their shareholders receive dividends on an equalised basis.

Unilever beats a takeover bid from Kraft

In 2017, the US-based Kraft Heinz Group made a US$143 billion takeover bid for Unilever. The Unilever board responded aggressively, with some hard-hitting statements against the bid, arguing that the offer did not fairly reflect the value of Unilever. Within two days of the bid becoming public knowledge it had failed.

The revised governance structure

Unilever planned to simplify its dual-share structure by creating a single share traded on the Amsterdam, London, and New York markets. Such an arrangement would require the approval of 75 per cent of its UK investors. The plan also involved moving its headquarters from London to the Netherlands. The London office would be responsible for Unilever beauty and homecare products.

However, problems were foreseen: a Dutch-based Unilever would not qualify for inclusion in the FTSE 100 index. That would mean that funds dedicated to tracking that index would have to sell their shares. Another fear in London was that the Dutch government might introduce a 15 per cent withholding tax on dividends, which could apply to foreign investors. Should that happen, Unilever

---

[27] www.unilever.com/investor-relations/agm-and-corporate-governance/our-corporate-governance/

said that it would offer them a 'dividend substitution' payment from its capital reserves, guaranteed for ten years. But some UK funds felt that the Unilever proposals did not do enough to persuade them, and could have unexpected tax implications.

Some in the CSR lobby also criticized the proposals for their emphasis on shareholders' interests, disregarding the implications for employees, consumers, sustainable manufacturing processes, and societal interests.

Why did the Unilever board propose the new governance structure?

Commentators were quick to suggest reasons for Unilever's proposals, including:

1. To reflect the reality of the way the Group actually operated, rather than continuing a fiction rooted in its historical development.

2. To avoid the additional costs and time involved in running the Group through two separate listed entities.

3. To reflect the reality of the shareholder base, with over half its shares held in the Netherlands. Savings would result from the reduction of administration and investor relations costs involved in the dual-share structure.

4. The uncertain effects of Britain's plan to leave the European Union (Brexit) in 2019.

5. A recognition, following the Kraft bid, of the exposure to predators offered by the dual-company structure.

6. Cost savings arising from reporting publicly on two separate corporate entities: although, with listings in Amsterdam, London, and New York the company would have to meet the listing requirements in London and Amsterdam (and thus the relevant corporate governance codes) and the SEC requirements in the United States.

7. The possible exposure of directors under UK company law if they failed to 'act in a way ... most likely to promote the success of a company for the benefit of its members as a whole'.[28] Some authorities suggest that this could mean that directors could be at risk if they failed to recommend a bid offer higher than the current share price (as had occurred in the Kraft case).

8. A long-term strategy to promote the Unilever Group as an international European-based business rather than an Anglo-Dutch enterprise.

9. Savings in directors' and staff time by eliminating one set of corporate meetings and reports (the directors are the same in both companies).

10. Cultural or nationalistic differences between members of the board.

Discussion Questions

1. What do you believe were the real reasons for the Unilever board proposing the fundamental change in the Group's governance structure?

2. In your opinion, are these reasons valid?

3. What are the pros and cons of the proposed changes to the Group's governance?

[28] Section 172, UK Companies Act 2006.

Self-test questions

1. List some drivers of change in corporate governance.

2. What did the NYSE-sponsored Commission on Corporate Governance have to say about the NYSE requirements relating to independent directors?

3. What schism has appeared between American and British concepts of corporate governance?

4. What is the key question in deciding whether the chief executive should also be chair of the board?

5. What is the first step to better corporate governance according to the CSIA?

6. What evidence suggests that society is no longer satisfied with corporate behaviour?

7. What might board-level information systems offer directors in the future?

8. What might be some of the interesting and more important developments in the future that could affect corporate governance?

9. What are the principal differences between corporate governance in China and the Western world?

10. What might the development of a philosophy of corporate governance achieve?

 For suggested answers to these self-test questions visit the online resources at: **www.oup.com/uk/tricker4e/**

Projects and exercises

1. Consider a corporate entity with which you are familiar. In the next ten or twenty years, what forces for change could occur that would cause the organization to change its approach to governance?

2. What will corporate governance look like in ten or twenty years' time? Prepare a report/presentation outlining your expectations.

3. In 2008, all public companies in Norway were obliged by law to ensure that at least 40 per cent of their board directors were women. Advance the arguments for and against such legislation in your country.

References and further reading

Boubaker, Sabri, Bang Dang Nguyen, and Duc Khuong Nguyen (eds) (2012) *Corporate Governance—Recent Developments and New Trends.* Springer, Berlin.

Carter, C. B and J. W. Lorsch (2004) *Back to the Drawing Board.* Harvard Business School Press, Boston, MA.

Chew, Donald H. and Stuart L. Gillan (2005) *Corporate Governance at the Crossroads: A Book of Readings.* McGraw-Hill, Boston, MA.

Clarke, Thomas and Douglas Branson (eds) (2012) *Handbook of Corporate Governance—The Limitations in Corporate Governance Best Practice.* Sage, London/Thousand Oaks, CA.

Denis, Diane K. and John J. McConnell (2004) 'International corporate governance', *Journal of Corporate Finance*, 10, 5, November.

Ferguson, Niall (2011) *Civilization: The West and the Rest.* Penguin Press, New York.

Journal of Financial Economics (2000) Special issue on international corporate governance, 58, 1–2.

La Porte, Rafael and Florencio Lopez-de-Silaries (2003) 'Investor protection and corporate governance', *Journal of Financial and Quantitative Analysis*, 38, 1, March.

Lipton M. (2007) *Some Thoughts for Boards of Directors.* Watchell, Lipton, Rosen & Katz, New York.

Lowery, Kellan V. (2008) *Corporate Governance in the 21st Century.* Nova Science Publishers Inc., Hauppage, NY.

MacAvoy, P. W. and I. M. Millstein (2003) *The Recurrent Crisis in Corporate Governance.* Palgrave Macmillan, Basingstoke, UK.

Mayer, Colin (2011) *Firm Commitment—Why the Corporation is Failing Us and How to Restore it.* Oxford University Press, Oxford.

Monks, Robert A. G. (2008) *Corpocracy: How CEOs and the Business Roundtable Hijacked the World's Greatest Wealth Machine—and How to Get it Back.* Wiley, Chichester.

Nordberg, Donald (2011) *Corporate Governance: Principles and Issues.* Sage, London.

Semple, Kirsty (2014) *The ICSA Charities Handbook.* ICSA, London.

Sun, William, Jim Stewart, and David Pollard (2011) *Corporate Governance and the Global Financial Crisis.* Cambridge University Press, Cambridge.

Tricker, Bob (2011) 'Reinventing the limited liability company', *Corporate Governance: An International Review*, 19, 4, July.

Zattoni, Alessandro and William Judge (2012) *Corporate Governance and Initial Public Offerings.* Cambridge University Press, Cambridge.

Zinkin, John (2014) *Rebuilding Trust in Banks—the Role of Leadership and Governance.* John Wiley, Singapore.

Corporate Governance Codes around the World

Africa

Ghana
https://thelawreviews.co.uk/edition/the-corporate-governance-review-edition-8/1168924/ghana

Kenya
www.ecgi.org/codes/documents/principles_2.pdf

Malawi
www.ecgi.org/codes/documents/malawi_codeii_1jun2010_en.pdf

Nigeria
www.ecgi.org/codes/documents/cg_code_nigeria_oct2003_en.pdf

South Africa
www.ecgi.org/codes/documents/king3.pdf

Tunisia
www.ecgi.org/codes/documents/guide_tunisia_2008_en.pdf

Asia

Australia
www.asx.com.au/documents/asx-compliance/cgc-principles-and-recommendations-3rd-edn.pdf

China (PRC)
www.ecgi.org/codes/documents/code_en.pdf

Hong Kong (SAR of China)
www.hkex.com.hk/-/media/hkex-market/listing/rules-and-guidance/listing-rules-contingency/main-board-listing-rules/appendices/appendix_14

India
www.ecgi.org/codes/documents/final_code_english.pdf

Indonesia
www.ifc.org/wps/wcm/connect/topics_ext_content/ifc_external_corporate_site/ifc+cg/resources/toolkits+and+manuals/indonesia+corporate+governance+manual%2C+2nd+edition

Japan
www.jpx.co.jp/english/equities/listing/cg/tvdi-vq0000008jdy-att/20180601.pdf

Malaysia
https://home.kpmg/content/dam/kpmg/my/pdf/External/mccg2017.pdf

New Zealand
https://fma.govt.nz/assets/Reports/141201-FMA-Corporate-Governance-Handbook-Principles-and-Guidelines2014.pdf

Pakistan
www.secp.gov.pk/corporate-governance/listed-companies/

Philippines
www.chanrobles.com/secmemorandumcircular-no022002.html#.XEQ64dL7SM8
(Take care if you Google for the official government code: it has had a Trojan problem.)

Singapore
www.mas.gov.sg/Regulations-and-Financial-Stability/Regulatory-and-Supervisory-Framework/Corporate-Governance/Corporate-Governance-of-Listed-Compa-nies/Code-of-Corporate-Governance.aspx

South Korea
www.ecgi.org/codes/documents/cbp_korea_2003_en.pdf

Sri Lanka
www.sec.gov.lk/wp-content/uploads/code%20of%20best%20practice%20-%202013.pdf

Taiwan
www.carrotsandsticks.net/regulation/corporate-gov-ernance-best-practice-principles-for-tsecgtsm-listed-companies/

Thailand
https://ecgi.global/node/6197

Europe

Austria
www.omv.com/pbd_download/430/490/corporate-governance-code-012018%20EN.pdf

Baltic States
https://ecgi.global/code/governance-state-owned-enterprises-baltic-states-2012

Belgium

www.corporategovernancecommittee.be/en/about-2009-code/2009-belgian-code-corporate-governance

Bosnia Herzegovina

http://documents.worldbank.org/curated/en/675461468202759670/Bosnia-and-Herzegovina-Report-on-the-Observance-of-Standards-and-Codes-ROSC-corporate-governance-country-assessment

Croatia

www.ebrd.com/news/2017/croatia-pushes-for-better-corporate-governance-standards.html

Cyprus

www.cse.com.cy/en-GB/regulated-market/listing/corporate-governance/

Czech Republic

www.ecgi.org/codes/documents/czech_code_2004_en.pdf

Denmark

www.ecgi.org/codes/documents/haa_kap05-01uk.pdf

Estonia

www.oecd.org/corporate/ca/corporategovernanceprinciples/1931752.pdf

European Union

https://ec.europa.eu/info/business-economy-euro/doing-business-eu/company-law-and-corporate-governance_en

Finland

https://cgfinland.fi/wp-content/uploads/sites/6/2012/01/finnish-cg-code-2010.pdf

France

https://rubis.fr/en/group/corporate-governance/french-corporate-governance-code/

Georgia

www.ecgi.org/codes/documents/cg_code_commercial_banks_georgia_sep2009_en.pdf

Germany

https://dcgk.de//files/dcgk/usercontent/en/download/code/170214_Code.pdf

Greece

www.ecgi.org/codes/documents/hellenic_cg_code_oct2013_en.pdf

Hungary

https://iclg.com/practice-areas/corporate-governance-laws-and-regulations/hungary

Iceland

www.ecgi.org/codes/documents/iceland_corporate_governance_guidelines_5th_edition_2015.pdf

Ireland

www.centralbank.ie/regulation/how-we-regulate/codes

Kazakhstan

www.ecgi.org/codes/documents/cg_code_kazakhstan_21feb2005_en.pdf

Latvia

www.oecd.org/corporate/corporate-governance-in-latvia-9789264268180-en.htm

Lithuania

www.ecgi.org/codes/documents/code_lithuania.pdf

Luxembourg

www.bourse.lu/corporate-governance

Malta

www.mfsa.com.mt/default.aspx

Montenegro

www.ecgi.org/codes/documents/montenegro_may2009.pdf

The Netherlands

www.mccg.nl/?page=3779

Norway

www.oslobors.no/ob_eng/Oslo-Boers/Listing/Shares-equity-certificates-and-rights-to-shares/Oslo-Boers-and-Oslo-Axess/Corporate-governance-CG/The-Norwegian-Code-of-Practice-for-Corporate-Governance

Poland

https://iclg.com/practice-areas/corporate-governance-laws-and-regulations/poland

Portugal

https://thelawreviews.co.uk/edition/the-corporate-governance-review-edition-7/1140926/portugal

Romania

https://bvb.ro/info/Rapoarte/Diverse/ENG_Corporate%20Governance%20Code_WEB_revised.pdf

Russia

www.ebrd.com/downloads/legal/corporate/russia_code.pdf

Serbia

www.ecgi.org/codes/documents/cg_code_serbia_jul2008_en.pdf

Slovakia

www.ecgi.org/codes/documents/cega_code_slovakia_jan2008_en.pdf

Slovenia

www.sdh.si/Data/Documents/asset-management/Slovenian_CG_Code_listed_companies_2016.pdf

Spain

www.cnmv.es/DocPortal/Publicaciones/CodigoGov/
Good_Governanceen.pdf

Sweden

www.corporategovernanceboard.se/UserFiles/
Archive/496/The_Swedish_Corporate_Governance_
Code_1_December_2016.pdf

Switzerland

www.ecgi.org/codes/documents/swiss_code_
26sep2014_en.pdf

Turkey

https://iclg.com/practice-areas/corporate-governance-
laws-and-regulations/turkey

Ukraine

www.oecd.org/daf/ca/corporategovernanceprinciples/
1930958.pdf

United Kingdom

(See the list of corporate governance reports and the
UK Corporate Governance Codes listed in Chapter 5.)

Middle East

Bahrain

www.cbb.gov.bh/page-p-the_corporate_governance_
code_of_the_kingdom_of_bahrain.htm

Israel

www.isa.gov.il/Download/IsaFile_1124.pdf

Lebanon

www.ecgi.org/codes/documents/lebanon_cgcode_
2010_en.pdf

Qatar

www.ecgi.org/codes/documents/cgcode_listed_compa-
nies_qatar_27jan2009_en.pdf

Saudi Arabia

https://ecgi.global/code/corporate-governance-
regulations-kingdom-saudi-arabia-1

United Arab Emirates

www.rna-cs.com/corporate-governance-code-for-
small-and-medium-enterprises-smes-of-united-arab-
emirates-uae/

North America

Canada

www.tsx.com/listings/tsx-and-tsxv-issuer-resources/tsx-
issuer-resources/corporate-governance

Mexico

www.ecgi.org/codes/documents/mexico_code_en.pdf

United States

(See the list of corporate governance reports and the US
Corporate Governance Codes listed in Chapter 5.)

South America and the West Indies

Argentina

www.oecd.org/corporate/ca/corporategovernanceprin-
ciples/37329786.pdf

Brazil

www.ibri.com.br/Upload/Arquivos/novidades/3877_
GT_Interagentes_Brazilian_Corporate_Governance_
Code_Listed_Companies.pdf

Colombia

www.oecd.org/countries/colombia/corporate-govern-
ance-in-colombia-9789264281134-en.htm
www.oecd.org/corporate/ca/corporategovernanceprin-
ciples/39741294.pdf

Jamaica

http://ocg.gov.jm/ocg/sites/default/files/Revised%20
Corporate%20Governance%20Framework%20
%28Oct%202012%29_0.pdf

Peru

www.oecd.org/daf/ca/corporategovernanceprinci-
ples/39741211

Trinidad and Tobago

www.caribbeangovernance.org/T&T-Corporate-Gov-
ernance-Code-2013-(TTCGC-2013)

Index

Tables and figures are indicated by an italic *t* and *f* following the page number.